Contemporary Issues in Psychological Assessment

Series Editor
Randy W. Kamphaus
Georgia State University College of Education
Atlanta, Georgia
USA

More information about this series at http://www.springer.com/series/7353

Anna P. Kroncke • Marcy Willard
Helena Huckabee

Assessment of Autism Spectrum Disorder

Critical Issues in Clinical, Forensic,
and School Settings

With Contributions from Jessica S. Reinhardt

 Springer

Anna P. Kroncke
Emerge: Professionals in Autism
Behavior and Personal Growth
Glendale, CO, USA

Marcy Willard
Emerge: Professionals in Autism
Behavior and Personal Growth
Glendale, CO, USA

Helena Huckabee
Emerge: Professionals in Autism
Behavior and Personal Growth
Glendale, CO, USA

Contemporary Issues in Psychological Assessment
ISBN 978-3-319-25502-6   ISBN 978-3-319-25504-0   (eBook)
DOI 10.1007/978-3-319-25504-0

Library of Congress Control Number: 2015960742

Springer Cham Heidelberg New York Dordrecht London

Springer International Publishing AG Switzerland is part of Springer Science+Business Media
(www.springer.com)

Acknowledgments

Thank you to our editor Randy Kamphaus, Ph.D., distinguished professor and Dean of the College of Education at the University of Oregon, who graciously accepted this book as a part of his Assessment Series and provided us the opportunity to write about what we love to do every day.

Thank you to our contributing author, Jessica Reinhardt, Ph.D., who provided a voice in our differential diagnosis and assessment parts of this book with insight into sensory processing, learning disabilities, AD/HD, and behavior and coauthored the school chapters. Thank you to Khalid Mohammad, B.S., who assisted with research and references, compiled tables of measures and appendices with psychometrics, and authored many case studies. We could not have completed this project and kept our clinic going without their support. It is essential to have exemplary team members with new perspectives and energy and we are so grateful for all they do.

Thank you to Kirsten Brown, Ph.D., who provided an essential peer review of our text.

Special thanks to Allison Margulies, Ph.D., who contributed to the cognitive assessment section and provided valuable information on the selection of intelligence measures.

We offer thanks to those researchers, authors, and teachers before us. There are so many individuals who influence our work. Thank you especially to Catherine Lord, Ivar Lovaas, Lorna Wing, Fred Volkmar, Deborah Fein, Sally Ozonoff, Tony Attwood, Robert and Lynn Koegel, Shahla Alai-Rosales, Susan Landry, Ami Klin, Judy Reaven, Susan Hepburn, the JFK Partners team, Richard Kelley and countless others who have taught us so much.

Thank you to the Autism community, to Temple Grandin, Stephen Shore, and many others who provide a guide and offer hope to our clients as they make their way in the world.

Thank you to the families and clients who have provided so much insight over the years and who have also enlightened us and remind us of the importance of early identification and intervention every day. They are forging a path that other families and individuals with autism can learn from and follow. Their strength, dedication, and love is inspiring always.

Thank you to our own families for their support and patience as we dedicated time to this project. Dr. Kroncke would like to thank her husband for his support in this line of work and in the intense research and effort that went into her authorship of this meaningful piece. Dr. Willard offers her appreciation to her husband and two boys, Brad and Brian, who monitored and marveled at the page and word count and gave seemingly endless hours of their mother's time for this important work. Dr. Huckabee would like to thank her husband and children, Kevin and Kimmy, for inspiring and supporting her to do this work and write this piece that will hopefully illuminate a brighter path for clinicians and the families they serve. She notes proudly that Kevin has her taught more than anyone ever has. Kevin will forever bring much joy, peace and contentment to all those who choose to get to know him.

All authors would like to express their sincere thanks to the researchers who came before us and the reader who comes after us and will build on this critical knowledge in order to diagnose and serve families on the autism spectrum.

Contents

About the Authors

Anna Kroncke, Ph.D., N.C.S.P. is the Director of Psychological Services at Emerge, a private practice in Denver, CO, specializing in the diagnosis and treatment of autism spectrum disorders as well as other mental health issues. She earned a bachelor's degree in Psychology from the University of North Carolina at Chapel Hill and a master's degree and a Ph.D. in School Psychology from the University of Georgia, where she was awarded a Presidential Fellowship. Her research and clinical interests are in psychological assessment, autism spectrum disorders, and early identification of emotional and behavior problems in children. She has coauthored various book chapters and professional presentations on learning disabilities, cognitive assessment, and social-emotional assessment while working with Randy Kamphaus, Ph.D., at the University of Georgia. She completed her postdoctoral work in psychological assessment in Atlanta, GA. Dr. Kroncke worked for 5 years as a school psychologist in diverse urban school districts and has been in private practice at Emerge specializing in autism assessment and treatment since August 2010.

Marcy Willard, Ph.D. is a Licensed School Psychologist and a Postdoctoral Fellow at Emerge. Dr. Willard completed a bachelor's degree at the University of Colorado, a master's degree in Psychology from Pepperdine University, and a Ph.D. in Child, Family, and School Psychology from the University of Denver. Dr. Willard's clinical specialty is in the area of autism evaluation and treatment. She has published in the field of electronic collaboration and peer review in academic research. She was awarded a fellowship with JFK Partners, Center of Excellence for Autism and Neurodevelopmental Disabilities at the University of Colorado Medical School and the Children's Hospital. She developed a proprietary assessment of visual imagery for children with autism for her dissertation under the supervision of Dr. Susan Hepburn, nationally recognized autism researcher, and Dr. Gloria Miller, an expert in school psychology. She completed her Predoctoral Psychology Internship for Emerge conducting psychological, neuropsychological, and forensic evaluations, providing therapy to clients, and consulting with schools. She now works as a school psychologist and postdoctoral clinician serving primarily pediatric populations.

Helena Huckabee, Ph.D., BCBA-D is a Pediatric Neuropsychologist, Clinical Psychologist, and Board Certified Behavior Analyst. She received her bachelor's degree in Geological Engineering from the Colorado School of Mines and master's and doctoral degrees in Clinical Psychology from the University of Houston. Dr. Huckabee completed an internship at Baylor College of Medicine with postdoctoral fellowships at DePelchin Children's Center and JFK Partners at the University of Colorado. Her research studies have involved understanding intelligence and language skills in children with autism, the role of serotonin in mood disorders, self-injurious behaviors, brain anoxia, and treatment outcome in autism. She has previously held administrative leadership positions at five clinics for autism spectrum disorders, including the Universities of Houston (TX) and Colorado. Ironically, Dr. Huckabee's son was diagnosed with autism when she was in graduate school. With compassion and competence, she provides counseling for individuals and couples as well as leads parent groups in the community.

Jessica S. Reinhardt, Ph.D., N.C.S.P. is a Nationally Certified School Psychologist, Postdoctoral Fellow at Emerge, and adjunct faculty at the University of Denver. She earned a B.A. in Journalism and Psychology and an M.A. in Psychology from the American University. Dr. Reinhardt completed her Ph.D. in Child, Family, and School Psychology at the University of Denver. She is an active member of a number of committees within the American Psychological Association and the National Association of School Psychologists. Her research studies have examined sports programming interventions for exceptional children. Her clinical experiences include working with autism, AD/HD, developmental disabilities, anxiety, and mood disorders in a variety of school environments, counseling centers, and higher education.

Part I
Understanding Autism

This part is a focus on the history and foundations of autism as a diagnosis. Research abounds to show that autism is on the rise. Included here is a broad strokes analysis of the prevailing thought as to why incidents of autism continue to increase. Questions have been raised about everything from pesticides, to enzymes, to obesity, to increased paternal and maternal age as potential causes for autism. Even though the causes for autism are yet to be firmly identified, children are now being diagnosed more clearly and promising treatments are emerging that offer hope to families. With adequate treatment, is it possible to be "cured" of one's autism? Although autism has no known cure, there are cases of children who were once diagnosed with autism and are later found to no longer meet criteria for the diagnosis. These cases are referred to as "optimal outcomes." Research is included here regarding evidence-based treatments as well as the factors generally present in cases of optimal outcomes. Finally the DSM-5 diagnostic criteria for an Autism Spectrum Disorder is reviewed and discussed in light of updates and changes that make the fifth version quite distinct from the fourth. In the parts that follow, clinicians are guided toward a practical, decisive, and dynamic approach to autism diagnosis.

Chapter 1
What Is Autism? History and Foundations

Abstract Increasing rates of autism have changed the face of child psychology, education, and family life. Clinicians and educators, in general education and special education alike, are challenged like never before to identify and treat children with autism. Autism assessment, school psychology, and forensic psychology fields are rapidly expanding to address critical issues in the ASD population. As children on the Autism Spectrum mature to adulthood, the community college and university system, as well as employment programs and adult service providers, encounter a new level of need for this expanding population. Although assessment and treatment technologies have advanced substantially over the past decade, there are a myriad of unanswered questions about the potential for people with ASD to function in school and the workplace, have families, and live fulfilling lives. Psychologists, scientists, and doctors feel a deep sense of urgency to find answers to these provoking questions that plague our time. This passion is ever increased through the continued deepening understanding of individuals with ASD who are often endearing, talented, intriguing and may see the world in a new way; offering us a window into the brain and to the breadth of human experience. In this chapter, the reader is invited to explore the meaning of the term "autism," the history since its early foundations as "Kanner's autism," and the currently increasing prevalence estimates.

Keywords What is autism? • What is the autism spectrum? • Autism spectrum disorder • What happened to "autistic"? • Theory of mind • Kanner's autism • High functioning autism • Autism prevalence rates • Intelligence in autism

What is Autism?

Considering that this book is dedicated primarily to providing an in-depth guide for diagnosing Autism Spectrum Disorders and associated comorbid diagnoses or differentially separate disorders, the information provided here is just a "warm up" to the big picture. The big picture, per se, is for readers to be able to understand autism diagnosis on a deep level, such that clinicians can offer clear and accurate diagnosis

© Springer International Publishing Switzerland 2016
A.P. Kroncke et al., *Assessment of Autism Spectrum Disorder*, Contemporary Issues in Psychological Assessment, DOI 10.1007/978-3-319-25504-0_1

to families, as early as is feasible. It is also important for readers to learn what autism is so that individuals in the greater community are equipped to identify and refer loved ones for a comprehensive evaluation. Finally, this deep understanding should allow readers to see the gravity of obtaining an autism diagnosis and also the hope for a bright future, given early diagnosis and effective treatment.

The new term Autism Spectrum Disorders was regularly used even before the Diagnostic and Statistical Manual, Fifth Edition (DSM-5) and refers to a set of common symptoms, although there is a great deal of variation in the presence and severity of those symptoms. A full description of the "Spectrum" is provided later in this book. For now, readers should know that the terms "autism" and "Autism Spectrum Disorder" refer to a continuum of symptoms, ranging from severe and pervasive to low severity level, or High Functioning. On another continuum are language and cognitive abilities. An individual may be very intelligent but demonstrate many symptoms of autism or he or she may be lower in cognitive domains and have a low symptoms severity level. The DSM-5 diagnosis requires a clinician to specify each individual symptom including severity, language, and cognition. Throughout the book, the term "autism" and "Autism Spectrum Disorder" are used interchangeably. Readers should know that the term "autistic" has largely been abandoned at present; as most clinicians prefer person-first language, referring to an individual with these symptoms as, "a child with autism" or "adolescent with ASD"; "individual with autism" or "adult with ASD."

Individuals with autism struggle primarily with social communication. They often show a limited range of facial expressions and their emotions are generally not well-integrated with the content of the dialogue. They often fail to share enjoyment, interests, or emotional experiences with others. Thus, conversations with individuals on the Spectrum are often flat or awkward in nature. Individuals with ASD may use repetitive or scripted language. They tend to use gestures less frequently than neurotypicals; perhaps, due in part to a limited social-communicative motivation. That is, some individuals with autism do not focus as much on engaging the listeners or "checking in" for understanding. They may speak in a robotic or a "sing-song" voice or use an overly formal style of communication with advanced vocabulary for their age and developmental level. Children with autism tend to use vocabulary that is beyond not only what is expected for their age, but also beyond what they understand themselves. That is, children with autism often show a unique pattern where expressive language skills are higher than receptive. While all of these things may be true for an individual with autism, they also may not be. Speaking with appropriate prosody and conversational fluency does not in reverse rule out the diagnosis.

Even very bright individuals on the Spectrum tend to show significant delays in comprehension, particularly comprehension within a social context. They may misread or fail to assess the intentions, perspectives, and feelings of others. Unfortunately, this deficit may render people with autism more vulnerable to bullying and victimization. They may struggle to comprehend metaphors, idioms, jokes, or sarcasm. This problem is, in part, due to limited "Theory of Mind," which is the understanding of another person's perspective. These comprehension difficulties may manifest in social relationships as well as academic endeavors. Sometimes individuals with autism have poor narrative coherence (meaning difficulty telling sensible stories) and poor reading and oral comprehension.

Individuals with this disability may avoid eye-contact and display sensory sensitivities or tactile-defensiveness, being highly sensitive to sights, smells, tastes, and touch. They may show significant rigidity and resist changes to familiar routines.

Children with autism may display repetitive behaviors such as hand flapping, rocking, and odd finger movements. They may have special or circumscribed interests. Although having passion or a focus area is generally considered a valuable personality trait, these interests are either not appropriate developmentally, or they are obsessive in nature (APA, 2000). Children with autism tend to "monologue" about their interests or ideas, whether or not it fits within the context of the conversation. They often appear more restricted in their play, using less imaginative, symbolic, or pretend play than typical children (Rutherford, Young, Hepburn & Rogers, 2007).

The most significant symptom of autism is a *lack of social reciprocity*. Individuals with autism tend to lack the understanding of the give-and-take nature of conversation and relationships. They do not take others' perspectives well. This difficulty can be so pervasive that they may not understand why seeking friendship is a useful endeavor. Often, even in highly intelligent children with autism, there is a failure to understand the concept of friendship. They tend to struggle to join peers in play or social exchanges; sometimes preferring to be alone, and other times avoiding social contact because of a history of frustration and failure in establishing relationships. Thus, children with autism sometimes appear to be withdrawn and this is often the feature that raises red-flags to parents and family members. Taken together, the term autism encompasses a set of symptoms manifested primarily in disordered social communication and reciprocity.

History and Foundations of ASD

Autism was originally discovered by Dr. Leo Kanner (1943). Prior to Dr. Kanner's discovery, children with autism symptoms were referred to as "feeble-minded, retarded, moronic, idiotic or schizoid" (Fischbach, 2007, p. 1). The term "autism" was actually borrowed from Eugene Bleuller, who used the term "infantile autism" to describe the introverted and self-absorbed aspects of patients with schizophrenia (2007).

In developing a construct for understanding autism, Dr. Kanner wrote a paper in 1943 where he drew symptom similarities between 11 case studies (Kanner, 1943). He became fascinated with one particular child named "David," who did not socialize with other children, repeated phrases from adults, and displayed repetitive behaviors. In his article, *Autistic Disorders of Affective Contact* (1943), Kanner writes about David,

> He seems to be self-satisfied...He does not observe the fact that anyone comes or goes, and does not seem glad to see father or mother or any playmate. He seems almost to draw within his shell and live within himself...In his second year he developed a mania for spinning blocks and pans and other round objects (218).

Soon after its recognition, the cause of Autism was erroneously attributed to detached parenting, a notion promoted by Bruno Bettelheim (Bettelheim: 1950–1960 in Solomon, 2012). Bettleheim accused mothers of children with autism of refusing to provide affection to their children (2011). Although Kanner had recognized parents of children with Autism as being professional, analytical, and organized, he perpetuated the belief that autism was due to "a genuine lack of maternal warmth" (Laidler, 2004; Solomon, 2012; Thomas, 1960). Thus, the popular notion of "Refrigerator Mothers" was insidiously published by Time Magazine (Thomas, 1960) based on an interview with Kanner, where he indicates parents of children with autism, "defrost just enough to produce a child" (Laidler, 2004; Thomas, 1960). It was likely that any "coldness" Kanner may have observed in his clients may have had more to do with the child's inhibition than warmth in parenting.

During Kanner's period (1950s), Temple Grandin's own mother, Eustacia Cutler, was called a refrigerator mother (Solomon, 2012, p. 274). More will be said about Temple Grandin in this book; for now, it is important to recognize that Temple's mother is known for the intensity of care she provided to "pull [Temple] out of the limbo of [her] self-absorption" (2012, p. 274). Her efforts combined with the consistent care of the family's nanny supported Temple in navigating a myriad of significant autism and mood symptoms to eventually go to college and make a meaningful contribution in her career (2012). She describes Temple's teen years thusly, "Adolescence is hard enough for any child, but autistic adolescence is something devised by the devil" (2012, p. 274). She then came to admire Temple for her willingness to work so adamantly to connect with other people and to participate in our world. She said about the refrigerator mothers hypothesis that, "We mothers would have liked an apology. We deserve it. And so do the fathers" (Solomon, 2012, p. 231). This example serves to show that in many ways parents in the 50s were not only left to fend for themselves in terms of securing a diagnosis and treatments for their children, they were often mistakenly blamed for their autism.

Kanner labeled the condition "infantile autism" based on the previously held understanding of childhood schizophrenia (Thomas, 1960), and for the next 50 years, the term remained similar to the qualitative diagnostic guidelines laid out by Kanner. During the 1950s–1970s, Infantile Autism was diagnosed through clinical observations noting a child who demonstrated a clear sense of aloneness consistent with the Latin root of the word Autism; "Auto," meaning one.

Kanner was the first to understand the biological basis of autism stating, "We must, then, assume that these children have come into the world with an innate inability to form the usual, biologically provided affective contact with people, just as other children come into the world with innate physical and intellectual handicaps" (Zimmerman, 2008). Thus, even in the early days, autism was primarily understood as a disorder of social-emotional understanding and connections. Today, although our understanding has increased, autism is still to be diagnosed as a disorder of social reciprocity; regardless of the level of functioning or intellectual capacity.

It was not necessarily understood in the 1960s–1970s that an autism diagnosis was distinct from a cognitive delay unless the child clearly lacked any communication and incessantly participated in repetitive behaviors such as banging their head or rocking back and forth. In these cases, a child was labeled autistic. It is reasonable to assume that children with autism were misdiagnosed if their intellectual impairment was prominent or not evaluated at all if their language was functional or fluent and they simply presented as odd or awkward. Indeed, a term called "diagnostic accretion" has been used to describe the increase in autism rates that is due to the fact that some children diagnosed with autism would have formerly been diagnosed with mental retardation (Seneff, 2014). Some recognition of children who did not clearly meet criteria for Infantile Autism or Mental Retardation; as it was archaically called, came in DSM IIIR with the addition of Developmental Disorder Not Otherwise Specified (DDNOS). This unfortunately misleading "slush category" was used diagnostically for children who did not clearly fit the autism diagnosis. It was later replaced by Pervasive Developmental Disorder Not Otherwise Specified in DSM IV. At this time, Asperger's disorder and PDD-NOS were included among pervasive the Developmental Disorders as separate diagnostic categories accounting for the high degree of variation in cognitive and symptom profiles in this population.

Asperger's Disorder was first discussed by Hans Asperger only 1 year after Kanner discovered Autism, in 1944, when he encountered a group of six young children who "were socially maladroit, developed bizarre obsessions and yet were highly verbal and seemingly quite bright" (Nash, 2002). Hans Asperger, a Viennese child psychologist, published the first definition of Asperger syndrome in 1944. Asperger died before his work became widely recognized, as his writings were mostly in German and not well-translated.

The term "Asperger's syndrome" was popularized in a paper by British researcher Lorna Wing, MD. Wing indicated that children with autism show disinterest and dislike of social behavior from a young age. The underlying problem is a lack of understanding of the give and take of social interactions. Wing and Gould (1979) explored three categories of abnormal social interactions for those with ASD. The three categories identified were: (1) aloof, (2) passive, and (3) active-but-odd. The *aloof group* represented the most traditional picture of autism, those who remain largely cut off from social contact and become agitated by it. Repetitive and stereotyped behaviors were common in this group (Wing & Gould, 1979). The *passive group* was marked by social inactivity and poor nonverbal communication. Members of the group are unlikely to make social advances or read subtle social cues. The passive group members were considered to be the best behaved of the three groups. The *active-but-odd group* differs from the other groups in social behavior. Those in the active-but-odd group may have reached out socially, but it tended to be about topics of their own interest with little regard for another's engagement in the conversation. This group was marked by "talking at" others. Behavior problems and repetitive communication or interests were also common in the active-but-odd-group (Stevens et al., 2000; Wing & Gould, 1979).

Although Hans Asperger identified Asperger's Disorder in 1944, and the idea was popularized by Lorna Wing in 1979, it was not an official diagnosis until 1994, approximately 50 years after the syndrome was first described (Nash, 2002, p. 50). By the year 2002, Asperger's syndrome made the cover of TIME magazine, but this time with a focus on concerns about increasing prevalence rates, rather than "refrigerator mothers" (1960). As of 2002, the rate had grown to 1 in 150 children who were aged ten and under; an estimated 300,000 children (Nash, 2002). There was a brief reference in TIME to the emerging new label for Asperger's as "Geek Syndrome" or "the little professor syndrome," citing one child's ability to provide great detail regarding astrophysics and supernovas to an unwittingly nonplussed audience (p. 50).

In 2006, Autism made the cover of TIME magazine again, exploring how genetic vulnerability and environmental factors may be the cause for Autism Spectrum Disorders (Wallis, 2006). Wallis (2006) indicated that enlarged frontal lobes, undersized corpus callosum, larger brains by the age of two, enlarged amygdala, a 10 % larger hippocampus, and extra white matter in the cerebellum may all be to blame for autism. This article included brain research from Marcel Just of Carnegie Mellon's Center for Cognitive Brain Imaging on the lack of synchronization and coordination across brain structures; and from Ami Klin of the Yale Child Study Center (now at Emory), who analyzed how the autistic brain tends to process information, such as letters and faces, in different areas than controls (2007). This small sampling of TIME articles serves to highlight how awareness in the popular media regarding the complexity of the autism diagnosis advanced from the year 1960–2007.

Primarily over the past decade, diagnostic criterion has tightened in large part due to the work of Catherine Lord and her colleagues at the University of Michigan and in New York to move to empirically-based diagnoses using standardized criteria. The principle instruments used now are reliable and valid as well as more sensitive to slight symptom variations. This increased clarity regarding differential diagnosis is most fortuitous given the rapidly increasing prevalence rates.

Concluding Remarks on the History and Prevalence of Autism

The global estimates for ASD are that rates have increased 20- to 30-fold since the 1970s (CDC, 2012). The authors on this work became involved in autism research, evaluation, and treatment, during a dynamic time, in the 1990s–2010s, when autism was just beginning to gain awareness in the general public. In just 10 short years, 1993–2003, some estimate that autism in schools in the United States rose by over 800 %. (Rudy, 2013) Rates of autism continued to rise over recent decades in the United States. Rates grew from 1 in 500 by 1995; to 1 in 150 by 2002; then to 1 in 110 by 2006; then to 1 in 88 by 2008 (CDC, 2012; Seneff, 2014). Today, prevalence rates have increased yet again to 1 in 68 (CDC, 2014; Seneff, 2014). The Center for Disease Control reports that, "Comparison of the 2008 findings with those for previous surveillance years showed an increase of approximately 23 % compared with the 2006 estimates and 78 % compared with 2002" (CDC, 2014, p. 2). Many community members wonder if the increased prevalence represents a true change or if it could be due to increased identification and diagnostic clarity. However, most researchers believe that the changing rates represent a real difference in the number of children who have autism; not just the significant advances in identification and diagnosis. This increase over the past few decades has resulted in most people in the general public now knowing someone in their family or immediate social group who is affected by autism. In August 2007, a Google search for the word "autism" produced 18,200,000 hits (Schwartz & Davis, 2008a, 2008b). In May 2015, a Google search for "autism" revealed 71,300,000 hits. The rates of autism have reached epidemic levels and are now higher than AIDS, pediatric cancer, and diabetes combined (Autism Speaks, 2010). Autism is now the fastest growing developmental disorder.

Chapter 2
The Causes of Autism

Abstract The surge in autism prevalence has led scientists to search evermore fervently for the cause of the disorder. Why is the number of American school children with autism seeming to dramatically increase every decade? Questions abound in terms of whether or not some of the factors predicting autism can be prevented. Autism does tend to run in families, and as such, genetic and inherited factors clearly have some influence on the development of autism. However, even identical twins do not express autism symptoms to the same degree, leading scientists to consider other potential causes. Although the precise cause is unknown, research points to a combination of genetic and environmental causes. It may be that there seems to be an epigenetic mechanism by which aberrant environmental factors trigger gene expression and the resultant appearance of autism symptoms. Other factors include dietary and digestive issues influencing the processing of certain enzymes, leading to the somewhat common use of the gluten-free, casein-free diet. Exposure to pesticides, either in utero or early childhood, has been proposed as a potential cause of autism as well. In this chapter, readers are invited to consider the prevailing thought as to the reasons autism prevalence continues to be on the rise. Risk factors for the disorder are discussed. The chapter concludes with information regarding signs that a diagnostic assessment may be warranted. Regardless of the cause, early identification and treatment provides the best potential for intervention and recovery.

Keywords Cause of autism • Genetics of autism • Epigenetics in autism • Pesticides and ASD • Genetic vulnerability • Vaccines and autism • Gluten-free • Casein-free diet • Do dietary restrictions help? • Leaky gut in autism • Intestinal permeability in ASD

Genetic Causes

Scientists have found that autism has an extremely high heritability rate of 0.80–0.90, which indicates that 80–90 % of the causal variance is genetic. This means that of all causes which are relevant to the manifested severity of each case, by far the majority of those factors are genetic. Approximately 90–100 genes have

© Springer International Publishing Switzerland 2016
A.P. Kroncke et al., *Assessment of Autism Spectrum Disorder*, Contemporary Issues in Psychological Assessment, DOI 10.1007/978-3-319-25504-0_2

been associated with the disorder (Broad Institute of MIT & Harvard, 2012, IMFAR, 2014). The human genome is highly complex involving hundreds of thousands of genes that can each be subject to any number of tiny deletions, substitutions, or abnormalities. Scientists are currently making progress toward identifying specific gene combinations that may increase the risk of certain forms of autism, often referred to as "The Autisms" (Corey Robinson: Director of JFK Partners Center of Excellence for Autism and Neurodevelopmental Disabilities, personal communications, 2012; Wallis, 2006: citing David Amaral of the MIND Institute at U.C. Davis). This means that at some point, it is predicted that blood tests may be able to reveal the genetic code for autism and predict the symptom profile for various forms of the disorder. But this possibility is likely a long way off in the future.

The genetic code for autism is not well understood. It is recognized that autism is highly heterogeneous from a genetic perspective and likely polygenetic (involving multiple genes), but there is no clear genetic pattern for this congenital neurologic disorder and many individuals with autism have no known genetic abnormalities at all. Demark (n.d.) explains, "A probable non-Mendelian model for autism is multi-factorial inheritance whereby a large number of genes and/or environmental factors contribute to the development of this disorder" (p. 30). Although the precise genetic variants are yet to be identified (Demark, n.d.; Wallis, 2006; Yurov et al., 2007), scientists know that autism heritability is based on a complex combination of genes, mutations, and chromosomal abnormalities (Veenstra-VanderWeele et al., 2004; Harmon, 2012; Sanders et al., 2012; Veenstra-VanderWeele et al., 2004).

Studies of twins and siblings with autism have revealed a significant risk for autism, representing a 50–70 % higher risk (Wallis, 2002) when a child in the family already has autism. Yet identical twins (monozygotic) who share 100 % of their genes do not manifest autism to the same degree. Monozygotic twins, however, have a pooled concordance level of .64 — indicating that roughly 64 % of the variance in incidence of autism was attributed to shared genes; whereas non-identical twins (sharing 50 % of their genes) have a pooled concordance level of only 0.09 (Demark, n.d.). Twin studies tell us that genetics play a significant yet complex role in the risk for development of autism.

Another way to understand the genetic sequences that may be implicated in autism is by understanding the relationship autism shares with entirely genetic syndromes. Fragile X, for example, is identified through genome sequencing and shares a complicated relationship with autism. One study found that as many as 47 % of individuals with Fragile X met criteria for autism (Demark, Feldman, & Holden, 2003). Studies have found rates of shared genes between individuals with both disorders to range from 0 to 12.5 %, with most studies finding about 3 % of cells in the autism group that code for Fragile X (Demark, n.d.). However, even though the genetic code for Fragile X and autism shares only a modest relationship, both disorders share common symptom profiles in certain domains. For example, people with Fragile X and autism tend to have attention problems, hyperactivity, anxiety in social settings, and limited eye contact. This serves as just one example of the complex relationship between the autism genotype (the genetic code) and the phenotype (the expression of symptoms) that can look similar to a variety of other disabilities not sharing that genetic code. This research again points to the strong genetic influence on risk for autism, as well as the fact that there is still a sizable percentage of cases that cannot be attributed to genetics alone.

Thus, it is generally accepted that autism has a genetic or inherited basis. It is also generally believed that children are born with autism; they do not "contract" it later in life. Even so, why the sudden surge in autism rates? To ignore genetic factors would be failing to see the whole ocean; however, to subsume all of the causal factors under genetics would be failing to notice the storms, waves, and the life teaming beneath the surface. Thus, researchers began to evaluate and find that autism could be caused by a combination of genetic and environmental factors (D'Amelio et al., 2005; Demark, n.d.; Horvath, Papadimitriou, Rabsztyn, Drachenberg, & Tildon, 1999; McCandless, 2002/2009; Nash, 2002; Reid, 2004; O'Hara & Szakacs, 2008; Wallis, 2006). Hair and tissue samples are currently under study around the country to identify whether or not pesticides or other environmental toxins could be to blame for autism (Wallis, 2006).

Vaccines: Not a Cause of Autism

Initially, vaccines were blamed for the surge in autism rates. This argument gained traction when the parents of Hannah Polling won a lawsuit in a federal court, claiming that their daughter's autism was caused by vaccines (Wallice, 2006). In this unique case, Polling's symptoms were reported to have increased dramatically after receiving a large dose of a variety of vaccines. Expert witnesses testified and indeed were victorious in showing that Polling's autism symptoms were either caused or increased significantly after receiving vaccinations.

Following this case, many families worried that their child's symptoms could be due to vaccines as well. One reason for this belief is that some symptoms of autism may not be evident until immediately following the vaccines administered at the 1-year or 2-year check-up. This sudden increase may be due to the fact that there are some regressive forms of autism where symptoms do tend to show around the second year of life which coincides with the timing of vaccines. Another rationale for the symptom increase during this phase of life is that many developmental language milestones tend to become more evident during that time and the absence of delay of speech is often a characteristic of autism. That is, it is possible that many of the signs of autism go unnoticed in infancy; however, when a child is not gesturing, sharing enjoyment, talking, or responding to his name at 2 years of age, parents and clinicians take notice. Thus, there may be a correlation between the timing of the symptoms surfacing and the shots being administered; however, this correlation does not necessarily indicate a causal relationship.

Although the potential relationship between vaccines and autism has been sensationalized in the media, researchers have repeatedly concluded that there is no clear relationship between vaccines and autism. The original research linking the MMR shot to autism was rejected when multiple flaws were uncovered, revealing their results were exaggerated and statistically unsubstantiated (Kaye, del Mar

Melero-Montes, & Jick, 2001). Salzberg (2015) indicates, "We're still spending vast amounts of time and money trying to counter the ill effects of a discredited, retracted paper from 1998 that claimed to find a link between the MMR (measles, mumps and rubella) vaccine and autism" (p. 1). Adding to this skepticism in the medical community is the fact that the allegedly dangerous preservatives in the MMR shot have been removed, and autism prevalence continues to be on the rise. Further problems with the vaccine argument were uncovered when a relatively sizable percentage of Americans stopped vaccinating their children, which might predict a co-occurring reduction in autism rates (Rosenberry Conference, 2010). Unfortunately, autism rates continued to skyrocket, thus further calling into question the plausibility of the relationship between autism and vaccines. Taken together, the medical community does not believe that vaccines cause autism. Salzberg lashes out against the hype around vaccines, "So: once again we have a large, carefully conducted study showing that the MMR vaccine does not cause autism… Let's hope this study helps to end the anti-vax movement, so that we can soon stop spending time and money trying to refute their long-discredited hypotheses and instead focus on trying to understand the true cause " (p. 1). Many also warn that the authors of the original study linking autism to vaccines have seriously endangered public health by creating fear around vaccines that could potentially have prevented a myriad of serious illnesses.

Genetic and Environment Interaction Effects

Inherited and Familial Factors

The belief that autism could be born from a combination of genetic and environmental causes is well-founded (D'Amelio et al., 2005; Demark, n.d.; Horvath et al., 1999; McCandless, 2002/2009; Nash, 2002; Reid, 2004; O'Hara & Szakacs, 2008; Wallis, 2006). Scientists believe that children are generally born with autism; however, is it possible that certain risk factors in pregnancy and early life are also implicated in development of the disorder. Preliminary research on the risk factors for autism includes parental age, maternal exposure to environmental toxins, and frequent illnesses in utero or in early infancy. Studies have shown a significantly high number of children with autism who are born to mothers who are obese or have metabolic conditions (Harmon, 2012; Krakowiak, et al., 2012). Paternal and maternal age is known to be an additional risk factor. There is a high correlation between older fathers and increased numbers of sons born with autism. That is, paternal age over 30 is linked with 50 % higher risk of having a child born with autism; age over 40 with a 500 % higher risk; age over 50 with a 900 % higher risk (Hnida, 2006; Deer, 2009). Harmon (2012) identified that the increased risk with paternal age may be due to the continual sperm division process which happens throughout a man's life and the resultant higher risk of mutation during continual DNA replications (Harmon, 2012; Schubert, 2008; Willard, 2013). There is also an increased risk of other developmental disorders associated with increased parental age, so this genetic variance is not necessarily unique.

Epigenetics

Autism is a complex disorder for which many models blending genetic and external factors have been proposed. Epigenetics research investigates the mechanism by which genes are expressed in individuals and by which gene expression is passed on through generations. Specifically, epigenetics considers environmental influences on gene expression (Lahiri et al., 2013). Although autism has a high heritability, the cause of autism is made ever more complicated by the fact that siblings and even twins do not always show signs of autism to the same degree. The science of epigenetics has been associated with autism as an additional mechanism to explain how genetics and environment interact and alter phenotypic expression. Epigenetics may provide some explanation as to why many children who are exposed to the same toxins do not develop autism; whereas some cases of autism seem to show a clear link to environmental or health insults.

Day and Sweatt (2011) explain how environmental conditions impact gene expression thusly, "we consider how aberrant epigenetic modifications may lead to cognitive disorders that affect learning and memory, and we review the therapeutic potential of epigenetic treatments for amelioration of these conditions" (Day & Sweatt, 2011, p. 813). This research points to the fact that the brain is plastic, as is our genetic expression of our brain's capacity, and both can be affected; either positively or negatively, by environmental factors. Pennington (2002) puts forth that the familial phenotype may be dimensional and that certain epigenetic factors can lead to expression of symptoms or traits. Even though a child may have the genetic "code" for autism, he may appear healthy and typical as a young child. Later, after exposure to certain toxins, the child may start showing symptoms. It is possible then, that it may appear the child's autism was "caused" by the environmental trigger. Could it be that children who are medically fragile or genetically vulnerable to certain viruses or toxins suddenly show symptoms after being exposed to toxins? Possibly; research has not provided clear conclusions. A whole book could be written on the science of epigenetics and whether or not autism symptoms could indeed be expressed (or not expressed) due to an epigenetic mechanism. It does stand to reason that understanding the complex epigenetic interaction of genes and environment may allow researchers to comb through and untangle the reasons why some children's symptoms emerge in response to environmental triggers while others do not.

Exposure to Toxins and Pesticides

The prevailing research on causes of autism points to the idea that it could be the result of genetic vulnerability coupled with environmental factors (D'Amelio et al., 2005; Demark, n.d.; Horvath et al., 1999; McCandless, 2002/2009; Nash, 2002; Reid, 2004; O'Hara & Szakacs, 2008; Wallis, 2006). This genetic vulnerability research was further understood in the book, *Children with Starving Brains* (McCandless, 2002/2009), where there is a thorough discussion of the impact of toxins such as heavy metals and pesticides on the immune function, the digestive system, and toxicity from the introduction of pathogens in children with autism.

Maternal exposure to neurotoxins may explain the link between genetics and environment in utero. Researchers in Italy published a study in the Journal of Molecular Psychiatry, identifying a link between autism and exposure to pesticides such as organophosphates (D'Amelio et al., 2005). The study included 177 Italian and 107 American subjects. The Paraoxanase gene (PON1) in children with ASD was defective; an enzyme involved in detoxification from pesticides called Organo-phosphates (OPs). The researchers found that children in Italy who are not regularly exposed to OPs did not have a defect on the PON1 gene. The children in the United States autism sample were significantly more likely to have a genetic mutation on the PON1 gene and toxicity from OPs. The authors postulate that prenatal exposure to OPs is harmful to children in the U.S. and can potentially halt brain development, resulting in autism. D'Amelio et al. (2005) conclude:

> Our prior work on Reelin and APOE delineated a gene-environment interactive model if autism pathogenesis, whereby genetically vulnerable individuals prenatally exposed to OPs during critical periods in neurodevelopment could undergo altered neuronal migration, resulting in autistic syndrome...These results are consistent with our model and provide further support for the hypothesis that genetic vulnerability and environmental OP exposure may possibly contribute to pathogenesis in a sizable group of North American individuals. (p. 1006)

Consistent with these results, new research is emerging considering the effect of pesticides, insecticides, and weed killers on the development of autism. Dr. Seneff (Meyer, 2014), a Senior Research Scientist from Massachusetts Institute for Technology (MIT), released a study at a presentation for the Autism One confer-ence indicating the danger of a particular pesticide. She found a high correlation between autism's rising prevalence and the rise in the use of a chemical called glyphosate, a highly popular weed killer and pesticide which is commonly used in a variety of foods and chemically treated crops in the United States. She cautions that aluminum and glyphosate play a synergistic role in the development of digestive problems and the liver functions that detoxify, resulting in a significant impact on neurological functioning, and potentially the development of autism. Seneff argues that some of the "biomarkers" for autism such as disrupted gut bacteria, low serum sulphate, zinc and iron deficiency, and urinary p-cresol, among others, may be the potential effect of glyphosate (Seneff, 2014). The study she references (Samsel & Seneff, 2013) found that glyphosate restricts production of an enzyme needed by the brain to produce serotonin and that limited serotonin is a problem in autism. She provided a graphic that shows an almost identical rise in the use of glyphosate (and associated pathogens that are used in pesticides with glyphosate) and the rates of autism in schools. She claims the correlation to be $R = .9972$, which is considered to be extremely high. This correlation means that more than 99 % of the variance in one variable (autism rates) may be associated with a 1 point raise in the other variable (glyphosate use). Seneff cites stats from US Department of Agriculture to show the increase in rates of pesticide use and the Seneff, 2014 for the data regarding autism's increasing rates (Seneff, 2014). Bear in mind that the educational data only encompasses the number of children who have been currently identified under the IDEA (Individuals with Disabilities in Education Act) and this number is lower than the actual number of diagnosed cases in the general population of children. She cites the finding that glyphosate has been discovered at "dangerously" high levels in the breast milk of mothers in the United States, 760–1600 times higher than allowed in drinking water in European countries. There is also evidence presented that urine tests show 10 times high concentrations of glyphosate in individuals in the United States as compared to Europeans (Meyer, 2014). Dr. Seneff (2014) argues that if the use of pesticides continues at the current rate, autism prevalence will increase to an alarming 50 % by 2025 (10 years from this writing).

It is critically important when reviewing this research to be clear that this is a study based on correlation. Correlation does not indicate causality and many studies have shown how correlations can make it appear that two variables are related to each other, when indeed the relationship is spurious; or when no true relationship exists. Thus, there is not a claim made by the authors here that this correlation study provides "proof" of the cause for autism. It is compelling work, however, in light of the other research presented in this section about epigenetics, enzyme problems in autism, and the research on organophosphate exposure being implicated in autism prevalence in the United States (D'Amelio et al., 2005).

Although this research is only emerging and is correlational in nature, it may be wise for parents of medically fragile or genetically vulnerable children to carefully consider their child's nutrition and the degree to which their symptoms may change in response to certain foods. Pregnant mothers might carefully consider this research and consult with their doctors regarding whether or not it would be advisable to avoid foods that have been treated with pesticides and weed killers. It is the author's hope that if indeed an environmental cause exists, such as pesticide use, the research will advance rapidly enough for parents to be informed; and many children and families will be spared the struggles that an autism diagnosis presents. Autism advocacy organizations are well-advised to continue to stay abreast of emerging research of this nature so that community members can be informed of environmental toxins, where they are found, and any associated risk of autism to individuals and their children.

Enzymes and Digestive Problems

Research regarding autism risk factors and genetic vulnerability often points to problems in digestion, particularly in digestion of certain enzymes (DeFelice, 2008; Horvath et al., 1999; Reid, 2004; O'Hara & Szakacs, 2008). Dr. Timothy Buie, a pediatric gastroenterologist from Harvard Mass General Hospital, researched the enzymes of 89 children with autism through endoscopies and biopsies (Author, 2005). He found that most of the children had lactase deficiencies, causing difficulties breaking down milk, and deficiencies of the enzyme Sucrase, causing problems digesting sugar (2005). Reid (2004) claims that children with autism do not have the same ability to process proteins into peptides, such as the casein in milk. The casein in the milk interacts with the brain's opiate receptors, producing a calming effect, explaining why a warm glass of milk might be given to children to help them sleep (p. 25). Reid explains,

> While this peptide-receptor interaction is a normal part of the way the body works, many children with autism seem to be much more dramatically affected by it than the rest of us. In some cases, the peptides may create such a strong reaction in the child's brain that it is difficult for him to focus on things or be entirely aware of her surroundings. Reactions to peptides derived from gluten and casein can also cause severe headaches, prompting some children to engage in head-banging or other harmful behaviors. (Reid, 2004, p. 25)

The use of enzyme supplements has been supported in some preliminary research in that it may help children with autism digest gluten and casein into the same small units needed for absorption, such that the "offending peptides are not formed," inducing almost an immediate alleviation of autism symptoms (Dr. Devin Houston in Reid, 2004, p. 26). Dr. Hovarth and Dr. Papadimitriou at the University of Maryland researched 36 children with ASD, using gastrointestinal endoscopy and biopsy, enzyme analysis, and bacterial cultures (Horvath et al., 1999). They found that children with ASD had Reflux, Chronic Gastritis, Chronic Duotentis, and significantly elevated Pathen's cells as compared to the control group. Similar to the findings of Dr. Buie, they also found that the children had lower enzyme levels and low lactase levels (1999). In one case study, Dr. O'Hara and Dr. Szakas followed a child with PDD-NOS through various stages of enzyme therapy and dietary restriction. At his 1-year follow-up, he was no longer considered to have an ASD (O'Hara & Szakacs, 2008). Taken together, there exists continually emerging literature on the idea of children with autism having a "leaky gut," (D'Eufemia et al., 1996; Reid, 2004), meaning that their stomach lining is more permeable than controls, impairing their ability to break down enzymes properly, and in some cases leading to increased symptom levels in autism.

It is important to note that although support for dietary restrictions or enzyme supplement therapy has been found in these studies (D'Eufemia et al., 1996; Horvath et al., 1999; Reid, 2004; O'Hara & Szacks, 2008; Uhlmann et al., 2002), dietary restriction would only be supported for children who suffer from this "leaky gut" condition. D'Eufemia et al. (1996) indicate that 43 % of children with ASD may have digestive problems; Uhlmann et al. (2002) suggest that 75 of 91 children in the study or 82 % had gut problems, and Author (2005) concluded that 50 % of children with ASD have intestinal permeability. Indeed, the research points to an estimate of 50 % or more children with ASD who could be impacted by digestive problems, "leaky gut" condition, or a difficulty processing certain proteins due to impaired interaction effects between peptides and opiate receptors in the brain.

This means that doctors can and should indeed carefully consider the child's digestion function before prescribing any dietary restrictions or enzyme therapies because in about half of the cases enzymes and digestive problems may not be relevant.

Risk Factors for Autism

Taken together, autism is largely inherited and there are some early genetic markers found in the research that could be implicated. However, the genetic "code" for autism is yet to be identified and this effect is further confounded by the fact that children with the same or similar genes (twins, for example) do not express autism symptoms at the same rate. Epigenetics may be an additional mechanism explaining why some children who are more genetically inclined toward autism may not show signs of autism; as there may be a genetic–environment interaction effect causing the genes to not express. Familial factors, such as paternal age, maternal obesity or metabolic conditions, and having a sibling or parent with autism present additional risk for autism. Dietary factors such as the digestion of enzymes and intestinal permeability may be to blame for autism in roughly half the cases where this "leaky gut" is relevant.

Additionally, pesticides digested by pregnant mothers, such as organophosphates, may increase autism risk in the United States. A commonly used pesticide and weed killer used in U.S. containing a chemical called glyphosate may cause digestive problems and toxicity effects which mirror those seen in autism. The American Psychiatric Association proposes that, "advanced paternal age, low birth weight, or fetal exposure to valproate [medication], may contribute to the risk of autism spectrum disorder" (APA, 2013, p. 56). Although there are no clear answers, families, and particularly pregnant mothers, are wise to consider the environmental impact on risk for autism. It may be important, in many cases, to avoid foods treated with pesticides and other chemicals, particularly if other genetic or familial concerns are present (having a sibling with autism for example). Parents of genetically fragile children might consider the effect of diet, digestion, enzyme absorption, and nutrition on their child's symptoms. It is the author's hope that as continued research on the genetic–environmental interaction is conducted, more and more families will be advised of their risk and provided with much needed answers to prevent autism and to minimize and treat symptoms that arise.

Early Identification Mitigates Autism Risk

Many of the signs of autism are present from an early age, and although sometimes subtle, can be identified during critical phases of development. Symptoms are most often observed at about 24 months of age, but may be seen in children under 12 months if symptoms are severe (APA, 2013). In children under the age of two, parents should note any delay in language or lack of social interest as potential signs. A child who knows the alphabet but does not respond to his or her name, for example, may be showing early signs of autism (APA, 2013). Children who display odd play behaviors such as carrying toys around but not playing with them (APA, 2013); repetitively flipping a doll's eyes, spinning objects, or lacking the ability to play symbolically or imaginatively with toys may be displaying symptoms. Another red flag may be a child with abnormal communication patterns such as grabbing the hand of an adult (APA, 2013) or using an adult's hand as a tool; rather than making appropriate requests. In children aged 18 months to 3 years, the following may be signs of autism:

- Less likely to look at others
- Less likely to show objects to others
- Less likely to point to an object
- Less likely to orient to name
- Less likely to follow attention

These features are not diagnostic; rather, should be seen as markers or red flags that an autism assessment is warranted (Charmain and Baird, 2002; Cox et al., 1999; Osterling and Dawson, 1994; Stone et al., 1999 as cited in Hepburn & Katz, 2009). In addition to these signs, children who appear withdrawn, avoid social interaction, and lack typical play skills should be evaluated if symptoms persist. Children who have meltdowns over changes in routine or sensory defensiveness may be at high risk.

For infants and young toddlers, there are sometimes significant red-flags evident that should not be missed. In the early life, although there is a great deal of variation in development, these features should be considered "absolute indicators" that a developmental assessment is needed:

- No Babbling by 12 months
- No Gesturing by 12 months
- No Single words by 16 months
- No 2 Word Spontaneous Phrases by 24 months
- Any loss of language or social skills at any time

The features listed above are again not diagnostic; however, should be taken seriously and indicate that an assessment is warranted (Johnson & Meyers 2007; Centers for Disease Control and Prevention 2014). In addition to these, parents and clinicians should watch for extreme sensitivity; such as an infant who becomes quickly overwhelmed by mild sensory input. Parents who wonder if the child can hear but the hearing test comes out normal may have a child on the Spectrum. Disturbed patterns of sleeping (Reaven, 2015) and eating are common in autism; although these problems exist with a variety of disorders. A significant early sign of autism is limited joint attention, including failure to follow the pointing or eye gaze of an adult or caregiver (APA, 2013).

The authors of this text are firm believers, as are the majority of professionals in various treatment disciplines, in the importance of early intervention. Given the markers above, parents and clinicians are well advised to take concerns seriously. If these developmental areas do not appear to be on track, it is important to talk to a pediatrician or psychologist, early and often. Sometimes parents are hesitant to get an evaluation in part because there is a slight stigma about the notion that they are in essence "looking for problems" and in that process might stumble upon symptoms that are not truly there. Alternately, parents express that they have been concerned for some time but their pediatricians told them to "wait and see." Unfortunately, if parents do not push past these obstacles, valuable time is wasted. The authors hope that in reading a text of this nature, readers will be clear on the fact that diagnostic tools are sensitive enough not only to determine if there is a diagnosis present, but also to rule out diagnoses and ideally send the client home with a clean bill of health. Of course, sometimes even healthy clients have skills to work on that can be identified during an evaluation. In either case, clients are well-served by a comprehensive evaluation as it provides critical information regarding developmental progress and offers the best potential opportunity for optimal outcomes.

Chapter 3
Optimal Outcomes and Recovery

Abstract There is currently no "cure" for autism; although, treatment technologies are rapidly improving and there are reasons to have hope that children with autism can be alleviated of most of their symptoms and enabled to live fulfilling lives. Although there is some debate over this, research is consistent that some individuals do indeed recover from autism. Recovery means that the individual who once had autism is now able to reach average or better developmental levels. Knowing that this "optimal outcome" is possible, readers are invited to learn about the factors that generally predict such a recovery. Most research indicates intelligence, language skills, early intervention, and certain adaptive personal characteristics as the primary factors in recovery for children on the autism spectrum. Individual factors or intervention alone do not tend to be directly predict ASD symptom severity; rather, there are a specific set of adaptive and personal characteristics that, when present, and combined with best practice treatment, lead to optimal outcomes. Models for fostering optimal outcomes for children with ASD are discussed in this chapter.

Keywords Reaching optimal outcomes in Autism • Recovery rates in ASD • Adaptive skills predict recovery in ASD • Language skills predict recovery in ASD • Intelligence predicts recovery in ASD • Early identification in ASD • Early intervention predicts recovery in ASD • Do people with autism recover? • Severity levels in ASD • Will my child with ASD get better?

There are many well-documented instances where individuals who once had an autism diagnosis no longer meet criteria later in life (Fein et al., 2013; Helt et al., 2008; Kelley et al., 2010; Sutera et al., 2007; Tyson et al., 2014). These instances are referred to as "optimal outcomes" (Hepburn & Katz, 2009; Kelley et al., 2010; Sutera et al., 2007). There is debate about whether or not children can actually "recover" from autism or achieve an optimal outcome (Suh et al., 2014) and the degree to which they reach typical developmental levels. However, most researchers who study autism have found that recovery or optimal outcomes are indeed obtained by many children with autism (Helt et al., 2008; Hepburn & Katz, 2009; Kelley et al., 2010; Sutera et al., 2007; Tyson et al., 2014).

© Springer International Publishing Switzerland 2016

A.P. Kroncke et al., *Assessment of Autism Spectrum Disorder*, Contemporary Issues in Psychological Assessment, DOI 10.1007/978-3-319-25504-0_3

Research reveals that the rate of "recovery" is 3–25 % of individuals diagnosed with ASD (Helt et al., 2008, p. 339) for children who receive effective intervention at an adequate dose. Some researchers have found higher rates of recovery, even over 50 %, with intensive best-practice intervention such as the Early Start Denver Model (Rogers, 2015). This rate varies across studies (Sutera et al., 2007) in part because of the criteria used to define optimal outcomes. Helt et al. (2008) define recovery as (a) a "convincing history of ASD" is present, and (b) "the child must now be learning and applying a set of core skills that reaches the trajectory of typical development in most or all areas" (Helt et al., 2008, p. 340). Optimal outcomes have also been defined thusly, "(1) initially meeting criteria for ASD or PDD-NOS, (2) no longer meeting criteria as determined by experts in ASD, and (3) average skills demonstrated in cognition, language, and adaptive domains" (Sutera et al., 2007, p. 100). Even for children who qualify as recovered, it is commonly seen that approximately 50 % often have persisting psychiatric problems not present in neurotypical peers. For example, ADHD (or subclinical attention problems) (Troyb et al., 2014), depression, anxiety (or subclinical worry), and some odd or atypical social behaviors are common in children who have achieved optimal outcomes (Helt et al., 2008). The research shows that although it was previously thought to be adequate for a child with autism to be integrated into the general education classroom and demonstrate an average IQ, this is now believed to be insufficient to demonstrate the child has moved off of the Spectrum (Kelley et al., 2010, p. 527). Indeed, it is generally believed that the child must reach typical levels of communication, social, and adaptive skills to be considered "recovered" or to have Optimal Outcomes (Helt et al., 2008; Kelley et al., 2010).

What factors lead to optimal outcomes and how do clinicians and parents go about the process of fostering these factors in the children who are capable of making great contributions to our world and are held back by a mix of challenging symptoms? The authors have identified a number of significant factors in autism outcomes, finding the most important to be: intelligence, language skills, early intervention, especially when combined with certain adaptive personal characteristics and behaviors. Most studies show that intervention itself does not predict better outcomes; however, intervention in combination with certain individual factors maximizes outcomes in children on the Spectrum. Fortunately, the individual factors do not tend to be directly related to ASD symptom severity; rather, there are a specific set of adaptive and personal characteristics that, when present, and combined with best practice treatment, lead to optimal outcomes. Functional toy play and the presence of at least a single word in their repertoire (or a word approximation) can be predictive of better outcomes. Individual factors such as early positive social skills in certain areas are strongly related optimal outcomes (Fein et al., 2013). It is promising that some features of autism are not related in the research to outcomes. For example, repetitive behaviors at the time of diagnosis bear no relationship to outcomes later in life (Fein et al., 2013). Thus, even families who may see scarce hope for their child's prospect of recovery are well advised to remember that optimal outcomes do exist. Fortunately,

Fig. 3.1 Primary
predictors of optimal
outcomes

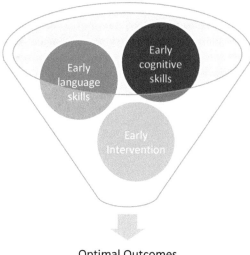

Optimal Outcomes

researchers have made significant progress in outcome research. Below is a description of the three variables the authors find are most significantly associated with optimal outcomes (Fig. 3.1).

Intelligence

One important factor in outcomes (Helt et al., 2008; Stevens et al., 2000), and likely the most important factor, is intelligence. Indeed, a large number of studies have found either IQ and early language or IQ alone to be the most significant factor in outcomes (Schreibman et al., 2011). Bearing in mind that children with autism do not necessarily have cognitive deficits at all, it is important to understand the effect of cognitive ability on later outcomes (31–37 % have intellectual disabilities, 23 % borderline range, 46 % have average or above IQs; Centers for Disease Control and Prevention, p. 6; Trammell et al., 2013). Research generally shows that children with higher IQs tend to respond more readily to treatment (Stevens et al., 2000). It is unknown as to whether the high cognitive ability actually moderates the treatment response, or rather, if cognitive ability alone is a factor in resilience and success in a variety of domains. One treatment utilized for ASD is Cognitive Behavioral Therapy (CBT) which has strong evidence in the literature for treating emotional symptoms, such as anxiety, which are often associated with ASD. Therapeutic outcome in CBT depends to a degree on intelligence (CNNH, 2015; Doubleday et al., 2002). In order to respond to CBT, clients need to be able to consider their own thinking process, evaluate core beliefs, cognitively reframe events, and to respond to feedback. Although some benefit may be achieved at various cognitive levels, treatment outcome is increased for patients with higher cognitive levels and intellectual maturity (CNNH, 2015). Stevens et al. conducted a study on 138 children with autism considering subgroups of the Spectrum and which preschool factors predicted later outcomes. They reported that cognitive ability was perhaps the most significant factor on outcomes, explaining their findings thusly,

"The outcome of cognitive status are far reaching, as outcome seems to depend significantly on cognitive ability. Although it has been shown that aggressive early intervention can circumvent some of the abnormalities of autistic children, it is not currently known whether IQ itself can be influenced by therapies that capitalize on existing cognitive strengths for treatment." (Stevens et al., 2000, p. 351).

Thus, intelligence seems to play a significant role in response to treatment because children with greater cognitive capacity are more capable of responding to certain types of therapeutic interventions. Helt et al. explain the relationship between treatment, IQ, and optimal outcomes, "All of the children in the studies that reported participants with optimal outcome were receiving some level of treatment and thus it is possible that the treatment, in combination with the potential for normal levels of cognition, was responsible for their improvements" (Helt et al., 2008, p. 349). Thus, it is not clear whether the treatment or the IQ or both are the primary factor in optimal outcomes. It has also been discovered that effective treatment in children with autism actually increases IQ scores (Rogers, 2015).

There is often found in longitudinal research an effect referred to as "catch-up intellectual development," in the ASD population, meaning that many children with ASD have lower IQ scores in preschool, particularly in language development, tend to show improved abilities in elementary school (Dietz et al., 2007; Mayes & Calhoun, 2003). This raise in IQ shares a complex relationship with IQ; often, a raise in IQ occurs regardless of the amount or type of treatment. However, as previously discussed, best practice treatment tends to influence IQ and generally IQ is one of the factors considered as an outcome measure when a child is said to have "recovered" from autism. This means that intelligence does show some plasticity in the ASD population, which is a good sign for children who may show some early cognitive delays. Thus, IQ shares a cyclical relationship with IQ in that intelligence impacts the treatment effects and adequate treatment may increase IQ. Taken together, research points to the notion that children with higher IQs who receive effective intervention tend to have the best outcomes.

A further model to understand the potential for children with various IQ levels and autism to achieve optimal outcomes is to see autism symptoms and intelligence on a continuum (see Fig. 3.2).

This model intends to highlight that children in the Low IQ and High Symptoms group have a poorer prognosis than other groups. However, other combinations such as Low IQ and Low Symptom Levels or High Symptom Levels and High IQ would show more variation in treatment outcomes. This model highlights the importance of the fact that autism falls on a continuum, a "spectrum," and that each child's strengths are unique. It takes into account the fact that although early symptom levels may appear to be the primary indicator of later success, the research points to the idea autism symptoms alone are not necessarily predictive of later outcomes.

Fig. 3.2 Orthogonal
model of symptom severity

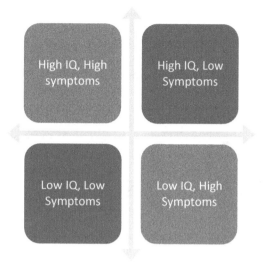

Rather, individual factors including IQ, language, and certain early social skills tend to have a complex and dynamic relationship with symptom levels and optimal outcomes.

Intelligence is inversely related to the age of diagnosis, which in itself plays a negative role in optimal outcomes. That is, children who are intelligent are often diagnosed later (Mayes & Calhoun, 2003), because higher IQ may mask symptoms in younger children. This later diagnosis factor unfortunately leads to later diagnosis and later intervention. Sometimes, patterns of rigidity and poor reciprocity are resistant to treatment in children who are diagnosed later. There is some evidence that a more even cognitive profile leads to better outcomes; children with a greater discrepancy between nonverbal and verbal IQ scores show poorer social skills later in childhood (Joseph et al., 2002). However, the fact that children with higher IQs are more responsive to treatment can moderate that effect and provide an opportunity for better outcomes. Overall, research in resiliency and response to treatment shows a positive effect of IQ as a significant factor in optimal outcomes.

Language Skills

Optimal outcomes for children with autism are linked in the research to children with strong language skills. The fact that language is a significant factor is not surprising as a language delay or communication deficit has always been a defining feature of the disorder (APA, 2000a, 2000b). One of the authors of this text found in a large-scale study ($N=272$) over 15 years at the University of Texas that the percentage of variance (r^2) of IQ accounted for by language was 27 % in the ASD population (without significant intervention) (Huckabee, 2003). Language alone or language combined with IQ is generally considered the best predictor of outcomes (Sutera et al., 2007, p. 100, Schreibman et al., 2011, p. 295). Indeed, researchers claim, "Early language ability and cognitive ability have emerged as the most robust predictors of overall prognosis for autism during childhood, adolescence and adulthood" (Schreibman et al., 2011, p. 295). Thus, most researchers who study the outcomes of children on the Spectrum believe that language is a significant factor. It is a factor in two ways. First, children with better language skills in certain areas tend to have better outcomes later in life because language in itself is a resilience factor, and because early language often predicts better language acquisition developmentally as language abilities have a cumulative "building" effect over time. Second, when studying children with optimal outcomes, researchers tend to find that one of the major differences between the optimal outcome group and the typically developing group is language skills. Generally, high functioning children, typically developing children, and children with optimal outcomes, all tend to have generally average language skills rather than significant language deficits. However, the type of skills can be differentiated by group. Premier optimal outcome researchers describe it thusly,

> Employing an extensive language evaluation we found that standard scores on language tasks were all in the normal range but probing with more complex language and social cognitive tasks such as comprehension of second order theory of mind and mental state verbs, ability to construct narratives, and ability to reason inductively about animate things, still showed residual difficulties (Sutera et al., 2007, p. 99).

Thus, in children with autism who achieve optimal outcomes, it is commonly found that although their language skills may move into the average range, complex language skills may be "residually" impaired (Sutera et al., 2007, p. 99). Abstract, metaphorical, emotional content, and pragmatic language skills tend to be weak areas in ASD.

It has oft been found that children with autism have significant weaknesses in narrative coherence (storytelling) in spite of average IQ scores (Losh & Capps, 2003; Suh et al., 2014; Willard, 2013). Children with optimal outcomes are more likely to use overly formal language, scripted speech, or unusual references to TV shows and movies than typically developing children, in their storytelling (Suh et al., 2014). When telling a story, children with optimal outcomes are able to include as many story elements as typical children, whereas children with High Functioning Autism produce significantly fewer (Suh et al., 2014). Taken together, although children with optimal outcomes in general have language skills in the average range, there are residual factors often present in their language production; one of the most significant of these is impaired narrative coherence. However, even while evidencing these somewhat subtle residual language differences in children with optimal outcomes, it is important to understand that strong language development, especially when combined with average or high IQ scores, tends to strongly predict better outcomes in children with autism.

Early Intervention

Early intervention shows a promising correlation with optimal outcomes. Early intervention is defined as treatment that begins by the age of two or three, and continues for a minimum of 2–4 years. In fact, "Autism experts agree that early behavioral intervention is crucial to maximizing outcomes" (Schreibman et al., 2011, p. 297). Hence in Autism, as with other disorders like Reading Disorder, there appears to be a critical window during which effective intervention at an adequate dose must occur in order to capitalize on limited neurodevelopmental opportunities. Rogers (2015) reports that behavioral treatment and the learning opportunities therein change the brain: the brain wiring, brain functioning, and brain structure. She states (regarding language, intelligence, and adaptive skills), "these are flexible skills and they are built on learning opportunities." Thus, although there are a variety of factors that impact outcomes for autism, and even though there is vast disagreement about the types and dosage of treatment that is best, people who know autism almost exclusively believe in early intervention. Schreibman et al. explain, "The results of a growing amount of research show that with early behavioral intervention a large number of children with autism show substantial improvement... The finding that early intervention can make a significant difference in treatment outcome presents us with an opportunity to greatly improve the overall positive outcome rate for these children" (Schreibman et al., 2009, p. 163). Kelley, Naigles, and Fein (2010) studied a group of 13 children with Optimal Outcomes (OO), 14 children who are typically developing (TD), and 14 children who still retained their ASD diagnosis (HFA), 8 years after their original diagnosis. They found that early diagnosis and early intensive intervention predicted optimal outcomes. Unfortunately, even though treatment is a factor in outcomes, effective intervention alone does NOT predict optimal outcomes (Sutera et al., 2007, p. 99). Most studies show that instead, treatment is important in concert with positive characteristics within the child such as early language, joint attention, the amount of intervention (Sutera et al., 2007), and intelligence (Helt et al., 2008).

Many studies have examined treatment as a predictor of better outcomes, finding that although the precise amount of treatment needed is unclear, children who achieved better outcomes received 40+ h more per month of therapy, compared to controls who did not achieve the same positive outcome from treatment (Helt et al., 2008). However, other researchers including Sally Rogers's colleagues have found that even 15 h per week of early intervention can create optimal outcomes (Rogers, 2015). Isabell Smith of the Halifax research group has an impressive body of research to show that treatment (even at 15 h per week) in a community setting can have significant impact on outcomes. Unfortunately, this is a hard number to verify in the broader community because children with more treatment hours tend to be more impaired in the first place, confounding the effect of treatment as a variable in outcomes (2008). Most research verifies behavioral treatment as efficacious for autism (Schreibman et al., 2009). There are several unique manualized interventions with evidenced positive outcomes. For example, Pivotal Response training, Early Start Denver Model, and TEACCH are generally found to show promise in treatment of core autism symptoms (Schreibman et al., 2009). Taken together, research is pointing to early effective intervention as a significant factor in treatment. However, larger scale parametric studies need to be done in order to show the relative contribution of treatment to further optimize outcomes.

Another important consideration when evaluating whether or not treatment is a significant factor in optimal outcomes is looking at epigenetic factors and the degree to which certain symptoms of autism tend not to develop at all in response to early intervention. That is, it is possible that treatment actually changes the brain's structure and the capacity for the child to develop stronger social skills due to changes impacting the neuronal connections, pruning process, and the longer-range social-cognitive intellectual development. Day & Sweatt (2011) provide research to show that epigenetic factors change the way the brain is formed and moderate the treatment response. They explain, "We discuss evidence for an 'epigenetic code' in the central nervous system that mediates synaptic plasticity, learning, and memory" (p. 812). This means that the cognitive and behavioral memories and patterns may actually lead to permanent improvement in brain functioning and indeed impact the child's potential for positive outcomes. Fein et al. (2013) explain this phenomenon, "A pressing theoretical question is to what extent brain structure and function have normalized in the OO children. It is possible that effective early intervention plus maturation have resulted in normalization of the pathways and functions or even anatomical structure" (Fein et al., 2013, p. 203). Sally Rogers (2015) tells us that recovery is an expected outcome and that indeed the reason for people to believe in best outcomes rests on high quality intervention. This research lends strong support to the idea that even if the child is genetically predisposed to have certain features of autism, and even if the symptoms appear pervasive and significant, early intervention could change the child's brain and the resultant potential for optimal outcomes.

A word on personal factors: As noted throughout this discussion on optimal outcomes, most of the research points to the notion that certain predictive factors, such as high IQ, solid language skills, or early intervention, may not alone predict best outcomes. Rather, these positive factors when combined with resilient personal characteristics and personality traits predict best outcomes in children on the Spectrum. As such, it is interesting to consider which personal factors are most indicative of maximal opportunities for children on the spectrum to achieve recovery or optimal outcomes. One such concept is put forth by Hepburn and Katz (2009) and illuminated in Fig. 3.3, below.

As noted in this graphic, autism's core feature is "qualitative impairment in social communication." This means that children with autism have a core deficit in their ability to understand and relate to peers socially, to communicate their feelings and needs with others, and to socially reciprocate in conversations and play. This often manifests into difficulty making and maintaining friendships and tends to interfere with participation in school or community activities. However, children with autism may not suffer as much from these symptoms due to the "moderating

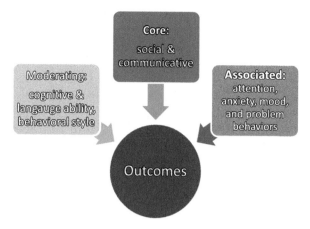

Fig. 3.3 Core, moderating, and associated features model of outcomes

features" such as higher cognitive ability, stronger language skills, or a more *adaptive behavioral style (see next section)*. Alternately, symptoms may indeed appear more significant and pervasive due to "associated features," which are not symptoms of autism but tend to commonly co-occur with an autism diagnosis. These are emotional conditions such as anxiety and depression, extreme difficulties with attention and impulsivity, and challenging behaviors. Positive personal factors such as high IQ, strong language skills, adaptive behavior, and emotional health tend to lead to optimal outcomes, especially when combined with effective early intervention.

Adaptive Behaviors

A personal factor mentioned in the model above is "behavioral style." Many children with autism symptoms also have significant maladaptive behaviors. Maladaptive behavior patterns such as aggression, outbursts or meltdowns, and conduct problems interfere with their relationships and functioning. This is one of the reasons why behavioral approaches are often critical for children on the Spectrum. Early behavioral intervention in the toddler and preschool years can reverse negative patterns such that they do not become somewhat "hardwired" and continue to cause struggles socially, academically, and in treatment.

One way parents can promote positive behavior is through the requirement that children do chores. Simplistic as it sounds, children who are required to do daily chores have greater success in life, whether or not they have disabilities. Psychologists measure a child's positive developmental behaviors as a part of any thorough diagnostic assessment, terming them, "Activities of Daily Living" or "ADLs." Adaptive behavior is often considered a significant factor in optimal outcomes.

Activities of Daily Living (ADLs) include *self-care* skills like self-dressing, toileting, and brushing teeth; *community living skills* like crossing the street safely, taking care around strangers, and alerting an adult of dangers in the environment; and *domestic skills* such as picking up toys, sweeping, or clearing the dinner table. Interestingly, scores on measures such as the Vineland these ADLs are often found more important in predicting positive outcomes than the level of symptoms found on an ADOS (Autism Diagnostic Observation Schedule) (Helt et al., 2008; Klin et al., 2007; Sutera et al., 2007). This means that it matters more whether or not children have basic life skills than it does if they have significant autism symptoms (poor social reciprocity, repetitive behaviors, and restricted interests).

One measure of ADLs in younger children is motor skills, both gross and fine motor, which are included on the Vineland Scales of Adaptive Behavior (Sparrow, 2005/2006/2008). Sutera et al. (2007) found that strong motor skills at the age of two on the Vineland were the most significant factor in predicting optimal outcomes (Sutera et al., 2007, p. 98). Looking at individual items on the Vineland, Sutera et al. found that with a stringent alpha level only two items were significant in differentiating children who obtain optimal outcomes from those who do not at the preschool level. These items are: opening doors by turning door knobs and helping with chores. With a less stringent alpha level, children who could listen to a story for more than 5 min, bathe themselves with some assistance, help with extra chores when asked, and show a desire to please their caregiver (Sutera et al., 2007, p. 104) had a greater potential for optimal outcomes. Stevens et al. (2000) found that nonverbal IQ, receptive language, and adaptive functioning were the most important factors in outcomes. This research is somewhat encouraging in that ADLs are life skills that can be taught to individuals of various ages and abilities, as opposed to treating symptoms, which is more complex to identify and treat.

Taken together, although autism is a serious and often pervasive, long-term neurological disorder, optimal outcomes and recovery are possible. Factors that predict optimal outcomes are intelligence, language ability, early intervention, and individual characteristics (including behavioral style). Research shows that although early intervention is critical and may actually have a direct effect on gene expression and structural brain changes, early intervention alone does not directly predict best outcomes. Rather, effective early intervention for children with the other factors in place, such as intelligence, adequate language ability, and resilient personality traits, leads to the best outcomes. It may be that in the decades to come, specifically prescribed treatments for the various types of autism, considering individual characteristics, outcome factors such as IQ and language, and symptom severity, could be provided such that the rates of optimal outcomes will continue to increase.

Neurodiversity and Strength-Based ASD Models

The new "neurodiversity" model sees autism as a different way of thinking, worthy of celebration in its own right, not a malady to be cured (Solomon, 2012). This term was founded by Judy Singer, a sociologist who is on the Spectrum. Her own mother and child share an ASD diagnosis as well. She explains, "I was interested in the liberatory activist aspects of it—to do for people who were neurologically different what feminism and gay rights had done for their constituencies" (Solomon, 2012, p. 278). The foundations of the neurodiversity movement rest in the notion that "curing" autism may be in fact only an attempt to eradicate the unique aspects of their diagnosed condition that, while different than the norm, are valuable and intrinsically rewarding. Further, some significant figures in the ASD community such as John Elder Robison claim that his specialized skills are somehow dulled or limited when he focuses attention on developing similar social skills to neurotypicals. Camille Clark, once known for her blog as the Autism Diva, explains, Parents shouldn't expect that their kid is ever going to be "normal." Autistic people are value as they are. They don't have value only if they can be transformed into less obviously autistic people (Solomon, 2012, p. 279). There are many opponents to neurodiversity, as well, concerned parties feel the neurodiversity movement vastly underestimates the debilitating aspects and sells short the message that research and treatment efforts are needed (Solomon, 2012, p. 279).

In the author's view, neither way of viewing autism is dismissible. Rather, symptoms should only be viewed as problematic enough to require treatment when they "get in the way" of a major life activity or interfere with the individuals obtainment of personal goals and objectives. Thus, each individual with autism has symptoms, but also individuality and uniqueness which are to be respected and valued. There is an ethical requirement in the psychology field for clients (even young children) to maintain their autonomy and for the psychologist to serve as an agent of support so that clients can utilize their talents to pursue their own dreams and live happy, productive, and fulfilling lives, on their time and on their own terms.

The idea of "growing from strengths" is promoted by a popular figure in the autism community, Temple Grandin, and by the school that bears her name in Boulder Colorado, The Temple Grandin School. The school's founder and director, Jennifer Wilger jests that Temple Grandin is constantly pressing her staff to "make sure these kids get to work…get them jobs." Although this advice is easier understood than implemented, Grandin's model for success is very much in line with the evidence shown in the aforementioned studies revealing ADLs as a critical ingredient for success, rather than alleviation of symptoms. Grandin has built her own career by utilizing her passion and specialized understanding of animals in the cattle and livestock industry to develop more humane practices. In keeping with that philosophy, the Temple Grandin School approaches autism from a strength-based perspective. Their educational philosophy involves "rethinking" each child's strengths as opportunities for education, enrichment, and a brighter future (See Case Study, Chap. 9: Judy). Models such as this one at the Temple Grandin School are finding a great deal of success for children with higher functioning autism. These gains are due to not only sound educational practices but also developing a community of like-minded individuals who are working hard to live with their disabilities and become well-educated and productive members of society.

Chapter 4
Autism in the DSM-5

Abstract Clinical assessment is crucial for it is not only about diagnosis, but also a guide regarding treatment and prognosis. Classification is an important tool for communication between researchers, clinicians, and policy makers to ensure that they are referring to the same features, symptoms, and traits, when making a diagnosis (J Child Psychol Psychiatry 52(6):647–660, 2011a; J Autism Dev Disord 41(4):395–404, 2011b). Planning for the Diagnostic and Statistical Manual, Fifth Edition, (DSM-5) began in 2003 and included a series of conferences and work groups with experts from many disciplines and from locations all around the world. In his research review written in 2011, Rutter notes that a better attempt was made to review the science for DSM-5 than for DSM-IV or ICD 10. This review focuses only on one aspect of DSM-5, the diagnosis of ASDs. Rutter cites that subcategories of ASD "manifestly do not work" and argues for their elimination. Much research was reviewed in writing this text citing a substantial body of evidence that Asperger's and Autism are not qualitatively distinct; rather different quantitative manifestations of the same disorder (J Autism Dev Disord 40(8): 921–929, 2010; J Child Psychol Psychiatry 40(2): 219–226, 1999; J Autism Dev Disord 34(4): 367–378, 2004; J Am Acad Child Adolesc Psychiatry 37(3): 271–277, 1998). This chapter examines the new severity classifications for diagnosing ASD which are different from the previous classification of Autism versus Asperger's Disorder. The new criteria introduced in DSM-5 for identifying Social (Pragmatic) Communication Disorder is included in this chapter as well. Diagnostic criteria for ASD, including severity levels on a continuum of cognitive, language, and other skills, are discussed.

Keywords ASD in the DSM-5 • Severity levels in ASD • Cognitive impairments in ASD • Social impairments in ASD • Social Communication Disorder vs. ASD • What happened to Asperger's? • Can you keep your Asperger's diagnosis? • Diagnosing autism today

Studies on the diagnostic criteria for separate conditions along the Autism Spectrum date back to the late 1990s, suggesting that researchers have been considering whether or not to segment the Spectrum in this way for some time. This research is consistent with Rutter's argument to eliminate subcategories, which the DSM-5

© Springer International Publishing Switzerland 2016   35
A.P. Kroncke et al., *Assessment of Autism Spectrum Disorder*, Contemporary
Issues in Psychological Assessment, DOI 10.1007/978-3-319-25504-0_4

subcommittee did in 2013. Szatmari's et al. (2009) for a lack of structural language impairment being the differentiating factor in Asperger's and Tsai's argument that PDD-NOS is distinctly different from Autism do argue against such a change, but seem to be in the minority. Some researchers in 2014 argue for an even broader categorization under neurodevelopmental disabilities because of the vast heterogeneity within Autism Spectrum Disorders. While this may work on some level, we need diagnosis to inform treatment and in order for third party payers to cover a portion of treatment cost. The steps DSM-5 takes to align diagnosis with the research seem to be appropriate. As clinicians become more familiar and learn to apply the new criteria appropriately, less controversy will remain. The International Meeting for Autism Research (IMFAR) is evidence of this phenomenon as the discussion of DSM-5 was minimal at IMFAR 2014 and much more prominent 2 years earlier in 2012. Volkmar, Klin, and McPartland (2014) argue that research and practice would benefit most if within this overarching category of "autisms" homogeneous subtypes of the disorder could be identified (p. 28 Eds. Volkmar et al., 2014). For now the authors remind us that DSM-5 states that those who met criteria under DSM-IV should continue to maintain the diagnosis and receive services (American Psychiatric Association, 2013).

Changes in Diagnostic Criteria: Pervasive Developmental Disorders to Autism Spectrum Disorder

First, discussion will focus on what seems to be the less controversial change in DSM-5 classification of ASD and is related to the factor structure and symptoms required to make a diagnosis. The DSM-5, released in 2013, includes a two-factor structure for identification of an Autism Spectrum Disorder instead of the three-factor structure included in DSM-IV-TR. The DSM-5 (2013) criterion A (first factor) states that social communication and social interaction deficits across multiple contexts must be present noting that the three criteria are "illustrative not exhaustive" and include deficits in social emotional reciprocity, nonverbal communicative behaviors, and in developing, maintaining, and understanding relationships. The second factor, criterion B, is restricted or repetitive patterns of behavior, interests, or activities noting that two of four criteria need be met. These include repetitive or stereotyped movements, insistence on sameness and routine, restricted and fixated interests, and hyper or hypo-reactivity to sensory input. Symptoms must be present in early development, though they may not be obvious until social demands increase. Finally, like all DSM diagnoses, symptoms must cause clinically significant impairment in functioning. In DSM-5, the social and communication domains become one factor, while these domains were two different factors in DSM-IV-TR. This change is supported by many research studies with factor analytic data showing that this improves the model (Mandy, Charman, & Skuse, 2012; Rutter, 2011a, 2011b). Additionally, severity scales and specifiers allow the clinician to provide more information on co-occurring conditions and level of symptom severity (and these will be discussed later in the review).

The more controversial change in DSM-5, as mentioned in the introduction, has to do not with factor structure, but with combining the PDDs into one ASD. DSM-IV-TR provided five diagnoses falling under Pervasive Developmental Disorders including Autistic Disorder, Asperger's Disorder, Pervasive Developmental Disorder- Not Otherwise Specified, Childhood Disintegrative Disorder, and Rett's Syndrome. Ongoing research on these different PDDs allowed the team of experts on the DSM-5 subcommittee to determine that one diagnosis would better conceptualize Autism Spectrum Disorder and in fact the differences in Autism/Asperger's/PDD-NOS came down more to clinical preference/familiarity than actual differences in disorder. As Sally Ozonoff, author and expert Autism researcher and clinician, noted in her editorial on DSM-5 (Ozonoff, 2012) the changes have empirical basis from extensive literature reviews and data analysis and are not "capricious or arbitrary." Dr. Ozonoff shared that the concept "Autism Spectrum Disorders" came about in a 1991 article by Happe and Frith. From the early 90s, studies on the difference between Autism and Asperger's failed to find empirical differences between the diagnoses (Frith 2004) and in fact differences were quantitative (Prior et al, 1998).

The degree of impairment, severity of symptoms, and level of cognitive functioning were the most common differences between Asperger's and autism leading to a dimensional classification removing subcategories (Eaves & Ho, 2004; Kamp-Becker et al., 2010; Prior et al., 1998; Stone et al., 1999; Tanguay, Robertson, & Derrick, 1998; Volkmar et al. 1994). Lord and Jones (2012) wrote that individuals receive diagnoses of autism, Asperger's, and PDDNOS based on knowledge and biases of the clinician. If these are indeed on a severity continuum, it is logical to use one label. Rett's Syndrome now has a known genetic cause, thus it is recognizable on a genetic level and no longer falls under ASD. As early as 1998, Volkmar discusses Rett's inclusion in the neurological section. Researchers argue that little is known about Childhood Disintegrative Disorder to determine its relation to the rest of the Spectrum and it has a different outcome than Autism (Volkmar, 1998). As for the other disorders on the Spectrum evidence supports the "broader phenotype" of Autism (Bailey et al. 1998; Rutter, 2011a, 2011b; Yirmiya & Chairman 2010), the DSM-5 purports to include all those with clinically sound diagnoses under the new diagnosis ASD.

While individuals on the Spectrum have reported to the authors of this text that "Asperger's" the word and the label is important as a piece of their identity, the research does support DSM-5's attempt to combine dimensional and categorical models (Rutter, 2011a, 2011b). Encouraging clients to continue to use Asperger's as a part of their identity, even when ASD is the diagnostic label, can help with discontent regarding the change. Let us recall that individuals with ASDs do not always adapt well to change. Helping clients understand that they are still "Aspies" may be helpful in some cases. Diagnostically, Asperger's is subsumed on the Spectrum, but this does not mean that individuals should feel the need to give up the term "Aspie." Rutter suggests that some individuals with Asperger's do not view themselves as having a "disorder," and when coping well, intervention may not be needed. He offers the title "Autism Spectrum Patterns" to include these individuals. Further investigation of research on DSM-5 and the continued "controversy" follows.

Controversies Surrounding DSM-5

As the Autism community waited for the release of DSM-5 in 2013, many articles were published in mainstream newspapers and magazines discussing the fear that changes in DSM criteria for Autism would lead to different diagnoses and in some cases a loss of services for those who previously met criteria for one of the Autism Spectrum Disorders (Autistic Disorder, Asperger's Disorder, Pervasive Developmental Disorder- Not Otherwise Specified, Childhood Disintegrative Disorder, Rett's Syndrome). Papers were published noting the proposed changes confusing and poorly justified (Ghaziuddin, 2011). A literature review by Kulage, Smaldone, and Cohn (2014)) reported that out of 14 studies reviewed, more than 7 demonstrated reduction rates in diagnosis from 25 to 68 % when using DSM-5 criteria. Four studies included those with Asperger's diagnoses and while a reduction in diagnosis was noted, it was not significant (Kulage et al., 2014). Kulage et al. conclude that the DSM-5 should establish a "gold standard" for diagnosis and criteria thresholds for receipt of services may have most implications for those formerly captured by the PDDNOS diagnostic label. The authors of this book believe that the "gold standard" is achieved when expert clinicians use appropriate diagnostic tools and evaluate comprehensively. Stone et al. (1999) agrees that "extensive experience" improves diagnostic clarification. Structured interviews as well as observations are very important in research (Rutter, 2011a, 2011b) and it is a loss to exclude one or the other.

Other research reports that DSM-5 can lead to as sensitive and specific of a diagnosis as the DSM-IV-TR (Kent et al., 2013). The majority of studies reviewed the DSM-5 criteria; one by Kent et al. (a paper including researchers Ann LeCouteur and Lorna Wing) reported either good sensitivity or good specificity (only one study reported both). One purported reason for inconsistencies was that data in all studies was collected according to DSM-IV-TR. Kent et al. used the Diagnostic Interview for Social and Communication Disorders (DISCO) developed by Wing and Gould, a semi-structured interview measure with solid reliability and validity. The study suggests that DSM-5 can achieve both sensitivity and specificity. The sensitivity was lower than specificity, particularly for PDDNOS, but authors found that by relaxing thresholds increased sensitivity could be achieved without hurting the improved specificity of DSM-5 over DSM-IV. Kent et al. additionally suggests careful consideration of all symptom information to increase sensitivity of the criteria. This research group continues to collect data on use of the DISCO to assess Autism Symptoms using DSM-5 and the data as of 2014 continues to be very promising with regard to DSM-5 diagnosis (IMFAR presentation "In search of Essential Behaviours for Diagnosis" Leekam et al.). This research is consistent with the viewpoint of the authors of this text and points to a need for expert assessment and diagnosis.

Wing et al. (2011) explored the degree to which the newest version of the DSM V covers all of the important issues in autism, finding it lacking regarding diagnosing infants and adults, and the unique presentation in girls (Wing, Gould, & Gillberg, 2011).

The authors on this text agree that diagnosis across the lifespan requires specific expertise beyond what is readily available in terms of diagnostic criteria and updated research. Thus, the book has been developed to guide clinicians through a practical and clear approach from the time of the referral to an accurate diagnosis; as well as, to rule out or dually diagnose other conditions during an autism evaluation.

Another group of researchers, Huerta et al., used the ADI-R and ADOS to compare to DSM-5 criteria. The clinical diagnoses were determined by experienced psychologists and psychiatrists using DSM-5 criteria. Using over 4000 children who received DSM-IV diagnoses of PDDs, they found that 91 % continued to have an ASD diagnosis on DSM-5. The adequate sensitivity of diagnosis came across all groups including young children, girls, and cognitively "higher functioning" individuals. Researchers note that most children previously diagnosed would continue to be diagnosed and the specificity of diagnosis is improved (over DSM-IV-TR) particularly taking both clinical and parent report data into account (Huerta, Bishop, Duncan, Hus, & Lord, 2012). This study went on to examine the individuals who did not continue to meet criteria for a DSM-5 diagnosis. Those who did not meet did not demonstrate the required impairments in social and communication functioning and most did meet for restricted and repetitive behaviors (Huerta et al., 2012). The study showed that criteria A1 and A3 were most challenging to interpret and assign items effectively. This data was provided to the DSM-5 subcommittee as they refined the wording of the diagnostic criteria before DSM-5 was published.

In an editorial response to this article by Tsai and Ghaziuddin, researchers conclude from literature review that PDDNOS is qualitatively and quantitatively different from autism and thus cannot lie on a continuum (Tsai & Ghaziuddin, 2014). This is not consistent with the research cited above noting that severity of symptoms differentiates the diagnoses of Asperger's, PDD, and Autism—indicating that a dimensional model removing subcategories works best. Further review of the literature supports the idea that Asperger's is not distinct from Autism beyond severity, IQ, and language differences. Research on PDDNOS emphasizes that it is different only in that it is less severe than Autism and over time individuals may switch back and forth from classification of Autism to PDDNOS. Eaves and Ho (2004) go on to state that PDDNOS is less stable and "not well defined." The debate continued on; however, the research was leaning heavily toward support of a severity model, rather than diagnosing separate and distinct disorders along the Spectrum.

A study by Young and Rodi (2014) included psychologists, speech pathologists, and teams including both and utilized DSM-5 criteria to reassess and confirm diagnoses. This study found high specificity and low sensitivity. It is noted that one difference between Huerta et al. and Young & Rodi is the use of "experienced psychologists and psychiatrists" versus "psychologists and speech pathologists and teams of both trained in the ADI-R." As noted earlier in the text, a speech pathologist is not trained to independently diagnose an autism Spectrum disorder. However, of course, speech pathologists are often critical members of the diagnostic team, providing necessary insights about language discrepancies and delays that are part of diagnostic decision making. The article concludes that perhaps the diagnosticians were "too stringent" in applying criteria and appropriate training is important to ensure consistency in DSM-5 application (Young & Rodi, 2014).

Articles focused on the loss of diagnosis seem to focus most on the PDD-NOS classification, which in DSM-IV-TR was assigned when an individual did not meet full criteria for another Pervasive Developmental Disorder including Autism and Asperger's. The DSM-5 states on p. 51 "Individuals with well-established DSM-IV diagnoses of autistic disorder, Asperger's Disorder or pervasive developmental disorder not otherwise specified should be given the diagnosis of autism Spectrum disorder." This statement appears to protect individuals from losing services they have been legitimately receiving. One article by Kent et al. states that sensitivity of the DSM-5 criteria could be improved by "relaxing" the standards and using sound clinical judgment when interpreting the "illustrative not exhaustive" criteria. This is echoed in Young & Rodi discussed above (2014). The authors of this text would agree that sound clinical experience and expertise in diagnosing and treating autism Spectrum disorders is crucial. The authors have not yet encountered a case for which the DSM-5 criteria changed or removed a diagnosis of an Autism Spectrum Disorder.

Examining factor structure, studies show that a two-factor structure has better psychometric data to support it than the three-factor structure did (Mandy et al., 2012). Mandy, Charman, and Skuse used confirmatory factor analysis on a sample size of 708 verbal children with mild to severe challenges to test the factor structure comparing DSM-IV to DSM-5. They found the DSM-5 to be superior with the removal of items measuring "play and imagination" and "stereotyped and repetitive use of language." The addition of a scale measuring sensory abnormalities also loaded well onto the restricted repetitive behavior factor. These researchers concluded that "the autism phenotype is inadequately described by DSM-IV-TR criteria, and that the proposed autism dyad of DSM-5 has greater validity, with the core impairments of ASD being manifestations of separable social communication and RRB dimensions (2012)."

Studies cite that the challenge in meeting both criteria for DSM-5 is in criterion A for social communication and social interaction, while most participants in studies have continued to meet criterion B for restricted repetitive patterns of behavior, interests, or activities. Under criterion A, Huerta et al. note that deficits in nonverbal communicative behaviors (criterion A3) are the most challenging to meet. Some of the challenges may be in the need to subtly assess symptoms in this domain. Just because an individual makes eye contact or uses gestures does not mean that he or she integrates nonverbal communication appropriately. This is an example of an area where experienced, expert clinicians can better assess symptoms to determine whether these impairments are evident and are significant.

Indicating Cognitive or Language Impairments

Looking further at the differences in DSM-5 classification of ASD versus DSM-IV-TR brings our discussion to the indication of cognitive and/or language impairments. The purpose of this addition to DSM-5 seems to be a clearer indication of severity of symptoms as most mental disorders are dimensional in their operation (Rutter, 2011a, 2011b). As in the medical community severity is noted in the degree of malignancy in a tumor, Michael Rutter (2011a, 2011b)) argues that denoting severity in diagnosis lends to a true picture of the clinical presentation for treatment. This approach reflects a combination of categorical and dimensional classification which is normal in most areas of medicine.

While DSM-5 does not specifically state cut scores or explain how to determine these skills in the context of a scattered profile, it does state this: "Regarding the specifier 'with or without accompanying intellectual impairment' understanding the (often uneven) intellectual profile of a child or adult with autism Spectrum disorder is necessary for interpreting diagnostic features. Separate estimates of verbal and nonverbal skills are necessary." It appears that the DSM-5 subcommittee defers to sound clinical judgment and interpretation by expert clinicians qualified to assess for ASDs to make these distinctions. This is true for both cognitive and language assessment. The authors of this text have found that using specific wording and qualifying statements, for example "Without cognitive impairment, with language impairments in the area of pragmatic language, speaks in full sentences," gives a clear picture of an individual's level of functioning.

One question that arises is related to indicating cognitive functioning for a very young child. Consider the profile of a young child, under age three, with a cognitive profile on the Mullen scales, DAS preschool, or WPPSI that falls around a standard score of 80 with various skills falling within the Average range and other skills Below Average. Taking into account that cognitive abilities are far from stable at age three and that behavioral compliance can be an issue in untreated Autism Spectrum Disorders, what is the level of cognitive "impairment"? For this, clinician thoughts turn to parents of a young child already faced with a diagnosis that is challenging to process and understand. Is it clinically indicated to report cognitive impairment when these scores in young children can be variable? It is known that cognitive ability tends to stabilize in children at approximately age seven, with more variability in the population of children diagnosed with Autism. Clinically, it is best practice to provide a more specific statement "without cognitive impairment in verbal abilities, with cognitive impairment in the area of nonverbal reasoning." The DSM-5 encourages assessing and describing functioning in a thorough manner for both cognitive and language skills. For example, considering expressive and receptive language separately and commenting on both or using untimed nonverbal tests to assess cognitive ability in this domain separately from verbal ability assessment. The DSM-5 leaves much to the clinician which may lead to different interpretations as to how to specify the diagnosis. For this reason, the final diagnosis may be confusing to an untrained clinician, teacher, or parent. It is the responsibility of the clinician to explain the diagnosis thoroughly and clearly to parents in the feedback session so that individuals are not confused about a diagnosis and what it means. This will be especially crucial now, as criteria is new and the final date to shift from DSM-IV-TR to DSM-5 for all settings was October 1, 2014. There continues to be some resistance even after this date has passed, but most settings have adopted the DSM-5 as this book is submitted for publication.

Another important point noted in DSM-5 is that severity may fluctuate across contexts and time. It should not be used to determine provision of services. "Services can only be developed at an individual level and through discussion of personal priorities and targets." This is also essential for service providers to understand. It would not be appropriate to determine services based on such a variable specifier that leaves much to clinical judgment. DSM-5 as a whole removes the Global Assessment of Functioning (GAF) for this reason, noting that it was too subjective and often it was used to determine eligibility for services. In practice, use of parent interview/ADI-R data and ADOS-2 data can best guide development of individual treatment goals.

Next, there will be a discussion of severity specifiers for the two domains of autism Spectrum social communication and restricted repetitive behaviors.

Severity Scales for Social Communication and Restricted Repetitive Behaviors

Additional specification regarding severity is required for a diagnosis of autism Spectrum disorder in each area assessed. This is consistent with Rutter (2011a, 2011b)) who indicates that noting severity is a common practice in medicine and can provide useful information for clinicians. This practice may be challenging particularly for young children just diagnosed as the severity table in DSM-5 does not appear to be written with toddlers in mind. These ratings should not be used to make determinations on who receives treatment and how much they receive according to the DSM-5. This is clinically an important point as the ratings are perhaps even more subjective than cognitive and language notations and these may change over time and across setting. Rutter suggests that the information may be useful to clinicians as part of a diagnostic picture. Ratings may guide a clinician to understand whether an individual is "high functioning" or more significantly impaired. The DSM-5 provides a chart with examples to guide ratings, level 1 being mild, 2 moderate, and 3 severe.

These three levels of severity indicate the level of support a clinician estimates an individual needs based on an evaluation. These are vague distinctions that note "requiring support," "requiring substantial support," and "requiring very substantial support." Here are examples of the application of these notations. Individuals who have challenges in social interaction and making friendships while speaking in full sentences may have social communication challenges that are level 1 and "require support." Level 1 for restricted repetitive behaviors may indicate difficulty with organization and planning (executive functioning) and with shifting attention from one activity to another. In other words, "difficulty with transitions" which is often indicated by parents or teachers as it is noticeable at school where there are many transitions during a given day. Level 2 or "requiring substantial support" refers to social communication challenges like having limited interaction with others, very narrow special interests, or use of simple language. For restricted repetitive behaviors, level 2 may indicate frequent repetitive behaviors or challenges like those noted in level 1 that are "obvious to the casual observer." Finally, level 3 indicates "requiring very substantial support." Severe deficits in verbal and nonverbal communication with little speech or response to social overtures are provided as examples. For restricted repetitive interests, "restricted repetitive behaviors markedly interfere with functioning in all spheres."

Studies investigating the use of severity levels and the consistency between severity in DSM-5 and the scales reported on the ADOS-2 (comparison scale) have found little correlation between measures. Weitlauf et al. reports that while qualitative differences are noted between severity levels, there are no quantitative methods to differentiate (2014). This study discusses the concern that discrepancies will indeed lead to implications for services and treatment. Weitlauf et al. uses the ADOS-2 severity scale to compare to DSM-5 severity in a descriptive study as the comparison score is a quantitative measure with severity ratings calculated from the ADOS-2 algorithm. Researchers found that there is inconsistency in assigning severity across a broad age range of individuals. Lord et al. (2012), consistent with Weitlauf et al., report that severity ratings depend on the individual preference, background, and training of a clinician.

Reszka et al. examined autism symptom severity categorization using the ADOS, CARS, and SRS, noting these are all reliable and valid measures. The study sought to determine whether these measures are in agreement because the DSM-5 asks clinicians to rate severity along a continuum. The results indicated that there is disagreement among these three measures, thus the DSM-5 specifier could impact services without providing a quantitative measure of services (2014). By qualitatively noting severity, clinician biases may impact services provided. This is important for clinicians to take into consideration and act in a manner that is careful and considerate of each individual's needs.

A Word on Social (Pragmatic) Communication Disorder

Social (pragmatic) Communication Disorder (SCD) is characterized by social and communication impairment in light of social rules and conventions and use of verbal and nonverbal behavior to communicate without the restricted or repetitive patterns of behavior that are evident in ASD. Specifically, the criteria indicate challenges in using communication for social purposes, not considering the context of communication, difficulty with rules of conversation and storytelling, and difficulty with inferences and nonliteral language. These challenges must impact relationships and occur in the early developmental period.

Many researchers have criticized this new disorder as lacking sound research and data to support its addition to the DSM-5, while others wonder whether SCD may be the new diagnosis for PDDNOS. Early studies examining reassignment of PDDNOS found that individuals failed to meet the full social communication criteria and met the restricted repetitive patterns of behavior only thus not meeting SCD. Early indications are that SCD is not the catch all for PDDNOS. It is yet to be seen whether this diagnosis will stand alone or whether it is simply ASD. Ozonoff (2012) writes in an editorial perspective that SCD may provide a diagnosis for some individuals with PDDNOS. She echoes the critical questions raised by Skuse (2012) and Tanguay (2011) wondering how SCD is really different from ASD. As we subsume Asperger's under ASD using a "pioneering" dimensional approach why introduce a separate category? Ozonoff notes that changes to DSM-5 "arise from empirical and conceptual forces at work for decades."

A Need for More Research and for Continued Comprehensive Assessment

One article published on the DSM-5 notes that the new criteria must be the "gold standard" for Autism Assessment (Kulage et al., 2014). The authors of this text feel that it is essential that expert clinicians continue to use comprehensive assessment including the ADOS-2 as the "gold standard" and not simply a set of criteria. Using comprehensive measures allows a clinician to appropriately assess the symptoms present without missing a more subtle presentation. This is crucial for diagnosis and for treatment. The purpose of the DSM-5 is to improve and clarify the diagnosis keeping up with years of research on the subject of ASDs. The implementation of a dimensional approach with less focus on subcategorical classification is supported by years of research (Rutter, 2011a, 2011b). While there are studies that question whether the DSM-5 criteria will limit diagnosis and lead individuals to lose services, much of the data points to careful and thorough assessment by expert clinicians. As this is possible, individuals diagnosed with autism Spectrum disorders will continue to be classified as meeting criteria and individuals newly assessed will be appropriately "categorized" so that they can access services. Rutter's point that autism Spectrum patterns would be a better name than ASD is interesting (2011a, 2011b). Rutter's argument suggests that in order to diagnose functional impairment should not be necessary. This differs from the DSM-5 approach which stresses functional impairment as a criterion for diagnosis. Rutter notes that individuals who meet criteria for ASD but have well-managed symptoms and are not impaired may benefit from not being labeled "disordered." Individuals may meet criteria and own the ASP label as many own "Aspie." As the DSM-5 continues to require impairment for diagnosis, ASP has not been adopted. The majority of data sources support the new criteria and its use in diagnosis of ASD. Factor analysis strongly supports the two-factor structure as statistically sound in comparison to the previous three-factor structure (Mandy et al., 2012). It is crucial that as a community we continue to make research-based decisions as we work to best serve individuals on the Autism Spectrum and meet their treatment needs for optimal outcomes.

Summary of Part 1: Understanding Autism

This concludes the part of this book dedicated to understanding autism, increasing prevalence rates, and the critical issues around potential causes and opportunity for recovery from the disorder. Readers are now familiar with the basic core features of autism; as well as the clinical diagnostic criteria. Individuals with autism struggle primarily with social communication and reciprocity. They often show a limited range of facial expressions and their emotions. They often fail to share enjoyment, interests, or emotional experiences with others. Autism is largely inherited. However, the genetic "code" for autism is yet to be identified and this effect is further confounded by the fact that children with the same or similar genes (twins, for example) do not express autism symptoms at the same rate. Epigenetics may be an additional mechanism explaining how the interaction of genes and environment may impact the presentation of symptoms. Familial factors, such as paternal age and having a sibling or parent with autism, present additional risk for autism. Although autism is a serious and often pervasive, long-term neurological disorder, optimal outcomes and recovery are possible. Factors that predict optimal outcomes are: intelligence, language ability, early intervention, and individual characteristics. Although early intervention is critical and may actually have a direct effect on gene expression and structural brain changes, early intervention alone does not directly predict best outcomes. Rather, effective early intervention for children with the other factors in place, such as intelligence, adequate language ability, and resilient personality traits, lead to the best outcomes. At the conclusion of this part of the book, readers learned about the specific criteria used to make a diagnosis. The DSM-5, released in 2013, includes a two-factor structure for identification of an Autism Spectrum Disorder. Criterion A addresses social communication and social interaction deficits across multiple contexts. Criterion B considers restricted or repetitive patterns of behavior, interests, or activities. Symptoms must be present in early development and must cause clinically significant impairment in functioning. Now that the critical issues surrounding an autism diagnosis have been introduced, as well as the importance of early diagnosis and intervention, it is time to take a close look at the assessment process.

Part II
Conducting an Evaluation

This part describes how to conduct a thorough diagnostic assessment as it applies to Autism Spectrum Disorders. A detailed outline is included which elaborates on the process from the time of the referral, including logistical issues such as paperwork and billing, to completion of a comprehensive evaluation. A sample set of questions and critical information to be gathered during the initial intake process for children and adults is provided. The observation guide assists examiners in watching for potential symptoms in the client's presentation such as: behavior, language, attention, social reciprocity, and mood. Guidelines are provided for addressing more challenging behaviors using ABA principles for reinforcement and motivation. A sample checklist of valid and reliable assessment instruments that clinicians may utilize is provided. These authors propose that the selection of the test battery should be dynamic and evolving, based on the needs and presentation of the client. This approach is consistent with the Luria-Nebraska Model and contrasts with models utilizing a fixed battery. In order to assist examiners in selecting testing instruments based on the client's needs, the "Dynamic Assessment Overview for ASD and Other Disorders" framework is provided. This conceptual model provides a roadmap for diagnosticians to use when considering the following types of assessment: autism diagnosis alone; autism and a comorbid condition(s); and other diagnoses. Through provision of tools for the entire assessment, from referral, to intake, to observations, to selection of measures, this chapter offers a prescriptive best-practice approach for a diagnostic assessment in consideration of ASD.

Chapter 5
Referral and Initial Consult

Abstract The first step in the comprehensive evaluation process is that a family member, friend, or clinician identifies a concern and makes a referral. Then, an initial consult is conducted which is an interview with the family to identify concerns, gather background information, and determine the type of evaluation that is needed. Depending on the concerns identified during the initial consult, the clinician determines if the evaluation will be brief, comprehensive, psychological, neuropsychological, academic, or forensic. Included in this chapter is a comprehensive set of questions that might be asked and domains that should be addressed during the initial consultation. The next step is to complete paperwork such as the intake packet, disclosures, and informed consent. This chapter provides sample intake packet questions for this purpose. From this initial consult, the clinician begins framing a picture of the client's testing needs, potential diagnostic considerations, and a list of areas to assess. Testing priorities are identified and a preliminary assessment plan is laid out. This chapter includes a sample checklist of the tests that might be utilized for individuals of various ages. Next, testing is scheduled and the clinician prepares the client by providing a timeline for the day of testing. Finally, the clinician sets up for a successful testing session by reviewing the intake packet, and additional information provided, pulling protocols, and assembling the members of the assessment team.

On the following page is a graphic depicting the entire assessment process which will begin in this chapter with the referral and initial consult (Chap. 5), proceed to testing day including taking observations and managing behaviors (Chap. 6), and then complete the assessment, including the dynamic selection of tests and priorities based on the client's presentation (Chap. 7). The next section (Chaps. 8–12) will review the data analysis process for evaluating the information collected during a diagnostic assessment. The differential diagnosis process will be covered next (Chaps. 13 and 14). Finally, the recommendations and report will be discussed (Chap. 15).

Keywords Initial intake for ASD • Intake interview questions • Clinical interview for ASD • Intake packet questions • Disclosures and financial agreements for ASD assessment • Arranging for third-party payments • Identifying assessment priorities in ASD

Figure 5.1

© Springer International Publishing Switzerland 2016   49
A.P. Kroncke et al., *Assessment of Autism Spectrum Disorder*, Contemporary
Issues in Psychological Assessment, DOI 10.1007/978-3-319-25504-0_5

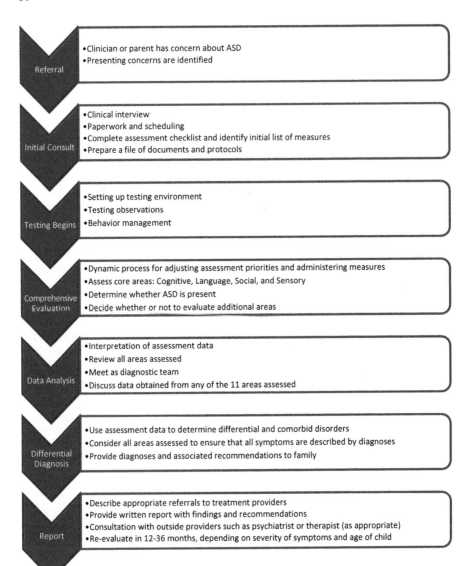

Referral
- Clinician or parent has concern about ASD
- Presenting concerns are identified

Initial Consult
- Clinical interview
- Paperwork and scheduling
- Complete assessment checklist and identify initial list of measures
- Prepare a file of documents and protocols

Testing Begins
- Setting up testing environment
- Testing observations
- Behavior management

Comprehensive Evaluation
- Dynamic process for adjusting assessment priorities and administering measures
- Assess core areas: Cognitive, Language, Social, and Sensory
- Determine whether ASD is present
- Decide whether or not to evaluate additional areas

Data Analysis
- Interpretation of assessment data
- Review all areas assessed
- Meet as diagnostic team
- Discuss data obtained from any of the 11 areas assessed

Differential Diagnosis
- Use assessment data to determine differential and comorbid disorders
- Consider all areas assessed to ensure that all symptoms are described by diagnoses
- Provide diagnoses and associated recommendations to family

Report
- Describe appropriate referrals to treatment providers
- Provide written report with findings and recommendations
- Consultation with outside providers such as psychiatrist or therapist (as appropriate)
- Re-evaluate in 12-36 months, depending on severity of symptoms and age of child

Fig. 5.1 A practical guide to comprehensive assessment

Making a Referral

- Clinical interview
- Paperwork and scheduling
- Complete assessment checklist and identify initial list of measures
- Prepare a file of documents and protocols

How Referrals are Made

The first step in the process of a comprehensive evaluation begins when some-one voices a concern. Often this is a parent speaking to a friend, family member, or perhaps a preschool teacher having a parent–teacher conference. A parent may ask, "Should I seek an evaluation?" and a teacher may respond with "You may want to speak with your pediatrician." Sometimes a concerned parent talks to the family doctor who recommends a neuropsychological evaluation to gather more information. Often, referrals are obtained from professionals in the field, including speech therapists, occupational therapists, and other clinicians. When qualified professionals make the referral, it can be helpful if they work with the family to identify the type of evaluation the client will need. Clinicians can fur-ther empower families by providing a letter to the clinic where the evaluation will occur or making a phone call to the psychologist conducting the assessment.

What Should Referring Professionals Know?

It is important for individuals and families who make referrals to have a basic understanding of the assessment process so that clients are directed to an appropriate source for a comprehensive evaluation. It is common to hear "I am having my child tested." This testing may look very different across settings. Parents sometimes mistakenly share that they have had "an evaluation" already when only an initial consultation occurred. Other times, the family may have obtained an evaluation from a clinic or other provider that does not diagnose autism. Some psychologists and testing centers focus primarily on testing for emotional conditions or learning needs. These centers are generally not equipped to test for autism. Hopefully, these clinics guide the family toward a more appropriate evaluation when potential symptoms of autism are evidenced.

Being Responsive to Concerns

Unfortunately, often when a parent has a concern, some well-meaning specialists from other disciplines may imply that a diagnosis is present or is unwarranted when they are not qualified to make diagnostic decisions. It is critical to be aware that when an individual is not qualified to diagnose an Autism Spectrum Disorder, he or she is also not qualified to rule out the diagnosis. At times, school professionals, counselors, occupational therapists, physical therapists, or other specialists without diagnostic training make comments such as, "He doesn't seem to have autism to me." Just as people who are not doctors cannot "rule out" cancer as the cause for certain symptoms, professionals who are untrained in ASD evaluations are not qualified to rule out autism. Well-meaning statements like "Don't worry I think he's just being a boy." Or "His eye contact is excellent, it can't be autism;" or (a comment made by a pediatrician to a mother) "He can talk so well; clearly it is not autism," can be incredibly damaging to families. Unfortunately, some doctors tell parents for years to "wait and see," often making families feel powerless to move forward with addressing their concerns. Bearing in mind that early intervention is critical, it is important that concerns are addressed by qualified professionals. Appropriate responses may include "It sounds like you have a few concerns about Johnny's development. As a parent you know your child best. Consider a consultation with a psychologist or pediatrician to further discuss your concerns." Or "I'm not qualified to diagnose but the following observations we've made in the classroom may be noteworthy. Why don't you share this information with your doctor?"

Finding an Appropriate Evaluation

Evaluations from qualified clinicians range from psychological or neuropsychological test batteries to parent consultation interviews that result in a diagnosis. Comprehensive evaluations may consist of comprehensive psychological or neuropsychological batteries including a wide range of standardized tests. Alternately, pediatricians or psychiatrists may provide a diagnosis based on a clinical consultation, potentially including rating scales or developmental screeners. Best practice comprehensive psychological evaluations for autism minimally include an initial consultation to prioritize areas of concern; an ADOS-2 and clinical interview; screening questionnaires; and formal assessment of cognitive, language, social, and sensory areas.

Referring to Clinics Qualified in Diagnosing ASD

Often parents who pursue evaluations have clinically significant concerns that are causing great distress to the family and to their child. Referring individuals can support families in identifying an appropriate place for an evaluation. In doing so, referring parties should consider that an appropriate evaluation can occur only when the clinicians are highly qualified in diagnosing ASD, as well as understanding potential comorbidities and differential diagnoses. Understanding what autism is *not* is as just as important as understanding what autism is. Diagnostic clarification by highly trained clinicians helps guide treatment recommendations in accordance with best practice standards and ultimately can be of great benefit to the individual and the family.

Elements of a Comprehensive Assessment

Research varies about the precise components of a comprehensive evaluation but the common themes are that assessment should include multiple assessment modalities and look at a variety of domain areas. Most clinicians agree that a comprehensive evaluation should address cognitive, language, motor skills, emotions, and attention in addition to the social skills deficits associated with ASD. The Autism Diagnostic Observation Schedule, Second Edition (henceforth known as the ADOS-2) manual states that the ADOS-2 is only one part of an evaluation and that it is not appropriate to make a diagnosis considering a score on an ADOS-2 algorithm alone (Lord et al., 2012). Cognitive assessment, adaptive assessment, an ADI-R or caregiver interview, and a parent-report screening measure like the SCQ should be a part of the battery (Gotham, Bishop, & Lord 2011 for best practice guidelines for assessing ASD).

Diagnosticians who work with children and adolescents should have a thorough understanding of typical development in a variety of domains, and particularly in social communication. Often, autism symptoms are best identified by seeing whether or not the milestones typically achieved by a child of that age are indeed present. That is, many of the symptoms associated with autism are called "negative symptoms," meaning essentially, that it is not necessarily what the child is doing, but what he or she is *not doing* that can be of concern. For example, a bright 7-year-old child, who does not play reciprocally or share enjoyment with others, may be showing important signs of ASD. Klin et al. in 1997 outlined a comprehensive developmental approach to Autism Assessment including assessment of multiple areas of functioning, adopting a developmental perspective. The approach emphasizes variability of skills, variability across settings, functional adjustment, and developmental delays. Kamphaus and Campbell (2006) discuss the use of this approach with assessment from clinicians in multiple disciplines in the book *Psychodiagnostic Assessment of Children* (Ed. Kamphaus & Campbell, 2006). These authors would argue that assessing multiple domains and incorporating various clinical perspectives are best practices. As shown in Chap. 7, there are four core areas that must be assessed for an ASD evaluation: cognitive, language, social, and sensory. There are seven associated areas that should be assessed if potential symptoms arise during the initial consultation or the evaluation of the core areas. The associated areas are visual–spatial, motor, attention, executive functioning, memory, emotional/behavioral, and adaptive. An evaluation that addresses (either formally or informally) all of these areas by way of screening instruments, interview, observations, and standardized testing is considered comprehensive.

Multidisciplinary/Arena Evaluations

Research shows that a multidisciplinary or "arena" evaluation is the best approach for assessing ASD. Multidisciplinary team evaluations *may* involve physicians, psychologists from various disciplines (clinical, neuropsychology, counseling, or school), speech therapists, occupational therapists, physical therapists, and educational specialists. It *will* involve, at minimum, a team of psychologists with consultation from other disciplines (i.e., referring doctor, OT, or SLP). An evaluation without a psychologist who is fully trained to administer the ADOS-2 cannot be considered comprehensive and does not meet the "gold standard" for autism assessment. A comprehensive literature review conducted in 2013 by Falkmer, Anderson, Falkmer, and Horlin indicated that while we refer to the ADOS and ADI-R as the "gold standard" a review of the literature supports this statement "…the true 'gold standard' classification and diagnosis of autism is still considered to be multidisciplinary team clinical assessment, including use of the ADOS and ADI-R, as well as other assessments with consensus clinical judgment" (Falkmer et al., 2013). This study supports use of the CARS rating scale, while qualifying that it is used in combination with a developmental evaluation including the ADOS and ADI-R, as well as the M-CHAT parent-report questionnaire (often provided by pediatricians). It is important for referring professionals to know that the research indicates best practice for autism assessment is a comprehensive, multidisciplinary team assessment. When these various clinicians are not within the same practice, consultation can be helpful. Often, clinicians conducting evaluations will call the child's therapist, teacher, psychiatrist, or medical doctor to obtain information and collaborate on the evaluation.

A referring clinician such as a speech therapist, pediatrician, or occupational therapist may reach out to the diagnostic team. The clinician may consult, write a letter, or provide screening data to the psychologist or team of professionals evaluating. A letter from a referring clinician can empower families as they pursue an evaluation. It may be the case that the family has cultural, language, or socioeconomic barriers, and the prospect of pursuing an evaluation for their child can be intimidating and daunting. A letter from a qualified professional who speaks the language of the evaluator, using clinical terminology to explain the referral concerns, can be a significant asset to families.

Comprehensive multidisciplinary evaluations are often provided by hospitals, outpatient clinics, and sometimes by private or group practices. Wait lists to receive these services can be long or there may not be such a provider in the area. Sometimes psychologists in independent private practice also provide evaluation services that are likely to cover fewer domains. While there are certainly drawbacks to a less comprehensive assessment, it is possible to rule out the presence of an Autism Spectrum Disorder if the necessary assessments are administered in the core areas of cognitive, language, social, and sensory. A quality referral from a clinician, doctor, teacher, or family member to a comprehensive, multidisciplinary evaluation can be the precise factor that turns the tides for families and allows a child to get critical treatment. When faced with a lengthy wait list (3 months to 1 year), clinicians recommend families make an effort to find comprehensive services that are more readily available. Especially with very young children, losing a year of potential treatment can be hugely detrimental.

- Clinical interview
- Paperwork and scheduling
- Complete assessment checklist and identify initial list of measures
- Prepare a file of documents and protocols

Initial
Consult

To summarize, clinical psychologists, neuropsychologists, medical doctors, and specialists, such as child psychiatrists, may diagnose an Autism Spectrum Disorder. Training of these clinicians varies and if they do not have extensive training in autism assessment they should refer out. If a parent or referring clinician is having difficulty finding a provider, it may be helpful to contact a local chapter of the Autism Society. This organization should have a list of local providers. Families and referral sources might also contact the community centered board, insurance company, or Autism Speaks chapter for referrals.

The Initial Consultation

Once a referral has been made, the next step of the comprehensive evaluation process is the initial consultation or intake interview. The initial consult looks much different depending on the age of the individual being evaluated. Often one or both parents of a toddler, child, or teenager seek a consultation to discuss a potential referral for an evaluation. At times, a medical doctor, school psychologist, teacher, or another service provider like a speech pathologist brings concerns to the family that are discussed during the initial consult. Referring clinicians may note symptoms regarding behavior, mood, attention, or social interaction skills. As noted before, it may be helpful to request that the referring specialist write a letter to the diagnostic team, complete rating scales, or offer to be interviewed to explain their rationale for the referral. Sometimes, this collaborative relationship between the referring clinician and the assessment team can allow for a more comprehensive evaluation, taking into perspective the symptoms present in multiple environments. For example, if a teacher or school psychologist referred a student for an evaluation, the school professional may have important information regarding social skills and academic history.

In some cases, parents may have an understanding of neurodevelopmental disabilities, such as autism. They may have completed screening questionnaires for an Autism Spectrum Disorder or another diagnosis like AD/HD or Depression with another professional. In that case, parents may come in with specific questions like, "My child has traits of an ASD. Is this diagnosis relevant and what treatment can we seek to best serve our child?" Clinicians are wise to carefully consider those concerns but not offer judgments or clinical impressions until the evaluation process is complete. It may be that the situation looks very different once the clinician meets the child and starts gathering data. As such, clinicians are advised to listen and clarify concerns without offering any information that may be perceived as diagnostic.

In other cases, the referral question is vague. Sometimes parents note symptoms observed but have not begun considering what disability may be potentially impacting their child. Parents or individuals may not have heard diagnostic terms like autism and may have little knowledge as to what an assessment entails. This initial interview can look much different from a consultation with parents or individuals who come in with more knowledge about the process.

When meeting with adults who are self-referred or physician referred, often individuals have completed an Internet questionnaire or read a book that seemed relevant to the symptoms they experience. Many adults have obtained a diagnosis in the past but wonder about the validity of the findings and hope for clarification to help with self-understanding and direction. They may seek specific recommendations through a reevaluation on how to approach life, career, and relationships. In the case of reevaluations, the diagnosis may be undisputed but the family or individual would like to update progress and receive information on treatment options and community resources.

Who Should Attend?

If the individual to be evaluated is a baby, young child, or younger adolescent, it is most helpful for one or both parents to attend this consultation without their child. This allows parents to speak more freely about concerns and limits distractions. When two parents are available and can attend this is ideal because parents are the experts on their children and each parent can provide a unique perspective. When this is not possible, a single parent can attend or one parent can come in on behalf of both. If both parents are not available to be present for the assessment, rating scales can be completed independently outside of the office to provide different perspectives. When families are blended or divorced, more or fewer members can attend the consultation. Further, if another family member is a primary caregiver for the child, this person's perspective is valuable, either in person or by way of rating scales. In some cases, when a divorce is contentious, parents may wish to schedule two sessions so that they can comfortably share perspective on their child.

When the individual referred is a teenager, parents can make the decision with their adolescent whether to come together or allow the parents to complete the initial consultation. Many adolescents play a part in the decision to seek an evaluation and can provide valuable information on their own experiences. It is also a chance for the clinician to view and understand family dynamics. Some adolescents do not feel comfortable participating in this meeting and it can be detrimental to force them to do something uncomfortable. Once a teenager has reached 18 he or she must sign paperwork and play a part in this initial meeting unless parents have legal guardianship. An adult seeking an evaluation may choose to bring a spouse, parent, other family member, or a roommate to an initial consultation for support and to offer additional perspective. Many adults also choose to come alone.

Conducting the Initial Consultation

This initial meeting typically lasts 50 min to an hour and may be simply a chance for clarification about the evaluation process. A clinician can listen, reflect, paraphrase, and summarize concerns and help to guide the individual or family in making a decision about proceeding with an evaluation. The clinician can provide information about what types of testing would be appropriate based on the concerns mentioned during the initial consultation. If a family or individual has directed questions and comes with knowledge about assessment, this meeting can be a chance for a clinical interview including a comprehensive developmental history or a chance for a structured interview such as an ADI-R. A clinician may choose to provide the parents or individual with screening rating scales to complete to obtain more detailed information.

Family members or individuals may present for a consultation with varying levels of emotional distress. Sometimes seeking a diagnosis provides satisfaction and validation of concerns and gives direction for action. Individuals may be eager to begin the assessment process and to receive diagnostic information and recommendations for services. Other individuals may be wary, grieving, or seeking an evaluation out of medical or legal necessity. These individuals may need to move more slowly, ask more clarifying questions, and may need to share emotions. Anger, fear, anxiety, denial, or sadness may permeate the initial session. It does not serve the client to move too fast in this process and so the approach must be tailored to the individual and to the referral question. One author recalls a parent who presented for an initial 25 min late was clearly stressed and overwhelmed and the first words out of her mouth were "I need you to diagnose my child (child was not present) with autism right now!" With 30 min of listening, reflecting, and explaining the process and diagnosis itself the parent was able to calm down and decided to schedule a full evaluation to address her concerns.

Questions Asked During the Initial Consultation

The initial consult should include client information such as date of birth and contact information, strengths and interests, developmental history, health history, clarification of concerns, developmental milestones, and psychological symptoms. Provided below are two examples of an interview structure that may be used in an initial consultation. This list should be seen as a dynamic and evolving guide that clinicians will need to adjust based on the needs of the client as presented during the intake interview (Tables 5.1 and 5.2).

Ultimately at the close of the initial session, a clinician can aim to clarify the process, answer questions, and suggest next steps. Some individuals or families may wish to schedule an evaluation immediately while others may take more time

Table 5.1 Sample items for initial consultation

Initial/intake of a child

1. Demographics
    (a) DOB
    (b) Age
    (c) Grade
    (d) Interview with
    (e) Who referred?

2. Present concerns
    (a) Tell us a little bit about why you are here—What brings you in today?
    (b) Language abilities?

3. History of concerns
    (a) Length? Intensity? Frequency? Change?
    (b) Diagnoses—past/present, when, by who

4. Family
    (a) Tell us a little bit about your family, family structure, and relationships—who lives at home?

5. Developmental history (pregnancy/infancy)
    (a) Born: at___weeks; at___weight
    (b) Complications with birth or pregnancy?
    (c) How was he/she as an infant?
    (i) Eat?
    (ii) Sleep?

6. Developmental history (infancy/toddlerhood)
    (a) Developmental milestones?
    (b) How did he/she let you know what he/she wanted? (nonverbal/verbal cues) Reach, gesture, grunt—words/repeat? Rephrase?
    (c) What kind of things did he/she play with?
    (d) How was he/she when you were in the room?
    (e) Second year of life
    (i) What did he/she do with other kids? At the park, b-day party?
    (ii) What did you notice there?
    (iii) How did he/she play with siblings?

7. Interests/behavior/development (toddler through present)
    (a) At home?
    (b) On playground, park (how to interact with other children?)

8. Current social interaction/behavior?
    (a) Interests?
    (b) Clubs/Activities?
    (c) Friendships?

9. Education
    (a) Preschool—how did that go?
    (b) Teacher comments?
    (c) Academic progress?

(continued)

Table 5.1 (continued)

Initial/intake of a child
(d) Setting—class size?
(e) Peers?
(f) Services at school?
10. Medical history
(a) Diagnosis?
(b) Illness?
(c) Injury, accident?
(d) Head injury? Hit head?
(e) Hospitalization?
(f) Allergies?
(g) Current medications?
(h) History of medications?
(i) Family medical history?
(i)Mother
(ii)Father
(j) Current Sleep?
(k) Current Eating?
11. Mental Health history
(a) Previous diagnosis?
(b) Past evaluations?
(i) When?
(ii) Where?
(c) Past or current treatment?
(i) When?
(ii) Where?
(iii) Duration?
(iv) Frequency?
(v) What worked? What didn't work?
12. Present mood/emotional
(a) Hurt self?
(b) How would you describe his/her mood?
(c) Feel nervous? Sweaty palms? Feel panicked? Short of breath?
(d) Any voices—See things?
(e) History of trauma or abuse?
13. Strengths
14. Summarize concerns, (so it sounds like)
(a) If applicable suggest an evaluation to clarify some of these issues and find out how to address them
(b) Probe on how do you feel/how did that feel? These are big issues (validate for family/individual)
(c) Next step guidance (when applicable)
(i) Contact your insurance

(continued)

Table 5.1 (continued)

Initial/intake of a child
(ii) Explain process of evaluation or therapy
(iii) 1–3 days, team, feedback, report
(iv) Evaluation (Brief, Comprehensive, Add on Academic?)
15. Questions?

Table 5.2 Initial/intake of an adult

1. Demographics
(a) DOB
(b) Age
(c) Grade/Job
(d) Interview with
(e) Who referred?
2. Present concerns
(a) Tell us a little bit about why you are here—What brings you in today?
3. History of concerns
(a) Length? Intensity? Frequency? Change?
(b) Diagnoses—past/present, when, by who?
4. Home life
(a) Romantic Relationships- Dating, Significant Other?
(b) Living Arrangement?
5. Developmental history (available knowledge)
(a) Developmental milestones?
6. History of interests/behavior/development
(a) Youth?
(b) Friendship History?
7. Current social interaction/behavior?
(a) Interests?
(b) Clubs/Activities?
(c) Friendships?
8. Education/employment
(a) Dates; Hard/Easy Activities across ages
(b) Elementary?
(c) Middle?
(d) High School?
(e) Post High School?
(f) Teacher comments?
(g) Academic progress?
(h) Setting—class size?
(i) Peers?
(j) Services at school?
(k) Job History?
(l) Job Currently?

(continued)

Table 5.2 (continued)

9. Medical history
(a) Diagnosis?
(b) Illness?
(c) Injury, accident?
(d) Head injury? Hit head?
(e) Hospitalization?
(f) Allergies?
(g) Current medications?
(h) History of medications?
(i) Family medical history?
(i) Mother
(ii) Father
(j) Current Sleep?
(k) Current Eating?
10. Mental health history
(a) Previous diagnosis?
(b) Past evaluations?
(i) When?
(ii) Where?
(c) Past or current treatment?
(i) When?
(ii) Where?
(iii) Duration?
(iv) Frequency?
(v) What worked? What didn't work?
11. Present mood/emotional
(a) History of trauma or abuse?
(b) Hurt self?
(c) How would you describe your mood?
(d) Anxiety or Panic Symptoms?
(e) Any voices—See things?
(f) Alcohol or Drug Use?
(g) How do you cope with stress?
12. Strengths
13. Summarize concerns, so it sounds like—
(a) If applicable suggest an evaluation to clarify some of these issues and find out how to address them
(b) Probe on how do you feel/how did that feel? These are big issues (validate for family/individual)
(c) Next step guidance (when applicable)
(i) Contact your insurance
(ii) Explain process of evaluation or therapy
(iii) 1–3 days, team, feedback, report
(iv) Evaluation
14. Questions?

to consider options and may choose to hold off on making additional plans or appointments. If the family decides to move forward with an evaluation, the clinician can provide information about the schedule for testing, snack breaks, lunchtime, and whether or not the parent's presence is required. The clinician should leave the session with diagnostic considerations and rule out information so that an assessment can follow. The clinician should have background information on the client, parent or client concerns, any data from the referral source (pediatrician, speech pathologist, school psychologist), an idea of the client's understanding of autism (did they ask specifically for a rule out or not), and an opinion about whether an evaluation is the next step. The clinician can now make recommendations to the family or individual about the type of assessment needed and, in his or her head, should have hypotheses for a number of rule out diagnoses.

Paperwork

Paperwork including consents and disclosures should be completed and logistics of scheduling the evaluation may be discussed with clients who are ready to move forward in the process of an assessment. At a minimum, informed consent, disclosures about the credentials of the clinicians, financial agreement and payment information, and exchange of information forms should be utilized during the initial consultation. Families should have the option to choose if they would like to have diagnostic information shared with other individuals. Sometimes families elect to have the clinician contact the school, the family doctor, or other referring professional. All of this should be discussed and agreed upon at the conclusion of the initial consultation.

Intake Packet

During the initial intake, it can be helpful to have parents complete a registration form or intake packet. The packet should minimally include Contact Information, Concerns and Strengths, Family History, Birth History, Nutritional History, Developmental History, Medical History, and Educational History. This packet provides a useful tool, allowing families to organize their thoughts and outline their concerns. The packet helps clinicians when preparing for the evaluation and writing the report at the conclusion of the assessment. A sample set of areas that might be included on an intake packet are included on the next page (Table 5.3).

At the conclusion of the intake, clinicians should feel prepared to lay out a plan for the assessment, with associated potential rule-out diagnoses. A comprehensive background history is obtained from the initial interview and the intake packet. At this point, the clinician is ready to begin identifying tests that will be administered. In so doing, financial considerations are critical. If this evaluation is forensic, it is likely to be more expensive and much of the financial burden will fall on the family. If the evaluation is academic, the assessment is typically self-pay and may be expen-

Table 5.3 Sample intake packet questions

1. Contact information for child
2. Contact info for both parents
(a) DOB
(b) Address
(c) Phone
(d) Occupation
(e) Highest level of education obtained
3. Family information
(a) Siblings
(b) Who lives in the home
(c) Primary care doctor
4. Concerns and strengths
(a) Specific concerns
(b) When concerns first evidenced
(c) Previous evaluations/consultations
(d) Child's strengths and interests
(e) Questions to be answered during evaluation
(f) Who referred
5. Family history
(a) Checklist of medical and psychological conditions
(b) Explain conditions on either side of the family
6. Pregnancy and birth history
(a) Birth weight
(b) Weeks gestation
(c) Complications
7. Nutritional history
(a) Breast Fed/Formula Fed
(b) Weight at 1 year
(c) Feeding and sleeping patterns
8. Developmental history
(a) Motor milestones
(b) Language milestones
(c) Development: Quickly, Typically, Slowly
(d) Temperament
(i) How active is child
(ii) How does child adjust to new places, people, things
(iii) Child's basic mood: happy, sad, angry, quiet, other
9. Medical history
(a) Checklist of medical conditions: abdominal, allergies, dental, ear infections, etc.
(b) Current weight and height
(c) Hospitalizations
(d) List all current medications

(continued)

Table 5.3 (continued)

(e) Checklist of behavior concerns: aggression, disobedience, poor concentration, etc.
(f) List any current behavioral concerns
(g) How does child do with the following?
(i)   Gets along well with others
(ii) Becomes easily upset or frustrated
(iii) Becomes angry or destructive
(iv) Becomes overactive
(v)   Prefers to be alone
(vi) Difficulty sitting still
(vii) Problems with clumsiness
(viii) Listens well
(ix) Follows directions
(h) List of current providers for mental and behavior health
(i) Disciplinary approach utilized
10. Educational profile
(a) List of schools attended in chronological order
(b) Any special education services
(c) Any current school programs
(d) Use of community resources
11. Goals for child
(a) Communication
(b) Social Skills and relationships
(c) Sensory integration and motor skills
(d) Structured learning and academic skills
12. Family
(a) Family involved in legal issues
(b) Family activities/places in the community family enjoys
(c) Ways evaluation can help family
(d) Additional information clinicians should know to help family

sive, depending on the extent of the testing needed to answer the referral questions. A brief evaluation may be much less expensive and may be covered by insurance. Often, for psychological evaluations, insurance coverage may dictate the type of evaluation and the tests that will be included. Families often may elect to self-pay for evaluation services that are not covered by insurance.

Next Steps: The Role of third-Party Payment (Insurance)

While in a perfect world the assessment that follows the initial interview would include every measure and consideration the clinician noted, insurance can limit the scope of the evaluation substantially. When a family wishes to use insurance to cover the cost of assessment, clinicians may have to complete pre-authorization forms and request assessment time by measure or by the hour. Some insurance providers may cover comprehensive evaluations and others may not cover an evaluation at all. As insurance billing can be cumbersome and limiting, some providers choose not to work with insurance companies and only offer self-pay evaluations. Providers who accept insurance often do this in an effort to make services as accessible to families as possible, even as it adds paperwork, and reimbursement for services is rarely a guarantee. In many cases, insurance providers may not decide until diagnoses are made whether to cover testing costs. When individuals are willing to self-pay a portion or all of the assessment, it is generally possible to collect more comprehensive data.

In order to provide services that align with third-party payers, some clinics offer both brief and comprehensive services. In the case of a brief evaluation, a single referral question can be answered, i.e., "Does my child have an Autism Spectrum Disorder?" Fitting with the research discussed in this book, screening measures, a comprehensive interview, an ADOS-2, and data regarding cognitive, language, social, and adaptive skills can provide information on whether an Autism Spectrum Disorder is present. However, the evaluation will not be considered comprehensive in that the clinician is unable to evaluate all areas of functioning that may be impacted. A brief battery may include a cognitive measure such as a WISC-V or DAS-2 Preschool form, an ADOS-2, clinical interview, and emotional and adaptive questionnaires.

Choosing Initial Assessments

At the concluding of the initial consult, the clinician should be able to complete a checklist noting the dynamic priorities for testing, considering the areas of concern identified during the initial consultation. The assessment should address all of the concerns identified during the initial meeting, given that this is not a "brief evaluation" to comply with insurance requirements. Choosing the correct testing instruments is critical to lead to diagnostic decision-making.

The table below illustrates some examples of presenting concerns that may arise in an initial consultation. Immediately following is a guide for choosing which measures should be used to address these concerns (Table 5.4).

The initial consultation often leaves a clinician with detailed stories and descriptions of the client and his/her behaviors and challenges across settings that will then lead to various areas for assessment. Take for example a child who spoke early and demonstrates advanced language. This child walked at 18 months and never crawled. Now, at age five he is struggling with hand–eye coordination, has an awkward gait when running, and is having "real trouble" with his T-ball team. These challenges are in motor, social, and sensory domains as he runs to hide when the crowd cheers and hates the feel of his uniform on his arms, legs, and torso. He cannot remember teammates' names, he appears not to hear his coach who is giving directions, and he often cries when it is time to go to practice or a game. This story may describe an individual with an ASD. It suggests that further evaluation in a number of areas may

Table 5.4 Presenting concerns identified in an initial consultation

Social	Inadequate or unsuccessful interactions/relationships
	Odd or awkward
Emotional	Withdrawn
	Unhappy
	Nervous
	Angry
Learning	Weak or deficient skills (speech, language, reading…)
	Academic underachievement
	Unsuccessful recreation
Behavior	Noncompliant (ignores, refuses, defies, argues)
	Excessive repetition
	Aggressive to self, other, materials

provide useful data for his parents in helping their child succeed. In addition to cognitive, language, and autism-specific assessment, these areas may include sensory processing (loud noises and clothing textures bother him), visual–spatial (challenges with hand–eye coordination and visual perception), motor (late to walk, never crawled, awkward gait), attention (does not hear his coach), memory (does not recall names), and emotional/behavioral domains (cries/attempts to avoid social situations). Maybe this little guy is not cut out for T-ball, or perhaps accommodations can allow him to be more successful and enjoy his extracurricular pursuits.

This example illustrates how a clinician may use data collected to prioritize measures for evaluation. In an ideal world, funding would always be available for a wholly comprehensive battery. As it is, we must prioritize based on the data provided and assemble a battery that addresses as many aspects of the referral question as possible.

Dynamic Assessment Battery

The authors recommend a dynamic process approach versus a fixed battery approach, meaning that measures can be selected initially, but the process is dynamic and the list will change based on data obtained. A full explanation of the dynamic process approach is provided in Chap. 7. In the same way in which a physician may run a number of tests and determine next steps based on each result, a diagnosing clinician may not ascribe to a fixed battery but rather selects measures that will provide the most useful data based on results of other measures. When autism seems to be a relevant concern, the clinician should plan to test the core areas of cognitive, language, social, and sensory. The other areas to be assessed, however, can dynamically evolve throughout the assessment process. This approach aligns with the

Luria-Nebraska neuropsychological battery approach (Ch. 9: Eds. Golden, 2003). It may be important to help some parents or clients to understand the process approach, as a rigid personality can lend to an individual asking for "a list of exactly what will be administered."

A clinician should never feel locked into a fixed battery. As the expert, it is the clinician's responsibility to explain to the family that he or she will choose to collect data that will help serve the client best and to explain that a fixed battery is not recommended. Limitations to the battery will also be influenced based on the type of assessment the client or family requests and insurance coverage. These limitations must be clearly explained to the family before testing is scheduled. Provided below is a sample checklist of valid assessment instruments that might be chosen as part of an evaluation. Using a process approach, the clinician concludes the intake with an initial checklist of measures and then adjusts that list, either adding or removing tests, based on the needs of the client. This list includes assessments for the following core areas: Cognitive, Language, Social, and Sensory. Also included are the areas that should be assessed if there are concerns evidenced during the initial consult or during assessment of the core areas. The associated areas are: Visual–Spatial, Motor, Attention, Executive Functions, Memory, Emotional/Behavioral, and Adaptive (Table 5.5).

Table 5.5 Sample checklist of measures list

Cognitive
Bayley infant (Bayley-iii)
Differential Ability Scales, Second Edition, Lower Early Years Record Form (DAS-II)
Differential Ability Scales, Second Edition, Upper Early Years Record Form (DAS-II)
Differential Ability Scales, Second Edition, School—Age Record Form
Kaufman Assessment Battery for Children (KABC-II)
Leiter International Performance Scale, Third Edition (Leiter-3)
Mullen Scales of Early Learning (MULLEN), AGS Edition
Stanford-Binet Intelligence Scales, Fifth Edition (SB5)
Universal Nonverbal Intelligence Test, Second Edition (UNIT 2)
Wechsler Adult Intelligence Scale, Fourth Edition (WAIS-IV)
Wechsler Intelligence Scales for Children, Fifth Edition (WISC-V)
Wechsler Preschool and Primary Scale of Intelligence, Fourth Edition (WPPSI-IV)
Woodcock-Johnson IV Tests of Cognitive Abilities (WJ-IV)
Language
Assessment of Basic Language and Learning Skills (ABLLS-R)
Clinical Evaluation of Language Fundamentals, Second Edition Preschool (CELF-PRE2)
Clinical Evaluation of Language Fundamentals, Fifth Edition (CELF-5)
Controlled Oral Word Association Test (COWA)
Expressive One-Word Picture Vocabulary Test, Fourth Edition (EOWPVT-4)
Expressive Vocabulary Test, Second Edition (EVT-2)
Peabody Picture Vocabulary Test, Fourth Edition (PPVT-4)

(continued)

Table 5.5 (continued)

Cognitive
Preschool Language Scale, Fourth Edition (PLS-4)
Test of Pragmatic Language, Second Edition (TOPL-2)
Verbal IQ scores on cognitive measures
Social
Autism Diagnostic Interview-Revised (ADI-R)
Autism Diagnostic Observation Schedule, Second Edition, Module T-4 (ADOS-2)
Autism Observation Scale for Infants (AOSI)
Social Communication Questionnaire (SCQ)
Social Responsiveness Scale (SRS)
Sensory
ADOS-2 Sensory Items & observations
Sensory Profile Caregiver Questionnaire
Short Sensory Profile
Visual–spatial
Beery-Buktenica Developmental Test of Visual–Motor Integration (VMI), Sixth Edition
Beery-Buktenica Developmental Test of Visual Perception, Sixth Edition
Beery-Buktenica Developmental Test of Motor Coordination, Sixth Edition
Comprehensive Trail Making Test (CTMT)
Motor-Free Visual Perception Test, Third Edition (MVPT-III)
Picture Span Subtest on WISC-V
Tower of London, Second Edition (TOL-II)
Hooper Visual Organization Test (VOT)
Motor
Bayley Scales of Infant Development, Third Edition (Bayley-iii) (Motor Scales)
Beery-Buktenica Developmental Test of Motor Coordination, Sixth Edition
Grooved Pegboard
Test of Gross Motor Development, Second Edition (TGMD-2)
Mullen Scales of Early Learning (Motor Scales)
Vineland Scales of Adaptive Behavior (Vineland-II)
Attention
Conner's Rating Scale Third Edition (Conners 3)
Conner's Continuous Performance Test, Second Edition (CPT-II)
Conner's Kiddie Continuous Performance Test, (K-CPT)
Test of Variables of Attention (TOVA)
Wepman's Auditory Discrimination Test, Second Edition (ADT-II)
General attention observations during cognitive testing
Observations during ADOS-2 regarding attention during conversation/play
Results from Executive Functioning measures
Executive functioning
Behavior Rating Inventory of Executive Functioning (BRIEF)
Boston Naming Test, Second Edition (BNT-2)
Comprehensive Trail Making Test (CTMT)

(continued)

Table 5.5 (continued)

Cognitive
Tower of London, Second Edition (TOL-II)
Stroop Color and Word Test—Child/Adult Version
Paced Auditory Serial Addition Test (PASAT)
Wisconsin Card Sorting Test (WCST)
Memory
California Verbal Learning Test, Second Edition (CVLT-II)
Rey Auditory Verbal Learning Test (RAVLT)
Rey Complex Figure Test and Recognition Trial (RCFT)
Test of Memory and Learning (TOMAL)
Wechsler Memory Scale, Fourth Edition (WMS-IV)
Working Memory Scales on cognitive testing
Academic & learning
Gray Oral Reading Test, Fifth Edition—Form A/Form B (GORT-5)
Wechsler Individual Achievement Test, Third Edition (WIAT-III)
Woodcock-Johnson Tests of Achievement, Fourth Edition (WJ-IV)
Emotional/Behavioral
Behavior Assessment System for Children, Second Edition (BASC-II), Self, Parent & Teacher Reports
Beck Anxiety Inventory (BAI)
Beck Depression Inventory, Second Edition (BDI-II)
Children's Depression Inventory, Second Edition (CDI-2)
Minnesota Multiphasic Personality Inventory, Second Edition (MMPI-II)
Minnesota Multiphasic Personality Inventory, Adolescent (MMPI-A)
Post-Traumatic Stress Diagnostic Scale (PDS)
Revised Children's Manifest Anxiety Scale, Second Edition (RCMAS-II)
Sixteen Personality Factor Questionnaire (16PF) (Computer)
Projective measures
Rorschach
Human Figure Drawing Task
Brief Projective Measures (Animal Choice Test & Three Wishes)
Roberts, Second Edition (Roberts-II)
Thematic Apperception Test (TAT)
Sentence Completion for Children/Teens/Adults (SCT)
Validity
Validity Indicator Profile (VIP) Verbal Scales and Nonverbal Scales
Test of Memory Malingering (TOMM)
Adaptive behavior
Behavior Assessment System for Children, Second Edition (BASC-II), Self, Parent & Teacher Reports
Scales of Independent Behavior—Revised (SIB-R)
Vineland Adaptive Behavior Scale, Second Edition—Parent/Caregiver Rating Form (VABS-II)
Vineland Adaptive Behavior Scale, Second Edition—Survey Interview Form (VABS-II)

Checklists of Measures by age of Client

The checklist provided above spells out the measures often used by the clinic where the authors conduct assessments. When selecting the initial list of assessments, the clinician should determine which measures are most appropriate to evaluate all of the areas of concern identified during the initial consult, or a priority list of essential measures based to comply with financial limitations. It is important to consider the age of the client when selecting instruments. Most assessments have a range for which the test is considered appropriate. Below is a brief reference table that can be used when choosing measures for clients of various ages (Table 5.6).

As a clinician identifies priorities for testing, he or she should consider issues raised in the initial consultation that map onto areas or domains of assessment. These must include the core areas: cognition, language, social, and sensory. These areas will be discussed in detail in the following chapters on assessment. Autism-specific measures including the ADOS-2 are always part of a battery for ASD assessment, regardless of whether the evaluation planned is brief or more extensive.

Taking into account the funding challenges noted previously, additional areas on which an expert clinician will gather information during an initial interview include: visual–spatial, motor, attention, executive functioning, memory, emotional/behavioral, and adaptive domains. Individuals with ASD may have strengths or weaknesses across these domains and a thorough understanding of these areas will lead to better recommendations for treatment and support.

Table 5.6 Measures by age of client

Assessment area	Age		
	Child	Adolescent	Adult
Cognitive	WPPSI-IV	DAS-II	WAIS-IV
	MULLENS	WISC-V	WJ-IV
	DAS-II	WAIS-IV	SB5
	WISC-V	WJ-IV	
	WJ-IV	SB5	
	SB5		
Language	TOPL-2	TOPL-2	CELF-5
	CELF-PRE2	CELF-5	EOWPVT-4
	CELF-5	EOWPVT-4	PPVT-4
	EOWPVT-4	PPVT-4	COWA
	PPVT-4	COWA	
	COWA		
	PLS-4		
	ABLLS-R		
Social	SCQ	SCQ	SCQ
	ADOS-2	ADOS-2	ADOS-2
	SRS	SRS	ADI-R
	ADI-R	ADI-R	

(continued)

Table 5.6 (continued)

Assessment area	Age		
	Child	Adolescent	Adult
Sensory	Sensory Profile	Sensory Profile	
Visual–spatial and motor	MVPT-III	MVPT-III	MVPT-III
	GPBT	GPBT	GPBT
	Beery VMI	Beery VMI	VOT
	TGMD-2	VOT	
	VOT		
Attention	K-CPT	CPT-3	CPT-3
	CPT-3	TOVA	TOVA
	TOVA	Conners 3	
	ADT-II		
	Conners 3		
Executive functions	CTMT	CTMT	CTMT
	TOL-II	TOL-II	TOL-II
	WCST	WCST	WCST
	Stroop	Stroop	Stroop
	BRIEF	BNT-2	BNT-2
		PASAT	PASAT
		BRIEF	
Memory/learning	TOMAL	TOMAL	TOMAL
	RCFT	RAVLT	RAVLT
		RCFT	RCFT
		WMS-IV	WMS-IV
		MMSE	MMSE
		CDT	CDT
Academic	WJ-IV	WJ-IV	WJ-IV
	GORT-5	GORT-5	GORT-5
	WIAT-III	WIAT-III	WIAT-III
Emotional/behavioral	CDI-2	BAI	BAI
	RCMAS-II	BDI-II	BDI-II
	BASC-2	CDI-2	MMPI-II
		RCMAS-II	PDS
		MMPI-A	16PF
		16PF	
		BASC-2	
Projective	Human figure drawing test	Human figure drawing test	Sentence completion
	Animal choice	Animal choice	Rorschach
	Three wishes	Three wishes	Thematic Apperception Test (TAT)
	Roberts-II	Roberts-II	
		Sentence completion	
	Sentence completion	Rorschach	

(continued)

Table 5.6 (continued)

Assessment area	Age		
	Child	Adolescent	Adult
Validity		VIP	VIP
		TOMM	TOMM
Adaptive	BASC-II	BASC-II	BASC-II
	VABS-II	VABS-II	VABS-II
	SIB-R	SIB-R	SIB-R

Assessment Preparation

After completion of the initial consult, the clinician walks away with a list of initial concerns, associated domains, and a checklist of assessment measures. There may be documentation provided by the client including the initial packet and any previous assessments or records shared from school, pediatricians, or other clinicians. At this time, the clinician should review all background information and identify the timeline for testing as well as the planned order of administration of assessments. However, as presented in this chapter, the process is dynamic based on symptoms presented by the client and this plan can change. In order to be prepared, the psychologist or staff should compile the client file that includes all background information, checklist of measures, any additional documentation provided, consent forms, releases, and other paperwork with assessment materials including behavior observation forms, protocols, and any additional materials needed.

Helping parents consider how to tell their child about an upcoming assessment, discussing what snacks or favorite items (an I-Pad, for example, perhaps to be utilized as reinforcement) to bring to the assessment, and discussing the schedule for the day can be helpful. Some parents need to be present for standardized assessment (ADOS—Toddler Module, Mullen Scales, etc.) and/or for the child's comfort. Other parents may choose to wait in the waiting room and see their child for breaks as is standardized for other measures (ADOS—Module 3, WISC-V) or to leave a cell phone number and return at lunch time. Adults may come alone or at times bring a friend or family member to be present in the waiting room as the assessment is conducted. The authors of this text find that depending on the age and behavioral presentation of the client, between 2 and 5 h of testing in 1 day is enough, and most frequently clients come on 2 days for 3–4 h of testing each day. These testing schedules may change based on the limitations of the setting and needs of the client.

Once the client has been prepared for the assessment experience and the examiner has compiled all of the data gathered from the initial consultation, intake packet, and other important paperwork, it is time to begin testing. In order to ensure a successful first day of testing, the clinician should know how to take important behavioral observations, as well as how to manage challenging behaviors. The following chapter will provide clinicians with a guide for taking observations and successfully engaging the client such that the testing can ultimately provide an accurate measure of the individual's skills.

Chapter 6
Testing Begins

Abstract When the client presents for the first day of testing, psychologists should be prepared to take observations regarding the individual's affect, behavior, as well as social and communication skills. In an assessment for ASD, eye contact, gestures, facial expressions, and the integration of these are important considerations. Social interaction, play, and interests are critical to observe. It is best practice to have behavior observations from multiple raters who are trained in autism assessment. These observations answer questions like, "was the interaction comfortable or awkward?" "Was the child rigid, bossy, or resistant to testing?" Included in this chapter is a guide for taking such observations, as well as assessing the child's problem-solving approach during cognitive assessments. It can sometimes be helpful to consider first impressions of the client as compared to clinical impressions after a full diagnostic assessment. A careful look at the various perspectives of clinicians during different stages in the assessment process can provide rich data to be considered in diagnostic decisions. The chapter includes an instructive guide for managing behaviors during a diagnostic assessment. Through the utilization of ABA principles, clinicians are empowered to complete a comprehensive evaluation, even when others may have deemed the child "untestable." At the conclusion of this chapter, clinicians are prepared to set up for a successful testing session, manage challenging behavior, establish rapport with clients, and take valuable assessment observations.

Keywords Observation Protocol for ASD • Eye Contact • Gesture Use and Autism • Establishing rapport in ASD assessment • Observing play behaviors in ASD • Observing language skills in ASD • Observing reciprocity in ASD • Observing approach to task in ASD • Managing behavior during diagnostic assessments

© Springer International Publishing Switzerland 2016
A.P. Kroncke et al., *Assessment of Autism Spectrum Disorder*, Contemporary Issues in Psychological Assessment, DOI 10.1007/978-3-319-25504-0_6

Testing Begins

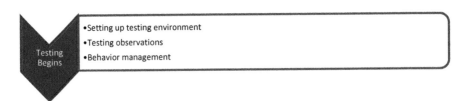

Testing
Begins

- Setting up testing environment
- Testing observations
- Behavior management

A clinician or team of clinicians will begin the assessment process with a general idea of what measures may provide the most useful data as discussed in the previous chapter. Clinicians should have a completed checklist nearby during the assessment. As the assessment progresses and data are collected in domains including cognitive and autism symptoms, sometimes a battery will be adjusted as measures are added or removed to answer the referral question(s). The referral questions of most interest in this text are of course "Do I/Does my child have an Autism Spectrum Disorder? If so/if not, what other diagnoses are relevant?" And "Where do we go from here?"

As will be explained in Chap. 7, the selection of tests is dynamic and evolving throughout the assessment. The clinician may plan to administer a cognitive measure and an ADOS-2 on the first day of testing and then will constantly review data from that testing as a basis for understanding results from other tests. Provided here are some basic examples of the way in which a clinician may adjust the battery as needed. A child with presenting social skills deficits who does not meet criteria on the ADOS-2 for an Autism Spectrum Disorder may benefit from assessments that consider attention, anxiety, and attachment. A child who very clearly does meet criteria on the ADOS-2 and is very rigid and literal may not benefit from taking projective assessments but a rating scale for emotions and/or play observation may provide more useful data on emotion and behavior. If a cognitive measure reveals very low verbal skills, this may impact the language measures selected. If tasks of visual perception or fine motor demonstrate weaknesses, then additional measures in these areas (VMI sequence, Grooved Pegs, MVPT) may be added to a battery. These examples here were provided to illuminate how the selection of measures evolves throughout the testing sessions. Again, a more thorough description of this process is provided in Chap. 7.

Observations During the Assessment Process

It is essential to take very thorough behavior observations during the testing process. *When assessing Autism Spectrum Disorders, it is necessary to pay close attention to eye contact, gestures, facial expressions, and the integration of these.* Social interaction, play, and interests are also critical to observe. It is best practice to have behavior observations from multiple raters who are trained in autism assessment. Observations should be conducted by each clinician who works directly with the child and ideally by other clinicians who are observing the interaction. These observations answer questions like, "was the interaction comfortable or awkward?" "Was the child rigid or flexible in his or her problem-solving approach?" It can sometimes be helpful to consider first impressions of the client as compared to clinical impressions after a full diagnostic assessment. A careful look at the various perspectives of clinicians in different stages in the assessment process can provide rich data to be considered in diagnostic decisions. Below are the areas specifically addressed in the authors' clinical practice in taking behavior observations. Each clinician who works with a client completes a behavior observation form and these forms are used as a piece of the data needed to formulate diagnostic impressions. Sometimes in practice clinicians may only note mood and behavior which is less comprehensive and limiting the valuable data comprehensive observations can provide. It is most helpful to be thorough in assessing each of the areas noted below.

Appearance

Appearance is considered including dress, physical stature, facial features, and hygiene. It is important to note atypical features that may relate to genetics such as big ears, a wide nasal bridge, facial dysmorphologies or skin abnormalities, or an especially small or large head. Fashionable attire, grooming, and cleanliness should be considered. These can speak to the level of appropriate care and indicate sensory sensitivities or awareness of social norms. For example, it is important to recognize an individual who wears the same clothes on multiple days, dresses only in soft sweat pants, or is disheveled in appearance. These could reflect rigidity, sensory sensitivities, or a lack of appropriate social awareness. In some cases, a child's dress may be overly formal or reflect restricted interests and rigidity. It should be noted when a child always wears neckties, vests, or hats. A child may dress in costumes, wear a cape, don shorts in the winter, or seem not to notice when his shoes are untied or shirt is unbuttoned. All of these atypical clothing preferences can indicate whether or not a child is aware of how he or she is perceived by peers or others in public. It can be helpful to notice if an individual wears excessive makeup, is overly accessorized, or dresses provocatively. Weight, height, and muscle tone can also provide useful information about diet and health.

Behavioral Presentation

Behavioral presentation is important to observe specifically looking at patterns of behavior and antecedents. For example, if behavior changes over the course of testing or if an individual presents differently on different days, it is helpful to take note and consider these shifts. For younger children, noting the response of the child to saying goodbye to or being without the caregiver and additionally noting the caregiver's response to spending time away from the child is helpful. For example, a child with ASD may run into the testing room completely forgetting to say goodbye to mom or dad and without taking a moment to meet the examiner. He or she may also cry, hide behind a parent, or avoid the testing room. It is useful to note whether the individual greeted the examiner appropriately, avoided gaze and hid in the corner, or perhaps started out with a statement like "Do you know how many planets are in our solar system?" As testing progresses, it is helpful to note whether the individual warms to testing or becomes increasingly active and distracted. Misbehaviors or reactions that are out of the ordinary should also be recorded.

Language

When making observations about language, include both receptive and expressive language skills. In children with ASDs, sometimes expressive language skills are better than receptive skills. In the receptive domain, it is important to note whether the client appears to listen, understand, and respond to others' comments or directions. It is important to observe the length of utterance, prosody, and tone of voice and note any formal or stereotyped statements. Particular speech patterns can signal autism symptoms such as a "sing-song" voice, or a staccato or robotic tone. Children with a sing-song tone tend to exaggerate certain sounds and syllables in an odd fashion, even at a young age. Children with a robotic speech pattern, sound overly serious, often use formal, overly high level vocabulary, and tend to be monotone. The typical inflection and expression expected of a child that age may be absent or delayed. Sometimes, the child seems to be on a monologue and is unaware of whether the "audience" is following the conversation. Other times, the child constantly tells jokes or talks incessantly. Formal language may be very advanced or professorial in nature, often feeling as though the individual is giving a lecture or academic discourse, seeming unable to participate in an informal social context.

Stereotyped language may sound like a quote from a television show, movie, or quote from a parent. It is sometimes helpful to write these phrases down and keep track of how many times the child says them. Repetitive comments are also important to consider. Some children may echo the examiner or their parent but struggle to produce language that is not echoic. Other children may repeat the same phrase over and over. With older children, teens, and adults it is also important to consider stereotyped, formal, or repetitive utterances. At times, individuals with ASD will make a repetitive comment, be too formal, or quote a parent or TV program without fully understanding the concept or saying. For example, a repetitive comment may be reporting "I'm happy when my grandmother is happy!" And then when further questioned, "My grandmother is happy when I'm happy!" This can become repetitive and indicate that the individual is unaware of or unsure of how to describe his or her feelings. A formal response may be like in one case of an 8-year old in response to "Why do people get married?" answered "To perpetuate the human species." Stereotyped language could include a comment like "Oh kids these days!" when asked about getting along with others at school. When taking language observations, we find it important to write down examples of these comments made by an individual because it can be very helpful when explaining differences in language skills to be able to provide parents or the individuals with examples of language differences that may be associated with ASD.

Eye Contact and Gesture in Communication

Other important behavior observations include the use of eye contact, gesture, and the integration of these with use of language. One common myth about Autism Spectrum is that an individual who makes eye contact cannot have Autism. While the quality of eye contact is important to note, an individual with appropriate eye contact may have Autism. Sometimes clinicians hear upon intake "I think my child may have an ASD but our pediatrician or classroom teacher says 'no' because my child has good eye contact." Many individuals with Autism Spectrum Disorders do make eye contact. One important practice when taking behavior observations is to reflect on the quality of eye contact. Eye contact that is too intense or not well integrated with other components of communication is as important to take note of as avoiding gaze.

Often upon intake, parents ask how we might differentiate between a young child with language delays and a child with an ASD. Children with language delays or severe articulation difficulties are relatively easy to distinguish from individuals with Autism Spectrum Disorders by their use of other methods of communication. Even more than a typically developing child, a child with a language disorder will rely on means of nonverbal communication. This child will make eye contact and use gesture as a means of communicating play, intent, wants, and needs. Children with language delays but not autism often involve the examiner in their play, both show and share objects, and display a sense of shared enjoyment. Some children are inflexible and unable to take the perspective of another child even when talking about their own interests. As noted before, many individuals on the Spectrum make less coordinated eye contact and use gesture only when it is specifically requested of them. Often these individuals have difficulty integrating these modes of communication. Again, ASD is a spectrum, and so it is important not to rule it out or in with a single characteristic.

Play/Interests

When observing a child's play or interests, it is helpful to note whether they are age appropriate and flexible versus narrow and repetitive. An individual may love Legos, for example, but when a friend visits who does not have an interest in Legos; he or she can ride bikes, play board games, or complete arts and crafts activities all the while taking turns and playing cooperatively. It is when an interest is so narrow that a child would rather do this alone and let his or her playmate be entertained by parents or siblings than try a different game, that it can be a concern.

Individuals who are so bossy and controlling that they can only play with a very passive sibling or peer may have social difficulties worth noting. For example, a child may obsessively line up or organize toys, rather than playing with them. If another child or parent attempts to change the order of the toys, and the child has a meltdown, he or she may be showing signs of autism (although this could also be due to anxiety or other condition). It can also be important to consider the age-appropriateness of the play. It should be noticed as peculiar and restricted when a child who is 15 years old shows an obsessive interest in Disney princesses or Thomas the Train. Further, a teenage girl who seems to have no interest in the latest music, styles, or celebrities, although not diagnostic in itself, may be considered atypical. In the evaluation, it is helpful to determine whether an individual can have conversations about areas of interests and about other topics introduced. An individual who ignores the examiner or makes a shift like "Well the spiders in Minecraft … ." may have difficulty conversing reciprocally. Each time a new topic is introduced, an individual may have challenges taking the perspective of others or being flexible. It also should be noted when the child is overly directive in play with the examiner. For example, he may only allow certain toys to be used in a precise manner, or refuse to share certain objects with the examiner. It is of note when a child will not use an object symbolically and can only use it as intended. For example, if the examiner tries to pretend that a fire truck is an ambulance or wants to make an animal talk and this is disallowed by the child, this pattern may be indicative of limited imagination or rigidity.

Social Reciprocity

Social reciprocity refers to an individual's ability to respond appropriately to comments or play initiation from the examiner. Often as evaluators, we find ourselves making comments such as "Today is my birthday!" or "My favorite fish passed away yesterday" so that we can evaluate a client's social and emotional reciprocity. We make note of the response and its relevance. Some children with ASD may ignore a comment completely or provide a very factual response like "What color fish?" They may offer their own perspective without taking the examiner's saying "My fish didn't die." Or "I don't even have a fish." A response considering the examiner's perspective might be "Oh no, what happened." Or "poor fish!" In response to "it's my birthday," an appropriate answer may be "Oh! How old are you?" or "Happy birthday!" while a response that fails to take perspective may be "Huh" or no response at all. In play, an examiner may take interest in a toy or do something silly with a character and look to see if the child laughs or plays along versus ignores or tells the examiner he or she is wrong. An example of a child struggling with flexibility and reciprocity in play would be "No, no he didn't slip on the banana he's over there reading the book!" "That dinosaur is a plant eater, he can't eat the hot dog." or "My guy (play figure) doesn't want to play that game." These responses could indicate challenges in reciprocity and perspective taking.

Attention

It is helpful to make notes on attention, even though this is a domain very frequently evaluated with direct measures and parent/teacher questionnaires. First, it is necessary to consider differences in attention across settings; to note observations of attention, and to compare these to testing and rating scale data. An individual who starts out the evaluation without focus but improves quickly may have been anxious at the start but has "warmed up" to testing. An individual who can attend to certain tasks but not others may have intermittent challenges with attention or motivation. Finally, an individual who maintains attention initially but this quickly wanes over the course of 3–4 h in office may have significant challenges with sustained attention. It is helpful to know whether an individual appeared attentive but made errors related to inattention or appeared inattentive but responded correctly. At times, evaluations assess attention only with rating scales. These authors suggest that it is important to consider rating scales, behavior observations of attention, and performance on direct measures to be thorough in the assessment of this domain.

Motor Skills

When observing gross and fine motor skills, it is helpful to consider gross motor movements like walking, jumping on the trampoline, running, and balancing. Fine motor skills are observed by watching pencil grip as well as grip on any utensils, considering the speed of writing, and noticing whether fine manipulative objects (beads, coins) are well managed or often dropped. Observe a child snacking and taking breaks to notice fine or gross motor challenges. Very active younger children may climb all over the testing room and it is noteworthy whether movements are clumsy or agile. Studying a child's hands, arms, and core strength (i.e., does he have good muscle tone or is he very thin and weak) can be very helpful. A clinician should note posture and stamina to complete tasks. Again this is an area to assess via rating scales and direct measures but observations can also provide useful information.

Mood and Affect

Mood and affect should be observed for congruence and integration, as well as the level of fluctuation in mood throughout testing the session(s). Individuals with ASD often have restricted or incongruent affect. An individual with restricted affect does not show typical appropriate levels of emotion when sharing personal stories or relating to the emotions of the examiner. A child with incongruent affect may discuss times when he or she has felt sad or angry while wearing a big smile. Other individuals may report feeling happy but affect is flat, sad, or anxious. The other issue examiners should look for is how consistent or fluctuating the affect is. It is important to note cheerful or depressed mood or inappropriately labile mood. Euthymic mood with congruent affect would indicate that an individual feels fine, and mood may not be of concern. Sometimes individuals may be initially anxious during an evaluation but become more comfortable as testing continues. Taken together, examiners should carefully note any time the individual's mood shifts suddenly or seems inappropriate to the situation or conversational content.

Naturalistic Observations

Taking observations outside of the office or assessment center may add credibility when providing diagnostic information to parents, families, or treatment teams. In some cases with complex presentation, it can be helpful diagnostically to observe an individual in more than one setting. Often rating scales from parents, teachers, tutors, or other familiar individuals provides useful and clear information about the individual's presentation in multiple environments. At other times, even with rating scales and interview data, the clinician feels unclear and may need to consider a naturalistic observation. Sometimes diagnostic clarification is not needed, but it may be helpful to observe an individual at home, work, or school to consider environmental variables or relationship dynamics that are impacting them. This can provide more information from which to tailor specific recommendations for best supporting a child or adult with an ASD. Collaboration between school and clinical teams, when this is possible, is very helpful for diagnosis and treatment. In the chapters on school-based assessment, authors revisit the value of school observations and clinician–teacher consultation in meeting a child's needs.

Now readers have been exposed to the primary areas required for observation during a comprehensive evaluation. These include: behavior, appearance, language, eye contact and gestures, play and interests, social reciprocity, attention, motor skills, mood and affect, and naturalistic. Sometimes, examiners mistakenly underutilize observation as a tool in assessment. Often the data obtained from watching the child complete the testing is every bit as important as the data obtained from the assessments. These authors suggest that observations should occur throughout testing, from the waiting room, to the time the individual goes home for the day.

Cognitive Testing Observations

Often, examiners conduct the cognitive evaluation first in the series of assessments administered. One reason for this is that cognitive testing provides a foundation from which each other assessment can be compared. The other potentially helpful reason to conduct cognitive testing first is to observe the child's approach to attacking test items, persevering on challenging tasks, and problem solving. To that aim, examiners should consider "Facilitators/Inhibitors" as a guide for making observations during cognitive testing.

Facilitators–Inhibitors

One valid measure of IQ is the Woodcock-Johnson Tests of Cognitive abilities, Fourth Edition (WJ-IV). A major contribution of the Woodcock-Johnson test development was the creation of what is called *"facilitators–inhibitors"* which are factors that influence performance on the Woodcock-Johnson-IV (Flanagan & Kaufman, 2004). Whether or not the examiner chooses the WJ-IV or another measure, these important factors should be evaluated for any cognitive assessment. Indeed, factors influencing performance are probably the most important pieces of clinical insight gained during a cognitive evaluation for ASD. It is critical to evaluate the influences of symptoms and other factors within the individual or test environment that influence the demonstration of skills.

Internal Facilitator–Inhibitors

Organic Integrity

The facilitators/inhibitors identified by Woodcock and Johnson include factors like *"organic integrity"* which refers to the client's general health, need for medications, and functioning of the sensory and nervous system (Flanagan & Kaufman, 2004, p. 110). During an assessment for autism, there may be the influence of neurological dysfunction or delays which affect performance. The child may have poor vision or hearing, may be heavily medicated, and may have sensory needs. Sometimes individuals with ASD unfortunately have been misdiagnosed with ADHD or Anxiety when in fact autism or a mood disorder may be the reason for their symptoms. In that case, medications may have a detrimental effect on the child's functioning during cognitive testing.

With regard to sensory needs, it is important to be "sensitive" to these during an assessment. If the noise is too loud during the testing session, the examiner should be sure to use a sound machine or other system to block out the distractions. If the light is too bright, close the blinds; if the smell is too strong, try another room, and if there are too many people, consider individualized administration. It is also important to not overestimate the impact of sensory issues on behavior, however. As will be explained in the next section, poor behaviors generally do not have a sensory basis in ASD so examiners must avoid such assumptions. Even when sensory accommodations are provided, examiners should make sure to note them, as they indicate that the child's sensory sensitivities are interfering with demonstration of skills; potentially in multiple environments.

Attention and Concentration

Other internal facilitator–inhibitors include motivation, attention, and concentration. These factors can be influenced by the child's general attitude toward testing, his or her level of effort, and his or perceived abilities on specific tasks. For example, some children with ASD will apply much more effort on the perceptual reasoning tasks than on verbal tasks due to higher levels of engagement and self-efficacy with these items. Some factors that may influence attention and concentration include distractibility and impulsivity. Examiners should watch carefully as the child is testing. Does a plane flying overhead completely derail his thinking process? Does the child respond too quickly, almost as if guessing, and does this result in the missing of items? Another sign of attention problems on a cognitive assessment for ASD is a pattern of missed items that proceeds thusly. A child misses item #19, correctly answers #20 and #21, misses item #22, and so forth. This pattern is often a sign of attention deficits. When this occurs, it is important to watch carefully to see whether or not the child really did not know the answer or if he or she just lost focus. At times, examiners may choose to "test the limit" and administer items past a ceiling to determine if the child has further knowledge that went undemonstrated due to attention problems. Although items answered correctly after a test ceiling do not impact the child's score, testing the limit can provide useful data regarding the impact attention is having on performance. Individuals with ASD often have attention problems, whether or not these problems occur in the context of a comorbid diagnosis with ADHD, so observations of attention are critical.

Further, it is important to consider factors like attitude and effort on these tasks. Did the child only miss items with less appealing graphics or particularly uninteresting subject matter? Sometimes individuals with ASD refuse items that are not highly motivating or repeatedly request to go back to a test enjoyed previously. They often have difficulty shifting mental set. During cognitive testing, this may appear when the individual answers the items on a new test incorrectly because he or she is following the directions of a previous subtest. Sometimes individuals with ASD perseverate on the test items, providing the same answer to multiple items.

Finally, consider whether or not impulsive responding actually results in missing of items. Sometimes children who are highly intelligent with a quick processing speed may answer quickly but not miss items, which may indicate giftedness, rather than attention problems. Sattler (2001) encourages examiners to consider attentional factors like the child's response to name, response to visual and auditory distractions, length of time on task, and the ability to regain a child's attention once distracted (p. 195). When assessing for ASD, the examiner should watch for flexibility in problem-solving approach as well as use of strategies. Often, individuals with ASD struggle with metacognition (thinking about one's thinking), and fail to use verbal mediation strategies or to self-correct on test items. They may rigidly adhere to answers that are clearly wrong or repetitively ask if answers are correct even when the examiner explains that no feedback can be given on the test. All of these observations are noteworthy in an assessment for ASD. Attention and concentration, attitude and effort, flexibility and metacognition, all may be impaired in individuals with ASD.

When testing a child with lower cognitive abilities who may have autism, it is especially important to engage the examinee such as to capture his or her attention and obtain the best sample of ability levels. Whenever necessary, examiners should start with the easiest items in the entire battery, or start with particularly engaging subtests, in order to gain behavioral momentum (using Premack principle) (Cooper, Heron, & Hewerd, 2013). Test administrators might choose to begin with more concrete tests that require less elaborate verbal responses. An example might be the Picture Concepts task of the WISC-IV where the child is asked only to point to items that share a common category, rather than the more abstract requirement of telling the examiner how two words are alike on Similarities. Clinicians should offer breaks, snacks, and consistent praise of effort. When testing a child of lower cognition, it can be exceedingly important to provide wait time, be patient, and to reward the child's efforts. Examiners should reduce distractions and sensory stimuli. Clinicians should be careful to limit language and noise. These mild adjustments can result in obtaining an accurate sample of a child's cognitive ability, even in more challenging cases. Sometimes children are judged to be "untestable" by other examiners when in fact the child can be tested successfully with the appropriate strategies and accommodations in place.

In one case at the Emerge clinic, it was necessary to administer the test as just described, with the utilization of two examiners and an assistant. The examiner administered the items, held the stimulus book, and recorded responses. The second examiner provided cues and praise for effort and offered sensory breaks. The assistant provided test materials, removed any unnecessary objects from the client's view, co-scored with the examiners, and took behavioral observations. This assessment resulted in valid results which were then extremely helpful to the family in securing resources and services.

Personality Style

The final internal facilitator–inhibitor factor to consider is *personality style* (Sattler, 2001, p. 110). This includes characteristics of personality that, although certainly changeable, are more stable over time, and impact the child's performance on cognitive tests (p. 110). One significant personality factor is problem-solving approach.

This includes the child's care and speed in responding and thinking style (convergent or divergent thinking patterns) (p. 110). Sattler (2001) recommends the evaluator consider if the child is shy, friendly, cooperative, or eager to please (Sattler, 2001, p. 195). During an assessment for ASD, personality factors are highly important to evaluate. Some individuals with autism are less motivated by pleasing the examiner and may thusly apply a lower degree of effort on tasks they find unengaging. To evaluate this, the examiner should consider how difficult or easy it is to motivate the child to finish the items of the cognitive assessment. Was there an inordinate need for administration strategies? Did the child attempt to distract the examiner with side-bar conversations and questions? Did the child need an excessive amount of breaks to complete the cognitive testing? The presence of these issues serves to inform the examiner that these same problems may interfere with functioning at school and at home.

Further personality factors that should be considered during a cognitive assessment include (Sattler, 2001, p. 195) the child's attitude toward test-taking; was he interested, withdrawn, or reluctant? The child's mood should be considered as well; was he anxious, angry, fearful, sad, or flat? (p. 195). How did he or she respond to time limits and queries? For example, a child may become anxious when the timer is used or become defensive when challenged to provide elaborations on verbal responses. In an assessment for ASD, it is particularly important to consider personality factors such as these that may be indicative of autism symptoms. Generally, it is a red flag for ASD when any personality issue results in reduced quality of rapport. The examiner should take note immediately when the test administration becomes challenging due to an inordinate need to apply test administration strategies, breaks, and encouragement to gain compliance with testing.

External Facilitator–Inhibitors

Clinic, Home, and Community Environmental Factors

There are also external facilitator–inhibitors that impact a child's performance on cognitive testing. External factors might include the physical setting of testing, as well as the stability and comfort of the individual's home and school environments (Flanagan & Kaufman, 2004, p. 110). It may be that the child lives in an unstable or emotionally intense home environment. The resultant stress may impact testing. Sometimes the child does not feel comfortable in the setting where the test is administered and this may impact performance. In this case, the examiner should make accommodations, if possible, as noted above. Alternately, some children perform far better in the clinic, in large part because of the structure, the 1-to-1 attention, and the limited distractions. When the examiner suspects an external factor may be impacting the child's performance, this should be noted and reported with the results. The examiner might note, "This cognitive assessment may be a low reflection of Joey's abilities because he was nervous and distracted often during testing."

Final Thoughts on Facilitators–Inhibitors

On the WJ-III: COG, NU protocol, there is a helpful list of test observations to consider: *conversational proficiency, cooperation, activity level, attention and concentration, self-confidence, care in responding, and response to difficult tasks* (Flanagan & Kaufman, 2004). When assessing children who are suspected of having autism, this short list alone provides a rich body of information about how ASD symptoms may interfere with demonstration of skills. For example, "conversational proficiency" is often a factor to evaluate during an autism evaluation. With regard to conversation, look at the quality of the child's speech, considering pitch and tone, loudness or softness, rhythm, and intonation (Sattler, 2001). Consider reciprocity of the communication, the child's tendency to go off on tangents or to monologue, and whether or not he or she attempts to engage the examiner in conversation. A thorough account of each of the assessment areas is provided in the chapters that follow. For now, it is important to understand that cognitive assessment goes well beyond interpretation of responses and scores. In addition to the facilitators–inhibitors and test observation areas mentioned above, the authors invite clinicians conducting cognitive assessment for ASD to consider overall engagement, tendency to fatigue and frustration tolerance, the use of strategies and verbal mediation, the ability to accept feedback, flexibility in problem-solving approach, humor and playfulness versus seriousness, and general quality of rapport. Clinical observations are critically important. An overly serious, nonreciprocal, easily fatigued or frustrated child who fails to use strategies and self-monitor may be showing signs of autism. The minute testing begins, the child is offering hints and clues about his/her "way of being in the world"—it is the examiner's job to tune into them.

Challenging Behavior: Behavior Management during a Diagnostic Evaluation

Utilizing ABA Principles

There are many reasons assessment results may underrepresent an individual's true abilities and skills. The participant may be anxious, tired, hungry, not wearing necessary eyeglasses, or unable to properly comprehend the instructions—just to name a few. When evaluating individuals who may have an ASD, the number of barriers to valid performance typically increases even further. The primary reason for this is that most elements of the assessment process represent a social interaction between the participant and the evaluator and interpersonal interactions are inherently more challenging for individuals with an ASD than their neurotypical peers. Furthermore, the evaluator and many aspects of the evaluation setting and materials are likely novel for the participant and individuals with an ASD are often likely to resist change. Individuals with an ASD especially enjoy routines and familiar people hence the skilled evaluator makes special accommodations to assist the client in feeling as calm and comfortable as possible so he or she can do his or her best. Not all individuals with ASD exhibit challenging behaviors during an assessment, but in such instances it is crucial to be competent in behavior management for the child and for best practices in data collection.

While some factors such as depression are constitutional and unlikely to vary significantly across the course of the assessment, very often challenging behaviors or emotions are transient and it's possible to minimize or eliminate their influence. The competent evaluator effectively minimizes the effects of barriers like sensory sensitivities, tantrums, social anxiety, and rigidity on measures designed to assess cognitive skills and abilities. Since assessment of social skills, behaviors, and emotions is also important, these variables are assessed directly on measures designed to evaluate them in a valid manner. By dissociating the assessment of different variables in this manner, valid assessment results can be determined in all areas. To achieve valid results, the evaluator must optimally harness the participant's attention and motivation so that the results truly represent his/her abilities and skills. Optimizing attention and motivation to complete the testing tasks can be divided into antecedents (things that happen before an item is presented) and consequences (the evaluator's responses following behaviors exhibited by the participant).

Managing Antecedents

Antecedents are conditions or events that occur before the testing and influence the behavior or performance of the individual being tested. Antecedents include customary practices like helping ensure the individual is well rested and well fed before the assessment. In addition, managing sensory experiences is often very relevant to obtain valid evaluation results. Finally, an individual may have persistent emotional problems like anxiety or depression or neurophysiological conditions such as psychosis or seizures which generally impact their functioning in a chronic manner.

Managing the testing environment can be thought of as proactively setting the stage to help the child perform optimally. Indeed, the environment is experienced through a variety of sensory receptors including our eyes, ears, nose as well as mast cells and proprioceptors in our skin. Mast cells receive input pertaining to our sense of touch while proprioceptors process input pertaining to where our limbs and body are in space. While any skilled evaluator or clinician is well aware of the importance of adequate lighting and a quiet environment for their participants, most do not consider the scent of the cleaning solvent used to wipe testing surfaces or the frequency of the air conditioner whir or the sound of the furnace that periodically cuts into the otherwise quiet environment. Sensory sensitivities for individuals with ASD can be a cause of behavior problems if the participant experiences them as highly aversive. This is particularly relevant for individuals who may have little or no functional language skills with which to communicate their needs.

Sensory Sensitivities

Individuals with autism very often experience marked sensory sensitivities as mentioned. Sensory sensitivities are conditions where the individual is significantly under- or overly-responsive to certain sensory input compared with the general population of people their age. Sometimes these sensitivities are always present and unvarying in strength but more often their impact varies based on factors, including stimulation, present in a given setting. In general, the evaluators should try to minimize the effects of sensory sensitivities because the goal in assessment is to help the individual do the best he or she is capable of on a given day. For example, many individuals with autism are sensitive to certain fabrics such as denim which can feel uncomfortable and be distracting for them. The participants should be permitted to wear preferred clothing for the assessment even if that means they show up in sweats or pajamas! Again, the goal of the assessment is to determine a valid representation of abilities and skills not just to observe a client emotionally meltdown. If a child is annoyed by his or her clothing because a parent wanted him or her to look presentable, chances are the findings will underrepresent capabilities. Similarly, participants may choose to turn off fluorescent lighting and do the entire evaluation in a naturally lighted room. Other participants may turn on a sound machine to cancel otherwise inaudible high frequency voices from an adjacent office that may distract them. Some evaluators may provide a yoga ball to provide beneficial proprioceptive input to the client while they work at a desk.

Similar to clients with AD/HD, many individuals with autism frequently need movement breaks to enable them to optimally focus their attention when working. These authors have a small trampoline in the evaluation room for such purposes. In addition, a small basketball game is available for participants to shoot hoops in between tasks and the evaluation room itself is an oversized office to permit easy movement and minimize tendencies to feel claustrophobic. These authors may also provide spandex tunnels made of thick Lycra fabric for children to crawl through to provide deep pressure somatosensory input which can feel comforting or calming for some individuals. Many younger participants enjoy an "egg chair" which consists of a low chair with a closable hood that can enclose a child inside. This chair can provide a functional method for the child to relax by allowing him or her to "hide" and temporarily escape the conversational demands of testing.

These authors recommend having a variety of chairs made of different materials and cushioning available in the testing room so that the participant can self-select furniture that is pleasing for him or her. The evaluator could offer up a favorite ergonomically designed chair if this is the seat the participant selects. Similarly there's no reason the participant can't complete test items seated on a couch as long as the materials are appropriately positioned in close proximity and centered on his/her midline as explained in the test manuals. It is further recommended that examiners deliberately keep the evaluation room particularly bare of any extraneous materials, including omitting unnecessary toys, that could be distracting or undesirable to the participant. All testing rooms can probably be enhanced by including high quality white-noise machines to hopefully cancel even the faintest sounds that might distract the participant. As previously mentioned, the evaluation room might include a yoga ball and small trampoline to provide additional options for seating and sensory breaks, respectively. Noting a child's sensory preferences is an important component of quality behavior observations.

While sensory processing differences are very significant for some people with ASD, it is vital to know and remember that sensory processing is rarely the primary cause of behavior problems. Far too many people mistakenly believe that individuals with ASD have a Sensory Processing Disorder or some form of sensory processing anomaly that solely causes them to behave badly. In fact, most behavior problems are maintained because the individual is trying to obtain attention or a tangible item; or because the individual is trying to avoid or escape something challenging; or because the individual just finds the behavior enjoyable. Even if a behavior functions as a communicative attempt to get or change something, individuals deserve to be taught more sophisticated ways of requesting than behaving badly.

While managing the environment to respect sensory experiences is important as just outlined, the entire front half of the brain is responsible for making choices in response to our experience. Even if an individual has limited intellectual abilities and no verbal speech, he/she still makes many choices constantly typically including how to behave. This point warrants emphasizing because inaccurately believing behavior problems are unavoidably caused by sensory processing differences likely ensures the individual will not receive services necessary to learn more sophisticated responses. In addition, inaccurately believing sensory issues cause poor behavior can actually make those very problems worse if pleasant experiences are provided whenever someone acts badly.

Managing Consequences

Sensory information reaches the brain through sensory nerves called efferents that transmit information to the posterior region of the brain located behind the central sulcus. Sensory signals ascend up the spinal cord and along cranial nerves in the face and head to be processed in the back portions of the brain. In contrast, all planned responses including speech originate in the frontal lobe generally residing in the forehead region. As stated, most behavior problems are not uncontrollable reflexes automatically executed in response to sensory experiences but instead are volitional actions which serve to have the individual get something or get out of something. The goal in sound behavior management applied to testing is to effectively have the individual motivated to get items correct and obtain breaks or rewards that the evaluator controls.

When assessing an individual who is suspected of having an ASD, it is very important to optimize his or her attention to the testing tasks as well as motivate the client to try and get the answers right. Unfortunately, many individuals with intellectual disabilities in general, but also with ASD and intellectual disabilities, are shortchanged by not being expected to complete any direct assessment of skills or abilities, and are inappropriately termed "untestable." Other times they're minimally evaluated by questionnaires administered to caregivers because evaluators are unskilled in harnessing their attention and motivation or effectively eliciting skills directly. Such practices are a gross underservice to these individuals especially when considering that if a clinician or teacher is unable to get them to pay attention and care about a testing task, they'll hardly be able to teach them anything either.

Knowledge and skills in getting the participant to attend and respond is essential for a valid assessment. When individuals have ASD, they are inherently less concerned with what the evaluator thinks about them, compared to people without ASD. This means that the usual strategies of conversation, complimenting, and praise may be insufficient. In fact, conversation is often very challenging and even aversive for people with ASD. More effective strategies for harnessing attention and motivation, as well as handling behavior problems, likely include classical conditioning, visually tracking progress, effective pacing of tasks, carefully selecting and providing reinforcers on an appropriate schedule, utilizing behavior momentum, and the Premack principle. These strategies can readily be implemented by the skilled evaluator while still preserving standardized administration procedures.

Classical Conditioning

Most people are familiar with classical conditioning from the age-old experiments that Pavlov performed in eliciting dogs to salivate at the sound of a bell or light after repeatedly pairing these stimuli with the presence of dog food (Pavlov, 1927). Those experiments worked because the dogs wanted their food (an unconditioned response). When considering the origin of many fears, one realizes that classical conditioning can also work in a problematic manner through repeated pairing of stimuli that immediately precede something undesirable such as fighter planes that precede bombs in a war, bees that may precede getting stung, or screeching tires that precede a car crash. By thinking about what individuals with ASD likely find pleasurable or aversive, principles of classical conditioning can be especially useful in testing and working with this population. Let's apply classical conditioning to examples of social interactions.

When we meet someone for the first time, most people in Western cultures typically say a standard "Hello" followed by "Nice to meet you" or something similar. If we're going to spend any amount of time with the person, almost invariably we begin to ask them questions like "Where do you go to school?" or "What's your favorite movie?" These questions are very often challenging for individuals with autism who inherently have communication difficulties. Conversing will likely challenge their weak language skills, create social anxiety, or both. Even if a test-taker has average or better intellectual ability, he or she is still meeting the evaluator for the first time, and the typical socially friendly conversations may be uncomfortable. What if the child doesn't know what "favorite" means or can't understand why you care what her favorite movie is because she obviously is not going to watch it today? This kind of logical thinking is typical of individuals with an ASD. In any event, the sequence of meeting someone immediately followed by being asked questions is a pairing that has already occurred numerous times in this participant's life. Evaluators are inevitably tripping into whatever positive or aversive response social conversations naturally evoke for this person. Because examiners likely don't know what response the questions are likely to evoke, it is recommended that questions be issued judiciously and sparingly. Examiners can adjust this precept as appropriate once it is determined whether the participant finds social questions pleasant or problematic. Many behavior problems are created because the expectations are set too high and the person is seemingly expected to endure such circumstances. Excess social communication may inadvertently serve to task the participant unnecessarily before the evaluation has formally even started! Examiners are wise to remember that this individual is likely less skilled in recognizing and asking for what he or she needs so it's up to the evaluator to optimally anticipate how to help the client do his or her best.

Now that readers have seen how classical conditioning can unknowingly hurt the evaluation process, it's helpful to consider how using its principles can be beneficial. It is recommended that examiners discern specifically what the individual enjoys before the client arrives for testing. It might be anything from playing with Legos to discussing airplane bathrooms or methods of recycling. Quite possibly it is something eccentric. By promptly pairing oneself with the activity or topic the client finds most pleasurable, the examiner is personally likely to become more reinforcing for the participant. This is important because examiners want the client to be motivated to do what is asked as well as find praise desirable. If the person has ASD, he or she is not likely to socially connect simply because the examiner is polite and kind. The important thing to remember is that by definition, individuals with an ASD have restricted interests so unless examiners provide what he/she finds pleasurable, the evaluator runs a serious risk of having the person remaining uncomfortable and disconnected. Such factors are likely to result in underperformance as well as increase the possibility of behavior problems.

Visually Tracking Progress

Individuals with ASD inherently have relative weaknesses or deficits in communication. Often they're unlikely to ask questions such as "How long is this task?" or "When do I get a break?" or even "What all are we going to do today?" Even with their communication challenges, providing such information could assist them in attending as well as reduce anxiety. In addition, they are known to relate better to isolated details and frequently have challenges in grasping the bigger picture. Information about exactly what's planned, how long it's expected to take, and when they will get a break and lunch should usually be provided proactively. This can be provided visually in a manner that's continually informative. It is recommended that a visual tracking chart be used that outlines the number of tasks planned as well as openly monitors progress. Such a chart can simply consist of 10 square boxes hastily drawn on a piece of paper with each box representing a subscale on a measure, for example. In this way, the participant can readily determine how much work remains until a break. For example, if stickers are being used in a form of token economy for reinforcement, these can be pasted directly on the visual tracking chart so the individual readily discerns how much has been completed. If an individual is nonverbal, simple pictures can be drawn to represent the planned reinforcement at the conclusion of sections of the assessment. Examiners should be sure to match the amount of work expected in each section with the duration the individual can successfully sustain attention to avoid behavior problems that can occur because of hyperactivity. Planned reinforcement at breaks can be a preferred snack or activity. As boxes are checked off or stickers pasted on the visual tracking chart to represent progress, the individual is likely to grasp the testing format even if speech or language is limited to nonverbal communication.

Effective Reinforcement

When working with individuals with an ASD, it is especially important to understand reinforcement because they are less motivated by social connections. Very often a young child with autism can be highly connected with a parent or another caregiver making it even harder for even a pleasant examiner to motivate him or her to comply with tasks. By knowing what preferred items, activities, or snacks the individual likes, the evaluator can utilize reinforcement.

Many people believe reinforcement is the same as a reward but they are different. A reward is something provided as a consequence that the giver believes the individual will *like*. Reinforcement is something provided as a consequence that *increases the probability of the proceeding behavior reoccurring*. For example, winning the Super Bowl and getting a trophy is definitely a reward but it really doesn't serve as reinforcement to play more football because the football season ends after the Super Bowl is played. Some players retire after winning the Super Bowl so for them it's definitely not a reinforcer because they quit playing football all together. Consider also how much football the NFL players would play if they got only trophies without their million-dollar salaries! For most employed adults, monetary compensation is the reinforcement for them to keep working. Back to assessment…

In order to keep an individual with autism doing tasks that are probably challenging with a person he or she has just met and may not necessarily like, it's essential to master provision of reinforcement on a schedule that sustains compliance. Most evaluators are familiar with providing access to a treasure chest at the end of the evaluation, but such a lean schedule of reinforcement is not likely to be effective for an individual with an ASD. In all likelihood, the client needs frequent reinforcement or a token, such as a checkmark or sticker, to signal subsequent provision of reinforcement. By using the visual tracking chart previously described, a checkmark or sticker can be provided often to maintain motivation to comply and put forth best effort. Possible schedules of reinforcement could be a sticker at the completion of each subscale representing about 6+ items for each token. The risk of providing reinforcement too infrequently is the individual's attention can wane, and he or she may begin to fidget with distracting materials (such as hair, the window blinds, or pencils) and even bigger behavior problems can arise such as defiance or elopement. Many times these behavior problems are some of the primary reasons the client was referred for the assessment in the first place, so observing concrete evidence that he or she can behave in a problematic way accomplishes little. After all, clients are coming to be assessed to determine what they *can do* not what they *can avoid* doing because they're not motivated to try.

Reinforcer preference assessments can be regularly used to ensure the evaluator is providing something the participant actually wants. Such a preference assessment is conducted by holding or placing two items on the table or tray equidistant in front of the participant and directly observing for what the client reaches. Information from parents or a caregiver can be used to determine which two objects or snacks to try in the preference assessment but the evaluator is responsible for determining that the reinforcer used is actually effective. Remember the Super Bowl trophy that's nice but not necessarily reinforcing? Now try taking away their salaries and see how well they play football. Those NFL players are likely to quit and try another sport if the NFL stops paying them. A professional athlete changing sports may seem silly save a few notable examples. That said, a professional athlete that changes teams during free agency to receive a higher salary, is not that much different than the participant changing activities to something they find more pleasurable instead of doing the assessment.

After observing what the individual physically selects as a reinforcer, examiners should either provide that regularly at an appropriate schedule or use a token to symbolize the reinforcement and then provide access to the selected toy or item for several minutes at a break. Examiners must be sure to teach the client that a checkmark or sticker symbolizes a reinforcer by describing this for an individual with adequate language skills to understand. If language skills are weak, it may be necessary to provide several pairings of making a checkmark followed by providing a Skittle or whatever was selected before beginning the formal assessment begins.

Because people satiate on different reinforcers whereby the item loses its effectiveness as a reinforcer with time, it's important to conduct a reinforcer preference assessment any time the examiner suspects the individual no longer wants the reinforcer being provided. After all, how many gummy bears does one person really want to eat in a given setting? Yes, an individual will tire as the day goes on but the examiner must be sure that there are no losses in cooperation and effort because the client is satiated on the current reinforcement. If a client is assessed across 2 days and on the second day motivation is significantly weaker than on day one, examiners should suspect that the strength or frequency of reinforcement may have been inadequate on the first day or the person would be motivated to come back and try again. After all, at the beginning of day two the participant is likely well rested so fatigue is probably not the issue.

Reinforcement Schedules

Reinforcement schedule pertains to the contingency basis and frequency that the evaluator uses to reinforce the participant's effort. Much research on schedules of reinforcement has shown that ratio schedules of reinforcement afford the highest rates of responding. (Cooper et al., 2013). A ratio schedule is one that provides a reinforcer after a given number of test items or test subscales have been completed. When the individual is struggling to maintain motivation and or appears to find the assessment material hard, a more frequent ratio schedule such as FR1 (fixed ratio after 1 item) may be implemented. As the participant exhibits motivation for trying (note reinforcement should be afforded for effort not contingent on correct responding), the reinforcement schedule can be gradually leaned and made more variable while sustaining motivation and effort. If a new task is started which is pretty hard for the individual being assessed, the reinforcement schedule may again need to be made more frequent. The examiner should use the participant's demonstrated effort as an indicator of whether reinforcement should be more frequent or can be successfully faded and made more intermittent. Note that intermittent reinforcement has been found to maintain rates of responding more effectively than a consistent reinforcer schedule (Cooper et al., 2013) so examiners should be sure that the rate of responding is appropriate and stable before shifting to a more random schedule. In general, it's best not to verbalize the reinforcer schedule since the individual can readily become rigidly fixated on whether or not he or she gets the edible or token rather than appropriately attending to the assessment tasks. In addition, be sure not to repeat phrases or words that would be inappropriate for the participant to echo or the parents won't be happy that a problematic behavior was actually learned during testing! Note that a reinforcer schedule is different from visual tracking of progress which simply depicts how much the participant has completed and how much of the evaluation remains. Many great books and articles have been written on the choice of reinforcement schedules to optimize motivation and performance. The interested reader is referred to Cooper et al. (2013) or the *Journal of Applied Behavior Analysis* for further information in this regard.

Premack Principle

The Premack Principle is the technology of reinforcing a low preference task such as a challenging assessment scale with a high preference activity as opposed to using a more tangible reinforcer like a desirable edible (Cooper et al., 2013). Use of a high preference activity which also has some clear sensory or motor components can not only serve as a reinforcer for successful completion of a section of the assessment but it can also provide valuable opportunities for necessary sensory input such as deep pressure, movement breaks, or other preferred sensory input. It is well known that individuals with ASD can greatly benefit from unique sensory activities and these can serve as a lovely reinforcer in exchange for tokens or checkmarks accumulated on a visual tracking sheet. Sensory activities that these authors have readily observed as enjoyable for clients with ASD include jumping on the trampoline, lying on the couch, floor or table, or hiding in the "egg chair."

It's very important that a preferred sensory activity is not offered "reactively" when the participant ignores instructions, tantrums, or performs any other undesirable behavior because the undesirable behavior will very likely be reinforced and subsequently become more intense or more frequent. This is a common mistake among novice caregivers and clinicians who reactively assume that if a child with ASD misbehaves it's because he or she has some unmet sensory need. At the very worst, someone may even give a child food upon misbehaving naively believing hunger is causing misbehavior. If a caregiver does suddenly recognize that indeed the child is hungry, the adult can simply illicit appropriate requesting from the child before feeding him or her. A request can be as elementary as an openhanded reach. Requiring the child to request, thereby avoids reinforcing undesirable behavior with such strong primary reinforcement as food which does not even necessitate learning to be reinforcing.

The careful evaluator should ask the parent or caregiver a priori, before any assessment tasks are presented, if the child or individual needs anything provided proactively to help him or her feel most comfortable. Having first met any needs in this regard, the evaluator can then proceed confidently, striving to maximize performance through more frequent and consistent reinforcement schedules and effective activities as discussed above.

Behavioral Momentum

Behavioral momentum is the technique of presenting test items or questions at a quick pace to optimally assist the responding in "maintaining set" without getting distracted. Maintaining set is a fancy way of saying the participant keeps doing the same type of task over and over again as when labeling simple pictures depicting nouns or selecting designs to complete a matrix. After successfully harnessing the participant's attention, the skilled and experienced evaluator proceeds promptly from one item to the next without hesitation such that the participant has little opportunity to get distracted. When using the technique of behavioral momentum, it is typically necessary to present the next item immediately after the participant has responded and before recording the response. The evaluator then records the response while the participant is answering the next item. Obviously, use of behavioral momentum requires substantial familiarity with each measure being given as well as much experience and comfort in working with individuals with ASD.

Unfortunately, while the successful harnessing of the participant's motivation and attention enables him or her to perform optimally, the reverse is also true. An unsuccessful management of behavior can result in an assessment that underrepresents the individual's skills and abilities to some or a large degree. An evaluation done under these circumstances all but guarantees that the recommended services and supports following the assessment will be inappropriate and potentially even hinders growth and development. In our opinion, this situation is completely unacceptable especially since individuals with ASD are by definition weak communicators and typically lack the skills necessary to self-advocate. By successfully harnessing behavioral momentum, it is typically possible to obtain the best performance an individual can offer.

Concluding Remarks on Observations and Behavior Management

In this section of the text, the assessment process has been introduced with an emphasis on initiating the process of assessment and observing behavior over the course of the evaluation process. Establishing rapport with a client on his or her terms (be it talking about airplane bathrooms or baseball statistics) ensures a more positive experience and a higher, more valid assessment of the child's skills. When taking observations, it is important to note factors like mood, language, reciprocity, and behavior throughout testing. During the cognitive portion of the evaluation, examiners should consider external and internal facilitators/inhibitors, such as attention and concentration; attitude and effort; personality and social interest. When assessing individuals with particularly challenging behaviors, examiners must carefully manage the environment and the client's behavior in order to obtain the best estimate of skills across domains. Examiners should utilize ABA principles by providing appropriate reinforcement, visually tracking progress, and taking advantage of behavioral momentum to maximize motivation, compliance, and performance.

In the chapter that follows, the next phase of the assessment process is introduced. This chapter follows a prescriptive approach called "Dynamic Assessment Overview of ASD and Other Disorders." This process allows for clinicians to dynamically adjust assessment priorities and selected tests based on the needs, behavior, and symptoms evident in the client's presentation. At the conclusion of the next chapter, readers have a comprehensive overview of the assessment process, from the initial intake to the time the client leaves the clinic. Following this part of the book, readers will learn how to evaluate the data collected and make differential diagnoses.

Chapter 7
Comprehensive Evaluation

Abstract Contrary to alternative models using a fixed battery approach to neuropsychological assessment, these authors propose that clinicians choose the assessment battery based on the client's data as testing progresses. This is consistent with the Nebraska—Luria model for neuropsychological assessment where the assessment evolves based on the needs of the client. To do so, this chapter provides the Dynamic Assessment Overview for ASD and Other Disorders. These authors propose that the first set of measures is based on the referral concern. The clinician must first use clinical judgment and careful analysis of all information presented during the intake interview to determine which areas must initially be assessed during the evaluation. If the initial concern is autism, the Core assessment Areas of: Cognitive, Language, Social, and Sensory must be evaluated. Once the client presents for testing, the examiner should consider the scope of the evaluation and referral questions as well as the data collected to determine whether or not to assess additional areas. The examiner may evaluate any number of Additional assessment Areas including: Visual Spatial, Motor, Attention, Executive Functions, Memory, Emotions/Behavior, and Adaptive. Then, the clinician or team of clinicians reviews these data from interviews, rating scales, observations, and a variety of direct measures to make a diagnosis. In the framework provided, that diagnosis may be ASD, ASD and comorbid condition (s), or Other Disorder (s). The process concludes with the feedback session, recommendations, and comprehensive report.

Keywords Diagnostic framework for ASD • Dynamic assessment battery • Clinical assessment process for ASD • Valid tests for autism assessment • Ruling-out ASD • Assessing disordered social interactions without autism • Should I keep testing? ASD and other conditions • Four important areas in ASD • Cognitive and language in ASD • Social and sensory in ASD

Referral

The "referral concern" noted here is the clinician's impressions formed during the initial consult, which may or may not be the same as the referral concern voiced by the client. For example, it has been the author's experience that often a client may voice concerns about attention or ADHD, and then describe symptoms that appear to be more consistent with an autism spectrum disorder. The clinician should use clinical judgment to determine which areas must be assessed to address all of the symptoms discussed during the initial intake. When issues with social reciprocity are expressed during the initial consult, autism should be considered. In Fig. 7.1a of the framework, the process begins with a referral for ASD. Any referral in consideration of autism necessitates that the following areas be assessed: Cognitive, Language, Social, and Sensory.

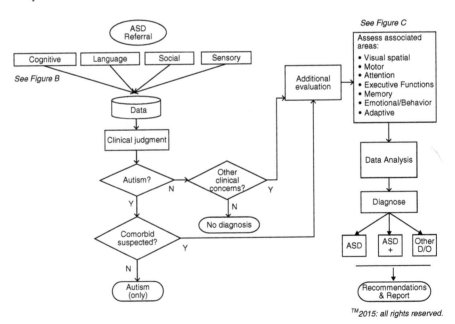

Fig. 7.1 Dynamic assessment framework for ASD and other disorders. (**a**) Dynamic assessment overview for ASD and other disorders. (**b**) Core areas. (**c**) Associated areas. (**d**) Diagnosing disordered examiner–client interactions in the absence of ASD

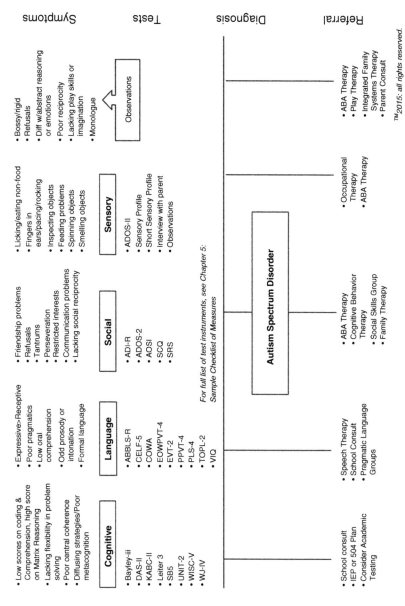

b Core Areas

Fig. 7.1 continued

c Associated Areas

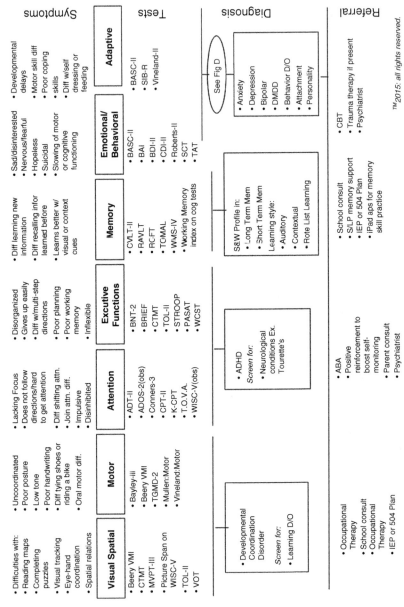

Fig. 7.1 continued

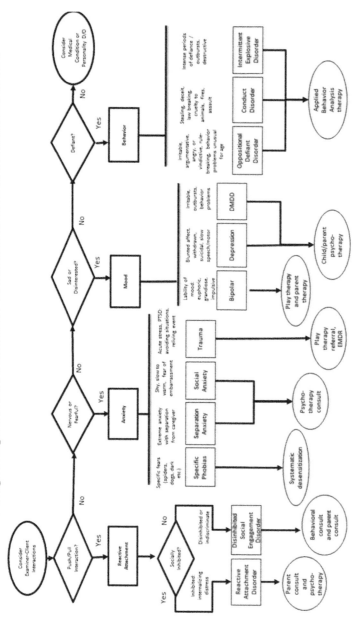

d Diagnosing Disordered Examiner-Client Interactions in the Absence of ASD

Fig. 7.1 continued

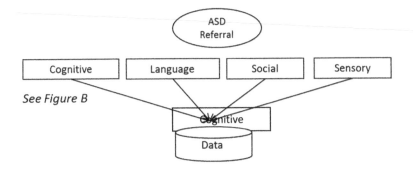

Assessing Core Areas

Cognitive

Cognitive assessment in consideration of ASD should include a careful look at overall cognitive ability compared to social understanding and comprehension. A bright child with adequate language skills, who cannot tell the examiner about simple relationship dynamics such as how a friend differs from any other classmate, is showing signs of autism. Clinicians may notice that a child on the Spectrum scores highest on nonverbal, untimed tests such as Matrix Reasoning. Often Block Design is a favorite subtest for individuals with ASD. Children with autism tend to score lowest on comprehension subtests. As stated in the previous chapter, approach to task should be considered with autism. Examiners should assess the child's overall engagement, use of strategies and verbal mediation, the ability to accept feedback, flexibility in problem-solving approach, significant difficulties establishing rapport and connecting with a child can be observed during cognitive testing.

> Language

Language

When assessing language in consideration of ASD, clinicians should loo losely at pragmatic language. Does the conversation have a give-and-take, to-and-fro quality? Children who struggle to converse, share ideas, and show interest in the topics shared by others may be showing signs of autism. Next, clinicians should consider whether the child's speech is overly formal; potentially comprises vocabulary that is beyond what is generally used in a child's developmental vernacular. For example, the child who seems like a "little professor," appearing to "talk at" the clinician, may be showing signs of autism. The clinician should take note of any monologue the individual may embark on, especially when centered around a restricted interest. Children with autism may use words they do not understand. Language testing may reveal a pattern where expressive language is especially high, relative to lower receptive language. All of these signs point to the notion that an ASD may be relevant.

```
┌─────────────────────────┐
│         Social          │
└─────────────────────────┘
```

Social

When assessing for social needs, clinicians utilize the ADOS-2, observations, clinical interview, and rating scales. Clinicians should look primarily at social reciprocity. Children with autism tend to lack empathy and perspective taking in their communication. When conversational bids are offered, such as, "oh, and then I broke my leg" a child with autism may not know how to respond. Children on the Spectrum may struggle with imaginative, reciprocal, and symbolic play. They may struggle with joint attention, and with following the pointing and eye-gaze of the examiner. Sometimes, a child on the Spectrum will simply walk away during a conversation with the examiner. Other times, the child may refuse tasks or throw tantrums during the evaluation. Any sense of rigidity or bossiness during the evaluation should be noted. Often, a child on the Spectrum fails to offer information and to provide narrative descriptions of events in his or her life. The overall rapport of the interaction is critical to assess as well. If the conversations or play feel awkward, flat, or stunted, the examiner should consider this as a sign autism may be relevant.

```
┌─────────────────────────┐
│        Sensory          │
└─────────────────────────┘
```

Sensory

Children with a previous diagnosis of "Sensory Processing Disorder" should be carefully evaluated for signs of ASD. Often, unfortunately, families have been misled to see that their child's sensory symptoms occur in isolation; when in fact, they may occur in the context of an Autism Spectrum Disorder. Children with sensory sensitivities may show odd behaviors during the evaluation. They may visually inspect toys or objects. At times, children with ASD are observed playing with the wheels of the car or flipping the eyes of a toy doll, rather than playing with the toy in a functional manner. They may lick or eat non-food items. Sometimes, children with sensory problems walk on their toes, rigidly refuse eye contact, and fail to habituate to sounds, smells, and textures in the evaluation environment. Parents may report that the child is sensory seeking, sensory avoidant, or has sensory meltdowns. Sometimes, children with sensory defensiveness have feeding problems, avoiding a wide variety of foods due to problems with certain texture or smells. Sometimes, children with sensory problems avoid certain clothes, preferring to wear only elastic waistbands, collarless shirts, and refusing to wear socks or certain types of shoes. All of these sensitivities should be observed and considered, in concert with all of the evaluation data, as potential signs of autism.

Data Analysis

Clinicians reviewing Cognitive, Language, Social, and Sensory data from interviews, rating scales, observations, and rating scales are well equipped to make an autism diagnosis. Clinicians should consider data from all four areas together and certainly not use the ADOS-2 alone as the sole reason for making a diagnosis. When reviewing data in detail, readers are invited to the comprehensive sections in the next section (Part 3: Data Analysis). Chapter 8 is a comprehensive review of Cognitive and Language assessment data in an assessment for ASD. Chapter 9 provides a clear explanation of the data analysis process for the Social and Sensory areas. All of these data together should answer first, "does the child show impairments in social reciprocity?" Children with limited social reciprocity, poor communication skills (given adequate verbal skills), and restricted interests or behaviors meet the general criteria for an autism diagnosis (Fig. 7.2).

Fig. 7.2 Clinical judgment

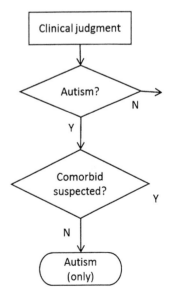

Autism Alone or Comorbid?

Throughout the assessment and certainly toward the end of the first set of measures, clinicians should be able to decide whether to make a diagnosis of autism and to rule autism out. If the client has autism, the clinician must then begin to ask, is it autism alone or are there other concerns? For example, a clinician might observe that the client is clumsy or has poor posture, or handwriting, and consider running additional motor tests. The client might present with grandiosity and flight of ideas, and additional emotional and personality tests might be included in the assessment battery. Clients who present as disinhibited and unorganized might require attention or executive functioning measures. In this way, the clinician reviews the initial data collected in addition to the way the client presents as a way of determining what other assessments should be completed. When conducting the additional measures, clinicians are able to assess other potential diagnoses such as ADHD, Mood, Motor, and Behavior.

See Figure C

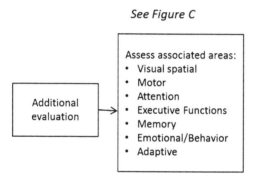

Assessing Additional Areas

If the clinician suspects the child may have additional concerns beyond autism, it may be necessary to do additional formal evaluation. Often, the clinician can screen for the above Associated Areas while looking at Core areas such as Cognitive and Language. The framework provided in Fig. 7.1c allows clinicians to consider all of the major Associated Areas: Visual Spatial, Motor, Attention, Executive Functions, Memory, Mood, Behavior, and Adaptive. Interested readers are again guided to the chapters in the next section (Part 3: Data Analysis) for a comprehensive overview of each area. Visual Spatial and Motor are covered in Chap. 10, Attention, Executive Functions, and Memory are covered in Chap. 11, and Emotions, Mood, Behavior, and Attachment are covered in Chap. 12. The next section here provides readers with a brief overview of each area in order to illuminate the process shown in the Diagnostic Overview framework.

```
┌─────────────────────────────┐
│        Visual Spatial       │
└─────────────────────────────┘
```

Visual Spatial

Examiners should consider evaluating visual–spatial when clients present with poor visual planning skills. They may struggle with assembling visual puzzles or have trouble reading maps. They may have poor eye–hand coordination or problems with visual tracking. Sometimes, individuals with visual spatial problems may have trouble assessing their body's position in the physical space, bumping into walls or door frames. Young children with visual spatial problems may not be able to navigate tunnels and other play equipment in the school-yard. If some of these symptoms appear while assessing the Core Areas, clinicians should evaluate Visual Spatial and may consider instruments such as the Motor-Free Visual Perception Test or the Beery Visual Motor Integration sequence or the Comprehensive Trail Making Test (CTMT).

```
┌─────────────────────────────┐
│            Motor            │
└─────────────────────────────┘
```

Motor

Children who present with poor coordination, poor posture, or poor drawing skills may require motor assessment. They may appear to have low muscle tone, and may struggle with climbing stairs, jumping, or riding a bike. Young children on the Mullen Scales may struggle with stringing beads, stacking blocks, or placing a penny in the bank. Parents might report that they cannot tie their shoes, struggle in sports, or are clumsy around the house. In this case, clinicians should consider tests like the Beery VMI, Grooved Peg Board, and scores on the Vineland Scales of Adaptive Behavior or Mullen Scales in the motor domains.

```
┌─────────────────────────────┐
│          Attention          │
└─────────────────────────────┘
```

Attention

Individuals who present as disinhibited, impulsive, or disorganized may require testing for attention. People with attention problems may struggle with initiation of tasks or in shifting their attention between tasks. They may lack focus or only seem to be able to sustain attention for short periods. Sometimes during a cognitive assessment, an individual with attention problems will fatigue quickly during early items of the subtests. They may also show a pattern of getting one item right, missing one or two items, and then getting another couple items correct. Given that items generally increase in difficulty throughout cognitive subtests, this pattern is a red flag for attention problems. Clinicians with concerns about attention should consider administration of a continuous performance measure like the Test of Variable Attention (TOVA), as well as response patterns during cognitive and language measures, executive functioning measures, joint attention skills on social tests, and working memory assessments.

```
Executive
Functions
```

Executive Functions

One important screener for executive functioning weaknesses is the Working Memory scales of cognitive or memory assessments. Working memory regulates attentional cognitive control processes to permit the simultaneous storage and processing of information while performing cognitive tasks. People with ASD struggle to manipulate stimuli compared to neurotypicals, while they can adequately store visual and verbal information. Individuals who present with poor planning and organization skills (common in ASD) may require executive functioning assessment. Children who struggle to initiate tasks, self-monitor their progress or their comprehension of assignments, and regulate their movements or emotions often have problems with executive functions. Examiners should consider results from the Tower of London, BRIEF, TOVA, and CTMT.

```
Memory
```

Memory

Individuals with memory impairments may struggle in school as they may forget information learned even minutes earlier, or reportedly "space out" during class. Parents may report that their child does not follow multi-step directions. If the child requires both visual and contextual cues to learn from lectures, memory may be an area that requires further assessment. Long-term memory may be impaired if the child struggles with background knowledge, word and information retrieval, and vocabulary. Often memory can be strengthened by associated newly learned information with background knowledge. Examiners may consider results from measures such as the Rey Auditory Verbal Learning Test, Wechsler Memory Scale, Fourth Edition (WMS-IV), or the Working Memory scales on the WISC-V.

```
┌─────────────────┐
│   Emotional/    │
│   Behavioral    │
└─────────────────┘
```

Emotional/Behavioral

Clients present as withdrawn, nervous, angry, or fearful may be showing signs that emotional or behavioral testing is warranted. Later, in this section is a more detailed review of how to use examiner–client interactions to consider symptoms of specific mood, trauma related, and behavior issues. Examiners might consider utilizing measures such as the Behavior Assessment Scales for Children (BASC-II), the Revised Manifest Anxiety Scale (RCMAS), the Children's Depression Inventory (CDI), or the Beck Depression Inventory (BDI) to evaluate emotional conditions. Sometimes, projective tests such as the Thematic Apperception Test, the Roberts-II, or the Human Figure Drawing provide useful data.

```
┌─────────────────┐
│    Adaptive     │
└─────────────────┘
```

Adaptive

It is often helpful to use an adaptive measure for any diagnostic assessment in order to get an overview of the child's skills and development. Common adaptive skill deficits in autism are coping skills, communication skills, and interpersonal relations. On the Vineland Scales, some children with ASD struggle with motor skills. Often children with autism tend to favor domestic over communication and other adaptive areas. One commonly low item in ASD is in following multiple step directions. Children who present as delayed, or who have difficulties with self-dressing or self-feeding may require adaptive assessment. Clinicians should consider results from the Vineland Scales of Adaptive Behavior, Second Edition, or the Scales of Independent Behavior (SIB-R) (Table 7.1).

Table 7.1 Absence of ASD characteristics

Adequate communication skills	Descriptive facial expressions and gestures
	Audible, intelligible, and rhythmic speech
	Communication amount and quality consistent with IQ
Reciprocal play and/or conversation	Expands on other's play or topics
	Eye contact, gestures, expressions synchronized with speech
	Empathic
Varied interests	Absence of nonfunctional, repetitive behaviors
	Absence of perseverative topics
	Fluent and flexible in ideas and activities

Ruling Autism Out

As diagnosticians who are looking at autism as the referral question, our job is multidimensional. The first question to answer is whether or not the diagnosis is ASD. Then, the question becomes what to do if it is NOT ASD but the child's social interactions are disordered, delayed, awkward, or impaired. For the first question, there are graphics here and much more in the differential diagnosis chapter with regard to diagnosing autism. However, how does a clinician rule it out?

Absence of ASD Characteristics

Adequate Communication Skills:	Descriptive facial expressions & gestures
	Audible, intelligible, and rhythmic speech
	Communication amount & quality consistent w IQ
Reciprocal Play &/or Conversation	Expands on other's play or topics
	Eye contact, gestures, expressions synchronized w speech
	Empathic
Varied Interests	Absence of nonfunctional, repetitive behaviors
	Absence of perseverative topics
	Fluent & flexible in ideas and activities

As shown in the figure above, there are three major factors to consider when ruling out autism: Communication Skills, Reciprocal Play or Reciprocal Communication, and Varied Interests. Listed below is a quick reference to determine if autism can be confidently ruled out.

Adequate Communication Skills

Children with descriptive facial expression and gestures tend to show a communication style inconsistent with an autism diagnosis. Descriptive facial expressions may include appropriate social smiles, laughter at comedic parts of conversations, and empathic expressions when the examiner discusses sad or concerning events. When conversational bids are provided during the assessment, such as "then something terrible happened," a child without autism is likely to show a concerned facial expression and to ask for an elaboration by saying, "what happened?" or a comment of that nature. Thus, the ability to take another's perspective and provide an empathetic response is inconsistent with autism. Children without autism can use adequate communication skills such as audible, intelligible speech, having appropriate pitch, tone, and rhythm. Thus, individuals that do not have autism tend to be able to converse clearly and understandably throughout the evaluation. The speech generally does not include odd prosody, robotic voice quality, or repetitive phrasing. Finally, children without autism tend to have the ability to show verbal skills and conversation quality that is consistent with intelligence. Thus, even a child with a lower IQ who has limited verbal skills would generally be able to communicate commensurate with his or her intellectual capacity. The child may still show gestures and facial expressions that are appropriate to the situation. Whereas, children with autism tend to show communication skills that are far behind what the IQ score would predict. A child with ASD and a 115 Verbal IQ, for example, may show stunted communication skills, leading to depravity in the conversational content and an awkwardness in the overall interaction. However, children for whom an autism diagnosis can be ruled out show fluid, natural, and comfortable communication skills.

Appropriate Social and Communicative Reciprocity

Individuals with strong social reciprocity do not have autism. It is important to note here that some children may present with poor language skills but still may have social and communicative reciprocity. In this case, the child likely has a language disorder, not autism. For example, a child with a language disorder may show appropriate social smiles and gestures, eye contact, and expressions, offer information or support to others, and display adequate play skills. Similarly, children with appropriate communicative reciprocity link their facial expressions with gestures and eye contact. Another skill that would fall into this category is the ability to expand on the topics, interests, or play sequence of the examiner. Children with social reciprocity are able to follow along with the conversation rather than going off on tangents or focusing exclusively on their own interests or ideas. Of all of the ASD symptoms to explore during an evaluation, social reciprocity is the most important. As the examiner, the rapport building process and making a clear judgment about the child's social reciprocity is critical to making accurate diagnostic decisions. Children, who are reciprocal, empathetic, and willing to follow along with the examiner's topics and affective presentation, are unlikely to have an autism diagnosis.

Varied Interests

Children without autism tend to demonstrate varied interests. This may be evidenced in the evaluation through the parent interview, child interview, or during administration of the assessments. The child may be interested in sports, computers, and animals, for example. The place where a circumscribed interest might appear is when the examiner attempts to change the topic of conversation and the child keeps coming back to the same interest, almost as if he or she doesn't notice the examiner is no longer engaging with that topic. Children without autism can flexibly transition between their interests, both during the evaluation, and in different areas of the child's life. They also do not display nonfunctional rituals or repetitive behaviors. Repetitive behaviors may include using the same phrase over and over during the evaluation, or flapping, tapping, pacing, and lining up objects. Children without this flexibility may be rigid during the evaluation, saying "I have to finish this" before he or she can move onto another item or activity. Children without autism have a flexible style that allows for the interaction to flow and the relationship to become more comfortable and relaxed over the time of the evaluation.

Diagnosing Disordered Social Interactions in the Absence of ASD

At this point, clinicians have decided if autism is to be diagnosed and are able to make comorbid diagnoses. The clinician is also now clear on how to rule autism out. There is another issue that may come up during an evaluation. Sometimes, autism has been ruled out but the clinician is still concerned about the quality of the individual's social interactions. In that case, the clinician should utilize Fig. 7.1d and take a careful look at the practitioner–client interactions.

As shown in Fig. 7.1d, often, after ruling out autism, the clinician still has concerns about the child's social skills. In this case, it is necessary to carefully examine the nature of the social interaction to determine a diagnosis. The decision tree in Fig. 7.1d is intended to be a tool for clinicians and diagnostic teams to use as a guide for discussions in terms of the direction to go during the data review process, and potential rule-outs to consider. Of course, this is not an exhaustive list. Rather, this is intended as a quick reference of the major categories to consider for children who do not have autism but do show poor social interaction skills. Further, this tree is set up in a "yes/no" format for the sake of simplicity. There certainly can be times where a yes or no answer is not appropriate, such as comorbid conditions or gray areas requiring clinical judgment and expertise. As in any assessment, this guide is no substitute for clinical judgment or the use of the DSM-5 diagnostic criteria. Clinically, to use this guide…start with asking the following questions.

- Is this a push–pull interaction?

Interaction Style

Push–Pull Interactions

Although sometimes subtle, children with attachment disorders will show the examiner that there are issues connecting with others during the evaluation through this push–pull style. The evaluation may proceed thusly. The child presents as hesitant, shy, or defiant. He or she may refuse test items or conversation. Then, after a warm-up period, the child may connect more than normal, provide too much personal information, and demand constant attention from the examiner. He or she may lean on the examiner, sit on her lap, stroke her hair or clothing, and will show poor boundaries overall. Then, if the examiner has to leave the room, the child may be distressed, refusing to say goodbye or insisting that she is not separated from the child. Alternately, the child may show a sweet and endearing demeanor 1 min and then suddenly switch to being stubborn or rude. In this case, the child is displaying a push–pull style, and an Attachment Disorder should be considered.

Once a push–pull interaction has been identified, the examiner must determine whether the child shows signs of Internalizing Distress or Externalizing Distress. Children with *Internalizing Distress* are inhibited, withdrawn, and rarely seek comfort or respond to comfort when distressed, have persistent emotional disturbance, with a history of neglect or inconsistent caregiving likely have a diagnosis of REACTIVE ATTACHMENT DISORDER. It is recommended that a *referral* be made for Parent Consult and Psychotherapy for child (depending on child's mental age). Children with *Externalizing Distress or Indiscriminate Attachment* seem to lack boundaries or do not change interactions based on the familiarity of the relationship. The diagnosis is likely to be: DISINHIBITED SOCIAL ENGAGEMENT DISORDER. The recommended *referral* is ABA Parent Consult and Behavioral Consult or Behavioral Therapy.

- Is the child worried or nervous?

Interaction Style

Anxious Interactions

Children with an anxious style may appear worried, hesitant, or anxious about their performance. This may be evidenced during timed tasks. The child might ask, "Are you going to time me again?" Or, incessantly ask whether or not the answer was right. Similarly, children with an anxious style might appear impatient, wanting to get the evaluation over with, or wanting to avoid any challenging items. Alternately, their anxiety may show up more in the child interview. When asked, "how do you feel most days?" a child with anxiety can typically report back, "worried" or "nervous." The child may show outward signs of anxiety such as foot tapping, finger drumming, or a consistently anxious facial expression. Any of these presentations are likely to be consistent with an anxiety disorder.

Once an anxious interaction style has been identified, the examiner must determine the type of anxiety. If the child shows a strong reaction to *Specific fears* of dogs, dark, spiders, or other items, he or she may have a SPECIFIC PHOBIA. Children with highly specific phobias or may show symptoms like crying, freezing, sudden distress, and avoidance of the stressful object. The child may be afraid of animals (F40.218), natural environment (F40.228), blood (F40.230), and other (F40.298). The recommended referral is Systematic Desensitization. Alternately, the child may display extreme distress over being separated from parents in the waiting room. Although some nervousness when separating from the caregiver is normal, most children will eventually grow comfortable without the parent in the room. Children showing *extreme distress over separation from parents may meet criteria for* SEPARATION ANXIETY and the recommended *referral* is Psychotherapy Consult for parents.

Some children may present as *shy, slow to warm, having a fear of embarrassment.* Children with social anxiety show fear about social interactions and the potential to be evaluated or criticized by other people. They may tantrum, freeze, avoid participating in, or refuse to speak in social settings. The diagnosis is SOCIAL ANXIETY DISORDER. The referral is for psychotherapy or therapy consult. Another potential presentation would be children who suffer from *Acute Stress (tied to specific trauma)* that was either witnessed or experienced involving death, serious injury, sexual assault; *PTSD, (reliving of a stressful event*, and consistent avoiding of situations related to event). The diagnosis is ACUTE STRESS DISORDER and the referral recommended for the client is Play Therapy and EMDR.

Other Anxiety Disorders to Rule Out (not covered in the Decision Tree):

PANIC DISORDER (sweating, trembling, shortness of breath, chest pain, numbness, etc.)

AGORAPHOBIA (public places, enclosed places, crowds)

GENERALIZED ANXIETY DISORDER (restlessness, irritability, tension, sleep problems)

- Is the child sad or disinterested?

  Interaction Style

Disengaged or Blunted Interactions

If a child without autism displays flat or blunted affect, it is likely that a mood disorder is present. Children with mood disorders may appear disinterested in the conversation, the items administered, or the entire assessment. Contrary to anxious examinees, children with mood disorders may appear to not care whether or not they answer items correctly. When asked how he or she feels most days, the response may be "sad," "down," or "I don't know." Remember that sometimes depressed individuals feel numb and may not be aware of their emotional experiences or symptoms. Depressed children may be irritable and angry. They may lack energy or report being tired. They will have disorganized patterns of sleep and eating, often reporting that they used to like certain foods or activities that they now find uninteresting. Motor slowing, slower speech, and drastically lower processing speed or working memory are signs of depression as well. Taken together, if the child seems sad or disinterested, a mood disorder should be considered.

An individual showing *lability of mood, euphoric, grandiose, irritability, and impulsivity may have* BIPOLAR DISORDER, and the referral would be for Play Therapy and Parent Therapy. Finally, children who present as *irritable, with angry outbursts, behavior problems, and persistent depression* may meet criteria for Disruptive Mood Dysregulation Disorder, and the referral recommendation is Child and Parent Psychotherapy or Consult.

- Is the child defiant?

Angry, Defiant, or Irritable Interactions

During the assessment, if a child is especially difficult and argumentative, there may be a behavior disorder present. Children with behavior disorders may require extensive strategies in order to encourage them to complete the test items. They may bore easily and constantly ask when the tests will be over. Parents will report that the child has outbursts at home or school, refusing to listen or follow directions. Children with behavior disorders may have a history of serious problems including criminal activity, lying, cheating, stealing, or assault. In the case where there are concerns about behavior disorders, it is important to rule out or consider ADHD and Disruptive Mood Dysregulation Disorder. A child can have both ADHD and a behavior disorder; especially, in light of the impulsivity and the consistent problems with disinhibition in ADHD that may lead to poor behavior choices. However, a child can NOT be diagnosed with DMDD and a behavior disorder because in DMDD the behaviors are considered to be subsumed under the mood disorder.

Children who present as *irritable, angry, arguing, and rule-breaking* may meet criteria for OPPOSITIONAL DEFIANT DISORDER, and the referral would be for Applied Behavioral Analysis Therapy. When a client shows such symptoms as stealing, deceit, law-breaking, cruelty to animals, setting fires, and assault on others (either physical or sexual), the diagnosis is likely to be CONDUCT DISORDER, and the *referral* is Applied Behavioral Analysis therapy. Another potential symptom profile may *be intense periods of defiance and outbursts, destruction of property,* and the diagnosis may be INTERMITTENT EXPLOSIVE DISORDER, for which Applied Behavioral Analysis therapy is recommended.

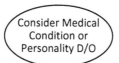

- Social interactions impaired but none of these seem to fit?

Consider a *Major Medical Condition*. Children with chronic health problems encounter frequent stress and may experience trauma at the hands of medical doctors. Although the care may be provided by competent and caring health professionals, children who are regularly experiencing surgeries or hospitalizations can be intensely afraid, violated, lonely, exhausted, and some may show signs of acute or long-term trauma. Other conditions may occur in response to changes in medication such as Antidepressant Discontinuation Syndrome (995.29) or Other Adverse Effect of Medication (995.20). Taken together, medical conditions should always be ruled out when there are unexplained concerns from the evaluation or the medical history shows significant health problems.

As stated at the beginning of this section, the framework provided and the description here are simplified in order to provide a roadmap for diagnosticians and clinical teams to use in the case that an autism diagnosis has been ruled out and the

Fig. 7.3 Data analysis and
differential diagnosis

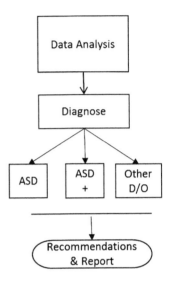

child's social skills show significant impairment. The purpose for this guide is to provide a consistent orthogonal methodology for determining the meaning of diagnostic data and ultimately making an accurate determination. If none of the diagnoses presented in this section area appropriate, it is possible that the individual has ADHD, a Personality Disorder, or other medical or psychiatric problem (Fig. 7.3).

Concluding Remarks on Comprehensive Evaluations

At this point in the assessment framework provided here, the clinician is guided to review all assessment data, and to make a diagnosis of either ASD, ASD, and other comorbid condition (s) or other disorder. For a comprehensive guide to data analysis, the reader is guided to Part 3: Data Analysis. For a clear guide to differential diagnosis, the reader is invited to review Part 4: Differential diagnosis. Generally, clinical teams meet as a group and consider all of the data gathered during a comprehensive evaluation, make diagnoses, and begin assembling a list of recommendations. Clinicians often have an in-person or phone meeting to share the results of the evaluation. The comprehensive assessment concludes with the written report which should be provided in a timely manner to families. A guide for choosing recommendations and writing reports is provided in Chap. 15: Feedback, Report, and Recommendations. It is the author's hope that clinicians conducting autism assessments will find this guide helpful in conducting a dynamic and comprehensive assessment and making a definitive and accurate diagnosis (Table 7.2).

Table 7.2 Summary of evaluation process

I. Referral
(a) Professional, family member or friend has concern about autism
(b) Referral to comprehensive evaluation (may include letter or consult)
II. Initial Consultation
(a) Clinician conducts clinical interview (parents/guardians or client)
(b) Clinician identifies presenting concern
(c) Choose type of evaluation that is needed to answer referral question
i. Brief
ii. Comprehensive
iii. Academic
iv. Forensic
(d) Complete paperwork to initiate evaluation
i. Clinician and services disclosure: providing information about credentials, scope of service, client rights, confidentiality
ii. Financial disclosure and agreement
iii. Exchange of information forms to confer with other providers or school
iv. Intake packet
(e) Schedule testing
III. Choose initial measures using Sample Checklist of Measures
IV. Assessment preparation
(a) Review documents and initial intake packet
(b) Select measures and pull protocols
(c) Assemble and schedule assessment team
V. Testing begins
(a) Observations
i. Appearance
ii. Behavioral presentation
iii. Language
iv. Eye contact and gestures
v. Play interest
vi. Social reciprocity
vii. Attention
viii. Motor skills
ix. Emotions and affect
x. Naturalistic observations
(b) Behavior management using ABA principles
VI. Comprehensive evaluation
(a) Dynamic assessment overview for ASD and other disorders (Framework)
i. Begin Day 1 measures:
ii. Cognitive (DAS-II, Leiter 3, SB5, UNIT-IV, WISC-V, WJ-IV)
iii. Language (CELF-5, COWA, EVT-2, PPVT-4, PLS-4, TOPL-2)
iv. Social (ADOS-2-chose module based on speech fluency, ADI-R)

(continued)

Table 7.2 (continued)

v. Sensory (observations, sensory profile)	
(b) Score and review data from Day 1	
(c) Consider results from:	
i. Cognitive and language	
ii. Social and sensory	
(d) Consider whether to administer additional measures:	
i. Visual spatial and motor (Beery VMI, MVPT-III, VOT)	
ii. Attention, executive functioning and memory (CTMT, TOL-III, STROOP, PASAT, T.O.V.A., WCST)	
iii. Emotions, mood, behavior, and adaptive (BASC-II, BDI-II, CDI-II, Roberts-II, SCT, TAT)	
(e) End of Day 2: Schedule feedback	
(f) Score and discuss initial conclusions after completion of Day 2	
VII. Data analysis with diagnostic team	
(a) Review data from any of the 11 areas assessed	
(b) Review observations	
(c) Discuss clinical impressions from various clinician's perspectives	
VIII. Differential and comorbid diagnosis	
(a) Develop list of referrals for therapy or further evaluation	
IX. Feedback and recommendations	
X. Report	

Summary of Part 2: Conducting an Evaluation

This part has set a foundation for the assessment process. Readers have now been introduced to the beginning of the evaluation, including the referral, and initial consult. The first chapter of this part had an emphasis on initiating the process of assessment, assessing behavior over the course of the evaluation process, and managing the environment and client behavior in order to obtain the best estimate of an individual's skills across domains. Establishing rapport with a client on his or her terms and helping parents and families to feel comfortable with the assessment process enhances the assessment experience. Helping parents consider how to tell their child about an upcoming assessment, discussing what snacks or favorite items to bring to the assessment and discussing the schedule for the day can be helpful. Some parents need to be present for the standardized assessment in order to follow test guidelines or for the child's comfort. Other parents may choose to wait in the waiting room and see their child for breaks or to not be present during the evaluation. Adults may come alone or at times bring a friend or family member to be present in the waiting room.

As it was noted earlier, clinicians complete a referral checklist after the evaluation is scheduled and indicate measures to give in an assessment based on the referral question or questions, age of the client, and scope of the evaluation based on insurance or self-pay. On the first day of testing, observations should be taken in the following areas: appearance, behavior, language, eye contact and gesture use, play and interests, social reciprocity, attention, motor skills, mood and affect, and naturalistic observations. If challenging behaviors are present, the examiner should utilize ABA principles, including managing antecedents such as the sensory environment and building rapport with the examiner; and managing consequences, including effective reinforcement on an appropriate schedule, utilizing Premack Principle and behavioral momentum. These techniques allow examiner to harness the client's motivation and engagement, even in the most challenging behavioral presentations.

After the initial day of testing evaluators consider preliminary results and add or remove measures based on data obtained. It is helpful to administer a cognitive measure on day one, as well as Language, ADOS-2, and Sensory screener, if possible so that this data can be utilized to guide day two of the assessment. The authors of this text find that 2–5 h of testing per day, over two testing days, is sufficient to complete a comprehensive evaluation. At the end of the first day of testing, the team should meet briefly to consider the data and determine what needs to be collected on the second and possibly third days of testing. Once the assessment is complete the clinician should schedule a feedback session to meet with the parents and provide data, diagnoses, and recommendations for treatment. This should be scheduled with enough time for the assessment team to score and consider all data, meet to discuss, and analyze data and to form diagnostic impressions and create recommendations. The process concludes with a comprehensive report which can be either provided during the feedback session or sent in the mail.

This part has provided a guide for the comprehensive evaluation process. The next part will be a prescriptive guide to data analysis in a comprehensive evaluation for an Autism Spectrum Disorder. It is not possible to be wholly comprehensive in discussing the broad category of neuropsychological assessment in a single book; thus, the authors of this text strive to present assessment as it relates to Autism Spectrum Disorders and associated profiles. We hope that the presented case examples interwoven with the discussion of primary assessment areas as they relate to autism are helpful to clinicians in understanding and applying the information presented. The Data Analysis Framework will help clinicians understand all data obtained during the evaluation. The figures and tables will guide diagnostic decision-making. The assessment in applied settings will guide clinicians to assess individuals of different ages in the various locations, where evaluation of ASD is relevant.

Part III
Data Analysis

This part of the text is a detailed guide for analyzing assessment data in consideration of ASD. These authors advance 11 specific areas to assess during a comprehensive assessment; organized by "Core Areas" and "Associated Areas." As previously explained, the selection of assessment instruments should be dynamic to determine which areas require a screening as compared to an in-depth assessment. The Core Areas are: Cognitive, Language, Social Communication/ASD Core Symptoms, and Sensory Processing. The Associated Areas include: Visual-Spatial, Motor Skills, Attention, Executive Functions, Memory, Emotional/Behavioral, and Adaptive. In assessing the Core Areas, *Cognitive* assessment provides the foundation for the data analysis process. Assessing *Language* development is crucial as communication is a core deficit of autism. Evaluation of the *ASD Core Symptoms* includes: social interaction and reciprocity; play and imaginative use of materials; and restricted or repetitive behaviors. Within the Associated Areas, recommended Attention and Memory instruments are provided for examiners; as well as, how to specifically analyze symptoms in these domains that are common to individuals with ASD. *Mood and Behavior* are crucial components of a comprehensive evaluation in terms of both differential and comorbid diagnostic considerations. Assessing *Adaptive Skills* is essential because adaptive strengths and deficits can guide treatment. Through a thorough examination of these 11 areas as they relate to autism, the reader is able to clearly understand how to collect and analyze data for a comprehensive diagnostic assessment in consideration of ASD.

1.1   Data Analysis

- •Interpretation of assessment data
- •Review areas assessed
- •Meet as diagnostic team
- •Consider data obtained from any of the 11 areas

Data Analysis

It is now time to gather all of the data collected in the assessment and evaluate the meaning in terms of symptoms that are associated with specific conditions. This section of the book includes the four Core Areas and the seven Associated Areas in detail; with an associated guide for how symptoms are evaluated. Provided on the following pages is a Data Analysis Framework that structures this part of the book, guiding clinicians through a comprehensive evaluation process. The areas included are: Cognitive and Language (Chap. 8), Social and Sensory (Chap. 9); Visual-Spatial and Motor (Chap. 10), Attention, Executive Functions and Memory (Chap. 11); and Emotions, Mood, Behavior, and Adaptive (Chap. 12). The testing instruments are abbreviated in the Framework; however, there is a full list in the Sample Checklist, provided in Chap. 5. In order to guide clinicians, each assessment area includes a copy of that section of the Framework and the associated assessments that are included in the Sample Checklist. Appendix A at the end of this book provides a more detailed description of many of the instruments, including psychometric properties. Readers are invited to review and reference the Data Analysis Framework as a guide through these chapters.

Table P3.1 Data analysis framework

Core areas
1. Cognitive
• *FSIQ* has the most reliability and validity as a composite score: stable and predictive
• *Variation among indexes*: baseline of skill strengths and weaknesses (both relative and absolute strengths and weaknesses profile. Bear in mind that the GAI is much more common in ASD intellectual profiles on WISC-IV (no GAI info on WISC-V as of this writing)
• *Verbal IQ*: compare VIQ overall to social and language—look for significant discrepancies
• *Note highest and lowest subtest score*:
○ Comprehension subtest score is likely to be low score (particularly lowest within VIQ) in ASD
■ Even though Comprehension is not a core test in WISC-V, it is essential this test be administered for ASD evaluations
○ Low scores on Coding subtest is common in ASD
○ Highest score on Matrix Reasoning, followed by Picture Concepts, and Block Design (due to timed test)

(continued)

Table P3.1 (continued)

• Consider results from: Bayley-III/Mullen, DAS-2, KABC-II, Leiter-3, SB5, UNIT-2, WISC-V, WAIS-IV, WJ-IV

2. Language

- *Core language*—compared to VIQ (concerning if Core Language is much lower)
- *Expressive vs. receptive* language discrepancies
- *Pragmatic language* (in ASD pragmatic language scores may be lower)
- *Ideational fluency and word retrieval* (concerning when low compared to VIQ)
- *Reporting of events and narrative coherence*: following consistent plot line and share main idea
- Consider results from: ABLLS-R, CELF-5, COWA, EOWPVT, EVT, PLS-4, PPVT, TOPL-2, Verbal IQ

3. Social and ASD symptoms

- Overall score on ADOS algorithm (consider scores only valid if administered by qualified clinician)
- Consider major symptom areas in light of entire evaluation
- Review screening instruments: SCQ, GARS, CARS, M-CHAT, feedback from pediatrician
- Behavior observations: appearance, behavioral presentation, language, eye contact and gesture use in communication, play/interests, social reciprocity, attention, motor skills, mood and affect
- Rating scales and interview on child's social communication, behaviors, and overall functioning
- Consider developmental milestones, social communication, and emotional regulation
- Toddler: communication, reciprocal social interaction, restrictive and repetitive behavior
- Module 1–3: social affect, communication, reciprocal social interaction; restricted and repetitive behavior
- Module 4: communication, reciprocal social interaction, imagination/creativity, stereotyped behaviors and restricted interests
- Consider results from ADI-R, ADOS-2, AOSI SCQ, SRS; clinical interview/observations

4. Sensory processing

- Diagnosis of "Sensory Processing Disorder"
- *Odd sensory behaviors*—smelling toys, visual examination of objects, spinning of objects, overwhelmed by noise in the room, walks on toes, repetitively jumping off of high places (seeking proprioceptive input), clumsy
- Seven senses: sight, hearing, taste, smell, touch, balance and motion (vestibular), muscle and joint (proprioceptive), hunger and need for elimination (can be considered also in sensory needs)
- Consider results from ADOS-2 Sensory items, Sensory Profile, Short Sensory Profile

Associated areas

5. Visual-spatial

- *Visual perception*: consider WISC-IV Perceptual Reasoning or WISC-V Visual-Spatial Index Score, Motor-Free Visual Perception Test (MVPT): visual closure, visual figure ground, visual rotation

(continued)

Table P3.1 (continued)

- *Visual memory*: visual working memory, picture span test on WISC-V, WMS, MVPT visual memory items, VMI—Visual Perception test
- *Visual planning*: consider performance on Tower of London, and CTMT (Trails)
- *Central coherence (local vs. global Processing)*
- *Consider discrepancies between Language and Visual-Spatial*: visual develops before language in ASD
- *Consider results from*: Beery VMI, CTMT, MVPT, Picture Span: WISC-V, TOL-II, VOT

6. Motor skills
- *Oral motor*: swallowing, drooling, chewing
- *Visual motor*: integration of visual and motor skills, performance on Beery VMI
- *Fine motor*: dexterity, handwriting, and drawing; Mullen: stringing beads, stacking blocks, placing penny in bank
- *Gross motor*: hypotonia, motor apraxia, poor posture, clumsy
- *Stereotyped motor behaviors*
- Consider performance on: Bayley-III, Beery VMI, TGMD-2, Mullen, Vineland-II

7. Attention
- *Focused*: typically focused attention is a deficit in ADHD; adults may have difficulty obtaining attention of people with ASD as they may prefer to attend to objects or ideas of their own interest and ignore the environmental stimuli
- *Selective and overselective*: individuals with ASD tend to focus on restricted interests more—may have overselective attention, perseverating on specific interests
- *Sustained*: often sustained attention okay in ASD but more difficulty with shifting
- *Shifting*: challenges with multitasking, establishing, and maintaining mental set
- *Joint attention*: a process of engaging and shifting attention for social interaction (often impaired in ASD)
- In ASD alone and not ADHD: better inhibition, flexibility, working memory, and planning skills
- Consider results from: ADT-II, Conners, T.O.V.A. and Observations: ADOS-II WISC-V

8. Executive functions
- *Inhibition*: difficulty getting individuals with ASD to stop preferred activities and transition to another less preferred activity (do not inhibit their desire to focus on other activities)
- *Planning*: complex cognitive skill requiring the identification and organization of steps towards a goal (often difficult for individuals with ASD)
- *Flexibility*: shifting one's response set or update cognitive strategy in response to new information
- *Working memory*: regulates attentional and cognitive control processes to permit the simultaneous storage and processing of information while performing cognitive tasks. People with ASD struggle to manipulate stimuli compared with neurotypicals, while they can adequately store visual and verbal information
- Consider results from: BNT-2, BRIEF, CTMT, TOL-II, STROOP, PASAT, WCST, and observed ability to inhibit prepotent responses

(continued)

Table P3.1 (continued)

9. Memory	
	• *Short-term memory*: ability to hold information for short term or immediate retrieval (without requirement of acting on the information)
	• *Long-term memory*: can be strengthened by associating information from short-term memory with background information, semantic memory, and cultural knowledge
	• Consider results on: CVLT-II, RAVLT, RCFT, TOMAL, WMS-IV, WMI on cognitive tests
10. Emotional/behavioral	
	• *Anxiety*: behavior during testing such as performance anxiety, self-deprecating comments; display anxious movements (foot tapping, drumming fingers, shaking); may report physiological symptoms such as: tummy aches, chest pain, trouble falling asleep; may report problems with: restlessness, excessive worries, adherence to nonfunctional rituals
	Consider: BAI, BASC-2, RCMAS, client interview, PTSD Diagnostic scales, MMPI-2
	• *Depression*: test behaviors such as poor eye contact, minimal response to questions, slower processing speed, appear to be on the edge of tears, crying, sense of hopelessness; may report loneliness, suicidality, lack of interest in previously pleasurable activities
	Consider: BDI-II, BASC-2, CDI, client interview, Roberts, TAT, SCT, and MMPI-2
	• *Bipolar*: racing thoughts, pressured speech, grandiosity, flight of ideas, history of mood swings, suicidality, irritability in children, self-injury, explosive temper, high-risk behavior
	Consider: BASC (depression, hyperactivity, and aggression), BDI-II (depression)
	• *Frozen profile*: across emotional measures is a sign of ASD: Alexithymia (not identifying own emotions)
	• *Behavior*: Functional Analysis, and Functional Behavior Analysis, rating scales, behavior observations, questionnaires, and interviews
	Consider results from: BAI, BASC-II, BDI-II, CDI-II, MMPI-II, PDS, 16PF, Roberts-II, SCT, TAT
11. Adaptive	
	• Overall *Adaptive Composite* on Vineland or SIB-R
	• *Communication*—Expressive > Receptive, Written (discrepancies)
	• *Internalizing and externalizing behaviors*
	• *Social skills*
	• *Consider results from*: BASC-II, SIB-R, Vineland-II

Chapter 8
Cognitive and Language Assessment

Abstract Cognition is an important area of assessment in ASD and other disorders because cognitive performance provides the foundation to which all other assessment data are compared. Cognitive testing reveals strengths and weaknesses in verbal, nonverbal, working memory, and fluency domains. When diagnosing an ASD, DSM-5 requires comment on the level of cognitive impairment or lack thereof (American Psychiatric Association, Diagnostic and statistical manual of mental disorders (5th edn). Arlington, VA, 2013). Language is crucial to assess as communication is a core feature of an ASD. Parent report of challenges with expressive, receptive, or pragmatic language helps guide the selection of appropriate language measures that may address important areas such as core language, language fluency, language memory, or language content. One of the authors of this text found that in ASD, the percentage of variance of IQ accounted for by language was 27 % (without significant intervention) (Huckabee, Correspondence of DSM-IV criteria for autistic spectrum disorders with standardized language measures of intelligence and language. University of Houston, Unpublished dissertation, Presented April 2003). Language alone or language combined with IQ is generally considered the best predictor of outcomes (Sutera et al., J Autism Dev Disord 37(1), 2007, p. 100; Schreibman et al., International handbook of autism and pervasive developmental disorders. Springer, New York, 2011, p. 295). Indeed researchers claim, "Early language ability and cognitive ability have emerged as the most robust predictors of overall prognosis for autism during childhood, adolescence and adulthood" (Schreibman et al., International handbook of autism and pervasive developmental disorders. Springer, New York, 2011, p. 295). Given these considerations, effective and thorough cognitive and language testing are essential to a comprehensive evaluation for ASD. This chapter provides a best-practice guide for assessing cognition and language, including some of the common intellectual profiles evidenced in children and adults with ASD.

Keywords Cognitive assessment in ASD • Language assessment in ASD • Test behaviors in ASD • Processing speed in ASD • Verbal comprehension in ASD • Perceptual reasoning in ASD • Expressive language in ASD • Receptive language in ASD • Pragmatic impairment in ASD • Central coherence theory

© Springer International Publishing Switzerland 2016   127
A.P. Kroncke et al., *Assessment of Autism Spectrum Disorder*, Contemporary Issues in Psychological Assessment, DOI 10.1007/978-3-319-25504-0_8

Assessing for Cognition

With Contributions from Allison Margulies, Ph.D.

Cognitive assessment is generally the first assessment given during a diagnostic evaluation. It provides the foundation for the data analysis process. Provided below are two vignettes highlighting the potential findings that may be uncovered while completing an evaluation for Autism with cognitive concerns as part of the referral question. The remaining sections of Part III shall procedure thusly, a vignette highlighting the area to be assessed will open the section and a description of that assessment area will follow (Table 8.1).

Table 8.1 Assessing for cognition

Core area
1. *Cognitive*
• *FSIQ* has the most reliability and validity as a composite score: stable and predictive
• *Variation among indexes*: Baseline of skill strengths and weaknesses (both relative and absolute strengths and weaknesses profile). Bear in mind that the GAI is much more common in ASD intellectual profiles on WISC-IV (no GAI info on WISC-V as of this writing)
• *Verbal IQ*: compare VIQ overall to social and language—look for significant discrepancies
• *Note highest and lowest subtest score:*
– Comprehension subtest score is likely to be low score (particularly lowest within VIQ) in ASD
Even though Comprehension is not a core test in WISC-V, it is essential this test be administered for ASD evaluations
– Low scores on Coding subtest is common in ASD
– Highest score on Matrix Reasoning, followed by Picture Concepts, and Block Design (due to timed test)
• Consider results from: Bayley-iii/Mullen, DAS-2, KABC-II, Leiter-3, SB5, UNIT-2, WISC-V, WAIS-IV, WJ-IV
Full measure names:
Bayley Scales of Infant Development, Third Edition (Bayley-iii)
Differential Ability Scales, Second Edition, Lower Early Years Record Form (DAS-II)
Differential Ability Scales, Second Edition, Upper Early Years Record Form (DAS-II)
Differential Ability Scales, Second Edition, School-Age Record Form
Kaufman Assessment Battery for Children (KABC-II)
Leiter International Performance Scale, Third Edition (Leiter-3)
Mullen Scales of Early Learning (MULLEN), AGS Edition
Stanford-Binet Intelligence Scales, Fifth Edition (SB5)
Universal Nonverbal Intelligence Test, Second Edition (UNIT 2)
Wechsler Adult Intelligence Scale, Fourth Edition (WAIS-IV)
Wechsler Intelligence Scales for Children, Fifth Edition (WISC-V)
Wechsler Preschool and Primary Scale of Intelligence, Fourth Edition (WPPSI-IV)
Woodcock Johnson IV Tests of Cognitive Abilities (WJ-IV)

Vignette #1 Derick: Cognitive Assessment of a Child with a Language Delay

Derick was 3 years old when he came to Emerge for an evaluation for language delay and behavior problems. He was administered the Mullen Scales of Early Learning (MULLEN), AGS Edition (select sections); Differential Ability Scales, Second Edition, Lower Early Years Record Form (DAS-II); Autism Diagnostic Observation Schedule, Second Edition, Module 2 (ADOS-2); Behavior Assessment System for Children, Second Edition (BASC-II), Parent and Teacher Reports; and Vineland Adaptive Behavior Scales, Second Edition—Parent/Caregiver Rating Form (VABS-II).

Derick's parents reported that they struggled to communicate with their son. Specifically, he did not understand them, had limited vocabulary, and threw violent tantrums, which were disruptive at home and in his half-day preschool environment. Derick's parents were often called to pick him up from preschool due to tantrum behavior and his teacher's inability to communicate with him. Assessments indicated Derick's language was significant for articulation challenges, echoing, and he had not yet developed conversation skills. His cognitive ability score was a general conceptual ability score of 70. Derick's intellectual ability fell into the Borderline Impaired Range. His language core standard score was 65; he spoke in sentences but was not responsive to questions or conversational statements. His pattern of expressive language skills higher than receptive language and difficulty with conversational reciprocity is consistent with a diagnosis of an Autism Spectrum Disorder. Derick was diagnosed with autism and then referred for behavioral therapy at Emerge and speech therapy in the community where he made significant progress, grew in his compliance with adult requests, and was able to interact with others socially. Derick's tantrums have been reduced significantly and he is now able to spend a full day at preschool. He will be reevaluated in 12 months to assess progress. As cognitive abilities stabilize around age seven, clinicians are hopeful about gains that may be made through therapy and supports.

Vignette #2 Clark: Cognitive Assessment of a Teenager with a Gifted Intellectual Profile

Clark was 13 years old when he came to Emerge for an evaluation for social skills challenges and executive functioning problems. He was administered the Wechsler Intelligence Scale for Children (WISC-IV); Autism Diagnostic Observation Schedule, Second Edition, Module 3 (ADOS-2); Tower of London-II; Test of Variables of Attention (TOVA); Behavior Assessment System for Children, Second Edition (BASC-II), Parent and Teacher Reports; Vineland Adaptive Behavior Scales, Second Edition—Parent/Caregiver Rating Form (VABS-II).

Clark's parents reported that they believed he was very smart but that they struggled to communicate with their son. Specifically, he did not respond at length to questions about his day saying it was "fine" or "I don't remember." Clark spent hours in his room on Lego creations or video games and he forgot to turn in his homework. Clark's parents were often called to meet with the teacher about his motivation. Assessments indicated Clark could sustain attention but he did have challenges with executive functioning and his processing speed was poor relative to his other cognitive abilities. His cognitive ability score was a General Ability Index (GAI) score of 142 with a processing speed index of 105. Clark's intellectual ability fell into the Very Superior Range, but he had challenges with organization, planning, completing work, and processing speed. His ADOS-2, ADI-R, and observations are consistent with a diagnosis of an Autism Spectrum Disorder. Specifically, Clark could converse on topics he enjoyed but demonstrated limited reciprocity for topics or conversational bids offered by the examiner. He enjoyed talking about World War II and often turned the topic of conversation to his research. Clark made good eye contact but it could be intense at times and he used limited gestures. He was creative in his play only within the realm of his areas of interest. He did not describe his own emotions or relationships well. Clark was diagnosed with Autism Spectrum Disorder and Gifted and Talented. He was referred for a social skills group and an advanced learning plan addresses his need for academic differentiation and extensions, as well as support for his executive functioning challenges. He was advanced to eighth grade classes in math, language arts, and history commensurate with his Very Superior cognitive abilities and his interests.

Cognitive Assessment as It Applies to Autism

Cognitive evaluation is essential to any comprehensive assessment as it provides a basis and foundation for understanding the child's capabilities in a variety of domains. Cognitive assessment provides critical information regarding verbal abilities, nonverbal reasoning skills, spatial skills, processing speed or cognitive efficiency, fluid reasoning, crystallized intelligence, and long-term and short-term memory. Research on optimal outcomes for individuals diagnosed with ASD points to strong cognitive profiles, adaptive skills and language being indicative of positive outcomes (Chlebowski, Fein, & Robins, 2014). With this in mind, assessing cognitive skills provides one metric regarding the child's potential for optimal outcomes, as well as a list of skill areas to build on when providing recommendations. It is generally considered best practice that every comprehensive battery include some form of cognitive assessment although this may be simply an examination of recent cognitive scores from a previous evaluation. In the context of an evaluation for autism, it is generally recommended that the cognitive evaluation come first in the battery as this provides the clinician with a wide variety of important information about the child's skills, symptoms, personality traits, behavior, and of general intellectual functioning. Further, observations on facilitators and inhibitors to performance during cognitive testing (discussed in Chap. 6) can provide important data on the individual's ability to demonstrate his or her understanding, knowledge, and cognitive ability.

Usefulness of FSIQ Scores in ASD

The cognitive profile and full scale IQ score allows for important comparisons with performance in other domains. Social skills and language data obtained in other parts of the evaluation should be consistent with cognitive ability. A child with strong cognitive abilities is expected to be able to perform well on other areas of an assessment; if performance is not congruent, this raises clinical concern. For example, a child with a FSIQ of 135 who is not able to answer the question, "what is a friend?" or "how is a friend different than a classmate?" raises red flags in a clinician's mind. A very bright child, who does not know what a friend is, likely has significant deficits in social understanding relative to many strengths in other cognitive areas. Further, a child with a 135 IQ should be able to use toys symbolically during play, have an engaging discussion with the examiner, and to report accurately on events in his life. If these abilities are absent or delayed in a bright child, it is possible the child has autism or another neurodevelopmental disability. In this way, cognitive assessment provides a basis for analyzing all other data collected during an evaluation. During feedback meetings with families, a clinician generally provides results from the cognitive assessment first and uses these data as a framework to discuss strengths and weaknesses in a child's neuropsychological profile and how these relate to the remainder of data collected and diagnostic conclusions.

Cognitive abilities are generally measured using intelligence tests, or tests of "cognitive abilities." It is important to note that although the use and misuse of intelligence tests has come under scrutiny over the years (Gould, 1996), intelligence or "IQ tests" remain one of the most psychometrically robust and predictive instruments psychologists have during an evaluation. With this in mind, there are a few cautions clinicians should consider during an assessment for ASD. One is that it is generally the case that test developers are unable to capture a large sample of children with Autism in the clinical sample during the norming process. Further complicating the matter, children with ASD fall on such a wide spectrum, it can be quite difficult to evaluate their performance as a group (see the next section regarding norms for the WISC-IV). For example, although the psychometric properties of the WISC-IV are considered excellent (Sattler, 2001), the developers struggled to obtain a clinical sample for ASD.

Even with this potential challenge in terms of developing ASD specific norms, cognitive testing *does* provide clinicians with information about how this child performs on school-related novel tasks, *relative to peers* his or her age. This, of course, is highly important information for evaluators to collect and to impart to families. That is, a child with a 75 full scale IQ and an Autism diagnosis is going to struggle relative to typical peers in a general education classroom. Thus, although there may be some limitations of intelligence test scores, this metric alone can provide a context for understanding a child's challenges relative to typically developing peers which can be a key to helping the family evaluate placement decisions and support needs.

The next word of caution is that, although the Full Scale IQ has value, and the soundest psychometric data to support its use, this score is only one piece of data. It is an overall measure to characterize an individual's ability but does not necessarily speak to an entire skill set. It may underestimate a child's potential in the case of a profile with significantly discrepant index scores. Intelligence testing can provide data that is useful considering both a full scale score and index scores independently. Overall, using a composite IQ score has psychometric support but an individual subtest score may be telling also. For example, one child at the Emerge clinic with a 120 Full Scale IQ score obtained a scaled score of "2" on the comprehension test of the WISC-IV. Although not diagnostic, relatively low scores on the comprehension subtest are a red flag for autism.

Intelligence tests are often utilized to inform about a collection of strengths and weaknesses, as well as for the rich body of data that can be obtained through observations. The clinical observations obtained during a cognitive evaluation are of great value when assessing for autism. A thorough explanation of the key factors for clinicians to consider during an ASD evaluation was provided in Chap. 6: Testing Begins.

Cattell–Horn–Carroll Theory of Intelligence

With cautions clearly stated, IQ testing as a practice is reliable, valid, and has a high degree of clinical utility, largely due to the extensive work of Raymond B. Cattell, John Horn, and John Carroll (Sattler, 2001). The Cattell–Horn–Carroll (CHC) model of intelligence is the most widely used and respected model for understanding cognitive ability (Flanagan & Kaufman, 2004). The model includes two primary forms of intelligence: Fluid Intelligence (Gf) and Crystalized Intelligence (Gc). Fluid intelligence generally involves mental efficiency for novel tasks, or abilities that are not encountered in school or daily life. In CHC theory, Fluid Intelligence includes symbolic classification, concept formation, inductive reasoning, and similar nonverbal tasks. Crystallized Intelligence involves knowledge and acquired understanding that tend to have been learned in school, are influenced heavily by cultural factors, and may have a verbal component. Skills such as general information, verbal comprehension, and semantic relationships fall within this cognitive ability. Also included in the comprehensive CHC theory is a three-stratum factor structure, whereby Stratum I consists of narrow abilities; Stratum II includes broad abilities; and Stratum III includes general ability. Narrow abilities are skills in specific areas such as Reading Comprehension. Broad abilities include fluid and crystallized intelligence as well as retrieval, memory, processing speed, and learning. Finally, the third stratum is represented by (g) and represents overall ability or General Intelligence (Sattler, 2001).

Intelligence testing in ASD can occur by using a variety of valid and reliable measures. For very young infants and toddlers, the Bayley-iii is often used. For children who are toddlers or preschoolers, examiners may prefer the Mullen Scales or Early Learning. Assessment of children who are beyond the age limits for the Mullen but too young for the WISC-V may be assessed using the Differential Ability Scales, Second Edition (DAS-II). The Stanford-Binet, Fifth edition is often a preferred instrument in cognitive testing for ASD. Often, individuals with autism struggle to demonstrate their intelligence on a test that primarily taps language skills; which is often a weakness area. It also may be that the child is from another cultural background or is an English language learner. In these cases, it may be helpful to utilize a nonverbal assessment such as the Leiter-3 or the UNIT-2. As was noted in the beginning of this chapter, examiners may consider results from the following instruments:

• Consider results from Bayley-iii/Mullen, DAS-2, KABC-II, Leiter-3, SB5, UNIT-2, WISC-V, WAIS-IV, and WJ-IV

A full list of these instruments, spelling out the full names and separating assessments by area, is provided in the "Sample Checklist" chart in Chap. 5. This explanation of the cognitive profile in ASD is not intended to be comprehensive of all of the potential tests that could be used. Instead, these authors prescribe an approach for some of the major assessments commonly used in an evaluation for ASD. Research shows that individuals with ASD have unique cognitive profiles, requiring specific supports and interventions (Coolican, Bryson, & Zwaigenbaum, 2008; Mayes & Calhoun, 2003; Matthews et al., 2015; Saulnier & Ventola, 2012; Siegel, Minshew, & Goldstein, 1996). Therefore, when choosing an assessment tool, it is imperative to consider the individuals' overall level of functioning, language ability, and any motor challenges, not just chronological age, especially for those suspected of having ASD.

Mullen Scales of Early Learning (MULLEN)

The MULLEN test provides an effective opportunity to assess young children using engaging materials and quickly administered items. This test does not directly measure cognitive ability; however, it is an excellent assessment of development in a variety of domains that align closely with areas of intelligence, such as visual reception, and expressive and receptive language. In the examiner's experience, it can be very helpful to utilize multiple examiners in the administration of the MULLEN. One examiner might administer the items, while the other organizes materials and ensures that all of the necessary items are administered. In the author's experience, individuals with ASD tend to be more engaged in the Visual Reception tasks and may perform much better, relative to the language and/or motor scales. Due to the language problems in ASD, it is often the case that Receptive or Expressive Language scales are the lowest scores of the assessment. Bearing in mind that individuals with ASD tend to favor expressive language over receptive, it stands to reason that the receptive language score may be relatively low as compared to other areas when autism is present. It is important when testing children this young to remind families that cognitive abilities do not stabilize until about the age of seven (Schneider, Niklas, & Schmiedeler, 2014) so this is simply an estimate at this point, and certainly should not be seen as set in stone.

As in other assessments, examiners should note the child's test behaviors. If the examinee refuses items, tantrums, runs away, hides on mom's lap, or gives up easily, these observations should be seen as red flags. If the child shows great confidence and effort on Visual Reception but suddenly disengages on language items, examiners should take note. Overall, any delay in any area may be a sign of ASD or another neurodevelopmental disability and should be carefully analyzed.

DAS-II

The *Differential Ability Scales, Second Edition* (DAS-II; Elliott, 2007) is an assessment modeled after the CHC theory of intelligence and allows for the identification and interpretation of cognitive profiles of strengths and weaknesses, rather than an overall intelligence quotient (i.e., "*g*"). This is an essential consideration for the assessment of individuals with ASD, given their tendency to display variable cognitive profiles. In fact, with respect to the DAS-II normative sample, significantly more children with ASD demonstrated a discrepancy indicating better developed nonverbal than verbal abilities. Such findings are consistent with existing research using the *Wechsler* scales and the SB5. The DAS-II includes teaching items on each subtest, which, for individuals with ASD, is beneficial given their difficulty completing novel tasks without concrete directions, explanations, models, and demonstrations. The DAS-II also includes norms to accommodate those whose cognitive abilities fall in the extremes of the bell curve. The Early Years battery has extended norms through age 8, and the School-Age battery has extended norms down to age 5. Lastly, clinicians can discontinue a subtest based on two options, by either reaching a ceiling or by completing a set block of items. This option allows clinicians to alleviate the frustration that children may experience with designated ceiling rules.

The DAS-II measures cognitive abilities in children ranging in age from 2 years, 6 months to 17 years, 11 months. It comprises two batteries, the Early Years battery (2 years, 6 months to 8 years, 11 months) and the School-Age battery (5–17 years, 11 months). The Early Years battery is composed of the Lower Level (2 years, 6 months to 3 years, 5 months) and the Upper Level (3 years, 6 months to 8 years, 11 months). Regarding the Early Years Lower Level, four subtests yield an overall ability score, as well as two domain scores. The Verbal domain is composed of the *Verbal Comprehension* and *Naming Vocabulary* subtests, and the Nonverbal domain is composed of the *Picture Similarities* and *Pattern Construction* subtests. The Early Years Upper Level battery is made up of six subtests that also yield an overall ability score, as well as three domain scores. The Verbal domain includes the *Verbal Comprehension* and *Naming Vocabulary* subtests, the Nonverbal domain includes the *Picture Similarities* and *Matrices* subtests, and the Spatial domain includes the *Pattern Construction* and *Copying* subtests. The School-Age battery also composes six subtests and three domains, including Verbal Reasoning (*Similarities* and *Word Definitions*), Nonverbal Reasoning (*Matrices* and *Sequential and Quantitative Reasoning*), and Spatial (*Recall of Designs* and *Pattern Construction*). For the Early Years Upper Level and School-Age batteries, the Nonverbal and Spatial domain scores are combined to formulate a Special Nonverbal Composite. The Verbal domain score is then compared to the Special Nonverbal Composite to identify the presence of a discrepancy.

Although much research regarding the cognitive profiles of individuals with ASD is based on the *Wechsler* scales and the SB5, more research is beginning to surface using other assessment tools, such as the DAS-II. It is noteworthy that cognitive profiles also were explored with the predecessor of the DAS-II. Joseph, Tager-Flusberg, and Lord (2002) examined the cognitive profiles of 120 children administered the Differential Ability Scales. Seventy-three of the participants were given the DAS Preschool Battery (now called the DAS-II Early Years battery) and 47 were given the School-Age battery. Of the 73 participants who completed the DAS Preschool Battery, discrepancies were noted with more participants demonstrating verbal domain scores that were significantly lower than nonverbal domain scores. For those who completed the DAS School-Age battery, more participants also demonstrated a variable profile that favored nonverbal reasoning abilities. Further, results indicated that the larger the discrepancy, the more significant the level of social impairment (Joseph et al., 2002).

Research using the DAS-II is limited but is beginning to surface due to large scale studies such as the Simons Simplex Collection (SSC) through the Simons Foundation Autism Research Initiative (SFARI). Ankenman, Elgin, Sullivan, Vincent, and Bernier (2014) examined cognitive profile discrepancies using the DAS-II in a sample of children with ASD. The sample included 1954 children with ASD (1710 boys and 244 girls) between the ages of 4 and 17 years from the SSC. Results indicated that approximately 60 % of participants did not display a significant discrepancy, whereas 28 % showed a cognitive split favoring the nonverbal domain and 14 % showed a cognitive split favoring the verbal domain. Additionally, when compared to the DAS-II normative sample, a greater frequency of significant discrepancies favoring nonverbal reasoning was observed in the sample of individuals with ASD. Results also highlighted more severe symptomatology in those with a profile favoring nonverbal reasoning, which is consistent with findings from Joseph et al. (2002). Nowell, Schanding, Kanne, and Goin-Kochel (2015) also used the DAS-II to examine cognitive profiles of children with ASD and to explore discrepancies between verbal and nonverbal reasoning. Results indicated that a larger proportion of individuals in the ASD sample had significant discrepancies between the VIQ and NVIQ, compared to the normative sample.

Stanford-Binet 5

Stanford-Binet Intelligence Scales, Fifth Edition (SB5)

The *Stanford-Binet Intelligence Scales, Fifth Edition* (SB5; Roid, 2003) is an individually administered assessment of intelligence and cognitive abilities used for a variety of clinical (e.g., diagnostic and psychological assessments, neuropsychological assessments, and special education assessments) and research purposes. Distinctive patterns of strengths and weaknesses have been identified on assessments of intelligence for individuals with ASD (Coolican et al., 2008; Matthews et al., 2015; Mayes & Calhoun, 2003; Siegel, Minshew, & Goldstein, 1996). The SB5 offers clinicians an opportunity to assess these patterns in ASD, taking into consideration mental age and verbal abilities. The SB5 differs from its predecessors in that the number of subtests has changed; there are now five instead of four cognitive ability dimensions; there are two routing subtests to determine start points, and half of the test items require only a nonverbal response. There also are a variety of engaging materials (e.g., toys, manipulatives, and pictures), and an increased range of test items and norms to accommodate a wide range of ages (2–85 years) and ability levels. Assessment time ranges from 15 to 75 min, depending on the number of subtests administered.

The SB5 yields a Full Scale IQ (FSIQ), a Nonverbal IQ (NVIQ), a Verbal IQ (VIQ), and an Abbreviated Battery IQ (ABIQ). The SB5 also includes measures of five important dimensions of cognitive ability (Fluid Reasoning, Knowledge, Quantitative Reasoning, Visual–Spatial Processing, and Working Memory), and tools to examine narrower abilities at the subtest level that parallel the CHC theory of intelligence. The CHC model, referenced previously, proposes that intelligence has a hierarchical structure with three levels (narrow abilities, broad cognitive abilities, and a general measure of ability [g]). The ability to use the SB5 to analyze skills at all three levels of the CHC model enhances decision making related to instructional style, accommodations and modifications, and choice of curricula. For example, if results highlight a deficit in categorical reasoning (feature, function, class), then a recommendation is made to support the development of such skills using appropriate strategies across a variety of contexts and activities.

Although much cognitive profile research related to ASD has been completed using the *Wechsler* scales, research utilizing the SB5 is available and consistent with the cognitive profile research discussed throughout this section. Coolican et al. (2008) completed a study with 63 participants (12 girls and 51 boys) with diagnoses of Autistic Disorder, Asperger's Disorder, and Pervasive Developmental Disorder Not Otherwise Specified (PDD NOS). Results highlighted an overall profile characterized by a FSIQ and NVIQ in the Below Average range, whereas the VIQ fell in the Borderline range. Regarding diagnostic subgroups, those with Asperger's Disorder obtained higher FSIQ, NVIQ, and VIQ scores (Average, High Average, and Average, respectively), as did those with PDD NOS (Below Average and Borderline), than those with Autistic Disorder (Borderline).

Matthews et al. (2015) conducted a study with 73 children and adolescents with ASD, and reported similar findings.

It is this author's experience that, when assessing individuals with ASD using the SB5, more often than not cognitive profiles are in line with those just described. The SB5 provides a more comprehensive profile of abilities across nonverbal and verbal domains. Therefore, given variability in profiles in ASD across domains, the FSIQ, although meaningful and robust, is important to consider in the context of the individual profiles of domain and subtest scores. Clinicians should clearly state information in psychological reports highlighting that the entire profile of strengths and weaknesses should be considered, as opposed to global ability in isolation.

The SB5 FSIQ comprises ten subtests, and different pairings or groupings of these subtests yield additional verbal and nonverbal domain scores, as well as factor index scores. The NVIQ and the VIQ, each, are composed of five corresponding subtests that represent the five factors measured by the SB5. The ABIQ is composed of two routing subtests (Object Series/Matrices and Vocabulary). The Fluid Reasoning factor index assesses verbal and nonverbal inductive and deductive reasoning. Knowledge provides an assessment of learned information acquired at home, school, and in the community. Often times, these subtests appear to be areas of relative strength for individuals with ASD due their strong memory for details and facts. The Quantitative Reasoning factor index measures understanding and application of numerals and number concepts. These subtests also appear to represent areas of relative strength due to the concrete nature of the math problems. It is noteworthy, though, that some individuals with ASD may experience difficulty with the word problems due to language delays (including pragmatics). This difficulty can be evidenced during story problems in mathematics (see Chap. 18: School-Based Assessment for ASD). Visual–Spatial Processing assesses the ability to see patterns, relationships, spatial orientations, and the gestalt among visual displays. Lastly, the Working Memory factor index assesses the ability to store and manipulate verbal and visual information in short-term memory. Individuals with ASD may appear more successful on rote memorization tasks compared to those that require the active manipulation of information while holding it in short-term memory on this instrument.

The routing subtests, nonverbal Fluid Reasoning (*Object Series/Matrices*) and verbal Knowledge (*Vocabulary*), are administered at the beginning of the SB5 and identify the developmental starting point for all other subtests. The clinician, then, administers appropriate levels of nonverbal and/or verbal items, based on the predetermined starting points. If an individual has language or communication difficulties, including those associated with ASD, the examiner may choose to administer only the nonverbal subtests because language demands may yield a distorted profile, as evidenced by the aforementioned research. Additionally, examinees may experience undue frustration, which, in turn, may impact their performance on other subtests, again yielding an inaccurate representation of their profiles. However, if the verbal subtests are administered, clinicians are encouraged to be sensitive to the individual's behavior and provide breaks, as needed. The clinician also may consider "testing the limits" once standardized administration is completed to determine effective accommodations and modifications. For example, if an examinee is unable to complete a task successfully within a specified time limit, the clinician may read-minister the item without time constraints to determine if it can be completed successfully. If so, the clinician can determine if the time failure is related to a lack of ability or due to processing speed weaknesses.

The SB5 subtests contain a variety of items and difficulty levels, which is necessary because of the wide range of ages and abilities measured. An activity that works well with a preschool-age child may not be the most appropriate activity for an adolescent or young adult. For example, on the nonverbal *Visual–Spatial Processing* subtest, younger examinees are initially presented with form board activities using basic shapes, whereas older examinees are presented with form patterns that they must duplicate using a variety of geometric shapes. Each subtest contains training/demonstration items at several points to teach examinees tasks as they become more challenging. These items help examinees, particularly those with special needs, understand the requirements and expectations. Such training items also are helpful to individuals with ASD, as they benefit from the use of models and demonstrations when learning new concepts and ideas. As noted earlier, the SB5 also helps clinicians analyze narrow abilities so a more detailed profile of strengths and weaknesses related to information processing and problem solving can be obtained (Roid, 2003). In turn, this information should be used for therapeutic and educational programming, development of accommodations and modifications, and choice of curricula based on an individual's learning profile.

WISC-V

Substantial changes to the content, structure, and scoring were made in the fifth edition of the Wechsler Intelligence Scales for Children (WISC-V). Although normative data for ASD populations did not exist at the time of publishing, a brief overview of some critical components of the WISC-V will be discussed. At the composite level, there exist five composite indices, one more than the fourth edition. Within composites, primary subtests factor into Index score, and secondary subtests do not. Further, the FSIQ is made up of only some primary subtests. Additionally, ancillary and supplemental subtests factor into new ancillary composites.

The Verbal Comprehension Index comprises primary subtests Similarities and Vocabulary, both of which load into the FSIQ; Information and Comprehension are secondary subtests. Indeed, Comprehension has been removed from the core. This shift in core indices is exceptionally important in the assessment and diagnosis of ASD as Comprehension on the WISC-IV tended to be the lowest scoring subtests for persons with autism (Mayes & Calhoun, 2008). As such, it is highly recommended that clinicians assessing persons suspected of having an ASD administer Comprehension on the WISC-V, due to the well-established trend in subtest scoring patterns. Another substantial change from the WISC-IV is the replacement of Perceptual Reasoning with two arguably better defined indices: Visual Spatial and

Fluid Reasoning. The Visual Spatial Index measures the child's ability construct visual designs from a model and understanding of visual–spatial relationships. Whereas, the Fluid Reasoning Index reports on the child's ability to identify conceptual relationship among visual objects and use reasoning to identify and utilize apply rules to said relationships. Visual Spatial comprises primary subtests Block Design and Visual Puzzles; Block Design factors into the FSIQ.

Fluid Reasoning comprises Matrix Reasoning and Figure Weights, both which factor into the FSIQ; Picture Concepts and Arithmetic are secondary subtests.

The Working Memory Index underwent important changes as well in the WISC-V. Rather than the previous version which included Digit Span, and Letter-Number Sequencing only, the WISC-V includes Digit Span and Picture Span. Picture Span is a visual working memory subtest. Digit Span is factored into the FSIQ; wheras, Letter-Number Sequencing is a secondary subtest. The Processing Speed Index in the WISC-V retains its three subtests: Coding, Symbol Search, and Cancellation. Coding and Symbol Search are included as primary scales; whereas, Cancellation is a secondary scale. Coding factors into the Full Scale IQ.

The WISC-V contains a number of Ancillary Index Scales which provide scores for targeted areas of cognition, which may be of interest when conducting and assessment for ASDs. These scales are made up of a mixture of primary and secondary subtests. Ancillary Indices included on the WISC-V include: Quantitative Reasoning (Figure Weights and Arithmetic), Auditory Working Memory (Digit Span, Letter-Number Sequencing), Nonverbal (Block Design, Visual Puzzles, Matrix Reasoning, Figure Weights, Picture Span, and Coding) The GAI shifted significantly, GAI which is a composite of Verbal Comprehension, Fluid Reasoning and the Block Design subtest from Visual Spatial. The Cognitive Proficiency Index comprises the following: Digit Span, Coding, Picture Span, and Symbol Search.

QRI measures mathematical capacities including understanding of quantitative relationships, and working memory, abstract, conceptual reasoning.

The WMI teases those components of immediate working memory associated with verbal input including auditory sequential processing, memory span, mental manipulation, and more. The Nonverbal Index is useful when examining persons with ASD who have impaired language capacities (Maccow, 2015). It emphasizes visual–spatial processing but similar to the FSIQ is impacted by processing speed abilities. The CPI examines proficiency in information processing, as with the WISV-IV it can be a point of comparison to the GAI, as it is made up of strictly working memory and processing speed tasks.

Finally, the WISC-V offers a number of Complementary Index Scales, which assist in the assessment of children with learning challenges. Naming Speed (Naming Speed Literacy, Naming Speed Quantity) provides "broad estimate of automaticity of basic naming ability drawn from a variety of tasks" (Maccow, 2015). Symbol Translation (Immediate Symbol Translation, Delayed Symbol Translation, Recognition Symbol Translation) examines associative memory. Storage and Retrieval (Naming Speed Index, Symbol Translation Index) looks at long-term storage and retrieval precision and fluency.

As previously noted, normative data for populations with ASD was unavailable at the time of publication. The following are observations made by the authors regarding the WISC-V's role in assessing for ASDs. As such, the following qualitative observations require future research to determine any significant patterns and trends. First, it has been the author's experience that when assessing persons with ASD, the FSIQ is more often statistically appropriate to interpret in the fifth edition of the WISC compared to the fourth edition. That is, on the WISC-IV significant discrepancies among index scores often required the use of the GAI when reporting an intelligence quotient. Additionally, the inclusion of a measure of visual working memory (Picture Span) in the Working Memory Index provides a more balanced representation of Working Memory, especially for persons with language and/or cognitive impairments. The separation of PRI into VSI and FRI provides practitioners with the opportunity to better explain to parents the differences in skills when providing feedback regarding assessment results.

The present authors speculate that Verbal Comprehension Index scores are higher among populations with autism diagnoses since Comprehension was removed as a primary subtest.

Cognitive Assessment Using Q-Interactive Technology

The publishers of the WISC-V, Pearson Inc., have released a format for test administration using iPads. The WISC-IV became available first on Q-interactive in August of 2012 (Daniel, 2013). Other tests have since been included in the available battery on Q interactive, such as D-KEFS, NEPSY, CMS, and WIAT-III (Daniel, 2013). The Q-interactive now includes the WISC-V. This test format includes two iPad devices that are connected to each other using Bluetooth. The one iPad is the "clinician" device. The screen provides instructions from the test manual, such as "See these blocks? They are all alike…" The clinician device enables the examiner to then present the stimulus, such as the picture for the block design items. The examinee provides responses, either orally or through "clicking" on the iPad, as is the case with many of the nonverbal subtests. The developers of the Q-interactive application took care to ensure that this is still entirely directed and scored by the examiner; it is *not* a "computer-based" assessment.

As such, the examiner selects the score for each item before scrolling to the next item in the test. There is also the ability to track "events" like Queries, Prompts, the scrambling of blocks, or the response "don't know." It is the authors' impression that the administration process is quite similar to the pencil and paper administration; however, the device enables quicker scoring, and may improve standardization due to built-in ceilings, reverse rules, prompt reminders, and computer scoring. Equivalency studies reveal that the Q-interactive administration method reveals scores on the tests that are generally the same as the traditional format. Some examinees score higher on Similarities; however, the overall effect size of test format is less than .20 (Wahlstrom, 2014).

Regarding use of the Q-interactive test format for cognitive assessment in ASD populations, the preliminary research is encouraging. The developers of Q-interactive conducted user surveys to evaluate the effect of test format on examinee test behaviors. The survey was primarily completed by WISC-IV users, but the users of other tests were included as well (Daniel, 2013). Users were asked general questions about the test format, as well as specific questions regarding clinical populations. In terms of assessing clients on the iPad in certain clinical populations, examiners were asked, "Do you find clients with [diagnosed condition] respond differently to the stimuli presented on the iPad versus paper and pencil tests?" Examiners also responded to the following, "Please describe any other nuances you have observed when using Q-interactive with clients diagnosed with [condition]?" (Daniel, 2013, p. 3). The majority of examiners (59 %), who have administered to children with ASD using Q-interactive indicate that it had an effect on examinee behaviors (Daniel, 2013). Of these examiners, 85 % of the examiners felt that the children who had autism were more engaged in testing with the use of the Q-interactive technology format. Of the users who assessed children with ASD using Q-interactive, 15 % said the effect was neutral or inconsistent (Daniel, 2013).

These generally positive results would stand to reason, as many children with autism are technologically motivated or inclined. It may be that the iPad administration is somewhat less invasive in terms of assessing children with ASD, because a slightly lesser degree of eye contact and direct communication is required to complete the assessment. For example, on some nonverbal tests, examinees can simply click their responses on the iPad without the need to orally provide a response or make eye contact with the examiner. Indeed, none of the examiners in the equivalency studies indicated the children with ASD were less engaged on the Q-interactive format. Taken together, early research indicates that children with ASD seem to generally respond favorably to the Q-interactive test format. The authors wonder whether or not some children with ASD would perseverate on the device, which may reduce the quality of rapport. Presently, this does not appear to be the case. The device is basically disabled from typical uses during administration, as the only stimulus shown on the screen is that of the test item. This may perhaps reduce the desire to play games or perseverate on preferred iPad activities. Overall, the Q-Interactive test format appears to be effective for assessing children with ASD, based on the results of preliminary user surveys from Q-Interactive customers.

Previous Versions of the WISC

One of the most widely recognized IQ tests is the Wechsler Intelligence Scales for Children, Fifth Edition (WISC-V). As of this writing, there were not any equivalency studies for children with ASD (Wahstrom, 2015). There have fortunately been a variety of studies examining the performance of individuals with ASD on the WISC-IV. When reviewing performance for children with ASD on the WISC-IV however, it is necessary to state that multiple studies have found the norms for autism are inconsistent due to a variety of skills and symptom profile differences across the wide range of the Spectrum (Flanagan & Kaufman, 2004). Often the norms include smaller samples of children with ASD due to the fact that large clinical samples of children with autism are difficult to obtain; further, even clinical samples are not perfectly reliable in that the children may have been diagnosed in multiple sites by clinicians of various levels of experience. Adding to the difficulty in interpretation, children who were diagnosed with Autism (having a language delay) score differently than those diagnosed with Asperger's Disorder under DSM-IV criteria (not having a language delay). Thus, as a clinical sample, analysis can be daunting due to the differences among the groups that make up the Autism Spectrum. Considering these challenges, there are some consistent trends that tend to emerge in most studies.

Profile research indicates some modest trends in the skills demonstrated by persons with ASDs on cognitive assessment instruments as compared to neurotypicals. For example, children with High Functioning Autism (HFA) often score in the Average range on Perceptual Reasoning and Verbal Comprehension Index but below average on Working memory and Processing Speed (Mayes & Calhoun, 2008). Children with ASDs tend to score higher on tasks of visual reasoning (Mayes & Calhoun, 2008). They tend to struggle on the Coding test relative to the Symbol Search assessment. Mayes and Calhoun (2003) found in a sample of 163 3–15-year-olds with autism that visual reasoning exceeded grapho-motor skills. In preschool, children with ASDs tended to score lower on the verbal IQ index, relative to nonverbal; however, by school age, the difference between the two indexes was not significant.

Full Scale Intelligence Quotient or GAI

The full scale IQ score is a composite of all of the other indexes measuring cognitive ability. Studies repeatedly indicate that the Full Scale Intelligence Quotient (FSIQ) is the strongest predictor of successful outcomes (Mayes & Calhoun, 2008). This finding is promising news for children with high cognitive abilities. Generally, children with high IQs can demonstrate stronger skills in school which may lead to greater self-confidence, a lower degree of frustration, and potentially fewer issues with anxiety and depression later on in life. High IQ scores are generally correlated with high scores on achievement tests, although this may be due to similar test construction as opposed to true differences in academic achievement (Hazel, Personal Communications, 2012). Generally, children with higher cognitive abilities are more capable of responding to treatment such as Cognitive Behavioral Therapy. In this way, the FSIQ score of children with autism is a critical data point for all autism assessments and case reviews.

Profile research indicates some similar trends regarding the FSIQ or GAI in children with ASD (Mayes & Calhoun, 2008). In one study, the mean Full Scale

IQ score for children with HFA was 101 (SD = 19) (Mayes & Calhoun, 2008). Note that although the children had a mean score which is almost precisely average, the standard deviation is more than one full standard deviation of the Standard Scores used for the test (15 points). Thus, there was significant variation in performance overall. The mean score of the GAI was 113, which was higher than the FSIQ in 98 % of children with ASD in the study (effect size was large and significant: $t = 16.8$, $p < 0.0001$).

This means that children with autism struggled more than typical children on tests of Working Memory and Processing Speed which are not captured in the GAI. Indeed, while the mean score for Verbal Comprehension was 107 (Average) and for Perceptual Reasoning was 115 (High Average), the score on Working Memory was 89 (Low Average), and Processing Speed is 85 (Low Average). Taken together, the cognitive profile of children with autism on the WISC-IV (with an IQ score over 70) was that the FSIQ score was Average, although there was significant variation among test subjects and a significant scatter between the indexes that make up the FSIQ, necessitating often the use of the GAI. Similar to the Mayes and Calhoun research, studies in Colorado have found that the children with Autism ($N = 34$), who had IQs of 75 or higher, had a mean IQ of 100 (SD = 20), which is Average and at the 50th percentile, for the mean of the population at large (Willard, 2013). When including all of the children in this study with autism, even those with lower cognitive ability than 75 ($N = 84$), the mean IQ score was 90 (SD = 22), which is still in the average range. This means that although there is significant variation among children with autism in terms of their performance on IQ tests overall, there was not a significant difference between the IQs of children in these studies with autism compared to neurotypicals.

Verbal Comprehension

The Verbal Comprehension Index on the Wechsler Intelligence Scale for Children includes the test of Vocabulary, Comprehension, and Similarities (WISC-IV; note the WISC-V has been released at the time of this writing but data were not available so the WISC-IV was used for this section). Vocabulary is a test where children are asked to define words. Similarities is a test of assessing two items to evaluate what the words share in common. Finally, the Comprehension test measures a child's ability to understand and evaluate what to do in everyday social situations. Taken together, performance on all of these tests gives the examiner a basis for understanding the child's receptive and expressive cognitive skills; however, to assess a language disability, a true language test should also be administered such as the Clinical Evaluation of Language Fundamentals (CELF-V)—see the next section on Language Assessment.

Lowest Verbal Comprehension Score: Comprehension

Interestingly, children with autism struggle with the Comprehension subtest more than any other subtest on the WISC-IV. On the WISC-V, the Comprehension test is not a required test in the core battery. However, these authors strongly recommend administering Comprehension for any child suspected of an ASD because of the rich data it offers to examiners. In order to understand cognitive profiles in autism, Mayes and Calhoun (2008) analyzed cognitive profiles for 54 children aged 6–14, with a Full Scale IQ of 70 or higher. Results indicated that relative to other verbal skills, scores on the Comprehension test come out *lowest* in 94 % of the cases in this study. This finding points to the understanding that Autism is primarily a qualitative deficit in social skills (which includes social understanding as well as communication). That is, children with autism tend not to understand social cues and situations, and with this deficit might be expected to score lower on tests of Comprehension. Research is overwhelmingly consistent about Comprehension being the lowest score for ASD (Barnhill, 2000; Flanagan & Kaufman, 2004). Many hypothesize that low scores on Comprehension are likely due to the fact that social understanding is an essential component of a diagnosis of autism (Flanagan and Kaufman, 2004). In fact, clinically, this is one of the first signs that an autism diagnosis may be present. Children with autism may look as though they are cognitively quite adept on all of the previous subtests, but when the child attempts comprehension, he or she struggles significantly and obtains a very low score on Comprehension. Clinicians are wise to note any scatter among subtests but particularly a large deficit in Comprehension relative to other strong abilities.

In some studies, the difference between Verbal Comprehension and Perceptual Reasoning was statistically significant with a small to medium effect size ($p=0.001$ and $d=0.4$) (Mayes & Calhoun, 2008). This finding where Perceptual Reasoning scores are higher than Verbal Comprehension scores in children with autism is important to note. This is consistent with most research on the cognitive profiles of children with autism favoring nonverbal problem solving over verbal tasks (2008). Although not necessarily diagnostic, clinicians might consider a significant discrepancy between Perceptual Reasoning and Verbal Comprehension as a potential sign that an autism diagnosis may be relevant. In some cases, it may not be possible to obtain an FSIQ score at all because the child is not verbal enough to complete the items. In this case, the Leiter-3 or UNIT-II may be appropriate. In some circles, the NVIQ (Nonverbal IQ) may be adequate for the purposes of understanding cognitive ability; however, it may be necessary to assess language through observation, adaptive behavior scale scores, and work samples.

Perceptual Reasoning

Perceptual reasoning refers to nonverbal problem solving. Many of these tests, although the stimulus and response are presented nonverbally, still are amenable to verbal mediation. For example, on the Picture Concepts subtest of the WISC-IV, children are asked to look through a group of pictures and determine which pictures share a common category. A child may say, "This stapler is a school supply, and this paper clip is also a school supply. Ah, there it is, I chose these two." This is called verbal mediation. Thus, although it is important to evaluate nonverbal reasoning apart from verbal skills, it is not entirely possible to completely isolate the effects of verbal skills on perceptual reasoning scores. Within the Perceptual Reasoning Index, there is a subtest called Matrix Reasoning in which test subjects are expected to evaluate a series of patterns and identify which item comes next in the series. Finally, the WISC-IV and WISC-V include a test called Block Design where a child is expected to use blocks to match a printed design.

Lowest Score on Perceptual Reasoning Index: Block Design

On the Perceptual Reasoning Index, children with autism have the most difficult time with Block Design (although anecdotally they tend to enjoy the task, and they score higher on Block Design than many other subtests such as Coding). Mayes and Calhoun (2008) found that children with Autism scored lowest on Block Design as compared to Picture Concepts and Matrix Reasoning in 91 % of cases. The mean score was 11 (SD=3) (t=2.6, $p<0.01$, and d=0.3). Other studies have found that Block Design is actually a stronger score in ASD. The *WISC-IV Technical and Interpretive Manual* includes findings from a variety of studies showing Block Design as the highest score and Comprehension as the lowest (Flanagan & Kaufman, 2004). The highest mean score for the WISC-IV sample reported in the manual for children with Autistic Disorder was 7.9 on Block Design. Barnhill et al. (2000) found that in 19 of 20 studies on children with ASD, that Block Design was the highest score, whereas Comprehension was found to be the lowest. Although there could be various reasons for these apparent discrepancies, it is likely due to the factors mentioned previously about the extreme variation in profiles and skills across the Spectrum. Also, much of the research that is done for the WISC-IV is conducted on the WISC-III because generally at the release date there is not a body of available data on clinical samples for the new instrument. This test is also timed, which will be discussed later in this section as a common weakness area in ASD. It is sometimes hypothesized that some children with ASD may struggle on Block Design difficulties with Central Coherence, which means getting the main idea or putting all of the details together into a coherent picture.

Mayes and Calhoun (2008) report that Block Design was initially one of the highest scores for children with autism on the WISC-III but that this no longer holds true on the WISC-IV due to the fact that the WSIC-IV has two untimed tests requiring visual motor skills (Matrix Reasoning and Picture Concepts). The researchers indicate that the significant visual processing skills in children with autism were not shown on the WISC III because they tended to struggle with timed nonverbal tests like Object Assembly and Picture Arrangement. If indeed this is the reason, it could be due to problems with processing speed, rather than to difficulties with the tasks.

This research also points to stronger skills shown by children with autism on the untimed visual tasks on other tests such as the Leiter (Mayes & Calhoun, 2003).

Working Memory

Working Memory is a measure of a child's ability to hold information in the short-term memory and perform a mental operation with it. Working Memory is an Index score used in both the WISC-IV and WISC-V. For example, a child is asked to hold a series of letters and numbers in her memory and then repeat the numbers back in numerical order and then the letters in alphabetical order in the Letter-Number Sequencing subtest. On the Digit Span subtest, children are first asked to repeat numbers first in order and then in reverse order. The WISC-V adds a sequencing domain in which children are asked to put a group of numbers in numerical order. Working memory skills are impacted by attention and executive functioning (see Executive Functioning and Memory sections in Chap. 11). This is due to the fact that Working Memory involves multiple cognitive processes including paying careful attention to the stimulus and planning or organizing one's response.

Lowest Score in Working Memory: Letter-Number Sequencing

Of the Working Memory subtests, children with autism struggled the most with Letter-Number sequencing, having a mean of 8.4, whereas the mean was 12.5 for Picture Concepts and 13.1 for Matrix Reasoning for the Mayes and Calhoun study (2008). This means that children with autism struggled to listen to a series of numbers and letters and then retell the series in alphabetical and numerical order. As previously stated, this difficulty is likely due to difficulties with executive functions such as attention, planning, and sequencing.

Processing Speed

Processing Speed tests are a measure of quick thinking or cognitive efficiency. In other words, these tests measure how fast a child can do something. In general, children with autism struggle most with processing speed relative to strong skills in other areas (Mayes & Calhoun, 2008). One test on the WISC-IV, Coding asks the child to copy symbols given a visual key. The other, Symbol Search, asks children to answer "yes" or "no" as to whether or not a specific target symbol is present in a group of distracting symbols. Although the tests have been changed in terms of the precise items and presentation in the response booklet, the WISC-V also includes Coding and Symbol Search.

Lowest Score on Processing Speed Index: Coding

Children with autism tend to score lowest on Coding relative to all other tests on the WISC-IV. The average score for coding was 6.6 on the Mayes and Calhoun study (2008). This score of 6 is not only below average but represents a 7 point difference between the highest score mean for Matrix Reasoning ($M = 13$, SD = 3). There could be various reasons for this difficulty in autism. One may be due to impaired executive functions in general, causing a child to perhaps struggle to plan out how to approach the task of identifying and copying the symbols (i.e., memorize the symbols vs. checking the key each time). Executive functions are also involved in "shifting mental set" which may impair a child's ability on the coding subtest. It is also timed, which may cause undue anxiety in some children. Finally, there is a fine motor component involved in copying the symbols which is not present on the Symbol Search test. Children with autism struggle with writing tests in general on achievement tests (2008) and may also have fine motor delays.

Stability of IQ Scores in ASD

While IQ scores are predictive and tend to remain relatively stable over time, it is important to note that research continues to show the brain is plastic and malleable. Research demonstrates that IQ is a stable construct; however, cognitive abilities are not static, and children with lower IQ scores can learn and grow into higher functioning individuals. Sattler (2001) provides that approximately 50 % of the variation in IQ scores is due to genetic factors, while the other 50 % is correlated with other factors outside of genetics or heritability. This does not mean that IQ is inherited; rather, a certain genetic makeup is inherited which is a child's genotype. The phenotype (actual expression or presentation of those genes) is influenced by factors including environment and genetics. Sattler explains, "Genes set the upper and lower limits of the phenotype, but the environment determines where this range of intellectual functioning will fall. The current nature-nurture controversy is reducible to the single issue of how wide the range of reaction is" (p. 162). This can be seen as encouraging news and more evidence for the need for enrichment opportunities for children with cognitive difficulties, in light of the plasticity of the brain. Sattler (2001) indicates that the following factors contribute to IQ: genetic factors (child's genetic makeup), familial factors (parent's IQ, parent's education, quality of home environment), educational factors (quality of school, teacher characteristics), and non-familial factors (best friend's IQ, quality of community) (Sattler, 2001, p. 162).

Factors impacting IQ increase in ASD

IQ scores can be impacted by: access to enriching experiences, access to sources of knowledge, high level of social support and encouragement, cultural beliefs that foster learning, secure attachment to caregivers, rich and responsive language environment, good school attendance, parents who are involved with child's education, non-impoverished living conditions, and good nutrition (Sattler, 2001, p. 163). In the evaluation of children with ASD, the "good nutrition" factor should be considered due to research indicating that children with ASD often have comorbid difficulties with digestion, and metabolism referred to in the seminal work, *Starving Brains*. For a more thorough treatment of these issues, see Chap. 2. In light of this research, the importance of nutrition cannot be overstated. It is highly possible that the child has much higher cognitive abilities but struggles to demonstrate them due to problems with adequate metabolism, digestion, and nutrition. It is also possible that the child's cognitive development is stunted, at least temporarily due to inadequate nutrition.

Regarding the malleability of IQ in the ASD population, Dietz, Swinkels, Buitelaar, van Daalen, and van Engeland (2007) provide encouraging news. In a longitudinal study of children with ASD at ages 25 months and 43 months ($N=39$), Dietz and colleagues found that although IQ scores were relatively stable, about one third of children in the sample showed a 15 point increase in IQ scores at Time 2. The authors claim that "Findings suggest that some children with ASD show catch-up intellectual development" (p. 405). The authors indicate that IQ scores as young as 25 months are predictive of scores later in life (correlation = .81, $p < .01$); however, many children in the study do show improvements over time. The study *did not* find treatment effects to be correlated with these increases. Rather, the two factors implicated in increased IQ were: lower levels of symptoms at Time 1, and higher expressive language abilities at Time 2. This means that children who initially did not have as many significant autism symptoms and who later had higher language skills showed an increased IQ, relative to children without these factors.

Although "intensity of treatment" was not a factor in the change, it is important to consider that treatment intensity may offer up a spurious relationship. That is, children with higher needs at young ages tend to have a higher intensity of treatment. As such, the sample may a bit skewed in that children who have highly intensive treatment may be more impacted to begin with, and as such, may be less likely to show improvements later in life. Thus, it may be difficult to determine the effects of treatment on cognitive functioning differences at later times in development.

Similarly encouraging news comes from Mayes and Calhoun (2003) who studied a sample of 163, 3–15-year olds with autism, finding that IQ increased with age. Mayes and Calhoun postulate that this increase likely indicates both a true increase in IQ and the fact that children with lower IQs are more likely to be diagnosed younger. Also encouraging, Mayes and Calhoun cite a previous study (Mayes & Calhoun, 2008) finding that children with autism who were tested 1 year later had an increased IQ of up to 15 points, and further cite Freeman (1985) who found that children with autism tended to show increased IQ scores from age four to age seven. The VIQ mean increased from 82 to 96 and the PIQ mean raised from 92 to 109 (in the group of children who were not classified as intellectually disabled). These findings point to the notion that children with autism may have average to high cognitive abilities that can be essentially "tapped into" with intervention, education, and adult support. A potential hypothesis for these changing IQ scores is that children who receive support and interventions may increase their ability to demonstrate skills due to increased compliance, improved language abilities, more developed executive functioning and problem-solving skills, and increased positive attitude toward testing.

Another potential reason for these findings is that the interventions targeting specific skill deficits essentially "light up" brain connections that are further strengthened by educational and environmental supports, thus resulting in higher cognitive functioning overall. A final hypothesis for this "catch up" intellectual development was provided by Rogers (2015) when she states from repeated trials using the Early Start Denver Model that early and effective intervention actually changes the brain's structure and functioning, and results in IQ increases. Roger's results are certainly consistent with the early seminal work by Lovaas in 1987, finding that many children with autism showed increased IQ scores after intensive early intervention (Cited in Cohen, Amerine-Dickens, and Smith (2006), Rogers and Vismara (2008)). Although the precise reasons for this increased IQ potential in the ASD population are unknown, these results provide promising hope for families who have children with cognitive delays, as well as further support for enhanced research and implementation of evidence-based early intervention.

Assessing for Language

Vignette #2 Sam: Language Assessment in a Gifted Child with Autism Spectrum

Sam, age 6, was referred for an evaluation at Emerge to rule out the presence of an Autism Spectrum Disorder. Parents reported significant "giftedness" academically as Sam had a history of speaking and reading early and met pre-academic goals in preschool ahead of his peers. Sam's parents reported that he is kind, caring, and a bit anxious, and has some difficulty with complex pretend play. He reportedly has a tendency to watch the same movies over and quote them in his play with his sisters. Sam scored in the Superior range on the WISC-IV, consistent with parent report, and was administered the CELF-4 to assess language abilities. Sam demonstrated impulsivity in his responding on Concepts and Following Directions and frequently had to self-correct when he caught his mistakes. He ignored and misunderstood the directions more frequently than expected given his superior verbal skills. In the area of Word Structure, Sam consistently omitted pronouns and struggled with irregular plurals, irregular past tenses, comparatives, and superlatives. For example, Sam said "mouse" instead of "mice" and "drawed" instead of drew. He also said "goodest" instead of "best" and "this girl is happy" instead of "she is happy," seemingly to avoid using a pronoun. Sam earned a scaled score of 8 on Word Structure which is not commensurate with his Superior cognitive ability. Sam exhibited advanced vocabulary skills and sometimes used formal language. He scored a scaled score of 13 on Expressive Vocabulary. Overall his CELF-4 score was Average. Sam additionally demonstrated subtle challenges in unstructured conversation on the ADOS-2 and challenges with pretend play. Taken together, Sam's consistent omission of pronouns and the discrepancy between Sam's Core Language composite score and his Verbal Reasoning score are best explained in the context of an Autism Spectrum Disorder. Sam began Cognitive Behavioral Therapy with an Emerge clinician who was also able to do direct social skills training with Sam at school and on playdates. Sam's subtle symptoms of Autism Spectrum Disorder were addressed and he has made steady progress across language and social communication domains. Now, as a fourth grader he is excelling in school and has friends to sit with at lunch. He has fewer playdates than most children his age but Sam is happy and successful in school and socially by his own report (Table 8.2).

Table 8.2 Assessing for language

Core area
1. *Language*
• *Core Language*—compared to VIQ (concerning if Core Language is much lower)
• *Expressive* vs. *Receptive* language discrepancies
• *Pragmatic language* (in ASD pragmatic language scores may be lower)
• *Ideational fluency and word retrieval* (concerning when low compared to VIQ)
• *Reporting of events and narrative coherence*: following consistent plot line and share main idea
• Consider results from: ABLLS-R, CELF-5, COWA, EOWPVT, EVT, PPVT, PLS-4, TOPL-2, Verbal IQ
Full measure names
Assessment of Basic Language and Learning Skills (ABLLS-R)
Clinical Evaluation of Language Fundamentals, Second Edition Preschool (CELF-PRE2)
Clinical Evaluation of Language Fundamentals, Fifth Edition (CELF-5)
Controlled Oral Word Association Test (COWA)
Expressive One-Word Picture Vocabulary Test, Fourth Edition (EOWPVT-4)
Expressive Vocabulary Test, Second Edition (EVT-2)
Peabody Picture Vocabulary Test, Fourth Edition (PPVT-4)
Preschool Language Scale, Fourth Edition (PLS-4)
Test of Pragmatic Language, Second Edition (TOPL-2)
Verbal IQ scores on cognitive measures

Language Assessment as It Applies to Autism: Expressive, Receptive, and Pragmatics

Assessing language development particularly in young children and school-aged children is an essential part of the diagnostic assessment for ASD. Communication is a core deficit of Autism Spectrum Disorders and is an area that should be assessed directly and indirectly in a variety of ways for a comprehensive assessment. There are various cognitive theories of Autism presented in the research that can assist in explaining the language deficits associated with Autism Spectrum Disorders. These are Empathizing and Systemizing, Executive Dysfunction, and Central Coherence (Baron-Cohen & Belmonte, 2005). Theory of Mind is another cognitive theory with support in providing information on how Autism impacts cognition. Much has been written from these cognitive perspectives in recent years.

The theory of Central Coherence refers to the idea that those with ASD process information more locally and with a detail-oriented framework than they do globally (Baron-Cohen, 2004). This theory would apply to language; for example, explaining why specific areas like grammar may develop more easily than complicated aspects of language such as pragmatics which utilizes global processing. This then impacts how an individual interprets language. On the CELF-4, the Semantic Knowledge subtest assesses understanding of complex statements that involve perspective taking and global understanding of the meaning of the statements presented. Individuals must select statements that are true based on what is originally asserted. This can be very difficult for individuals on the spectrum, taking both Central Coherence and Theory of Mind into account. Theory of Mind proposes that individuals with ASD are not able to understand, as typical persons do, that others have interests, beliefs, and ideas different from their own. For example, take pronoun reversals, as noted in the case study. This could be an inability to take perspective. A child hears an adult say "Do you want to swing?" It is to be inferred that the answer should be something like, "I want to swing." Young children with ASD may mix up these pronouns, making requests, such as, "You want a cookie" to mean "I want a cookie." An older individual may misunderstand the meaning of language because he or she assumes the speaker's perspective does not differ from one's own.

While some individuals may have particularly high scores across language measures, many individuals may have more varied patterns of language development. When Verbal Comprehension abilities are Very Superior, and are equally high across subtests, a language measure like the CELF can be less discriminating than it would be for an individual with a more varied cognitive profile. In the case of a very intelligent individual, noting the prosody, tone, and formality of language is most useful. Also assessing use of jargon, metaphors, or neologisms may be diagnostic. The ADOS-2 provides structure and an opportunity to assess these skills that may be evident in conversation.

The Creating a Story task on the ADOS-2 provides an opportunity to assess an individual's skills in creating plot, drawing events together, using emphasis, and correctly interpreting actions and emotions. Research has shown that data from this task alone, or similar narrative construction tasks, can provide rich diagnostic information (Losh & Capps, 2003; Suh et al., 2014; Willard, 2013). Those with ASD do not identify or reference emotions; their narratives tend to be more simplistic, particularly in their explanations of the action seen in pictures; they tend to fail to tie the story together with a concrete plot (Happé & Frith, 2006; Willard, 2013).

The TOPL-2, a pragmatic language measure, may be useful in assessing a child's ability to understand the perspective of another individual, comprehend language that is figurative, and use language and social problem-solving skills to resolve or avoid conflict. Pragmatic language requires some level of reciprocity in the communication. There should be a to-and-fro quality to interactions, a fluidity between topics, and a comfort level in the conversation. If some of these pragmatic elements are missing, the examiner should consider the presence of autism.

Sometimes when assessing young children with high scores across cognitive measures and language composites on the Mullen Scales or the CELF-2 Preschool, it is important to assess in relation to joint attention. Joint attention, or referencing a toy or object jointly with another, is related to use of language. Often children who have challenges with joint attention use language primarily to make requests and gain help from others but not to socialize and share. A child's language may be grammatically correct and even advanced in verbal knowledge but the social aspects are delayed. Utilizing the ADOS-2, we can assess both joint attention and social and conversational language.

When an individual has lower comprehension scores or a varied cognitive profile, it may be helpful to assess areas like expressive language, receptive language, language content, and language memory. All of these scales are available on the CELF-5 for use with those aged 3–19. Younger children can be assessed using the Mullen Scales or Preschool Language Scale providing expressive and receptive language data below the age of three. The CELF-5, language structure, and specifically, the word structure task administered to children aged 3–8 may provide useful information on language errors like pronoun reversal which may be attributed to Theory of Mind.

One profile commonly seen in young children diagnosed with Autism Spectrum Disorders involves expressive language skills higher than receptive language. This is not always the case, but when it is, children are often very good at naming objects or sharing information but they are not fluent in conversation skills. Deficits may be present in a child's ability to recall what others' say, take perspective of the others, or to comprehend what is shared or asked. These difficulties are perhaps related to Theory of Mind. These problems often co-occur with language structure challenges like those observed in the case study. Sam reversed pronouns, had trouble with verb tense, and generally struggled with the structure of his language in addition to problems in perspective taking during conversations.

Another area of language and speech worthy of mention is related to articulation and the production of language which some theorize is oral motor dyspraxia or challenges with fine motor control of the mouth and tongue (Belmonte et al., 2013). Another theory is that delayed language of any sort may be related to joint attention and the social means we use to establish language. Applied Behavior Analysis therapy and Speech/Language Therapy by a clinician with experience working with ASD are often prescribed to treat language weaknesses.

Ideational Fluency and Language

Ideational fluency pertains to the speed with which a person can generate ideas. "Ideational Dysfluency" refers to problems generating ideas in ASD. Dr. Huckabee, a clinician and author of this text, often uses this term to explain how individuals with ASD often struggle to think of things to say. Ideational dysfluency can be seen as an index of creativity and flexibility (Eigsti, de Marchena, Schuh, & Kelley, 2011). Research suggests this is indeed a dissociable skill separate from overall cognitive ability (Vannorsdall, Maroof, Gordon, & Schretlen, 2012) and individuals with ASD typically have marked difficulty in this area across a variety of ages. These results shed light on one reason most individuals with ASD either have little to share socially or incessantly talk about their restricted interests. Clearly, the ability to think of a variety of things to share is a necessary precursor to sophisticated conversation.

While much research is still needed on this budding construct, assessment of ideational fluency can be done using the Controlled Oral Word Association Test (COWA), formerly the FAS Fluency test. This measure requires the participant to separately list as many words as possible that start with three different letters in 1-min intervals. Next, the participant is asked to list as many words as possible within a category like "animals" or "foods" in a 1-min interval. Since animals may be a high preference topic for a person with ASD, this selective interest should be considered when interpreting results of the COWA. Additional research with the COWA or similar measures will likely reveal much needed normative information on fluency for individuals with ASD. While it seems logical that listing animals, for instance, is ecologically relevant to sustain a conversation on animals, it's less clear how ecologically valid it is to list phonologically similar words as are typically assessed with the letters F, A, and S. Clinically, some individuals with ASD have extreme challenges in thinking of what to say, while others seem verbally disinhibited and loquaciously provide information on topics that capture their own interests.

Administering the COWA can shed light on verbal and perhaps ideational fluency which could assess requisite skills for conversation. It seems reasonable to deduce that weak or deficit skills on the COWA would predict impairments in conversations that may involve much less structure than that afforded on the test. Listing words within a 1-min time frame is highly consistent and structured, and is thus a prerequisite skill for effective conversational fluency. Clinical observations of the individual's conversation with the examiner are also highly relevant in assessing communication and social skills. However, results are somewhat different than typically would be observed in other settings because the examiner is an unfamiliar person and the examinee's performance may suffer as a result of social anxiety.

Information on verbal and ideational fluency is also relevant. If a person is deficient in ideational fluency, he or she may exhibit poor conversational skills than expected in many areas. Examiners could reasonably conclude the person needs remediation or compensatory strategies to support weak fluency as reflected in the limited ability to think of topics and related comments to share in conversation.

Language and Optimal Outcomes

Early language development is commonly found as a primary predictor of optimal outcomes. When assessing young children who have a high risk for ASD, based on their status as a sibling of an individual with ASD, one study found that language development predicted ASD status at 36 months of age better than early eye tracking, social engagement, and eye contact (Edwards, Masyn, Luyster, & Nelson, 2014). Those with high language scores were less likely to be diagnosed with ASD at age 3 (Edwards et al., 2014). Another study of individuals diagnosed at 24 months of age assessed predictors of a non-spectrum diagnosis 2 years later at age four and found that better language and adaptive skills predicted optimal progress in up to 37 % of individuals (Moulton, Fein, Barton, & Robins, 2014). It has oft been found that children with autism have significant weaknesses in narrative coherence (story telling), in spite of average IQ scores (Losh & Capps, 2003; Suh et al., 2014; Willard, 2013). When telling a story, children with optimal outcomes are able to include as many story elements as typical children, whereas children with HFA produce significantly fewer (Suh et al., 2014). Taken together, strong language development, especially when combined with average or high IQ scores, tends to strongly predict better outcomes in children with autism.

Concluding Remarks on Assessment of Cognition and Language

It is valuable to assess for cognitive deficits because the most common comorbid condition for individuals with ASDs is an Intellectual Disability (Trammell, Wilczynski, Dale, & McIntosh, 2013); however, many children with ASDs have average or superior IQs. Assessment of intellectual functioning allows for discussion of cognitive strengths and weaknesses and can lend to recommendations for both academic and community supports depending on areas of strength and weakness identified. Cognitive profiles tend to be more scattered in individuals with ASDs than in the general population (Kim et al., 2011). It is important to note that cognitive abilities do not become stable until approximately age 7 (Schneider et al., 2014) and there is more instability in IQ scores in the ASD population. However, cognitive measures provide information on skills and abilities at the time of assessment, in comparison to the performance of typical peers. Assessing for cognition generally includes an evaluation of verbal or language skills. In ASD, language skills tend to lag behind perceptual reasoning and in some studies, the Verbal Comprehension Index was clinically significantly lower than the Perceptual Reasoning Index (although this effect tends to dissipate with maturation). Cognitive ability or the combination of cognitive and language ability tends to be important factor in optimal outcomes.

Research on optimal outcomes for ASD identifies language development as a strong predictor. Those with high early language skills are less likely to be diagnosed with ASD at age three. Individuals with strong language and cognitive skills in the toddler years tend to achieve optimal outcomes more often than those with weaker skills in these areas during early development. Thus, cognitive ability and language skills are strongly associated with better outcomes for children with ASD in a variety of studies. Taken together, the evaluation of Cognitive and Language skills is *Core Areas* of assessment. These authors recommend assessing for cognitive skills early in the evaluation so that clinicians have a basis for comparison for other measures. Cognitive and Language scores provide the foundation of understanding a child's skills, as well as predict optimal outcomes.

Chapter 9
Social and Sensory Assessment

Abstract The autism phenotype includes social communication, inflexible language and behavior, and repetitive sensory and motor behavior. Our discussion will address these essential areas: assessment of communication, social interaction, play/imaginative use of materials, and restricted or repetitive behaviors. In discussing ASD assessment, it is important to carefully review the "Gold Standard" for observational assessment of autism spectrum disorders (Kanne, Randolph, & Farmer, 2008; Ozonoff, Goodlin-Jones, & Solomon, 2005) the ADOS, now in its second version (ADOS-2), and the ADI-R or diagnostic caregiver interview. Evaluation will be discussed across the domains of social communication and restricted repetitive behaviors, as well as sensory processing. This chapter provides examples of the assessments that might be used in all of these social and sensory areas. Assessment of core autism symptoms, explanation of the ADOS-2 items and algorithm, description of the ADI-R clinical interview, review of screening instruments, and review of sensory measures are included in this chapter. This chapter discusses sensory processing in the context of autism and other diagnoses instead of as a stand-alone diagnosis. These areas of assessment complete the core assessment of ASD while the following chapters include associated areas for comprehensive assessment.

Keywords Social assessment of ASD • Social reciprocity in ASD • ADOS-2 • Assessing joint attention in ASD • Assessing play behaviors • Assessing restricted interests in ASD • Repetitive behavior in ASD • Sensory sensitivity in ASD • Sensory processing disorder? Is it real? • Odd sensory behaviors

Assessing for Social and Core Autism Symptoms

Vignette #3 Alex: Autism Assessment in a Child with Social Interaction Challenges

Alex is 6 years old who was evaluated at Emerge for mood, social interaction, sensory, and behavioral challenges. He scored in the Superior range of intellectual ability on the WISC-IV and was reported to be bright, clever, and kind to others in class. Alex does not like it when his first grade classmates break rules and he wants to play the same pretend game "puppies" on the playground day after day. Alex has huge meltdowns at home over small things like disagreements with his sister. He is a bed wetter, seemingly unaware when he has to "go" and thus he often does not make it to the bathroom on time (Table 9.1).

Alex demonstrated an unusual style of communication and social interaction throughout the ADOS-2 and during other parts of testing. His speech was occasionally formal and advanced, and his utterances were sometimes characterized by an odd use of words or phrases. Though he occasionally offered information to the examiner during conversations, what he disclosed appeared to be blatant fabrications or events that were unlikely to be true. It seemed that Alex was unsure of how to respond to the examiner, and he dealt with this uncertainty by making up stories. For instance, he told stories about his dog catching ten squirrels at once, being on Fox News, and having a pet tiger. When asked follow-up questions about his pet tiger, he said the tiger is currently one inch long and is about to "turn two inches." He seemed to lack any awareness of how the information he shared would be received by the examiner (i.e., that she would know he was being untruthful).

Alex occasionally asked the examiner about her ideas or experiences; however, he dropped several of the examiner's conversational bids for him to ask questions and simply ignored her comments. Alex exhibited good eye contact and he directed some facial expressions appropriately at the examiner such as raising his eyebrows and smiling. Alex demonstrated extremely limited insight into typical social situations and relationships. For instance, he could not identify any of his friends' names, and he shrugged when asked, "What makes someone a friend?" or "How is a friend different from someone whom you just go to school with?" Alex's difficulty answering these questions is not commensurate with his strong verbal abilities, as evidenced by his performance on the WISC-IV.

Alex's play was typified by unusual sensory interests and a highly specific focus on certain aspects of the play characters. For instance, when asked to play with several different objects, Alex first picked up a piece of cotton, held it in his hand, and said, "It's a fluffy rock." He also laid down the human figures, covered up their faces with plates, and said, "I don't want to see their bald eyes." Alex was diagnosed with ASD; and through the cognitive behavioral treatment that followed, Alex began to work on social perspective taking skills. He is becoming less bossy with his peers and his tantrums are reduced in frequency because his emotional awareness and coping skills have improved.

Table 9.1 Assessing for social and core autism symptoms

Core area
1. *Social communication and core ASD symptoms*
• Overall score on ADOS algorithm (consider scores only valid if administered by qualified clinician)
• Consider major symptom areas in light of entire evaluation
• Review screening instruments: SCQ, GARS, CARS, M-CHAT, feedback from pediatrician
• Behavior observations: appearance, behavioral presentation, language, eye contact and gesture use in communication, play/interests, social reciprocity, attention, motor skills, mood, and affect
• Rating scales and interview on child's social communication, behaviors, and overall functioning
• Consider developmental milestones, social communication, and emotional regulation
• Toddler: communication, reciprocal social interaction, restrictive and repetitive behavior
• Module 1–3: social affect, communication, reciprocal social interaction; restricted and repetitive behavior
• Module 4: communication, reciprocal social interaction, imagination/creativity, stereotyped behaviors, and restricted interests
• Consider results from ADI-R, ADOS-2, AOSI, SCQ, SRS; clinical interview/observations
Full measure names
Autism Diagnostic Interview-Revised (ADI-R)
Autism Diagnostic Observation Schedule, Second Edition, Module T-4 (ADOS-2)
Autism Observation Scale for Infants (AOSI)
Social Communication Questionnaire (SCQ)
Social Responsiveness Scale (SRS)

Assessing the Core Symptoms of Autism

Our discussion of core autism symptoms will address these essential areas: assessment of communication, social interaction, play/imaginative use of materials, and restricted repetitive behaviors. Georgiades et al. (2007) identified a factor structure for the autism phenotype that included social communication, inflexible language and behavior, and repetitive sensory and motor behavior. All of these factors associated with ASD are reviewed in this section. In discussing ASD assessment, it is important to carefully review the "Gold Standard" for observational assessment of autism spectrum disorders (Kanne, Randolph, & Farmer, 2008; Ozonoff, Goodlin-Jones, & Solomon, 2005) the ADOS, now in its second version (ADOS-2). The Autism Diagnostic Interview, Revised (ADI-R) parent or caregiver diagnostic interview is also discussed as a Gold Standard instrument. Evaluation will be discussed across the domains of social communication and restricted repetitive behaviors.

ADOS and ADI-R

Gold Standard Instruments

A review of the research indicates that the Autism Diagnostic Observation Schedule, Second Edition (ADOS: Lord & Schopler, 1989) and the Autism Diagnostic Interview-Revised (ADI-R: Lord, Rutter, & Le Couteur, 1994) are the tools generally recommended for autism evaluations and research (Tanguay, 2000). The ADOS-2 is an observation scale whereby a clinician assesses a child's play and communicative behaviors through a naturalistic observation, using a defined set of activities and assessment criteria (approximately 14 activities, 26 items, and 3 domains). The ADI-R is a semi-structured interview, administered to parents (over 70 items, summarized into an algorithm that includes three domains/dimensions). Some studies name the ADOS as the "gold standard" (Klin et al., 2007) for diagnostic assessment of autism spectrum disorders. However, others refer to the ADI-R as the gold standard (Matson, Nebel-Schwalm, & Matson, 2007). Matson and colleagues claim, "The ADI-R is considered to be the *gold standard* for assessment scales used in the diagnosis of autism by many at this time. It has a broader age range of norms, more published psychometric data, and is a best fit with DSM and ICD criteria relative to other scales…" (Matson et al., 2007, p. 43).

Finally, other studies suggest the use of both instruments as the *gold standard*. A comprehensive literature review conducted in 2013 by Falkmer, Anderson, Falkmer, and Horlin found that "…the true 'gold standard' classification and diagnosis of autism is still considered to be multi-disciplinary team clinical assessment, including use of the ADOS and ADI-R, as well as other assessments with consensus clinical judgment" (Falkmer, Anderson, Falkmer, & Horlin, 2013, published online no page number). Research on the usefulness of the ADOS and ADI-R in populations with co-occurring intellectual disabilities shows that these measures are valuable diagnostic tools (Sappok et al., 2013). Robertson and colleagues report that the ADOS and ADI-R measure slightly different aspects of manifestations of the disorder and the combination is a conservative approach to diagnose Autism Spectrum Disorders (Robertson, Tanguay, L'Ecuyer, Sims, & Waltrip, 1999). Another study focused on using these measures to assess preschool children and found good agreement between the two instruments (Dover & Le Couteur 2007). Research on the use of both instruments found approximately 75 % agreement between the ADI-R and ADOS (in 2006) (Dover & Le Couteur 2007). The authors of this text agree with the research claiming that the ADOS-2 and the ADI-R are both considered gold standard instruments, but argue that the purpose and usefulness of the instruments can be differentiated.

In looking at the utility of both the ADOS and ADI-R, both considered Gold Standard instruments, it is useful to consider sensitivity and specificity. For clarification, specificity measures the proportion of negatives (no diagnosis) correctly identified as such and sensitivity measures the proportion of actual positives (those with the diagnosis) correctly identified as such. Sappok and Diefenbacher's findings indicate that the ADOS is a very sensitive measure with 100 % sensitivity but is lower in differentiating between diagnoses (45 % specificity) (Sappok et al., 2013). The study also utilized the ADI-R which had 88 % sensitivity and 80 % specificity. In the intellectually disabled population, it was more feasible to do the ADOS and less so to do the ADI-R, based on the number of caregivers available to be interviewed.

Studies have examined the relative practicality of utilizing both measures during an autism assessment. Both Filipek et al. (1999) and De Bildt et al. (2004) noted that the time to train on and administer both measures is extensive. In these authors' experience, practicality is often discovered as the reason why some clinicians do not utilize both instruments consistently during diagnostic evaluations. Le Couteur et al. (2007) notes that for clinical and research settings the Autism Spectrum has broadened and a clear assessment framework is needed. As previously mentioned, the ADOS-2 offers observational data, whereas the ADI-R offers diagnostic interview information. Both interviews and observations have advantages and limitations. One advantage of using both is to "gather clinically relevant information in a systematic and comparable fashion." These authors advance that the ADOS-2 is mandatory to include; however, most ADI-R data can be obtained through a comprehensive diagnostic interview meeting with parents. In more involved cases with diagnostic uncertainty, it is valuable to record behavior with both the ADOS-2 and ADI-R (Le Couteur et al., 2007).

History and Development of the ADOS-2 and ADI-R

According to the ADOS-2 manual, the first version of the ADOS was introduced in 1989 and intended for administration with children ages 5–12 with expressive language at least at a 3-year-old level. This measure was proposed to complement the Autism Diagnostic Interview, known as the ADI (Le Coutuer et al., 1989). The combination of the two measures was offered as having adequate reliability and validity for research diagnosis. For administration of the original ADOS, specific training was required. According to the manual, after the ADOS was released, it became evident that there was a need for a version of the measure appropriate for younger children and those with less language. The PL-ADOS was developed with this population in mind. At that time, the ADOS authors were participating in a longitudinal study that referred children at age two and further necessitated the development of this measure. The PL-ADOS, which came out in 1995, was more flexible and included more use of play materials (DiLavore, Lord, & Rutter, 1995). The ADI-R was released including more questions about social interaction and communication for younger children (Lord et al., 1994) making it a better companion measure.

The PL-ADOS was useful for assessing younger children with very limited speech but researchers found it still excluded two subsets of individuals. It did not identify young children with autism who also had some expressive language skills.

It also failed to provide a method to assess and identify older adolescents and adults with autism. Test developers set to resolve these issues and the ADOS-G was developed. The ADOS-G is what we now know of as the ADOS. This version of the ADOS included Module 1 based on the PL-ADOS and Module 3 based on the original ADOS (1989). It included a "new" Module 2 developed for "phrase speakers" in the preschool age range and a Module 4 for assessing adolescents and adults. This module was less play based and included more questions about daily living, personal responsibility, and job skills. With the development of the ADOS-2, the original algorithms for Modules 1–3 were revised; a comparison score was created for Modules 1–3, and the ADOS protocols were improved to clarify administration guidelines. A fifth Module, the Toddler Module, was created with associated algorithms designed to assess children with limited expressive language who are aged from 12 to 30 months (Lord et al., 2012). For detailed psychometric data on reliability and validity of the measure see Appendix.

ADOS-2 Administration and Training Requirements

The ADOS-2 was originally released in May of 2012. It contains five assessment modules to evaluate varying developmental levels at different chronological ages. The modules assess skills in communication, reciprocal social interaction, and restricted and repetitive behaviors or interests. The ADOS-2 is a semi-structured measure including open-ended and creative tasks. The goal of the revision was to make the algorithm fit with continued research and provide increased specificity in lower functioning populations, as well as provide a uniform basis of comparison and maintain the strong predictive validity of the measure (Lord et al., 2012). Research findings indicated a need for a unitary social-communication factor (Constantino et al., 2004; Lord, Rutter, DiLavore, & Risi, 1999, 2000; Robertson, Tanguay, L'Ecuyer, Sims, & Waltrip, 1999). Modules 1–3 of the ADOS-2 include "social affect" or SA which is a composite of social and communication skills, and "restricted repetitive behavior" or RRB. The Module 4 algorithm was not revised because of limited available samples of older adolescents and adults, an area needing further study (Lord et al., 2012). Research on the ADOS Module 1 found it to be over-inclusive of those with a mental age of 15 months or below (Gotham et al., 2007) and thus the Toddler Module was developed for those 12–30 months old with play activities, codes, and an algorithm that is better aligned with this population.

In order to administer the ADOS-2, a clinician must be appropriately trained in assessment (i.e., have licensure and credentialing in psychology or medicine), have adequate practice with administration, and read the manuals thoroughly. Additionally, he or she must attend a workshop with an independent trainer or complete the video training program. It is crucial that a clinician has extensive experience in giving the measure and scoring the algorithm and this can take varying amounts of time depending on the clinician. In the authors' clinical practice, administrators of the ADOS-2 should have completed the training and have co-scored the measure watching a reliable clinician and consistently achieving at least 70 % agreement on the algorithm overall. Additionally, it is required that trainees achieve the same diagnostic conclusion, with 100 % agreement, from the algorithm. This standard is consistent with what Dr. Lord's team recommended for clinical practice at the ADOS training workshop (WPS, Ann Arbor, Michigan, June 2011). Those trained in the ADOS do not need an additional training for ADOS-2, only a thorough review of the manual, and completion of the ADOS-2 training video program for the Toddler Module. For research reliability, an individual must attend a research reliability workshop and achieve a greater interrater reliability than what is required for clinical work (WPS ADOS training workshop Ann Arbor Michigan, 2011).

ADOS-2 Administering and Readministering the Test

An important benefit of ADOS-2 administration is that, in addition to providing diagnostic information, it is excellent for guiding treatment planning. The ADOS-2 provides valuable information on pretend play, joint attention, flexibility, conversation and communication with others, restricted interests, unusual sensory interests, emotional awareness, and emotion regulation. Those with ASDs often have much more difficulty and sometimes present with resistance to ADOS-2 activities versus concrete cognitive or language testing. It is interesting to note whether a child preferred the ADOS-2 or other assessment measures. When introducing pretend play with toys, acting or demonstrating tasks, and conversations, often those who do not have ASDs are more excited or engaged with these measures than they are with cognitive measures.

In contrast, individuals with ASD may refuse to play with toys, citing their preference for video games, sports, books, etc. They often make excuses to avoid "acting" tasks; or they may say that they cannot do it or are too embarrassed. At other times, individuals with ASD might engage with the toys or books but have play skills that are not commensurate with cognitive and language abilities.

They may make up a story in a picture book but with no plot, character development or emotional response. In the authors' experience, and consistent with past research, their responses on the storybook task alone can offer rich diagnostic data. Children with ASD often struggle to tell stories, fail to identify characters, struggle to describe the sequence of events, and cannot provide the main idea of the story (Suh et al., 2014; Willard, 2013) Some studies have found that children with autism actually perform similarly to neurotypical children when telling stories from picture books, but struggle with more challenging tasks requiring narrative recall (Losh & Gordon, 2014). Children with optimal outcomes may actually show improved narrative production over time, sometimes similar to neurotypical children. Thus, examiners should carefully consider the child's narrative quality during the storybook task of the ADOS-2, particularly over repeated administrations.

Discussion of friendships and other relationships may be less sophisticated than expected or a child might often respond "I don't know" or "I can't remember." Readministering the ADOS-2 periodically can provide nice data on progress, as goals for treatment may be improving pretend play skills, conversation or joint attention; the ADOS-2 can provide a measure of skill development over time. The authors recommend reevaluations every 1–2 years to provide progress data and direct treatment.

ADOS-2 Modules

Each module of the ADOS-2 provides the evaluator an opportunity to use a semi-structured approach to assess social communication and restricted, repetitive behaviors. The algorithm information provided in this section is from the ADOS-2 protocols and manual (Lord et al., 2012). Certain elements that fall under each domain are assessed and given a score that contributes to the overall ADOS-2 algorithm. Items are scored 0, 1, 2, or 3 based on what is observed during testing. A score of 0 indicates that the skill is present and consistent with typical development. A score of 1 indicates partial proficiency on a skill. A score of 2 or 3 indicates challenges with the item or an absence of the skill. Some items may be scored 7 or 8 indicating another challenge with language or behavior, for example. A score of 3 is recalculated as a 2 in the algorithm and 7 or 8 are scored as 0. The ADOS-2 takes approximately an hour to administer and should be scored within an hour after administration. Not all elements scored fall into the algorithm. These items not included in the algorithm vary to some degree based on the module administered.

The Toddler Module is administered to those falling from 12 to 30 months old. Toddlers can have "few to no words" or "some words" and items fall into the algorithm depending on the level of language. The Toddler Module focuses on responses to interaction from parents/caregivers and evaluators. Module 1 also provides a different scoring algorithm for those with limited words and with "few to no words." Module 2 is administered to those with phrase speech and Module 3 is for individuals with an expressive language level of 4 years old or above. Module 3 is administered to those through childhood and into adolescence while Module 4 is intended for those who are teenagers, adults, and have more independence. Module 4 is less play based and more focused on conversation, responsibility, and emotional communication. In the section that follows, readers find a discussion of each module and the assessment of social interaction/communication and restricted/repetitive behaviors.

ADOS-2 T

Communication

Frequency of Spontaneous Vocalization Directed to Others

This item is scored for children with few to no words and focuses on the amount of spontaneous vocalization. This vocal production may include sounds and partial words that are directed to another person for the purpose of engagement. For example, a child may say "da!" and clearly direct that communication to another person as a form of communication (smile, point, touching another). This type of utterance counts as a vocalization. However, any sounds that are directed to a toy, other object, or to the child himself or herself (back turned to adults, no eye contact or attempt to involve a person) would not be included as a directed vocalization in an examiner's assessment of this skill.

Pointing

This item is scored for young children who do use language and refers to whether the child points distally to an object, toy, person, snack, or other object to reference it when it is out of reach. Coordinated pointing indicates a score of 0. Pointing only to an object within reach or using an open-handed grab is not considered coordinated, and may be assessed here as a 1 or 2.

Gestures

Gestures can be informational, descriptive, instrumental, or conventional and refer to whether a toddler communicated nonverbally during the assessment. The authors' experience is that many clinicians struggle with understanding the subtle differences in type of gesture. As a clear understanding is critical to scoring, clinicians are advised to review the ADOS-2 manual in depth and consult with trainers and expert administrators to clarify nuances in gestures. In short, descriptive gestures include "the giraffe was this big!" (with an obvious wide reaching hand motion) and "the ant was tiny" (with a small reach or coordinated finger gesture to indicate small). Informational gestures may indicate how many of something (a show of fingers). Instrumental may include shrugging, nodding, shaking the head, waving, putting up a hand for stop, pointing or shushing (Attwood, Frith, & Hamelin, 1988), and conventional refers to clapping for "well done," showing, and pointing (Kientz, Goodwin, Hayes, & Abowd, 2013). Gestures must contribute to the understanding of a communicative intent. Gestures are assessed in play and in engagement with parents and evaluators. Nodding or shaking one's head no is a gesture, though it is not as advanced as descriptive gestures used to explain or clarify something for the listener. Spontaneous use of gesture receives more credit than gestures that are prompted and occur in response to a task.

Reciprocal Social Interaction

Unusual Eye Contact

The eye contact item refers to eye gaze that is too intense or the avoiding of eye gaze. A child who is constantly looking down or to the side is generally not making eye contact with the evaluator. Some may avoid eye contact because of shyness so the extent to which this improves over the course of testing is considered. Eye contact that is consistently poor or inconsistent, with the child looking away or looking at the examiner sometimes while avoiding eye gaze completely at other times is considered unusual, and should be scored a 2. Clinically, most examiners note that if there is any sense that eye contact was awkward or not integrated to facilitate communication, then this item should automatically be coded a 2.

Facial Expression Directed to Others

Facial expressions are important considerations in autism. The examiner must consider if the facial expressions are typical and congruent with the conversational context. They must further consider whether or not the client's facial expressions are directed at the examiner. A facial expression that is accompanied by vocalization and eye contact certainly would qualify as directed to someone. Generally speaking, any facial expression that is directed, even a puzzled look toward the examiner when "blocked" toy play is going on, would be a directed facial expression. An individual who maintains a flat affect, whose expression is unusual or inappropriate, or who does not direct facial expressions to another person would receive a score of 2.

Integration of Gaze and Other Behaviors During Social Overtures

The examiner is now required to code the integration of gaze and gestures with any social overtures that occur during administration of the ADOS-2 T. When young children integrate their gaze, speech, and facial expression, this item would be coded 0. Toddlers who use these communication modalities separately (not in an integrated fashion) or show less consistency with the integration of them would receive a 1 or a 2.

Shared Enjoyment in Interaction

Throughout the ADOS-2, skilled examiners are constantly assessing the quality of the interaction. Individuals who are reciprocal and seem to share enjoyment with the examiner likely do not have autism. When administering toy-play items on the ADOS-2 T, it is extremely important to pay attention to whether the child is sharing enjoyment in the *interaction* or only likes the *toy*. Some children really enjoy play and will squeal delightfully while playing with a pop-up toy, play characters, or letter blocks. This is a lovely play skill but does not indicate shared enjoyment. The same child may continue to face his or her back toward the examiner, try to use the examiner's hand as a tool, or take the toy away from the examiner. This is a particularly crucial item to attend to during the ADOS-2 T. It can be very helpful to watch how hard the parents are used to working in order to gain their child's attention in general.

Response to Name

Response to name involves calling a child's name up to four times when he or she is engaged in something else, though not overly engaged. If there is no response, the parents or caregivers are asked to call the child's name twice. If this does not work, parents are asked to indicate how they might get their child's attention without touching him or her. If none of these are effective, it can be helpful to see how a parent engages their child even if this may be by tickling, swinging them around, or hugging them.

Ignore

The "ignore condition" refers to a situation where the behavior of a child is evaluated while when he or she is ignored or blocked from accessing a toy by the examiner. It is important to note whether the child cries or cares at all about being ignored and the general kind of response that is present. A child may not respond at all, simply moving onto something else or he or she may try to move the examiner like an object. If a child makes eye contact or says something like "hey!" or "no!" then, he or she would receive a score of 0. Those who do not respond to the ignore condition receive a higher score.

Requesting

One potential impairment in autism is making requests. The term "manding" at it applies to autism, refers to verbal requests in order to obtain reinforcement. On the ADOS-2 T, young children may request a toy, snack, interaction, or other involvement from the parent or caregiver. A child can request with a gesture, words, or eye contact. Note, only partial credit is given for requesting only during the snack time.

Showing

The "showing" item refers to whether or not a child shows a toy, snack, anything of interest to a parent or an evaluator. Showing involves holding something up where another person can see it, not for the purpose of getting help, but only for the purpose of engaging the other person.

Spontaneous Initiation of Joint Attention

Spontaneous initiation of joint attention means that the individual being evaluated attempts to gain the attention or engagement of the examiner. Initiating joint attention is less frequently seen in young toddlers and so response to joint attention is often of more interest in this module. Initiation of joint attention requires the child say something like "look" or point and reference something for the parent or caregiver in order to get that person's attention. A multiple point initiation would then involve looking at the target of interest, and then looking back at the caregiver or examiner.

Response to Joint Attention

This involves responding to an evaluator's attempt to get attention just with his or her eyes. A child may see an evaluator looking at something and follow his or her gaze to check out what is being looked at. In this case, a toy bunny is placed across the room in triangular position to the child and examiner without the child seeing the object before the examiner calls attention to it. If the child sees the bunny first, the item is spoiled. The examiner has four chances to say "Johnny, look" or "Johnny look at that!" while only drawing attention with the eyes and face. If the evaluator has to point to the object of interest to draw attention, then the item only receives partial credit. A child who looks at something the examiner references with "Hey (child) look!" and then looks back at the examiner to laugh or share a reaction is doing this very well and receives a 0. If an individual ignores the examiner, or only looks once the toy is activated, he or she is scored 2 or 3.

Quality of Social Overtures

Quality of social overtures is an assessment of the quality of the efforts made by the child to get someone's attention. Initiating to get something like a snack is less valuable than initiating to share toys, play a game, or give a hug.

Amount of Social Overtures Parent/Caregiver

This refers to the amount of social interaction indicated toward the parent or caregiver who is in the room. It is very helpful to see how a child interacts with his or her parents and how hard a parent must work to scaffold a social interaction with the child. Some children talk reciprocally with their parents (0) and others ignore their parents entirely (2).

Overall Quality of Rapport

Quality of rapport takes into account the overall feel of the session and interaction between the examiner and child. An individual who refused every task, seemed to want to get away from the evaluator, or had an awkward interaction style may have challenges with rapport. If the examiner has to modify the administration beyond typical limits, this is significant. If toys must be removed from the room to shift a child's attention, this is significant. A "0" score is noted for a good quality of rapport while a "2" would be given if toys needed to be removed from the room to accomplish tasks. If the assessment went relatively well but felt very awkward and stilted, a "1" may be assigned.

Restricted and Repetitive Behavior

Intonation of Vocalizations or Verbalizations

It is important to note the intonation of verbalizations and any difficulties or unusual sounds or phrases in this area. A child who speaks in a particularly shrill tone of voice, mechanical tone, or is stilted in vocal prosody will score a "1" or "2."

Unusual Sensory Interest in Play Material or Person

A child who sniffs, rubs, licks, or is particularly interested in a part of a toy or object may have a sensory interest that is unusual. Children who cry with loud noises, cover ears, or stop everything to search for a fire engine from the siren heard two miles away may have unusual sensory interest(s) or sensitivities. It is noteworthy that this is a coded item on the ADOS-2. Often parents are surprised to learn that sensory differences may be associated with Autism.

Hand and Finger Movements/Posturing

The "Hand and Finger Movements/Posturing" item may refer to flapping, rocking, tensing, finger flicking, or anything unusual in movement that may be associated with the body. It is helpful to note on the protocol any particularly unusual finger movements or repetitive body motions.

Unusually Repetitive Interests or Stereotyped Behaviors

Unusually repetitive interests can refer to excessive mention of numbers or letters, or only playing with a truck or a pop-up toy, and having a tantrum or meltdown when that toy is removed from the room. Making statements that appear to be echolalia, or delayed echoing of another person, is coded as repetitive. A child who quotes a movie or a song may all fall under this category.

Obtains a Range of Concern Mild, Moderate, Severe

At the conclusion of the ADOS-2 T, scores are totaled and a level of concern is decided upon. Higher scores on these totals are indicative of more concern for an Autism Spectrum Disorder using the Toddler Module. The protocol provides suggested cut scores for mild, moderate, and severe concern for ASD and is a piece of data considered in the overall consideration of whether autism will be diagnosed. This module provides a range of concern instead of a diagnostic cutoff because it can be used to assess children as young as 12 months. An older child or adult with no language or very limited language would be administered Module 1 and not the Toddler Module as it is only administered through 30 months. After 30 months age, maturity and expressive language play into the decision about what module to give. Modules 1–3 provide an Autism Severity Scale and cut scores for Autism Spectrum and Autism. Module 4 does not have a severity score at this time. Modules 1–4 are discussed in the section that follows, expanding on algorithm items not already explained.

ADOS-2 Module 1

Social Affect (SA)
Communication

> *Frequency of Spontaneous Vocalization Directed to Others*
> *Pointing*
> *Gestures*

These items on Module 1 are consistent with what was discussed for the Toddler Module; again here children or adults may have more or less language, characterized by "few to no words" or "some words." Those with the expressive language level that includes phrased speech, or who are speaking in a few words or language units at once, can be administered Module 2.

Reciprocal Social Interaction

Unusual Eye Contact

Consistent with the toddler module, assessing for avoiding gaze, staring to the side, looking at the examiner's forehead while speaking, or having inconsistent gaze is remarkable. An individual whose eye contact improves markedly over testing can receive a score of "0" as examiners want to look at social engagement and not penalize for anxiety. Overly intense gaze is also problematic because this item is assessing for eye contact that is used to regulate social interaction.

Facial Expression Directed to Others

Facial expressions directed to others to convey feelings, interest, apprehension, excitement, frustration, etc. are a huge part of communication. It is important to note if an individual lacks a range of facial expression or directs them only to objects and not to people.

Integration of Gaze and Other Behaviors during Social Overtures

It is important to note whether an individual integrates eye contact with other behaviors for the purpose of social engagement. Integrating gaze with facial expression or gesture lends to more fluid communication and is useful in social interaction. It is remarkable if an individual cannot do this. Those who use one communicative modality, almost exclusively, receive partial credit.

Shared Enjoyment in Interaction

Like in the Toddler Module, sharing enjoyment in interaction (or not) is a crucial piece of information. For example, take a child with little language who enjoys a video game. This can be solitary and a child can easily ignore others and play alone. A child who gives another person a turn, wants someone to see him play, and looks to others to enjoy an interaction with a smile, eye contact and clapping is showing that he or she is sharing enjoyment. In play with toys: clapping, looking at another person, and sharing the toys, indicates enjoyment in the interaction.

Showing

Showing is another way of sharing enjoyment and interacting socially with another person. It is possible to show partially by placing an object in front of another person. Showing skills are not in place if the child only shows items in order to get help. Rather, if the child shows items and makes eye contact or engages fully with the person, this would be coded a "0."

Spontaneous Initiation of Joint Attention

In play, a child who references bubbles the examiner is blowing, looks then at mom, smiles and claps, and looks back at the bubbles is initiating joint attention and sharing enjoyment with mom in the game. A child that says "mom" then looks at a toy and back at the parent is also initiating joint attention.

Response to Joint Attention

As in the Toddler Module, this is assessed with a task using a remote control bunny. If the evaluator can get the child to follow his or her gaze, without needing to point to the out of reach toy, then the child is responding to joint attention, or paying attention to something because another person initiates with gaze. If the child needs to see the examiner point to the object in order to attend, he or she is partially responding. If the examiner must activate the toy or is unable to direct the child's attention at all, he or she is not responding to joint attention.

Quality of Social Overtures

The Quality of Social Overtures item is an assessment of the quality, not the amount, of the overtures. Examiners are to note whether the overtures are repetitive and restricted or appropriate to the context. A child, who shows a number of toys to others, names the toys, or plays with caregivers and evaluators, is displaying a good quality interaction style.

Restricted and Repetitive Behavior

Intonation of Vocalizations or Verbalizations

Stereotyped/Idiosyncratic Use of Words or Phrases
Unusual Sensory Interest in Play Material/Person
Hand and Finger and Other Complex Mannerisms
Unusual Repetitive Interests or Stereotyped Behaviors
These items are consistent with those noted for the Toddler Module. It is important to note the tone of verbalizations and to observe anything with an unusual pitch or prosody. Similarly, it is important to pay attention to what is said and note whether the language is meaningful or repetitive. For example, a child who says "it's a letter __" thirty-two times during the hour ADOS-2 is being repetitive and demonstrating a restricted interest.

ADOS-2 Score

This module provides a cut score indicating whether an individual meets criteria, does not meet criteria, or meets broader spectrum criteria for ASD. Again it is important to use this score with other information in order to determine whether or not to make the diagnosis of an Autism Spectrum Disorder.

ADOS-2 Module 2

Social Affect

Communication

Pointing
Descriptive, Conventional, Instrumental, or Informational Gestures

These items are consistent with the nonverbal communication discussed above for the other two modules. Similar to the previous modules, a thorough understanding of the nuances between the types of gestures is critical to effective scoring of the ADOS-2.

Reciprocal Social Interaction

Unusual Eye Contact

Consistent with the Toddler Module and Module 1, assessing for avoidance of eye gaze, staring to the side, or looking at the examiner's forehead while speaking is remarkable. An individual whose eye contact improves markedly over testing can receive a score of "0" as we want to look at social engagement and not penalize for anxiety. Children who stare blankly at the examiner or who are highly inconsistent in their eye contact obtain a score of "2."

Facial Expression Directed to Others

This item is consistent with Module 1. The examiner is assessing whether or not the individual displays appropriate facial expressions and uses expressions as a means of reciprocal communication with the examiner.

Shared Enjoyment in Interaction

As in the other modules, sharing enjoyment in interaction is a crucial piece of information for an ASD assessment. Children who display shared enjoyment may laugh with the examiner at appropriate times, appear to be engaged throughout the assessment, show care and interest in the examiner's thoughts or ideas, and may want to continue testing, whether or not the examination is over. Any of these signs are positive and indicate that the child has the ability to share enjoyment with the examiner.

Showing

This item is similar to the Toddler Module and Module 1. The showing of objects is coded as to whether the child attempts to gain the attention of another through the presentation of items to the examiner. As with the other modules, if the child only shows objects for the purpose of seeking help (for example, requesting help opening a container or operating a toy), this receives less credit in the scoring.

Spontaneous Initiation of Joint Attention

In play, a child who references an object the examiner is holding, looks at mom, and then looks back at the examiner is initiating joint attention and sharing enjoyment. A child receives full credit for this item when he or she spontaneously initiates the interaction. This would mean that the child attempts to engage or interact with the examiner, without a prompt from the caregiver or examiner to do so.

Quality of Social Overtures

This item looks at the quality and not the number of social overtures. Consistent with Module 1, a child who shows a number of toys to others, names the toys, or plays with caregivers and evaluators is interacting appropriately.

Amount of Reciprocal Social Communication

This item conversely looks at the amount and not the quality of overtures. A child who consistently attempts to engage with the examiner, with a number of reciprocal communication attempts, would earn a score of "0" here.

Overall Quality of Rapport

This item refers to the interaction between the child and the examiner. Is the interaction stilted or uncomfortable? Does the child throw a temper tantrum, scream refuse, or try to run out of the room? Does the examiner need to modify the structure of the ADOS-2 in a remarkable way to maintain the child's attention? If problems such as these are present, the quality of the rapport is diminished and the child should receive a higher score on this item.

Restricted and Repetitive Behavior

Stereotyped/Idiosyncratic Use of Words or Phrases
Unusual Sensory Interest in Play Material/Person
Hand and Finger and Other Complex Mannerisms
Unusual Repetitive Interests or Stereotyped Behaviors

These items are consistent with those noted for the Toddler Module and Module 1.

ADOS-2 Score

This module provides a cut score indicating whether an individual meets criteria, does not meet criteria, or meets broader spectrum criteria for ASD. Again it is important to use this score with other information in order to determine whether or not to make the diagnosis of an Autism Spectrum Disorder.

ADOS-2 Module 3

Social Affect (SA)

Communication

Reporting of Events

Reporting of events is an important skill to assess on the Module 3. Here the individual is evaluated based on his or her ability to report an event in an understandable manner that is likely to be true. Some individuals with autism may report an event that sounds unlikely to be true and not be aware of the misstep. A child who shares "I always almost get bit by sharks. Every day in Florida, a shark tries to bite me" may have shared this story in an effort to interact without knowing how to gain attention appropriately. Other individuals may tell a partial story that makes it less comprehensible. A child who talks extensively about Betty, without saying who Betty is, and appears surprised when you ask, may have trouble taking perspective and reporting events. Similarly, if the child tries to tell about his last birthday party by providing some ambiguous detail, such as the color of the clown's hair, he is showing poor event reporting. A child who can report an event that seems to be true without scaffolding (though questions may be asked) and with enough detail to convey the story receives a score of "0." A child who needs extensive scaffolding, who makes something up or who cannot report an event gets a "1" or "2."

Conversation

This item in Modules 3 and 4 assesses an individual's ability to have a back and forth conversation. This exchange may be on a particular topic and must involve the examiner talking and the child responding, with up to four elements. Elements are described as the number of reciprocal exchanges that occur during one part of a conversation. For example, the child may say, "I like bugs" and the examiner may say, "I think bugs are cool too. I like to see them in my garden" and the child may say "I think bees are very important to the flowers" and then the examiner may conclude, "I do too." This would be an appropriate conversation that includes four elements. The examinee does not have to ask questions of the examiner; rather, simply talking about a subject and participating in a back-and-forth exchange is enough.

Descriptive, Conventional, Instrumental, or Informational Gestures

The gesture use coded in Module 3 was described in the section on Module 2. Using gestures is assessed for spontaneous gestures, as well as gesturing when asked to "show" the examiner in the context of storytelling, acting, or a demonstrating task. Children are asked to "show and tell", or "teach" the examiner how to brush teeth. This task taps into the child's ability and comfort level with gestures, eye contact, and language, as well as the integration of these. Washing hands or driving a car could also be used as a task to assess the skill.

Reciprocal Social Interaction

Unusual Eye Contact

Consistent with the other modules, any unusual eye contact is coded a "2." A child, who warms up over time or modulates eye contact effectively for communication, receives a score of "0."

Facial Expression Directed to Examiner

As with the other ADOS-2 modules, this item is coded as to the degree an individual can direct appropriately ranging facial expressions toward the examiner for the purpose of engagement and communication.

Shared Enjoyment in Interaction

Assessment of "shared enjoyment" in the interaction provides a crucial piece of information. A child or teen who laughs at the examiners' joke or comment, shares a story of his or her own, finds the "tell a story" book funny and enjoys a laugh with the examiner, is sharing enjoyment. Someone who really enjoys the "create a story" task and engages with the examiner in it is sharing enjoyment. On the cartoon task, some children or adolescents may really enjoy acting out the characters and effectively conveying the story. One examiner recalls a child who asked when the examiner's birthday was. Upon finding out her birthday was a few days away, she asked about the examiner's plans and expressed happiness about the upcoming event. Later the child made a card and brought it on day two of testing for the examiner (this part was not scored as it was not within the ADOS-2 but just further shows the way children may share enjoyment and connect with others.) These sort of positive and engaging interactions demonstrate shared enjoyment.

Quality of Social Overtures

This item looks at the quality and not the amount of overtures. A child who will talk about a number of topics, expresses interest in things the examiner says, and shares information for the purpose of sharing (not solely to talk about restricted interests) is engaging in quality social overtures.

Quality of Social Response

This refers to the quality of the response to things the examiner shares. If she shares that she recently fell on the ski slope and sprained her ankle and the examinee says "Better luck next time!" he is not demonstrating a high quality social response. Another example would be when the examiner reports that her pet fish died and the examinee says "That's just the life cycle!" In these examples, the child is not responding in a socially appropriate way. Eye contact, exclamations like "Oh no!" "That must have hurt." or "I'm sorry about your fish" indicate quality social responses.

Amount of Reciprocal Social Communication

Overall Quality of Rapport

As previously noted, these refer to the amount of communication that appears to have reciprocal intent, not a lecture but conversation, and the overall impressions about the rapport during the session. The interaction with a child may feel strained, uncomfortable, or awkward. The child may respond to questions, by saying "I don't know" twenty times, complaining, or refusing questions. The child may say, "I'm not answering that" or "That's personal!" when it is not personal. In this case, the child is not engaging in a high quality of rapport interaction.

Restricted and Repetitive Behavior

Stereotyped/Idiosyncratic Use of Words or Phrases
Unusual Sensory Interest in Play Material/Person
Hand and Finger and Other Complex Mannerisms
Excessive Interest in Unusual or Highly Specific Topics/Objects or Repetitive Behaviors

These items regarding excessive interest in highly specific topics or repetitive behaviors are diagnostically quite important. The items are consistent with those noted in other modules. The examiner is continually assessing sensory differences, actions like sniffing a book or touching objects of a certain texture repeatedly. In this section, we are looking more at language-based repetitive behaviors like getting stuck on a topic, saying the same thing over and over or using a certain phrase or expression that is unusual. An examinee may reverse pronouns or have an unusual structure to his or her language. He or she may talk only about truck driving, trains, How to Train Your Dragon, or Megalodon.

ADOS-2 Score

This module provides a cut score indicating whether an individual meets criteria, does not meet criteria, or meets broader spectrum criteria for ASD. Again it is important to use this score with other information in order to determine whether or not to make the diagnosis of an Autism Spectrum Disorder. A severity score is also provided to further explain symptoms consistent with autism. Severity scores offer utility when re-testing an individual to demonstrate the response to interventions. Often an individual will maintain a score consistent with an ASD diagnosis but the severity score will go down after intensive ABA and other therapeutic interventions.

ADOS-2 Module 4

Communication

Stereotyped/Idiosyncratic Use of Words or Phrases
Conversation

Descriptive, Conventional, Instrumental, or Informational Gestures
Emphatic or Emotional Gestures

Module 4 is coded as to the communication skills and interaction style expected of an adult. There is the addition of Emphatic or Emotional Gestures because it is expected that as an individual gets older he or she will use facial expression and gesture to demonstrate an even wider array of nonverbal cues that make it possible to understand the emotional and conversational context.

Reciprocal Social Interaction

Unusual Eye Contact

Consistent with the other modules, examiners consider whether or not the individual avoids eye gaze or is too persistent with eye gaze, rendering the conversation awkward. That is, an adult who stares blankly at the examiner is considered to have inappropriate eye contact. Similarly, someone who constantly avoids eye gaze is displaying poor eye contact. Finally, someone who intermittently struggles to use eye contact to maintain the interaction is struggling with eye contact. Individuals who gradually provide more appropriate eye contact as the assessment continues, should receive full credit because this can be typical, particularly in individuals with anxiety.

Facial Expression Directed to Examiner

Facial expressions directed to others in adults should be particularly integrated and include a wider range of expressions. Adults should be able to display more complex emotions such as being "perplexed," "intrigued," "amazed," "put-off or offended," "delighted," or "impassioned." In adults without ASD, these emotions should be clearly expressed such that the interaction flows naturally, and both parties are engaging reciprocally. Alternately, examiners may observe flat or restricted affect that refers to the fact that the emotional reactions a person makes are nonexistent or just very narrow in range. In that case, the individual may have ASD. Sometimes flat or blunted affect may occur in the context of a mood disorder (see Chap. 7, Dynamic Assessment Overview for ASD and Other Disorders, Fig. 7.1d).

Comments on Another's Emotions/Empathy

In Module 4, the "Comments on Another's Emotions/Empathy" item refers to the individual's ability to comment on the emotional experiences of others. This may occur during the storybook task, in creating a story, or in acting out a cartoon. It also may be evidenced during the ADOS-2, Module 4, when the individual is discussing with family members, friends, and relationships. Finally, an individual may demonstrate this skill by responding appropriately to comments of the examiner during a conversation.

Responsibility

The Responsibility item refers to the individual's ability to act responsible in the context of his or her own life. Doing laundry, paying bills, having realistic goals, keeping a job, and planning for the future indicate responsibility.

Quality of Social Overtures
Quality of Social Response
Amount of Reciprocal Social Communication

These remaining items of Module 4 were discussed in the Module 3 section above. As with the other modules, social reciprocity is of paramount importance. As individuals mature, their reciprocal social interactions should grow in complexity and conversational fluency. Adults should be able to start and respond to conversation cues and bids in an appropriate manner. It is important to note the amount of overtures, the quality of these, and the amount of social response the examinee provides. Any awkwardness or reduced quality of rapport should be carefully noted as critical observation data when assessing adults suspected of having an ASD.

Imagination/Creativity

This item on Module 4 refers to the examinee's ability to be imaginative and creative in storytelling and in using objects beyond their functional use, in order to tell a story. As "creating a story" is modeled first by the examiner, it is important to note whether the examinee simply retells a version of the examiner's story or sets the stage in an awkward manner without adding any plot. It should also be noted if the examinee suddenly becomes very nervous or uncomfortable when asked to tell a story. The individual may say something like, "I'm not good at this" or "I don't really like to tell stories." These sorts of responses may indicate an ASD is present.

Stereotyped Behaviors and Restricted Interests

Unusual Sensory Interest in Play Material/Person
Hand and Finger and Other Complex Mannerisms
Excessive Interest in Unusual or Highly Specific Topics/Objects or Repetitive Behaviors

Compulsions or Rituals

These items are consistent with those noted for Module 3.

ADOS-2 Score

This module provides a cut score indicating whether an individual meets criteria, does not meet criteria, or meets broader spectrum criteria for ASD. Again it is important to use this score with other information in order to determine whether or not to make the diagnosis of an Autism Spectrum Disorder. No severity score is provided for Module 4 at this time. Research by Lord et al. provides a suggested cut score of 10 for a diagnosis of autism (2012).

For more detailed information on ADOS-2 tasks, see the administration guidelines in the manual (Lord et al., 2012). It is the authors' practice to use a sizeable room for ADOS-2 administration and store materials in a locking cabinet where they can be easily accessed or put away. In some cases, administration may take 45 min. That said, examiners should reserve a full hour in case it takes longer, and to allow for time to score the items, immediately following administration. With younger children an assisting clinician aids the primary examiner in providing materials, helping to set up tasks, promoting engagement, and preventing elopement.

ADI-R Administration

The ADI-R is a parent or caregiver interview that is frequently used in combination with the ADOS-2. Studies show it is "largely accurate" but a discrepancy has been noted indicating that parents may underreport early difficulties (Noterdaeme, Mildenberger, Minow, & Amorosa, 2002). The parent interview is divided into five sections that include opening questions, communication questions, social development and play questions, repetitive and restricted behavior questions, and questions about general behavior problems. In some clinical practices, the administration time between 1 and 2 h may be too lengthy and impractical. As was discussed in Chap. 5, the discussion of third-party payers, administration time may be at a premium. When minimal time is allotted for an assessment, the administration of the ADOS-2 and ADI-R may not be feasible. Thus, a combination of a 45 min parent interview, developmental history questionnaire, and the Social Communication Questionnaire (SCQ) may be adequate. This provides a detailed developmental history with special attention to the social and communication domains and the restricted repetitive behaviors, which are essential to the diagnosis of ASD.

Screening Instruments versus Instruments that Provide Definitive Diagnoses

Falkmer et al. (2013) conducted a systematic literature review and included analysis of 19 tools utilized to evaluate for Autism Spectrum Disorders. Only three instruments had enough supporting evidence in the literature review and these are the ADOS, ADI-R, and CARS parent rating scale. As noted earlier, the CARS is used in combination with other measures. Other rating scales that are found to have high sensitivity and specificity are the RAADS, PDDBI, ASD-DC, ASDS, VISS, CASD, GADS, and 3Di. The GARS was discovered to be low on both specificity and sensitivity (Falkmer et al., 2013). These specific screeners need more research to support their use.

Studies comparing the use of rating scales to the ADOS and ADI-R, not surprisingly, found the rating scales to be less effective. Examiners using the ADOS and ADI R were found to have "fairly high" rates of agreement with team diagnosis. The GARS was not very effective in discriminating between children with various team diagnoses and it underestimated the likelihood of autism (Mazefsky & Oswald, 2006). Data supports the conclusion that rating scales can provide valuable information when they are part of a comprehensive assessment. While direct instruments including the ADOS and comprehensive parent interview like ADI-R should be utilized as part of an evaluation to diagnose, rating scales can be very valuable in guiding a physician, clinical or school psychologist to refer for further testing. The MCHAT is most frequently used in pediatric practices while other rating scales like the CARS may be used in a school or clinical settings to help determine whether an evaluation is warranted.

Criterion Versus Normative Referenced Measures

The measures discussed thus far in this section include normative data. That is, the individuals evaluated are compared to peers or others of the same age when we assess their performance. The tests measure the progress of a population as a whole (Cronbach, 1970). In contrast, a criterion referenced measure looks at performance on a given skill or standard. Often school-based assessments given to individuals identified as having Autism Spectrum Disorders include criterion referenced measures. These measures do not assess whether a diagnosis is present but rather can be used to monitor progress in skill areas. The ABLLs (Assessment of Basic Language and Learning Skills) and VB-MAPP (Verbal Behavior Milestones Assessment and Placement Program) are assessments often used with individuals on the Autism Spectrum, particularly in early grades, to assess progress. The VB-MAPP was developed by Mark Sundberg and is to be used by individuals who have training in Applied Behavior Analysis (ABA) to identify strengths and weaknesses in skills and behaviors that might impact language and social development. These tests are indicated to help to prioritize intervention needs, provide feedback to parents and other professionals, guide curriculum planning, and track skill acquisition (Sundberg, 2008).

Assessing for Sensory Processing

Vignette #4: Tricia

Assessment of a Child with Sensory Challenges

Tricia, age three, was referred to Emerge for odd sensory preferences and behavior problems. She was administered the Mullen Scales of Early Learning (MULLEN), AGS Edition (select sections); Differential Ability Scales, Second Edition, Lower Early Years Record Form (DAS-II); Autism Diagnostic Observation Schedule, Second Edition, Module 2 (ADOS-2); Behavior Assessment System for Children, Second Edition (BASC-II), Parent and Teacher Reports; Vineland Adaptive Behavior Scales, Second Edition—Parent/Caregiver Rating Form (VABS-II); and Short Sensory Profile, by Winnie Dunn, Ph.D.

Tricia's parents indicated concerns about her behavior, sound sensitivities, and motor activities. Tricia was previously classified as having "sensory processing disorder" and had been receiving speech therapy and occupational therapy for 10 months, with little reported improvement. Tricia has two brothers, both of whom are diagnosed with Autism Spectrum Disorders. Tricia used few gestures during the assessment and did not consistently coordinate her vocalizations with her gaze. Her play tended to be repetitive, simply labeling objects or repeating the examiner's directions (Table 9.2).

In addition to cognitive and play-based assessments, both fine motor and gross motor skills were assessed as parents indicated these as an area of concern. Tricia demonstrated some weaknesses in both fine motor and gross motor skills, but results were interpreted with caution, as she was non-compliant during motor tasks. Her parents indicated that Tricia does not enjoy gross motor activities such as climbing at the park and dancing. She is largely disinterested in fine motor activities such as coloring and play dough. Tricia's sensory and motor vulnerabilities were characterized under the rigidity symptoms associated with autism. She was diagnosed with autism and referred for behavioral therapy, as occupational therapy and speech services alone were not successful. Additionally, it was recommended that a BCBA collaborate directly with her speech and occupational therapists, for coordinated comprehensive care. At a 1-year follow-up, parents reported marked improvements in social interactions, tolerance of highly sensory situations, and overall behavioral compliance.

Table 9.2 Assessing for sensory processing

Core area
2. Sensory processing
• Diagnosis of "Sensory Processing Disorder"
• *Odd Sensory behaviors* — smelling toys, visual examination of objects, spinning of objects, overwhelmed by noise in the room, walks on toes, repetitively jumping off of high places (seeking proprioceptive input), clumsy
• Seven senses: sight, hearing, taste, smell, touch, balance and motion (vestibular), muscle and joint (proprioceptive), hunger and need for elimination (can be considered also in sensory needs)
• Consider results from ADOS-2 Sensory items, Sensory Profile, Short Sensory Profile
Full measure names
ADOS-2 Sensory Items and observations
Sensory Profile Caregiver Questionnaire
Short Sensory Profile

Sensory Processing Assessment as It Applies to Autism

Sensory sensitivities are common in both ASDs and AD/HD. So frequently individuals present for an evaluation between ages 5 and 10 with a "diagnosis" of "Sensory Processing Disorder." While sensory sensitivities are real and have a significant impact on day-to-day functioning for many individuals, the DSM-V does not contain such a diagnosis. Rather, sensory sensitivities are recognized as occurring in the context of other diagnoses.

It would be ideal if professionals treating individuals for sensory impairments at a young age would refer those individuals for comprehensive evaluations. If this was standard practice, many children would receive the early intervention that is associated in the research with optimal outcomes. Many occupational therapists do make these referrals and thus children may receive OT, Speech and ABA therapy, which are so critically needed to treat the sensory and other impairments associated with ASD. These providers are to be championed. Sadly, there are still providers who discourage parents from seeking other evaluations stating that occupational therapy for "sensory" "sensory processing disorder" or "SPD" must occur "first" and will "cure" these behavior problems. Some children even self-identify with this fictitious label, claiming, "I have sensory processing disorder" so I am unable to do this or that. This uninformed practice, identifying sensory needs as a primary and singular condition, hurts young children who could be receiving comprehensive services.

The authors' experience is that frequently parents seek evaluations after months or years of OT services that they express did not address all concerns or problem behaviors. While a diagnosis of SPD is not supported by the research, comprehensive assessment of sensory sensitivities is a part of the comprehensive assessment process provided here, because individuals with ASD do very frequently have sensory processing differences. Sometimes this makes concentrating in a busy classroom difficult. A large, crowded, noisy lunch room can be nearly impossible when an individual experiences sensory sensitivities. Certain clothing, lighting, or art materials may be overwhelming and uncomfortable to some individuals. In providing tools for success, occupational therapy or OT consultations at school can be very valuable to assess the environment and make sensory modifications that may help these individuals. Use of the Sensory Profile Questionnaire, Short Sensory Profile, direct questioning during parent and child interview, and observations can provide data that is useful in a comprehensive assessment.

Another thought on sensory processing is that for many parents it is much easier to hear and process that a child has sensory processing difficulties than it is to hear ASD or even AD/HD because of the stigma related to these diagnosed conditions. However, generally, children with sensory problems have a host of other symptoms associated with other neurological conditions, and to ignore these other areas is damaging for kids who so need additional therapies and supports.

It is so crucial for parents to understand that occupational therapy can play a valuable role in a child's treatment in a variety of areas. For example, children who struggle with feeding and self-dressing are well served by occupational therapists. Participation with peers at recess, lunch, and P.E. is commonly a primary goal in OT. Adaptive skills such as developing personal responsibility around the house and in the community can be treated in the context of physical or occupational therapy. However, unless the challenges are solely in motor, adaptive, handwriting, and sensory areas, OT alone is rarely enough.

In a Policy Statement, The American Academy of Pediatrics notes the behavioral differences of ASD, AD/HD, and developmental coordination overlap with the so-called sensory processing disorders (Zimmer & Desch, 2012). Specifically stating, "Studies to date have not demonstrated that sensory integration dysfunction exists as a separate disorder distinct from these other developmental disabilities" (p. 1187). The Academy reports that sensory and occupational therapies are not well researched and in fact much research suggests that traditional behavior focused therapies are more effective than sensory therapies in eliciting desired behavior outcomes.

A systematic review of twenty-five studies exploring the efficacy of sensory integration therapy (SIT) did not support the treatment modality (Lang et al., 2012). Specifically, 14 studies demonstrated no benefits, eight studies had mixed results, and only three studies put forth positive outcomes. That said, the authors note "serious methodological flaws" with the three positive outcome studies and advise that SIT is not considered a scientifically based intervention (Lang et al., 2012). Finally, the American Academy of Pediatrics does not support using sensory processing disorder as a diagnosis and encourages pediatricians to educate families on selecting evidence-based treatments, considering occupational therapy in isolation, a "limited resource"(p. 1188). The 2012 Statement put forth that occupational therapy including sensory-based treatments is an acceptable component of a "comprehensive treatment plan."

The authors of this book do not discourage parents from utilizing treatments that they feel are helping their children. That said, providers must impart to families that occupational therapy, particularly in the treatment of sensory needs alone, is not considered best practice. Parents should further be informed of the evidence suggesting sensory dysfunction is not a separate disorder. With these considerations carefully noted, these authors still advance that sensory impairments should be evaluated during any assessment for ASD due to the inclusion of these symptoms in the diagnostic criteria.

It is critical to examine sensory processing in the diagnostic process. There are seven named senses—vision (sight), audition (hearing), gustation (taste), olfaction (smell), tactile (touch), vestibular (balance and motion through space), and proprioception (muscle force and joint position). Additionally, there are internal sensations, such as hunger and the need for elimination, that some consider as an eighth sense. Challenges with sensory processing seem to be the most prevalent in persons with ASD. Specifically, both hypersensitivity and hyposensitivity to sensory inputs are common sensory processing problem associated with ASD (Baranek et al., 2007; Chen et al., 2009; Foss-Feig et al., 2012). Furthermore, a body of evidence suggests that an individual may be over-responsive to some sensations and under-responsive to others (Lane, Young, Baker, & Angley, 2010; Schoen, Miller, Brett-Green, & Nielsen, 2009). The authors have noted this pattern in their practice, and often children with ASD seem unaware of some sensations but overly impacted by others. Traits such as low muscle tone, poor handwriting, dyspraxia, light and sound sensitivities, and poor balance may all be indicative of ASD or other neurodevelopmental disorder. As it relates to ASD, there is some evidence that dyspraxia may be a defining marker for ASD (Dowell, Mahone, & Mostofsky, 2009; Mostofsky et al., 2006).

Use of the Sensory Profile Questionnaire, Short Sensory Profile, or direct questioning during parent and child interview can provide data related to hypersensitivities, hyposensitivities, and overall sensory processing that is useful in a comprehensive assessment.

Concluding Remarks on Assessment of Social and Sensory Areas

Taken together, assessment of social and sensory symptoms is core area in the evaluation of individuals suspected of having an ASD. A defining feature of autism is a significant deficit in, or lack of, social reciprocity. Individuals who are not socially reciprocal tend to struggle to share enjoyment with others, interact in a fluid and comfortable manner, spontaneously initiate joint attention with peers or caregivers, and to listen and comprehend conversations. The authors recommend the use of the ADOS-2 and either a thorough clinical interview or the ADI-R in the assessment of the social symptoms associated with ASD. Rating scales such as the SCQ, Vineland, and BASC-II, in addition to clinical observations, client or parent interview, and diagnostic impressions of multiple raters, are all elements of a comprehensive evaluation for ASD. Sensory impairments are often associated with ASD and must be considered part of any diagnostic assessment for the disorder. Sensory impairments are not considered distinct from other disabilities, rather, can be associated features. It is not recommended that individuals be treated for sensory needs in isolation but occupational therapy for such challenges might be part of a more comprehensive treatment program for ASD that also includes ABA, psychotherapy, and potentially psychopharmacological treatments. This concludes the assessment of Core Areas of ASD. The following chapters will provide data analysis information on the Associated Areas.

Chapter 10
Visual, Spatial, and Motor Assessment

Abstract Visual, Spatial, and Motor Assessment are associated areas of a comprehensive evaluation for an Autism Spectrum Disorder. Visual Spatial skills include visual perception, visual closure, visual processing, and visual figure ground. Impairments may include visual tracking and planning, hand eye coordination, and reading a map. Measures often used to assess visual-spatial skills in ASD include the MVPT-3, Perceptual Reasoning tasks on the WISC-IV, Visual Spatial tasks on the WISC-V, Spatial tasks on the DAS-2 Preschool, The Beery Test of Visual Perception and the Rey Complex Figure Test (RCFT) copy trial, or WMS-IV copy trial for Visual Reproduction. In the motor domain, children may have challenges with oral motor skills related to muscle tone that may include chewing, swallowing, and drooling. Fine motor deficits may relate to fine motor dexterity, handwriting, manipulation of beads or coins and can be assessed by a number of measures. In younger children, cognitive measures like the Mullen Scales include motor skills assessment. The Vineland-2 also provides sections for parents to report motor skills from birth to age six. Additional assessments like the Beery VMI Sequence, informal drawing and writing tasks, and the Grooved Pegboard can provide information on fine motor skills. By assessing these Associated Areas, a clinician can offer more targeted recommendations for treatment of these symptoms that may be present in an individual with ASD.

Keywords Visual-motor in ASD • Visual planning in ASD • Visual memory in ASD • Fine motor in ASD • Gross motor in ASD • Low tone in ASD • Handwriting in ASD • Local vs. global processing in ASD

Assessing for Visual-Spatial Skills

Vignette #5 Tom: Visual-Spatial Assessment in a Child with a Scattered Verbal/Nonverbal Profile

Tom, age 10, was referred for an evaluation at Emerge to rule out the presence of an Autism Spectrum Disorder (Table 10.1). Parents reported a significantly scattered academic and cognitive profile for Tom that seemed to provide immense challenges

Table 10.1 Assessing for visual-spatial skills

Associated area
1. *Visual spatial*
• *Visual Perception:* Consider WISC-IV Perceptual Reasoning or WISC-V Visual Spatial Index Score, Motor-Free Visual Perception Test (MVPT): visual closure, visual figure ground, visual rotation
• *Visual Memory:* visual working memory, picture span test on WISC-V, WMS, MVPT visual memory items, VMI-Visual Perception test
• *Visual Planning:* consider performance on Tower of London, and CTMT (Trails)
• *Central Coherence (Local* vs. *Global Processing)*
• *Consider discrepancies between Language and Visual Spatial:* visual develops before language in ASD
• *Consider Results from:* Beery VMI, CTMT, MVPT-III, Picture Span: WISC-V, TOL-II, VOT
Full measure names
Beery—Buktenica Developmental Test of Visual—Motor Integration (VMI), Sixth Ed.
Beery—Buktenica Developmental Test of Visual Perception, Sixth Ed.
Beery—Buktenica Developmental Test of Motor Coordination, Sixth Ed.
Comprehensive Trail Making Test (CTMT)
Motor-Free Visual Perception Test, Third Ed. (MVPT-III)
Picture Span Subtest on WISC-V
Tower of London, Second Ed. (TOL-II)
Hooper Visual Organization Test (VOT)

to educators as they worked with him. Tom had a history of not speaking in sentences until first grade and not reading until third grade. He used sign language to communicate as a young child and he had challenges with peers, biting others in prekindergarten, for example. Tom's parents reported that he uses many gestures, enjoys pretend play, and is quiet and sweet at home. He had sensory sensitivities to taste and texture that sometimes caused challenges with meal time and dressing. Tom displayed a restricted interest in Legos .

Tom scored in the Superior range for Perceptual Reasoning on the WISC-IV and his Verbal Comprehension abilities were Mildly Impaired. This clinically significant differential in scores occurs in less than one percent of the population. Tom scored in the Superior range on Motor Free Visual Perception (MVPT-3) and Visual Memory (TOMAL), but his CELF-4 score fell in the Mildly Impaired range. Tom was somewhat impulsive at times and needed frequent breaks to maintain focus. He did not speak spontaneously during the first 30 min of testing. However, he was able to answer questions like "What do you like to do for fun?" (I play with Legos) and "Where do you live?" (I live in a duplex with my family.). On The ADOS-2, he did well with gesture and pretend play, but struggled to tell a story from a book, have a reciprocal conversation, or describe relationships. His reported "best friend" was the child who most often teased him at school.

Taken together, Tom's profile was indicative of an Autism Spectrum Disorder. Tom had been underserved in school as teachers did not realize he had such strengths in Visual Spatial skills and nonverbal domains. His parents decided to pursue private schooling based on this unique profile and Tom began to make progress particularly in math and science. Tom started ABA therapy to address his communication and social interaction weaknesses and he has begun to make friends with common interests like Legos and drawing.

A 1-year follow-up evaluation revealed much improved verbal skills. Anecdotally, he talked with examiners the whole time he was being assessed during this follow-up session. He also showed a significant improvement in verbal skills as evidenced on standardized language testing.

Visual-Spatial Assessment as It Applies to Autism

As introduced in the Language section of Chap. 8, weak Central-Coherence theory refers to an inability to integrate information from the environment into a meaningful whole, focusing on local stimuli and not on global meaning. Individuals with weak coherence have a detail-focused style of processing that is often characteristic of ASD (Happé & Frith, 2006, p. 5). When we think of visual-spatial assessment as it applies to ASD, we often think of that characterization of "Rain Man," an individual with very specific strengths in the visual-spatial realm but an inability to integrate these skills in a more global manner. Of course, this is only one very specific example of an individual with significant impairment and in no way represents the variation of presentations across the Spectrum.

Individuals with ASD who have weak language skills may present with exceptional talent in artistic areas. Deborah Fein writes in her book *The Neuropsychology of Autism* (2011) that the visual-spatial cortex develops earlier than the language cortex and thus may be spared in individuals with ASD. This is also consistent with Piaget and Vygotsky's models for development. Studies have shown that tasks requiring local processing are often easier or skills are at minimum intact in individuals with ASD while global processing deficits are noted. Attention to detail on a task like Block Design may lead to high scores initially as the individual can look at each block and the individual pattern. As the figures are more complex and it is helpful to see the figure as a whole and not as a sum of parts, performance may decline. Fein (2011) notes (p. 100) that a cognitive style favoring detail-oriented processing has been found in family members of those diagnosed with ASD.

This weak Central-Coherence theory fits with neuroimaging data highlighting under-connectivity in the white matter of the brain, which may cause problems with global or higher order processing (Fein, 2011, p. 101). Just, Cherkassky, Keller, Kana, and Minshew (2007) completed a study utilizing the Tower of London, an executive functioning measure, and found that individuals with ASD exhibited underactivity between the frontal and parietal areas of the brain. The way brain function was altered indicated less communication across cortical areas. A cross-section of the corpus callosum showed that relevant parts utilized in the autistic brain were smaller than in controls. The study concluded that there is a deficit in integration of information at neural and cortical levels in ASD (Just et al., 2007). Studies including individuals with ASD and a comparison group of neurotypical children, matched for IQ, show that individuals with ASD struggle with integration across the language and imagery functions of the brain (Willard, 2013).

Connectivity may be characterized by local over-connectivity and long distance under-connectivity or weaker long range connections between brain regions. In 40 adolescents and young adults, Anderson, Nielsen et al. (2011) found differences in connectivity in the brain between control subjects and those with autism. Unaffected siblings' brains were more similar to controls than to the individuals diagnosed on the Spectrum (Anderson, Druzgal et al., 2011). These data support the idea that we may find localized strengths in areas like visual-spatial skills for those with ASD. We may also find that global processing is impaired, so a task that draws on many brain regions to complete is likely to be more difficult for an individual on the spectrum.

Another theory worth reviewing is that of *systemizing* and *empathizing* introduced by Simon Baron-Cohen and detailed in Baron-Cohen and Sally Wheelwright's chapter in the *Neuropsychology of Autism*, edited by Deborah Fein (2011). While a *systematizing* approach involves understanding the system and looking at the specifics, an *empathizing* perspective includes making sense of the behaviors of others and encompasses Theory of Mind. Empathy involves attributing mental states to oneself and others and having an emotional reaction like sympathy (Baron-Cohen, 2004).

Systemizing is a drive to analyzing systems (Baron-Cohen, 2004). Strong visual-spatial skills in recalling or reproducing detail may be part of a systemizing approach. There are rules and clear structures that can be relied on when understanding visual patterns. Patterns have detail, involve concrete elements, and tend to have clear and logical solutions. The emotions and perspectives of others do not lend well to such logical algorithms and systematic analysis. Billington, Baron-Cohen, and Wheelwright (2007) propose that individuals with ASD take a systemizing approach to the world thus making social understanding very difficult because it does not have an exact recipe.

The chef metaphor is pertinent here. Someone who is systemizing will consistently produce dishes that follow the recipe precisely every time. This exacting approach is very useful in some situations. A non-systemizing approach would look much different in the culinary arts. A chef may change ingredients, throw this or that, until it 'tastes right.' The consequences of such spontaneity could be delicious or disastrous, but they are not predictable. In the chef metaphor here, individuals with ASD would generally prefer the precise recipe approach over the dynamic style of the more spontaneous chef.

As theorized, if individuals with ASD are systemizing, they may be very good with a detail-oriented skill like drawing while predicting social responses can be a different story. A study of spatial navigation in autism by Lind, Williams, Raber, Peel, and Bowler (2013) hypothesized that considering the systemizing brain, those with ASD should be better at spatial navigation, a visual-spatial skill. Lind and colleagues predicted that, in contrast, those with ASD would perform below a control group in navigation. Navigation involves spatial skills but also perhaps an ability to switch routes and to tolerate the unpredictable, and thus, may be a more global task. The researchers noted that some visual-spatial skills may not be strong in individuals with ASD (Lind et al., 2013).

Caron, Mottron, Berthiaume, and Dawson (2006) proposed that perception may be reorganized in ASD. When those with high-functioning autism were given a task involving block design, participants did not have a deficit in constructing global representations which is inconsistent with the 'weak central coherence' hypothesis. Participants with autism also demonstrated strong locally oriented processing though, which is more consistent with the systemizing and weak central coherence hypotheses. Across all research reviewed on visual spatial processing, superior visual processing skills were noted in both local and global tasks. This provides some evidence for a systemizing approach and some evidence for weak central coherence. Data reviewed indicates a need for continued research to further assess visual spatial processing strengths and weaknesses in individuals with Autism Spectrum Disorders.

Measures often used to assess visual-spatial skills in ASD include the MVPT-3, Perceptual Reasoning tasks on the WISC-IV, Visual Spatial tasks on the WISC-V, Spatial tasks on the DAS-2 Preschool, The Beery Test of Visual Perception and the Rey Complex Figure Test (RCFT) copy trial, or WMS-IV copy trial for Visual Reproduction. Evaluators can assess an individual's approach to these tasks and note orientation to detail. For a task like the Beery Visual Perception Test, attention to detail is crucial. Depending on an individual's approach to a task, it is possible to obtain significantly scattered results across these measures.

On the MVPT-3, visual perception is assessed considering visual closure, visual figure ground, visual rotation, and visual memory. Visual closure refers to the ability to see what a picture or figure will look like from an incomplete version of the full image. Visual figure ground involves seeing a figure within a larger or cluttered visual image (imagine Where's Waldo or Photo Hunt). Visual rotation refers to being able to rotate an image or flip an image in your mind and could relate to reading a map or graph. Visual memory refers to seeing an image and being able to hold it in working memory or store it in long-term memory. These skills may be advanced or they may be impaired in ASD; perhaps because of impacted executive functioning skills that lead to challenges with flexibility and attention, particularly sustained attention. Some tasks of executive functioning can provide information on visual processing, considering the ability to visually plan and sequence including the Tower of London-II (TOL) and the Comprehensive Trail Making Test (CTMT).

Performance on the Rey Complex Figure Test and Recognition Trial has been studied for individuals with ASD. Kuschner, Bodner, and Minshew (2009) looked at local versus global approaches to reproducing the RCFT in children, adolescents, and adults with ASD. Differences in Rey performance were noted for adolescents and adults but not for children. Adolescents and adults did not develop visual spatial skills on the same trajectory as expected; thus differences were noted later but not seen in children. There is an altered pattern of visual processing in autism that can be noted across the Spectrum if sensitive methods of assessment are employed (Kuschner et al., 2009).

Researchers agree that it is crucial to assess visual spatial skills because the visual processing centers tend to be impacted less primarily in ASD. It may be that visual spatial skills are a hidden area of strength, as was seen in the vignette. In this case, failing to assess for visual-spatial skills would have done a major disservice to this individual as his skills would have gone unidentified. As shown in the vignette, acknowledgment of Tom's Superior skills in visual-spatial domains helped clinicians recommend strategies for how to teach Tom and maximize his learning. A child who was virtually unchallenged because of his language weaknesses was able to learn and excel utilizing a visual learning style. It is critical that examiners consider all of the potential strengths and weaknesses that may be evident in an individual's cognitive style (Happé & Frith, 2006); particularly when the individual has ASD or another disorder that has significant impact on various areas of cognition and development.

Assessing for Motor Skills

Vignette #6 Pablo: Fine and Gross Motor Assessment in a Child with Autism

Table 10.2 Assessing for motor skills

Associated area
1. Motor skills
• Oral Motor: swallowing, drooling, chewing
• Visual motor: integration of visual and motor skills, performance on Beery VMI
• Fine motor: dexterity, handwriting, and drawing; Mullen: stringing beads, stacking blocks, placing penny in bank
• Gross motor: hypotonia, motor apraxia, poor posture, clumsy
• Stereotyped motor behaviors
• Consider performance on: Bayley-iii, Beery VMI, TGMD-2, Mullen, Vineland-II
Full measure names
Bayley Scales of Infant Development, Third Edition (Bayley-iii) (Motor Scales)
Beery—Buktenica Developmental Test of Motor Coordination, Sixth Edition
Grooved Pegboard
Test of Gross Motor Development, Second Edition (TGMD-2)
Mullen Scales of Early Learning (Motor Scales)
Vineland Scales of Adaptive Behavior (Vineland-II)

Pablo, age four, was referred for an evaluation at Emerge based on significant gross and fine motor deficits (Table 10.2). Pablo was identified by his pediatrician at age three as likely having an Autism Spectrum Disorder, but no formal diagnosis had been made. Parents reported that Pablo walked late, at 18 months, was not riding a tricycle, had difficulty throwing and catching a ball, and threw tantrums in preschool when it was time to draw or write. Pablo's parents were concerned because he was entering pre-kindergarten in the fall and had no interest in writing, drawing, or cutting. Additionally, he was somewhat clumsy and while he could walk and run, he was not demonstrating appropriate motor coordination. When he became overly excited, Pablo flapped his hands by his sides and rocked on his toes. Pablo's parents reported that he had sensory sensitivities and really enjoyed his iPad and looking at books. He could name all of his colors, letters, and numbers. Pablo scored in the Superior range on the DAS-2 for Verbal and Nonverbal domains, but Below Average in the spatial domain. He refused many of the copying designs figures. Consistent with the model presented in Chap. 7, these early signs of motor deficits led the examiner to consider a more comprehensive assessment of the motor domain.

Pablo also scored poorly on the Mullen Gross and Fine Motor scales and the Beery Tests of Visual Motor Integration and Motor Coordination. He did well on Visual Perception when pointing to his responses, not circling them. Pablo fell out of his chair during the assessment and he was uncoordinated when bouncing on the trampoline. He could not complete the Grooved Pegboard as he continued to drop the pegs. He scored in the Average range for language on the CELF-2 Preschool, but his conversation skills were not on par with his Superior cognitive functioning.

Taken together, Pablo's profile was indicative of an Autism Spectrum Disorder, as expected by his parents and doctor. Pablo was diagnosed with Developmental Coordination Disorder, based on fine motor deficits, and Occupational Therapy was recommended both privately and at school. Pablo began ABA services and his flexibility to try new tasks, like drawing, improved as well as his play and conversation skills. He enrolled in a swimming course that helped with gross motor coordination. His ABA therapist helped Pablo's parents teach him to ride a tricycle and then a bike. Pablo's private OT reports that he is more willing to cut with scissors, play with molding dough, and make crafts. She has seen great improvement in his flexibility and willingness to try new tasks since he began ABA. While Pablo still flaps his hands when excited, he has also learned he can take a jump break on his small trampoline and this behavior has partially replaced hand flapping with support of his ABA therapist. Pablo's parents are pleased with his progress.

Motor Skill Assessment as It Applies to Autism

Visual Motor Integration and Fine and Gross Motor Coordination skills, oral motor abilities as well as visuo-motor information processing skills have been found to be impacted in individuals with ASDs (Belmonte et al., 2013; Freitag, Kleser, Schneider, & von Gontard, 2007; Green et al., 2009; Sachse et al., 2013). Children may have challenges with oral motor related to muscle tone that may include chewing, swallowing, and drooling. Fine motor deficits may relate to fine motor dexterity, handwriting, manipulation of beads or coins and can be assessed by a number of measures. In younger children, cognitive measures like the Mullen Scales include motor skills assessment. The Vineland-2 also provides sections for parents to report motor skills from birth to age 6. Additional assessments like the Beery VMI Sequence, informal drawing and writing tasks, and the Grooved Pegboard can provide information on fine motor skills. The ADOS-2 directly assesses gesture use which involves integrating motor movements with language in order to communicate and requires some degree of motor skill. As these skills have an impact on academics, social engagement, and athletic pursuits, these assessments can provide data that is helpful in understanding learning styles and perhaps explaining problem behaviors. In some cases, individuals may escape/avoid tasks that involve motor skills because this is an area of weakness.

Leo Kanner described clumsiness in gait as well as gross motor delays in his first cohort of 11 children with autism (Kanner, 1943). Ming, Brimacombe, and Wagner (2007) used review of clinical records to study motor deficits in ASD. Hypotonia, motor apraxia, toe walking, and gross motor delay were the most reported areas of motor impairment. It can be important to watch a child's posture, clumsiness, and the way he or she sits, stands, or carries himself. The first two, posture and clumsiness, were found in this research, to improve significantly with age. These researchers noted that fine motor deficits commonly co-occur in ASD. Sutera et al. (2007) found motor impairment at age two to be the best predictor of later testing off of the Autism Spectrum at age four. In a very early study completed in 1969, Wing and colleagues note that "clumsy" children with ASD have trouble learning organized patterns of movement (Fein, 2011; Wing, 1969). Impaired imitation and impaired motor learning can impact many areas of functioning. Research shows that the mirror neuron system in the brain is involved as we look at others performing movements and are able to interpret the actions and how to perform them (Fein, 2011, p. 210).

Research shows that children with ASD often have delays in motor skills. Dowd, McGinley, Taffe, and Rinehart (2012) addressed motor planning in a study of 3–7 year olds, finding ASD is associated with challenges using visual information to prime movements in response to environmental demands. Lloyd, MacDonald, and Lord (2013) found that the motor deficits associated with autism only become more marked in comparison to the skills of typical peers. That is, as the skills of peers grow, the trajectory for children with ASD may flatline or remain parallel. Thus, it is crucial to assess and treat motor delay in young children before these challenges become even more pronounced. Although motor deficits are not diagnostic, they do occur frequently in ASD, and challenges can become more pronounced in relation to peers over time. Therefore, it is useful to understand how these skills are developing in individuals referred for assessment. One researcher explains the importance of motor development thusly, "...Motor skills contribute to overall developmental outcomes for children" (Lloyd et al., 2013). Taken together, motor impairments are evidenced more often in ASD than in the general population. Remediation and treatment for motor skill deficits, primarily through Occupational Therapy and athletic pursuits, can greatly enhance functioning and positive behaviors for individuals with ASD.

Stereotyped Motor Behaviors

Often stereotyped motor behaviors are part of a diagnosis of ASD. Parents and individuals report that these behaviors are at times linked to levels of stress or excitement and sometimes they just appear to be self-reinforcing. The Basal Ganglia contribute to movement and to the movement abnormalities often associated with autism (Fein, 2011). Stereotyped movements also play a role in motivation, repetitive behaviors, and obsessiveness (p. 66). Stereotyped behaviors like arm flapping, toe walking, and finger flicking are not present in all individuals with ASD; but sometimes repetitive interests and behaviors are diagnostic. Repetitive motor movements are obvious to the casual observer and for that reason are often first associated with ASD and of first concern to parents who wonder about the cause and treatment for these difficulties. The cause is not definitively established (Fein, 2011, p. 367). The behaviors serve to self-regulate and they are reinforcing, so additional motivations to continue such behaviors may develop over time (Fein, 2011, p. 387; Willemsen-Swinkels, Buitelaar, Dekker, & van Engeland, 1998). Repetitive movements are likely related to over-arousal (Fein, 2011, p. 388), but researchers are not entirely certain of how this works. These behaviors are assessed via clinical observations, rating scales, and direct measure including the ADOS-2.

Concluding Remarks on the Assessment of Visual-Spatial and Motor Areas

Visual-spatial and motor skills are often impacted in autism. Visual-spatial problems may be evident during such activities as reading maps, completing puzzles, or in general eye-hand coordination. Strong visual-spatial skills require the integration of many parts into a coherent whole, which can often be difficult for individuals with autism. Often the executive functions of planning and organizing a strategy to solve a visual problem are impaired in autism, which may also impact scores on visual-spatial assessments. Visual-spatial tests can evaluate such areas as: visual closure, visual figure ground, visual rotation, and visual memory. Due to research indicating that the non-verbal abilities may emerge first in children with autism, while the verbal skills develop later, some individuals with autism may be spared such difficulties with visual-spatial skills. However, weaknesses in attention, executive functioning, and central coherence can interfere with visual-spatial processing; and as such, should be assessed when the clinician notices potential problems during the evaluation (see Chap. 7: Dynamic Assessment Overview for ASD and Other Disorders). In the motor domain, children may have trouble with oral motor, fine motor, or gross motor skills. Oral motor problems would be evidenced by issues with chewing, swallowing, or drooling. Fine motor challenges can be seen in poor handwriting, difficulty stringing beads, tying shoes, or turning the pages of a book. Gross motor problems may appear during an assessment if the individual is uncoordinated, has poor posture, low muscle tone, awkward gait, or difficulty riding a bike. Although not diagnostic for ASD, delays in motor skills may signal a neurodevelopmental disability such as autism. Clinicians are advised to carefully observe potential difficulties with visual-spatial and motor skills throughout the assessment, and if concerns are evident, further assessment of these areas is warranted.

Chapter 11
Attention, Executive Functions, and Memory Assessment

Abstract While individuals with ASD are characterized by challenges communicating and reciprocally interacting with others, it is often weaknesses in attention, memory, or executive functioning that underlie difficulties with academic or vocational success. Specifically, persons with autism typically manifest with selective attention to particular stimuli of most interest and have difficulty shifting their attention required to multitask. Of profound importance is the fact that it's essential to attend to something in order to encode the event or item and be able to remember it later. In this manner, attending is the first step required to potentially learn something new. Subsequently, weaknesses in memory include remembering complex information (Neuropsychology 20:21–29, 2006), spatial working memory, relational memory (Neuropsychology 27:615–627, 2013), episodic memory, and time-based prospective memory. These memory difficulties significantly impact what an individual learns. Executive functioning pertains to an important cluster of skills which, like attention, are mediated by the frontal lobe and include initiating, organizing, and sequencing information. Frequent challenges in these areas associated with autism include problems generating ideas, responding inflexibility or perseverating, as well as deficits in planning. Challenges in these areas can often be just as debilitating as social weaknesses for an individual with autism. Hence, the importance of assessing, remediating, or compensating for these challenges cannot be overstated in order to help promote success at home, in school, and the workplace.

Keywords Attention in ASD • Executive functions in ASD • Memory in ASD • Splinter skills: an outdated term • Exceptional abilities: an updated term • Sustained attention in ASD • Shifting attention in ASD • Focused attention in ASD • Joint attention in ASD • Neuropsychological assessment of autism • Can you have ASD and ADHD?

Table 11.1 Assessing for attention

Associated area
1. *Attention*
• *Focused:* adults may have difficulty obtaining attention of people with ASD as they may prefer to attend to objects or ideas of their own interest and ignore the social or environmental stimuli
• *Selective and Over-Selective:* individuals with ASD tend to predominantly focus on restricted interests—may have over-selective attention, perseverating on specific interests for prolonged periods
• *Sustained:* sustained attention may or may not be okay in ASD Typically sustained attention is a deficit in ADHD
• *Shifting:* challenges with multi-tasking, establishing, and maintaining mental set This is typically challenging with ASD
• *Joint Attention:* a process of engaging and shifting attention for social interaction (typically impaired in ASD)
• Consider results from: ADT-II, Conners, T.O.V.A., and Observations of behaviors on the ADOS-II and WISC-V; Executive Functioning Measures
Full measure names
Conner's Rating Scale Third Edition (Conners 3)
Conner's Continuous Performance Test, Second Edition (CPT II)
Conner's Kiddie Continuous Performance Test, (K-CPT)
Test of Variables of Attention (TOVA)
Wepman's Auditory Discrimination Test, Second Edition (ADT-II)
General attention observations during cognitive testing
Observations during ADOS-2 regarding attention during conversation/play
Results from Executive Functioning measures

Assessing for Attention

Vignette #7 Madeline: Assessment of Focused, Sustained, and Shifting Attention in a Child with Social Skills Deficits

Madeline, age 7, was referred for an evaluation at Emerge to rule out the presence of AD/HD. Her school recommended testing as Madeline had difficulty paying attention, was impulsive, and had meltdowns as she became easily upset with peers in the classroom. Madeline often claimed "nobody likes me!" but when asked "why do you think that is?" she seemed confused and remarked "Because I have a red scratch on my leg!" Parents reported that Madeline had an excellent memory but sometimes appeared to be "checked out" and did not pay attention. She had particular difficulty when she was engaged in a game or movie, and it was time to transition to another activity. In testing, Madeline presented with a High Average cognitive profile across all domains. She was very active and impulsive but maintained her attention with breaks every half hour. On the Test of Variables of Attention (TOVA), a test of sustained attention in the absence of immediate reinforcement, Madeline scored Above Average across all domains, even while she complained, "I made 12 mistakes!" (Table 11.1).

Madeline had difficulty on a task of shifting and sequencing, the Comprehensive Trail Making Test (CTMT), and worked more slowly than would be expected. On the Tower of London (TOL-2), Madeline broke rules on three of ten puzzles and presented with inflexibility in her attempts to solve problems. She also had some perseveration and difficulty shifting set on the Wisconsin Card Sort Test (WCST), but this score was within age expected ranges.

Madeline was given the ADOS-2 based on her reported social struggles. While she played and conversed; making eye contact, and enjoying social interaction, she was inflexible in her play. Madeline had trouble taking a character as an agent of action and spent more time setting up the toys. She was a bit bossy with the examiner, telling her who to be and what to do. Madeline demonstrated significant challenges in understanding social relationships and told many stories about her experiences that seemed unlikely to be true. When the examiner shared something about herself, Madeline often responded with "I know." Madeline's own stories included reporting owning a leopard as a pet. These responses indicate that she does not know how to interact reciprocally; spontaneously share, and relate to the experiences of others.

Taken together, Madeline's profile was indicative of an Autism Spectrum Disorder and not AD/HD. Her challenges were not in sustained or focused attention at all, though shifting attention and flexibility were problems, consistent with ASD. Madeline began to receive ABA support at school through her district's Board Certified Behavior Analyst (BCBA) and a Functional Analysis aided in the development of a behavior support plan. She began to participate in social skills training in a group setting. Her behavior improved substantially across social and school settings.

Attention Assessment

The recognition of co-occurrence of AD/HD with ASD is aptly captured in DSM-5 which permits comorbid diagnoses of both conditions. Indeed, studies have found similar structural brain abnormalities in those with ASD and AD/HD when compared to controls (Matson, Rieske, & Williams, 2013). In contrast to this literature, diagnostic criteria in the DSM-IV reflected the historical view that a diagnosis of ASD preempts and therefore precludes an additional diagnosis of AD/HD. This historical assumption is no longer considered valid as it was revisited and changed in the DSM-5 which permits comorbid diagnosis (Matson et al., 2013). Research indicates that AD/HD and ASDs are co-occurring 14–78 % (Gargaro et al., 2011). This is a wide range but indicates that many individuals with ASD struggle with attention problems. For this reason, it is very important to thoroughly assess attention skills when evaluating for an ASD.

As will be comprehensively reviewed in the Chap. 13, differential diagnosis of AD/HD requires an assessment of disinhibition and social reciprocity. If the child is disinhibited and lacks social reciprocity, he or she likely has both AD/HD and ASD. Mayes et al. (2012) state that ASD and AD/HD are "neurobiological disorders with similar underlying neuropsychological deficits." (p. 283) Children with comorbid symptoms have more difficulty inhibiting inappropriate responses when compared with children who have ASD alone (Mannion & Leader, 2013). Those with ASD alone demonstrate better inhibition, flexibility, working memory, and planning skills than those with comorbid diagnosis (Sinzig, Bruning, Morsch, & Lehmkuhl, 2008) although these skills are still often challenging. Deprey and Ozonoff & Corbett et al. (2009) found that hyper vigilant attention and internal distractibility are more common in ASD while lack of focus and distractibility by external stimuli is characteristic of AD/HD.

The authors of this text observe that many children with ASD exhibit intermittent challenges with attention and executive functioning skills while those with comorbid diagnoses have significant deficits in sustained attention, inhibition, and focus. Individuals with AD/HD who do not have ASD may have some social challenges influenced by impulsivity, inattention, and hyperactivity. However, when focused, individuals with only AD/HD should be able to engage in pretend play and creative activities like telling a story or acting out a cartoon. Children with ASD alone tend to have less pervasive problems with attention. They can attend when given appropriate reinforcement. Sustained attention can be assessed via continuous performance testing and with rating scales completed by parents, teachers, and individuals. These may include the TOVA, BASC-2, BRIEF, or Conners AD/HD scales.

Attention Assessment as It Applies to Autism

Attention can be broadly defined as information processing mechanisms that mediate perceptual selectivity (Keehn, Shih, Brenner, Townsend, & Müller, 2013). Problems with attention have historically been considered as an associated or secondary deficit when present with ASD. Research reveals, however, that impairments represent early and lifelong abnormalities in efficiently modulating attention networks for individuals with ASD (Keehn, Müller & Townsend, 2013).

Attention mechanisms represent the confluence of external stimuli processed through bottom-up, sensory afferent nerve signals received in the posterior brain regions as well as internal, goal-directed processes originating in the anterior/frontal brain regions and executed through efferent, top-down signals (Kandel, Schwartz, & Jessell, 1991). Sensory processing assessment and therapies (Ayres, 2005) focus on the former bottom-up processes while behavior analytic assessments (Iwata et al., 1990) and therapies focus on both processes through classical and operant conditioning paradigms (Barlow, 2002; Cooper, Heron, & Hewerd, 2013).

In light of the fact that millions of brain fibers are sensory processing assessment and therapies (Ayres, 2005) focus on the former bottom-up processes while behavior analytic assessments (Iwata et al., 1990) and therapies focus on both processes through classical and operant conditioning paradigms. In light of the fact that millions of brain fibers are connecting the posterior and anterior cortical regions, perceptual selectivity or attention rarely consists exclusively of top-down or bottom-up processes but rather successful and adaptive information processing requires the integration of both processes (Keehn et al., 2013).

As previously mentioned, AD/HD and ASDs co-occur in a wide range of 14–78 % of the population diagnosed with ASD (Gargaro et al., 2011). Such a range in findings likely reflects that, in addition to the wide ASD span of various symptoms and severities, attention problems are multifaceted and responsible for a distinct set of cognitive processes. These processes include alerting, orienting, and executive control networks (Petersen & Posner, 2012; Posner & Petersen, 1989). Furthermore, research on attention indicates that attention networks each have their own developmental trajectories resulting in the emergence and strengthening of various attention skills into adulthood. Often these trajectories are delayed or attention skills may be present but significantly less efficient for individuals with ASD. All these complexities emphasize the importance of individually assessing for the occurrence and nature of attention deficits when evaluating for an ASD.

The authors of this text observe that most individuals with ASD exhibit challenges with attention and executive functioning skills evidenced in selective attention to highly preferred interests or activities and/or problems with flexibility, ideational fluency, planning, or central coherence. Nonetheless, those with ASD and not AD/HD demonstrate better inhibition, flexibility, working memory, and planning skills than those with both ASD and AD/HD (Sinzig et al., 2008). Individuals with comorbid diagnoses of ASD and AD/HD have additional deficits in sustaining attention in the absence of immediate reinforcement. Individuals with AD/HD but not ASD may exhibit some social challenges as a result of being impulsive, inattentive, or hyperactive. Such social difficulties look different and may appear like obnoxiousness, impulsive aggressive acts toward peers, and a lack of body awareness that could interfere with social functioning. Some children with AD/HD may have some difficulty understanding emotions, challenges with rejection or academic punishment for over-active behavior, or even failed friendships from impulsive aggression. When focused, however, individuals with only AD/HD should be able to engage in reciprocal activities such as pretend play or conversation and they should exhibit synchronized verbal and gestural communication in creative activities such as telling a story or acting out a cartoon. The following discussion provides further details on attentional networks, skills, developmental trajectories, and comorbid deficits found with ASD. In addition, assessment measures appropriate for each attention process as well as recommendations for associated weaknesses or deficits are included.

Alerting Network

The alerting network is responsible for achieving and maintaining a state of sensitivity to incoming information (Keehn et al., 2013). Parents can attest to the fact that newborn infants respond only to internal information such as hunger or pain and often actually sleep best when there is a high level of external noise or activity. Such endogenous wakefulness is referred to as tonic alertness and describes general arousal. Tonic alertness in infants develops rapidly between 2 and 24 weeks. Subsequently, the autonomic nervous system continues to develop across the life span. Research on persons with ASD indicates the possibility of separate subgroups representing individuals with either hyper- or hypo-arousal. These two disparate subgroups are captured in the ADOS assessment where the examiner may observe and record the participant's overall level of engagement, attention, excitability, and alertness ranging from over-responsive to lethargic. Clinically, individuals with ASD and hyperarousal are subject to being easily distracted by any form of internal or external stimuli and likely also meet criteria for AD/HD. Deprey and Ozonoff & Corbett et al. (2009) found that lack of *focused attention* skills and distractibility by external stimuli is characteristic of AD/HD. Furthermore, Mayes et al. (2012) found that children with comorbid symptoms of both ASD and AD/HD have more difficulty with inhibitory performance when compared with children who have ASD alone (Mannion & Leader, 2013) which may again reflect the hyperarousal subgroup. Alternately, some have hypothesized that chronic hyperarousal may actually result in increased *overselective attention* (Liss, Saulnier, Fein, & Kinsbourne, 2006); a tendency to perseveratively regard, review or rehearse high preference internal or external stimuli.

The second component of the alerting network is phasic alertness which refers to a transient response to a behavioral or experimental cue (Keehn et al., 2013). This is a reflexive physiological response to a change in the environment rather than a volitional reaction. Phasic alertness is modulated by the level of tonic alertness and tonic alertness or overall arousal influences task performance. Phasic orienting responses develop rapidly during the first year of life, efficiency, and speed of phasic alerting appear to develop into early school-age years, and may reach adult levels by age 7–8 years of age (Cycowicz, Friedman, & Rothstein, 1996). Electrophysiological measures have demonstrated atypical phasic alerting in individuals with ASD and findings suggest modulation of phasic alerting mechanisms may be dysfunctional in ASD (Keehn et al., 2013). This in turn is likely related to marked insensitivity to novel stimuli often seen in individuals with ASD.

Assessment of response to novel stimuli can be gleaned from the Wechsler Cancellation and Symbol Search tasks. Like most assessment tasks or protocols, these measures assess multiple constructs; the Symbol Search also being a measure of processing speed. Nonetheless, observation and review of the quality of performance, specifically, any errors, and the type of errors, can shed light on whether they are insensitive to novel stimuli. Parents or family members may also express concern that the individual with ASD ignores presents under the Christmas tree or fails to notice a new student in the classroom. A partner may complain their mate with ASD does not notice droopy plants that need watering or a special outfit they wear. These challenges may reflect problems with phasic orienting.

Conversation activities from the ADOS as well as clinical observations to the examiner's verbal efforts to build rapport can shed light on the participant's response to novel auditory stimuli. If a verbally fluent participant fails to comment appropriately or at all when the topic of conversation changes, even in the absence of emotional content, it may be indicative of a fundamental impairment in phasic orienting. The Cancellation and Symbol Search subtests combine with other measures to assist in assessing focused attention skills more generally. The Comprehensive Trail Making Test may yield valuable information on the participant's distractibility to various visual stimuli.

The voluntary maintenance of alertness in the absence of immediate reinforcement is called *sustained attention*. Sustained attention increases rapidly from 2 to 6 months of age (Richards, 1997); and then increases significantly again from 3 to 6 years of age; continuing to develop into late childhood and adolescence, and reaching adult-like levels around 12 years of age (Lin, Hsiao, & Chen, 1999). Deficits in sustaining attention are often present within the population of individuals with ASD and, when present, warrant the added diagnosis of AD/HD either Inattentive or Combined Type. Sustained attention can be assessed directly via continuous performance testing (CPT) using the TOVA or Gordon. Subjective rating scales can be helpful; completed by parents, teachers, and individuals, including: BASC-2 or Conners' AD/HD scales or the CBCL. Continuous performance testing measures are advantageous for providing computer captured reaction time, variations in reaction time as well as errors of omission and commission. While rating scales are clearly influenced by the perceptions of the rater, they do afford the possibility of obtaining information about the participant in other environments beyond the testing room.

Attention Recommendations

Strategies to boost or calm alertness in the face of hypo- or hyper-arousal, respectively, could include the following: sensory integration therapy, a rich sensory diet to improve bottom-up responsiveness to external stimuli, removal of irrelevant stimuli to reduce distractibility, having a consistent and predictable schedule to reduce uncertainty which may heighten arousal, and therapies to promote calming or soothing techniques. These calming techniques might include deep breathing, frequent breaks, and sensory activities often involving deep pressure. Further treatments might include cognitive and behavioral therapies to promote top-down goal-directed activities and responses. Pharmacological therapies may also be considered for problems with hypo- or hyper-arousal (Ozonoff & Corbett et al., 2009). Clearly, stimulant medications are likely to enhance arousal while benzodiazepines, neuro-leptic medications, or antihypertensive drugs, for example, would be expected to reduce arousal levels. A psychiatrist can best advise individuals interested in considering these biophysiological strategies.

Strategies to boost weak or deficient phasic alerting are likely to focus on enhancing the relevant behavioral or environmental cues. Parents and teachers of children with ASD who have problems with phasic orienting should be aware that they are likely to require multiple visual and/or auditory prompts to respond to relevant or novel changes in the environment. Text books or reading material that employs bold print to highlighted vocabulary words or side bars to emphasize key concepts may be especially helpful to such individuals. Spouses, partners, or roommates may choose to adopt patient and deliberate strategies to orient their loved ones attention to important environmental cues to avoid being disappointed or incensed when special details are repeatedly overlooked.

Strategies to improve sustained attention skills include consideration of pharmacological therapies mentioned above as well as behavioral therapies and environmental modifications. Behavioral strategies can take on many dimensions from provision of tangible or social positive reinforcement designed to boost arousal and enhance learning as well as self-awareness and self-monitoring strategies to build skills in reviewing performance or scanning the environment. Environmental modifications include simplification of work or domestic settings to minimize clutter that could otherwise be distracting as well as implementing regular and frequent breaks to provide opportunities for movement or selective sensory stimulation to boost arousal and improve attention. Histogram data from the TOVA or other CPT task can suggest the maximum duration the individual is likely to be able to sustain attention for before they begin to miss information, respond impulsively, or attend sporadically.

Orienting Network

Shifting Attention

Posner, Walker, Friedrich, and Rafal (1984) defined visuospatial orienting as disengaging, shifting, and reengaging attention; or more parsimoniously as *shifting attention*. While phasic alerting mechanisms respond homogeneously across the visual field, orienting visual attention involves processing over a localized area (Mangun & Hillyand, 1988). Orienting is associated with the neurotransmitter acetylcholine (ACh) and improves proportionally to ACh levels (Thiel, Zilles & Fink, 2005). Orienting efficiency increases between the ages of 4 and 7 years (Mezzacappa, 2004), however, some research indicates no improvement from age 6 to adulthood (Rueda, Fan et al., 2004).

Individuals with ASD have consistently demonstrated deficits in orienting visual attention including findings that infants later diagnosed with ASD did not orient to visual stimuli as often (Baranek, 1999), did not orient to people or their voices as frequently (Maestro et al., 2002), and did not orient to their name as often as either typical controls or a developmental disability control group (Osterling & Dawson, 1994; Osterling et al., 2002). More research also found that children and adolescents with ASD were slower to shift attention (Keehn et al., 2010). Additional research found that individuals with ASD can use volitional control to orient attention, but this skill is also atypical compared with typical peers (Haist et al., 2005).

Research on disengagement of attention as the preliminary component involved in shifting attention shows individuals with ASD exhibit significantly increased latencies to disengage visual attention compared with matched children with Down syndrome or typical development (Landry & Bryson, 2004). In other words, children with ASD do not efficiently shift attention. Alarmingly, studies of infants at high risk for developing ASD, because of an older sibling with ASD, found that every single child that exhibited increased difficulties disengaging attention between 6 and 12 months received an ASD diagnosis at 24 months (Zwaigenbaum et al., 2005). Not all results are consistent yet it appears that disengagement of attention in ASD, when present, persists across the life span.

Problems shifting attention are readily assessed as part of a comprehensive evaluation. ADOS tasks including Response to Name, Initiating Joint Attention and Responding to Joint Attention clearly involve disengaging and shifting attention skills in both the auditory and visual domains. *Joint attention* is a three-part process involving engaging attention to an object of interest, shifting attention to another person, and then shifting back to the object for the purpose of socially connecting with someone about the object. Further assessment of the ability to shift attention can be gathered through additional ecologically valid approaches including observing the participant's response to the examiner's introduction in the waiting room, the examiner's interruption to resume testing following a snack or break, as well as transitions between different testing tasks. Parent and teacher reports or concerns from other family members also provide valuable information about the individual's skills for shifting attention in response to visual or auditory stimuli.

Often challenges shifting attention may be construed as rigidity, poor transitions, and/or perseveration on preferred activities. While these characteristics may apply, deficits in shifting attention are likely primordial. Specifically, it is likely that the individual will still exhibit problems shifting attention even if an adult interrupts carrying balloons or ice cream or some other highly desired object. In addition, many loving parents routinely complain that their child with ASD ignores them, and yet there is often a strong bond between the child and their nurturing parent. Recognizing weaknesses or deficits is especially important in reducing or eliminating academic problems because naïve teachers are rarely sympathetic to students who appear to ignore their instructions and carry on doing their own thing.

Recommendations for Shifting Attention

Recommendations for individuals who exhibit problems disengaging or shifting attention involve pharmacotherapy that would target ACh levels as well as behavioral interventions which primarily emphasize antecedent strategies occurring before the desired attention shift. Such antecedent strategies include priming the participant for what to expect using a visual or textual schedule, timer, or auditory warnings such as "in 5 minutes we're going to do ___." Since individuals with ASD are known not to shift attention efficiently, it is necessary to provide extra time for them to disengage and shift to a new activity or conversation. Individuals with ASD, including those with intellectual disabilities, may especially benefit from prompts or cues in other sensory modalities including a gentle tap on the hand or shoulder to help them shift attention. Some persons with ASD seem particularly acute in attending to music. Timing a transition from an activity with the end or beginning of a musical selection may also afford a creative approach to aiding in shifting attention.

Executive Control Network

Posner and Petersen (1989) included the executive control networks in their conceptualization of attention. Clearly, many elements of executive control including set-shifting, inhibition, and working memory are relevant in any discussion on attention. These constructs are included in the discussion on Executive Functioning.

Assessing for Executive Functioning

Vignette #8 DeShawn: Executive Functioning Assessment in an Adult with Romantic Relationship Challenges

DeShawn is a 30-year-old man previously diagnosed with depression who was referred for an evaluation for an Autism Spectrum Disorder as he was having self-reported difficulty at home. DeShawn is married and has an interest in music. He and his wife play together in a band and occasionally socialize with bandmates and other musicians in quiet settings. DeShawn relies on his wife to plan and organize their life including paying bills, shopping, and planning social and musical engagements. She feels he struggles to provide her with emotional support though he is a calm and trustworthy husband. DeShawn is a software engineer by trade and reports feeling successful at work though he keeps to himself and does not really know his coworkers well. He often needs to write things down at work to remember his daily schedule and addresses the projects one at a time (Table 11.2).

DeShawn met criteria on the ADOS-2 for ASD. In light of the model presented in Chap. 7, evaluators decided to pursue additional tests beyond the Core Areas of cognitive, language, social, and sensory, based on the results of the assessment of core areas; as well as, the findings during the initial consult. Thus, examiners also

Table 11.2 Assessing for executive functioning

Associated area
2. Executive functions
• *Inhibition*: difficulty getting individuals with ASD to stop preferred activities and transition to another less preferred activity (do not inhibit their desire to focus on other activities)
• *Planning*: complex cognitive skill requiring the identification and organization of steps toward a goal (often difficult for individuals with ASD)
• *Flexibility*: shifting one's response set or update cognitive strategy in response to new information
• *Working Memory*: regulates attentional and cognitive control processes to permit the simultaneous storage and processing of information while performing cognitive tasks. People with ASD struggle to manipulate stimuli compared with neurotypicals, while they can adequately store visual and verbal information
• Consider results from: BNT-2, BRIEF, CTMT, TOL-II, STROOP, PASAT, WCST, and observed ability to inhibit prepotent responses
Full measure names
Behavior Rating Inventory of Executive Functioning (BRIEF)
Boston Naming Test, Second Edition (BNT-2)
Comprehensive Trail Making Test (CTMT)
Tower of London, Second Edition (TOL-II)
Stroop Color and Word Test—Child/Adult Version
Paced Auditory Serial Addition Test (PASAT)
Wisconsin Card Sorting Test (WCST)

assessed memory, attention, and executive functioning, based on DeShawn and his wife's reported concerns. Memory and attention results were Average and DeShawn had High Average cognitive abilities on the WAIS-IV in Verbal and Nonverbal while Working Memory which was Low Average. DeShawn's processing speed was Below Average. On the CTMT, Stroop, WCST, and TOL-2, DeShawn demonstrated difficulty planning, shifting, and inhibiting his responses. Overall, results of tests of executive functioning indicate deficient skills in planning, organizing, sequencing, and problem solving.

DeShawn's performance is well below what would be predicted from his High Average vocabulary and knowledge mentioned above. His executive functioning skills are very slow, as a result of, his poor processing speed. DeShawn's skills in this area contribute to his challenges in helping his wife manage the household and in multitasking at home and at work. Therapy was suggested with a focus on addressing DeShawn's organization, planning, and problem solving, and implementing strategies to help at home. This was successful and his therapist was able to move to working with DeShawn on his emotional awareness and in providing emotional support to his wife.

Executive Functioning Assessment as It Applies to Autism

Foundations and Assessment of Executive Functioning

The term executive function (EF) is a vague concept referring to a multitude of self-directed cognitive processes (Barkley, 1998, 2006; Barkley & Lombroso, 2000). EF comprises a set of complex cognitive skills believed to be mediated by frontal lobe brain structures including inhibition, fluency, planning, flexibility, cognitive control, and working memory. In short, EF can be defined as neurocognitive processes that uphold an appropriate problem-solving set to attain a later goal. As such, these skills are integrally involved in successfully working toward a goal and are usually, though not always, compromised in individuals with Autism Spectrum Disorders. Indeed, many have postulated that executive functioning impairment plays a primary causal role in the manifestation of ASD.

Indication of possible weakness or impairment in executive functioning can be gleaned from parent, teacher, or spouse reports that the individual does not initiate important tasks without being told, that they cannot finish tasks on their own, they don't know how to use their time wisely, they are rigid or intolerant of others' ideas, or they can perform only one activity at a time. While these complaints can also be present in an individual with an attention deficit, executive functioning impairment is not just a problem getting distracted. Additionally, it is not surprising that these problems sound similar to someone who may have AD/HD because both impairment in sustained attention and executive functioning impairment appear to implicate some compromise of the prefrontal cortex.

Individuals with ASD are more likely to have certain EF deficits than others which may be spared these challenges. In addition, there is evidence that EF-related problems worsen with age in the individuals with ASD as assessed by parent report (Rosenthal et al., 2013). By including measures of executive functioning in the assessment, it is possible to determine which skills are impacted and to what degree. This information then becomes pivotal in formulating a comprehensive and effective plan for remediation, compensation, and support. As with other skills and abilities, a weakness is determined by comparing scores on EF measures with relevant results on standardized measures of intellectual ability such as the WISC-V, Stanford-Binet-V, or Differential Ability Scales-II. A weakness is identified when an EF score is more than 1 standard deviation below the overall intellectual ability as reflected in a Full Scale IQ (FSIQ), Global Ability Index (GAI), or General Conceptual Ability (GCA) score on the Differential Ability Scales, as appropriate (see assessment of Intellectual Ability for further discussion on assessing overall cognitive ability).

It should be noted that if an individual has Borderline or Deficient intellectual ability as reflected by a FSIQ below 70–80 (and associated adaptive impairments), it may not be possible to quantify EF skills precisely because the individual likely lacks the language or reading skills necessary to understand the instructions and complete most measures of EF. For such individuals with overall low cognitive abilities, it can be accurately assumed that they will also have low or deficient EF skills and recommendations for EF weaknesses would likely be appropriate.

EF skills can be temporally conceptualized in a related order, outlining the skills involved in successfully progressing toward a goal. Comprehensive assessment of executive functions can clarify intact skills and identify skill deficits. Accurate and specific assessment of EF is necessary to effectively remediate or compensate skills so that an individual can be successful in completing tasks. The following discussion lists skills typically included within the realm of executive functioning, including different measures which tap these skills, and reviewing characteristic patterns of results for individuals with ASD.

Inhibition

Weakness or deficiencies in inhibition can be the cause of problems stopping a preferred activity because such cessation requires inhibition of responding. Examples include refraining from studying the designs on the floor when a student is supposed to be doing homework, refraining from tapping on the table at mealtime, or refraining from only talking only about football scores in a conversation. Weaknesses in inhibition can be detected on a variety of tests and subscales including but not limited to the Color-Word score on the Stroop Color and Word Test (Stroop), the Kiddie Stroop (Russell, Jarrold, & Hood, 1999) and commission errors on the Test of Variables of Attention (TOVA). Furthermore, inhibition can be categorized into prepotent and flanker visual inhibition, as well as proactive interference as discussed below.

One type of inhibition pertains to the capacity to refrain from responding in a prepotent manner in any mode of sensory output including speech, motor movement, or visual regard. A prepotent response is one that is notably stronger or more instinctive than other responses. Research indicates that individuals with ASD do not typically have problems inhibiting a prepotent response compared to neurotypical individuals when the stimuli are either words or numbers. Inhibition of prepotent responses can be assessed with either the Stroop Color-Word subscale or a modified version of the Stroop using incongruent and congruent numbers. In these tasks, the participant is asked to say the color of the printed ink used for an incongruent color word (e.g., "blue"; answer "red") or say the number of typed digits which is incongruent with the number used to type the digits (e.g., "33"; answer "2"). The Stroop, or modified Stroop can be used to assess problems with prepotent inhibition. It has been argued that inhibition deficits are evident in individuals with ASD when rules are arbitrary and must be verbally encoded (Eigsti, 2011). Neither of these conditions are true in the Stroop, hence a hypothesis why individuals with ASD usually exhibit intact inhibitory skills on this task.

Research using flanker visual tasks with individuals with ASD indicates weaknesses or deficits in inhibition of responding to irrelevant stimuli that is visually placed on the side of target stimuli. Specifically, individuals with ASD were unable to disregard "fish" depicted as "<" or ">" signs that were laterally adjacent to target fish located in the center of a set of five fish (e.g., "<<><<" was often erroneously read as "<" for the target center fish). These research results suggest individuals with ASD may have difficulty disregarding other visual flanker stimuli (Christ, Kester, Bodner, & Miles, 2011).

Process analysis of performance on tasks like the Digit Span or Cancellation subscales of the Wechsler intelligence tests, both of which present lateral rows of visual stimuli, may be helpful in assessing flanker visual inhibition skills. Careful review of item responses could provide qualitative information as to whether the participant responded to irrelevant lateral stimuli thereby deducing possible problems with flanker visual inhibition. Clearly, more measures developed to assess flanker inhibition would be helpful.

Assessment of inhibition can be assessed with the T.O.V.A. Commission error score. On this go/no-go task, an individual is asked to inhibit responding to a box appearing in the bottom of a square on the computer screen yet push a button when the box appears in the top of the square. This measure of motor disinhibition is characteristically used to assess impulsive responding in individuals suspected of having AD/HD. It can similarly be used to assess motor inhibition skills in participants suspected of having ASD. The TOVA is a nice addition to the assessment battery not just to assess inhibition but also to evaluate for difficulties sustaining attention associated with possible comorbid AD/HD. Note that a comprehensive guide for assessing comorbid AD/HD and ASD is included in Chap. 13. The combination of significant disinhibition and poor social reciprocity generally indicates comorbid diagnosis of ASD and AD/HD is warranted.

Interesting research on an emotional go/no-go task using emotional versus neutral facial expressions (Yerys, Kenworthy, Jankowski, Strang, & Wallace, 2013) found individuals with autism were notably faster in responding to the emotional go items compared with typical individuals and participants with AD/HD. Individuals with ASD were more impulsive on these stimuli than typical individuals on both emotional and neutral faces. These intriguing results suggest differences in inhibition as well as speed of processing emotional stimuli which could shed valuable light on significant characteristics relating to affective responding in social interactions; as well as, potentially the increased frequency or intensity of tantrums often seen with ASD.

A third type of inhibition pertains to the capacity to inhibit proactive interference of information recently stored in memory. Examples of proactive memory interference come from verbal list-learning tasks like the Rey Auditory Verbal Learning Test (RAVLT) or California Verbal Learning Test (CVLT) or similar word list-learning tests that include an "interference" trial. List-learning tasks typically consist of a list of 8 or 12 words (depending on the participant's age) which are read aloud to the participants who are aware they will have to say the words back from memory. The "interference" trial consists of the same number of semantically related but different words that are read after about five trials of the target words. Assessment of proactive interference is determined from how well the participant can inhibit recall of the target words which were initially read five times. Research indicates that individuals with ASD do not evidence any more difficulty with proactive interference than neurotypical individuals. Administration of such a list-learning task can assess if the individual with ASD indeed follows predictable patterns of proactive inhibition or, rather, evidences uncharacteristic intrusive errors.

Planning

Planning is a complex cognitive skill which requires the identification and organization of steps toward a goal. It is most commonly assessed using the Tower of London (TOL-2) or Tower of Hanoi (TOH) tests. These tests require the participant to manipulate colored balls (TOL-2) or discs (TOH) on pegs one at a time from the same start position to create visually depicted target patterns of increasing difficulty within a time limit. Individuals with ASD frequently have difficulty with planning. These authors have noted that individuals with ASD often demonstrate a rigid problem-solving style, and will "get stuck" on trials during completion of these measures.

Incorporation of planning measures in the evaluation can assess for possible deficits in planning; but also, may provide more detailed information on how and where deficits occur for the individual tested. For example, results on the TOL-2 consist of several variables including total initiation time (time to get started), total problem-solving time, total move score (number of moves taken), total items correct, as well as scores of time and rule violations. Different score results combined with clinical observations made during the administration can yield valuable information for characterizing the individual's planning skills as well as assessing for possible comorbid conditions often seen in autism. Examples of these patterns are outlined in Table 11.3.

Table 11.3 Tower of London-2 planning and problem solving

Weak or deficient score	Challenges suggested
Low total correct score	Weak or deficient problem-solving ability with visual/spatial tasks or high anxiety
Brief total initiation time score	Impulsive; could suggest comorbid AD/HD
High-time violation score with good total correct score	Slow processing speed or Motor Coordination Disorder but intact problem-solving ability
High total rule violation score	Oppositional Defiant Disorder or disinhibition (possible problem with working memory)
High total move score with good total correct score	Inefficient planning but persistent response style

By analyzing process information and specific patterns of scores, much information about the individual's problem-solving skills as well as potential comorbidity can be gleaned from instruments measuring planning which is expected to be difficult for people with ASD.

Flexibility

Flexibility pertains to the ability to "shift" one's response set or update one's cognitive strategy in response to information in the environment. Flexibility is also often referred to as "set-shifting." The term flexibility is used here as it may be more digestible for parents and other healthcare professionals for whom evaluation reports are primarily written. The term flexibility is familiar and readily understood by most whereas set-shifting sounds a bit technical or confusing.

The most common measure of flexibility is the Wisconsin Card Sorting Test (WCST). The WCST consists of four target cards to which the participant is asked to match a deck of cards (64 or 128) based on either the shape pictured, the number of shapes pictured, or the color of those shapes. After each match (card placed) the participant is given simple feedback regarding whether his or her match was "correct" or "incorrect." The goal is for the participant to deduce the correct criteria for matching the cards (by color, form, and then number of shapes). The participant is further tested on the ability to maintain the correct match criteria for ten consecutive matches; after which, the criteria changes without warning. Upon completion of another ten successful matches based on the current criteria, the participant will again have to deduce the new criteria using only the simple feedback about the success of his or her matches.

Several studies have shown impairments on the WCST in autism across a variety of ages. Impairment is especially evident in perseverate responding whereby the individual, despite adequate intelligence, continues to match their cards using color, form, or number of shapes, despite receiving repeated feedback that the responses are incorrect. Such perseverate responding may be rooted in deficits in inhibition discussed above; or rather, such a pattern is consistent with the rigidity or lack of flexibility often observed in autism. This task can be administered in the traditional manner, with an examiner, or a computerized version is also available. Interestingly, some research indicates less impairment in participants with ASD relative to typical control subjects on the computerized version suggesting alternate forms of the WCST may not be equivalent for this group (Ozonoff, 1995). These findings hint that individuals with ASD perform better on cognitive tasks when human interaction is minimized or eliminated which is what parents and caregivers often report. These results are consistent with the user surveys for examiners who use the iPad format for IQ tests, called Q-interactive; finding that generally children with ASD preferred the electronic format. The precise reason for these differences is unclear; however, if participants lack the social drive and motivation to attend to verbal feedback provided in the context of a social interaction, they may prefer the visual feedback from the computer screen or electronic device.

Administration of the WCST can provide valuable information about the individual in a number of domains in addition to flexibility. An individual can be assessed with regard to their reaction to "incorrect" responses. Some rigid individuals may have extreme reactions or immediately refuse to continue. It is also possible to assess the degree to which they are motivated to respond to social feedback versus continuing to respond in a perseverative manner. It is interesting to note if the child continues with wrong responses despite often vocalizing an alternate correct matching strategy. This demonstrates in effect, the individual's ability to "hold-set" versus "losing-set" (answering correctly three times in a row but then matching incorrectly). Difficulties with losing set suggest problems with working memory. The other area that this test allows for consideration is how persistent an individual with ASD is when the environmental contingencies keep unpredictably changing.

Working Memory

Working memory has been construed in a variety of ways over the past three decades and can be included in EF skills. It is also, reasonably included within the topics of attention or memory because of the involvement with learning. Working memory (WM) can be described as the skill that regulates attentional and cognitive control processes to permit the simultaneous storage and processing of information while performing cognitive tasks (Eigsti, de Marchena, Schuh, & Kelley, 2011). Others have described it as following closely behind inhibition and alongside analysis and synthesis of information as essential elements involving in sustaining attention (Barkley, 2006). Working memory can also be divided into verbal input or nonverbal input. In either case, working memory involves brief retention and processing of information (less than 2 min) compared with short-term and long-term memory which typically refer to retention of input for at least 2 or 20 min, respectively.

When considering individuals with ASD, it is valuable to separate simple WM tasks from complex WM tasks because research supports the latter being significantly more challenging for this population (Gabig, 2008). Specifically, it appears that participants with ASD can adequately store both visual and verbal information that is not overly complex but struggle to manipulate even simple stimuli compared with neurotypical controls. This finding of deficits in storage of complex information may seem at odds with family members' report of the child's excellent memory for movie scripts, navigation routes to favorite places, or photographic memory in artwork. Such examples, however, more aptly describe recall of highly preferred information from long-term storage which has probably been repetitively rehearsed either overtly (as in echoic language) or covertly. Another reasonable hypothesis for how a person with ASD manages to perfectly recall more complex information (such as the DFW airport configuration) after only a single presentation of stimuli likely has to do with flashbulb memory phenomena whereby the individual with ASD will indeed accurately recall more complex information when it is highly emotionally salient *for them* in the same way we can likely visually recall the twin towers crumbling on 9/11 even after a single video exposure. Note also that exceptional recall of highly preferred material, even if complex, does not involve manipulation of the information. The point to understand here is that even though individuals with ASD may have strong long-term memory skills for certain preferred topics, their working memory is often impaired.

Individuals with ASD have also characteristically been found to have deficits in facial processing and young children with ASD statistically fix their eye gaze more on the mouth of a speaker rather than their eyes (Zwaigenbaum et al., 2005). The reason for this may be the fact that a person's mouth moves when one speaks (similar to a cause-and-effect toy) compared with someone's eyes which predominantly convey emotional content. Considering that brief storage and manipulation of facial expressions is impaired in ASD, and bearing in mind that nonvocal cues are essential in proper encoding and interpretation of social exchanges; it stands to reason that establishing and maintaining more intimate relationships is consistently challenging for this population. While faces indeed involve complex visual information, fMRI research has found evidence of neural connectivity differences indicating individuals with ASD process facial features more as objects and less in terms of their human significance (Koshino et al., 2008). These important neurophysiological findings offer further insight as to why family members of persons with ASD often lament feeling more like an object to be managed rather than a person who's emotionally understood and cared about.

In contrast to the limited number of other EF measures, there exist many tests of both simple and complex working memory in visual and verbal domains. Note again that simple working memory tasks typically involve brief storage of information while complex tasks typically involve both storage and manipulation—or storage of complex information. Several working memory assessment measures and scales are outlined in Table 11.4.

Table 11.4 Scales assessing working memory

Assessment measure	Verbal scales	Visual scales
Simple working memory tasks assessing brief storage		
Wechsler Intelligence Scales	Digits Forward	
California Verbal Learning Tests (CVLT-2)	Trial 1	
Rey Auditory Verbal Learning Test (RAVLT)	Trial 1	
Mullen Scales of Early Learning		Visual Memory items within the Visual Reception Scale
Differential Abilities Scales (DAS-II)		Copying (also assesses Visual Spatial and Fine Motor skills)
Comprehensive Trail Making Tests		Trails 1–4
Wechsler Memory Scale	Logical Memory I, Verbal Paired Associates I	Designs I, Visual Reproduction I
Complex working memory tasks assessing brief complex storage or mental manipulation		
Wechsler Intelligence Scales	Digits Backward, Letter Number Sequencing, Arithmetic	
Clinical Evaluation of Language Fundamentals (CELF)	Recalling Sentences, Concepts and Following Directions	
Test of Memory and Learning (TOMAL-2)		Facial Memory, Visual Selective Reminding
Rey Complex Figure		Immediate Recall
Wechsler Memory Scale	Logical Memory II, Verbal Paired Associates II	Spatial Addition, Symbol Span, Designs II, Visual Reproduction II

Assessing for Memory

Vignette #8 Kimmy: Memory Assessment in an Adult Enrolling in College Courses

Kimmy, age 19, was referred for a reevaluation of ASD symptoms for educational planning as she made the transition to college. Memory, attention, and cognitive functioning were of interest to Kimmy as she worked to understand her own neuropsychological profile. Kimmy had been diagnosed at 15 with ASD after having social interaction difficulties that became particularly traumatizing her freshman year of high school. Kimmy reported significant anxiety, particularly in social situations and she felt overwhelmed during her first semester of college, so she dropped her classes and decided to take a year off of school before re-enrolling (Table 11.5).

Kimmy demonstrated a WAIS-IV General Ability Index in the Very Superior range, Standard Score 146, with Very Superior Verbal Abilities and Superior Nonverbal Reasoning. Her RAVLT score fell in the Superior range suggesting

Table 11.5 Assessing for memory

Associated area
3. *Memory*
• *Short-Term Memory*: ability to hold information for immediate or short-term retrieval
• *Long-Term Memory*: skills involving longer term storage (over 20 minutes) and retrieval of information - can be strengthened by associating information from short-term memory with background information, semantic memory, and cultural knowledge
• Consider results on: CVLT-II, RAVLT, RCFT, TOMAL, WMS-IV, WMI on cognitive tests
Full measure names
California Verbal Learning Test, Second Edition (CVLT-II)
Rey Auditory Verbal Learning Test (RAVLT)
Rey Complex Figure Test and Recognition Trial (RCFT)
Test of Memory and Learning (TOMAL)
Wechsler Memory Scale, Fourth Edition (WMS-IV)
Working Memory Scales on cognitive testing

advanced skills in learning and memory. These skills were confirmed with the WMS-IV Long-term and Immediate Memory scores across verbal and visual domains. Kimmy presented with Low Average to Average visual and auditory working memory assessed by the WAIS-IV and WMS-IV. She confirmed that she learns with repetition and really needs to take her time with new material. Kimmy also has Average processing speed which contrasts with her Very Superior abilities in many domains. She plans to enroll in classes soon and wishes to become a professor perhaps in a science field like genetics.

Kimmy understands that once she is able to learn new information, she retains it very well. Her weaknesses in working memory indicate that she has intermittent challenges with attention and needs adequate time to read and learn new material. She particularly benefits from a chance to dialogue with professors and ask questions as she processes. Kimmy has a tendency to be a perfectionist and to be hard on herself. She has learned that this contributes to academic struggles. Kimmy was pleasantly surprised to learn how advanced her General Ability and her long-term memory skills are. She continues to work on anxiety in CBT sessions with her therapist and plans to re-enroll in classes in the winter.

Memory Assessment as It Applies to Autism

Assessment of memory for individuals with ASD is very important as memory is fundamental to learning, and some form of learning is always challenging for people with ASD. Based on the neuropsychological areas known to be compromised in ASD, some characteristic patterns of memory strengths and weaknesses are likely. Weaknesses include memory for complex information (Williams, Goldstein, & Minshew, 2006), spatial working memory, relational memory (Maister, Simons, & Plaisted-Grant, 2013), episodic memory, and time-based prospective memory.

Memory strengths in ASD often include rote learning particularly for highly preferred visual or verbal information such as movie scripts, routes to favorite destinations, logos, and other information that may frequently be repeated like class rosters or the pledge of allegiance. Additional memory strengths can include semantic memory, associate learning, verbal working memory, and recognition memory. Memory taxonomy and characteristic profiles are discussed further below.

It is important to differentiate memory skills for people with ASD who have comorbid intellectual disability compared with those with ASD and not ID. Research supports fundamental differences in memory skills between these two subgroups. Unfortunately, much research needs to be done particularly for individuals with lower intellectual abilities as these persons are often underrepresented in study samples. While generalities frequently apply, it is important to carefully assess memory for each individual client or student to discern his or her unique profile. In some instances, memory measures require significant executive functioning skills (such as the Wechsler digits backward subscale or the Wechsler Memory scale spatial addition subtest) and a participant can score poorly on the measure because of weak EF skills rather than weak memory. Reviewing results on EF measures alongside results on memory assessments will aid in interpreting both neuropsychological aspects of functioning. Often, the amount and quality of intervention received can also alter memory skills beyond what would be predicted given their age and diagnosis. These and other factors discussed below should be considered when interpreting results on memory measures.

Unfortunately any discussion on memory quickly dissolves into a jargon soup seasoned with all kinds of terms that are easily confusing to anyone but the mature memory researcher. To aide in understanding memory as it applies to ASD, a brief description of important terms is provided here. The first distinction to be drawn is between verbal and visual memory as these two types of information directly map onto separate and discrete brain regions. Review of verbal and visual memory assessment performance should stem from consideration of the individual's verbal and perceptual or nonverbal intellectual abilities previously discussed noting consistencies or discrepancies where they occur. Specifically, verbal memory skills should generally be commensurate with scores predicted from verbal intellectual abilities. Similarly, visual memory skills should generally be commensurate with nonverbal intellectual abilities. However, memory weaknesses can result from anxiety, depression, and fatigue as well as other factors. From verbal and visual memory, taxonomy of memory readily branches into terms that describe the duration of storage and the psychology underlying what's being encoded.

Memory Taxonomy and ASD

Working memory is the shortest duration of information storage and the term primarily pertains to short-term maintenance, manipulation, and use of the information in thinking and reasoning (Boucher & Mayes, 2012). Working memory is implicated in successful inhibition necessary for sustaining attention as well as believed to play an important role in executive functions; hence, it is often included in discussions of the latter construct. Working memory for auditory information is assessed directly in the Wechsler Digits, Letter-Number, and Arithmetic subtests. Research on high functioning individuals with ASD generally reveals that verbal working memory appears to be predominantly intact (Ozonoff & Strayer, 2001; Pennington et al., 1997); however, impairments in visuospatial working memory have been identified in most studies (Minshew, Luna, & Sweeney, 1999; Steele, Minshew, Luna, & Sweeney, 2007). Individuals with ASD and comorbid AD/HD may well have deficits in both verbal and visual working memory and assessment can discern if this is the case. Working memory is believed to be fundamental to the ability to inhibit responding and sustain attention as is well described by Barkley.

Long-term memory pertains to information that is successfully encoded and retained for at least 20 or 30 min. Types of long-term memory skills are assessed in numerous measures that involve assessment of stimuli following a delay. Long-term memory can be further subdivided according to Tulving's (1984) taxonomy into *procedural memory* (involved in the acquisition of sensorimotor and cognitive skills and habits), *perceptual memory* (for discrete single items), *semantic memory* (for factual information including word meanings), and *episodic memory* (for unique events experienced by the individual). Sometimes, semantic and episodic memories are combined into declarative (explicit) memory verses nondeclarative memory combining perceptual and procedural memory. Noting the challenges of individuals with ASD in encoding and recalling personal events, some professionals characterize ASD as an explicit learning disorder. While it is true that individuals with ASD typically have weaknesses or impairment in explicit memory, such a simplistic conceptualization fails to describe the pervasiveness of ASD involving so many other areas of functioning as discussed in this text.

Research findings suggest that most but not all forms of nondeclarative memory are unimpaired in people with high-functioning ASD (Boucher, Mayes, & Bigham, 2012). Procedural memory also includes simple conditioning, however, and there is evidence that fear conditioning and memory for emotionally significant material generally is impaired among all individuals with ASD (Gaigg & Bowler, 2008). Relatively intact procedural memory in individuals with ASD is frequently capitalized on in effective intervention techniques. *Strategies for procedural memory include:* error-free learning, physical guidance, and hand-over-hand procedures, whereby a therapist ensures successful completion of a skill by assisting the individual with ASD in actually moving through the activity.

Long-term declarative recognition for either visual or verbal stimuli has been shown to be relatively intact in individuals with high-functioning ASD (Boucher & Mayes, 2012). One study that showed superior skills in recognizing pictures in ASD (Blair, Frith, Smith, Abell, & Cipolotti, 2002). Indeed superior visual recognition memory skills are likely involved in those individuals with ASD who demonstrate precocious skills in letter recognition as well as hyperlexia. Similarly, studies show superior memory for the physical, as opposed to semantic, characteristics of words involved in word recognition (Toichi, 2008; Toichi & Kamio, 2002).

This phenomenon of relatively strong visual declarative memory seems inevitably involved when an assessment participant obtains significantly higher scores on reading accuracy or reading fluency compared with reading comprehension. These specific comprehension problems in ASD are well founded in the research (Huemer & Mann, 2009; Mayes & Calhoun, 2007; O'Connor & Klein, 2004; Snowling & Frith, 1986; Tager-Flusberg, 2006; Willard, 2013); and will be discussed more thoroughly in Chap. 18, the School-Based Assessment chapter.

Relative strengths in visual recognition for individuals with ASD do not extend to faces, however. Numerous researchers have demonstrated impaired recognition of previously unfamiliar faces (Boucher & Mayes, 2012), and the visual complexity of faces seems relevant in these findings for individuals with ASD. In addition, research on very young children who go on to develop ASD shows that very often such toddlers are actually looking more at peoples' mouths rather than their eyes when listening to others speak (as previously described). Clearly, such differences in the attentional focus of these toddlers' influences what the youngsters encode as well as their brain development for processing facial information generally.

In memory recall tasks, distinction between "cued" versus "free" is typically drawn even though all recall memory tasks are essentially "cued" in some way through prior experiences and learning. Individuals with ASD typically do best on tasks of recalling supraspan lists of unrelated items such as everyday pictures or single words (Boucher & Mayes, 2012). These memory strengths are generally evident on both immediate and delayed memory tasks (Minshew & Goldstein, 1993, 2001; Williams, Goldstein, & Minshew, 2006). On recall tasks of supraspan word lists, weaknesses in semantic declarative memory are again often evident as individuals with ASD group words idiosyncratically compared with neurotypical participants. Individuals with ASD do not evidence improved primacy effect on word list tasks; whereby the words at the beginning of the list would increasingly be better recalled (Bowler, Gaigg, & Gardiner, 2009). The Wechsler Information subtest performance can provide further information on free recall of overlearned factual information. Overall, however, free recall, especially for semantically or syntactically structured verbal material, is somewhat fragile for individuals with ASD.

High-functioning individuals with ASD are generally better on cued-recall tasks involving provision of a letter or category (Boucher & Mayes, 2012). This fact can obviously be capitalized on in recommendations for improved academic performance including keywords or topic outlines to facilitate oral or written expression. On tasks requiring recall of the source of information, people with ASD typically perform poorly unless the source is available and recognizably from context. Results and patterns discerned from memory assessment can be used to determine characteristic profiles consistent with ASD and such information will likely be valuable to the participant or parents. Specifically, individuals typically like to know which of their challenges can be attributed directly to ASD symptomatology. Since memory is integral to learning, results of memory assessment should give clear guidance for recommendations to aide in skill acquisition and academic success.

Individuals with ASD and ID

Many times parents of younger children with a suspected ASD will comment to the evaluator about how smart their toddler or preschooler is. Such comments often reflect parents' observations of their seemingly precocious skills in letter-recognition, precise memory for the directions to an amusement park, or incredible recollection of dinosaur types, elevator manufacturers, or sports statistics. As always, it is important for the evaluator not to dash parents' enthusiasm even while clinicians may correctly discern the child has significant weaknesses in important academic or social domains.

Exceptional Abilities (EAs): When meeting with families who have a child with ASD and ID, the use of the term "splinter skills" is strongly discouraged by these authors. The term is antiquated and implies children or individuals with ASD are not worthy of having their talents appropriately labelled as such. A splinter is a term applied to something made of wood and individuals with ASD are people not forestry products. These authors prefer the term "exceptional abilities" or *"EAs"* which more adequately characterizes some of the unique and amazing skills individuals with ASD may have in a variety of areas. Although these *EAs* are not shown in the research to be common in the general population of ASD, sometimes individuals with ASD may show *Exceptional Abilities* in art, math, music, science, or architecture. Clinicians are well advised to support parents in celebrating, cherishing, and capitalizing on these *Exceptional Abilities.*

As with higher functioning individuals with ASD, people with substantially lower cognitive ability (lower functioning) also exhibit strength in nondeclarative memory and procedural learning (Gordon & Stark, 2007). In fact, some research indicates that individuals with ASD in this more cognitively compromised group rely on procedural learning to an unusual extent (Russell, Jarrold, & Hood, 1999) and that learning through conditioning is also intact (with an exception for emotion-related conditioning). When it comes to research on memory span in ASD, findings show intact skills in immediate serial recall of digits, use of verbal rehearsal to aid recall, and use of visual shaped cues to order a sequence (Boucher & Mayes, 2012). When it comes to memory recognition, provisional research suggests fragile skills in this area for lower-functioning individuals compared with their cognitively stronger ASD peers (Boucher & Mayes, 2012).

Recognition skills can be further compromised for individuals with ASD through the introduction of a delay or increased complexity of the material presented. Specifically on tasks of free recall, there is evidence of intact or improved recency effects whereby the individual better recalls items presented later in a sequence combined with reduced primacy effects. Furthermore, some research indicates potential for improved recall through handling of items to be remembered (Summers & Craik, 1994). Intact procedural memory and improved recall through handling items are similar in that they capitalize on sensorimotor input of stimuli rather than verbal input which is likely a weak area for individuals with ASD and lower cognitive abilities. Consistent with likely weakness for verbal material, recall was found not to be improved by semantic meaningfulness or syntactic structure for this subgroup and they tended not to use a clustering strategy in recall (Tager-Flusberg, 1991). This research is consistent with all of the comprehension challenges often seen for individuals with ASD (Huemer & Mann, 2009; Mayes & Calhoun, 2007; O'Connor & Klein, 2004; Snowling & Frith, 1986; Tager-Flusberg, 2006; Willard, 2013). Delayed recall for all types of material including personally experienced events has also been found for individuals with ASD and lower cognitive skills (Boucher & Mayes, 2012). Finally, a relative memory strength has been found on tasks involving recently cued recall using words (Tager-Flusberg, 1991), shapes, non-meaningful features, or actions to prompt recall (Hare, Mellor, & Azmi, 2007).

Overall, memory patterns for individuals with ASD and lower cognitive abilities are commensurate with their deficient language development leading to weak semantic memory. Still other memory challenges such as episodic learning, emotion-related conditioning, and weak or impaired recall of personally experienced events remain common to all individuals with ASD. Strengths in procedural learning, cued recall, and generally intact short-term memory are important to capitalize on for these more cognitively challenged individuals with ASD. In cases where assessment results concur with strengths in these areas for a particular individual, the astute clinician should be sure to include corresponding recommendations to promote use of strategies such as verbal rehearsal and tactile or visual cues to aide in learning and academic performance.

Individuals with ASD and IQ Over 70

Characteristic patterns of memory strengths and weaknesses in individuals with ASD and Verbal IQ greater than a standard score of 70, in many cases, parallel the patterns of other neuropsychological skills seen in these individuals. For example, it is recognized that individuals with ASD often have difficulty shifting attention (discussed in Attention) and, similarly, their memory for complex verbal and visual information represents a relative weakness (Williams, Goldstein, & Minshew, 2006).

These tasks seemingly require simultaneous mental processes such as tasks requiring shifting attention. "Children with ASD do not use organizational strategies or context to support memory" (Williams et al., 2006, p. 21) resulting in increased difficulty remembering complex information including stories, pictures, and faces. Weakness or inability to use context hurts the participant's capacity to preactivate related concepts and schemas which could otherwise aide in verbal memory of complex information. These memory difficulties for complex verbal information could manifest in tasks such as a Story Memory task (on the Woodcock-Johnson Tests of Achievement or the Wide Range Assessment of Memory and Learning), where the participant has to recall elements of a story immediately after hearing it and then following a 20 or 30 min delay. On such tasks, the stories are novel and less likely to pertain to the participant's area of interest. Often times, the results on story memory are significantly below what would be predicted from their verbal IQ or receptive language skills. Sometimes, participants have been observed to remember more details on the delayed trial than on the immediate recall trial as if consolidation of information improved with time. This clinical finding has apparently yet to be researched.

Difficulty remembering complex visual or verbal information is also often evident when parents routinely ask their ASD child, "How was your day?" Despite this being a high frequency question, most individuals with ASD have difficulty answering in any substantive way or, alternately, provide an unusual account or esoteric details about an experience that others are not likely to find interesting. No doubt this clinical phenomenon is related to what individuals with ASD attend to based on their interests; however, it also likely reflects a real-life (ecologically valid) account of marked difficulty remembering complex information.

Research has been done regarding how memory difficulties in individuals with ASD manifest in everyday life largely pertaining to prospective memory tasks (Jones et al., 2011; Williams, Jarrold, Grainger, & Lind, 2014). In a large study of 94 adolescents with ASD across a wide IQ span (50–119), Jones et al. (2011) found significant difficulties in event-related prospective memory (including remembering to retrieve a belonging, to inquire about an appointment, re-walk an observed route and deliver a message) compared with typically developing peers. However, later research has replicated the findings that individuals with ASD actually have more difficulty with time-related prospective events whereby they are tasked with remembering to do something at a certain time. In contrast to earlier research findings, later studies actually support the results that both children and adults with ASD are capable of event-related prospective memory tasks especially when they are able to engage in verbal rehearsal strategies (Williams et al., 2014).

It appears that citizens with ASD have particular difficulty with time-related prospective memory tasks because of difficulties with limitations on complex visual memory span as well as difficulty projecting themselves into the future consistent with theory-of-mind deficits common to ASD. Congruent with this hypothesis are findings by Jones et al. (2011) indicating an inverse relationship between prospective memory and the ADOS Social and Communication score. In addition, researchers have found that individuals with ASD are inaccurate in predicting their prospective memory ability on episodic memory tasks (Wojcik, Moulin, & Souchay, 2013). Prospective memory tasks are fairly new on the assessment front, and additional work is necessary to satisfactorily move such tasks from the research to clinical and school evaluation arenas. Nonetheless, it is possible to assess visual memory storage capacity through a variety of measures for children (WRAML or TOMAL), adolescents, and adults (Rey Complex Figure or WMS).

Studies have assessed correlations between language skills in individuals with ASDs and verbal memory (Tyson et al., 2014) with significant findings. Specifically, distinguishing features between those who lose their ASD diagnosis (Optimal Outcome) and those who are high-functioning include significant differences on the CELF Formulated Sentences subtest (a measure of expressive language production) as well as the CELF Recalling Sentences subtest (a measure of rote verbal short-term memory) and the CVLT recognition memory task. The social implications of these weaknesses in language and verbal memory should be evident as Formulated Sentences relates to making comments in conversation and Recalling Sentences relates to skills in remembering others' statements and thereby listening well. In reviewing assessment results on language and verbal memory measures, the astute clinician will draw these connections for the participant and/or their parents on how measured weaknesses relate to difficulties sustaining conversation and subsequently deepening relationships.

While the CELF-4 and the WAIS-IV/WISC-IV, discussed elsewhere in this text, provide some assessment of verbal and visual memory, more focused memory measures can provide important information particularly when memory is an area of reported difficulty. Measures like the CVLT and RAVLT are relatively brief verbal memory measures that provide useful information on auditory learning and memory for items presented in a list. Analysis of the pattern of responses on these list-learning tasks can also shed light on the individual's tendency to perseverate (repeat the same answer) or confabulate (provide responses not part of the list itself) as well as their use of memory strategies which may be revealed from spurious comments made during the test itself. Interestingly, there is some research that individuals with high-functioning ASD provide less intrusions (Tyson et al., 2014) on these list-learning tasks than typical peers consistent with challenges with verbal production. Measures that are likely to be more time consuming but provide comprehensive data on working memory, learning, and delayed memory include the WMS-IV, WRAML, and the TOMAL. The participant's memory profile can provide guidance for treatment especially as the individual gains insight about his or her memory strengths and can develop ways to cope with deficits including strategies such as verbal rehearsal, reliance on visual aids, and pairing events to be remembered with existing steps in mastered routines.

Concluding Remarks on Attention, Executive Functions, and Memory in ASD

Impairments in attention represent a significant and pervasive problem for individuals with ASD. In addition to the wide range of ASD symptoms, attention problems are multifaceted and responsible for processes that include alerting, orienting, and executive control networks (Petersen & Posner, 2012; Posner & Petersen, 1989). Impairments in these functions impact an individual's education and career achievement substantially. Executive functioning pertains to an important cluster of skills which, like attention, are mediated by the frontal lobe and include initiating, organizing, and sequencing information. In short, EF can be defined as neurocognitive processes that uphold an appropriate problem-solving set to attain a goal. As such, these skills are integrally involved in successfully working toward personal objectives. Executive functions and are usually, though not always, compromised in individuals with Autism Spectrum Disorders. Indeed, many have postulated that executive functioning impairment plays a primary causal role in the manifestation of ASD. Research on high-functioning individuals with ASD generally reveals that verbal working memory appears to be predominantly intact. However, impairments in visuospatial working memory have been found in most studies (Minshew, Luna, & Sweeney, 1999; Steele, Minshew, Luna, & Sweeney, 2007). Taken together, attention, executive functioning, and memory are often impaired in ASD, and problems in these domains present significant obstacles in educational and career endeavors. Thus, interventions designed to support individuals with ASD should be designed in consideration of remediating deficits in these areas and supporting enhanced brain functioning such that clients on the spectrum can meet personal goals and objectives and thrive in their career pursuits.

Chapter 12
Emotions, Mood, Behavior, and Adaptive Assessment

Abstract Emotional, Mood, and Adaptive Assessment are associated areas of a comprehensive evaluation for an Autism Spectrum Disorder. Emotional, mood, and behavioral diagnoses may include anxiety, depression, bipolar disorder, DMDD, and behavioral disorders to name a few. Symptoms may include restlessness, excessive worries, adherence to nonfunctional rituals, poor eye contact, minimal response to questions, slow processing speed, individuals may appear to be on the edge of tears, crying, have a sense of hopelessness, may report loneliness, suicidality, lack of interest in previously pleasurable activities, racing thoughts, pressured speech, grandiosity, flight of ideas, history of mood swings, suicidality, irritability, self-injury, explosive temper, and high risk behavior. Adaptive challenges include difficulties with daily routines, hygiene, self-care, chores, community living, and social relationships. A clinician may assess these emotional and adaptive areas using measures and interviews including the BDI-II, BASC-2, CDI, BAI, RCMAS, client or parent interview, Roberts, TAT, MMPI-2, Vineland-II, and SIB-R. By assessing these associated areas, a clinician can offer more targeted recommendations for treatment of other symptoms and conditions that may be present in an individual with ASD.

Keywords Mood in ASD • Anxiety in ASD • Behavior problems in ASD • Adaptive behavior deficits in ASD • Severity level 2: requiring substantial support • Huckabee's frozen profile • Frozen profile in ASD • Alexithymia in ASD • Functional analysis in ASD • Four conditions of functional analysis

Assessing for Emotional and Behavioral Symptoms

Vignette #9: Adam

Assessment of a Child with Mood, Anxiety, and Aggressive Behaviors
    Adam is an 8-year-old referred primarily for tantrum behaviors and aggression. He was assessed using the Wechsler Intelligence Scales for Children, 4th Edition (WISC-IV), Clinical Evaluation of Language Fundamentals, 4th Edition (CELF-4), Vineland Adaptive Behavior Scale—Parent/Caregiver Rating Form (VABS-II),

© Springer International Publishing Switzerland 2016   227
A.P. Kroncke et al., *Assessment of Autism Spectrum Disorder*, Contemporary
Issues in Psychological Assessment, DOI 10.1007/978-3-319-25504-0_12

Test of Variables of Attention (TOVA), Sensory Profile, Behavior Assessment Scales for Children, 2nd Edition (BASC-II), Parent and Teacher Reports, Social Communication Questionnaire (SCQ), Autism Diagnostic Observation Schedule, Module 3 (ADOS) Children's Depression Inventory, 2nd Edition (CDI 2), Revised Children's Manifest Anxiety Scale, 2nd Edition (RCMAS-II), Sentence Completion for Children (Table 12.1).

Table 12.1 Assessing for emotional and behavioral symptoms

Associated area
1. *Emotional/behavioral*
• *Anxiety*: behavior during testing such as performance anxiety, self-deprecating comments; display anxious movements (foot tapping, drumming fingers, shaking); may report physiological symptoms such as tummy aches, chest pain, trouble falling asleep; may report problems with restlessness, excessive worries, adherence to nonfunctional rituals
Consider BAI, BASC-2, RCMAS, client interview, PTSD Diagnostic scales, MMPI-2
• *Depression*: test behaviors such as poor eye contact, minimal response to questions, slower processing speed appear to be on the edge of tears, crying, sense of hopelessness; may report loneliness, suicidality, lack of interest in previously pleasurable activities
Consider BDI-II, BASC-2, CDI, client interview, Roberts, TAT, SCT, and MMPI-2
• *Bipolar*: racing thoughts, pressured speech, grandiosity, flight of ideas, history of mood swings, suicidality, irritability in children, self-injury, explosive temper, high risk behavior
Consider BASC (depression, hyperactivity, and aggression), BDI-II (depression)
• *Frozen Profile*: across emotional measures is a sign of ASD: Alexithymia (not identifying own emotions)
• *Behavior*: Functional Analysis and Functional Behavior Analysis, rating scales, behavior observations, questionnaires, and interviews
Consider results from BAI, BASC-II, BDI-II, CDI-II, MMPI-II, PDS, 16PF, RCMAS-II, Roberts-II, SCT, and TAT
Full measure names
Behavior Assessment System for Children, Second Edition (BASC-II), Self, Parent, and Teacher Reports
Beck Anxiety Inventory (BAI)
Beck Depression Inventory, Second Edition (BDI-II)
Children's Depression Inventory, Second Edition (CDI-2)
Minnesota Multiphasic Personality Inventory, Second Edition (MMPI-II)
Minnesota Multiphasic Personality Inventory, Adolescent (MMPI-A)
Post-Traumatic Stress Diagnostic Scale (PDS)
Revised Children's Manifest Anxiety Scale, Second Edition (RCMAS-II)
Sixteen Personality Factor Questionnaire (16PF) (Computer)
Projective measures
Rorschach
Human Figure Drawing Task
Brief Projective Measures (Animal Choice Test and Three Wishes)
Roberts, Second Edition (Roberts-II)
Thematic Apperception Test (TAT)
Sentence Completion for Children/Teens/Adults (SCT)

Adam's parents reported that he was noncompliant toward directions, had mood swings and frequent violent tantrums, and had excessive fears of thunderstorms and flushing toilets. He was reportedly aggressive toward his parent and siblings. Modifications were required to complete testing, such as sitting on the floor, receiving back scratches and back-rubs as a reward, eating small snacks, and having frequent breaks. Adam frequently cried and screamed and often asked his parents or the examiners to help him lower his hand from his face. This behavior seemed to be related to context and appeared to occur more frequently during questions that either were challenging or were emotional in nature. School and home observations indicated this behavior to be consistent across environments. Adam presented with impaired social interaction and social communication as well as a restricted interest in the planets. Everything in his room and all books he read were related to outer space.

His profile was found to be consistent with a diagnosis of an Autism Spectrum Disorder with significant problem behaviors and Generalized Anxiety. Adam was diagnosed with ASD and an anxiety disorder and then referred for behavioral therapy at Emerge, psychotherapy, and services in his school. His school was unable to provide the appropriate services, and he eventually received an out-of-district placement at a school specializing in the treatment of ASD. Adam received significant school and home-based treatment. Adam's violent behaviors have been reduced significantly; he demonstrates better compliance with requests, has less anxiety, and his family reports a significant improvement in quality of life.

Emotional and Behavioral Assessment as It Applies to Autism

Mood and Anxiety

Research indicates that mood and anxiety disorders are commonly prevalent comorbid psychological diagnoses among those with ASD (Trammell, Wilczynski, Dale, & McIntosh, 2013); further, outcomes research indicates that individuals with such comorbidities struggle more to achieve positive outcomes than those with ASD alone. Measures used to assess psychopathology like the MMPI-2, Beck Depression Inventory, and other valid measures often do not include individuals with ASDs in the standardization sample resulting in poor discriminant and predictive validity (Trammell et al., 2013). Trammell et al. (2013) describe that the lack of instruments intended to assess mood and anxiety in individuals with ASD poses a challenge for clinicians. Individuals with ASDs often lack insight into their emotions and/or internal thought processes. These challenges may be considered associated with theory of mind and related to thinking about one's own thoughts and feelings. Individuals with ASD tend to use more dichotomous adjectives like "always" or "never" to describe thought processes.

As has been shown throughout this book, it may be the case that emotional concerns are discovered during the initial consult or in administration of measures in the *Core Areas* (cognitive, language, social, and sensory). In this case, clinicians should look more closely at the *Associated Area* of Emotions/Mood in order to be comprehensive. Self-report measures must be used and interpreted with caution in this population (Deprey & Ozonoff, 2009). Even with those cautions considered, self-report measures provide helpful data for any diagnostic assessment. Self-report instruments that might be utilized to assess emotions include the BAI, BASC-2 self-report, BDI, CDI, MMPI-2, and RCMAS. These are just a few among many self-report measures available. The RCMAS contains a scale to assess an individual's response to dichotomous items like "I like everyone I meet." and "I never tell a lie." Often children with ASD have very elevated scores on this scale and lower self-reported symptoms of anxiety. Patterns of absolute thinking cause elevation on this defensiveness scale. While these measures, including the RCMAS, must be interpreted with caution, this pattern of elevated defensiveness may be an area for clinical attention. What is termed by Helena Huckabee, Ph.D. as a *"frozen profile"* may also be of clinical consideration. A *frozen profile* refers to a self-report profile of symptoms that is flat in nature and consistently much lower than the 50th percentile across a mood and anxiety scales. Generally, everyone experiences symptoms of worry or sadness at some point. Scores that are too low indicate either defensiveness or a limited ability to interpret one's own emotions.

Some individuals with ASD have difficulty offering perspective on how they generally feel, but they can provide information in the moment in response to what is currently happening in the environment. This could lead to a *frozen profile* as the individual feels "fine right now" and cannot reflect on past instances. A scale with extreme elevation may indicate that an individual is in emotional pain right now and so he or she is unable to reflect on times that things went well. Comparing self-report scales to parent and teacher scales can be helpful because it is noteworthy if other reporters see huge emotional and behavioral challenges while the individual reports nothing or vice versa. If parents and teachers paint a rosy picture but the individual reports elevated symptoms, it is likely that there are symptoms there in need of treatment; but it may also be that the individual is reporting elevation based on something happening presently. For example, often children with ASD are teased. If a child is reporting to the evaluator his history of being teased and bullied, and then completes a self-report scale, he might rate his emotions as elevated. If the same child has just finished reporting about a new module on Minecraft, he may rate a different emotional profile. This phenomenon is also likely related to local versus global processing of information, also known as, Central-Coherence theory.

Researchers looked at the association between ASD, anxiety, and a construct called *Alexithymia* or challenges identifying one's own emotions. They found that anxiety and Alexithymia are related to ASD as individuals have challenges identifying feelings. Research indicates that 40–50 % of individuals with ASDs have significant anxiety. Early face and emotion processing is delayed in ASD, but it does improve over time (Burner et al., 2014). Many individuals with autism have a breakdown in understanding the causes of the emotions they experience. These individuals better report physiological symptoms and specific phobias responding to a checklist of concrete fears instead of reporting worry or feelings independently. Researchers note that it can be counterintuitive to ask individuals who have difficulty identifying and speaking about their own emotions to do so (Gaigg, Bird, & Bowler, 2014). Indeed, these authors find that certain instruments, particularly projective tests (like the Roberts-II and the TAT) may not be practical to administer for individuals with severe difficulties identifying their own emotions. However, when there is some degree of emotional understanding present, certain self-report emotional measures can provide useful data.

For individuals with Anxiety and ASD, it seems that phobias and negative self-statements are particularly relevant. From a genetic standpoint, researchers find huge heterogeneity in autism (there are 92 known autism genes) and remark on a significant overlap of genetics of symptoms with other disorders (Autism Genome Project) including Bipolar, Major Depression, Schizophrenia, and AD/HD (Santangelo, 2014; Sweeney, 2014).

The authors' experiences indicate that using a variety of instruments is best. Collecting teacher and parent rating scales, interviewing parents, and taking behavior observations provide assessment of a child or adolescent's mood without asking them directly. Rating scales, interviews, sentence completion measures, projective drawing, or story measures can all provide insight into anxiety or depression if these are taken together and interpreted with caution.

Behavior Assessment

As it was discussed in detail in Chap. 6, assessing and managing challenging behavior can be essential in many diagnostic assessments for ASD. Unfortunately, some clients have been turned away from a comprehensive evaluation, hearing that their children are "untestable" when indeed a complete testing battery is quite achievable given that the appropriate behavioral supports are in place. In taking behavior observations and in implementing strategies to work with a child who has behavior problems, examiners are provided with a natural and immediate sampling of the very behaviors that may be interfering with the child's functioning in other settings.

Behavior is a crucial component of a comprehensive evaluation both as a piece of the referral question but also as it relates to being able to assess a child accurately and completely. As was provided in the *Dynamic Assessment Overview for ASD and Other Disorders* (Fig. 7.1d) in Chap. 7, individuals with ASD may require additional assessment for specific areas such Emotions/Mood and Behavior. Alternatively, some individuals without ASD may have impaired social interactions because of a behavioral disorder. In that case, a comprehensive evaluation must include a careful evaluation of behavior. Too often, examiners observe concerning social skills and forget to carefully consider the relative contribution of ASD, mood, and behavior to the overall presentation.

It is helpful to assess behavior and compliance over a variety of open-ended and more structured tasks. Sometimes, children behave very differently with different parameters or even with different evaluators. In assessing individuals with ASD, often children prefer more rote and concrete tasks to the open-ended tasks of the ADOS-2. Five and six-year-old children with ASD often say things like "No more questions!" "Stop talking!" or "What comes next?" to avoid completing the questions on friends, social interaction, and emotional experiences. At times, behavior problems like hiding, refusing, or even hitting may occur. Contrasting behavior may occur on cognitive tasks, where the same child may be more than willing to complete puzzle or concrete verbal task. Thus, it is critical to look at behavior across different tests or testing sessions.

Various questionnaires completed by parents, teachers, therapists, and other familiar individuals provide useful information on behavior. The Behavior Assessment System for Children (BASC-2) has forms for parents, teachers, and children (ages 6 and older) that assess behavior as well as emotional and adaptive domains. The BASC-2 also has a college form that assesses self-report for adults up to age 25. The Vineland-II interview or parent caregiver rating form also has a section that allows parents to rate behavior. Finally, the Scales of Independent Behavior-Revised (SIB-R) asks about problem behaviors including duration, frequency, and level of impairment. Behavior is often a large part of a referral question as parents whose children behave well may not refer them for testing. Even in the case of a purely academic referral often there are frustration, meltdowns, and sadness around school performance.

It is important to assess behavior across a variety of settings both directly and indirectly. Parents frequently come to an initial consultation and express concern that in a one-on-one setting, with no peers, evaluators will not see behavior problems, and this is often the case. Evaluators can note rating scales from a variety of settings to compare to behaviors observed in the office. Examiners may note low frustration tolerance or negative self-statements are that are more often seen in an evaluation than a full tantrum. That said, often children demonstrate problem behaviors in session and at times they show more behavior in an evaluation than they do at home because of the challenges inherent in a testing setting. Many very young children with ASD who are not used to having demands placed on them will cry, hit, or refuse in a testing setting. Assessment of behavior is an important piece of a comprehensive evaluation. In some cases, a home or school observation allows an evaluator to assess a child's behavior in multiple settings independently of parent, teacher, or therapist report and rating scales.

Functional Behavior Assessment (FBA): A successful home or school observation often utilizes an FBA and in many cases requires an analytical Functional Analysis (FA). An FBA is any systematic attempt to identify sources of reinforcement for a behavior. There are three tiers of an FBA: (a) descriptive assessment, (b) indirect assessment, and (c) functional analysis (FA). Descriptive and indirect assessments identify the structure of the behavior or what the behavior looks like (i.e., hitting, pushing, biting). This occurs through the use of direct observation, "ABC data" recording, standardized questionnaires, and parent or client interviews. The results of descriptive and indirect assessment provide information about the conditions under which behaviors are likely to occur, typical consequences of the behavior, potential frequency of the behavior, and other qualitative characteristics of the behavior. Limitations to using descriptive and indirect assessments include poor reliability and validity, biases, and insufficient information for treatment planning. That said, these methods do provide useful information for designing a functional analysis (FA).

Functional Analysis. Functional analyses are able to assess the function of a behavior more conclusively. They are often used when the target behavior is severe or when the function of the behavior cannot be determined via observations and interviews. Functional assessments can be a vital assessment tool to help clinicians diagnose and treat ASD and other neurodevelopmental disorders as well as determine the most appropriate treatment for a target behavior. Training in Functional Analyses is critical to accurate and successful use of this assessment method.

A functional analysis is a systematic behavioral assessment designed to identify the function, or purpose, of a particular behavior, in a rigorous manner. First, the behavior is identified for analysis. Next, a series of experimental conditions are used to determine the function of the behavior. The *four basic conditions* are: (1) *alone*, (2) *demand*, (3) *attention*, and (4) *tangible*. Based on the condition being assessed, environmental changes are made and unique, specific consequences are given based on the occurrence of the target behavior. By noting patterns of increased or decreased levels of the target behavior across different conditions, the function or reason for the behavior can often be determined.

In the *alone condition*, the child/client is alone (though supervised) without attention, access to preferred items, or any demands. Nothing is given to the child when the target behavior occurs. The occurrence of a behavior in this condition indicates that the behavior is *automatically* reinforcing or internally reinforcing. In the *demand condition*, the child is given a task to complete (e.g., spelling worksheets, puzzles, sorting tasks) without attention or access to preferred items. The child may stop an undesirable activity or demand when the behavior occurs. The occurrence of a behavior in this condition suggests that the behavior provides *escape* from demands/tasks. In the *attention (positive, social) condition*, attention is given to the child when the target behavior occurs. The occurrence of a behavior in this condition indicates the likelihood that the client's behavior will gain access to *attention* from a desired other (adult or peer). In the *tangible condition*, preferred items (toys, books, electronics, etc.) are given to the client when the target behavior occurs. The occurrence of a behavior in this condition indicates the likelihood that the behavior occurred because of the child's desired access for some preferred item (*tangible*).

Taken together, Functional Analysis can be a useful tool for assessing the behavioral patterns evidenced in many children with ASD. The four conditions that an analyst might utilize are alone, demand, attention, and tangible. The functions the behavior serves may be automatic, escape, attention, or tangible. Systematic experiments that utilize these conditions capitalize on objective data collection and avoid biased or subjective descriptive assessments. It is often the case that a child can make a dramatic change in behaviors when the function is identified, and the child is taught how to meet that same function with a more adaptive behavior. As was shared here and in previous chapters, effective behavior management, observation, and assessment are critical to the comprehensive assessment process for ASD.

Assessing for Adaptive Skills

Vignette #10: Mary Assessment of a Child with Adaptive Skill Deficits

Mary was 10 years old and referred for assessment due to language delay, self-injurious behavior (hitting her head), and repetitive gestures including hand flapping. She was assessed using the Wechsler Intelligence Scales for Children, 4th Edition (WISC-IV), Clinical Evaluation of Language Fundamentals, 4th Edition (CELF-4), Vineland Adaptive Behavior Scale—Parent/Caregiver Rating Form (VABS-II), Sensory Profile, Behavior Assessment Scales for Children, 2nd Edition (BASC-II), Parent and Teacher Reports, Social Communication Questionnaire (SCQ), Autism Diagnostic Observation Schedule, Module 3 (ADOS) Clinical Interview with parents, and Clinical Observations of Mary during testing (Table 12.2).

Mary's parents report that she is easily distracted and disorganized and does not seem to be aware of her hygiene (teeth, hair, toileting, etc.). She has impaired patterns of sleeping and eating; she is awake frequently through the night, has diet concerns, and only drinks water from a sports cap bottle (refuses cups). She has a pattern of elopement which is a significant concern. Modifications were required to complete testing, such as frequent breaks, sitting on the floor, and additional prompting.

Mary's parents completed The Vineland Adaptive Behavior Scales Parent/Caregiver Rating Scales (VABS-II) to assess Mary's adaptive behavior skills in the areas of *Communication, Daily Living Skills, Socialization,* and *Motor Skills.* Results indicate that Mary has significant deficits across all adaptive domains. Mary's Adaptive Behavior Composite score falls into the Low range with a Standard Score of 57 at the <1st percentile, and these scores are consistent with cognitive results discussed above. Testing indicated that Mary met criteria for *ASD with*

Table 12.2 Assessing for adaptive skills

Associated area
1. *Adaptive*
• Overall *Adaptive Composite* on Vineland or SIB-R
• *Communication*—Expressive>Receptive, Written (discrepancies)
• *Internalizing and Externalizing behaviors*
• *Social skills*
• *Consider results from BASC-II, SIB-R, Vineland-II*
Full measure names
Behavior Assessment System for Children, Second Edition (BASC-II), Self, Parent, and Teacher Reports
Scales of Independent Behavior-Revised (SIB-R)
Vineland Adaptive Behavior Scale, Second Edition—Parent/Caregiver Rating Form (VABS-II)
Vineland Adaptive Behavior Scale, Second Edition—Survey Interview Form (VABS-II)

Cognitive and Language Impairments, at a Severity Level 2 "Requiring Substantial Support" in Social Communication and Restricted, Repetitive Behavior as well as an Intellectual Disability with a mild severity level. Based on her cognitive profile, her adaptive scores as well as her sleep, diet, elopement, and self-care concerns including self-injurious behavior, it was recommended that Mary's family apply for government waivers to receive significant support and constant supervision.

Adaptive Skill Assessment as It Applies to Autism

Assessing adaptive skills domains is important in a comprehensive evaluation for ASD because information on adaptive skills strengths and deficits can be important in guiding treatment and in making diagnoses. Often parents state something along the lines of "I know my child but I don't know what is 'typical.'" Collecting parent report data and sometimes teacher report data on adaptive skills allows a clinician to provide normative information on adaptive skills and to inform parents of their child's developmental progress in relation to peers.

A typical pattern of adaptive behavior in ASD includes significant deficits in socialization, less severe deficits in communication, and relative strengths in daily living skills (Carter et al., 1998; Klin et al., 2007). In fact, cognitive skills tend to be significantly higher than adaptive skills, for individuals without a cognitive impairment and in those with cognitive impairment the discrepancy is beyond what would be expected given intellectual deficits (Klin et al., 2007; Volkmar et al., 1987). Furthermore, the level of adaptive impairment increases, in persons with ASD compared to same age peers through later childhood and into adolescence (Klin et al., 2007).

Adaptive skill assessments such as the Vineland-2, SIB-R, and ABAS-II allow parents or caregivers to report skills across communication, daily living skills, and social domains. The Vineland-II and SIB-R also collect data on problem behaviors. When completing an adaptive assessment, it is critical to tell parents that they are to report what the child *actually does,* not what he or she *is able to do.* For example, parents might report that their child could be independent in toileting but does not generally or spontaneously display this skill, has accidents often, or requires substantial support to use the bathroom. This would be considered a self-care deficit in the area of toileting.

An adaptive assessment is the most important piece of data in determining an intellectual impairment. The DSM 5 requires information on adaptive domains before specifying an Intellectual Disability. Adaptive skills also are important areas to target in treatment and can be predictive of later positive outcomes in individuals with ASD. Severity levels for ASD are also determined in part by considering deficits in adaptive functioning as adaptive functioning is considered when assessing cognitive impairments.

An adaptive skills assessment can provide specific data on weaknesses in domains like social interaction or personal self-care. Sometimes, very bright individuals with ASD have poor hygiene, community living skills, or receptive communication. It is also helpful to know when individuals do not have these deficits. Some well-meaning parents may have unrealistic expectations for their children. For example, a parent who expects a 2-year-old to eat a hamburger on a bun, without issue, when a plate is presented, may not realize that the child's performance is developmentally appropriate; it may be that he just needs to have food cut into small pieces. This parent may be comforted to see that their child has age appropriate daily living skills and to understand that more scaffolding of feeding is warranted. It is important to note that in many states, the presence of cognitive deficits alone is not sufficient to receive waivers for coordinated care. Most states require documentation cognitive and adaptive deficits to receive sufficient funding of services.

Concluding Remarks on Emotions, Mood, Behavior, and Adaptive Assessment

These associated areas are often a crucial part of an autism assessment because of the impact emotions, mood, behavior, and adaptive symptoms will have on the progress of an individual with an ASD. Coordinated care across providers and settings is very important as clinicians consider treatment outcomes for autism. In many cases, symptoms in the areas of emotional well-being, mood, behavior, and adaptive skills drive treatment. Applied behavior analysis, psychotherapy, and medications can be utilized to treat these symptoms. For example, an adult with an ASD may have significant anxiety around social interactions, and thus it is important to treat both the social deficit and the anxiety. A teenager may have poor self-care that leads to rejection and bullying. By treating adaptive skills this individual may be more accepted by peers. In a young child, problem behaviors may limit access to treatment of language or social skills. It is important to have a thorough assessment of these areas as they relate to the individual's well-being and progress. Treating the core symptoms of autism without addressing behavior, mood, emotions, and adaptive skills will not comprehensively address the needs of the client. Conversely, when clinicians can integrate this data and look at all areas that may be impacted in a given individual, there is greater hope of successfully treating the symptoms and allowing the client to live a more fulfilling life.

Summary of Part 3: Data Analysis

In this part of the text, authors have reviewed eleven areas of neuropsychological assessment data collected as these relate to Autism Spectrum Disorders. Each area uniquely offers up a vast amount of research and evidence to support its inclusion in a comprehensive psychological or neuropsychological assessment. A full review of each potential area is beyond the scope of this book. However, authors of this text put forth the most relevant topics relating to these primary domains. Through a thorough examination of these areas, clinicians can understand how to use data collected from all the relevant areas of a comprehensive evaluation put forth in this book. The *Core Areas* of cognitive, language, social, and sensory offer critical information that must be included in any ASD assessment. The *Associated Areas* of: visual–spatial, motor, attention, executive functioning, memory, emotions/mood/behavior, and adaptive domains should be included when the examiner has concerns about these symptoms during the initial consultation or the assessment of the Core Areas.

After these data are collected and scored, the multidisciplinary team meets as part of the assessment process, and normative information is compared across domains. The assessment team works to integrate findings and provide diagnostic clarification. During this process, clinicians must consider what data is clinically significant and what diagnoses can account for areas that are significant. In this process, ASD will be ruled in or out, based on the Core Areas; and other diagnoses may be considered, including those that may occur in the Associated Areas. For example, significant anxiety may lead to a secondary diagnosis of Generalized Anxiety Disorder in addition to ASD. As noted earlier, in DSM-IV (the previous version of the Diagnostic and Statistical Manual) ASD and AD/HD were thought to be mutually exclusive. We now understand that similar neural networks may be impacted and that in fact these disorders can co-occur. It is essential that clinicians are comprehensive in assessment and provide diagnostic information in a way that a primary diagnosis can guide treatment and secondary diagnoses can be addressed subsequently. Clinical judgment and a thorough review of the assessment data, considering all information obtained, such as observations, interviews, and rating scale data from family, teachers, and therapists, are crucial. This is why an assessment team must devote adequate time to data analysis and integration. This allows for adequate preparation for the feedback session with the individual or family in 1–3 weeks.

Once these data are integrated and understood, the assessment team is ready to make diagnostic decisions. Differential diagnosis is discussed in much detail in the next section to further explain the process of ruling autism in or out and to consider any relevant comorbidities, or differentially separate conditions. In order to guide clinicians, the following potential differentially relevant conditions are discussed in the next part of the text. These are disorders of: Intellectual, Genetic, Specific Learning, Language, Attention Disorders, Anxiety and OCD, Mood, Behavior, Trauma and Attachment, Personality, and Other Relevant Comorbidities.

Part IV
Differential Diagnosis

This part of the book illuminates the process of making differential diagnoses in Assessment of Autism Spectrum Disorders. A thorough evaluation for ASD must include both comorbid and differential diagnosis. In a diagnostic assessment, it is essential to realize when autism is *not* the appropriate diagnosis. In other words, ruling autism out is as important as ruling it in. A second focus of this section is comorbidity. There are a number of intellectual, mood, anxiety, behavior, and neurodevelopmental diagnoses that are identified as frequently co-occurring with ASD. This section includes a clear explanation of the presentation of autism when other comorbid conditions are present; as well as, how to differentiate between autism and other conditions that may share common symptoms. Diagnostic clarification is essential because it paves the way for effective treatment. Included in this section is a clear approach for determining whether or not symptoms are present that interfere with an individual's functioning. Diagnostically, it is crucial to start by first answering the question, "Is there something wrong?" If problems are evident, it must be determined "Is it pathologic or nonpathologic?" The following disorders which may co-occur or require differential diagnosis from autism are discussed: Intellectual disabilities, genetic, learning, language, attention, anxiety, mood, psychotic, behavioral, trauma related, attachment, personality, and other potentially relevant disorders. Although not an exhaustive list, this text intends to serve as a comprehensive guide for making an accurate diagnosis in light of the most common differential and comorbid conditions for individuals suspected of having an ASD.

1.1   Differential Diagnosis

- •Use assessment data to determine differential and comorbid disorders
- •Consider all assessed areas to ensure that symptoms are described by diagnoses
- •Provide diagnoses and recommendations to family
- •Refer to treatment providers

In this part of the text, Chaps. 13 and 14 will cover areas of differential and comorbid diagnosis. Chapter 13 will review disorders of neurodevelopment and brain functioning while Chap. 14 will cover Emotional, Mood, and Behavioral diagnoses. It is essential to carefully consider all symptoms presented and determine whether an Autism Spectrum Disorder is relevant. Does ASD explain all clinically significant symptoms? If not, what other symptoms are present and which diagnoses can account for these? In considering carefully all comorbid and differential diagnoses a clinician can ensure that the diagnosis or diagnoses will capture the clinical needs of the client. These diagnoses and the report will then be used to guide treatment. In order to be certain that best and research-based treatment options are explored, diagnoses must be accurate and comprehensive. For this reason, differential and comorbid diagnosis is crucial to the assessment process.

Chapter 13
Disorders of Neurodevelopment and Brain Functioning

Abstract Differential diagnosis of neurodevelopment and brain functioning includes the differential and comorbid diagnosis of intellectual disabilities, exceptional cognitive profiles, genetic disorders, specific learning disorders, language disorders, and attention disorders. As ASD is a diagnosis based on social communication and restricted repetitive behaviors or patterns, it is important to look at these areas in the context of other diagnoses. Intellectual disabilities include challenges in language, reasoning, knowledge, interpersonal skills, and adaptive skills. These may occur comorbid with ASD. When differentiating between giftedness and ASD, the clinician should evaluate social communication. Children who are gifted but do not have ASD will show strengths in verbal and nonverbal communication. There are numerous environmental and genetic disorders that may have ramifications for intellectual abilities and may need to be differentiated from or co-occur with ASD. These are FAS, Down syndrome, Turner syndrome, Williams syndrome, Rett syndrome, and Fragile X. Dyslexia; dysgraphia and dyscalculia are important diagnoses to consider in the assessment of ASD. A Specific Learning Disorder is performance in an academic area below what would be expected based on cognition, age, and/or grade level. A language disorder is characterized by difficulties in acquisition and use of language across modalities. These must be differentially diagnosed from ASD. While symptoms of inattention may lead to failure to read social cues and communicate effectively with others, social communication weakness is not a core deficit of AD/HD. Thus, individuals with AD/HD alone are likely to make eye contact, gesture, and exhibit ease in connecting socially with others.

Keywords Differential diagnosis in ASD • Diagnosing intellectual disabilities in ASD • Twice exceptional profiles in ASD • Giftedness and ASD • Genetic syndromes and ASD • Learning disabilities and ASD • Language disorders in ASD • Comorbid ADHD and ASD

Intellectual Disabilities and Exceptional Intellectual Profiles

One of the most common comorbid diagnoses with an Autism Spectrum Disorder is an intellectual impairment (only superseded by anxiety). This is defined as conceptual, practical and social skills two standard deviations or more below the mean.

© Springer International Publishing Switzerland 2016   241
A.P. Kroncke et al., *Assessment of Autism Spectrum Disorder*, Contemporary
Issues in Psychological Assessment, DOI 10.1007/978-3-319-25504-0_13

DSM-5 defines Intellectual Disability as hinging on Adaptive skills assessed by a measure such as the Vineland-II or SIB-R (APA, 2013). In order to diagnose an intellectual disability, the clinician considers IQ scores and adaptive scores less than or equal to a standard score of 70. Thus, with both conditions of adaptive and intellectual impairment satisfied, an individual will be diagnosed with an intellectual disability.

According to the CDC, 35 % of individuals diagnosed with ASD have a co-occurring Intellectual Disability. This is a downward trend as it was previously reported in 2001 that as many as 70 % of individuals with ASD were intellectually disabled (Trammell, Wilczynski, Dale, & McIntosh, 2013). The CDC notes 1 in 68 children are now diagnosed with autism; given current trends, it is likely that a larger percentage of these individuals have Average or better intellectual profiles. Particularly, high cognitive scores are more common in domains of Verbal Comprehension and Perceptual Reasoning relative to Working Memory and Processing Speed (Foley-Nicpon, Assouline, & Stinson, 2012). For this reason, the General Ability Index (GAI) composite may better reflect giftedness while a Full Scale IQ score may be deflated by significantly lower working memory and/or processing speed. (Foley-Nicpon et al, 2012).

Differentiating Between ASD and an Intellectual Disability

While individuals with ASD have an intellectual disability in 35 % of cases, it is important to be able to rule out an Autism Spectrum Disorder when evaluating a child with an Intellectual Disability. As ASD is a diagnosis based on social communication and reciprocity and restricted repetitive behaviors or patterns, it is important to look at these areas in the context of ID. Intellectual disabilities are defined as including deficits in conceptual, social, and practical domains (APA, 2013; Trammell et al., 2013). These would include challenges in language, reasoning, knowledge, interpersonal skills, and adaptive skills. An individual with an intellectual disability is likely to have impaired social skills and impaired communication and may be repetitive speech or restricted interests. It is essential to discern when these characteristics are consistent with autism. When differentiating between autism and intellectual disability, the clinician must consider features of autism including social reciprocity, gesture, and play skills. Individuals who have limited conceptual skills like language and verbal communication, but do not have ASD, may use gestures and nonverbal communication, even more frequently than the typical child. Children with ASD may not make such efforts to communicate even when they have the intellectual ability to do so. A child with an intellectual disability may be repetitive and concrete in creating a play sequence, but he or she is likely to make eye contact, watch for the examiner's reaction to play, share enjoyment, and work to connect on some level with the examiner. Thus, gestures, eye contact, nonverbally watching, connecting, and communicating, can be clear differentiating factors ruling out an ASD in children suspected of intellectual disabilities. Trammell et al. (2013) reports that adaptive skill deficits may be more pronounced in an individual with ASD and

ID than in ID alone. Thus, adaptive skills can be compared to cognitive abilities to provide additional insight when differentiating autism and intellectual disabilities (Matson & Shoemaker, 2009; Trammell et al., 2013).

Differentiating ASD and Giftedness

When differentiating between giftedness and ASD, the clinician should evaluate social communication including eye contact, facial expression, use of nonverbal communication, and reciprocal conversation. Children who are gifted but do not have ASD will show strengths in verbal and nonverbal communication rather than impairment. Although children with ASD tend to use formal language more than neurotypicals, gifted children may also use formal language because of their extensive vocabulary. However, gifted children tend to have strong receptive language and comprehension such that they understand the complex vocabulary they use, while children with autism may use words they do not understand. Children with autism may enjoy nonfiction more than fiction and may prefer reading to playing with toys. Gifted children may also show such preferences; however, this is likely due to the fact that they have a high proclivity for certain cognitively sophisticated topics and may have limited interest in playing games that do not call on this intellectual curiosity. Similarly, children with autism may prefer interacting with adults over peers. Gifted children may also prefer interacting with adults, but this is most likely due to the fact that adults may be more able to understand the intellectual complexity inherent in their communication. Alternatively, children with autism prefer socializing with adults because of their deficits in socializing with peers. Gifted children who do not have ASD will show appropriate social skills, adequate communication, and will not have restricted interests or repetitive behaviors.

Comorbid ASD and Intellectual Disability

Intellectual Disability is highly comorbid with ASD. As it was previously discussed, 35 % of individuals with ASD have Intellectual Disabilities. This means that in addition to having an intellectual disability, these individuals also show significant social communication weaknesses and restricted and repetitive behaviors. As noted above, it is possible that overall adaptive functioning is lower when Autism Spectrum Disorders and Intellectual Disabilities are comorbid. When considering comorbidity of ID and ASD, one important point is to reassess cognitive skills frequently as cognitive ability is more likely to change in those with Autism Spectrum Disorders and is particularly unstable at a young age (APA, 2013, p. 40).

In typically developing children, IQ scores are reported to become stable around age seven, but there may be more variability in autism. A study by Mayes and Calhoun in 1999 suggested that 33 % of young children with ASD who had IQ testing a year apart experienced significant change in IQ scores over time (in Mayes & Calhoun, 2003). A second study in 2013 found similar results showing that 32 % of children with ASD had a significant change of 15 IQ points or more from approximately age four to age seven (Barry, Moran, Anglim, Conway, & Guerin, 2013). In this study, researchers did not control for the intervention received; however, at time two 68 % were receiving ASD-specific educational supports which may have impacted their IQ.

Research consistently shows that high cognitive ability predicts optimal outcomes in ASD; however, IQ does not necessarily impact the severity of symptoms. Researchers found 2 years of early intensive behavioral intervention (EIBI) decreased Autism severity in both ID and non-ID groups (46 participants, mean age of 2) according to Ben-Itzchak, Watson, and Zachor (2014). The difference between ID and non-ID group was in their adaptive social and communication skills. Children with higher IQs had an increased rate of adaptive skill acquisition over 2 years. The study also found improvement in adaptive skills only occurred after 2 years of intervention suggesting that applying the skills required extensive practice before children could transfer them to day-to-day settings. Taken together, children who have a comorbid intellectual disability and autism show significantly more impairment across adaptive, social, and communicative domains.

Comorbid ASD and Giftedness

Giftedness can also be "comorbid" with ASD. Giftedness for the purpose of this book is defined as an IQ score at or above the 90th to 95th percentile (or an IQ score in the superior to very superior range). Some school districts utilize a profile approach to consider other aspects of giftedness beyond IQ; in clinical settings, this model is seldom used. Individuals with this profile are often termed *twice exceptional* (*also called* "2E"). Gifted children with ASD have challenges in social communication and restricted/repetitive interests. They tend to have strong rote reading and math skills as well as exceptional skills in problem solving, analyzing, and conceptualizing.

This profile is highly complex, difficult to treat, and worthy of special consideration in clinical and educational settings. Often gifted individuals with ASD have significant emotional and behavioral symptoms due to a high level of intellectual understanding coupled with lagging emotional and social development. Treatment programs for twice exceptional individuals must teach skills relevant to the child's developmental age (not chronological); and must consider these discrepant skills across domains. A gifted child may be able to access highly sophisticated academic materials; however, may require social skills groups to focus on very basic skills such as eye contact, active listening, conducting a to-and-fro conversation, and expanding on the topics that are important to others. Clinicians may worry, and indeed initially the child might claim, that such ideas are too simplistic; but after some time working on social communication, the child often will come to find this type of skill practice engaging and helpful. Generally, gifted children with ASD tend to come to an understanding of these skill deficits and may desire to improve in order to make friends and participate socially.

Gifted children or adults with ASD may have difficulty with abstract reasoning and making inferences. These difficulties tend to show up academically in poor reading comprehension and written expression. Sometimes, individuals with weaknesses in comprehension and writing may prefer careers in engineering, architecture, science, or mathematics. These careers may allow them to utilize their strengths in problem solving without relying on social communication and inferencing.

Comorbidity rates for children with Autism Spectrum Disorders who meet the criteria to be considered "gifted" are difficult to find in the research. A Korean study with a target population of over 55,000 school-aged children found that approximately 2 % of the sample met criteria for an Autism Spectrum Disorder. This is slightly higher than the CDC proposed rate of 1 in 68 children impacted in the United States. Seven to 12 % of the children who met criteria for ASD also had an IQ in the Superior range as measured by the Korean WISC-III or the Leiter, a nonverbal intelligence test (Kim et al, 2011). These data would indicate that Superior IQ scores are approximately equally present in individuals with Autism Spectrum Disorders as they are in the population as a whole. Taken together, based on the research available, individuals with Autism Spectrum Disorders are much more likely to have an Intellectual Disability than the general population data would suggest (approximately 35 % to the general population 2.5 %), but those with Autism Spectrum Disorder are just as likely to be gifted as any other individual (approximately 9 % in the general population to 7–12 % in those with ASD). This research clearly suggests that IQ scores among ASD are highly variable and much more so than in the general population. A greater number of individuals with ASD have low intellectual ability and fewer individuals are Average. In conclusion, the authors of this text find that although it is reported that IQ scores are more variable and less stable in the ASD group relative to the general population, further research is needed.

Measures for cognitive assessment should be considered based on the language level of the child as this will impact performance. Children with average or advanced language are able to be assessed via measures such as the WISV-V, WJ-Cog, and K-ABC, while children with more limited language abilities may be assessed with the Leiter, UNIT Stanford Binet-5, or DAS-2 preschool (Fig. 13.1).

This table provides IQ scores with qualitative descriptions that adequately assess a child's intellectual ability. Examiners must always consider IQ score in light of all other assessment data. For intellectual disabilities, an adaptive measure must also be administered with scores falling below 70 in order to meet criteria. Gifted individuals generally have either a Full Scale IQ score or an Index score in the Superior or Very Superior range. Some gifted schools accept children with an IQ score at or above the 90th or 95th percentile. Schools may also use a profile approach for assessing giftedness, which evaluates academic skills and other exceptional abilities, in addition to IQ. Clinically, this profile approach for giftedness is rarely used (Fig. 13.2).

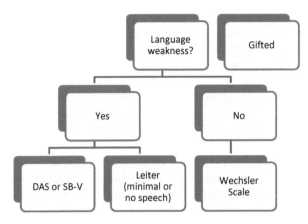

Fig. 13.1 Assessing intellectual abilities based on language level

Classifying Intellectual Ability

Genius	• IQ ≥ 130
Superior	• IQ 120-129
High Average	• IQ 115-119
Average	• IQ 85-114
Low Average	• IQ 80-84
Borderline	• IQ 70-79
Intellectual Disability	• IQ < 70

Fig. 13.2 Classifying intellectual ability

An Environmental Impact on Cognitive Abilities: Fetal Alcohol Syndrome

There are numerous genetic disorders, to be discussed below, that may have ramifications for intellectual abilities and at times may need to be differentiated from or co-occur with ASD. However, first it is useful to mention a syndrome with purely environmental influence that may impact cognitive ability and could co-occur with or require differentiation from ASD. Fetal Alcohol Syndrome (FAS) is a pattern of mental and physical deficits that can develop when a mother consumes alcohol during pregnancy. Drinking can cause damage to the fetal brain and result in an intellectual disability and/or physical, behavioral, and emotional challenges. Cognition, attention, executive functioning, and adaptive skills can be impacted in FAS, and thus at times a child with FAS may be referred for an ASD evaluation. Clinicians should familiarize themselves with the physical features associated with FAS and take a thorough history including information on prenatal care, birth weight, and growth information. Low birth weight and growth deficiencies are often associated with FAS. This can be a tough diagnosis to make, particularly in a case where the biological mother may deny that alcohol was used during the prenatal period. In other cases a family who has adopted a child they suspect may have been exposed to alcohol may seek a comprehensive evaluation to include a rule out of FAS. FAS could occur with an Autism Spectrum Disorder, but in this case the clinician will need to give careful consideration to the primary symptoms of ASD (social communication and restricted/repetitive behaviors and interests). The assessment should include consideration of facial expression, eye contact, gesture, quality of speech, and social skills relative to an individual's IQ. Play, empathy, and the absence of restricted topics or repetitive behaviors are all important areas to assess. Often significant behavior problems, executive functioning weaknesses, and attention problems can be secondarily present in ASD. In the case of FAS, these are also associated symptoms. Without clear core symptoms of autism present, it is not possible to make comorbid diagnoses of ASD and FAS.

Genetic Disorders

Genetic Disorders to consider for differentiation from ASD and possibly for comorbidity with ASD include Down syndrome, Turner syndrome, Rett syndrome, Williams syndrome, and Fragile X.

Down Syndrome

Down syndrome occurs when an individual has an extra full or partial chromosome 21. Individuals with Down syndrome are often compared to those with ASD in research studies. Studies often look at the impact of intervention or examine adult outcomes because of the relatively high occurrence of Down syndrome in the population and the rate of intellectual disabilities occurring in both DS and ASD. Down syndrome is associated with cognitive delays that range from very mild to severe with most individuals born with Down syndrome having mild to moderate cognitive impairment. One study in 691 children is born with Down syndrome in the United States, making it the most common genetic condition (National Down Syndrome Society, webpage copyright 2012).

Individuals with Down syndrome may have low muscle tone, small stature, and upward slanting eyes. All have some level of cognitive impairment. Down syndrome is associated with physical growth delays and physical features. Differentiating ASD and DS would include a careful assessment of social communication similar to that noted in the ID section. Down syndrome alone does not result in impacted social communication, though cognitive delays can make this more difficult to differentiate.

Autism and Down syndrome can co-occur in a small percentage of children and the research would suggest that those with dual diagnoses have more severe cognitive delays (Howlin, Wing, and Gould, 1995). Between 1 and 10 % of children with Down syndrome may also have an ASD (Capone 1999). Dr. Capone notes that through Kennedy Krieger's research studies on DS-ASD children with dual diagnoses had regression of language and social skills, poorer communication skills than other DS children, repetitive behaviors, self-injurious behaviors, unusual vocalization, unusual sensory responses, feeding challenges, increased anxiety, irritability, sleep disturbance, attention problems, and difficulty with transitions. Children with DS-ASD had less challenge with "social relatedness" than children with ASD alone but had more severe cognitive impairments on the whole (national Down syndrome society webpage 2012).

Dr. Susan Hepburn (2015), a recognized expert in the dual diagnosis of ASD and Down syndrome, describes that families often feel excluded in the greater community because their children do not share the same profile as would be expected for the stand alone disabilities. For example, children with Down syndrome generally do not have social deficits; however, children with comorbid ASD have significant social symptoms. These differences can make individuals feel as though they do not properly belong to either group. Further research is needed on treatment for individuals who have both disorders; as well as, advocacy efforts so that they can be appropriately included in the greater community of individuals with developmental disabilities.

Turner Syndrome

Turner syndrome is a genetic condition caused by complete or partial absence of the second sex chromosome in women. It occurs in one in 2000 births and may be associated with nonverbal memory and attention deficits and challenges with spatial temporal processing. These may lead to impaired nonverbal learning and social skills. Physical signs and symptoms may include short stature, webbed neck, droopy eyes, strabismus, a broad chest, and flat feet (Turner syndrome society of the United States webpage 2013). Turner syndrome can be definitively ruled in or out with genetic testing.

Because Turner syndrome and autism have some commonalities, genetic research has been funded by the National Alliance for Autism Research (NAAR). Studies by Eric Lander, Ph.D. and David Skuse, Ph.D. research the inability to recognize facial expressions that may be common to both disorders. Turner syndrome has a clear genetic makeup while ASD is genetically more complex but researchers feel that with some similar characteristics, looking at genes of those with Turner syndrome can help isolate genes involved in ASD. A study by Feigenberg et al. suggests that individuals with Turner syndrome should be routinely screened for ASD. Research indicates that as many as 25 % of women with Turner met criteria for a diagnosis on the Spectrum and 5 % met full autism criteria. This study found that 50 % of the 28 patients screened had at least mild Autism Spectrum symptoms (Inbar-Feigenberg et al., 2013). While Turner syndrome is relatively easy to diagnose, the presence may warrant an evaluation for ASD because of a high comorbidity rate.

Rett Syndrome

Rett syndrome was once classified a neurodevelopmental disorder caused by a gene mutation on the X chromosome that almost exclusively affects females. It is rare and was, before DSM-5, classified as an Autism Spectrum Disorder. Because of the known etiology of Rett syndrome, it has been removed from the category Neurodevelopmental Disorders. It is characterized by developmental regression of language and motor milestones impacting movement, speech, and cognitive development. It is also characterized by reduced head circumference and repetitive hand movements. Individuals with Rett syndrome often live until adulthood but need significant 24 h care and support with activities of daily living including feeding, dressing, bathing, and toileting. Rett syndrome is not an Autism Spectrum Disorder as classified by the DSM-5 (International Rett Syndrome Foundation).

Williams Syndrome

Williams syndrome is a genetic condition impacting 1 in 10,000 people worldwide. It stems from a deletion of genetic material from chromosome 7. According to the NIH, it is characterized by medical problems, developmental delays, intellectual disabilities, and learning disabilities. Those with Williams syndrome may have "elfin"-like features and are said to be "social, friendly, and endearing." Some have called Williams syndrome the "anti-autism," and research has found differences in the amygdala, with greater activation in those with Williams, which is associated with emotional and social functioning (Coe et al., 1999, Insights for Autism from Williams Syndrome SFARI). Autism Spectrum Disorders are not comorbid with Williams syndrome. Careful assessment of social communication should make the disorders fairly easy to differentiate. Research into genetics related to Williams syndrome may provide insights into genetics and ASD because of the "opposite" symptom profile and clear genetic makeup of Williams syndrome.

Fragile X

Fragile X is a genetic condition causing intellectual disability, behavioral and learning challenges, and occurring more frequently in males. There are physical and behavioral characteristics and Fragile X can include characteristics of AD/

HD, Autism Spectrum Disorders and Anxiety (National Fragile X Foundation 2014). Fragile X is identified through genome sequencing and shares a complicated relationship with autism. One study found that as many as 47 % of individuals with Fragile X met criteria for autism (Demark, Feldman, & Holden, 2003). Rates of shared genes between individuals with both disorders to range from 0 to 12.5 %, with most studies finding about 3 % of cells in the autism group that code for Fragile X (Demark, n.d.). Although the disorders share some common features, individuals with Fragile X display symptoms that are distinctly different from the typical presentation of ASD and can be differentially diagnosed (Jessica Wright, author for SFARI, wrote in 2014 that the director of the UC Davis MIND Institute in Sacramento, Leonard Abbeduto). Researchers Joseph Piven and Stephen Warren note that extreme social anxiety, hand flapping behaviors, and low IQ scores are characteristic of Fragile X and autism. However, the more complex autism symptoms such as lining up toys and restricted interests are seldom seen in Fragile X. Children with Fragile X have fewer social deficits when compared to their cognitive abilities than do those diagnosed with Autism Spectrum Disorder (Simon's Foundation 2014).

In conclusion, genetic disorders can be comorbid with Autism Spectrum Disorders including Down syndrome, Turner syndrome, and Fragile X. Studying genetic conditions and their relationship to Autism Spectrum Disorders may lead researchers to better understand the genetic mechanisms involved in ASD. Autism Spectrum Disorders are not thought to co-occur with Rett syndrome or Williams syndrome.

Specific Learning Disorders

Specific Learning Disorders, also known as dyslexia, dysgraphia, and dyscalculia, are important diagnoses to consider in the assessment of ASD. A Specific Learning Disorder is performance in an academic area below what would be expected based on cognition, age, and/or grade level. The deficit must be accompanied by stronger skills in one or more of other academic areas. Academic challenges cannot be due to a lack of appropriate education or a lack of school attendance or the presence of English as a second language (APA, 2013). The DSM-5 currently specifies three categories of learning disorders: Specific Learning Disorder, With Impairment in Reading (315.00) dyslexia; Specific Learning Disorder, With Impairment in Writing (315.2) dysgraphia; Specific Learning Disorder, With Impairment in Mathematics (315.1) dyscalculia. Additionally, the DSM-5 requires notation of the associated deficit and severity, which may include Mild, Moderate, or Severe. For example, the diagnosis may be reported Specific Learning Disorder, With Impairment in Mathematics, Accurate and Fluent Calculation, Moderate (315.1). These may be diagnosed comorbid with ASD but are not often a differential diagnosis during autism evaluations. This section will present information on comorbid diagnoses of Learning Disorders and Autism Spectrum Disorders.

Comorbid ASD and Specific Learning Disorders

Dyslexia

The DSM 5 puts forth three areas of Specific Learning Disorder, With Impairment in Reading: (1) Word reading accuracy, (2) Reading rate or fluency, and (3) Reading comprehension (APA, 2013). Children with ASD often present with reading challenges. The typical dyslexia profile is different than the profile of reading challenges associated with ASD alone. At large, persons with ASD perform weakest in reading comprehension as compared to all other academic areas (Chiang & Lin, 2007; Minshew et al., 1994; Nation, Clarke, Wright, & Williams, 2006). Furthermore, comprehension skills tend to fall below basic decoding skills (Minshew et al. 1994; Nation et al., 2006; O'Connor & Klein, 2004). When children with ASD have significant challenges in decoding and reading fluency, then it is important to consider an additional diagnosis of a Specific Learning Disorder in Reading.

A large-scale study compared the performance of children with ASD alone to children with dyslexia on groups' performance during nine standardized tests. Results indicated that those with ASD achieved lower scores on all comprehension measures compared to those with dyslexia. Additionally, those with dyslexia had lower scores on decoding measures than those with ASD. Regarding comprehension, many children with ASD may not be able to form a coherent mental model of a reading; specifically, they cannot mentally represent the text (Nation et al., 2006; Huemer & Mann, 2009). Children with ASD may be able to read a text fluently, as evidenced by scores on the WIAT-III, WJ-III, or GORT. Despite fluent reading, a child with ASD often lacks basic understanding of the main idea of the passage, story, or book. In many ways, this pattern is the opposite of "dyslexic" profile, in which children typically struggle to decode passages but comprehend readings at a much higher level than their basic reading skills would predict.

This is not to say that an individual with ASD cannot have a deficit in decoding, as it is possible to have both dyslexia and ASD. Rather, the pattern can assist practitioners in making an accurate diagnosis. As such, it is recommended that practitioners use multiple academic measures of language and reading including but not limited to: WIAT-III, WJ-IV, GORT, CELF-V, CBMs, and work samples from school. The GORT-V offers five different scores which can assist in the comorbid diagnosis of ASD alone vs. ASD and dyslexia. Specifically: *Rate*, the amount of time it takes an individual to read a story; *Accuracy*, measure of an individual's capacity to pronounce each of the words in the stories correctly; *Fluency*, measure of an individual's capacity to pronounce each of the words in the stories correctly; *Comprehension*, a score based on the correctness of an individual's responses to questions about the content of each story read; Oral Reading Quotient (ORQ), the overall best measure of an individual's reading ability. Very often students with dyslexia alone will demonstrate deficits in Rate and Accuracy but may have Average Comprehension scores. Conversely, individuals with autism alone tend to have Average or better scores on Rate, Accuracy, and Fluency but deficits in Comprehension. Taken together with other academic measures, work samples, and school information, the GORT-5 profile can often determine if the reading challenges of a child are related to autism, or warrant a comorbid diagnosis of dyslexia.

The WIAT-III provides three composites relevant for understanding a pattern of reading challenges: Total Reading, Basic Reading, Reading Comprehension, and Fluency. Similarly, the WJ-IV offers Reading, Broad Reading, Basic Reading Skills, Reading Comprehension, Reading Fluency, Reading Rate, scores. Additionally, Chap. 18 will present an overview of the Willard Imagery Observation Scales (WIOS: Willard, 2013), a recommended screener incorporated into the ADOS-2. This screener can be used along with clinical observation and reading assessments to (1) clarify whether or not the child's reading pattern is characteristic of autism and (2) whether or not the child's reading comprehension skills are likely to be affected by their disability of autism.

Dyscalculia

The DSM-5 puts forth four areas of Specific Learning Disorder, With Impairment in Mathematics: (1) Number sense, (2) Memorization of arithmetic facts, (3) Acute of fluent calculation, (4) Accurate math reasoning (APA, 2013). There is little research to suggest that the challenges associated with a Specific Learning Disorder with impairment in mathematics are unique to those with autism. That said, the aforementioned challenges with reading comprehension can present difficulties when solving mathematics word problems. Research on children with High Functioning Autism has shown that children tend to have math ability in the average range, but may have overall lower cognitive ability (Troyb et al, 2014). However, the significant rigidity, attention problems, and inflexibility often associated with ASD can impact the acquisition of math skills. The authors have assessed children who present with the comprehension-related symptoms of a math disability, who do not meet criteria for an SLD. For example, a child who appears to have a deficit in mathematics fluency can be a child with significant rigidity who insists on double checking each answer before moving to the next. Another example, a child who is asked to solve questions using a specific mathematics method in school, may receive poor marks. This same child, when allowed to solve problems using any means, is correct and efficient in math reasoning. The child may not have and SLD but rather rigidly stick to his/her own method of computation. A comprehensive evaluation of academic skills will utilize standardized achievement tests, work samples, IEP or 504 Plans (if available), teacher report and when possible classroom observations, parent report (specifically regarding homework challenges). Of note, mathematics is often an area of strength for children with ASD. It is possible to make a diagnosis of Dyscalculia in an individual with an Autism Spectrum Disorder if actual math knowledge and performance, not rigid thinking or reading comprehension weaknesses, are significantly lower than would be expected by age, grade, cognition, or other academic skills. Further research is needed to clarify the intricacies of mathematics strengths and weaknesses in the ASD population.

Dysgraphia

The DSM-5 puts forth three areas of Specific Learning Disorder, With Impairment in Written Expression: (1) Spelling accuracy, (2) Grammar and punctuation accuracy, (3) Clarity of organization of written expression (APA, 2013). In ruling out dysgraphia, an important consideration is language ability. An ASD diagnosis is accompanied by a specifier pertaining to language (i.e., With Language Impairments or Without Language Impairments). A language impairment associated with ASD may impact the clarity of organization of written expression, but may not meet criteria for a separate writing disorder. In making such a decision, it is important to consider the context in which challenges occur. For example, if a child's oral language, language memory, and receptive language are average, but scores on the WIAT-III or WJ-II indicate a weakness in spelling accuracy and grammar and punctuation, one could diagnose a Specific Learning Disorder, With Impairment in Written Expression comorbid with autism. On the contrary, if standardized performance on writing tasks are Below Average but consistent with a documented language impairment, challenges with writing may be subsumed under an ASD diagnosis. Additionally, the production of written language may be a challenge for some children with ASD, as it involves concurrent processing of motor and cognitive demands. The following section will review and provide a more in-depth overview of motor challenges in populations with ASD.

Developmental Coordination Disorder

Deficits in fine motor skills, manual dexterity, gross motor, dyspraxia, and movement planning control are highly prevalent in individuals with ASD (Dziuk et al., 2007; Kushki Chau, & Anagnostou, 2011). Such fine motor challenges contribute to acquisition and performance of skilled fine motor tasks, such as handwriting, use of utensils, and fastening buttons and clasps. Common gross motor challenges include awkward gait, challenges crossing midline, clumsiness, and general luck of fluidity in gross motor movements. In fact, these challenges are often early signs of ASD. Although motor disorders can occur in isolation, these are important to consider in the assessment of ASD. Presently, few researchers have examined the handwriting difficulties of children with ASD. However, Kushki et al. (2011) summarized the findings of seven studies on the topic. The research indicated that children with ASD tended to have deficits in pen control, letter formation, spacing, and alignment. Deficits in writing and fine motor coordination are known as Developmental Coordination Disorder, defined in DSM-5 as performance in daily activities that require motor coordination is below what is expected based on age or intelligence.

The consensus in the literature is that the handwriting challenges associated with ASD are related to motor coordination deficits in ASD, which begs the question, "how does one proceed diagnostically?" Not every child with ASD will meet criteria for developmental coordination disorder. These authors advocate for the dual diagnosis of ASD and Developmental Coordination Disorder if there are clear motor difficulties. If a child meets criteria for Developmental Coordination Disorder, it should be diagnosed as the secondary diagnosis as it will increase the likelihood of critical service delivery at school that may include occupational therapy and assistive technology supports.

In conclusion, learning disorders can be comorbid with Autism Spectrum Disorders including dyslexia, dysgraphia, dyscalculia, and Developmental Coordination Disorder. Studying learning disorders and their relationship to Autism Spectrum Disorders may lead researchers to better understand how to support those with ASD in achieving broader academic success whether they meet full criteria for both diagnoses or rather have some learning challenges that are related more to the core symptoms of autism.

Language Disorders

A language disorder is characterized by difficulties in acquisition and use of language across modalities. Diagnosis can be nuanced and difficult to differentiate because of the inherent language difficulties that many children with autism display. The criteria include reduced vocabulary, limited sentence structure, and impairments in discourse (APA, 2013 p. 42). The DSM-5 further explains that language abilities are below what is expected for an individual's age and must result in deficits in communication, social, academic, or occupational performance. This delay has onset during development and cannot be explained in the context of another neurological condition.

Differentiating Between ASD and a Language Disorder

Language Disorder (formerly known as Expressive/Receptive Language Disorder) is often a rule out in an assessment for ASD because Autism Spectrum Disorder criteria specify social *communication* deficits. In turn, a Language Disorder may lead to some social impact as challenges with language can make socialization challenging. The DSM-5 states "specific language disorder is not usually associated with abnormal nonverbal communication, nor with the presence of restricted, repetitive patterns of behavior, interests or activities." (DSM-5 p. 58). Like with ID a thorough assessment of nonverbal communication is crucial in making this rule out. When a child makes good eye contact, shares enjoyment with the examiner, initiates joint attention, participates in cooperative toy play, and is socially motivated to participate in tasks and activities, ASD can usually be ruled out.

In Language Disorder, frequently an individual will present with either equally delayed expressive and receptive skills or better receptive skills than expressive skills. Also language delays tend to be consistent, rather than intermittent. For example, a young child with ASD may speak in sentences one day and offer no verbal comment the next. In ASD, more frequently individuals have better expressive language skills than receptive language skills relating back to deficits in social communication. A child who is not attending to others and learning from social interaction in the environment may present with Average or advanced expressive language but deficits in receptive skills. Another language marker for ASD is related to word and sentence structure and the use of pronouns. Pronoun reversals, made-up words and phrases or stereotyped, formal, and odd use of language, are at times associated with ASD. Stereotyped language is a repetitive statement or a repeated quote from another person, television, or a book. For example, a child who says "It's a W or an M!" "It's a B or a D!" or repeats a phrase consistently like "Oh my Lord!" or "Do you think?" is presenting with stereotyped language. Formal language sounds as if a professor, parent, or grandparent made the comment instead of a young child. For example, "He's a naughty lad, that Jack." may be formal language. Odd or unusual use of language may include odd or made up phrasing, for example, "He said you're a gooey jerk!" or may reflect an unusual perspective (Question: "What do you like to do together?") "Oh we enjoy finding a nearby ditch or trench in order to reenact the Soviet Storm."

Social Communication Disorder, a new diagnosis in DSM-5, is by definition the presence of social communication symptoms of an Autism Spectrum Disorder without the restricted repetitive behaviors or interests. These differentiating factors include repetitive speech or motor movements, insistence on sameness, inflexible adherence to routine, rigid thinking patterns, restricted interests, and hypo- or hyperreactivity to sensory input (DSM-5 p. 50). With careful consideration of present and historical factors in this domain, a child who has never exhibited any of these patterns or interests would meet criteria for a language disorder and not ASD. A diagnosis of ASD supersedes Social (pragmatic) Communication Disorder if any restricted, repetitive patterns of behavior or interest are present.

Differential Diagnosis of Social (pragmatic) Communication Disorder and ASD

A graphic depiction on the next page guides clinicians in the complex differential diagnosis of Social Communication Disorder as compared to ASD.

Social Communication Disorder: Children with Social (pragmatic) communication disorder have impaired social skills but do not have any restricted or repetitive behaviors. They lack understanding of social rules and conventions. Children with SCD struggle to understand and use verbal and nonverbal cues for communication. They have challenges in communication for different purposes, such as not understanding how talking to a peer might be different than talking to a parent or teacher. Individuals with SCD fail to consider conversational context, and may struggle in their storytelling. They tend to struggle frequently with inferences and nonliteral language. However, children with this disorder do *not* seek environmental consistency and rigidly adhere to routines like is seen in ASD. The referral would be for social skills groups and speech therapy.

ASD (not SCD)

Children with ASD have pragmatic deficits; but also, significant rigidity, and restricted interests or repetitive behaviors. They may be withdrawn and tend to have behavior problems (which may not be experienced with those who have SCD). They show a limited range of emotional expression and emotions are poorly integrated with other forms of communication, such as gestures and eye contact. Children with ASD may have emotional symptoms and may not be interested in social engagement. This looks somewhat different than in SCD, where there may be adequate emotional regulation and expression; may be appropriate behaviors, and there will not be any restricted interests or repetitive behaviors. For this reason, both SCD and ASD are not diagnosed comorbidly. These are separate and distinct disorders. The referrals for ASD may include speech therapy; however, other therapies such as ABA therapy are generally recommended that will not be required typically for SCD (Fig. 13.3).

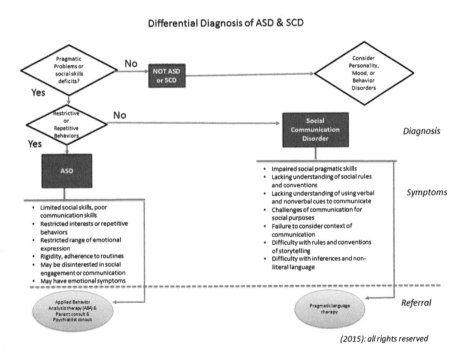

Fig. 13.3 Differential diagnosis of ASD and SCD

Comorbid ASD and Language Disorders

As language disorders occur in the context of ASD, it is a practice to specify language impairment as part of the diagnosis for ASD. Language Disorders are not diagnosed comorbid with Autism Spectrum Disorders. For example, if an individual meets criteria for ASD it would not be necessary to make a diagnosis of Language Disorder (formerly known as Expressive/Receptive Language Disorder). As noted above, ASD would also not be diagnosed comorbid with Social Communication Disorder. It is important when specifying the language impairment associated with ASD to give a detailed and specific description of the language abilities of a child. For example, a language specifier may entail "with associated language impairments in receptive language, pragmatic language and fluency; without associated language impairments in expressive language."

With communication disorders including Speech Sound Disorder and Childhood-Onset Fluency Disorder (Stuttering) having an oral motor deficit or another neurological condition rules out the diagnosis. Oftentimes, individuals with ASD have oral motor deficits that are linked to challenges in speech production, fluency, and clarity (Belmonte et al., 2013). While low tone in the face is a motor deficit, it can have an impact on articulation which can be quite debilitating. Children may have trouble with certain sound production or may tend to drop first or last syllables of a word. Additionally, vocal prosody may have a sing-song note with longer consonants or vowel sounds. These language differences can occur within the context of ASD and so Stuttering or Speech Sound Disorder should only be diagnosed if an individual does *not* have an Autism Spectrum Disorder.

Attention Disorders

Attention Deficit Hyperactivity Disorder (AD/HD) is a pattern of inattention and/or hyperactivity and impulsivity that interferes with functioning or development, is present prior to age 12, is present in more than one setting and interferes with social, academic, or occupational functioning (and cannot be explained by another mental or psychotic disorder) (APA, 2013 pp. 59–60). Prevalence estimates of AD/HD in school-aged children have ranged from 2 to 18 % in community samples, with most estimates between 3 and 10 % (Barkley, 2006; Pastor & Reuben, 2008). The Diagnostic and Statistical Manual of Mental Disorders, 5th Edition, reports a 5 % rate for children with AD/HD in the general population and identifies three subtypes of AD/HD: combined type, predominantly inattentive type, and predominantly hyperactive/impulsive type. Similar to autism, AD/HD is more frequently diagnosed in males than in females. The ratio is approximately 2:1 in children (Polanczyk, Silva, Bernardo, Biederman, & Rohde, 2007). Furthermore, females are more likely to present with inattentive symptoms (APA, 2013).

Symptoms of inattention include poor attention to detail, difficulty sustaining attention in tasks that are not otherwise reinforcing, failure to listen, failure to follow through with tasks, difficulty with organization, difficulty engaging in tasks that require sustained mental effort, tendency to lose necessary materials, distractibility, and forgetfulness. Children with AD/HD can demonstrate carelessness, academic skill deficits, impulsivity, and poor problem-solving techniques (DuPaul & Stoner, 2003). Barkley (1998, 2006) outlines four specific executive functions: (1) Nonverbal working memory, (2) Internalization of speech (verbal working memory), (3) Self-regulation of affect/motivation/arousal, (4) Reconstitution (planning and generalizing.) Although these four categories are distinct, Barkley puts forth that they are highly related and a deficit in any one area will produce a deficit in another. Any deficits will likely present as challenges with self-regulation, which is a central symptom of AD/HD (Barkley, 1998, 2006).

Research has long indicated that children with AD/HD generally show multiple deficits on measures of executive functioning; the most pronounced deficits are seen on measures of inhibition, verbal working memory, and planning ability (Barkley, 1998; Pennington & Ozonoff, 1996). A meta-analysis by Wilcutt and colleagues (2005) demonstrated that significant differences between AD/HD-diagnosed groups and control groups were most consistent on performance-based measures of response inhibition, vigilance, planning, and working memory.

Symptoms of hyperactivity and impulsivity include fidgeting, difficulty remaining seated, restlessness, running and climbing when inappropriate, lack of quiet play, acting as if "driven by a motor," excessive talking, blurting out answers, difficulty waiting his/her turn, and interrupting (APA, 2013 pp. 59–60). Behavior challenges are inherently at the root of AD/HD diagnoses. Traditionally, AD/HD has been assessed through multiple behavior rating scales, completed by multiple observers, namely parents and teachers. Diagnostic criteria in the current DSM-5 as well as previous editions clearly identify behaviors that negatively impact social and academic/occupational activities. In children, problem behaviors are most often evident during academic tasks, both in school and at home. These problems can become so pervasive that parents pursue diagnostic testing. DuPaul and Stoner (2003) reported that challenges with attention and behavioral control are two major reasons for referral to school and clinical psychologists. Academically, specific behavior challenges in children with AD/HD include listening, following directions, sitting still, organizing materials and spaces, and cooperating with classmates (Barkley, 1998, 2006).

While symptoms of inattention in particular may lead to failure to read social cues and communicate effectively with others, social communication weakness is not a core deficit of AD/HD. Rather, individuals with AD/HD alone are more likely to make eye contact, gesture, and exhibit ease in connecting socially with others than those with ASD. Those with ASD must have social communication problems and restricted repetitive behaviors and are likely to have deficits in executive functioning. They may exhibit a large number of symptoms of AD/HD or perhaps just a few, thus not meeting criteria for both diagnoses. It is possible to have AD/HD, ASD, or both; thus, making differential or comorbidity determination challenging and complex.

Much has been written about the differential diagnosis and comorbidity between ASD and AD/HD. Mannion and Leader (2013) report that prevalence data indicate that 14–78 % if individuals with ASD have co-occurring AD/HD, while Simonoff and colleagues report that 31 % of those with ASD also meet criteria for AD/HD (2008). This is a very wide range and may indicate the clinical challenges inherent in differential diagnosis for these commonly linked disorders.

Until the release of DSM-5, clinicians were informed by DSM-IV-TR not to diagnose AD/HD with ASD as attention problems in ASD were common and a part of the diagnosis of autism. DSM-5 states (p. 58) "A diagnosis of AD/HD should be considered when attentional difficulties or hyperactivity exceeds that typically seen in individuals of comparable mental age (APA, 2013)."

Differentiating Between ASD and AD/HD

Personal experience has revealed that many individuals referred for ASD evaluations already have diagnoses of AD/HD, some of which are supported by parent and teacher report, rating scale data and continuous performance testing of sustained attention, and others which are not. There is certainly a large percentage of individuals with ASD who do not meet criteria for AD/HD.

Catherine Lord's group reported research looking at the ADOS and ADI-R to determine items that best distinguish or differentiate between ASD and AD/HD. The study found that the ADOS was better at differentiating between the two diagnoses than the ADI-R. Four social communication items on the ADOS were good discriminators between AD/HD and ASD. Those with ASD had higher scores (indicating poorer performance) on the items "quality of social overtures," "facial expressions directed toward others," "unusual eye contact," and "amount of reciprocal social communication" than did the AD/HD group. The results of the study led researchers to caution against abbreviated measures or batteries because distinguishing between ASD and AD/HD is complex (Grzadzinski, Lord & Bishop poster Symptoms of ASD in ADHD: Distinguishing between high functioning ASD and ADHD).

Researchers Mayes, Calhoun, Mayes, and Molitoris (2012) examined distinct and overlapping symptoms of ASD and AD/HD (In Mannion & Leader, 2013). They found that ASD is distinct in reference to social communication deficits and restricted, repetitive behaviors, while attention deficits, hyperactivity, and impulsivity are (often) part of autism. They note these are "neurobiological disorders with similar underlying neuropsychological deficits" (p. 283). While those with AD/HD and ASD both have challenges with executive functioning, Tye and colleagues (2013) demonstrated that children with AD/HD alone have challenges in attentional orienting and inhibitory control. This is consistent with Mannion and Leader (2013) reporting problems in inhibitory performance for those with AD/HD when compared to children with ASD. Tye et al. found that children who have ASD and not AD/HD have differences in conflict monitoring and response preparation (2014).

In Deborah Fein and colleagues' keystone book, *The Neuropsychology of Autism* (2011) authors write that individuals with ASD alone have challenges shifting and sequencing. For example, they may struggle to: change tasks quickly, switch attention, transition, plan, and organize; however, may not have difficulty sustaining attention (Garretson, Fein and Waterhouse 1990; Courchesne et al. 1994). Translating this to neuropsychological testing, an individual with ASD alone may struggle with tasks like the WCST, TOL-2, Stroop, and CTMT but may have Average to Above Average performance on a continuous performance task like the TOVA. Conversely, an individual with AD/HD will have difficulty sustaining attention in the absence of immediate reinforcement. Deprey and Ozonoff (2009) note that attention problems, while common in ASD may be more related to internal distractibility while lack of focus and external distractibility are more consistently apparent in AD/HD. Matson, Rieske, and Williams (2013) additionally notes that sensory sensitivities may look like attention problems and be misinterpreted. Sensory sensitivities may be present in either diagnosis or in ASD, AD/HD, or both.

Comorbid ASD and AD/HD

As noted above, AD/HD is one of the most common comorbid disorders in those diagnosed with ASD (Jang et al., 2013). Additionally, ASD and AD/HD may share some genetic and biological risk factors (Jang et al., 2013). Research across numerous studies indicates that having both AD/HD and ASD results in more significant symptoms, or additive effects, than having one or the other (Tye et al., 2013; Jang et al, 2013; Matson et al., 2013). Individuals with both diagnoses are likely to have more attention problems and more behavior problems than those with ASD alone. A number of brain structures are implicated in both disorders, though the symptom patterns are distinct. These include the medial frontal and prefrontal cortex abnormalities (Jang et al., 2013). Jang et al. found more tantrum behaviors, conduct problems and more anxiety in the group they assessed with comorbid diagnosis than in either group with only ASD or AD/HD. They report that these findings are consistent with previous studies examining comorbid symptoms. Researchers suggest that there are differences on neurodevelopmental level between the three groups including ASD, AD/HD, and those with ASD+AD/HD (Matson et al., 2013). Social skills, executive functioning skills, and verbal and spatial working memory are more impacted in individuals with both ASD and AD/HD than those with either alone (Matson et al., 2013).

In conclusion, careful and comprehensive assessment is crucial when evaluating for the presence of ASD, AD/HD, or comorbid diagnosis. AD/HD co-occurs in a high number of individuals with ASD and is related to more significant symptom profiles. Understanding the complex presentation of each individual can lead to better treatment for both conditions and better treatment outcomes.

Differential and Comorbid Diagnosis of AD/HD and ASD

Differential Diagnosis between AD/HD and ASD can be a difficult task. Reviewing the graph on the next page, clinicians are invited to consider the different profiles in the following diagnostic categories: ASD alone, ADHD alone, and ADHD and ASD comorbid.

AD/HD Alone: *The primary feature used to determine if the child has AD/HD is disinhibition.* Clinicians can test disinhibition through observations, a continuous performance measure like the T.O.V.A., rating scales from parents such as the Conners, BASC-II, and BRIEF, as well as interview history. If the child is persistently inattentive and lacks inhibition, the child has AD/HD. As shown in the figure, children with AD/HD tend to show hyperactivity, impulsivity, and distractibility (of course, there is variation in the subtypes of AD/HD: Combined Presentation, Predominately Inattentive Presentation, and Predominately Hyperactive/Impulsive Presentation). Children with AD/HD have persistent attention problems and significant difficulties with impulse control. Children with AD/HD may blurt out in class, and may be seen as socially obnoxious. They may have a history of social rejection and "social dysfunction" (APA, 2013), but these problems tend to originate from challenging behavior, and poor self-control that are characteristic of the disorder. Children with AD/HD may impulsively hit other children, interrupt, or barge into conversations. These deficits tend to show up socially but look quite different from the "social disengagement" and "isolation" characteristic of ASD (APA, 2013). Unlike in ASD, children with AD/HD alone tend to have the skills to be socially reciprocal; they may be able to assess the emotions of others and recognize emotions in themselves, and they do not tend to have repetitive behaviors or restricted interests.

ASD Alone: *The primary feature in autism is poor social reciprocity.* Individuals with ASD cannot adequately initiate or engage in reciprocal play and communication. The DSM-5 differentiates the social and behavioral challenges seen in ASD compared to AD/HD, claiming that although both groups may have tantrums; the AD/HD group tantrums due to difficulty with poor self-control, whereas the ASD group tantrums due to "an inability to tolerate change from the expected course of events" (APA, 2013, p. 64). Those with ASD alone demonstrate better inhibition, flexibility, working memory, and planning skills than those with comorbid diagnosis (Sinzig, Bruning, Morsch, & Lehmkuhl, 2008). Although individuals with ASD may have attention problems, generally they have "selective attention," rather than the persistent attention problems seen in AD/HD. Children with ASD can attend with appropriate reinforcement but may prefer to attend to their special interest, rather than the stimulus being presented. In ASD alone, the child is likely to be socially withdrawn, have poor communication skills, limited emotional insight, or understanding, and lack awareness of social cues, repetitive behaviors, and significant rigidity.

ASD and ADHD: *The primary determining feature of ASD and AD/HD combined is that they are disinhibited and lack social reciprocity.* AD/HD and ASDs co-occur in 14–78 % of the population diagnosed with ASD (Gargaro et al. 2011). Children with comorbid symptoms of both ASD and AD/HD have more difficulty with inhibitory performance when compared with children who have ASD alone (Mannion & Leader, 2013; Mayes et al., 2012). Children with both disorders have poor social and communication skills. They tend to be socially disinhibited, impulsive, and distractible. Children with both disorders are more prone to outbursts and tantrums due in part to rigidity (ASD) and in part to poor self-control (AD/HD). Children with both disorders fail a continuous performance test such as the T.O.V.A. and are highly emotionally dysregulated.

In the figure that follows, readers can see how the different diagnostic categories call for different referrals and recommendations. Children with AD/HD alone can benefit from ABA therapy, parent consult, and psychiatrist consult. Children with ASD can benefit from Social Skills Groups, Cognitive Behavioral Therapy, and ABA. Children with both disorders may benefit from all of these types of therapeutic interventions (Fig. 13.4).

Differential and Comorbid Diagnosis of ASD & ADHD

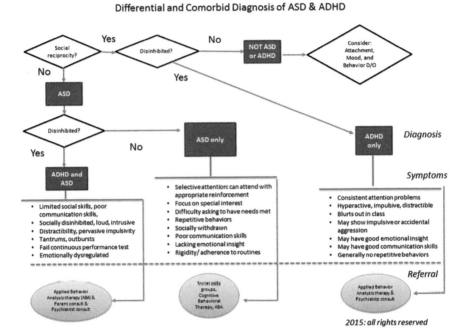

Fig. 13.4   Differential and comorbid diagnosis of ASD and SCD

Concluding Remarks on Disorders of Neurodevelopment and Brain Functioning

In this chapter, authors have reviewed comorbid diagnoses and differential diagnosis of a number of conditions that may occur with or be confused with Autism Spectrum Disorders. It is essential to complete a thorough assessment of cognition, language, learning, attention, and social interaction and to consider all significant symptoms present in an individual and possible diagnoses to explain an individual's presentation. With the DSM-5, clinicians are able to identify significant attention problems and make diagnoses of autism and AD/HD which is helpful in guiding treatment. Further research is needed in the area of comorbid diagnosis with ASD, but much ground has been gained in understanding symptoms and determining research-based approaches to treat each condition that is present. Now, discussion moves to disorders of emotion, mood, and behavior also commonly comorbid or confused with ASD.

Chapter 14
Disorders of Emotion, Mood, and Behavior

Abstract Differential diagnosis of emotion, mood, and behavioral conditions includes the differential and comorbid diagnosis of anxiety disorders, OCD, Mood Disorders, Psychosis, Behavioral Disorders, Trauma-related Disorders, Attachment Disorders, Personality Disorders, and other relevant comorbidities. As ASD is a diagnosis based on social communication and restricted, repetitive behaviors or patterns, it is important to look at these areas in the context of other diagnoses. For example, it is important to consider paucity of language in the context of depression versus autism where it occurs due to social communication difficulties. Social avoidance in the context of an anxiety disorder must be compared to the withdrawal symptoms often seen in ASD. The cognitive distortions associated with mood must be compared to the challenges with peer interaction found in autism. A lack of communication should be evaluated as to whether the child has trauma or the communication deficits associated with ASD. A push–pull interaction style could be a symptom of an attachment disorder or the lack of appropriate social reciprocity and social boundaries could indicate ASD. Sometimes the symptoms described occur in the context of multiple disorders; while at times, symptoms can be adequately subsumed under ASD or another disorder. This chapter will explore these other mood, behavior, and adaptive disorders in the context of ASD.

Keywords Differential diagnosis for autism and mood disorders • Comorbid diagnosis of autism and personality disorders • Autism and anxiety disorders • Autism and mood disorders • Autism and psychotic disorders; autism and behavior disorders • Autism and trauma disorders • Autism and attachment disorders • Autism and personality disorders • Prognosis of comorbid ASD and personality disorders

Anxiety Disorders and OCD

Anxiety Disorders are the most commonly comorbid condition(s) with Autism Spectrum Disorders. Although the rates vary across studies, the general consensus is that rates of occurrence are around 40 %. Reaven (2015) indicates Anxiety can be challenging to diagnose in individuals with ASD because of the unique presentation of ASD. One of the reasons it is so difficult to diagnose children on the Spectrum with anxiety is *diagnostic overshadowing* which is when a child's autism is erroneously assumed to encompass or subsume the anxiety symptoms. A second is *psychosocial masking*, when a child with autism is not able to identify and report his or her own symptoms of anxiety (similar to a frozen profile and alexithymia problems previously discussed). A third issue is *diagnostic overlap* as there are some common symptoms shared by autism and anxiety. There are also *problem behaviors* in ASD that may disguise anxiety problems. Finally, the symptoms may *present differently* in children with ASD and an Intellectual Disability (Reaven, 2015, citing Fuller & Sabatino, 1998; Reiss & Szyszko, 1983).

Anxiety Disorders share characteristics including excessive fear and worry and related behavioral disturbances (APA, 2013, p. 189). Cervantes et al. reported that 70 % of individuals with ASD have a comorbid psychological diagnosis and 41 % meet criteria for two or more comorbid diagnoses (2013). Anxiety Disorders, of various types, are some of the more commonly co-occurring diagnoses with prevalence estimates that range from 11 to 84 % in individuals with ASD. Simonoff et al. report 44 % of those with ASD have a specific phobia (like a fear of flushing toilets or dogs) and 37 % of those with ASD also meet criteria for OCD (2008). This represents a much higher occurrence of anxiety in those with ASD than within the general population (Cervantes, Matson, Tureck, & Adams, 2013).

This discussion will focus on Specific Phobia, Generalized Anxiety Disorder, Social Anxiety Disorder, Separation Anxiety Disorder, and Obsessive Compulsive Disorder (while not classified as an anxiety disorder, OCD does involve anxiety symptoms).

Generalized Anxiety is characterized by excessive worry occurring more days than not. Worry is difficult to control and must be characterized by at least one of these in children and three in adults: restlessness, fatigue, difficulty concentrating, irritability, muscle tension, and/or sleep disturbance. GAD can be diagnosed comorbid with ASD.

Social Anxiety includes anxiety related to social situations and cannot be comorbid with an ASD. *Separation Anxiety* is excessive fear concerning separation from an attachment figure not better explained by another mental disorder. Separation Anxiety can co-occur with ASD provided that the fear is not related to an adherence to routine or insistence on sameness and is indeed related to separation from a caregiver. *Obsessive Compulsive Disorder* is characterized by the presence of obsessions, compulsions, or both. Intrusive and unwanted thoughts or images causing marked anxiety followed by repetitive behaviors aimed at preventing or reducing anxiety define this disorder. OCD obsessions and compulsions do not involve real-life concerns as do the worries and anxieties associated with anxiety disorders. OCD can co-occur with ASD assuming repetitive patterns of behavior can be differentiated from obsessions and compulsions (APA, 2013).

Differentiating Between ASD and Anxiety Disorders

When examining the differentiation of an Anxiety Disorder and an Autism Spectrum Disorder, it is again pertinent to look closely at the social communication weaknesses and restricted repetitive behaviors. Does an individual struggle with social communication, avoid situations and complete routines or rituals because of anxiety, because of ASD, or could it be both? An individual with an ASD who does not suffer from anxiety may avoid social situations because of a lack of interest in social interaction. Conversely, he or she may enjoy social interactions, but deficits in social communication will have some impact on his or her ability to read social cues, interpret the perspective of others, and engage in reciprocal social interaction at an age appropriate level. Many individuals with ASD do not have co-occurring anxiety. Anywhere from 16 to 89 % of individuals who have ASD do not meet criteria for an Anxiety Disorder (Cervantes et al., 2013).

An individual who has Social Anxiety and not ASD will likely have very different behavior at home with siblings, family members, or close friends (playing cooperatively, making eye contact, initiating joint attention, conversing reciprocally) than he or she in a social setting like at school or at a party. This individual will fear embarrassment or rejection and try to avoid certain settings that may lead to these experiences. If forced into social settings, an anxious individual may freeze, cling to a parent, fail to speak, or throw a tantrum. An individual with an ASD is more likely to wander alone, ignore others, play independently, or misread nonverbal and social cues of others leading to disagreements or challenges. An individual with ASD will have some level of social communication challenges across settings, while an individual with an anxiety disorder should be able to interact appropriately in the absence of fear and anxiety. In the clinic evaluation setting, individuals who warm up considerably, show a marked change in eye contact, conversation, and engagement (social communication) over time, and who have insight into their own anxiety are likely to be diagnosed with an anxiety disorder, rather than ASD.

OCD can be more challenging to differentiate and is often diagnosed instead of autism in children with Autism Spectrum Disorders by practitioners who are not familiar with ASD. OCD is intrusive and *unwanted* thoughts or images causing marked anxiety followed by repetitive behaviors *aimed at preventing or reducing anxiety*. Those with ASD who have specialized interests in dinosaurs, trucks, trash, the solar system, or WWII and subsequently have routines based around their interests enjoy talking about these topics. Individuals report they like completing routines related to the topic. A child with ASD who lines up his or her cars does this because he or she likes to line up and look at the cars, not to reduce anxiety. A child with ASD may throw tantrum or demonstrate rigidity when prevented from completing such a routine, but the point of the routine is not to reduce anxiety. This is very important to differentiate during the assessment process. Westphal, Kober, Voos, and Volkmar (2014) put it well when they reported "… the obsessions and compulsions that occur with OCD are generally egodystonic, at odds with the idealized self-image a person may have. The circumscribed interests and rituals that accompany ASD, on the other hand, tend to be egosyntonic, in harmony with the subject's self-image" (p. 294).

Can an individual with ASD develop OCD? Yes. However, individuals who complete their repetitive routines and rituals because they want to, and are not trying to decrease or prevent anxiety, do not have OCD.

Comorbid ASD and Anxiety Disorders

A Specific Phobia, Generalized Anxiety Disorder, Separation Anxiety Disorder, and OCD can co-occur with Autism Spectrum Disorders. It can be challenging at times to make the comorbid diagnosis of anxiety, however, because of limited emotional insight in individuals with autism. Trammell, Wilczynski, Dale, and McIntosh (2013)) states that symptoms of anxiety are very common in ASD, but an anxiety disorder is only diagnosed if anxiety has a significant impact on an individual's daily functioning.

Clinically, the authors of this text find that anxiety commonly co-occurs in untreated Autism Spectrum Disorders. Bright individuals often overlooked for assessment until late elementary school, middle school, or at times even high school often present with significant symptoms of anxiety or depression based on a realization that they are different from peers and an inability to establish meaningful relationships. Worry about school performance, social situations, and peer rejection are common. In these cases, anxiety may or may not be reported on rating scales by the individual but frequently anxiety is evident in an individual's presentation, his or her stories, projective measures, and parent and teacher questionnaires. A child may deny symptoms when asked directly, but he or she may hyperventilate as questions become difficult or cry when a task does not come easily. A child may need frequent contact with a parent or even require a parent to be present at all times. It is important to determine whether anxiety is present because treating these symptoms can make a huge difference to the individual. Psychotherapy combined with a social skills group and at times medication management can help a struggling child, adolescent, or adult regain footing and find success socially, academically, and/or occupationally. It is important to note that anxiety is readily contagious and so a child with very anxious parents is more likely to exhibit symptoms than a child whose caregivers are psychologically more stable.

Mood Disorders

Many clinicians fail to consider the comorbid diagnosis of Mood Disorders and ASD. It can be complex to rule out ASD when an individual has a significant Mood Disorder. Mood Disorders include Depressive and Bipolar Disorders. Depressive Disorders encompass a variety of disorders that involve sad or irritable mood, while Bipolar Disorders include periods of sadness and irritability and periods of mania or hypomania. Manic symptoms may include inflated self-esteem, decreased need for sleep, excessive talking, distractibility, increased goal-directed activity, and involvement in risky or dangerous activities (APA, 2013, p. 124). These symptoms must be observable and cause clinically significant distress that impacts functioning. The DSM-5 classifies Mood Disorders as Bipolar and Related Disorders and Depressive Disorders. Simonoff et al. report that 24 % of individuals with ASD also suffer from depression (2008).

Another mood disorder of interest is the Depressive Disorder: Disruptive Mood Dysregulation Disorder (DMDD). DMDD is a new diagnosis that incorporates mood and behavioral symptoms and is diagnosed only in childhood and adolescence, from ages 6 to 18 (APA, 2013, p. 156). DMDD is defined as irritable and angry mood nearly every day present in two or more settings with severe and recurrent temper outbursts. DMDD differs from Oppositional Defiant Disorder because there is mood disturbance underlying the temper tantrums that occur. The DSM-5 notes that if DMDD and ODD are present DMDD supersedes ODD, which is a behavioral diagnosis. This disorder is important to note because often children with ASD develop behavior problems to escape or avoid non-preferred activities. These behavioral symptoms are secondary to autism, but some individuals may have underlying depressive symptoms along with tantrum behavior. In this case, the clinician must consider whether the behaviors occur in the context of ASD and ODD, or a mood disorder such as DMDD. It is possible to have both ASD and ODD, but DMDD and ODD are not comorbidly diagnosed.

Differentiating Between ASD and Mood Disorders

Determining whether an Autism Spectrum Disorder, Mood Disorder, or both are impacting social communication can be challenging, particularly in adolescents and adults. A process of identifying all symptoms that are pathologic and then examining these in the context of mood and autism is recommended. In adults, symptoms of withdrawal and interpersonal impairment are associated with both Depression and Autism Spectrum Disorders (Trammell et al., 2013). In the context of ASD, these impairments are secondary to challenges initiating conversation, taking others' perspectives and understanding relationship dynamics. It can be challenging when assessing a depressed adult or adolescent to determine whether ASD is present. It can also be difficult to differentiate between withdrawal, lack of eye contact, and lack of conversational reciprocity in ASD and these symptoms in Depression. Assessing for the presence of pathologic symptoms that only occur in ASD like stereotyped language, repetitive behaviors or interests, lack of creativity, and insight into the nature of relationships can help make a differential diagnosis. An individual with severe depression may present with impaired conversation skills, nonverbal skills, and even impaired emotional awareness. The same individual who does not have ASD should be able to describe what a friend is and discuss the nature of social relationships. An individual with ASD would likely have more difficulty discussing these or might sound as if he or she were reciting a definition from a textbook.

Stereotyped language and repetitive behaviors cannot be subsumed under depression or explained in the context of a Mood Disorder; thus these are pathologic symptoms that must be explained with another diagnosis. Creative ADOS-2 tasks like "Telling a Story from a Book" or "Description of a Picture" (discussing the cartoon map) can provide a nice arena to evaluate for stereotyped or repetitive language. Individuals who list states and capitols, remark on the size of the cartoon figures in relation to states, or provide an exhaustive list of cheeses produced in Wisconsin are exhibiting pathologic symptoms not associated with depression. An individual who exhibits no pathologic symptoms outside of those associated with a Mood Disorder, and has appropriate social reciprocity, would be diagnosed with the corresponding Mood Disorder and not ASD. With adequate treatment of an individual's depression, it may be advised to reevaluate for ASD. This may be recommended if an individual was so withdrawn that little language or conversation was offered. Conversely, an individual who does not report sadness, presents as neutral or incongruent in mood and affect, and who has impairments in social communication and poor reciprocity may have ASD alone, given his or her tendency to withdraw and avoid social interaction.

In children, when considering mood and autism, often tasks of creativity in play can aide in differentiating. A depressed child may exhibit depression symptoms or share emotions during play. For example, a child who acts out a scenario involving multiple character deaths and then demonstrates mourning and honoring these individuals with appropriate mood and affect usually does not have autism. Children who demonstrate the ability to symbolically represent characters in play, understand emotions, take another character's perspective, and express complex emotions generally do not meet criteria for ASD, but might indeed for a mood disorder. Character play that is immature, unreasonably violent or careless, not well-integrated, and lacking perspective taking may signal ASD.

Comorbid ASD and Mood Disorders

While emotional disturbance and difficulty regulating emotions are not core features of ASD, mood disturbances are surprisingly common in individuals diagnosed with Autism Spectrum Disorders (Mazefsky et al., 2013). Lehnhardt et al. report that when patients are diagnosed later with ASD, they are diagnosed with Depressive disorders in 53 % of cases (2013). The DSM-5 indicates the importance of determining whether mood symptoms such as irritability or temper outbursts occur in the context of ASD. An example for ASD would be when the tantrums occur in response to a routine being disturbed. Alternately, a child who meets full criteria for ASD and also exhibits crying, irritability, suicidal statements, and reports a lack of friendship and acceptance among peers may receive a diagnosis of depression in addition to ASD. When a child is overly active, has racing thoughts, and exhibits periods of grandiosity, pressured speech, flight of ideas, and engages in dangerous behavior in addition to having an Autism Spectrum Disorder, he or she may have a comorbid Bipolar Disorder. As with Anxiety Disorders, there may be a common ideology between Bipolar and ASD. Those with DMDD often have irritability and tantrums not related to the ASD symptoms, but do not have the elevated mood symptoms that would be consistent with Bipolar.

As individuals with ASD often have poor emotional insight, researchers suggest it is important to evaluate mood criteria with observable behaviors. While scales like the Beck Depression Inventory (BDI) may not be elevated, property destruction, aggression, or self-injury may be behavioral equivalents of depression (Witwer & Lecavalier, 2010). Researchers suggest that excessive giddiness, an increase in talking, and excessive noisemaking may be behavioral equivalents for mania. Witwer and Lecavalier (2010) note the importance of assessing these behavioral symptoms that may signal a mood disorder with multiple methods. This hypothesized use of behavioral indicators alone, rather than requiring self-report indicators for mood disorders, has not been validated to date. When evaluating children, it can be most useful to consider parent and teacher rating scales of emotions and compare these to self-report. The "frozen profile" termed by Helena Huckabee PhD, BCBA-D, suggests that often children with autism report fewer emotional symptoms than average. When individuals present with this profile, it suggests that the self-reporter does not have appropriate insight into his or her own emotions and is unlikely to adequately assess these internal emotional experiences. Taken together, it is recommended that clinicians consider self-report with caution, utilizing clinical judgment, observable behaviors, and rating scales from multiple sources to diagnose a mood disorder comorbid with ASD.

A study of emotion dysregulation in children and adolescents with ASD evaluated the use of various cognitive techniques including cognitive reappraisal and emotion suppression in those with and without autism. Individuals with ASD who had solid problem-solving and emotion-regulation skills benefitted equally from the use of cognitive strategies in regulating their emotions. While no significant difference was found in problem-solving, avoidance, and relaxation skills, Samson, Hardan, Podell, Phillips, and Gross (2014) found those with ASD suppressed emotions more frequently and were less likely to engage in cognitive reappraisal. Cognitive reappraisal involves modifying thoughts about an event so that the emotional response is altered. When prompted to do this, individuals with ASD had more difficulty using the strategy; however, when taught to generate cognitive reappraisals, individuals with ASD benefitted equally from using them. This study indicates that explicit teaching of skills for emotion regulation can benefit those with ASD. These researched differences in emotion regulation and suppression for those with ASD are perhaps a contributor to greater mood symptoms (Lehnhardt et al., 2013; Samson et al., 2014).

Psychotic Disorders

Psychotic disorders are not as commonly differentially diagnosed from ASD and attention disorders, and clinically, when psychosis is indeed present, diagnosis can be complex. Psychotic Disorders include Schizophrenia Spectrum Disorders and Bipolar or Depressive Disorders with Psychotic Features. Features of a Psychotic Disorder include: Delusions, Hallucinations, Disorganized Thinking, Grossly Disorganized or Abnormal Motor Behavior, and Negative Symptoms. To diagnose Schizophrenia, two of these features *may be* present and one *must* be: Delusions,

Hallucinations, or Disorganized Thinking (APA, 2013). When considering a diagnosis on the Schizophrenia Spectrum in an individual with developmental delays, and a diagnosis of Autism Spectrum Disorder, the individual must have prominent Delusions or Hallucinations present for more than a month. A Bipolar or Depressive Disorder with Psychotic Features is diagnosed if these features occur only in the context of Depressive or Manic episodes. Psychotic Disorders can be diagnosed with ASD; however, symptoms must be considered carefully as those without a full understanding of ASD may mistakenly identify psychosis. When clinicians are unsure if disorganized thinking and delusional conversational content occur in the context of ASD, it is advised to consider a consultation with an ASD diagnostic clinician and to clearly denote in the report whether or not these diagnoses can be differentially diagnosed or ruled out.

Differentiating Between ASD and Psychotic Disorders

In order to differentiate between Bipolar or Depression With Psychotic Features or a diagnosis on the Schizophrenia Spectrum and ASD, it is crucial to fully understand what is a Delusion or Hallucination and what is stereotyped language or a repetitive behavior or interest. The DSM-5 states on p. 105 "These (ASDs) may also have symptoms resembling a psychotic episode but are distinguished by their respective deficits in social interaction with repetitive and restricted behaviors and other cognitive and communication deficits." As prominent Delusions or Hallucinations must be present, making a differential diagnosis or a comorbid diagnosis involves understanding these features. "Delusions are fixed beliefs not amendable to change in light of conflicting evidence" (APA, 2013 p. 87). The degree of conviction in light of evidence that contradicts differentiates a Delusion from a strong belief. Themes can be persecutory (belief that one will be harmed), referential (belief that comments or cues are directed at oneself), somatic (regarding health), religious, grandiose (belief that the individual possesses exceptional abilities, wealth etc.), erotomanic (false belief that another is in love with the individual), Nihilistic (belief that a major catastrophe will occur), and bizarre (implausible and not culturally understandable) (APA, 2013). "Hallucinations are perception-like experiences that occur without an external stimulus" (APA, 2013 p. 87). These can occur in any sensory modality. The DSM-5 notes that auditory hallucinations are most common in the Schizophrenia Spectrum. These are voices distinct from an individual's thoughts.

A client told one of the authors of this text "An air conditioner used to talk to me and tell me I was a bad person." This client presented with diagnoses of psychosis and ASD, having had developmental delays and an early diagnosis of autism. This client did not have a perseverative interest in air conditioners and did not quote books or movies with relative themes. If in fact air conditioners were a restricted interest, this would indicate ASD is the appropriate diagnosis, rather than psychosis. She seemed to respond well to her antipsychotic medication and at the time was "in full remission" of symptoms.

Another client presented with significant stereotyped language around Star Wars movies, speaking of "Jedi Mind Tricks," "Light-sabers," and quoting sections of dialogue from Star Wars movies and books. This client expressed his frustration through the use of Star Wars analogies "I'm like Darth Mal in this scenario!" While professionals in the past had reported psychosis, this individual was presenting with restricted repetitive interests associated with autism. When pressed, he understood that Star Wars was a creation of a writer, producer, and director and could provide extensive historical information on the making of the series including set, score, and actors. In this case, Star Wars was a restricted interest and stereotyped language included quotes and reenactments. The client offered at one time that he really wished fictional characters were real because he understood them and knew in those scenarios what was going to happen next. These characters provided predictability and routine as well as entertainment. He remarked that real people were not so predictable. This client was not presenting with a grandiose delusion, but rather his symptoms occurred in the context of autism.

Hallucinations can be challenging for an individual with ASD to distinguish from a thought. At times, children express concerns about "hearing voices" and describe an internal dialogue or conscience. For example, "I shouldn't have a cookie, mom said to wait until after dinner" is an internal thought process and not a hallucination. Providers considering rating scale data like the BASC-2 self-report must clarify with the child what is meant by "I hear things that others cannot hear" when a child says "often" or "almost always." The literal nature of many children with ASD often leads to an elevation in scales and requires clarification.

Considering the need to differentiate between Schizophrenia and ASD, it is also helpful to consider the developmental period. Those later diagnosed with Schizophrenia would not be expected to have significant social communication challenges or restricted, repetitive behaviors as children. Disorganized thinking in schizophrenia is often inferred from how an individual speaks including changing topics and making little sense. Individuals with ASD may follow their own train of thought and share stories without regard for the perspective of the listener. This can make language hard to follow if statements are made without context. An individual with ASD may go on and on about "Mary," for example, without saying who she is. This is related to challenges in taking perspective and considering that the examiner does not know Mary. Stereotyped language may also sound disorganized as a client may make a comment like "There's cling-ons on the starboard bow!," which seems random but is actually a quote from Star Trek. Another client may remark out of the blue "Seaweed or spinach?" Comments may be related to an individual's own train of thought and offered in an effort to think of something to say but without considering the listener. A clinician can work to differentiate disorganized speech from stereotyped language by considering the context. Sometimes asking "Now which character said that?" allows the client to clarify the statement. If indeed the client is quoting movie lines or simply failing to take the perspective of the listener in communication, these symptoms signal ASD, *not* psychosis.

Two other features of psychosis include negative symptoms, like diminished emotional expression and disorganized or abnormal motor behavior. These symptoms

272 14 Disorders of Emotion, Mood, and Behavior

could be confused with restricted repetitive behaviors and nonverbal communication deficits. Diminished emotional expression occurring in psychotic disorders could easily be confused with flat or restricted affect or mood and affect incongruence. Those with ASD may have less varied facial expression, use fewer gestures, and avoid eye contact. They also may have unusual motor behaviors. Lord et al. (2000) suggested that when differentiating ASD from Schizophrenia, while this can be challenging, those with ASD have less reciprocal communication, use more stereotyped language, and demonstrate poorer rapport and fewer social responses (Trammell et al., 2013). Lord suggests evaluating directed facial expressions and shared enjoyment in differentiating the two (Trammell et al., 2013).

Because onset of Schizophrenia prior to adolescence is rare, the age of onset can be a very useful factor in differentiating Schizophrenia from ASD (APA, 2013; Lehnhardt et al., 2013). On average, Schizophrenia has onset in the mid-twenties for males and late-twenties for females. Autism Spectrum Disorders are evident much earlier. Taking a detailed history of an adult presenting for an evaluation can help to determine whether symptoms have been present across the lifespan or are later to onset. Less than 1 % of the population will be diagnosed with Schizophrenia (APA, 2013, p. 102).

While it is rare, it is relevant to mention Childhood-Onset Schizophrenia (COS) and the differentiation of these symptoms from ASD. Reaven, Hepburn, and Ross (2008) studied the use of the ADOS and ADI-R in differentiating between ASD and COS. They found that the ADOS and ADI-R alone were insufficient in making these to differentiations. Those with COS did have notable delays in language, motor, and social domains. Further, those with COS presented with grossly disorganized behaviors, hallucinations, delusions, and disordered thinking. Researchers suggest that specifically asking parents about delusions, hallucinations, ideas of reference, and unprovoked, serious aggressive behaviors can help to differentiate. The COS cases discussed by Reaven et al. (2008) provided report of hallucinatory experiences that included "things crawling on me," voices directing a child to "kill his mother," and hearing "Lucifer's voice."(p. 89). These bizarre reports are clearly psychotic in nature, while a child who shares "SpongeBob is real" is illogical and symptoms may be related to a preoccupation. Such an individual may have ASD, but does not have schizophrenia. In cases where Schizophrenia is present in children, it is possible to distinguish between ASD and COS with thorough observation of symptoms, clinical interviews, and careful consideration of a child's performance on the ADOS or ADI-R (Reaven et al., 2008).

Comorbid ASD and Psychotic Disorders

Comorbid psychotic disorders diagnosed with ASD signal poorer prognosis and greater functional deficits in areas including adaptive, executive functioning, social and attention domains (Wilson et al., 2014). Wilson et al.'s (2014) sample included individuals diagnosed with ASD and endorsing at least one Schizophrenia Spectrum symptom. Researchers reported that negative symptoms of schizophrenia tend to overlap with symptoms of ASD, which can make diagnosis challenging (Trammell et al., 2013, quoting Lord et al., 2000). Toal et al. (2009) used MRI technology to study brain regions implicated in ASD comorbid with psychosis and ASD or psychosis alone. The study reports that 7 % of those with ASD also have a diagnosis of Bipolar with Psychotic Features and 7.8 % have a diagnosis on the Schizophrenia Spectrum. Individuals with ASD, but without psychosis, differed in brain regions impacted. Those with comorbid conditions had differences in the right insular cortex and cerebellum extending to the fusiform gyrus. This is not consistent with typical differences in the brain studying psychosis in a non-autistic population. Researchers note that these brain regions are responsible for inhibitory control and face processing; hypothesizing that those with ASD may only require subtle additional brain abnormalities to develop positive symptoms of psychosis. Those with autism and those with Schizophrenia show similar deficits in social functioning and social cognition when considering theory of mind. These diagnoses can be comorbid and require careful consideration of both ASD symptoms and features of psychosis to make the diagnoses.

Behavior Disorders

People who do not know autism well might describe ASD as: reduced language, repetitive behaviors like head banging or lining up toys, and behavior problems. In reality, while restricted, repetitive patterns of behavior and routines are core symptoms of autism, *significant misbehavior is not.* Individuals with autism may become frustrated at a change in schedule or alteration of the regular routine; or because communication deficits impact his or her ability to communicate wants and needs; but behavior problems that develop in response to rigidity, adherence to routine, or communication challenges are not core features of autism. Researchers note that problem behaviors serve a purpose for the child and can be treated effectively if the highly trained clinician can determine the function of behavior. Brian Iwata, researcher and lecturer, describes the process of Functional Analysis or FA to determine the function of a problem behavior. He writes that behaviors can serve to escape or avoid an aversive situation or stimulus, to get access to something tangible (toy), to get attention, or to serve an internal purpose (hitting something because it feels good to the hitter in a sensory modality) (Iwata et al., 1994). An FA is the gold standard for assessing the function of a problem behavior because it does provide an assessment of causation instead of the correlation data that is available with a Functional Behavioral Assessment (FBA) (Trammell et al., 2013). These assessments are complex and should be conducted or supervised by a clinician with a BCBA or Board Certification in Behavior Analysis.

Children with Autism Spectrum Disorders may be more likely to develop problem behaviors than peers because of communication deficits that make it harder to express wants and needs in words and because of adherence to routine and sameness, thus eliciting frustration more easily as things happen and change in ways that are unexpected. For example, a child who does not have verbal means to communicate a desire to play with a toy (i.e. "Can I have a turn?") may grab, bite, or hit another child as a means to take the toy. If the child is successful and gets access to a preferred item in this way, then the behavior is reinforced. A school-aged child who is overwhelmed by the noise of the cafeteria, and the elevated social demands, may find that by misbehaving at the lunch table, throwing food perhaps, he or she is "punished" by having to eat lunch in the office. This provides an escape from the cafeteria, a quiet place, and perhaps adult attention. The behavior of throwing food is reinforced. As undesirable and misbehaviors are reinforced, they increase in frequency and a child (or an adult) may be at risk for developing a behavior disorder.

Behavior Disorders include disruptive, impulse-control, and conduct disorders in the DSM-5. Emotion and behavior regulation challenges are present in depressive and bipolar disorders previously discussed, but behavior disorders involve self-control and violate in some way the rights of others. Diagnosis of Disruptive Mood Dysregulation Disorder, DMDD, would not be made with a behavior disorder as DMDD would supersede a diagnosis of a behavior disorder. Behavior disorders are more common in males. Additionally, to some degree the behaviors noted in Oppositional Defiant Disorder (ODD) or Intermittent Explosive Disorder (IED) occur in typically developing individuals. It is important to consider the impact of these behaviors. BDs are generally diagnosed first in childhood or adolescence when the frequency and persistence are significant when compared to others at the same developmental level (APA, 2013, pp. 461–462). For the purpose of this chapter, ODD, CD, and IED will be discussed in the context of differentiating between these BDs and autism as well as the comorbid diagnosis.

Oppositional Defiant Disorder is often diagnosed first in childhood, and without proper treatment, could lead to the development of Conduct Disorder or Intermittent Explosive Disorder. ODD is described as a pattern of angry or irritable mood, defiant behavior, or vindictiveness lasting at least 6 months and with evidence of four of eight symptoms. These include losing temper, being easily annoyed, being angry or resentful, arguing with adults, refusing to follow rules, annoying others, blaming others for mistakes or misbehaviors, and being spiteful or vindictive. If a child is under five, these behaviors must occur most days and not be part of depression or bipolar disorders. For a child five and older, behaviors must be weekly. These behaviors cannot be solely directed at a sibling.

Conduct Disorder involves the violation of rights of others and/or societal norms with 3 of 15 criteria in categories including: aggression to people or animals, destruction of property, deceitfulness or theft, and serious violation of rules. A clinician can specify childhood or adolescent onset and this frequently follows an earlier diagnosis of ODD.

Intermittent Explosive Disorder requires a chronological age of six; includes aggressive outbursts not explained by a mood disorder and involves verbal and/or physical aggression not resulting in injury to people or animals; occurring twice weekly for 3 months; or aggressive outbursts that do result in injury to others three times within a year. IED would not be diagnosed if Depression, Bipolar Disorder, or DMDD are diagnosed (APA, 2013).

Differentiating Between ASD and Behavior Disorders

Individuals with Autism Spectrum Disorders may develop behavior problems that result from restricted and repetitive behaviors and routines and impairment in social communication. These behaviors may not necessarily meet criteria for a Behavior Disorder. When attempting to differentiate between ASD and BD, it is important to carefully assess for the presence of an Autism Spectrum Disorder. Individuals with ASD demonstrate significant difficulty with social reciprocity; often exhibit poor social perspective taking, poor problem solving, and impulsivity in social situations. They also may have a strong desire to avoid certain interactions or environments that are unpredictable or largely social in nature. Individuals with ASD do not tend to be vindictive or calculating in their behaviors. Parents describe children with ASD who may be rough with pets and younger siblings by rubbing a baby's head, pulling a dog's tail, seeming to misunderstand "gentle behavior." Thus, the presence of poor perspective taking, miscalculated "aggression" toward siblings and pets, and lack of bodily awareness in ASD would not alone meet criteria for ODD. Conversely, an individual who can be socially savvy in some situations, plays reciprocally with others, and follows directions at school, but argues, breaks rules, annoys others, and blames others for his or her mistakes at home may have ODD and not ASD. Children with ASD display symptoms across settings. One setting may be much easier to navigate and symptoms may appear much more subtle, but as a neuroanatomical change in brain structure, ASD is not transient and symptoms are present across settings. ODD is likely to be more volitional, and thus, symptoms may be present when an individual is in one setting, but not in another.

When treating ODD alone, behavioral modification and parent training are efficacious because generally parents have been unknowingly reinforcing bad behavior by allowing the child access to what he or she wants. For example, if a child demands, yells, whines, and complains for a snack, it can be reinforcing for a parent to eventually give in because these unpleasant behaviors go away. The bad behavior is then reinforced in the child, while the giving in behavior is reinforced in the parent. Eventually with enough disruptive and disrespectful behavior, the child is getting what he or she wants and the behavior disorder is ignited onto a perilous trajectory. When this reinforcement comes intermittently, the behaviors become more entrenched. Even for parents who are mostly consistent, the occasional reinforcing of bad behavior can lead to more significant problems. With consistent parenting that provides opportunities for success and reinforcement for appropriate behaviors, ODD alone should be relatively easy to treat.

Comorbid ASD and Behavior Disorders

ASD and BDs can co-occur under the following three conditions. First, criteria are met for ASD. Secondly, there is no additional Mood Disorder present. Finally, behavioral symptoms are reported that meet criteria for ODD, CD, or IED. Simonoff et al.

(2008) published a study estimating that 28 % of individuals with ASD have a comorbid Oppositional Defiant Disorder (Simonoff et al., 2008). This statistic represents results from only one study, but suggests significant comorbidity. In another study using a questionnaire, but not direct assessment, comorbidity ranged from 7 to 25 % (cited by Simonoff et al., 2008). Conduct Disorder was present in 3.2 % of Simonoff et al.'s sample (2008). These comorbid diagnoses tend to be more common with a later diagnosis of ASD, perhaps late elementary school. Unfortunately, through repeated reinforcement, these patterns become entrenched in older children. A persistent pattern of behavior intended to escape and avoid non-preferred activities, get attention, or receive a tangible item, unintentionally reinforced over the years, creates damaging behavior problems, requiring significant intervention to remediate.

Children with ASD are, in many cases, challenging to parent. As a result, parents are more likely to allow their children to have too much control in an effort to "keep the peace." An example of a comorbid ASD and ODD diagnosis is Sarah, age 11. Sarah is an only child who is rigid in her routine, loves My Little Ponies, enjoys playing alone, has few friends, and enjoys "lecturing adults" about the books she reads on horses, ponies, and their care. Sarah was diagnosed with ASD at 11 as it became harder and harder to accommodate for. She yells at her parents if routines change, insists on the same daily schedule, and hits others if she finds a pony out of place. Sarah has become defiant at school and is bossy with the other children in an effort to control her setting. When things are going her way she is happy. However, when she is not in charge, she becomes volatile, and she blames the other children for "making [her] mad" by touching her desk or making too much noise. As a bright child with autism Sarah was doing okay, but as she developed ODD in an effort to control her environment her behavior symptoms became pervasive. At 5 years of age, Sarah's bossiness and refusals were cute, but at 11, these symptoms became problematic and treatment became essential for peace at home and school and to prevent the development of a mood disorder.

As demonstrated in "Sarah's" case, in situations in which a behavior disorder is comorbid with ASD, it is important to seek parenting support and often ABA services with an experienced clinician who can help parents find ways to reinforce desired behaviors while putting defiant and aggressive behaviors on extinction.

Trauma-Related Disorders: Posttraumatic Stress Disorder and Adjustment Disorders

Imagine a child, age six, who intermittently does not speak to other children or adults for hours or days at a time. He looks down or away when spoken to and he refuses activities other than organizing his Legos. When his dad leaves the house, he cries and at school he refuses to follow instructions and throws tantrums frequently. A child exhibiting these symptoms is likely to be referred for an evaluation to determine whether he has an Autism Spectrum Disorder. This same child scores significantly on the ADOS-2 with limited facial expression, gesture, eye contact, and a lack of shared enjoyment in interaction. He is repetitive in his language (once he begins to talk) and he lines up and arranges toys during the ADOS-2.

A closer analysis of the data indicates appropriate labelling and understanding emotions in others and insight into relationships. During character play, the little boy creates an elaborate play sequence with firemen and a building on fire. He lines up characters to attend a funeral and to mourn the victim of the fire. His repetitive stories relate to his mother, who has an addiction to drugs and only intermittently comes in and out of his life. Is this autism? The algorithm on the ADOS-2 is elevated; however, as stated repeatedly throughout this book, this elevation on the ADOS-2 is not sufficient to make a diagnosis. Rather, this little boy meets diagnostic criteria for PTSD. A detailed family history, and careful consideration of his presentation and symptoms, led examiners to classify a parent's overdose and hospitalization as traumatic and leading to the subsequent symptoms that others suggested may be related to the Autism Spectrum.

Trauma-Related Disorders include Attachment Disorders, PTSD, Acute Stress Disorder, and Adjustment Disorders. For the purpose of clarity and comprehensiveness, Attachment Disorders will be discussed in a separate section as the authors of this text frequently encounter Autism Spectrum/Attachment and ASD/PTSD rule-outs in evaluation. Attachment disorders concern early care of a child that is significant for neglect, abuse, or major inconsistencies that impact a child's attachment to his or her primary caregiver. PTSD is related to exposure to trauma including death, serious injury, or sexual violence. It may occur in young children, but is not related directly to building attachment with caregivers. In this section, Trauma-Related conditions for discussion include PTSD, Acute Stress Disorder, and Adjustment Disorders.

Posttraumatic Stress Disorder has somewhat different criteria for children and adults older than age six. For this population, individuals must experience the event themselves, witness the event, learn that the event happened to someone close to the individual, or experience repeated or extreme exposure to details of the traumatic event. After the event, the individual must experience an intrusion symptom, an avoidance symptom, alterations in cognition and mood, alterations in arousal and reactivity, and the symptoms must have a duration longer than 1 month (APA, 2013). In a young child either avoidance or alteration in cognition and mood must be present, but not both. Acute Stress Disorder includes PTSD symptoms that occur between 3 days after a trauma and for up to 1 month. Adjustment Disorders are a less severe reaction to a stressor, but in excess of normal bereavement (APA, 2013). Particularly in young children, it may be challenging to differentiate emotional symptoms related to trauma or stressors from social communication deficits and restricted repetitive patterns of behavior.

Differentiating Between ASD and Trauma-Related Disorders

Mehtar and Mukaddes (2011) published a study on PTSD and ASD. They note the following symptoms in a preschooler experiencing PTSD: regressive, antisocial, aggressive, and destructive behavior. Preschoolers may have increased fears, nightmares, and separation anxiety from primary caregivers. In older children and adolescents, there is an increase in physiological arousal; children re-experience the traumatic event and tend to avoid emotions. On the surface, some symptoms of PTSD, Acute Stress, or even an Adjustment Disorder may look like an Autism Spectrum Disorder. Taking a detailed history of the client's development, family, and life experiences can be most helpful in determining whether symptoms began in the developmental period or whether symptoms developed after exposure to trauma. Mood and anxiety symptoms can certainly develop in individuals with ASD, as was discussed above, but a presentation with most symptoms occurring around mood and anxiety is less likely to be ASD. In considering the core features of ASD, it is possible to determine social communication deficits versus intermittent skills or skills that were present but disappeared after trauma. Children with PTSD may be repetitive in play or speech as it pertains to traumatic events. Adults and adolescents should not have significant restricted, repetitive behaviors if they have PTSD alone.

In PTSD and Adjustment Disorders, it is important to consider the stressor or trauma. According to one study by Mehtar and Mukaddes (2011), trauma experience for those with ASD was most often related to witnessing or being a victim of accidents, disasters, or violence. Sexual abuse was less common in the cohort than in the general population.

Looking back to the client discussed at the beginning of this section, in differentiating between diagnoses, clinicians must strongly consider anxiety symptoms, behavioral change over the course of testing, and complex pretend play. This child warmed up to examiners considerably over testing and used language fluently, albeit repetitively, on the second day. This, taken along with developed symbolic and abstract play, led examiners to determine that significant anxiety accounted for many of the symptoms in the referral. Noting anxiety, physiological arousal, intermittent language challenges, and alteration in mood as primary symptoms related to a traumatic experience, this 6-year-old child was diagnosed with PTSD. If ASD was present, and not PTSD, language and social relatedness would likely have been more consistent across the evaluation. Additionally, emotional awareness, perspective taking, and symbolic play would have been impaired. Often young children demonstrate and begin to process trauma they have experienced through play. This young one's play sequence was a cue to clinicians to investigate in-depth the family history and experience with parental separation and divorce. In this case, PTSD was the only diagnosis and clinicians determined that the child did not meet criteria for comorbid ASD. In other cases, ASD may be comorbid with a Trauma-related Disorder, given that the problems with reciprocity are persistent across time and setting.

Comorbid ASD and Trauma-Related Disorders

Many people may postulate that individuals with ASD experience more trauma than the general population because of the degree of cognitive and social impairment that may be present. Mehtar and Mukaddes (2011) discuss the rate of comorbidity between ASD and trauma. This study showed that 26 % of a cohort of individuals with ASD had experienced an event classified as traumatic in their lifetime. In the cohort, 17 % met criteria for PTSD in addition to ASD. Mehtar and Mukaddes report that in the general population 25–45 % of individuals are exposed to trauma, but 6–8 % is the lifetime prevalence of PTSD in the population. They cite research that 5–45 % of individuals exposed to trauma develop PTSD; certainly a broad range (2011). These statistics indicate that while the incidence of trauma is comparable between those with ASD and those without, individuals with ASD may be more likely to develop PTSD after experiencing trauma than are other individuals. ASD can also co-occur with an Adjustment Disorder as long as the adjustment issue is not an exacerbation of ASD symptoms. If ASD does not explain the symptoms in response to the stressor, an individual could have both ASD and PTSD or an Adjustment Disorder.

Adjustment Disorders include emotional or behavioral reactions related to a stressor. For example, if a child with ASD who has social communication deficits is placed in a classroom setting that has particular stressors, the child may develop an adjustment disorder in addition to ASD. Such a stressor could include an unaccepting classroom setting, an unstructured or chaotic environment, or a particularly imperceptive teacher. Symptoms of aggression, anxiety, or depression in reaction to the stressor may then constitute an Adjustment Disorder. Similarly, sudden changes to family structure, frequent relocations, or recent separation from a significant friend or love interest can all cause adjustment disorders.

In cases that both ASD and PTSD were diagnosed, individuals had a marked increase in stereotypical behavior, a decline in language and social skills and greater aggression, distractibility, sleep disorders, agitation, hyperactivity, and self-injury (Mehtar & Mukaddes, 2011). When considering the presence of trauma or stressor-related symptoms in children with ASD, a clinician should take a careful history of experiences to determine whether a traumatic or stressful event occurred. If so, the clinician should consider the client's symptoms to determine whether there has been a marked change or increase in symptoms that may constitute the diagnosis of a Trauma-Related Disorder.

Attachment Disorders

Attachment theory postulates that parental consistency, reliability, and sensitivity impact a child's attachment security (Ainsworth et al., 1979). Because deficits in joint attention and in processing social information are biologically present in individuals with ASD, the development of attachments may be somewhat altered. Secure or insecure attachment can certainly develop, but may come later or have a different relationship to parental sensitivity (Van Ijzendoorn et al., 2007). When insecure or disorganized attachment develops as the result of absent, inconsistent, abusive, or neglectful care, a child may be diagnosed with an Attachment Disorder. When attachments between parent and child are difficult to form due to the aloof

and sometimes rigidly detached style of individuals with ASD, this does not indicate an attachment disorder is present. Given this somewhat subtle difference, it is
important that clinicians are familiar with the nuances that may appear when children show signs of difficulty forming attachments with caregivers.

   Reactive Attachment Disorder (RAD) and Disinhibited Social Engagement
Disorder are diagnoses in the DSM-5 that are considered Attachment Disorders.
For diagnosis, neglect or mistreatment must occur between birth and age two and
the child must have a developmental age of at least 9 months. Insufficient care is
defined as neglect or deprivation of basic needs or affection, repeated changes in
primary caregivers so that attachments cannot form, and rearing in settings that limit
opportunities for attachment. RAD, which used to be the term for both disorders,
includes a consistent pattern of inhibited and emotionally withdrawn behavior. The
child rarely seeks or responds to comfort when distressed, presents with minimal
social and emotional responsiveness, has limited positive effect, and demonstrates
unexplained irritability, sadness, or fearfulness. Symptoms must be evident before
five and the child must not meet criteria for autism (DSM-5). Disinhibited Social
Engagement Disorder symptoms include overly social behaviors instead of withdrawn behaviors. Disinhibited engagement is evidenced in diminished checking in
with a caregiver; as well as, reduced reticence in interacting with, poor boundaries
with, and willingness to go off with unfamiliar adults.

Differentiating Between ASD and Attachment Disorders

Like with other Trauma-Related Disorders, particular attention to early developmental history is crucial when differentiating between attachment and autism. The
DSM-5 suggests that differentiation relies on the presence or absence of severe
social neglect, restricted interests, and ritualized behaviors and attachment-related
behaviors. Children with ASD generally show attachment behavior that is typical
for developmental level, which is not the case in attachment disorders (APA, 2013).

   The authors of this text have frequently been called upon to differentiate between
autism and attachment. In using professional judgment, the two have a much different
feel. Children with attachment disorders may talk non-stop, ignore the examiner, and
present in a disorganized manner. The overall presentation is different in that restricted,
repetitive interests and behaviors are absent. Children with RAD may prefer a structured, clearly presented routine, but the feel is that this mediates anxiety instead of simply being repetitive. One child with DSED asked constant questions during her
evaluation, often not even waiting for the examiner to respond. This demonstrated
impaired social skills. The same child expressed constant interest in the whereabouts of
a particular examiner and quickly and indiscriminately formed an attachment to that
individual. This was consistent with her pattern of interaction with other adults. Even
while ADOS-2 scores were elevated, and play was bossy and controlling, diagnostic
impressions included attachment and not autism. This is consistent with research citing
that "Children with RAD appear to be at least as impaired as children with ASD in certain domains of social relatedness" (Sadiq et al., 2012, p. 267). Early history of neglect

and abuse prior to this child's adoption at 11 months combined with overly familiar behavior with adults and challenges forming meaningful and lasting friendships pointed to attachment as the diagnosis. Another very young child referred for aggressive behavior, tantrums, and head banging, around age two, presented with diminished checking in with his mother. He had a history of frequently changing caregivers and neither parent was emotionally available for him during the first year of his life. This bright 2-year-old quickly learned the names of his evaluators and was concerned when either exited the room. He made eye contact, demonstrated joint attention, and used social referencing with unfamiliar adults. With his parents he had a "push-pull" style of interaction and could become quickly aggressive with little provocation. What many professionals suggested may be autism turned out to be an attachment problem.

Comorbid ASD and Attachment Disorders

There is limited research on comorbid diagnosis of ASD and attachment. Studies investigating comorbid diagnoses with Autism Spectrum Disorders have not included Attachment Disorders in the Psychiatric Disorders for discussion. RAD may be diagnosed with AD/HD, for example, but the DSM-5 does not express an opinion on the comorbidity of ASD and attachment (APA, 2013). In the DSM-5 criteria for RAD, it states that for diagnosis, an ASD may **not** be present. In the authors' clinical experience, attachment does not cause autism, but autism can impact the attachment that forms between a child and one or more parent (s). Challenges with attachment that may be influenced by autism are not necessarily going to result in care that meets the severity of maladaptive care associated with RAD, but nonetheless the attachment that forms may have a strong impact on the child and on the family system.

For secure attachment, care must be responsive, sensitive, trusting, and proportional. Naturally with an Autism Spectrum Disorder, a parent will face greater challenges in establishing this attachment. Parents want to make their children happy; and children with autism may be happiest when playing alone and engaging with objects instead of people. Considering operant conditioning introduced years ago by B.F. Skinner, a parent is positively reinforced for disengaging with the child because this results in the child's happiness. Thus, it is much harder to establish a secure attachment in which a child forms a secure base, stays in proximity to the parent, sees the parent as a safe haven, and exhibits an appropriate amount of separation distress. Children with autism may have big emotional reactions to changes and transitions that in turn impact the parent and the attachment style. When a toddler has autism, he may be content to play alone, repetitively spin objects or pace the room, and to withdraw from interactions. Taking into account joint attention and joint referencing, sharing and showing, all assessed via the ADOS-2, an experienced clinician will consider whether or not the child cares what the parent is attending to, offers a response, and shows toys or shares toys.

Children must learn, whether they have autism or not, that someone will meet their needs, that the world is safe and nurturing, and that parents and caregivers are special people. When working with a child, whether he or she is neurotypical or not, it is important for a parent to meet their child's needs. This includes taking into account whether the child is hungry, wet, lonely or hurt. As the parent meets the need and talks to the child, a stronger emotional vocabulary can develop, which will help an autistic child or a neurotypical child. Recalling the Hart and Risley (1995) seminal study that found children whose mothers talked to them and read to them developed higher Verbal IQ scores than children whose parents did not, we can find a similar correlation here. If caregivers work to increase a child's emotional vocabulary, he or she can better access support from a parent and this influences the attachment relationship.

When early trauma and neglect are present in a young child and behaviors meet criteria for an Attachment Disorder, it is important to make attachment a matter of clinical consideration. This may or may not occur in the context of an Autism Spectrum Disorder. One study postulates that social deficits stemming from very severe neglect and abuse will remit more quickly when the environment is "more appropriate." (Filipek et al., 1999) This is promising and indicates that parents must strive to form a strong attachment with their children despite any environmental or neurological differences that may exist. When considering making the diagnosis of RAD, children with a clear insecure attachment and poor reciprocal play, joint attention, sharing, and showing may have both ASD and an attachment disorder. Although the DSM-5 does not specifically recognize comorbidity for ASD and attachment disorders, clinically these conditions coexist. Autism is neurodevelopmental while attachment disorders are created environmentally. A child with ASD who experiences poor caregiving, neglect, and abuse could potentially meet criteria for both disorders. Treatment can be very different depending on which diagnosis is made or if both attachment concerns and autism are present; thus an accurate diagnosis is crucial.

Differential and Comorbid Diagnosis of Attachment Disorders and ASD in toddlers

Differential and Comorbid Diagnosis of ASD and Attachment Disorders involves a close look at play behaviors. Readers are invited to consider the graphic on the following page when differentiating between young children who may have: ASD alone, RAD alone, or ASD and RAD comorbid conditions.

ASD Alone: *The primary differentiating feature for ASD in toddlers is lack of reciprocal play.* Children with ASD in young ages tend to lack reciprocal play, whereas children with Attachment Disorders may display intermittent reciprocal play. As discussed above, autism may certainly influence the attachment that forms between parent and child even in a situation with engaging, nurturing, and involved parents. Parents may be reinforced for giving the child space because young children with ASD may prefer playing alone. As shown in the figure, toddlers with ASD tend to prefer to play alone, may focus on objects rather than people, may tantrum, may pace around the room, and may use the examiner's hand as a tool. As discussed previously, young children with ASD tend to show less symbolic, imaginative, and creative play; they generally will not join in or build on the play sequences of others.

RAD Alone: *Children who have RAD alone have an insecure attachment but have the ability to play reciprocally.* Children with RAD are inhibited and emotionally withdrawn, but not because of a preference for objects over people, as is seen in young children with ASD. To have the diagnosis, there must be a period of neglect or mistreatment between birth and age two. Children with attachment disorders rarely seek comfort from parents, show a persistently sad or irritable affect, and minimal or drastically changing emotional responsiveness (push–pull interaction). Contrary to ASD, children with RAD/ DSED may share enjoyment in the interaction and may display indiscriminate relationships with adults, regardless of the level of familiarity. A toddler with RAD/ DSED may wander off with strangers. Children with attachment disorders tend to have significant behavior problems.

ASD and RAD: *Children with insecure attachment and poor reciprocal play could have both ASD and an attachment disorder* (see figure on the following page). Although comorbid diagnosis is currently disallowed in the DSM-5, clinically if there is a pattern, a clear insecure attachment, and significant patterns of poor reciprocity, the child can meet criteria for both disorders. Children with insecure attachment to caregivers, and poor joint attention, sharing, and showing may have both ASD and an attachment disorder. In play, the child may prefer to play alone, may ignore the examiner, will not elaborate on play sequences of the examiner, and may show indiscriminate attachment or engagement (Fig. 14.1).

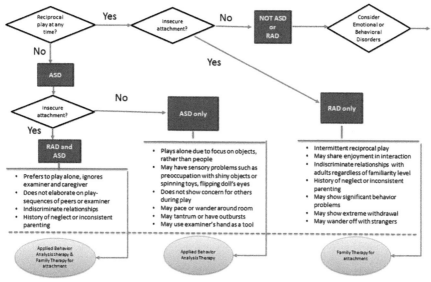

Fig. 14.1 Differential and comorbid diagnosis of ASD and RAD in toddlers

Personality Disorders

A 35-year-old man presented for an evaluation with a guardian from his group home. He was reportedly diagnosed with an intellectual disability as well as Antisocial and Schizoid Personality Disorders. He was considered dangerous and was not allowed to be without supervision. This man was prescribed a number of medications and given little freedom to leave his group home. In testing, he was quiet, polite, and expressed an interest in mystery novels and going for walks, which he was no longer allowed to do. He presented with repetitive and stereotyped language, interests, and behavior as well as deficits in social communication dating back to preschool. He had never been diagnosed with an Autism Spectrum Disorder and had never received treatment other than being educated in a special education setting. Because he had not been properly diagnosed, and treated, this man did not have the independence he could have possessed. He might otherwise have been able to hold a job or live at least semi-independently.

A personality disorder is an enduring pattern of inner experience and behavior that deviates markedly from the expectation of an individual's culture. It includes cognition, affectivity, interpersonal functioning, and impulse control. The pattern is inflexible and pervasive and leads to clinically significant distress or impairment in social occupational or other important areas of functioning. The pattern must be stable and can be traced to adolescence or early adulthood and it cannot be better explained as a manifestation of another mental disorder (APA, 2013, pp. 646–647). Personality Disorders are clustered thusly: A—odd and eccentric, B—dramatic, emotional, or erratic and C—anxious or fearful. At times, an individual may be diagnosed with a Personality Disorder without a thorough developmental assessment and another mental or neurodevelopmental diagnosis may be overlooked.

Differentiating Between ASD and Personality Disorders

Ozonoff et al. (2005) studied personality characteristics in individuals with Autism Spectrum Disorders and found phenotypic similarities between ASD and Schizoid PD (detachment from social relationships and a restricted range of emotional expression) as well as Obsessive Compulsive PD (a pattern of preoccupation with order, perfectionism, and control). The paper cites Baron-Cohen, noting that autism is often associated with a personality style including an orientation to detail and a drive to analyze and construct systems. These ASD symptoms may be consistent with the detachment or preoccupation with order seen in personality disorders. Researchers conclude that the MMPI-2 is a useful tool to assess psychopathology and relevant interaction styles in autism, noting that those with ASD are high on scales of social isolation, interpersonal difficulties, depressed mood, and coping deficits. Additionally, social reservation, shyness, social anxiety, and rigidity are frequently relevant for those on the Spectrum (Ozonoff, Garcia, Clark, & Lainhart, 2005). These data may suggest that it would be challenging to find Schizoid and OCPD not better accounted for by autism, indeed assuming the individual meets full criteria for ASD. Lugnegard et al. (2012) write that there may not be a pure Schizoid Personality Disorder without an Autism Spectrum Disorder. Schizoid PD may just be autism when a developmental trajectory cannot be supported for lack of data or recognition of early symptoms. The study notes that Schizotypal PD (acute discomfort in close relationships, cognitive or perceptual distortions, and eccentricities of behavior) includes the addition of psychosis, but is otherwise consistent with Schizoid and ASD. Lugnegard et al. further indicate that Obsessive Compulsive PD may be also related to the onset of behavior. A clinician could make a Personality Disorder diagnosis and miss a relevant diagnosis of an Autism Spectrum Disorder (2012). Another study by Hofvander found that OCPD, Antisocial PD, and Schizoid PD are more common in those with ASD than within the general population. In this study, each Personality Disorder was represented in the ASD cohort except Histrionic PD (a pattern of excessive emotionality and attention seeking) (Hofvander et al., 2009).

It is important for clinicians to remember that Personality Disorders manifest in adolescence or adulthood, while Autism Spectrum Disorders are present in the period of early development.

Comorbid ASD and Personality Disorders

It is possible to diagnose comorbid ASD and a personality disorder if some of the personality characteristics are not explained within the context of an Autism Spectrum Disorder. Research indicates that characteristics of any personality disorder could co-occur with an Autism Spectrum Disorder. The least diagnosed are Cluster B personality disorders including Antisocial, Borderline, Histrionic, and Narcissistic, with Histrionic being the least related to ASD. Lugnegard et al. (2012) suggest we should not rule out the possibility of co-occurrence in ASD and PDs, but a number of studies have not found Cluster B to commonly co-occur with ASD. Avoidant PD may exist without a person meeting ASD criteria, though the symptom of avoiding social relationships may often be present in ASD. While many individuals with ASD may be dependent on support, Dependent PD dependency cannot be caused by another mental disorder and thus must be differentiated from ASD.

One study by Ryden and Bejerot (2008) included a clinical sample of individuals with both ASD and psychiatric diagnosis(es). Researchers found that Schizotypal PD and Avoidant PD traits existed in the ASD group at a greater rate than the general population (Ryden & Bejerot, 2008). The cohort met criteria overall for four personality disorders, while a control group met criteria for two. Generally researchers found lower social and occupational functioning in adults with ASD even if they had the same education. In the study, only 27 % of those with ASD lived independently from age 23. Ryden and Bejerot suggest best outcomes have been linked to early childhood diagnosis. The ASD cohort demonstrated a lack of insight into symptoms and 17 % of the sample had attempted suicide. The researchers concluded that many bright females go undiagnosed with ASD until adulthood and may present in psychiatric settings. They are then diagnosed with a personality disorder or other psychiatric illness and are not identified as having autism. Ryden and Bejerot looked specifically at comorbid diagnoses of ASD and Borderline Personality Disorder, often thought to be uncommon. Of 41 adult patients, 15 % met criteria for both Borderline and ASD. The study suggests co-occurring relationship challenges and an increased risk for suicide when these diagnoses are comorbid (2008).

In conclusion, it appears that there is some disagreement as to whether it is appropriate to diagnose a Personality Disorder in an individual with an Autism Spectrum Disorder. A clinician must pay careful attention to whether the symptoms may be better explained by autism. The authors of this book would agree with research stating that Schizoid Personality Disorder should not be diagnosed comorbid with an ASD. Dependent Personality Disorder also needs to be differentiated. It does seem that in those with less severe symptoms, it may be easy to miss a diagnosis of an Autism Spectrum Disorder even when one is warranted. As Personality Disorders may carry more stigmas in social and occupational settings than Autism Spectrum Disorders, it will be most helpful to take a detailed history and fully consider all diagnostic rule-outs before diagnosing a Personality Disorder.

Other Relevant Comorbidities for Clinical Attention

There are additional comorbidities that can co-occur with an ASD. It is important to look at all symptoms that are causing clinically significant distress and to consider comorbid diagnoses. Clinicians may provide resources and referrals to families as needed to treat additional diagnoses. Areas that may lead to clinical concern and co-occur with Autism Spectrum Disorders are Traumatic Brain Injury, Sexual Dysfunction, Elimination Disorders, and Eating Disorders. Taking a detailed clinical interview, considering not only an adult or child's developmental history but also comprehensive medical history, considering patterns of eating, sleeping, toileting, and sexual behavior are important. These considerations may lead to recommendations for treatment. This is certainly not an exhaustive list, but may provide considerations for clinicians who work with individuals diagnosed with Autism Spectrum Disorders.

With regard to eating, those with ASD often have more selectivity by type and texture, but refuse food less on the whole than others with eating challenges. Highly selective eating can lead to long-term health consequences (Bachmeyer, 2009). In addition, Mannion and Leader (2013) report that gastrointestinal problems are present in between 9 and 91 % of children with Autism Spectrum Disorders. Studies are vastly different in their results which according to Mannion and Leader may be related to a lack of research using appropriate control groups. Further, problems with enzyme absorption digestion and leaky gut have been found in about 50 % of the cases of ASD (D'Eufemia et al., 1996; Reid, 2004). Constipation and feeding issues/selectivity may be related to behavioral rigidity and the type of foods preferred. Gastrointestinal symptoms should be evaluated thoroughly as they may lead to pain that causes sleep disturbance, irritability, and non-compliance (Mannion & Leader, 2013).

Mannion and Leader (2013) found that 80 % of children and adolescents with ASD presented with sleep problems. The study found that abdominal pain predicted sleep anxiety. Sleep problems may decrease the effectiveness of interventions as they can have a pervasive impact on mood and executive functioning. Toileting challenges significantly impact the quality of life for individuals and families impacted by ASD. Encopresis, toileting, and constipation are an area for further research. It seems that diet, sleep, and toileting are related and may have a huge impact on quality of life. It is important to assess these areas so that treatment can be more effective. (Mannion & Leader, 2013) In conclusion, while there may not be a need to differentiate diagnoses here, children and adults with Autism Spectrum Disorders may have a number of co-occurring challenges in feeding, toileting, and general gastrointestinal health that should be an area of clinical attention.

Summary of Part IV: Differential and Comorbid Diagnosis

The clinical presentation of those presenting for an Autism Assessment may be quite complex. It is essential that psychologists be comprehensive in their assessment, take a detailed medical and developmental history, and consider all relevant rule-out diagnoses. Understanding Autism Spectrum Disorders and being able to accurately diagnose these also requires knowledge, study, and experience in evaluating for many other neurodevelopmental and mental health diagnoses. Being an expert in ruling out an Autism Spectrum Disorder, and identifying potential comorbid conditions (most commonly Anxiety and AD/HD), is every bit as important as being an expert in assessing autism.

Part V
Concluding the Assessment Process

Chapter 15
Feedback, Report, and Recommendations

Abstract The recommendations for home, school, and the community included in an assessment report typically contain the most important information for parents, physicians, or school personnel. When to recommend various therapies including Applied Behavior Analysis, speech or occupational therapies as well as psychotherapy or psychiatric services is clarified for different individuals. How to respond to sensory defensiveness as well as academic challenges with reading or writing is important to handle properly so as not to create or worsen behavioral challenges. When individuals with autism have comorbid conditions like anxiety or AD/HD, additional recommendations are needed and vary depending on the severity of ASD as well as the intellectual capacity of each participant. Promoting emotional and social development is not just as simple as providing access to a social skills group especially given the language, attentional, and memory challenges that typically accompany autism. When behavioral challenges exist, it is important to determine whether rigidity, maladaptive learning history, or seizures underlay the difficulty as recommendations typically vary depending on the cause. Even setting up the homework environment and completing assignments can be challenging when an individual with autism lacks motivation to please others. These and other situations are addressed with comprehensive recommendations for each area of weakness or deficit.

Keywords ABA recommendations for autism • Therapy and autism spectrum disorders • Medication and autism • Behavior problems and autism • Weakness in ASD • Deficit recommendations in ASD • Speech and autism • Sensory needs and autism • AD/HD and autism spectrum disorders • Anxiety and autism spectrum disorders

© Springer International Publishing Switzerland 2016   291
A.P. Kroncke et al., *Assessment of Autism Spectrum Disorder*, Contemporary
Issues in Psychological Assessment, DOI 10.1007/978-3-319-25504-0_15

Feedback and Report

- •Provide written report with findings and recommendations
- •Consultation with outside providers such as psychiatrist or therapist (as appropriate)
- •Follow up session or further consultation as needed
- •Re-evaluate in 12-36 months, depending on severity of symptoms and age of child

Feedback &
Report

Recommendations are a crucial part of the assessment process and essential components of the written report. As discussed later in this section, parents are likely to accept and respond to relevant diagnoses in a dynamic manner requiring time to process and adjust. Accepting a diagnosis of ASD is more likely a journey than a milestone. Written recommendations are likely to serve as a permanent reference document to which the client or parents can repeatedly refer back to on their own timetable. Because reports are often shared with different individuals including pediatricians, teachers, or other family members, it is advised that recommendations be divided into relevant categories including: Further Evaluations, School, and Home. In this way, the user can more efficiently grasp the information they need. It is also recommended that clinicians clarify at the time of the feedback if there are professionals that the client or parents would like the report forwarded to, so the clinician can efficiently aid in disseminating the findings.

To maximize the utility of this book, many sample recommendations are included along with text discussing when such a recommendation should be considered. These recommendations are worded in a general manner here from which they should be tailored for a particular client's presentation and needs. While some may feel "canned" recommendations of this type are less professional, the truth is that diagnostic characteristics and associated empirically supported treatments generally do not change rapidly. As such, appropriate and sensitively worded recommendations, such as those presented here, are not likely to go out of date quickly. Rather, these recommendations are either relevant to the client's presentation and symptom profile and should be tailored and included; or alternately, are irrelevant to the child's condition, and therefore should be omitted. Finally, in this day and age of increasingly tighter healthcare budgets, fiscally responsible clinicians must develop such recommendation "banks" as implied here in order to avoid spending excess time that will not likely be reimbursed. The inclusion of such sample recommendations will never preempt the need for competent administration of tests, experienced integration and interpretation of findings, and pensive inclusion of appropriate recommendations.

Further Evaluations

The need for any additional evaluations should be presented first under Recommendations. Furthermore, it is recommended that subsequent evaluations with physicians should precede evaluations with other types of professionals given the important priority placed on any necessary medical diagnostics or treatments that may be warranted. Note that whenever there is a referral to another professional, it's very important that the professional have experience and competence in Autistic Spectrum Disorders. This may not always be possible especially in more remote locations where there is only one neurologist for instance. Every effort should be made, however, to locate professionals who will be effective given that ASD is often debilitating and typically lifelong. It may also seem that if a professional is competent with ASD, then the amount of experience he or she has is not that important. The challenge is that the Autism Spectrum is very wide and deep. As the saying goes, "If you've met one person with autism, you've met one person with autism." As such, just because a professional was competent with a very intelligent, mildly affected teenager with ASD doesn't mean they'll be remotely effective with a mute kindergartener who apparently has comorbid Intellectual Disability, seizures, and Generalized Anxiety Disorder.

Neurology

If a child under age 6 has a new diagnosis of ASD, a referral to a Neurologist should be seriously considered. The parents may wish to have a full neurologic workup to assess for genetic abnormalities, seizures, and/or neurophysiological problems although many would feel a neurological consult is not critical since it is not necessary for the diagnosis. When the client has any of the following additional conditions or symptoms, however, a referral to a Neurologist is recommended:

1. *Seizures* may be evidenced by the client staring vacantly for a few seconds without any explanation.
2. *Tics* can readily accompany other conditions and may be evident as eye blinks, sniffing, or other sudden/reflexive movement.
3. Clear evidence of *regression* compared with valid, standardized testing previously administered.
4. Any report of *numbness, tingling, or asymmetric motor movements* observed.
5. Recent report of a *head injury* as manifest by loss of consciousness, vomiting, dizziness, or other concerns.
6. Evidence of any *dysmorphic features* most notably in the face or hands. Note that Down syndrome, which has characteristic dysmorphic features, does co-occur with ASD in about 3 % of individuals with Down syndrome.

Psychiatry

If a client has any of the following conditions, a referral to a psychiatrist is in order:

1. *Attention deficit*, stimulant medication is usually the treatment of choice; however, such medication may need to be modified in the presence of significant anxiety.
2. *Hyperactivity* may be improved with a stimulant or antihypertensive like Intuniv.
3. *Aggression* to self, others, or property that risks injury or is otherwise poorly managed. Risperdone is one of few medications that are FDA approved for treatment of aggression, sleep problems, and such symptoms in persons with ASD. Risperdone is frequently accompanied by weight gain, however.
4. Serious *sleep problems*. Note that sleep disorders are highly comorbid with ASD. While many over-the-counter products are often tried, such as melatonin, moderate to severe sleep disorders readily compromise cognitive functioning as well as potentially impair quality of life for the whole family.
5. Clinically significant *anxiety or depression*. Typically treated with a Selective Serotonin Reuptake Inhibitor (SSRI) but may respond better to an atypical antidepressant. Occasionally, an anxiolytic (such as a benzodiazepine) may be prescribed for short-term relief of anxiety but these are generally prescribed in a more conservative manner because they can be habit-forming.
6. Any evidence of *psychosis* including but not limited to visual or auditory hallucinations or delusional thinking. While comorbid ASD and psychosis is rare, it is possible for them to co-occur (as discussed in detail in Chap. 14).
7. Any evidence of *mania*. Given the symptoms of ASD which often include hyperactivity or an attention deficit, it can be difficult to recognize comorbid bipolar disorder. Nonetheless, symptoms including grandiosity, marked mood swings, euphoria, and/or racing thoughts could signal the diagnosis of bipolar.
8. If the client is *already taking medications*, the recommendation should suggest a *review* of medications in light of the evaluation findings.
9. Many times clients will have their pediatrician or family doctor prescribe psychotropic medications as discussed above. This may be successful especially when prescribed by a Developmental Pediatrician or Neurologist. The facts are, however, that psychiatrists have substantial training in psychotropic medications and the treatment of psychiatric conditions. In addition, ASD is a tough condition to treat or manage and family physicians rarely have the experience to competently manage psychotropic medications for ASD.

Applied Behavior Analyst

Whenever the client presents with moderate to severe behavior problems, and especially when those behaviors are self-injurious or threaten the safety of others, it is essential to refer or consult regularly with a Board Certified Behavior Analyst (BCBA) for either an analytical Functional Behavior Analysis (FBA) or for intervention services as discussed further under *School* or *Home* below.

Unfortunately, many people are not fully aware of the importance of involving a BCBA in the treatment of moderate to severe behavior problems and such an omission readily results in delay or ultimate failure of effective behavioral management. It is truly sad when professionals who are incompetent in the treatment of moderate to severe problem behaviors foolishly embark on unsound and even harmful strategies when their professional training and credentials are actually in a completely different discipline.

In general, although some alternative treatments have their place, therapies without a clear research base should not be used. Methods such as simple dietary restrictions, "neurological massage," and isolated sensory treatments that are promised to families as an alteration or cure for behavior problems are misleading at the least. These "therapies" may not directly harm their clients; however, indirect harm is done when families waste time and money that could be spent on therapies that work. "Treatments" such as hyperbaric chambers, chelation, unsupervised supplements and off-label medications, and punitive behavior measures can be extremely harmful, abusive, or potentially fatal. Frankly, the world will be a happier place for individuals with ASD and their families when professionals who are unqualified to treat problem behaviors, and erroneously lead the family toward a harmful treatment, rightly face severe disciplinary consequences including but not limited to legal and professional sanctions as a result of the behavioral and psychological harm inflicted on clients and their families when such professionals practice beyond their domain of competency. Many times clients have suffered significantly, even developing symptoms of Post-Traumatic Stress Disorder, through the needless and ignorant practice of professions unqualified to treat problem behaviors. Such practice has to stop.

An analytical FBA is a series of experimental procedures designed to validly determine the cause of problem behavior(s) whereby a behavior is maintained by either positive (tangible, social, or internal/automatic) reinforcement or negative (escape or avoidance of something undesirable) reinforcement (Iwata, Vollmer, & Zarcone, 1990; Iwata et al., 1994). Since reinforcement is defined as a consequence that increases the probability of the preceding behavior reoccurring, a problem behavior is being reinforced by something and a necessary step in treating the problem behavior is validly determining that causal variable(s). Note that reinforcement is not the same as a reward or prize and this ABA definition of reinforcement is objectively based purely on mathematical principles of probability. If a behavior persists or increases, it is being reinforced. Once the reinforcing consequences are identified, effective steps can be taken to reduce or eliminate those problem behaviors and cultivate more adaptive responses for the benefit of the individual and their loved ones.

Like ABA in general, the concept of reinforcement is widely misunderstood. For example, many people mistakenly believe negative reinforcement refers to providing attention for undesirable behaviors. In fact, negative reinforcement refers to the removal of something aversive such as turning off a loud air conditioner and observing an individual to be more productive as a result.

Most FBAs are only descriptive in nature. In a descriptive or correlational FBA, the observer notes events or situations co-occurring with problem behaviors and presumes that some combination of these co-occurring variables is also causing the behavior problems. ~~Significant research has proven that descriptive FBAs are not valid for determining the cause of such problems.~~ In addition, substantial time can easily be lost in haphazardly attempting to change parameters in the classroom or work environment only to discover no improvement or even worsening of the problem behavior. In an analytical FBA, careful experiments are set up to determine definitively what variables are causing the problem behaviors, so effective intervention can be planned from the FBA results. While this is not a book on intervention, nonetheless the critical nature of promptly remediating moderate to severe problem behaviors warrants this limited dialogue on the importance of referring the client to persons competent in performing an analytical FBA. In many cases, when even moderate problem behaviors are not treated promptly, they readily worsen only to subsequently require the individual to be placed in more restricted home and school settings; sometimes including possibly having to change schools, or even placement in residential care facilities. In the worst cases, client can suffer permanent disfigurement from severe self-injury. Every effort should be made to refer the client to a BCBA competent in performing an analytical FBA or treating the problem behaviors as discussed further below.

Nutrition and/or Feeding therapy

1. Many times individuals with ASD are very picky eaters resulting in poor nutrition or insufficient weight gain or maintenance. For reasons that are not entirely clear, individuals with ASD often have a propensity to eat carbohydrates and little else. Some toddlers have been reported to eat only McDonald's French fries or Hostess Twinkies, for example. When very poor diet is reported and/or insufficient weight, a referral to a Registered Dietician is recommended.
2. When parents report that their child is an extremely picky eater, perhaps excluding all unprocessed meats, nuts, and/or fruits or vegetables, it may be necessary to refer to a professional who is competent in treating feeding difficulties. The discipline of such a professional can vary but is typically a BCBA or Psychologist with training and experience in treating feeding problems or a Speech and Language Pathologist with training and experience in Oral Motor Therapy.

Metabolic Specialist

Evidence exists to support the co-occurrence of compromised mitochondrial functioning and ASD (Weissman, Kelley et al., 2008). Mitochondria are responsible for the storage and maintenance of energy (among other functions), and persons with primary or secondary mitochondrial disorders often manifest with widely fluctuating energy levels. In addition, there are numerous cases of individuals with ASD who experience marked cognitive decline both before and after an illness.

Such individuals may exhibit substantial cognitive regression for days before an illnesses and even weeks after an illness. In some rare cases, patients with ASD have even been hospitalized for notable cognitive degeneration, including loss of speech and motor skills, co-occurring with an illness. When parents or clients report such events in their history, it is prudent to refer them to a physician who specializes in mitochondrial disorders for further assessment of these symptoms.

Occupational Therapy

If a client exhibits gross or fine motor impairments or complains of significant sensory sensitivities, it is helpful to refer them to an occupational therapist for further evaluation. When the evaluation team includes a neuropsychologist, physical therapist, or occupational therapist, assessment of motor skills is typically included and determination of the degree of weakness or impairment in this area is possible. Most young clients with ASD will benefit from occupational therapy to assist them in strengthening play skills and learning adaptive behaviors (tying shoes, cutting meat, and brushing teeth for example). Referral to an occupational therapist is reiterated under Home recommendations discussed below. In the USA, Occupational therapy is available for qualified children through the use of public funds under the Individuals with Disabilities in Education Act (IDEA).

School Recommendations

Individuals with ASD from preschool through 21 (maybe older or younger depending on state laws) should be eligible for appropriate services through their public school district. When a diagnosis of ASD is made, it is recommended that the individual be referred to their public school district for consideration of an Individualized Educational Plan (IEP). An IEP is the instrument under which school services, as well as any associated modifications or accommodations, are provided to students who qualify under different educational labels including "autism" for an ASD. Other educational labels that are recognized as qualifying for an IEP include "SLD" (specific learning disorder), "S/L" (speech language impaired), "OHI" (other health impaired for conditions such as epilepsy, and sometimes including autism), "TBI" (traumatic brain injury), "SIED" (significantly identifiable emotionally disability), and "PD" (preschooler with a disability). Students with other, less severe challenges, including those with high functioning ASD or AD/HD, may be provided with accommodations and educationally related services, in the general education classroom, under a 504 Plan. Educational eligibility will be explained in great detail in Chap. 18: School-Based Assessment for ASD.

    At times, public school districts who do not embark on a thorough evaluation process such as that described in Chap. 18 will erroneously decide a student with

ASD does not qualify for an IEP if grades are satisfactory. This can be a perilous situation because a student with ASD may still face significant social and emotional challenges which need support and accommodations even if academic achievement is on par with peers. The law does NOT require that the child's academics be impacted by the disability.

Under the IDEA §300.8 1(i), "Autism" is defined as such: "Autism means a developmental disability significantly affecting verbal and nonverbal communication and social interaction, generally evident before age three that *adversely affects a child's educational performance.*(see Chap. 18)" These adverse effects might include behavior, social, emotional, and adaptive performance. Thus, a child who can obtain high marks on tests is not necessarily excluded from an IEP. The questions that school IEP teams must ask are, "Can the child receive reasonable benefit from general education alone?" If so, the child does not qualify for an IEP. Another question is does the child require specialized instruction to access the learning environment and receive a free and appropriate education? If so, the child does require an IEP. It may seem that the answer to these questions is somewhat subjective; again this can be substantially improved by following an evidence-based approach such as that provided in Chap. 18.

It is often superior to follow an RtI process, such as is described in this book, when concerns are evident, and if through a process of increasingly intensive interventions, the child does not make adequate progress, conduct an IEP evaluation. It is generally most appropriate to provide an IEP proactively, even if the required services are limited to counseling or a lunch-bunch group, than to wait until a student is experiencing substantial emotional distress and accompanied academic problems and then decide to reactively provide services. Additionally, there have been numerous cases where students with ASD did not qualify for an IEP, according to their public school district, only to subsequently attempt college and fail miserably because necessary and sufficient accommodations or services were not provided. In a few tragic cases, students with ASD and very good grades, yet no friends for years, went on to college hopelessly ill-equipped to handle the social and sexual aspects of college life and subsequently face criminal charges for failing to maintain appropriate boundaries (see Forensic evaluations).

Provision of an IEP or 504 Plan would likely have accustomed the student and parents to the importance and familiarity with educational accommodations such that college success would be more likely for students with the requisite intellectual abilities and academic skills. In a 14-year study of 406 individuals with ASD being followed into and through adulthood, only 25 % had positive outcomes defined by supported employment or a post-high school education. The participants had much slower improvement after high school, experienced an early plateau in skills, and a loss of skills in their thirties as services and supports were even less available (and these individuals did not have intellectual disabilities). The women in this study were 15 times less independent than the men. Those who were employed, or had higher education, experienced much better outcomes (Mailick, Waisman Center University of Wisconsin, Madison). Clearly, there is a need to improve in effectively equipping qualified students with ASD for post-high school success. Much will be said about the Child Find mandate in Chap. 18. For now, suffice to say that school districts are charged with finding, identifying, and providing services to those suspected of having a disability from birth to 21. This includes provision of services that are required for educational and vocational success beyond high school. Appropriate services provided under an IEP could include the following as relevant:

Class Placement

A statement about class placement should be included under school recommendations. This determination comes largely from the results of assessment of Intellectual Ability (discussed above). In addition to noting the Full Scale IQ, General Cognitive Ability or General Cognitive Index, for example, particular emphasis should be placed on review of the client's verbal abilities because most regular education classrooms rely heavily on verbal means of instruction including oral lecture, group discussion, and reading of verbal information. If a client's verbal abilities or language skills are weak or deficient, placement in small group instruction or self-contained classroom, respectively, may be warranted. Note that all regular and Gifted and Talented (G/T) classroom placements are typically contingent upon the limited or absent problem behaviors including but not limited to any aggression toward self, others or property, as well as unmanaged elopement. Hence, the critical importance of effective evaluation and treatment of such moderate to severe problem behaviors cannot be overstated. In addition, any relevant modification and accommodations as outlined in Tables 15.1 and 15.2 below must also be appropriately provided for the student's success. This table also outlines guidelines for class placement:

Table 15.1 Classroom placement recommended guidelines

Intellectual ability	Class placement
Verbal and full scale IQ ≥ 120	Gifted and talented classroom
Verbal and full scale IQ ≥ 115	Consideration of advanced academic class placement. Review Grade Equivalent Scores from academic testing
Verbal IQ < 115 and ≥ 85	Regular classroom placement with possible select advanced instruction, as appropriate, only in any advanced academic areas as determined from Grade Equivalent scores on academic testing
Verbal IQ < 85 and ≥ 70	Integrated Learning (≤14 students in a class) placement with possible Regular class instruction, as appropriate, only in any Average academic areas as determined from Grade Equivalent scores on academic testing
Verbal and full scale IQ < 70 and ≥ 55	Integrated Learning Classroom or small group instruction (≤6 students) with Regular education participation in electives and select subjects contingent upon minimal or absent problem behaviors
Verbal or full scale IQ < 55	Self-contained/special education classroom with Regular education participation in electives and select subjects contingent upon minimal or absent problem behaviors

Table 15.2 School accommodations, modifications, and services summary

Presenting problems	Accommodations or modifications	School services recommended
Autism spectrum disorder	Select all relevant accommodations and modifications from Presenting Problems listed below	ABA, Speech therapy, Occupational therapy and/or Psychological services as discussed above
Intellectual disability	Reduced amount and difficulty of work assigned in class and for homework	Class placement: Integrated Learning Center or self-contained
Problem behaviors	Opportunity to work in a location free from problematic antecedents such as punitive feedback, talkative students, or loud noises.	ABA services provided or supervised by a Board Certified ABA professional
Slow processing speed	Reduced amount of work as well as additional time to complete assignments and tests	Match class placement with the processing speed of the student or they'll be unable to keep up
Distractible	Opportunity to work in an environment free from distractions, check for understanding by requesting repetition of instructions, opportunity to refer to information in written or picture form not just hear orally	Provide frequent breaks for movement or quiet fidgeting depending on what improves concentration and attention
Gross motor weaknesses	Additional time for transition between activities and/or classes as needed	Physical Therapy, Adaptive Physical Education
Fine motor weaknesses or poor handwriting	Opportunity to obtain class notes from teacher or a stellar classmate	Occupational Therapy, Consider "Handwriting Without Tears," accelerated keyboarding instruction
Hyperactivity	Opportunity to wiggle or fidget quietly while working, frequent breaks as needed following on-task behavior, opportunity to chew gum, or use a fidget toy if helpful	
Anxiety	Provision of teachers who have a warm and nurturing style with avoidance of punishment. Provide praise on a 5:1 ratio to corrective feedback. Opportunity to fidget, chew gum, or suck on sugar-free candies for comfort	Opportunity to meet regularly or intermittently with school counseling staff
Depression	Reduced amount of work assigned in class and for homework as needed	Opportunity to meet regularly or intermittently with school counseling staff
Inflexibility	Provision of a daily schedule in picture or written form. Provide advance notice of changes or special events whenever possible	Be careful to introduce routines judiciously in areas like social skills where the natural environment is governed by spontaneity and change. Plan for generalization or increased anxiety can easily ensue

(continued)

Table 15.2 (continued)

Presenting problems	Accommodations or modifications	School services recommended
Sensory sensitivities	Opportunity to learn and work in sensory-modified environments whenever possible including but not limited to quiet environment, low level lighting, avoidance of undesired fabrics for PE or other activities, alternate furniture for seating such as a yoga ball or "squishy seat" as helpful. Modify fire drill procedures appropriately whenever possible	Sensory breaks, rich sensory diet, Occupational Therapy services. Be careful not to provide fun sensory activities as a consequence for behavior problems or such problems will only worsen. Strive to program pro-actively
Language disorder (language skills ≥ 15 points below IQ)	Provision of materials to aide comprehension of concepts including but not limited to pictures, diagrams, charts, and written text or notes.	Speech therapy for expressive > receptive deficits, articulation, pragmatic language
Language impairment (Language skills ≥ 70 standard score)	Provision of materials to aide comprehension of concepts including but not limited to manipulatives, pictures, diagrams, charts, and written text or notes	Class placement: Integrated Learning Center or self-contained as appropriate. Provision of augmentative communication device, PECS, or ASL and associated language services to ensure learning and mastery
Reading disorder	Provision of materials to aide comprehension of concepts including but not limited to pictures, diagrams, and charts. Provide visual imagery strategies, practice story-retells and narratives with modeling and feedback	Specialized instruction from Learning Specialist or Special Education Teacher using Lindamood Bell or Orton Gillingham methods
Mathematics disorder	Provide curriculums that include conceptual simplicity, repetition, and concrete language necessary for effective learning	Show Me Math, K5 Learning, or TouchMath could be considered
Disorder for written expression	Provision of outlines, graphic organizers, electronic templates, or other materials to assist with writing assignments as appropriate. Additional time to complete written assignments and homework	Consideration of accelerated keyboarding instruction
Seizures	Provision of materials to aide comprehension of concepts that may have been missed including but not limited to manipulatives, pictures, diagrams, charts, and written text or notes. Provision of teachers who have a warm and nurturing style and are trained to respond appropriately when seizures are present	Medical support services from school nurse

Applied Behavior Analysis

Behavioral and educational interventions are currently the main treatments for individuals with ASD. Of these interventions, approaches based on applied behavior analysis (ABA) have received the most extensive research. ABA can be described as a science devoted to the acquisition of socially relevant skills and/or remediation of problem behaviors (www.abainternational.org). Goals for which ABA should be recommended include, but are not limited to, improved learning in the wake of intellectual deficits, improving communication and social skills, reducing repetitive behaviors, and reduction or elimination of behavior problems. Additionally, it is highly effective for expediting learning in general especially for persons with ASD (www.asatonline.org). Because it is a science requiring the acquisition and analysis of valid data taken on target behaviors, it readily reveals how successful or useless any particular intervention is; even treatments not based on ABA principles can be evaluated with ABA techniques.

Almost all expert reviewers conclude that early intensive behavioral intervention (sometimes called EIBI), based on ABA, is shown to be effective in increasing IQ and/or adaptive behavior. While the core characteristics of ASD are neither IQ nor behavioral deficits per se, it is not possible for individuals with ASD to independently access either regular education classes or most opportunities in the community if they have intellectual deficits or significant impairment in adaptive behavior. Additionally, language skills have been shown to account for a significant amount of the variance in IQ (Huckabee, 2003), and communication challenges are a core characteristic of ASD. In other words, it is very difficult for a person with ASD to learn to effectively communicate and socially interact with others as long as IQ or adaptive behavior remains impaired. Because of these issues, ABA should be included as a recommendation for all young children with ASD as well as any person with an intellectual disability or problematic behaviors.

While ABA is arguably one of the most effective interventions for individuals with ASD, the truth is that many individuals and school districts provide the so-called ABA services by unqualified or inadequately trained or supervised staff. If a school-based clinician finds himself or herself in the position of managing challenging behaviors without adequate training or support, it is generally possible to obtain consultation from a qualified BCBA for minimal cost. When school staff or clinicians do not receive support and training on how to assess and manage behavior, results are inevitably diluted or ineffective. Many times, children have acquired very bad habits such as irritatingly echoing instructions completely out of context, sitting docilely without ever using their skills because they are dependent on being told what to do, or even acquiring self-injurious behaviors. Sometimes, school districts will profess to provide effective ABA services for students; however, minimal standards of staff supervision are barely maintained. In many instances, paraprofessional aides are left desperately attempting to teach skills or manage severe behavior problems without remotely having the knowledge and skills to be successful. Such conditions are woefully inadequate. Parents or professionals who are seeking to identify qualified ABA services should first locate a BCBA or Board Certified Associate

Behavior Analyst (BCABA) through the Behavior Analyst Certification Board (www.BACB.org) who can properly supervise the intervention. The BACB does an excellent job of ensuring minimal standards are achieved by Board Certified personnel. When including a recommendation for ABA intervention, the evaluating clinician can apprise the parents or guardians of these important teaching parameters and strive to ensure referrals are appropriate.

Questions about the amount of ABA services and whether it should be in individual or group format are relevant. While there are countless peer-reviewed studies on the effectiveness of ABA for teaching a plethora of skills documented in the Journal for Applied Behavioral Analysis (JABA) and other scientific publications, there are few parametric studies precisely outlining the amount and format of ABA necessary to achieve optimal results covaried for age, ASD severity, and skill profile. Compelling research was presented which outlined the amount of time students with ASD were engaged in the classroom as a function of class size (Dykstra, 2014). These results showed a loss of coordinated joint engagement with each additional peer in the class. One can generally assume that individual or small group (3–6 students) settings will be more effective for *teaching* new communication or other social skills while emphasis on generalization (using skills in more complex settings, etc.) and maintenance of existing skills can be targeted in larger groups or a full class of 20 or more students. Most problem behaviors need to be addressed through individual instruction until at least low levels of intensity or frequency are achieved. Again, if individualized instruction is provided by a paraprofessional or teaching assistant, such a staff member *must* be properly trained and supervised to achieve successful results.

Sample ABA Recommendation for School

In the case of severe behaviors, it may be necessary to recommend the following. In order for (student) to satisfactorily acquire (specific academic, communication and/or social skills) and/or remediate/eliminate (specific problem behaviors), student should receive ABA services provided or supervised by a BCBA or BCABA. Communication and social skill deficits are best remediated in an individual or small group setting. To reduce or eliminate behavior problems, individual daily ABA intervention may be required. A Board Certified ABA professional (www.bacb.org) can acquire baseline data, select empirically supported techniques, and write and supervise an intervention plan with an adequate number of service hours for timely success in these areas.

Speech Therapy

Speech therapy is recommended whenever the individual has significant weaknesses or impairments in intelligibility such as problems with sound production, substitutions, or omissions. Other speech problems which frequently occur in ASD including problems with prosody (speech rhythm) or volume may also be addressed with a recommendation for speech therapy. Some speech pathologists can also assist with expressive and receptive language weaknesses for persons with ASD such as deficits in comprehension, vocabulary, syntax, grammar, and sentence formulation. It should be remembered, however, that many people with ASD also have problems sustaining attention and motivation to learn from others thereby requiring that the referred speech therapist be competent at addressing both these issues if necessary.

Speech therapy can be appropriately recommended, as discussed above, in both the school and/or home settings. Speech therapy in the school will be provided based on "academic necessity" which is a fancy way of saying such therapy will address skills necessary for school success. School success is only a fraction of the scope of skills necessary for success in life and therefore private speech therapy may be recommended as well. When it is determined that a student qualifies for speech therapy services in the school, such services are provided free of charge and range in frequency from about 1 h per month to 2 h per week depending on the severity of the need. It is recommended that the evaluating clinician specify the amount of speech therapy required, based on severity of speech and language deficits. Speech therapy services and/or consultation provided by the school needs to be included in the student's IEP discussed above.

Occupational Therapy

Occupational therapy should be recommended specifically when clients have problems including fine or gross motor coordination weaknesses, hand writing problems, or marked sensory sensitivities such as tactile defensiveness. These motor and sensory challenges are not part of the core characteristics of ASD but frequently co-occur with ASD. Many students with ASD enjoy and may benefit from "sensory breaks" or a sensory rich diet, including regular opportunities to access a variety of proprioceptive activities like swinging or bouncing, weight bearing activities as well as activities that stimulate light touch and deep pressure sensors such as playing in a sand tray or crawling through a tight lycra tunnel, respectively. These sensory activities are often professed to indirectly assist the student to subsequently sustain attention, sit quietly, concentrate, or decrease response latency, for example. It should be noted that these skills are foundational prerequisites to learning rather than academic or intellectual outcomes reflected in grades. For these reasons, and because each individual with ASD is highly unique, it is valuable to empirically assess through the acquisition of ABA or other empirical data, the degree to which sensory breaks are benefitting the student versus simply representing a fun break from academic instruction. It is imperative to ensure that any sensory breaks are provided *proactively* so they don't inadvertently serve to reinforce off-task or otherwise disruptive classroom behaviors by reactively taking the student for a fun sensory break in response to inappropriate behavior. Occupational therapy services and/or consultation provided by the school needs to be included in the student's IEP discussed above.

Physical Therapy

Physical therapy services or consultation should be recommended for clients who present with motor weaknesses or other related challenges. Unless a neuropsychologist, physical or occupational therapist is included on the assessment team, direct assessment of muscle strength is probably not included in the assessment. Motor weaknesses can be suspected, however, if the client physically appears to have low muscle tone as evidenced by small muscle mass, the client is clumsy and/or motor speed or dexterity is poor (see Chap. 10: Assessing for Visual Spatial and Motor). Motor weaknesses are not part of the core characteristics of ASD but frequently co-occur with ASD. When in doubt, it is best to refer at least for a physical therapy consult. If the physical therapist determines services are not necessary, at least the client has received thorough evaluation in this area. Physical therapy services and/or consultation provided by the school needs to be included in the student's IEP discussed above.

Psychological Services

Psychological services provided by the school vary in nature and scope. (For a full review of the types of supports that can be helpful to students with ASD, see Chap. 18: School-Based Assessment for ASD). Generally, psychologists in schools work on coping skills, social skills, and promote participation with peers. This may occur weekly in individual counseling sessions or in social skills groups.

When a client with ASD has Low Average or higher verbal abilities, provision of a social skills group by the school is always recommended. Social skills groups may also be recommended for ASD clients with weaker verbal abilities at the clinician's discretion or parents' preference, but the expectations for participation may need to be modified. Some schools may not readily provide social skills groups, but this does preclude the inclusion of this recommendation because all students with ASD have social weaknesses. Increasingly, it is apparent that when students with ASD attend college they are most likely to struggle to fit in socially and often fail or withdraw prematurely for this reason. As such, it is important for regular social skills groups or other social interventions (such as focused skills training) to be provided at school to strengthen the student with ASD in this area. Appropriate social skill interventions such as: Integrated Playgroup model, Superflex, Second Step, Peers, can be helpful for students with ASD (see Chap. 18 for a full list of social skills interventions). Social skills groups provided by the school need to be included in the student's IEP discussed above.

Some form of school services for emotional support of the student with ASD is often recommended. If the client has a comorbid anxiety or mood disorder or another serious psychiatric problem such as psychosis or substance dependence, emotional services should include weekly meetings of at least 30–60 min duration with a school psychologist, counselor, or social worker to help build and maintain emotional coping skills at school. This is obviously a more circumscribed scope than provision of private therapy services which would be expected to ameliorate or manage such comorbid conditions. If a student's presentation is limited to emotional challenges associated with ASD that do not meet criteria for another diagnosis, then emotional services should minimally include provision of psychological or counseling support as needed so that the student at least meets the school staff available for counseling to whom they can turn for assistance intermittently.

Other areas of psychological intervention for ASD include the direct teaching of social rules, body space, and boundaries for peers and adults. These authors have experience in providing explicit instructions for appropriate touching of staff and students. For example, a side hug can replace an inappropriately close front hug. If the child hugs too much, a child could be taught that one hug is enough for the day and then replaced with high-fives or fist-bumps. Similarly, a pat on the back or high five with a peer can replace inappropriate physical closeness with peers. As simple as this may sound, children with ASD can benefit greatly from such explicit teaching, tend to respect these rules and boundaries, and can find more social success this way. Regular or intermittent counseling services provided by the school needs to be included in the student's IEP discussed above.

Tutoring/Targeted Intervention

Sometimes individuals with ASD also have comorbid Reading Disorders or other Learning Disorders as previously discussed. Many persons with ASD have language deficits that compromise the prerequisite skills necessary for reading comprehension. When a Reading Disorder or other Learning Disorders are present, it is recommended that the student receive appropriate intervention such as instruction based on Lindamood Bell or Orton Gillingham programs. Again such services should be provided by the school district at no cost for the qualified student. Reading intervention services need to be included in the student's IEP discussed above. Often, when reading deficits are severe, it is also necessary for parents to seek additional tutoring supports for children. Local chapters of the International Dyslexia Association (IDA) can often provide parents with resources and names of tutors certified in research-based methods like those mentioned above.

Accommodations and Modifications

Many times students with ASD need and benefit from classroom or instructional accommodations and modifications. Often times, accommodations and modifications are simply included in the IEP as an exhaustive list. However, it is important to know what each specific accommodations or modification is designed to remediate. Accommodations may also be needed to prepare the environment so that the student can find more success; in this case, the IEP should clearly illuminate that purpose. The following table outlines accommodations and modifications frequently recommended for students with ASD and the presenting conditions for which they are appropriate. School services as relevant are reiterated in the table for clarity.

Recommendations for Home and Community

While there are many effective and meaningful interventions that have been scientifically proven to be valid treatments for individuals with autism, there is no cure. Autism is typically a lifelong disorder. Bearing in mind that early intervention, high cognitive ability, high language ability, and high adaptive behavior skills lead are the best predictors of optimal outcomes, parents can provide interventions to promote these abilities. Parents want their children to lead healthy and fulfilling lives; and as such, are highly vulnerable to countless, seemingly well-meaning individuals who profess to offer valuable solutions often at great cost yet with no scientific evidence or even theoretical basis for success. As previously described, these "therapies" waste valuable time and money. Sometimes, these "therapeutic" activities or exercises are fun for the children and may appear to have more efficacy than is truly evidenced.

Other times, recommended practices actually worsen ASD characteristics because they promote extensive repetition or rigid structure that is not functional in everyday life yet repetitive behaviors are some of the very symptoms that treatment should be ameliorating. Clinicians can be an awkward position when parents insist on pursuit of treatments that have scant evidence. It can be important to carefully explain the difference between evidence based and emerging treatments and compare these to treatments with no evidence. It also may be that clinicians help the family learn how to measure success in therapy. For example, the family might ask the therapist what the intended results are and in what time frame. If such results are not found, the parents should stop the treatment. Social psychology research has long proven that the more effort a person puts into a treatment or cure, the more he or she is inclined to swear by its usefulness or effectiveness if only because the alternative is to conclude that one has made a mistake. A helpful article from the Autism Science Foundation (www.autismsciencefoundation.org) describes how caregivers are highly vulnerable to:

"Duplicitous claims that encourage them to try unsafe, expensive, and ineffective non-evidence-based treatments… It is important to remember that anyone can start a journal or post a study on the Internet to tout the efficacy of dangerous or useless interventions. Healthcare fraud is a huge business in the USA, and parents of children with autism are often targeted. Fringe treatment providers prey on desperation and fear, and deceive parents with numerous unfounded claims." — With these unfortunate facts in mind, it is essential that assessment professionals stay current on the basics of treatment outcome literature for ASD and make recommendations that are grounded in scientific evidence of efficacy. The following discussions outline presenting diagnoses or problems and recommended treatments. Note that many of these interventions were also discussed under *School* recommendations above because they should be provided in the school setting as well when relevant. As previously mentioned, the scope of "Academic Need" is only a subset of the broader clinical needs of the client. Recommendations for the *Home* address the broader clinical need.

Core ASD Characteristics

In considering scientifically supported treatments for the core characteristics of ASD, including communication and social deficits as well as restricted interests and/or repetitive behaviors, the primary treatment disciplines recommended for consideration are ABA, Speech Language Therapy, Psychology and Occupational Therapy. As discussed elsewhere in this book, many other conditions frequently coexist with ASD, such as: Intellectual Disability, Sensory Sensitivities, Motor weaknesses, Anxiety or Mood Disorders, Phonological Disorders, and Disruptive Behavior Disorders including Oppositional Defiant Disorder or even Conduct Disorder. These ancillary conditions and associated treatment recommendations are discussed following interventions for ASD.

Interventions for Autism Spectrum Disorder

Applied Behavior Analysis

ABA is also discussed under *School* recommendations above. ABA is widely effective for many challenges associated with ASD but is also widely misunderstood. For this reason, some brief historical facts about ABA are included here.

Behavior Analysis emerged from the field of psychology in the 1960s as some psychologists of that day became increasingly disillusioned with psychological theories based on concepts that were neither observable nor measurable. The 1960s marked a period when psychoanalytic theories were flourishing; not just with respect to reasonable consequences of trauma such as projecting hatred onto adults who resembled perpetrators, but extending widely to include the "Refrigerator Mother" hypotheses promulgated by Bruno Bettelheim and others as a false cause of autism. Such mentalistic concepts such as repression, perception of phallic symbols, and neurosis were apparently being used for virtually any number of intractable psychological problems often in a pernicious circular argument rather than acknowledging inadequate theories and unknown causes that had yet to be discovered for mental problems. Such unsound scientific conclusions led to many persons being tragically blamed for causing problems in their loved ones as well as pursuit of damaging interventions. Furthermore, such unsubstantiated dogma likely fueled the stagnation of science in searching for valid explanations and successful treatments for many debilitating conditions. It was from this environment that Behavioral Analysis, with its grounding in observing and measuring what people and animals *actually do*, was born. The science of ABA emerged subsequently to focus only on socially meaningful behaviors which today include widely diverse goals from helping employees to be more productive to smoking cessation and treatment of obesity as well as efficiently building cognitive skills in a person with ASD. As referred to in ABA, a "behavior" is anything a person or animal actually does including making eye contact, carrying on a conversation, or typing an essay. Note the difference between this definition and how most people refer to "behavior" to imply actions that are problematic.

In the 1970s, early treatment for autism was being attempted by Ivar Lovaas and his students Robert Koegel, Darlene Grampeesah, and Laura Schreibman and others in California. While many strategies were crude, highly repetitious, and even questionably humane, it should be noted that there *largely was no treatment offered for people with autism at that time*, and it may have been more humane to try something rather than resign such individuals to chronic institutionalized care with increasingly few options for enjoyment and likely worsening of their physical and mental condition. Remember too that at one time medical doctors cut off limbs bearing shrapnel with no anesthesia, mothers frequently died in childbirth, and measles readily resulted in death (in many places in the world it still does) before medical technology advanced. ABA has similarly advanced and come a long way since the 1970s. State-of-the-art ABA treatment is now typically fun, naturalistic, flexible, and ecologically valid. The prudent evaluator should be aware, however, that some clinicians and facilities still use archaic and highly aversive punishment even including electric shock in teaching persons with ASD. Evaluators are strongly encouraged to assess the competency and ethical values of their referral sources. With these points in mind, the following table lists some conditions for which ABA strategies have proved to be widely effective and should be recommended (Table 15.3):

Speech Language Therapy

When an individual has a speech delay, is markedly difficult to understand, or has ASD with a Communication Impairment, a referral to a Speech Language Pathologist (SLP), *who is competent in treating autism*, is recommended. Note the added qualification that the SLP be competent and experienced in working with individuals with autism. This qualification is important because of the frequent challenges with attention and motivation that can accompany ASD. Speech therapists who know autism well can be extremely helpful in supporting students with ASD at school, at home, and in clinical settings. Speech therapists can provide intervention for articulation problems, speech dysfluency (stuttering), and speech intelligibility.

Pragmatic language therapies that are directed at turn taking, perspective taking, active listening, sharing and reporting of events, giving compliments, and participating in social conversations, can be especially impactful. National speech therapy conferences now include specific sessions for treatment of the social deficits in ASD (for both school and clinical settings). These programs include skills like asking for help, sharing interests, playing games, and appropriately joining peers in play and conversation. Speech therapy technologies are advancing to include systematic approaches to pragmatic language assessment as well as, intervention. Speech therapists can utilize iPad applications such as: http://www.virtualspeechcenter.com/Resources/talking_together_app.aspxs that aide in teaching social skills, and in weekly progress monitoring. Speech therapists with experience in ASD can support

Table 15.3 Sample ABA technologies for ASD problems

Presenting problem	ABA technology	Originating professionals
ASD in toddlers or preschool children	Early Intensive Behavior Intervention (EIBI)	Koegel & Koegel, Shreibman, Rogers, Bryson & Smith and many others
Weak or limited engagement of preschool or prekindergarten children with ASD in an inclusive classroom	Incidental learning	Gaile McGee, Emory University
Limited or absence of spontaneous communication	Pivotal response therapy	Lynn and Robert Koegel and Laura Schreibman, University of California
Poor stimulus & response generalization	Behavioral cusps	Jesus Rosales, University of North Texas
Dysfluent use of cognitive skills	Precision teaching	Fabrizio & Moor and others
Minimal behavioral success in inclusive community settings	Positive behavioral support	Lynn and Robert Koegel, University of California, Santa Barbara
Chronic failure to learn critical life skills in an older child, adolescent, or adult with an Intellectual Disability	Discrete trial training	Ivar Lovaas
Unclear preferences in a nonverbal adolescent or adult	Strategies for self-determination	Don Baer
Moderate to severe problem behaviors	Functional behavioral analysis and treatment	Brian Iwata, Florida State University

classroom participation, communication with peers, and with family members. Many highly trained speech therapists also provide interventions for cognitive deficits that impact language, including ideational fluency, working memory, and word retrieval.

Most ABA professionals who work with individuals with ASD are trained and competent in helping to remediate communication deficits since communication is a cardinal characteristic of ASD. Expressive and receptive language skills are foundational in communicating and therefore ABA as a treatment for ASD will include treatment goals to remediate deficits or weaknesses in communication.

SLPs are trained in the phonological production of sounds and are typically competent in treating sound omissions, substitutions, and stuttering in speech. SLPs who specialize in treating ASDs may also have been trained in PROMPT therapy techniques involving physical facial cues to the lips or cheeks to aid in the production of vowel and consonant sounds. ABA clinicians, even those who specialize in treating ASD, rarely have significant training in sound production. Hence, one way of thinking about speech and language therapies for individuals with ASD is that SLPs may be competent to treat both speech and language problems in ASD and ABA professionals and are likely competent to help treat language and communication problems. Note that ABA is broad technology used for treating a multitude of conditions so clarification about the ABA's training and experience as it relates to the communication problems inherent in ASD is necessary.

Occupational Therapy

As discussed, further under *Additional Evaluations* and *School* above, occupational therapy is valuable for assisting with many challenges often found in persons with ASD including but not limited to building toy play skills, developing adaptive behaviors to promote hygiene and self-care, improving community safety, managing sensory sensitivities, and strengthening motor skills. It should be noted that occupational therapy primarily targets ancillary problems that can co-occur with ASD rather than treating the core characteristics of ASD including impairment in communication and social reciprocity. Professionals reasonably argue that it is important for a person to be comfortable with their sensory experiences in order to optimally learn, however, it is false to deduce that effectively managing their sensory experiences *ensures* learning. When recommended, occupational therapy should not be seen as a substitute for provision of sound behavioral and educational learning opportunities. In addition, occupational therapy sessions are typically only 30–60 min in length and occur 1–2 times per week. Much research shows that children with ASD need to be successfully engaged with materials or other people a majority of the time to make optimal progress.

Psychotherapy

Psychotherapy is recommended whenever a client presents with significant anxiety or a mood disorder as well as relationship problems between the client and peers or caregivers. Clients who present with disruptive behavior disorders including Oppositional Defiant Disorder or Conduct Disorder should also be referred to a psychologist who is competent in treating these conditions when they co-occur with ASD. Note that tantrums, oppositional behavior, and aggression are not included in the core characteristics of ASD and therefore should be successfully treated. In general, such behavioral problems are learned and therefore successful intervention likely requires training for parents and caregivers as well. If a client has unfortunately also experienced trauma, he or she should also be referred to a clinician competent in utilizing proven trauma treatments such as play therapy, EMDR (Eye Movement Desensitization and Reprocessing), or IFS (Internal Family Systems) therapies.

Group Interventions

Group therapy can be effective for individuals with ASD in treating anxiety. For example, the "Face Your Fears" program at JFK Partners in Colorado (Reaven, 2015) is an evidence-based group therapy approach for treating comorbid anxiety and ASD. Group therapy can also help individuals with social skill deficits provided the leaders are knowledgeable and competent in working with this population. Evaluating clinicians should be aware of group services available and whether the provider is competent or at least willing to strengthen skills in serving individuals with ASD.

Recreation

Comprehensive recommendations should include suggestions to strengthen leisure skills and provide recreational opportunities for persons with ASD. As stated, the core characteristics of ASD include repetitive behaviors and restricted interests. As such, individuals with ASD are likely to remain limited in their leisure and recreational skill repertoire if this is not targeted directly and ideally starting at a young age. Furthermore, because of their frequent challenges with Executive Functioning, persons with ASD are unlikely to think of and commence novel activities on their own.

In making recommendations to enhance participation in recreational and leisure activities, consider interests the client already demonstrates and emphasize opportunities to promote social engagement. For example, a client gifted in drawing could be encouraged to take art classes assuming the instructor is open to any necessary accommodations or modifications (such as omitting the pottery requirement because gooey clay makes them gag). A class or group activity is preferred to individual instruction, if possible, because the presence of other participants increases the chance to make friends or at least communicate occasionally with a peer. A client with a penchant for music could volunteer in a music store using his or her sorting skills to help straighten displays while maintaining opportunities for interacting with others and gaining confidence for later paid vocational work.

Sports and other types of camps are also strongly recommended for consideration especially if the leaders are trained in accommodating individuals with ASD. While an overnight camp might be a lofty idea at the time, specific steps to promote recreation and leisure activities should continually be recommended so that the client continually builds on their skills and confidence in these areas. Try to imagine, along with the parents, and caregivers, where the client would like to be in 5 years, and recommend deliberate activities and opportunities that will help him or her achieve that goal. The failure to make and pursue such deliberate recreation and leisure activities is unfortunately likely to have very dire consequences as the individual inevitably ages and faces an ever greater need to integrate into the community.

Book and Internet References for Autism Spectrum Disorders

A recommendation for books and services may look something like one of these with added organizations and supports in the area where the evaluation takes place. These authors keep a file of photocopied book jackets to share recommendations. Clinicians regularly read new books to determine what might best help the parents served at the Emerge clinic. Authors frequently recommended for parents include Sally Ozonoff, Fred Volkmar, Tony Atwood, Temple Grandin, Lynn Koegel, and many others. For adults, Temple Grandin, Stephen Shore, Nick Dubin, John Elder Robison, and others are often suggested.

The following books and resources may be of assistance to the family in parenting a child with an Autism Spectrum Disorder and to the client in understanding autism and the strengths and weaknesses associated:

(a) Autism Society of Colorado (or similar) www.autismcolorado.org/
(b) Autism Society of Boulder County (or similar association) offers a newsletter and a number of community groups and supports (or similar) www.autismboulder.org/
(c) JFK Partners offers seminars and training as well as resources www.jfk partners.org/
(d) For client to read—"Anything But Typical" by Nora Raleigh Baskin.
(e) A memoir of a bright man with Asperger's "Beyond the Wall" by Stephen Shore.
(f) Another memoir "Look Me in the Eye" by John Elder Robison.
(g) An advanced text with up to date research "The Neuropsychology of Autism" by Deborah A. Fein.
(h) "A Parent's Guide to Asperger Syndrome and High Functioning Autism: How to Meet the Challenges and Help Your Child Thrive" by Sally Ozonoff, Geraldine Dawson, and James McPartland.
(i) "Asperger Syndrome and Adolescence—Practical Solutions for School Success," by Myles and Adreon.
(j) "Growing Up on the Spectrum: A Guide to Life, Love, and Learning for Teens and Young Adults with Autism and Asperger's" by Claire LaZebnik & Lynn Koegel, Ph.D., 2014.
(k) Mom's on the Spectrum Support Group—http://www.momsonthespectrum.org
(l) "Overcoming Autism: Finding the answers, strategies, and hope that can transform a child's life" by Koegel & LaZebnik, Viking Penguin: New York, 2014.
(m) "Facing Autism: Giving parents reasons for hope and guidance for help" by Lynn Hamilton, Waterbrook Press: Colorado Springs, 2009.
(n) "Pivotal Response Therapy" by Robert and Lynn Koegel at CCSP Program, Graduate School of Ed., University of California, Santa Barbara, Ca 93106-9490.
(o) "More Than Words," Hanen Language program.
(p) "Behavioral Interventions for Young Children with Autism" by Maurice, Green & Luce, ProEd: Austin, TX, 1996.
(q) Hanen Language classes www.hanen.org
(r) The Arc of the United States, (301) 565–3842, 1010 Wayne Ave., Ste 650, Silver Spring, MD 20886, www.thearc.org.

Thoughts on the Report

As is made evident in this chapter, even if the report is shortened because of limited financial reimbursement for the evaluation, every effort should be made to keep recommendations comprehensive. Typically, clinicians who work in the autism field are extremely dedicated to this population and their families and will do just about anything to assist their clients. The fact is, however, that clinicians must be reimbursed for their time in order to receive competitive pay. Hence, reports generally need to be shorter when clients are using insurance benefits for the evaluation because insurance company reimbursement rates are typically low. Despite these logistical challenges, comprehensive recommendations are important and should always be included in a report.

Now, clinicians are prepared for every part of the evaluation process from the referral and initial consultation to taking observations and managing challenging behaviors during testing, to selecting measures and testing core and associated areas, to making a differential diagnosis, and to deciding on appropriate recommendations. At the conclusion of this process, clinicians should provide a comprehensive report, highlighting all of the findings from the evaluation as well as evidence-based recommendations, such as those provided in this chapter. In order to write a comprehensive report, the authors provide the following outline, which provides a list of the critical components. The report is ultimately "the product" of a comprehensive evaluation and should thus be clear, professional, and comprehensive (Table 15.4).

Sample Recommendations for ASD by Age Diagnosis

Sarah, Age 3
DIAGNOSTIC IMPRESSIONS:
Autism Spectrum Disorder (299.00)
Without Cognitive Impairments; With Language Impairments in Receptive Language
    Severity Level 1 "Requiring Support" in Restricted, Repetitive Behaviors
    Severity Level 2 "Requiring Substantial Support" in Social Communication
Fine Motor Weakness
RECOMMENDATIONS:
Recommendations for Further Evaluation and Treatment:

1. It is recommended that Sarah be reevaluated in approximately 12–24 months to assess progress and update goals.
2. It is recommended that Sarah's parents contact their community centered board to see if they qualify for additional funding for services including ABA hours, family support, and/or other community resources. Sarah may qualify for services with a Children With Autism (CWA) waiver.
3. *Applied Behavioral Analysis (ABA):* Sarah will benefit from in-home applied behavioral analytic therapy to support her use of language, her compliance with demands, her ability to interact reciprocally, and her social skills. This type of support is vital to Sarah's long-term success. This service is available at Emerge. Additional recommended ABA providers in the community include but are not limited to (list providers). The following general recommendations are offered for ABA treatment.

    (a) Skills are typically acquired most quickly through one-on-one interaction.

Table 15.4 Outline of a comprehensive report

1. Report
(a) Client info
i. Name
ii. Date of birth
iii. School
iv. Grade
v. Handedness
vi. Age
vii. Date of testing
viii. Date of report
(b) Reason for referral
(c) Background information
i. Developmental and health
ii. Social and adaptive
iii. Educational
iv. Previous evaluation data
v. Parental Impressions
(d) Behavioral observations
(e) Assessments administered
(f) Test results and conclusions for all areas assessed
i. Cognitive
ii. Attention and executive functions
iii. Motor
iv. Language
v. Academic
vi. Mood
vii. Behavior
viii. Adaptive
ix. Autism
(g) Diagnostic impressions
(h) Recommendations[a]
(i) Charts and tables of scores
Mail report and follow up with client as needed

[a]Sample recommendations are provided in the following pages

(b) Parents, therapists, and teachers will need to identify individualized reinforcement for Sarah consisting of motivating stimuli. A reinforcer is an item or activity that increases the probability of the preceding response reoccurring.

(c) Social praise will acquire more meaning as its presentation is paired with things Sarah clearly enjoys.

(d) Reinforcement of emerging skills should occur frequently and consistently. It is also important to initially reinforce attempts or approximations. As skills become mastered, reinforcement needs to be provided intermittently (fading) for the skill to be maintained.

(e) Use errorless learning (getting it right the first time) by effectively prompting (cuing) and reinforcing successive approximations of a targeted skill. This will allow Sarah to experience success at learning. Prompts need to ultimately be faded to establish independence.

(f) Alternate more challenging activities (e.g., reciprocal play and conversation) with pleasurable activities (e.g., toys, mechanical devices, letters, and numbers) to boost motivation.

(g) An ABA therapist can consult with Sarah's parents to learn the environmental supports that can help her to develop positive behaviors and coping skills in times of frustration. Use few words when Sarah is upset. Block access to dangerous activities with your body, lock doors, and put a pillow on the floor so that Sarah does not bump her head. Place breakable or over-stimulating items out of reach. Wait for even the most minimal sign of calming down and then provide support and comfort to aide in her efforts to modulate her emotions. Always look for opportunities to reinforce the positive and ignore negative behaviors whenever possible. These skills can be challenging at first and the family would be well served by regular consultation with an ABA therapist.

4. It is recommended that Sarah's parents consider providing her school district with the results of this evaluation. Sarah will be eligible for an Individualized Education Program (IEP) in Colorado after age 3 should she attend public school at any time. It is recommended that a plan be developed, recognizing a diagnosis of Autism Spectrum Disorder and providing supportive services aligned with her disability.

5. *Preschool:* There are both private and public preschool options for Sarah. It is recommended that she receive services in a setting with professionals who have expertise in ABA to address language, communication, and social interaction skills. Sarah would be best served in a classroom where she has significant interaction with typically developing peers who have strong language and social interaction skills. In a home school setting, community activities and extracurriculars that provide social interaction opportunities will be very beneficial. Sarah will benefit greatly from social interaction with her peers and an opportunity to learn skills through observation and modeling. There are several preschool programs for children with disabilities provided through the school district for the family's consideration. If Sarah were in a public preschool, it would best serve Sarah if her preschool classroom was not limited to children with developmental delays. A play-based learning approach, rather than the primary focus on pre-academic skills would be most helpful. Sarah's parents may wish to consider Sewall Learning Center located in Denver. For more information, visit—http://www.sewall.org/contact-us/.

6. *Speech Therapy:* Sarah should continue with speech therapy services to increase her expressive and receptive language as well as reciprocal conversation skills and pragmatic language abilities as her therapist may want to collaborate with Sarah's ABA therapist. Sarah would benefit from support to work on using language more functionally and in social contexts.

7. *Occupational Therapy* is recommended to help the family with sensory needs, as well as fine motor skills. Many families have benefited also substantially from OT support either at school or in an outside of school setting.

8. *Social Skills Group* Sarah may benefit from participation in a social skills group such as those offered by the Positive Early Learning Experiences Center (PELE) with the University of Colorado, Denver.

9. Research indicates that some individuals with Autism Spectrum Disorders have metabolic abnormalities or disease that is related to their autism symptoms. Although research has a long way to go to clarify which individual with autism this is relevant for and exactly who may benefit from treatment, referral to a metabolic specialist is recommended if the following occur:

    (a) Failure to have cognitive and other mental processes return to baseline after cessation of an illness.
    (b) Apparently inexplicable degradation of previously acquired cognitive skills including loss of some words or phrases, execution of previously routine tasks, and/or reduced responsiveness.
    (c) Prolonged mental deficits accompanied by persistent dietary shortcomings and/or diarrhea that suggests possible nutritional shortcomings without associated signs of malnutrition.
    (d) Persistent lack of energy in the absence of other satisfactory explanations such as inadequate sleep, inadequate nutrition, illness, or mood disorders (e.g., depression).

10. Sarah's parents may find the following community services beneficial in assisting them:

    (a) Autism Society of Colorado offers resource support as well as a parenting mentor program, http://www.autismcolorado.org.
    (b) Autism Society of Boulder County offers a newsletter and a number of community groups, parent support groups, presentations and fun activities for kids www.autismboulder.org/
    (c) JFK Partners offers seminars and training as well as resources www.jfk partners.org/
    (d) Peak Parent Center, Inc. (800) 284–0251, 6055 Lehman Drive, #101, Colorado Springs, CO 80918
    (e) Parent support groups may be available through the community via the Autism Society of Colorado or through a private practice like Emerge.

11. The following books and resources may be of assistance to Sarah's parents in parenting a child with autism:

    (a) "A Practical Guide to Autism: What Every Parent, Family Member, and Teacher Needs to Know." Volkmar & Wiesner (2009)
    (b) "A Parent's Guide to Asperger Syndrome and High Functioning Autism: How to Meet the Challenges and Help Your Child Thrive" by Sally Ozonoff, Geraldine Dawson, and James McPartland
    (c) "The Optimistic Child" by Martin Seligman.

(d) "Behavioral Intervention for Young Children with Autism: A Manual for Parents and Professionals by Catherine Maurice" by Catherine Maurice, Gina Green and Stephen C. Luce (May 1, 1996)

David, Age 12

DIAGNOSTIC IMPRESSIONS:

Autism Spectrum Disorder (299.00)

Major Depressive Disorder, Mild Recurrent (296.31)

Asthma, History of Esophageal Stricture

Social Stress, Behavior Problems at Home

RECOMMENDATIONS:

Recommendations for Further Evaluation and Treatment:

1. It is recommended that David be reevaluated in approximately 24 months to assess progress and update goals.
2. It is recommended that David participate in psychotherapy with a clinician competent in treating Autism Spectrum Disorders and Depression in order to improve emotional competence, decrease rigidity and need for control, increase social skills and social perspective taking, and improve coping skills. Such services are available through Emerge and elsewhere in the community.
3. It is recommended that David's parents consider implementing Applied Behavior Analytic (ABA) services at home to specifically address tantrum behaviors and improve adaptive and self-help skills at home. At this time, David is not proficient at maintaining good hygiene, and he is unwilling to follow directions or accept suggestions from others without meltdowns that cause significant challenges for his family. In home, ABA consultations from a clinician with a BCBA credential or BCaBA credential would be most appropriate. These services are available at Emerge and elsewhere in the community. If interested, the family could contact their insurance company for a list of other covered providers.
4. David would benefit from participation in a social skills group with other bright children within his age range to work on social skills and social perspective taking. This service may be available at his school through a counselor or school psychologist led lunch group or social skills group. This service is also available in the community.
5. If depressive symptoms and tantrum behaviors do not remit with treatment, David's parents may find it useful to consult with a psychiatrist to discuss medications to help reduce depression. A list of psychiatrists who are familiar with Autism Spectrum Disorders and emotional issues is available upon request.

Recommendations for Academic Settings:

1. David may be eligible to receive special services through his local school district under an Advanced Learning Plan and Section 504 Plan recognizing his diagno-

sis of Autism Spectrum Disorder and his giftedness. Specifically, David should be eligible to receive educational services as needed such as the following:

(a) Continued placement in a gifted education classroom/program as commensurate with his Very Superior intellectual functioning.
(b) A quiet setting to complete tests and assignments as needed.
(c) Permission to reference instructions/have instructions repeated as needed.
(d) Reminders and redirection in a manner that is neutral and does not seem punishing to David. Reinforcement should be given in a manner of 5:1 or five positive comments like "nice job listening" or "great answer David" to one negative comment.
(e) Opportunity to participate in a social skills group and/or obtain regular counseling services to improve his social interactions and decrease his significant rigidity and perfectionism at school.
(f) Assignment of a "home base" adult (like a mentor) to check in with weekly. This allows David to discuss frustrations and problem solve with his designated support person.
(g) Recess/breaks should not be removed as punishment as recess is an important component to help David develop and improve his social skills.
(h) School wide bully prevention programs are important in protecting all children. David may be susceptible to teasing so his teachers should monitor this and make efforts to foster positive social interactions and friendships.

Recommendations for Home and Recreational Settings:

1. To assist in continued development of David's social skills, the following recommendations are offered:

(a) David needs direct services to recognize and respond appropriately to subtle social cues including voice tone, sarcasm, and metaphor. This is best accomplished in a supportive and positive group environment, where social interactions can be discussed, reflected on, and role played.
(b) David needs assistance recognizing and understanding others emotions. Learning to discriminate facial expressions, body postures, and nonverbal gestures can aid David in responding empathically in more sophisticated situations.
(c) Use of didactic questioning can assist teachers and parents in assessing David's understanding of social and communication concepts and modifying approaches as necessary.
(d) Approaches and strategies that consider David's tendency to think concretely are likely to be most successful.

2. The following recommendations are offered for increasing behavioral compliance from David:

(a) Instructions should be issued judiciously. Presently, David's parents will want to pick battles carefully.
(b) Initially, try to make interactions with David pleasant and positive.

(c) Utilize single step instructions that are easily prompted for completion when it is necessary to give an instruction. An example may be "David we need to leave in 10 min" and "David, it's time to leave, please meet me at the car." These instructions should be issued in a normal tone of voice and with eye contact to ensure you have David's attention.

(d) Extinguish defiance when it occurs by removing negative attention. Do not respond to negative statements, refusals, or insults from David. Never argue. Just remind David that you would be happy to have a discussion when he feels calm and can speak respectfully and in a normal tone.

(e) When instructions or directions are given, it is necessary that David be required to complete the task so these should initially be issued judiciously.

(f) Set up a system of reinforcement to increase compliance. For example, allowance, computer time, or a family dinner out or a Lego could be earned through respectful behavior.

(g) Modify the environment when possible to decrease the likelihood of conflict. For example, if David is likely to tease his sister during homework time, provide separate spaces for their work so this is less likely to occur.

(h) Relationships with David can be developed or strengthened by commenting on and/or sharing activities that he is interested in such as watching movies, having dinner together, and discussing his interests.

(i) Always try to have some positive time together each day despite any disagreements or arguments that have occurred. Put the disagreement aside to do something David enjoys even if it is just having ice cream or talking about his day.

(j) Withholding positive consequences (e.g., video games/privileges) until David complies with the agreed upon requirement (i.e., take out the trash) will improve the likelihood of compliance again next time.

(k) **Do not reinforce** tantrum behavior; simply withdraw attention after commenting that you would be happy to have the discussion in a calm manner whenever David shows he is ready.

(l) Do **reinforce successive approximations** to calming down if David lowers his voice and attempts to communicate in a more appropriate manner, do respond immediately, and remain calm yourself.

(m) Seek outside behavioral support as needed if defiance and verbally aggressive behaviors continue. This is available through Emerge or elsewhere in the community.

3. Research indicates that some individuals with Autism Spectrum Disorders have metabolic abnormalities or disease which is related to their autism symptoms. While research has a long way to go to clarify which individual with autism this is relevant for and exactly who may benefit from treatment, referral to a metabolic specialist is recommended if the following occur:

(a) Failure to have cognitive and other mental processes return to baseline after cessation of an illness.

(b) Apparently inexplicable degradation of previously acquired cognitive skills including loss of some words or phrases, execution of previously routine tasks, and/or reduced responsiveness.

(c) Prolonged mental deficits accompanied by persistent dietary shortcomings and/or diarrhea that suggests possible nutritional shortcomings without associated signs of malnutrition.

(d) Persistent lack of energy in the absence of other satisfactory explanations such as inadequate sleep, inadequate nutrition, illness, or mood disorders (e.g., depression).

4. The following books and resources may be of assistance to the Cortez's in parenting a child with Autism Spectrum Disorder and to David in understanding Autism Spectrum Disorder and the strengths and weaknesses associated:

(a) Autism Society of Colorado www.autismcolorado.org/

(b) Autism Society of Boulder County offers a newsletter and a number of community groups and supports www.autismboulder.org/

(c) JFK Partners offers seminars and training as well as resources www.jfk partners.org/

(d) For David to read—"Anything But Typical" by Nora Raleigh Baskin

(e) A memoir of a bright man with Asperger's "Beyond the Wall" by Stephen Shore

(f) Another memoir "Look Me in the Eye" by John Elder Robison

(g) An advanced text with up to date research "The Neuropsychology of Autism" by Deborah A. Fein

(h) "A Parent's Guide to Asperger Syndrome and High Functioning Autism: How to Meet the Challenges and Help Your Child Thrive" by Sally Ozonoff, Geraldine Dawson, and James McPartland

(i) "Asperger Syndrome and Adolescence—Practical Solutions for School Success," by Myles and Adreon

(j) "Growing Up on the Spectrum: A Guide to Life, Love, and Learning for Teens and Young Adults with Autism and Asperger's" by Claire LaZebnik & Lynn Koegel, Ph.D., 2014

Sam, Age 16
DIAGNOSTIC IMPRESSIONS:
Autism Spectrum Disorder (299.00)
Without Cognitive or Language Impairments
Severity Level 1 "Requiring Support" in Social Communication and Restricted, Repetitive Behaviors
RECOMMENDATIONS:
Recommendations for Further Evaluation and Treatment:

1. It is recommended that Sam be reevaluated in approximately 24–36 months to assess progress and update goals.

2. It is recommended that Sam consider participating in psychotherapy with a clinician who has expertise in treating Autism Spectrum Disorders in order to work on his planning and organization including long-term planning for college. Additionally, Sam could work to improve emotional competence, social–emotional reciprocity, and improve coping skills; all of which were brought up as concerns during questionnaires and self-report. Such services are available through

Emerge and elsewhere in the community. Emerge clinicians who work with teens who have High Functioning Autism Spectrum Disorders and may be a good fit for Sam. Many have additional expertise in college planning and programs to consider at the college level. Sam should have a different therapist from his brother so that each can have a person to work with them individually and be an advocate.

3. It is recommended that Sam have his own feedback with a chance to see his data and ask questions about his diagnosis, strengths, and weaknesses. By taking more ownership of his own learning style and profile Sam may become more open to accessing the tools available. He could meet with an Emerge clinician for this individual session to review his data.

Recommendations for Academic Settings:

1. Sam should continue to be eligible to receive special services through his local school district under a Section 504 Plan, recognizing his diagnosis of Autism Spectrum Disorder, and his Superior intellectual reasoning abilities. Sam's current 504 plan provides accommodations including: extra time for standardized tests and classroom assignments, assignments accepted by email, use of laptop and/or use of recording device, preferential seating, provide copy of classroom notes, daily planner check in with teachers, and access to the counselor or his therapist as needed:

    (a) Sam should be provided a case manager and/or mentor to work with him in advocating for himself and to make sure that he is taking advantage of the appropriate accommodations his 504 plan provides. It is likely that Sam is not asking for copies of notes or taking advantage of the options he has to submit homework electronically. A weekly meeting with a support person who also knows his teachers would help him use his supports to be successful.

    (b) Research indicates that bright students with an Autism Spectrum Disorder can struggle significantly with emotional regulation, which directly impacts their success in school, college, and in the workplace. Sam will benefit from meetings with a school psychologist or school counselor who can help Sam identify and understand triggers he may have for stress and anger, and to help Sam implement techniques for emotional regulation in the school setting.

    (c) If a student is highly rigid in the school setting or more deliberate in his working style, he will struggle with changes to schedules, requirements, deviations from a typical day, and even the unpredictability of peer responses.

        • When possible, Sam will benefit from additional time to process information regarding schedule and personnel changes, so he should be made aware of significant changes ahead of time. Last-minute surprise changes should be kept to a minimum.

        • In the case of a last minute surprise or change to something without prior warning, professionals at Sam's school should allow him a break and some flexibility.

    (d) It is recommended that Sam become adept at managing materials and deadlines for classes as a high school student. Being able to independently achieve this level of organization as a high school student will prepare Sam for college. As organization and meeting deadlines can be challenging for Sam, these can be supported directly by his mentor or case manager who may be able to teach him how to organize and plan effectively. Again a weekly meeting should be enough time to help Sam maintain organization.

2. As Sam is nearing the end of high school, it is crucial to have a plan in place for post-high school. For Sam, it is important to consider his skill sets and current academic level when choosing a direction. Sam's interest in the sciences, engineering, art and strong intellectual abilities may best serve him in a smaller school where he can attend small class sizes, receive supports promptly and effectively, and be known and supported by his professors and fellow students in the college campus in a fairly supportive way.

   (a) Sam may want to start visiting schools and get some ideas about campus life. It is recommended that he speak directly with the campus disability service programs and learning centers and obtain information about how to initiate supports prior to starting the year.
   (b) All colleges have disability support offices. Some colleges offer additional support services, such a learning support programs/centers, beyond that required by law.

     • Locally, the University of Denver's, Learning Effectiveness Program (LEP) is one such program. The LEP can be reached at: 303-871-2372.

Recommendations for Home and Recreational Settings:

1. It will benefit Sam to begin now honing his independent skills in order to prepare for college life and employment after high school. Skills such as doing laundry, making healthy food choices, organizing his materials, planning for deadlines, and learning to ask for help when needed can benefit Sam in preparing for college.
2. It will benefit Sam to learn how to effectively ask for help, ask for further information, read and respond to schedules, and manage his responses when expectations or schedules suddenly change. For a young adult with an Autism Spectrum Disorder, these can be challenging, yet essential, workplace skills to master.
3. It is recommended that Sam, his parents and his younger brother spend time engaging in areas of common interest to continue building and strengthening their relationships. This could be as simple as dining out at a favorite restaurant, or watching sports together. For parents and siblings to be associated with a student's areas of interest can help strengthen the connections between family members, and contribute to a family's mutual enjoyment of activities and each other.
4. Sam would also benefit from participating in extracurricular activities that match his interests, where he could meet peers who share interests. Whether it be sports, games, or the arts, there are a variety of extracurricular activities where he could meet friends and build self-competence and self-confidence in a safe and supportive environment. These activities could occur through Sam school or elsewhere in the community. As Sam comes to understand his own learning and emotional profile more, he may be more willing to consider these steps.

5. As adequate sleep is essential to daily functioning, it is recommended that Sam practice good sleep hygiene practices. The following are a list of recommended sleep strategies:

   (a) Go to bed at the same time each day.
   (b) Get up from bed at the same time each day.
   (c) Get regular exercise each day, preferably in the morning or early afternoon.
   (d) *Avoid screens (phone, computer, television) for 30 min before bed.*
   (e) Use a relaxation exercise just before going to sleep (i.e., imagery, muscle relaxation, warm bath, lotion).
   (f) Use your bed only for sleep (i.e., not for watching television or reading books).
   (g) Do not command yourself to go to sleep as this will only make your mind and body more alert. If you lie in bed awake for more than 20–30 min, get up, go to a different room, participate in a quiet activity (e.g., reading), and then return to bed when you feel sleepy.

6. College Living Experience is a program in Denver that offers summer programs to orient students to independent living the summer before their senior year in high school. CLE also offers comprehensive services for students who need more social and organizational supports throughout college. Experiencecle.com.

7. The following books and resources may be of assistance to Sam and his parents in learning about Asperger's Disorder now known as Autism Spectrum Disorder:

   (a) Autism Society of Colorado www.autismcolorado.org/
   (b) Autism Society of Boulder County offers a newsletter and a number of community groups, teenager groups and supports www.autismboulder.org/
   (c) JFK Partners offers seminars and training as well as resources www.jfkpartners.org/
   (d) For Sam—A memoir of a bright man with Asperger's "Beyond the Wall" by Stephen Shore
   (e) Another memoir "Look Me in the Eye" by John Elder Robison
   (f) An advanced text with up to date research "The Neuropsychology of Autism" by Deborah A. Fein
   (g) "A Parent's Guide to Asperger Syndrome and High Functioning Autism: How to Meet the Challenges and Help Your Child Thrive" by Sally Ozonoff, Geraldine Dawson, and James McPartland
   (h) "Asperger Syndrome and Adolescence—Practical Solutions for School Success," by Myles and Adreon
   (i) "Growing Up on the Spectrum: A Guide to Life, Love, and Learning for Teens and Young Adults with Autism and Asperger's" by Claire LaZebnik & Lynn Koegel, Ph.D., 2014

Mr. Johnson, age 25
DIAGNOSTIC IMPRESSIONS:
Autism Spectrum Disorder (299.00)
Major Depressive Disorder, Recurrent, Severe Without Psychotic Features (296.33)

Post-Traumatic Stress Disorder, Chronic (309.81)
Personality Disorder, Not Otherwise Specified (301.9)
Suicidal Ideation, Unemployment, Problems in the Social Environment, Problems with Primary Support

RECOMMENDATIONS:
Recommendations for Further Evaluation/Treatment:

1. It is recommended that Mr. Johnson consult with a psychiatrist to discuss treatment options including medication and psychotherapy to treat his symptoms related to Post-Traumatic Stress Disorder and Depression. Mr. Johnson is referred to his primary care physician and/or his insurance company for recommended psychiatrists in his area. Generally, psychiatrists manage medication and a psychologist provides psychotherapy services. It will be important for Mr. Johnson to work with someone who specializes in the treatment of adults with autism, depression, and anxiety disorders.

2. If severe depression and suicidal ideation continue, Mr. Johnson should seriously consider inpatient hospitalization to treat his symptoms. If at any time Mr. Johnson or his parents feel he is unsafe, they should call 911 and/or take him to the nearest emergency room for more intensive care. Mr. Johnson could discuss the benefits of inpatient treatment with his medical doctor or psychiatrist and determine whether this would be beneficial for him.

3. It is recommended that Mr. Johnson receive a minimum of regular weekly psychotherapy from a clinician familiar with Autism, Post-Traumatic Stress Disorder, and Mood Disorders. Mr. Johnson would benefit from being taught multiple coping methods to deal with depression and anxiety, as well as strategies to improve his emotional understanding, manage his frustration and irritability, increase emotional tolerance, and improve interpersonal relationships. It will likely also be important for Mr. Johnson to work with his therapist to increase his understanding Post-Traumatic Stress Disorder and Depression as a means of empowering him to explain it to others in his life for validation and support. Treatment modalities that may work best for Mr. Johnson would include family systems therapy, cognitive behavioral therapy, and/or eye movement desensitization and reprocessing (EMDR). These services are available in the community. Mr. Johnson will want to speak with his doctor to determine providers in his area. It is of the utmost importance that Mr. Johnson identify a qualified provider who he feels he can trust and connect with.

4. At some point in the future, group therapy may be helpful to Mr. Johnson. The Kempe Center in Denver is a treatment center for Child Abuse and may have information on support groups in the area for adults who experienced abuse as children. Additionally, as Mr. Johnson's depression is managed, he may benefit from a group for adults with Autism Spectrum Disorders. Mr. Johnson should contact his local chapter of the Autism Society to learn more about groups in his area.

5. Mr. Johnson may find assistance through his current Community Centered Board. This organization may be helpful to Mr. Johnson in identifying resources like transportation, job assistance, etc. This organization may be helpful based on Mr. Johnson's Autism Spectrum Disorder diagnosis.

6. Considering Mr. Johnson's unemployment status, he could benefit from services offered by the Colorado Division of Vocational Rehabilitation. Mr. Johnson may also wish to look into job assistance through Ability Specialists — abilityspecialists.com located in Denver.

Recommendations for Home and Occupational Settings:

1. It will be important that Mr. Johnson move to a location where he can obtain regular employment and regular mental health services. As he does not drive, he will need to have close access to public transportation. This is essential in Mr. Johnson's recovery process.
2. Mr. Johnson may wish to consider working toward earning a driver's license as this will provide independence and increased mobility. This is likely to be very helpful in Mr. Johnson's process of seeking employment.
3. It will be important that those close to Mr. Johnson understand his diagnoses so they can support his recovery. It will also be important that they recognize the difficulties he experiences are real and are not intentional.
4. As adequate sleep is essential to daily functioning, it is recommended that Mr. Johnson practice good sleep hygiene practices. The following are recommended sleep strategies:

   (a) Go to bed at the same time each day.
   (b) Get up from bed at the same time each day.
   (c) *Avoid screens (phone, computer, television) for 30 min before bed.*
   (d) Get regular exercise each day, preferably in the morning or early afternoon.
   (e) Use a relaxation exercise just before going to sleep (i.e., imagery, muscle relaxation, or a warm bath).
   (f) Use your bed only for sleep (i.e., not for watching television or reading books).
   (g) Do not command yourself to go to sleep as this will only make your mind and body more alert. If you lie in bed awake for more than 20–30 min, get up, go to a different room, participate in a quiet activity (e.g., reading), and then return to bed when you feel sleepy.

5. Because Mr. Johnson's executive functions like planning and organizing are impacted by his emotional difficulties, he should utilize strategies such as a daily calendar, consistent schedule and routine, and use of notes. These strategies will help alleviate any difficulties relating to planning and organizing, as well as help alleviate any anxiety relating to these difficulties, and will support Mr. Johnson in attaining his occupational goals.
6. Specifically, Mr. Johnson should be allowed modifications in the workplace as needed such as the following:

   (a) Additional time to complete assignments due to executive functioning weaknesses.
   (b) A quiet setting to complete assignments as needed.

(c) Assignments should be provided one at a time giving Mr. Johnson adequate time to process and complete his work.

(d) Down time to regroup and relax that will help him refocus his attention and stay organized and productive.

(e) Permission to reference instructions/have instructions repeated as needed.

(f) A caring mentor who can help him in times that demands may be overwhelming.

7. Mr. Johnson would benefit from opportunities for positive recreational and social experiences. Possibilities include groups or activities sponsored by the National Alliance on Mental Illness. The website for Colorado is www.namicolorado.org. Other possibilities include outdoor recreation and participation in book clubs or other social groups. Mr. Johnson should also seek additional groups and social outlets through his church.

8. To learn more about Post-Traumatic Stress Disorder, Mr. Johnson may find it helpful to read material on this subject, such as *Trauma and Recovery* by Judith Herman.

9. To learn more about Autism Spectrum Disorders, it is recommended that Mr. Johnson read books by successful adults who have been diagnosed with autism. Temple Grandin, Nick Dubin, and Stephen Shore are three authors who have published one or more books on their experiences presently and growing up with autism.

Recommendations for Academic Settings:

1. Mr. Johnson is eligible to begin receiving special education services under section 504 of the Americans with Disabilities Act (ADA). A 504 plan and an educational classification recognizing his diagnoses of Major Depressive Disorder and PTSD should be developed. Specifically, Mr. Johnson should be eligible to receive educational services in college as needed such as the following:

(a) Additional time to complete assignments and standardized tests due to executive functioning weaknesses.

(b) A quiet setting to complete tests and assignments as needed.

(c) Permission to reference instructions/have instructions repeated as needed.

(d) Preferential seating in the lecture hall to assist him in sustaining attention.

(e) Copies of notes as needed for studying due to Mr. Johnson's organizational challenges.

(f) Opportunity to be assessed verbally due to processing speed, fine motor, and executive functioning challenges. The verbal domain is Mr. Johnson's strongest cognitive index, and he should be able to best demonstrate what he knows through verbal evaluations.

2. In addition, it would be most helpful for Mr. Johnson to receive mentoring support focused on helping him manage academic challenges and emotional demands of attending school.

Concluding Remarks on the Feedback, Report, and Recommendations

This concludes the chapter on the final stages of the assessment process which involve a feedback meeting with the family, a comprehensive psychological evaluation report, and appropriate recommendations. The feedback session with the family is the clinician's opportunity to educate and guide the family toward evidence-based treatments, as well as offer understanding and hope. As has been highlighted throughout this chapter and those preceding, an accurate and clear diagnosis, that covers all of the areas of impairment, is a critical precursor for making appropriate recommendations. Children with autism may have deficits in any of the 11 areas reviewed in this book or more and recommendations should be based on the area of need identified. All too often, in clinical practice, these authors find that parents have been guided toward a treatment that, although evidence based, is completely inappropriate for the child's needs. For example, a family called one of the authors asking if her child needs occupational therapy. In this case, this child with no motor, sensory, or adaptive skill deficits was unlikely to benefit from occupational therapy. Alternatively, the case study "Sarah (age 3)," presented in this chapter discusses a child who struggled with both fine and gross motor challenges delegating occupational therapy move to the top of the list of recommendations. As was shown in Table 15.2, the recommendation must be made based on the child's presenting problem. The assessment process is generally complete when the clinician provides a comprehensive report detailing the background information, behavioral observations, assessments administered, results, diagnostic impressions, and recommendations. This report becomes an advocacy tool for the family so it is critical to be thorough and clear about the reasons that the clinician arrived at the diagnosis, the major presenting problems in the client's profile, and in provision of resources for the recommended treatments.

Chapter 16
Case Examples from Referral to Recommendation

Abstract This chapter follows three case examples of individuals referred for evaluation with Autism Spectrum Disorder as a referral question. These cases follow from the referral through assessment to recommendations for treatment moving forward. Examples include brief and more comprehensive assessments of individuals of different ages and with different diagnostic outcomes. These case examples are a compilation of data from various clients evaluated over the past 7 years and identifying information has been changed. The individuals are introduced below with information provided that was obtained during initial consultation and completion of parent/individual screening measures and rating scales.

"Scott," the first case example, was developed to provide insight into an assessment with a child under 2 years of age. Early diagnosis leads to early intervention and optimal treatment outcomes. The ADOS-2 Toddler Module is designed to evaluate children as young as 12 months old. Provided is an example of an assessment with a 22-month-old.

"Sarah," the second case example, is provided to demonstrate what an adult evaluation battery could look like. It also provides helpful insight into a battery that includes assessment for mood, as often it is necessary to differentiate between mood and ASD. This provides an example of what that differential diagnosis looks like at very young ages.

"Sam," the third example, is a socially motivated 10-year-old who is very bright and very rigid behaviorally. This example provides a look at comorbidity as often individuals not diagnosed until late childhood have developed other mood and behavior disorders secondary to ASD.

Keywords Case examples of autism spectrum disorders • Assessing autism in a toddler • Assessing autism with mood symptoms • Assessing autism spectrum disorder in a gifted child • Autism and gifted assessment • Recommendations for treatment of autism

Assessing a Toddler with Mood Swings and Self-Injurious Behavior

"Scott" is a case example that provides insight into toddler assessment. Although it is often reported that other clinics have told families their child is too young for an assessment, early diagnosis can spur early intervention and optimal outcomes. The ADOS-2 Toddler Module is designed to evaluate children as young as 12 months old. Indeed, at the Emerge clinic, children have been diagnosed as young as 13 months, referred for behavioral therapy, and have already advanced their communication skills, adaptive behaviors, and social skills. Research suggests that we can reliably diagnose an Autism Spectrum Disorder at 18 months and early intervention is crucial as children with ASD have a declining trajectory if they go untreated (Ozonoff, 2014 IMFAR presentation). This case example will illustrate how to do a comprehensive assessment with a toddler, including choosing assessment instruments, diagnosis, and conclusions.

Referral Question and Background Information

Scott is a 22-month-old who was referred in order to understand his frequent mood swings, temper tantrums, and self-injurious behaviors. Scott's parents report that he was an "easy baby." His speech currently includes, "where are you," "snack please," "ma ma," "da da," and "woff woff." At 12–14 months of age, parents noted that Scott frustrates quickly and easily. When upset, he bangs his head and throws toys or food. Scott is described as active, independent, strong willed, stubborn, and "fearless." He loves to rough house, carry trains around, and play with the vacuum cleaner. Per parent report he has strengths in fine motor skills and in his memory for songs and lines from books and movies.

Testing Observations

Scott is a handsome, well-dressed toddler with blonde hair and blue eyes. Scott said "hi" in the waiting room. He separated from his mother with ease. Upon seeing the toys in the evaluation room, he was initially hesitant and displayed frustrated mood with congruent affect. After a short time, he warmed up and appeared to have fun playing on his own. He made minimal eye contact with others, and his attention was variable. He tended to move from object to object, without taking time to play with a toy or interact with examiners. His communication was limited to making requests, such as wanting to open locks, and make tracks for toys. Scott was easily discouraged on many of the cognitive and language tasks, and gave up easily on challenging items.

Assessments Administered

Mullen Scales of Early Learning

For a child of Scott's age, the Mullen provides information about a child's developmental level, and an assessment of critical skills in different domains. For an autism assessment, it is notable whether or not skills are average or advanced on tests that involve a lesser degree of social demand, such as the Visual Reception scale, but delays are seen in the Receptive or Expressive Language scales. Although, not diagnostic, many children with autism may have gross or fine motor delays, which can be assessed with this instrument. Of further interest for ASD evaluations, is the child's approach to task. In this case example, Scott refused certain items and did not show the desire to please the examiners with his efforts. For some examiners, the child's lack of effort on the Mullen can be disconcerting, in that the clinician may wonder if the child is capable of more than he demonstrates. However, this pure assessment of a child's ability in a novel testing situation is valid, as it shows the examiner the skills a child can demonstrate independently. The Mullen is a critical tool for clinicians evaluating young children. It is generally recommended that two or more examiners administer the instrument in order to move through the items rapidly, manage the materials, and maintain the child's attention to the tasks.

Autism Diagnostic Observation Schedule, Second Edition: Toddler Module

For a child Scott's age, the ADOS-2: Toddler is the Gold Standard for assessing autism. This module includes toys targeting a toddler's interest, such as a doll, balloons, bubbles, jack-in-the box, and a blanket. This module allows the examiner to play with the child and assess the interaction. Recall that autism is more about the negative symptoms; skills the child is expected to display that are absent or delayed, rather than positive symptoms, such as aggression or odd behaviors. During the ADOS-2: Toddler, examiners assess whether or not the child will make requests, for example, to blow up a balloon again. A typical child might point, gesture or say "again," whereas a child with autism might grab the balloon away from the examiner or become frustrated. This assessment allows for the clinician to obtain a language sample, play behaviors, interactions with caregivers compared to examiners, response to joint attention and participation in a social routine.

Other Assessments Administered: Vineland Adaptive Behavior Scale—Parent/ Caregiver Rating Form (VABS-II), Clinical Interview with Mr. and Mrs. Browne, Clinical Observations of Scott.

Test Results and Conclusions

On the Visual Reception scale, Scott scores in the Average range and the 50th percentile; with an age equivalent of 22 months. Scott is able to sort objects by category; correctly separating blocks and spoons into the specified box. He shows the ability to identify and place shapes into a board-puzzle. Scott's cognitive abilities are commensurate with peers his age. *This performance is typical for a child with autism in that a child on the Spectrum may have average or strong cognitive abilities paired with delays in language and motor skills.*

Scott shows delays on the Gross and Fine Motor assessment. On the Gross Motor scale, he obtained a T score of 22, which falls into the Very Low range and the 1st percentile. He is able to walk a straight line and jump with both feet. He can balance on one foot with one hand held but is not able to do so without support. He is able to run but tends to run stiffly and is not yet able to make a sharp turn while running. He struggled to walk five or six steps in a straight line. He can throw, catch, and kick a ball. His T score of 24 on Fine Motor falls into the 1st percentile and the 17 month age level. On fine motor tasks, Scott is able to put pennies in a slot, and to coordinate his movements from hand-to-hand. He could screw on a bolt and string beads. He was not interested in stacking blocks or drawing shapes. He is not yet able to fold, stack items, and build structures with blocks. Overall, Scott's motor skills are delayed for his age. *These delays in motor skills are not diagnostic but are often seen in children with autism. This is especially remarkable when it occurs in contrast with average or high cognitive abilities.*

Scott showed significant delays in both Expressive and Receptive language. There was a 16-point discrepancy favoring Expressive Language Skills over Receptive. On the Expressive Language Scale, Scott's T score of 36 falls just below the average range. Scott was able to say words like, "hi," "bye," "spoon," "girl," "milk," and "doggie." On the Receptive Language Scales, Scott displayed significant delays. His T score on the Receptive Language Scale of 20, falls into the Very Low range and 1st percentile. Scott has difficulty following directions. He is not yet able to look at a picture and discern, "where is baby eating" or "where is baby sleeping." He does not demonstrate the ability to identify the purpose of objects. *This profile of higher expressive language skills paired with lower receptive language skills is common in children with autism. This pattern is diagnostic in that children with other disabilities display the opposite pattern, tending to understand more than they can say. Further remarkable is that children with autism tend to use more advanced vocabulary than they understand and may be able to perform nonverbal cognitive tasks at a level that far exceeds their skills on receptive language tasks.*

Autism Diagnostic Observation Schedule: Toddler Module

Scott shows the ability to utilize a social-smile during a peek-a-boo game. Scott makes intermittent eye-contact. He is able to show objects to others effectively at times, but tends not to sustain that interaction. His facial expressions are generally flat or only indicative of extremes of emotions. He tends to focus on the toys and objects more than people. When prompted, he did not request the balloon or the bubbles through gesture or verbalizations. Instead, he became frustrated with the tasks and would rest on the floor and suck his thumb to express his discontent. He shows a repetitive interest in toys; becoming focused on activating a toy bunny, blowing bubbles, or blowing up the balloon, such that the toy has to be removed from sight. He did not show the ability to use toys as an agent of action. He had difficulty imitating the sounds of animals and was not able to pretend one object could represent another object. He effectively pretended that he was washing a toy doll during "bath time." He did not help dry or dress the doll and did not make bids for interaction. Scott was inconsistent in nonverbal communication such as limited or absent gesture use and lack of pointing to make requests. Generally, Scott's ability to maintain an interaction with examiners is limited, affecting the quality of rapport. Scott has repetitive interests and does not display the ability to initiate and interact reciprocally with others. *His symptoms are consistent with a diagnosis of Autism Spectrum Disorder (299.00).*

Overall, Scott displays a variety of protective factors which speak to the likelihood that he will respond to intervention. His parents are supportive and keenly aware of his needs and challenges. Scott also displays the protective factor of adequate cognitive ability and appears to have a strong memory. Although Scott struggles to express himself verbally, he has learned to use words to communicate, and this is a skill that can be developed and strengthened in therapy. Scott shows risk factors with his diagnosis of Autistic Disorder. With the support of his parents and early, evidence-based intervention, Scott shows a great deal of promise for progress in therapy and his long-term future.

Recommendations

For Scott, it was recommended that the family seek behavioral therapy for him and behavioral consultation for parental support. Scott may be eligible for an Individualized Family Service Plan (IFSP) in Colorado. In terms of services, he may benefit from public preschool, speech therapy to support his communication, Applied Behavioral Analysis to build compliance and adaptive skills, and Occupational Therapy specifically to improve mealtime behaviors, gross and fine motor skills, and to aide in potty training. The family was also referred to community resources such as parent support groups and autism advocacy groups in Colorado.

Assessing an Adult to Rule out Autism Spectrum and Mood Disorders

"Sarah" is a case example that provides insight into adult assessment. Many clinics evaluate children but feel less comfortable diagnosing ASDs in adults. The rule out between a Mood Disorder and ASD can be challenging as low emotional awareness, poor conversation skills, avoiding eye contact, and flat affect can be mood related symptoms. It is crucial to obtain a thorough clinical interview to obtain developmental, social, medical, and educational history that can help with this rule out. Other social communication challenges like difficulty with creative storytelling or obvious restricted interests can provide information to help with diagnostic clarification. This case example will illustrate how to do a comprehensive assessment with an adult, including choosing assessment instruments, diagnosis, and conclusions.

Referral Question and Background Information

Sarah, age 35, requested this evaluation in order to understand the nature of her cognitive, psychological, executive functioning, and emotional profile. Sarah indicates concerns about depressive symptoms that she first noticed in college and shares that she wonders if she has characteristics of an Autism Spectrum Disorder as social interactions are very difficult for her and she reports challenges communicating with others. Sarah's birth and early development were unremarkable, and she recalls being a quiet and introverted child and an average student in school. Her extended family medical history is significant for Autism Spectrum Disorder (in a nephew) and Mood Disorders. She first experienced symptoms of depression in college, and she has been prescribed medication for Depression for about 15 years. She is currently prescribed Wellbutrin to be taken with Lexapro. Of note, Sarah reports having experienced the following difficulties at some time in her life: sadness, concentration problems, distractibility, eating problems, mood swings, sleep difficulty; avoiding people, avoiding going into public, and avoiding having conversations with others. Sarah has concerns that she is becoming more and more antisocial, and she finds social interaction to be awkward and stilted. She shared that she took an online ASD questionnaire that indicated she has significant characteristics of autism. This led Sarah to seek a full evaluation.

Testing Observations

Sarah expressed herself well and presented with strong language skills. Her tone of voice and prosody of speech were unremarkable. Sarah presented with depressed to neutral mood and congruent affect. She made small talk and conversed reciprocally with examiners when spoken to but tended to be quiet and presented as introverted. She demonstrated appropriate eye contact and when answering questions she synchronized her speech nicely with facial expression and gesture. She has a warm smile and appropriate insight into her own emotions and relationships. *These testing observations are not consistent with an Autism Spectrum Disorder. Despite her depression, Sarah was appropriately reciprocal and conversed well with evaluators demonstrating skills in perspective taking and communicating her point utilizing eye contact, gesture, and facial expression.*

Assessments Administered

Wechsler Adult Intelligence Scale, Fourth Edition

Sarah's Full Scale IQ standard score is 115, at the 84th percentile and in the Above Average range. If this test was repeated nine times out of ten, Sarah's intellectual ability standard score would fall between 111 and 118. Her verbal and nonverbal abilities were not significantly different from one another but Verbal Comprehension skills fall in the Average range and Nonverbal Reasoning skills fall in the Above Average range. She demonstrates High Average ability in Working Memory and Superior Processing Speed. These results indicate that Sarah has significant cognitive strengths, particularly in her nonverbal reasoning skills and in the speed at which she processes new information. Her verbal skills in defining words, offering similarities and answering information-based questions are Average. When Sarah is feeling well, she should be able to recall new information, solve problems, and work quickly.

Autism Diagnostic Observation Schedule, Second Edition: Module 4

To further understand the nature of Sarah's difficulties in social interactions, she was evaluated for a disorder on the Autism Spectrum. Sarah's social reciprocity and communication were assessed through clinical observation, clinical interview, and the Autism Diagnostic Observation Schedule (ADOS-2). Sarah conversed reciprocally on a variety of topics as these were introduced by the examiner, and her discourse was appropriate. She presented with congruent mood and affect that ranged from depressed to neutral. She demonstrated appropriate eye contact with the examiner and integrated facial expression nicely with her comments. Emotionally, Sarah endorsed that she is feeling apathetic and numb in her day-to-day life. She feels that lately her symptoms may be worsening, though she hopes that a recent medication change may help. Overall, Sarah presented as dysthymic with periods of significant depression. She has characteristics of agoraphobia without meeting full criteria at this time. Sarah is withdrawn and frequently avoids social interaction, but she demonstrates appropriate emotional awareness, insight, and reciprocal communication thus ruling out the presence of an Autism Spectrum Disorder.

Other Assessments Administered: Wechsler Memory Scale, 4th Edition (WMS-IV) select subtests, Comprehensive Trail Making Test (CTMT), Tower of London-II (TOL), Rey Auditory Verbal Learning Test (RAVLT), Stroop Color Word Test, Beck Anxiety Inventory (BAI), Beck Depression Inventory-II (BDI-II), Minnesota Multiphasic Personality Inventory-II (MMPI-II), Validity Indicator Profile (VIP), Scales of Independent Behavior-Revised (SIB-R), Sentence Completion for Adults.

Emotional Assessment

Sarah's self-report ratings on the MMPI-2, BAI, and BDI indicate statistically significant scores for depression. Symptoms of severe depression include feeling like crying but being unable to, feeling irritable, having trouble-making decisions, having no appetite, no sex drive and having lost interest in people and activities. Sarah feels sad, fatigued, and discouraged much of the time. Her MMPI-2 profile additionally demonstrates that Sarah feels insecure, withdrawn and hopeless much of the time. Sarah's highest T-scores fall in the areas of Depression and Social Introversion confirming that in addition to feeling sad, she presents as shy, self-conscious, and often avoids social interactions. Her code type is consistent with that of an individual who is depressed and avoidant of social interactions. *Sarah has a history of mild depressive symptoms that have been present since her early twenties and periods of more significant depressive symptoms that meet criteria for a Major Depressive Episode.*

Sarah reports that her long-term memory is solid while she feels she has short-term memory weakness and often goes about her day feeling as if she is "in a fog." Sarah consistently scored in the Average to Superior range on tasks of executive functions including shifting attention, sequencing, sustaining attention, and problem solving. In memory, she scored in the Superior range for visual short-term memory, High Average range for auditory short-term memory, Average range for verbal immediate memory and Above Average range for verbal learning and memory for both single words and stories. It appears that any memory, attention, or concentration difficulties that impact her day-to-day life may be better explained by her emotional state, specifically related to symptoms of depression. *Sarah has a consistently strong profile in memory and executive functioning; she does not demonstrate weaknesses in shifting attention that we may see in an individual with ASD.*

Diagnostic Impressions

Major Depressive Disorder, Recurrent, Moderate (296.32)
Headaches, Sleep Difficulty, Seasonal Allergies
History of Significant Social Stress

Recommendations

For Sarah, it was recommended that she seek individual psychotherapy to improve her mood, self-esteem, and coping skills, while decreasing her level of stress and feelings of numbness and apathy. Cognitive Behavioral Therapy may also provide a venue to address social skills support as needed. Sarah was provided recommendations for social supports and outlets, encouraged to participate in exercise and pleasant events. Scheduling and planning of activities with people she enjoys is further recommended as a strategy to treat her depression symptoms. Sarah was also given recommendations for sleep hygiene and diet. Sarah provided her psychiatrist with the results of her evaluation in order to consider this information for continued medication management.

Assessing a Bright but Rigid Socially Motivated 10-Year-Old to Rule out Autism Spectrum and Look at Secondary Mood and Behavior Disorders

"Sam" is a case example that provides insight into childhood assessment. This will demonstrate what assessment may look like in a child who is intelligent and successful in school; and unfortunately therefore, missed early diagnosis and intervention. Subsequent behavior and mood challenges have developed secondary to his untreated Autism Spectrum Disorder. Thus, at age 10, his parents referred him for an assessment because his behaviors are becoming hard to manage and socially he has had subtle challenges with social reciprocity and perspective taking. This case example will illustrate how to do a comprehensive assessment with a child, including choosing assessment instruments, diagnosis, and conclusions.

Referral Question and Background Information

Sam, age 10, reportedly has social awkwardness, poor listening skills, anger problems, emotional symptoms, and a lack of self-control. Early history includes difficulty with weight gain at 9 months and the inability to transition to solid foods until 15 months. His parents feel that as a result of esophageal difficulties Sam learned to throw up his food; and this happened somewhat frequently, until he was approximately two. Sam met language and motor milestones early. He could name all 50 states when he was two and he took a significant interest in geography with a focus on flags and maps between the ages of two and five. Sam's parents had concern about his defiance beginning around age three and in kindergarten his teachers noticed difficulty with focus and attention. His eating and sleeping are significant for difficulty staying still for long enough to eat. Sam also has poor table manners. He seems not to get enough sleep at night because he often stays up late reading books in his bed. Sam's extended family medical history is significant for the presence of mood disorders. *Notice Sam's early milestones, specific interests, and difficulty eating and sleeping.*

As a young child Sam was not particularly social with other children. He had very early color, number, and letter sense, and his interests prior to age five were in flags, maps, and countries. In kindergarten, he tended to play with the girls in his class and became interested in engaging with boys his age around first grade. His parents describe that Sam liked rough and tumble play and developed an interest in sports. He has never been good at reading nonverbal social cues which has led to a number of disagreements with peers over the years. Sam can also be a very black and white thinker, likes to be in control and tends to get frustrated if he does not get his way. Sam's elementary school program is "gifted and talented," and he does have friends in his classes. He cares about these friends and can talk about their interests when they align with his. His parents described situations however, in which Sam did not read the cues of other students and their feelings were hurt.

Mr. and Mrs. Page also notice that Sam can get frustrated with his friends and struggles to take their perspective particularly when completing group work at school. *Notice social delays and challenges with nonverbal cues.*

Currently, Sam is irritable at home and he does not take suggestions, instructions, or criticism well. He yells and threatens when asked to do something as simple as shower or maintain hygiene. Sam says "I hate myself." and "I want to kill myself." Sam's parents wonder if he might meet the criteria for a diagnosis such as those suggested by his pediatrician: Oppositional Defiant Disorder, AD/HD, Depression or an Autism Spectrum Disorder. *Often children who go untreated for ASD develop depression and more prominent behavioral symptoms that lead families to seek support.*

Testing Observations

Upon meeting the examiner in the waiting room Sam was sitting in a crouched position in the corner of the room with a blanket over his head. He did not respond for a moment but then peeked out and listened as the examiner talked about what Sam could expect from the day. Sam came out willingly and was initially quiet during the evaluation. As Sam became more comfortable, he became more talkative. He spoke formally in a professorial tone of voice. Sam offered lots of smiles to the examiner, but his tone of voice remained formal and he spoke with an advanced vocabulary. Sam offered a few quirky expressions that are considered stereotyped language. These included "He's a real history nut." "They make a big fuss." "I can't have the slightest toe out of line." "He makes a big stink about it." Sam did very well on concrete tasks and liked cognitive activities more than open-ended social or emotional tasks. When conversation topics were introduced by the examiner, he displayed awkward social reciprocity, had blunted affect, and dropped both emotional and conversational bids. If Sam was not interested in the topic, he simply ignored another person's comment and moved on to something of his interest. He used nice coordinated gestures with his speech, but his eye contact was somewhat inconsistent. His mood was generally cheerful, but his affect was flat. *Sam is obviously very bright but significantly socially immature evidence by hiding from the examiner. He was formal and stereotyped in language and lacked insight and conversational reciprocity.*

Assessments Administered

Wechsler Intelligence Scale for Children, Fourth Edition

Sam's Full Scale IQ standard score is 136, at the 99th percentile and in the Very Superior range. His verbal and nonverbal abilities were significantly different with nonverbal skills falling in the Above Average range and verbal abilities falling in the Very Superior range. Sam did not demonstrate any intellectual weaknesses. Sam did not demonstrate symptoms of inattention on a computer-based continuous performance task. His executive functioning skills were further evaluated through measures of problem solving, sequencing, and shifting attention. Sam did equally well on these assessments. Sam's "selective listening" and attention difficulties are best explained in the context of an Autism Spectrum Disorder.

Autism Diagnostic Observation Schedule, Second Edition: Module 3

Sam demonstrates weaknesses in social reciprocity and social communication. His presentation, including his awkward social reciprocity, restricted affect, rigidity and perfectionistic tendencies, and his history of controlling and independent behavior is consistent with *Autism Spectrum Disorder* (299.00). Sam is able to use language in an advanced manner to construct sentences and interpret what others say. However, like many individuals with Autism Spectrum Disorders Sam struggles with the social give and take of language and social perspective taking which affects his ability to communicate socially and emotionally with others. Sam has a tendency to become frustrated with peers and friends as it is hard for him to exhibit patience and understand the different perspectives of his friends. Sam has a hard time reflecting on his own emotions, reporting feeling "irked," when this seems to be a significant understatement of the frustration he often feels.

Other Assessments Administered: Social Communication Questionnaire (SCQ), Test of Variables of Attention (TOVA), Comprehensive Trail-Making Test (CTMT), Tower of London, Second Edition, Child Profile (TOL-2), Sensory Profile, Behavior Assessment Scales for Children, 2nd Edition (BASC-II), Self, Parent & Teacher Reports, Children's Depression Inventory (CDI), Revised Children's Manifest Anxiety Scale, 2nd Edition (RCMAS-II), Draw a Person and Brief Projective Measures, Sentence Completion for Children, Vineland Adaptive Behavior Scale—Parent/Caregiver Rating Form (VABS-II), Clinical Interview with Mr. and Mrs. Page and with Sam.

Emotional Assessment

Emotionally, Sam is demonstrating weak emotional awareness and significant rigidity and perfectionism that can be associated with an Autism Spectrum Disorder. He reports very low symptom levels across all emotional measures which is inconsistent of the presentation his parents describe. *Note, this is the "frozen profile" these authors describe, where the child is unaware of his own emotional experiences and thus dramatically underreports symptoms on self-report screeners.*

Sam seems to have limited coping skills for when he becomes frustrated, sad, or angry noting that he "reads" when this happens. His self-report measures show significant rigid thinking and very high motivation. He is "committed to learning" and to music, and he expects the same level of dedication from his peers. He is kind and thoughtful indicating that he wishes for "world peace, kindness, and happiness for everyone." Sam's parents referred him for this evaluation because of his significant anger, frustration, and defiance at home. Their rating scales indicate significant anger, conduct problems, depression, and low adaptability. His teachers see the same symptoms at a slightly lesser degree. Sam's significant anger and irritability combined with decreased sleep and significant tantrums indicate that in addition to ASD Sam does struggle with emotional symptoms best characterized as depression. Because he does not self-report these symptoms Sam's presentation is currently consistent with *Depressive Disorder, Other Specified Depressive Disorder with Insufficient Symptoms* (311). These emotional symptoms combined with low emotional awareness are common in untreated Autism Spectrum Disorder.

Diagnostic Impressions

Autism Spectrum Disorder (299.00)
Depressive Disorder (311)
Social Stress, Behavior Problems at Home

Recommendations

For Sam, it was recommended that he participate in psychotherapy with a clinician with expertise in treating Autism Spectrum Disorder and Depression in order to improve emotional competence, decrease rigidity and need for control, increase social skills and social perspective taking, and improve coping skills. Additionally, it was recommended that Sam's parents consider implementing Applied Behavior Analytic (ABA) services at home to specifically address tantrum behaviors and improve adaptive and self-help skills at home. Sam was not proficient at maintaining good hygiene, and he was unwilling to follow directions or accept suggestions from others without meltdowns that caused significant challenges for his family. These adaptive skill deficits may be treated by an Occupational Therapist or Behavior Analyst. Another recommendation was a social skills group with other bright children his age to work on social skills and social perspective taking. Finally, it was suggested that Sam's parents consider a consultation with a psychiatrist should depression and behavioral symptoms increase or fail to respond sufficiently to treatment. The family was also referred to community resources such as parent support groups and autism advocacy groups in Colorado. *Because of Sam's significant level of need and the amount of stress; these authors provided a number of recommendations for support. Notice that a later diagnosis often involves more significant behavioral and emotional challenges.*

Summary of Part 5: Concluding the Assessment Process

Parts two through five of this text have provided an overview of clinical Autism Assessment from the initial referral question, through behavior management and observations, the selection and administration of measures and data collection and to the feedback process. Here, three case examples were discussed in detail. Now that a foundation for assessment has been established, the remainder of the text will discuss Autism Assessment in forensic and school settings to provide a comparison for how the assessment process may look outside of a clinic. Assessment across the lifespan including issues in adults and young children will be discussed in detail as the authors of this text find often that many professionals feel competent in assessing a school aged child while evaluation of adults and younger children can be difficult. Often adults are misdiagnosed or never assessed and frequently parents of young children share that they have been told to "wait and see" for many years.

Part VI
Assessment in Applied Settings and Special Testing Considerations

The following part of this text includes chapters devoted to forensic and school-based assessment considerations. The text to this point has focused on clinical assessment. While the assessment process can be quite similar across settings, there are a number of considerations and requirements that do vary when the purpose of an assessment is to address legal considerations or school placement and services. Additionally the authors of this text feel it is essential to address assessment across the lifespan. This final chapter of the book addresses the special considerations involved when assessing very young children and adults. Often clinicians are quite comfortable assessing school-aged children and teenagers but feel less confident working with very young children and adults. In the case of young children, making a diagnosis and directing a family to services when a child ranges in age from one to three, increases the likelihood that a child may meet optimal outcomes. It is crucial that clinicians feel comfortable working this population so that children can receive early intervention and perhaps even recover. On the other end of the age spectrum, adult assessment is important as there are many individuals ranging in age from their twenties to seventies who are seeking diagnostic clarification. Some individuals have felt "different" or "socially isolated" for years while others have researched and read about the Autism Spectrum and feel that it fits their conceptualization of their own neurodiversity. In order for clinicians to work competently with individuals on the Autism Spectrum it is essential that they possess knowledge and understanding of legal, school, and lifespan considerations. A clinician who can support individuals and families with a variety of needs, even just to direct them to appropriate services and supports, is working to ensure that no one is left unsupported in a journey to understand, treat, and reach optimal outcomes for those with ASD.

Chapter 17
Forensic Assessment for Autism Spectrum Disorder

Abstract Unfortunately, individuals with an Autism Spectrum Disorder are very vulnerable to encountering legal difficulties. From custody disputes following divorce to administrative law cases regarding appropriate education and even criminal trials resulting from social, emotional, or sexual challenges, ASD is increasingly arising in the court room. Even while substantial advances have occurred, students with autism are frequently underserved or inappropriately placed in school classrooms necessitating assistance from an attorney. Because people with autism inherently have more difficulty seeing others' perspectives and often interpret directions literally, any encounter with law enforcement is prone to be problematic. The demands on parents and caregivers are typically overwhelming and frequently break even strong marriages leaving parents to often disagree about custody and proper educational services or medical care. Since sexual interactions are also social encounters, an area of deficit in autism, adolescents or adults with autism can readily be charged with sexual offenses. Finally aggression or violence, resulting from rigidity or misunderstanding so characteristic of autism, can easily create legal problems in the school or community. These and other legal scenarios relevant to autism are discussed in detail. Recommendations are provided for writing definitive and parsimonious reports that can withstand fierce cross-examination and rebuttal. Coaching is also included for experts providing forensic consultation as well as testifying in a deposition or trial involving a citizen with autism.

Keywords Civil law and autism • Criminal law and autism • Testifying as an expert on autism spectrum • Forensic psychology and autism • Sex-offense and autism spectrum disorders • Custody and autism spectrum disorders • Divorce and autism • Free and appropriate public education and autism • Due process and autism spectrum disorders • Deposition and autism

As the prevalence of Autism Spectrum Disorder increases, so does the number of individuals with autism who interface with the legal system. This discussion is based on experience with numerous cases of individuals with ASD in the state or federal court over the past decade. Forensic evaluations of individuals with ASD can be divided according to the type of court that will hear their case. Specifically,

© Springer International Publishing Switzerland 2016   345
A.P. Kroncke et al., *Assessment of Autism Spectrum Disorder*, Contemporary
Issues in Psychological Assessment, DOI 10.1007/978-3-319-25504-0_17

four types of courts are discussed: Family, Administrative, Civil, and Criminal courts. While many different individuals with ASD have been represented in all of these four different types of courts, information and recommendations have also come from additional cases of individuals with other types of mental illness or related developmental disabilities for whom forensic services were performed. Drawing from these other cases, where helpful, is appropriate since many individuals with ASD may also have comorbidity with other mental illness and/or genetic abnormalities. Before discussing specific factors that apply to each type of courtroom, a brief discussion of different types of forensic services follows.

Forensic Evaluations

A forensic evaluation is any evaluation primarily done for legal purposes. Sometimes, a clinical or academic evaluation will subsequently be used in a legal proceeding, but this is different from an evaluation primarily done to address a legal question. Whenever possible, it is desirable to foresee probable legal disputes arising, but this is not always feasible and any case can technically subsequently become involved in a legal argument. Clinicians are well advised to consider a priori what policy they wish to maintain regarding forensic work and present such policies to clients in writing along with other initial paperwork such as consent and disclosures. For example, clinicians can choose to be open to participation in legal disputes; should they arise, and in this case a Forensic Agreement is necessary. Minimally, a written statement about policies and fees in the event a client becomes involved in a legal dispute should be provided. Alternately, clinicians may intend to avoid participation in legal disputes and state this policy in writing to their clients at the onset of their professional involvement. Of course, clinicians can be court ordered to testify or evaluate clients at a judge's discretion. Examples of legal disputes involving individuals with ASD may include:

- What parental skills and which home environment is best suited to the needs of a child with ASD (Family Law)?
- Did a student with ASD receive a Free and Appropriate Public Education (FAPE) in the public school system (Administrative Law)?
- Was the individual's civil rights violated when they were subject to this educational practice/work environment/law enforcement actions (Civil Law)?
- To what extent did a person's ASD influence their actions that resulted in them facing criminal charges (Criminal Law)?

When a forensic evaluation is requested, the scope of background information reviewed as well as the extent of testing completed is much more comprehensive than for other types of evaluations. This is because information that is neither obtained nor reviewed from the individual's background, or skills or abilities that are not assessed, remain unknown and can subsequently be obtained and used by the other side to refute findings and discredit the evaluating clinician's opinion. In other words, any information that the clinician is unaware of in completing a forensic evaluation can be used against him or her. When a psychologist is hired to assist in legal proceedings, he or she is typically hired as an expert. If that expert fails to obtain and consider important information about the client, then he or she can readily look more like an idiot than an expert. Since the whole point of completing a forensic evaluation is to render an opinion about the imminent legal question, it is recommended to complete a comprehensive assessment whenever possible. In rare cases, a psychologist may be hired as a fact witness, but this usually occurs due to some administrative technically since the client's attorney would most like their witnesses to be able to testify more broadly as an expert and not just as a reporter of facts like anyone else without such special credentials.

Many times, financial limitations are raised as a concern since almost inevitably forensic evaluations are much more expensive than other types of evaluations. Increased costs arise because forensic evaluations usually involve more testing and longer reports. If financial limitations are a primary concern, however, it is probably not feasible to pursue legal action in the first place because attorney fees far outweigh the roughly $3000–$8000 cost of a forensic evaluation. Evaluations typically end up being more expensive when the client has a lengthy history of medical, developmental, or academic challenges. If a family or law firm cannot afford the high, and typically unknown, extent of the legal costs, they probably should seriously reconsider before requesting a forensic evaluation. In a few tragic cases, parents have requested a forensic evaluation only to subsequently decide that they cannot afford their attorney's fees to pursue the case. In such situations, the family is still responsible for paying the psychologists' cost of the forensic evaluation since the work they requested was completed. It should also be kept in mind that the cost of expert testimony (discussed below) is usually even more expensive than the cost of the report.

Forensic reports have important differences compared to reports which accompany clinical or school evaluations. Many recommendations pertaining to forensic reports apply to the language used in describing the client and the assessment results. First, it should always be born in mind that a primary audience of the report is attorneys who often have limited knowledge of autism, psychological evaluations, and mental health issues in general. In this regard, it is ever more important to clearly state the findings in lay language that can readily be interpreted accurately by a psychological novice. For example, stating "the client has never had any significant friends" is much preferred to "the client exhibits social impairment." Similarly, describing "the client never initiated any conversation during the 6 h evaluation" is far more informative than "the client presented as quiet and guarded." Any psychological term should be defined or avoided altogether in preference for a simple description of the construct. For example, "Verbal Comprehension Index" could be further explained as "Verbal abilities" and "Perceptual Reasoning Index" further explained as "Nonverbal abilities."

Other psychological jargon needs to be explained or omitted entirely. For example, "emotional lability" could be stated as "rapidly fluctuating moods" or "stereotypical behavior" explained as "repeatedly mimicking actions or phrases the client had likely seen previously on TV." Similarly, the 90 % Confidence Interval should be explained as "9 times out of 10 the client's score would be expected to fall between this lower number and this upper number." Furthermore, it is recommended that percentile ranks are always included alongside standard scores because the former statistic is much more widely understood by professionals in other fields, including attorneys. All types of assessments should generally be written for clarity, but forensic reports should achieve an even higher standard in this regard or the writer is at grave risk of having his or her statements perilously misinterpreted and even used against the client in a manner that was never intended. The cost of misleading statements in a school assessment is that the student may not be seated in the best classroom location to permit maximum productivity. In contrast, the cost of a misleading statement in a forensic assessment is that the client may face serious jail time simply because he failed to understand and heed law enforcement's requests.

A second recommendation regarding language used in forensic reports pertains to omission of ambiguous findings. Sometimes, assessment report writers like to overtly opine about different explanations or hypothesis they have about the client or their results. For example, some authors tend to write things like, "A high score on the ADOS-2 can be achieved when an individual is very depressed or clearly has autism." While the preceding statement is true, including such a statement in an individual forensic report opens the door to all kinds of debate over what the client's high ADOS-2 score may actually mean. The report writer should bear in mind that attorneys and judges are not qualified to decide the meaning of a particular client's high ADOS-2 score or any other assessment results. It is the job of the professional performing the forensic assessment to clearly report the findings and decisively present their conclusions about those findings in an unambiguous manner. If after carefully reviewing all the results, the assessment professional concludes the client is severely depressed and does not have autism, then she should definitively state this opinion. It is advised to appropriately integrate all the findings that support the conclusions, but this too should be done in a decisive manner. Drawing clear conclusions about all psychological domains for the forensic client is necessary and such opinions should be presented resolutely.

Forensic Consultation

Sometimes, professionals in ASD are asked to provide information either verbally or in writing that is informal and does not constitute testimony. Examples of such forensic consultation include reviewing records or another professional's report regarding a client who is involved, or may become involved, in some legal proceeding. In such a case, an attorney is likely interested in a professional's opinion as to whether his client has enough grounds to potentially be successful in pursuing a legal case. Such informal consultation is best done from a position of experience regarding similar legal cases. Forensic consultation can save the client or law firm considerable money if a case lacks significant merit since forensic review of records will likely be significantly cheaper than completing an entire evaluation or testifying formally. A specific example of a case requesting forensic consultation might be a lawyer or parent who feels a student is grossly underserved in a particular public school placement. The referring party would like the evaluator to review an IEP and maybe a few medical reports to provide a preliminary opinion regarding the appropriateness and compliance of the school district in serving the student. To provide such an opinion, clear understanding of FAPE as it pertains to ASD, appropriate accommodations and modifications in a school setting, progress that can be expected based on abilities and skills of the student, and what constitutes sufficient evidence of progress is necessary.

Expert Testimony

ASD professionals can be asked to testify in a deposition, hearing or trial as part of a legal case. In each type of testimony, the professional is sworn to testify to the truth and every word of the testimony is probably recorded by a court reporter. While a deposition generally occurs in a conference room rather than a courtroom, the stress on the expert testifying is typically no less than the stress encountered in the courtroom. Often times, the cross-examination can be even nastier in a deposition because the attorneys have no judge or the presence of a jury to help curb the rudeness of their questioning. Attorneys have different styles and some attorneys can predictably be expected to be condescending or belligerent unless or until a judge admonishes them to behave otherwise. In order to be seen as a credible witness, it is very important that experts do not take any criticism or insults personally or worse, change or modify his position in response to often circuitous or surreptitious questioning by opposing counsel. Some experts even describe testifying as both stressful and boring because attorneys can have considerable latitude to belabor a point in an especially confusing and painstaking manner with the hope of ultimately tricking the witness into saying something they feel is beneficial. One attorney described the role of opposing counsel as analogous to attempting to "collect eggs in their basket" whereby each egg symbolizes a witness's statement that they feel is favorable to their argument. Following a deposition, the attorneys will then retain their "basket of eggs" until the trial when they again revisit each "egg" (issue) in the hope of getting a witness for the opposing side to contradict themselves. To avoid contradicting oneself as an expert witness, it is strongly advised that witnesses reread the deposition testimony before the trial.

It is valuable to bear in mind that the end product of testimony in a deposition is merely a written transcript. Such a transcript will likely never capture any visual or auditory events that occurred during the deposition unless they equated to spoken words. For example, an attorney who crosses their arms and scowls at the witness will never have these adversarial gestures captured in the transcript even though their effect on the witness could be pronounced. Similarly, rapid questioning that attempts to evoke defensiveness, and even verbal missteps on the part of the witness, will not be captured in the transcript which has no time reference. The point being that attorneys can spend considerable effort and training acquiring many techniques to derail the expert witness and if they evoke defensive statements like, "I don't like the way you're badgering me!" the defensiveness of the witness may be all that's captured in the transcript with all provocative actions omitted. If the case progresses from deposition to trial, then the expert witness will again be questioned on her previous deposition based only on the written transcript. In other words, the witness can expect to be questioned again at trial and asked to defend previous statements captured in the written transcript from the deposition. In this same manner, it is necessary that witnesses articulate clearly and avoid use of utterances such as "uh," "hmm," and "uh huh" because these are not real words. Furthermore, it is important that the witness avoid speaking excessively fast or she'll likely be asked to slow down and/or repeat her testimony.

In both a deposition and court testimony, the expert will likely be asked to testify about any number of things including but not limited to her expert opinion regarding the case, a review of another professional's report, results of their own forensic evaluation; knowledge of ASD in general, scientific research pertaining to ASD, and observations of the client. While it is possible to take notes into a deposition or courtroom, any written material the expert uses is likely to be entered as an exhibit in the case which is then open to questioning by all parties.

Because the expert can be asked such a wide range of questions, it is usually best to carefully review and memorize any and all information relevant to the case 2–3 days before testifying. While this pretrial cramming almost inevitably compromises the professional's schedule and even sleep, there's little alternative owing to the natural rate of forgetting and/or interference effects on one's memory if the witness attempts to memorize such a vast amount of information several days or weeks in advance. Accordingly, this review time should be scheduled and billed as it is typically demanding and stressful. Testifying as an expert witness is a bit like one's oral defense for an advanced degree, where one can be expected to have to eloquently answer a very wide range of professional questions off the top of one's head. In the event that the expert is concerned, his memory may fail to recall important facts or details pertaining to the case, the expert may elect to bring a copy of his report and supporting documents including patient records and supporting literature, or write a summary of key points ahead of time. This information could also be prepared and presented to the court as an affidavit. Any such documents can be reviewed by opposing counsel and become an exhibit that is then used to assist the expert in testifying in an accurate and thorough manner.

The American Psychological Association has clear guidelines regarding psychologists' role in legal proceedings. Professionals who accept referrals for work in forensic settings are advised to be familiar with these guidelines or comparable guidelines from their own professional associations. The APA guidelines state the importance of psychologists presenting their findings and opinions in an objective and scientifically supported manner without bias. Indeed, legal cases require that experts use traditional means of determining their findings about a client such as standardized testing or scientific literature review. It is not acceptable for experts to derive their own means of determining facts or evidence about a client unless those procedures are standard techniques or approaches in the profession generally.

Given the pressure that is typically experienced when testifying in a deposition or courtroom, it is strongly advised that the expert carefully determine her findings and opinions ahead of time in the comfort of her office and then strive to simply maintain that position. Many times a psychologist or other professional will simply decline a case after hearing the gist of the argument from an attorney or family member because the professional feels incompetent to adequately form an expert opinion, personally unwilling to delve into a case of that nature, or believes that the legal team she is being asked to represent has little or no chance of being successful. In this latter case, many professionals feel it is unethical to accept the work only to watch the family or attorney lose the case. If after a cursory review of the records, the professional feels the legal side who has contacted them has little or no chance of winning, it is recommended that such a professional promptly share that opinion at that time, thereby saving the family or law firm additional expense and sparing the tax payer the undesirable cost of covering a frivolous lawsuit. Obviously, the law firm or family is perfectly capable of contacting another professional if they disagree with an expert's initial perception.

Before proceeding to discuss the different types of courts and sample ASD cases that may arise in each, it is prudent to offer recommendations regarding testifying in any courtroom. Some of these recommendations are being passed on from law firms whose attorneys have coached this author as follows:

- It is recommended that the witness strive to adopt the same posture, voice tone, and response style with counsel on both sides of the issue. Obviously, the questioning is probably much friendly from the counsel that hired the witness, but it is important that the judge, and especially a jury, feel like they are hearing from the same person regardless of who is doing the questioning.
- While the questions are posed from an attorney at the stand, the witness' answers should be directed to the judge or jury. Juries reportedly appreciate the witness making eye contact with them and momentarily speaking directly to each member.
- The witness is encouraged to sit up straight and place his hands where they can be seen by the jury.
- However offensive, derogatory, insulting or invasive the opposing counsel may be the witness should strive to remain unperturbed. It will be almost impossible for the witness to be perceived as professional, credible, and objective if he stoops to some comparable level of slinging mud back at the counsel conducting cross-examination.
- Strive to answer the question and provide 2–4 sentences of supporting detail if appropriate. Answering in a lengthier manner can cause the jury to lose focus, become bored, or otherwise distracted.
- An effective response from the witness may be perceived as analogous to stating a headline and including a relevant caption such as one might find in a newspaper article.
- Allow the questioning counsel to follow up on the witness' answer if he or she would like more detail. In this way, the dialogue between the questioning counsel and the expert witness should ideally maintain a reciprocal flow.

- When peppered with questions from opposing counsel that appear designed to steer the judge or jury off the main facts of the case, the witness can strive to respond with answers designed to maintain focus on relevant issues such as the following:

  - "Yes/no and I considered that possibility in my conclusions."
  - "Yes/no but the main point is… (restate your opinion)."
  - "Yes/no but I think what's important is… (restate some aspect of your findings)."

- Too many attempts to redirect the jury to the main points, however, can result in the witness being labeled as "non responsive". As such, it is helpful to remember that the counsel who hired the witness can and should take the opportunity to rebut points as necessary.
- The witness may be questioned about additional matters of which she has no knowledge. In lieu of incessantly answering "no" and thereby potentially conveying significant ignorance, the witness may reply in the manner suggested below:

  - "I'm not sure how I would access that information."
  - "I don't see why I would be told that information."

- If the witness fails to satisfactorily answer enough questions, counsel can complain to the judge that "witness is nonresponsive." Even if the counsel complains that the witness is nonresponsive, it doesn't mean the witness necessarily was nonresponsive or that the judge will admonish the witness for being nonresponsive.

The following sections provide sample cases and relevant elements germane to the different types of courts.

Family Law

Family courts handle family legal matters including cases of divorce, child custody, and adoption. Unfortunately, the stress of parenting a child with ASD renders the frequency of marital problems even more prevalent for such families than in the general population. In addition, it is increasingly common to discover that one biological parent of a child with ASD has an Autism Spectrum Disorder himself or herself. Since adults with ASD inevitably have some combination of communication, social and emotional difficulties as well as frequent weaknesses in executive functioning (planning, organizing, initiating) and a high prevalence of attention difficulties, such parents with ASD are more vulnerable to marital problems and divorce than neurotypical parents. Furthermore, because children with ASD have unique needs both as a child and adolescent, as well as special needs that often must be provided for as he ages into adulthood, separating and divorcing parents of children with ASD typically face complicated future concerns. All these factors can make the family courtroom for parents of a child or children with ASD, a contentious situation. And when there's conflict, a parent, attorney, or judge may call for the assistance of an autism professional to serve as a witness in some capacity.

Frequently, the issues encountered in family law pertaining to a child or teen with ASD include:

- Disagreement between parents about whether the child has ASD at all
- Disagreement between divorcing parents pertaining to services the child with ASD requires including but not limited to:
  - Where they should go to school
  - What therapies they require
  - What type of long-term care are they likely to require
  - Whether they require legal guardianship as a result of their disability

When the question is whether or not the child actually has ASD, a clinician may be asked to perform a forensic evaluation knowing that another professional or clinic has also recently performed a comparable evaluation. Under such circumstances, the child or teen may even remark that some of the ADOS-2 materials look familiar. Other times, the client will remark that he has recently seen the ADOS-2 materials yet you as clinician are unaware that anyone else has done an evaluation. In such situations, it's prudent to note these comments and try to substitute the ADOS-2 materials for other comparable test materials. For example, different ADOS-2 kits actually have different toys and other items so another comparable set can be used, borrowed, or even purchased. Because of the pervasive neurophysiologic nature of ASD, whereby actual neuroanatomical differences exist between the brain of a person with ASD and a neurotypical brain, it's not possible to "teach the ADOS-2" such that ASD is no longer evident a few weeks or months later. Even if a parent observed her child perform the ADOS-2 one time, it's not possible to eradicate the effects of ASD a few months later by attempting to teach the activities to the child. This is especially so because the examiner plays a critical role in the administration of the ADOS-2 tasks in contrast to virtually every other psychological measure where the items are precisely written on the assessment protocol. For these assessments, the administration has very little to do with the interests, style, or mannerisms of the examiner (see Chapter 9: Social and Sensory Assessment).

Some may argue that there is less need for a comprehensive forensic evaluation when the question is whether or not ASD is relevant because comprehensive testing is not necessary to simply determine if ASD is the appropriate diagnosis. The wide spectrum across which ASD can present, however, with vastly different weaknesses and levels of severity, again points to the value of a comprehensive assessment. For example, if the parents are going to argue whether ASD is present or not and findings indicate it is, the parent who believes his child doesn't have ASD will probably want to diminish the services needed. Without comprehensive testing to determine the nature and extent of the client's deficits, it will likely be impossible to testify to the need for certain services because there exists little evidence of the degree to which ASD is affecting critical skills or abilities. In addition, comprehensive testing is necessary to determine additional conditions that may exist alongside ASD. In other words, even if ASD is present, unless there is convincing data indicating how the individual is struggling to succeed in school, manifesting anxiety of depression secondarily to social inadequacy, or presenting with language deficits which undermine all aspects of communication and reading skills, it will likely be difficult to testify about the need for services or supports.

Courts are typically wedded to the concept of, "No harm, no foul." This curt saying means that if there's no damage to be expected or no damage has occurred then there's no reason for financial or other compensation to be awarded even if findings are significant. In the case of whether a child has ASD and what services he'll need as it pertains to family court, comprehensive testing is necessary to determine exactly what the client requires in all areas of their functioning, the extent to which he struggles in those areas and how long he'll require such accommodations, services, or supports. Almost always in forensic situations, money plays some central role in the dispute. In family court as well, how much various services are likely to cost is probably at the root of the disagreement. In order to cogently testify for what the witness truly believes the client needs during the rest of his life, comprehensive test data, coupled with empirically supported research on individuals with ASD should form the foundation for all opinions. It can also be vital to determine if there are comorbid conditions such as depression or even conduct disorder as these variables obviously substantially influence whether a recommended placement or services are likely to be successful. Obviously, professionals with integrity want to testify to recommendations that will be effective.

Sometimes, clinicians who are treating an individual with ASD will be asked to testify in family court either as an expert witness or a fact witness. Again, the reason the parents or guardians are in family court is because they are arguing about something such as school services, needed therapies, appropriate residential placement, or child support payments—just to name a few. In such cases, the professional should be aware that agreeing to provide testimony is likely to change their relationship with one or both parents or guardians. If the professional feels comfortable with these relationships, he may not wish to testify at all. While a court order to testify cannot be declined without being in contempt of court, a subpoena to testify can often be quashed. When doing any forensic work, it is advisable to identify an attorney ahead of time with whom one can consult with regarding subpoena's, court orders, and any other legal questions that may arise. Such an attorney can be very helpful in refusing a subpoena.

Frequently, when providing treatment for an individual with ASD whose parents or guardians have divorced or separated, the clinician's relationship with one parent or guardian will be better than their relationship with the other. After all, if the parents or guardians were aligned on matters pertaining to their children, they would likely not be living separately and arguing in family court.

An example of such a situation is two parents long since divorced who are now arguing over placement of their adult daughter with ASD. The father feels his nonverbal adult daughter should live in residential care so that he can sell the family home while the mother strongly prefers to have her daughter continue to reside with her in her childhood home. When a professional disagrees with a parent or guardian's actions or plans for their child, she may even be pleased to testify if she is solicited by the parent or guardian who is aligned with her recommendations. Testifying in support of the parent or guardian whose perceptions and actions are aligned with empirically supported treatments, services, or placements may indeed benefit the client which is obviously the ultimate goal. Recognize, however, that after testifying in support of one parent or guardian, the other parent may no longer be willing to bring the child for therapy, and the court may also decide that the testifying professional no longer represents an impartial advocate for the child. If the professional feels strongly that the opposing parent's actions and plans are very likely to going to damage the child anyway, it may be beneficial to testify to these concerns even if therapy is subsequently discontinued. Sometimes, a parent is ignorant of the fact that a clinician does not support his or her perceptions, strategies, or plans for the child and may naively solicit the clinician to testify on his or her behalf. In this case, the clinician may commend herself for establishing and maintaining rapport with a parent or guardian with whom she disagrees. However, it is advised that the professional either seek to quash the subpoena or politely inform the soliciting parent of any are unwillingness to testify because she feels it is not in the best interest of her client. One may say something about stressing the importance of remaining an advocate for the child especially while the parents or guardians strongly disagree. It is possible to be persistent in this position even if vague about the specific details surrounding reticence to testify if the clinician believes she can continue to be most helpful as the client's clinician. It is unethical to accept a parent or attorney's request to testify only to surprise them publically that the child's clinician does not support the parent's legal argument.

Administrative Law

Administrative courts are set up to decide a number of procedural matters that pertain to interpretation of laws outside of civil, criminal, or family law (Kingsbury, 2009). Administrative courts generally handle disputes concerning the exercise of public power particularly with respect to appropriation of state and federal funds. Individuals with ASD can face legal proceedings in Administrative Court on matters including what constitutes FAPE or the individual's ability to access state services for persons with disabilities. These cases tend to be heard by a judge not a jury and the judges in Administrative Court are generally perceived to be less experienced than judges who sit on Civil or Criminal benches.

Disputes Involving Appropriate School Services

Because ASD is a pervasive developmental disorder that is typically lifelong, whether or not someone's educational services are appropriate or whether the family can access state of federal funds to support their disability is substantially important. Many would correctly argue that appropriate school placement is important for all students; however, most students fall within a predictable range of skills and abilities which the majority of public schools are well equipped to accommodate. When it comes to a student with ASD, a vast range of abilities and skills can occur, especially for students who are substantially impaired in multiple areas of learning. This often results in the fact that many schools and even big school districts may not be able to appropriately accommodate all students. For example, some students with ASD remain in diapers and completely nonverbal even into high school. When their essential needs to communicate, engage in meaningful activities, and have opportunities to make friends are not adequately supported, they are likely to become aggressive and/or destructive in other ways. Parents and guardians of such students can unfortunately find themselves having to fight their school district to provide these students access to the highly skilled teachers, aides, and therapists who can enable their children to learn essential life skills. These placement matters take on new meaning when considering the cost of appropriate private school tuition can set the family back over $65,000/year if they have to pay the cost themselves without school district support. Such placement disputes are likely heard in Administrative Courts.

In these types of Administrative Court cases pertaining to accessing FAPE, ASD professionals are frequently called to write or testify as an expert witness regarding:

1. Evidence the individual has ASD as determined by an evaluation or from records
2. The nature and severity of the student's condition as well as any comorbid diagnosis
3. Evidence the student's previous school placement did not meet FAPE
4. Evidence the student did not make progress in a previous placement
5. Evidence the student's Individual Educational Plan (IEP) was not reasonably calculated for success
6. Nature and extent of services, accommodations, and modifications required to meet FAPE
7. Expected progress for the student under FAPE
8. Progress expected for the individual with ASD if FAPE is not provided
9. Skills and qualifications of persons capable of teaching or assisting the individual

When the professional is writing or testifying as an expert witness, "evidence" as referenced above may be met simply by the professional's opinion. Far too often, however, the expert witness is expected to opine about the matters she is being questioned about. Frequently, scientific literature is also referred and discussed in reports or public testimony. The professional should take time with the family and the attorney to carefully understand the dispute and points of contention in order to best address the issues. While Special Education Law, including FAPE is rarely revised, every student and school situation is a little bit different.

Sometimes, professionals are approached by families and asked to support the position that appropriate school placement and supports were not provided when, in fact, the professional's opinion is that the school district was doing a decent job. Inevitably, some parents or guardians are easily disgruntled, and their child's school services appear to be one more thing that displeases them. Additionally, a certain number of parents unfortunately have Personality Disorders or other mental health challenges that compromise their ability to trust and successfully interact with their child's school personnel and exercise sound judgment. Again, if the professional cannot support the position he or she is being asked to write or testify to, he or she should decline the work. It is recommended that professionals respectfully state their opinions about the child's school services and potentially refer them for additional support and maybe even suggest counseling for the parents. Sometimes, parents or guardians do not appear open to anything but the professional's unwavering support of their argument, however. In these situations, professionals may graciously decline the work without providing their opinion or referrals because of the belief that the parents or guardians are not willing to hear the rationale for refusing the case.

Disputes Involving Accessing Funds

Most states have funded programs to aide individuals with disabilities to access essential supports and services such as therapies, respite, and even housekeeping. The naïve reader may erroneously believe such financial support is gratuitous since what family would not appreciate state funds to help their child and household thrive? It is essential to consider, however, how chronically debilitating moderate to severe ASD can be for the entire family. For example, when the individual with ASD only sleeps through the night once every 2 weeks year after year, he can become violent almost daily resulting in domestic vandalism, injury, and trauma to siblings. The necessary constant supervision requires at least one parent to quit his or her job so he or she can be a full-time caregiver, the vital need for outside support becomes clearer. State-funded programs can result in annual assistance ranging from a few hundred dollars to in excess of $75,000 per year for the most severely affected citizens. Almost inevitably some qualifying criteria are set to determine eligibility. When persons with ASD fail to meet qualifying criteria despite parents' or guardians' conviction that they are entitled to such assistance, legal disputes can arise. These disputes about accessing publically funded programs are likely to be settled in Administrative Court.

Similar arguments about accessing necessary funds to assist persons with ASD can arise regarding health insurance benefits. With the increasing incidence of autism and the high cost of therapies, many insurance companies seek to limit coverage for ASD, ABA therapy, or avoid providing benefits altogether in order to keep their shareholders happy. Such situations are indeed sad and often contentious states of affairs. When a family chooses to sue their health insurance company to try and secure benefits for their dependent with ASD, such cases are often heard in Administrative Court. These disputes may also be heard in an Arbiters Group.

In these types of Administrative Court cases pertaining to accessing disability or health insurance funds, ASD professionals are frequently called as an expert witness to testify regarding:

1. Evidence the individual has ASD
2. The nature and severity of the condition as well as any comorbid diagnosis
3. Evidence regarding empirically supported services or treatments for different symptoms

4. Evidence the client is benefitting from services received
5. Prognosis for the client and other family members involved
6. Prognosis for the individual with ASD if necessary therapies are not provided
7. Skills and qualifications of persons capable of supervising or treating the individual

Civil Law

Clients with ASD can be involved in civil law disputes on issues such as violation of constitutional rights, discrimination, and wrongful treatment. Sometimes, a case will be investigated on criminal grounds but then tried in civil court if criminal charges were unfounded. Examples of cases initially investigated on criminal grounds but then tried as civil suits can include mistreatment or even abuse by school district personnel such as:

- An active student with ASD and a seizure disorder was repeatedly strapped into an uncomfortable occupational therapy support seat for hours at a time while a less-skilled teacher struggled to maintain order in the classroom.
- An anxious student who struggled to manage transitions successfully was eventually dragged off the school bus by her impatient teacher with several colleagues who allegedly smelled alcohol on her breath. The student became entangled in her seatbelt which was wrapped around her neck resulting in choking.
- A student who tantrummed often was repeatedly placed in seclusion in a time-out room. On one occasion, he ended up completely disrobing and urinating on himself when educational staff neglected to monitor this consequence, seemingly forgot about him, and left him locked up for more than an hour.
- An insurance company needed assistance from an ASD expert in defending an adult client who was previously charged with DUI and moving vehicle violations when he caused a head-on collision with a car containing a toddler. The toddler subsequently developed ASD and the plaintiff contended the adult driver was responsible for all ensuing treatment and therapies for the duration of the child's life even though the child was only diagnosed with a concussion following the accident.

Many times such cases can readily evoke very strong feelings of disgust, anger, and even outrage toward the individuals being defended. Professionals involved with these cases, as well as criminal cases discussed below, should think carefully about whether they can remain appropriately objective and professional throughout the life of the suit. Legal activities that can be required of an assessment professional may include assessing the affected individual, writing a forensic report, being deposed by often hostile or even belligerent attorneys, and testifying in court before a judge or even a jury. It is typically not feasible for the family or counsel who hires an expert to change their expert mid-way through the suit so the expert professional needs to be willing to persevere to the end of the case. If the professional does not feel capable of doing all these tasks, he or she is advised to refer the case before ever performing a single professional service regarding the case.

Just because a professional feels capable of remaining appropriately objective on a case does not mean he or she will not be emotionally moved, sometimes even temporarily devastated, by what the client experienced. In fact, the expert may well serve the client better if she is notably moved emotionally because in such situations their report and testimony will likely better reflect the emotional gravity of the client's experience. The key is to successfully manage and appropriately compartmentalize one's emotions about the case to remain professional and effective. Toward this end, all professionals, including those performing forensic assessments, need to develop and maintain strong skills in recognizing and effectively processing their own emotional reactions.

The questions that arise in such civil suits largely pertain to the following issues:

- Is there convincing evidence that the client has autism or other mental disorders that should be considered when assessing damage?
- What is the nature and extent of autism and any other mental disorders present?
- Based on standard means of assessing the client, as well as typical review of the extant literature, is there evidence that the client was harmed by the actions alleged to represent a civil violation?
- What is the extent of the harm?
- Are there other causal explanations for the deficits or damage found in the client?
- Did the alleged civil violation more likely than not result in significant harm?
- How has the prognosis for the client changed or remained the same as a result of the alleged civil violation?
- What treatment, services, accommodations, or modifications are necessary to support the client? How are these services different from what the client required before the alleged offense?
- What is the cost of the recommended services? How are these costs different from the long-term expenses that were expected before the alleged offense?

When addressing the issues pertaining to how has the prognosis changed as a result of the alleged offense, it is especially important to consider historical background information including previous evaluations the client may have experienced. When a client has ASD, it is the norm rather than the exception that he has previously participated in a standardized psychological evaluation. Often parents or educators have significant concerns about a child's development no later than the early elementary school years. When comparing results from multiple evaluations, the evaluator can imagine she is creating a timeline representing skills and abilities as well as emotional and behavioral functioning for the period before the alleged violation compared with the results of the evaluation completed after the violation. The evaluator as an expert witness strives to address or eliminate other threats to the validity of the claim that the alleged violation had a detrimental effect on the client's prognosis if in fact that is what the results indicate. Alternate threats to the validity of this causal claim could include but not be limited to, expected maturation of the client, other adverse historical events unrelated to the alleged violation (such as parents' divorce), effects due to change in assessment measures contrasted (instrument effects), and statistical effects whereby the changes in the client noted between evaluations fall within the statistical error expected for those measures. The evaluator should make every effort to carefully review the records considering historical and maturational threats to validity as well as select assessment measures to minimize or eliminate instrument threats to the validity of all claims. Finally, keen understanding of confidence intervals, the Flynn effect, and practice effects are important when interpreting the statistical validity of differences in results between evaluations. Clearly, strong knowledge regarding principles of reliability and validity as well as statistics and threats to validity is valuable in serving as an expert witness in civil law suits.

Many times the psychologist who assesses the client in a civil suit will have the opportunity to work with professionals who specialize in life-planning. Such a life-planning expert can be especially helpful in determining long-term costs for care and living expenses adjusted for inflation and the time-value of money. Such life-planners are usually secured by attorneys associated with the case.

Many times in a particularly big case, attorney clients consist of co-counsel whereby attorneys from more than one law firm are working together. Co-counsel is typically established in order to satisfactorily involve attorneys who specialize in individuals with autism as well as provide access to adequate financial backing from a larger firm in order to see the case through. Understandably, when civil suits are tried and appealed on multiple occasions, the legal costs can become astronomical thereby necessitating access to deep pockets in order to keep up with expenses long before a decision is reached. In bigger cases, the associated attorneys will regularly prepare their experts regarding the types of questions to anticipate, material included in exhibits about which the expert can expect to be required to comment, and potential strategies of the opposing counsel. In smaller cases, preparation for deposition or trial may be marginal to nonexistent in order to minimize expenses.

Criminal Law

Unfortunately, the number of individuals with ASD who are involved in criminal cases is increasing substantially (Nick Dubin, Isabel Henault and Tony Attwood, 2014). Obviously as the incidence of autism rises, statistically, one can expect the number of individuals who have encounters with law enforcement will also increase. However, because of the inherent nature of individuals with autism to have difficulty communicating and socializing successfully as well as the typically literal and rigid interpretation of situations, not to mention the fact that many individuals with autism exhibit problematic behaviors, they are much more vulnerable to criminal involvement than citizens with other types of disabilities or handicaps. Examples of criminal cases involving individuals with ASD probably run the gamut of crimes in general nonetheless here are some hybrid examples conjured from actual cases:

1. A preadolescent boy with ASD is handcuffed and arrested for attempting to enter locked offices on a Saturday morning and then failing to respond to police offi-

cers. The boy wanted to ride the elevators and only answers to people he knows. The police thought the boy was trying to break into the offices.

2. A junior high school student with ASD is arrested and charged with criminal mischief for taking lithium strips to school and attempting to recreate chemical reactions with batteries similar to what he previously did in science class. The teen noted how much his classmates enjoyed the science experiment and thought it would help him have more friends by repeating the explosions on another occasion at school.

3. An adult with ASD is arrested and charged after being caught speeding and then proceeding to drive away after pulling over because he didn't understand he needed to remain stopped and answer police questions. After all, the police had clearly stated their instructions over the megaphone to "Pull over!" which he believed he had done.

4. A parent with ASD was charged with child abuse after his son with ASD is found naked and burned in the home. The son reportedly was playing with chemicals while under the supervision of his older brother. The parent failed to seek medical attention for his son's burns because the family had no health insurance and the parent didn't understand his son would be treated at the emergency room even without health insurance. The son with ASD was often naked because he finds most clothing feels unpleasant.

These hybrid examples of actual cases highlight how core deficits of ASD readily lend themselves to deficits in understanding societal expectations involving laws and safety as well as frequent misunderstanding by police officers regarding intentions of people with ASD.

The essence of these and other criminal cases involving an individual with autism comes down to one or more of the following issues:

- Does the accused actually have an ASD? What is the nature and severity of ASD as manifested in this particular individual.
- What additional diagnoses are present if any? How does the presence of anxiety or depression further effect the accused's ability to communicate or exercise sound judgment for example?
- Is there clear evidence of the presence of ASD before the time of the crime?
- To what degree, if any, does the presence of ASD mitigate the accused culpability in the crime? What exactly were the intentions of the accused given an autism diagnosis?
- Are the criminal actions of the accused related to the core characteristics of ASD and if so, in what way?
- Is the individual with ASD competent to stand trial? Does he or she understand the charges and can they aide their attorneys in their defense? Can they comprehend and keep pace with the proceedings of a trial?
- How does the presence of ASD affect the appropriateness/suitability of various punitive consequences if convicted? Are possible punitive consequences, in fact, likely to result in further cost to society?

As with the other types of forensic disputes discussed above, a thorough and comprehensive evaluation is typically necessary. Other times, however, the individual with ASD is represented by a public defender and state funds for paying for expert services are notably limited. In these instances, some expert services are deemed better than no expert input at all even while questions about additional diagnoses, a comprehensive background review or testing to discern other neuropsychological deficits will probably not be feasible on a restricted budget.

The psychologist involved in evaluating someone involved in a criminal case should pay particular attention to the vital need to educate the court about autism and has a unique role in this regard. It is not enough to simply do a comprehensive evaluation and present recommendations when the individual is facing the real possibility of being sentenced to challenging community service, loss of driving privileges, loss of child custody, court-ordered attendance at group therapies designed for neurotypical participants, or even jail or prison time where they are likely going to be regularly misunderstood if not scapegoated. It is critical that the evaluator take deliberate steps to instruct the readers of the evaluation report on important characteristics of autism and how such symptoms relate to the crime. Without such education, the attorneys, judge, and/or jury will simply interpret the accused actions through their naïve lenses of how anyone that age would be expected to act, what the accused should be expected to intuitively know, and how he or she is likely to respond to punishment based on how anybody else would respond. Statements designed to educate judicial staff or lay public should use straightforward language that is free of clinical jargon. The importance of such education about ASD cannot be overstated particularly because autism is so often an "invisible disorder" whereby the individual physically looks just like anyone else that age. Autism can easily be a subtle but profound disability that relies on the informed advocacy of experts to be spokespeople in educating the public at large and the justice system specifically regarding how citizens with autism interpret the world and the critical needs they have in order to be able live safe, meaningful, and dignified lives. The following are key characteristics worthy of serious consideration to include as educational points within a forensic evaluation and/or expert testimony:

Core Characteristics

- Individuals with autism typically interpret statements and questions with *concrete, literal processing*. For example, if they're told to "Put your hands up!" they are not likely going to understand that it's not okay to put them down again and then reach for their cell phone to call their mother and let her know they need help.
- Individuals with autism typically attend to and process one piece of information at a time. They are *linear, sequential thinkers* who are usually horrible at multitasking. When presented with complex instructions or questions as in an interrogation interview, they are likely to grasp only a small fraction of the content

and gist of the inquiry. Their responses are likely going to reflect the limited amount of communication they actually heard and understood. Such reactions may readily appear dismissive and even mocking to the naïve listener.

- Individuals with autism usually exhibit *selective attention* whereby they can become fixated on a topic or item of particular interest to them. Such preferred ideas and objects also easily distract them from other information and events that most people would consider far more important and captivating. For example, the young boy referenced above who wanted to enter tall office buildings and ride the elevators scarcely noticed the police uniforms being worn by the men asking him what he was doing.
- Individuals with autism often have significant mental *processing speed weaknesses*. This means that if a law enforcement officer repeats many demands in a rapid manner, they may not actually be able to process anything they've been told to do because the instructions were said far too fast for them.
- Individuals with autism are highly prone to *become anxious and can even panic* when confronted with yelling or other loud sounds. When panic ensues, they are likely to freeze and stop responding, rapidly attempt to leave the scene, or become disorganized and frantic behaving in a manner that appears irrational. When anxious, individuals with ASD are likely to process things even more slowly and have even more impairment in expressing themselves and communicating with others.
- Individuals with autism are prone to engage in *repetitive thinking and behaviors* even when such thinking is unnecessary and even inappropriate. This characteristic is called perseveration. For example, a man with ASD wrongfully "played doctor" with his juvenile niece and was charged with molestation. He was repeatedly instructed to always "Look down!" resulting in him constantly staring at the floor and being unable to hold a job.
- Individuals with autism frequently have *difficulty recalling events* in a sequential manner and with sufficient detail. These weaknesses in expressive language can result in them appearing uncooperative and even nonresponsive upon being questioned by police, attorneys, or judges. This difficulty is also compounded by selective attention discussed above whereby it's not possible to recall information that was never attended to and encoded in memory in the first place.
- All individuals with autism have *weaknesses or deficits in social skills*. This means they frequently ignore or misinterpret nonverbal communication which is critical for them to respond appropriately to others' cues that they are bored, irritated, or rejected in a conversation or game. Furthermore, because many individuals with autism have few or no friends, they can easily over interpret others' actions to mean they are included or invited when in fact their actions constitute harassment or even trespassing.
- Individuals with autism typically have *marked difficulty with perspective taking* resulting in them expecting and believing others see things the way they do. This deficit often manifests in highly impaired judgment as the individual with ASD erroneously interprets others' actions and intentions in a narrow, singular manner consistent with his perceptions. For example, an individual with ASD facing

police with guns drawn disastrously believed they needed to flee the scene rather than comply with police instructions because they thought the police were trying to kill them and they needed to try and escape.

Unfortunately, research shows that individuals with ASD are often charged and even sentenced for crimes that directly involved or resulted from core deficits of autism (Dubin et al., 2014 and Attwood, 2014). Clearly, there are plenty of police officers, attorneys, and even judges who are naïve and unsympathetic toward the needs of these vulnerable members of society. One callous district attorney was heard to comment, "What's wrong with incarcerating people with mental illness? We do it all the time!"

Despite these discouraging facts, there are also many accounts of individuals with ASD who were successfully rescued from what would have constituted harsh and unfair treatment as a result of successful education and advocacy. The following are some of those victories:

- The boy handcuffed for trying to enter locked office buildings was released promptly and suffered only temporary trauma from being strapped into a police cruiser and bruised wrists from the handcuffs. All charges were dropped following information about autism being provided to police and advocacy on the child's behalf.
- The man on probation for playing doctor with his niece was released from sex offender treatment designed for neurotypical offenders and effectively taught to conduct his daily routines away from children. He became gainfully employed and was considered a model employee because he liked doing a good job over and over again.
- The underemployed parent with no health insurance accused of child neglect regained child custody, thanks to the valiant efforts of an educated public defender and sympathetic judge. The parent was able to get much needed therapeutic services for him and his partner as well as his sons, thanks to the comprehensive treatment plan from an expert.

These and other positive and encouraging stories will hopefully spur professionals, advocates, and stakeholders reading this book to redouble on their efforts to educate society and effectively represent individuals with autism facing legal challenges.

Case Studies: Family, Administration, Civil, and Criminal

Disclaimer: these cases are works of fiction adapted loosely from clinician's experiences with various clients. All identifying information has been changed.

By Khalid Mohammad B.S. and Jessica Reinhardt Ph.D.

Ethan

Family Law Case

Age: 13 years, 4 months

Assessments Administered:

Behavior Assessment System for Children—Second Edition, (BASC-2) Self, Parent & Teacher Reports

Children's Depression Inventory, Second Edition (CDI-2)
Revised Children's Manifest Anxiety Scale, Second Edition (RCMAS-II)
Roberts, Second Edition (Roberts-II)
Sentence Completion for Teens
Vineland Adaptive Behavior Scales—Second Edition, (VABS-II) Parent/
Caregiver Rating Form
Clinical Interview with Ethan and his Parents
Clinical Observations of Ethan
Review of Records provided by Ethan's parents
Consultation with School Administrators

Ethan, a 13-year-old seventh grader, was referred for a forensic psychological evaluation at the behest of both his parents, the court system as well as school administrators following social difficulties and problem behaviors during a school trip. This trip occurred during legal proceedings for his parents' divorce which included a report by a child and family investigator (CFI) to make recommendations on permanent custody arrangements. As behaviors seemed to be escalating, the CFI made a recommendation to Ethan's parents that they seek a comprehensive forensic evaluation to present to the courts regarding Ethan's mental health. Areas of concern included emotional symptoms, social awkwardness, difficulties with transition and change, and safety for himself and his peers. Ethan was previously diagnosed with Generalized Anxiety Disorder and a suspected Autism Spectrum Disorder his psychiatrist prescribed Risperidone, Clonidine, Lexapro, and Abilify.

Ethan's parents were in the midst of a highly contentious separation, and the entire family participated in weekly family therapy to address the emotional challenges each family member faced and the transition Ethan and his two siblings faced in light of their parents' recent separation and current legal involvement. Ethan's parents were working to improve their communication in the best interest of their children but disagreed on the best custody arrangement for the children. At the time of the evaluation, Ethan lived primarily with his mother but his father had regular visitation with the children as well as weekend custody. Ethan additionally participated in therapy with his father in an effort to build a better relationship between the two focused on improving respectful communication and defusing arguments. Family therapy services noted above were implemented following a court recommendation after an altercation between Ethan and his father in which Child Protective Services were called to investigate the possibility of child abuse. Allegations of child abuse were determined to be unfounded and dismissed and family therapy was prescribed to support all members.

Background information and consultation with school administrators provided information on the problem behaviors Ethan displayed at school and during the fieldtrip. These behaviors included past verbal and physical aggression toward peers in third through sixth grades, current aggression, and threatening remarks toward other students and teachers during the aforementioned trip and continued defiance and elopement when requests were made during times of transition.

A school evaluation was conducted prior to this forensic evaluation as part of a triennial reevaluation for special education services. Ethan struggled in areas involving nonverbal communication, social relationships, and processing speed. Additionally, academic testing showed weakness in academic fluency as timed tasks are challenging given his poor processing speed. Ethan displayed great strength in verbal skills, perceptual reasoning, and working memory. Academic areas of reading, math, and writing were also Average to Above Average. From this profile Ethan qualified for special education services for the educational classifications Autism Spectrum Disorder and Speech/Language impairment. During this time, a Speech and Language Pathologist observed Ethan during lunch period at school. It was noteworthy that Ethan ate his lunch alone and appeared uncomfortable around peers. Ethan walked around the lunch room until allowed to leave while avoiding interaction with others. This school evaluation included rating scales from parents and teachers which indicated elevations in depression, withdrawal, anxiety, and low adaptability.

During the forensic evaluation at Emerge, Ethan was observed to be socially awkward with the examiners and showed little variation in his affect despite reporting depressive symptoms and making comments that conveyed his agitation. His speech was remarkable for stilted language and a lack of vocal prosody. During conversation, Ethan used little gesture and paced back and forth when discussing social concerns and school events. Results indicated that Ethan demonstrated weak adaptive skills and significant depression with poor emotional awareness, low self-esteem, sense of inadequacy, and ineffectiveness in solving problems. Aggression and conduct problems were significant as Ethan threatened peers and became angry quickly when he had few choices or little control over situations. Based on these findings and history, Ethan was diagnosed with Oppositional Defiant Disorder (313.81), Major Depressive Disorder, Recurrent, Moderate (296.32), and Autism Spectrum Disorder (299.00). Ethan's relationships at school, struggles with his parent's separation, and relationship with his father were significant social and family stressors. Emerge recommendations included individual psychotherapy to improve emotional competence, decrease depressive symptoms, increase social skills, and improve coping skills; continued family therapy to strengthen his relationship with his parents; a medication review; a Board Certified Behavior Analyst to manage defiant behaviors at school; and a social skills group to improve social coping skills. Evaluators did not have concerns about abuse and found both parents to be equally important in Ethan's life from his perspective. While in a forensic evaluation, these evaluators do not make specific parenting plan/custody recommendations, it was recommended that both parents have an active role in Ethan's life and transitions be planned and structured so as to minimize the stress for Ethan.

The family implemented treatment recommendations and continued legal proceedings to determine a parenting plan. Through the implementation of treatment recommendations, small occasional gains were made in reducing Ethan's agitation, depression, and aggression although the severity of problem behaviors worsened. While parents cared greatly for Ethan, they struggled to be consistent in holding boundaries and implementing the behavior plan. Specifically, Ethan verbalized ideas of killing others and physically assaulting behavior therapists and his father (who more consistently held boundaries). Ethan was repeatedly hospitalized for aggression and/or hostile intent. These behaviors would arise during situations when Ethan was denied access to preferred activities due to his inappropriate behavior or as a means to escape simple demands. The challenge of co-parenting Ethan using the outlined treatment protocol between both of his parents resulted in Ethan being intermittently rewarded for his behaviors by his mother; since he could aggress toward others and subsequently be allowed to receive or do what he pleased. Through intensive ABA therapy, family therapy, individual therapy, and continued medication management Ethan began to improve. His parents continued to disagree on many fronts but were able to put aside their differences and consistently implement a behavior plan that after the initial extinction burst began to work for Ethan. The court took recommendations from the forensic evaluation into account and parents were granted shared custody with week on/week off structure that allowed for consistency. Ethan's mother was granted educational decision-making and his father medical decision-making, and thus they did not have to constantly work to make joint decisions.

Ethan's case illustrates how children struggling with an ASD and comorbid disorders which lead to severe behavior problems are impacted within a family dynamic. Family stressors such as marital conflict and divorce exacerbate the mental health of bright children with such disorders and are frequently seen in family court when issues such as mandated therapy, custody, or parental decision-making arise. When family members are at odds in parenting struggling children such as Ethan, effective treatment and progress can be difficult to achieve. Additionally, the management of Ethan's several diagnoses highly disrupts the functioning and well-being of each family member. This case is provided to stress the crucial importance of accurate and early diagnosis and intervention and the progress that can be made with consistent treatment and parents who work together despite their differences in the best interest of their child.

Farah

Administrative Law Case

Age: 8 years, 5 months

Assessments:

Differential Ability Scales—Second Edition, Upper Early Years Record Form (DAS-2)

Mullen Scales of Early Learning (Out of Level) Expressive and Receptive Language Indexes Autism Diagnostic Observation Schedule—Second Edition, Module 1 (ADOS-2) *Select Module 2 tasks attempted*

Beery—Buktenica Developmental Test of Visual–Motor Integration (VMI)

Beery—Buktenica Developmental Test of Visual Perception

Beery—Buktenica Developmental Test of Motor Coordination

Behavior Assessment System for Children—Second Edition, (BASC-2) Parent Report

Vineland Adaptive Behavior Scales—Second Edition, (VABS-II) Parent/ Caregiver Rating Form

Clinical Interview with Farah's Parents

Clinical Observations of Farah

Review of Records provided by Farah's Parents

Farah received a forensic neuropsychological evaluation at the request of her parents who shared with clinicians their concerns surrounding her academic progress, behavior, and cognitive development. Her parents felt strongly that the school district failed to provide an FAPE to their daughter and pulled her from her public school to place her in a private school with expertise in teaching students with autism. Along with assessing her current neuropsychological functioning and making academic recommendations, Farah's parents wondered what, if any, therapeutic services were appropriate for her continued progress.

Farah received an initial diagnosis of autism at age two and worked with many speech, occupational, and behavioral therapists. Farah's parents reported struggles with changes in routine and transitions, meltdowns during times when she couldn't control her environment, as well as challenges with communication, social interaction, and academic skills. To improve communication, Farah began using a Picture Exchange Communication System (PECS). A prior school placement was unsuccessful as her maladaptive behaviors increased. During this public school placement, Farah displayed frequent elopement from the school environment and increased defiance. Farah's progress was found to be nominal when her IEP goals were compared to her baseline data which was collected by her new private school. Additionally, her parents reported very low skill levels at home. The available IEP data from her public school placement suggested that goals were rewritten from more advanced goals to address very basic skills because progress was not being made. Goals were also phrased in an ambiguous way or presented without a clear modality in which to achieve them. Additionally, benchmarks for goals were vague and hard to assess. No evidence was available from the public school outlining improvements in areas such as adaptive skills, behavior management, academic skills, nor the core characteristics of autism (social communication and reciprocity, and restricted interests and repetitive behaviors). When IEP data was compared to the initial assessment from Farah's new private school (at the time of her initial enrollment) and her parent's report of skills at home, inconsistencies were apparent indicating that Farah's IEP team reported that she mastered goals while the evidence and data to support mastery was not available in the new placement. Farah was not able to complete skills like writing her first name and last initial, copying a simple three-to-five-step picture, wiping her face and blowing her nose, toileting, cleaning up, speaking in three-word sentences, and verbally making requests by putting three to four words together; while her IEP suggested at her previous public school she could complete these skills.

Following Farah's placement in the new school which specializes in the treatment of autism, there was a marked improvement in her behavior and adaptive skills. A school observation at this placement revealed that Farah was able to successfully use spoken language and her PECS to communicate and engage socially with teachers and staff. Farah could use simple expressive language to make requests, answer questions, and label objects and pictures. Other strengths included appropriately following directions, improvements in toileting skills, and decreased aggression. Furthermore, school staff reported a substantial decrease in elopement and during the observation Farah did not attempt to elope from the classroom even when the classroom door was open.

During the forensic evaluation, Farah vocalized by making squealing noises when happy or frustrated and she spoke in short words and phrases. Farah echoed the examiners speech and often used her hands to guide the hands of others toward or away from objects. Other observations included poor eye contact, stomping, flapping her hands, increased distractibility when tasks became difficult, and attempts to avoid answering questions by either siting on the floor or attempting to open the door to the evaluation room. Behavioral support was provided throughout the evaluation as were frequent breaks and Farah was successfully redirected back to completing tasks. It is noteworthy that Farah appeared more comfortable toward the end of the evaluation and during tasks which were easier for her and tasks that she enjoyed.

Results from Farah's forensic neuropsychological evaluation confirmed her previous diagnosis of an Autism Spectrum Disorder. Farah displayed challenges in the core characteristics of autism which remained substantial with little appropriate progress made in these areas. Along with her diagnosis of autism, Farah received a diagnosis of Intermittent Explosive Disorder due to her frequent behavioral defiance and outbursts as well as an Intellectual Disability based on her cognitive profile. Recommendations included continued work within her current school on managing challenging behaviors and implementing ABA principles, ABA therapy in the family's home, and IEP modifications and accommodations for continued success at school.

Farah's case describes an instance in which an individual with an Autism Spectrum Disorder is inappropriately served by her school. It profiles how in such cases an ill-equipped placement can yield inaccurate and inflated reporting of progress and sometimes an actual decline in progress in targeted areas or skills. With appropriate placement the school team was better able to decrease Farah's problem behaviors and increase her adaptive skills. Along with proper school placement, a comprehensive forensic neuropsychological evaluation allowed clinicians to assess Farah's present level of functioning, make appropriate diagnoses, and tailor recommendations accordingly. As a result, Farah continues to improve and make demonstrable progress.

The legal outcome from this case which went to trial was a ruling by a judge that the school did provide an FAPE despite elopement, regression of skills, and evidence of a lack of progress. Farah's case illustrates that the burden lies with families to prove that their child was denied what is deemed necessary for a school to provide under FAPE. It is very difficult in such cases to prove that a school is not providing FAPE to a student. This highlights the need for better collaboration between school and home teams and the need for schools to hire professionals with expertise in Applied Behavior Analysis and those with expertise in working with children who have Autism Spectrum Disorders. Additionally, it provides evidence to support the need for better in-service training and support for teachers by providing adequate tools to help them instruct children with special needs. In such cases, both parties are impacted with no real winner since the school district as well as families expects that FAPE be properly implemented. Schools and families wish to see students meet goals, grow, develop new skills, and meet their potential.

Louisa

Civil Law Case

Age: 9 years 5 months

Referral: To assess current abilities, skill levels to assess the long-term impacts of the use of restraint, as court proceedings continue.

Assessments: Autism Diagnostic Observation Schedule—Second Edition, Module 2 (ADOS-2)

Differential Ability Scales, School Age, Second Edition (DAS-II);

Differential Ability Scales, Early Years, Second Edition (DAS-II); Clinical Evaluation of Language Fundamentals, Fourth Edition (CELF-4) Clinical Evaluation of Language Fundamentals Preschool, Second Edition (CELF-2, Pre); Woodcock Johnson Tests of Achievement, Third Edition with Normative Update (WJ-III); Beery Buktenica Developmental Test of Visual–Motor Integration (Beery VMI); Beery Buktenica Developmental Test of Visual Perception (Beery VP); Beery Buktenica Developmental Test of Motor Coordination (Beery MC); Short Sensory Profile, by Winnie Dunn PhD; Grooved Pegboard; Behavior Assessment System for Children, Second Edition (BASC-II) Parent & Teacher Rating Forms; Vineland Adaptive Behavior Scales, Second Edition—Survey Interview Form Report (VABS-II); Clinical Interview with Ms. Brock; Clinical Observations of Louisa

Background Summary: Louisa is a student with multiple disabilities including ASD, she attended several schools within the County School District. Her IEPs from these schools indicate that she had a long history of behavioral problems including hitting, kicking, and biting. School staff found that Louisa's behavior problems were manageable with a behavior plan that included providing options, providing time outs, removing Louisa to another area, prompting, 1:1 staff and using positive reinforcers such as edibles, high-fives and toys. Assessment results from Spring 2005 indicate Louisa obtained a Receptive Language age equivalency score of 24 months on the Mullen Scales of Early Learning, Expressive Language age equivalency score of 22 months, a Gross Motor age equivalency score of 25 months. and a Visual Reception age equivalency score of 25 months. Her Adaptive Behavior skills were assessed with the Vineland Adaptive Behavior Scales and were judged to be in the Low range overall, with relative strengths in Gross Motor skills. Louisa was provided with a classroom appropriate to her abilities, a behavior support plan, occupational and physical therapies.

In August, 2005 Louisa was transferred to a different placement. Louisa's IEPs are devoid of much useful information about her behavior, her abilities. and her progress. Notes are typically restricted to comments on her schedule and transportation, and no behavior plan was put in place, as had been the case at her previous schools. Even though the staff felt a behavior plan was not necessary for Louisa, they apparently did wish to use excessive physical restraint. No documentation was provided that indicated her mother had agreed to this in writing and documentation that indicates verbal permission for such a restraint. Other school notes include statements that suggest Louisa's maladaptive behaviors increased while at her previous school and began to include screaming, crying, spitting, and throwing things in addition to her already apparent hitting, kicking, and biting. Such behaviors increase in children when they are in emotional distress, physical distress or are forced to do tasks beyond their capacity. Despite this increase in behaviors, no changes appear to have been made to her IEP or treatment in the classroom.

Louisa later transferred to another school. Her IEPs from these placements indicate that her behavior continued to be challenging initially, but she was able to be redirected and to learn through use of Applied Behavior Analysis techniques. Initially, permission for physical holds was signed by her mother, and this was later removed from her plan to be replaced with time away from group in the event that Louisa escalated. These notes indicate that Louisa was again able to do well in school, participate in activities, and reduce maladaptive behaviors when she was provided with support from her staff in the form of nonrestrictive behavioral interventions and positive reinforcement, indicating that physical restraint was an unnecessary intervention.

A report offered following their investigation of charges of restraint found that improper restraint had in fact been used on multiple occasions with multiple children, including Louisa. These incidents of restraint were consistent with abuse and neglect and violated the Colorado Department of Education's rules for restraint and seclusion

Conclusions

Louisa Brock is an 8-year-old girl who has ASD. She was referred for this evaluation to provide updated information regarding her skills, abilities, and functioning. Overall, Louisa's cognitive abilities as measured by the DAS-II resulted in a General Conceptual Ability in the Moderately Impaired Range. Her responses on the CELF-4 resulted in a Core Language below the 0.1 percentile, and in the Moderately Impaired Range. Results on the Beery VMI indicate her visual–motor integration skills, visual perception, and motor coordination skills are all Moderately Impaired. Louisa exhibited declines in sensory modulation over time, as evidenced by her scores on the Short Sensory Profile. Responses on rating scales indicate that Louisa's social–emotional functioning is clinically significant in many areas including Hyperactivity, Aggression, Conduct Problems, Attention Problems, and Atypicality. Louisa continues to exhibit symptoms of anxiety, heightened worry when her mother is not present, and aggression toward adults, particularly in the school environment. These characteristics are consistent with diagnoses of ASD, Oppositional Defiant Disorder, Intellectual Disability (Moderate), Generalized Anxiety Disorder.

It was recommended that Louisa receive consistent, nurturing care across all environments in order to help her maximize her opportunity to recover from her early pathological care experiences. It is important to recognize that provision of consistently intense and effective services for a child-like Louisa is categorically more challenging than what would be required for most children with problem behaviors. Data from this 2012 evaluation indicate that Louisa's maladaptive and aggressive behaviors have continued and that her development in key areas including language, academic skills, and sensory modulation have stagnated or declined. She continues to act out in school settings, to the degree that the staff who work with Louisa must essentially focus on managing her behavior. Therefore, Louisa is denied important educational opportunities.

It was hoped that if Louisa received the comprehensive services recommended in her 2008 report that her anxiety and problem behaviors would remit and result in improved skills and behaviors when comparing her evaluations in 2008 and 2012. Unfortunately, Louisa's anxiety remains very high and her consistently problematic behaviors represent substantial barriers to learning and academic growth. When comparing her language and visual–motor skills over the past 4 years, there is evidence of only a few months growth. This is most discouraging and suggests that Louisa has hardly learned anything since her last evaluation. At this time, Louisa is best classified as a nonreader and academic and community opportunities are enormously limited for illiterate persons. It is ever more essential that Louisa's anxiety and problematic behaviors be effectively managed or eliminated to permit her to make academic progress including learning to read. Unfortunately, it is now expected to be significantly more expensive to accomplish these goals because Louisa is now older and learns more slowly and her problem behaviors are even more entrenched as a result of persisting for years. Louisa's case continues to be appealed and such processes can take years.

Mark

Criminal Law Forensic Evaluation

Age: 20 years 9 months

Referral: To assess current neuropsychological functioning, attaining diagnostic clarification, and providing recommendations for appropriate supports and services in light of criminal charges

Assessments: Wechsler Adult Intelligence Scales, Fourth Edition (WAIS-IV); Wechsler Memory Scale, Fourth Edition (WMS-IV);Autism Diagnostic Observation Schedule, Second Edition, Module 4 (ADOS-2); Clinical Evaluation of Language Fundamentals, Fourth Edition (CELF-4); Tower of London, Second Edition (TOL-II) Adult Form; Beck Depression Inventory, Second Edition (BDI-II); Behavior Assessment System for Children, Second Edition (BASC-II), Self-Report; Test of Variables of Attention (TOVA); Validity Indicator Profile (VIP); Test of Memory and Malingering (TOMM); STROOP Color and Word Test — Adult Version

Sentence Completion for Adults; Wisconsin Card Sorting Test (WCST)

Comprehensive Trail-Making Test (CTMT); Controlled Oral Word Association Test (COWA); Scales of Independent Behavior — Revised (SIB-R) — parent report

Clinical Interviews with Mark and parents; Clinical Observations of Mark;

Review of Educational, Psychological, and Police Records Provided

Background Summary: Mark, a 20-year-old college student, came to Emerge for a forensic evaluation after being charged with second-degree sexual assault during his freshman year of college. Mark has history of learning disabilities including an educational diagnosis of auditory processing disorder, noted speech and language impairment, and fine motor delay. He received speech therapy, occupational therapy, tutoring, and academic accommodations from kindergarten with academic accommodations continuing into his first semester of college. Previous reports document weaknesses in attention, processing speed, and executive functioning and note a possible "neurological link" but no formal diagnosis was provided to the Hallinan family.

Mark spent countless hours completing homework during middle school and high school years. He reports no friends, no exposure to social norms such as relationships, courting, etc. In college, Mark watched pornography with a roommate for the first time. Having no exposure to appropriate social interactions with girls, Mark's framework for sex was based on this experience. He reenacted a sexual behavior typified in pornography against a sleeping person and was later charged with second-degree sexual assault.

Forensic Assessment

Mark participated in a full neuropsychological battery of tests. He presents with generally Low Average to Average intellectual abilities coupled with Average vocabulary and knowledge, Average nonverbal reasoning but poor Processing Speed. His language skills fall at 8–13-year-old age levels, not at all consistent of what is expected of a college freshman. Similarly, he presented with language skills below what would be expected from a college student. On measures of memory, Mark demonstrated the ability to hear and recall information both immediately and at a later time. His challenges appear to be in comprehension and interpretation of language. His deficient language comprehension skills were clearly evident in the police interrogation video in which metaphors were repeatedly used, and Mark does not understand the conversation. Overall, Mark displayed marked difficulties in communication, reciprocal social interaction, and attention. He also displays sensory difficulties, repetitive behavior, and highly restricted interests and has significant impairments in social interaction. He had great difficulty completing open-ended tasks about himself and his feelings. He was literal and concrete, worked very slowly, and left many items blank.

Mark was diagnosed with an Autism Spectrum Disorder, AD/HD, and Major Depressive Disorder. Regarding sexual beliefs, he demonstrated poor perspective taking, no knowledge of social norms, limited knowledge of sexual behavior norms, and general confusion about these matters. These characteristics are all consistent with an undiagnosed and untreated Autism Spectrum Disorder. The Emerge forensic report put forth that Mark's legal problems were undoubtedly influenced by his poor perspective taking, pitiful social skills, prepubescent adaptive skills, and abhorrent knowledge of social and sexual norms. These factors result from social communication weaknesses and restricted interests associated with autism and led to Mark's poor judgments.

Results

Mark was initially charged with second-degree sexual assault. Subsequent to the forensic evaluation charges were later lessened to attempt to commit criminal invasion of privacy. The forensic evaluation was a critical component of Mark's legal results. The report and testimony from Emerge provided critical information regarding persons with autism and the role autism played in Mark's legal troubles. Mark was sentenced to 15 years probation, has tracking software on his computer and was required complete Sex Offender Intensive Probation. Modifications to traditional sex offender treatment were made as a result of testimony from that traditional sex offender treatment programs, in isolation, would not be successful for Mark. Therefore, Mark participated in individual sex offender treated instead of a group modality. Additionally, he was required to participate in psychotherapy with a clinician who specializes in Autism Spectrum Disorders.

Chapter 18
School-Based Assessment

Abstract This chapter is a discussion of school-based assessment for Autism Spectrum Disorders. Although often misunderstood, the legal statutes are clear that school teams can and must conduct comprehensive evaluations in order to determine whether a child suspected of having an Autism Spectrum Disorder is eligible for services under the ASD criteria outlined for educational settings. An educational eligibility is in no way equivalent to the clinical diagnosis process, which is described in other chapters of this book. This chapter will delineate and differentiate between evaluations for eligibility as compared to the process used for clinical diagnosis. The term "educational diagnosis of autism" is considered misleading and the authors propose that there are only two potential appropriate terms to use for school teams: (a) Educational Identification of an Autism Spectrum Disorder, and (b) Eligibility Review for services under the ASD Criteria.

A clear discussion of the legal requirements for school teams in terms of eligibility, as well as best practice approaches to assessment in compliance with these laws, will be covered. Although the Response to Intervention (RtI) or Multi-Tiered Systems of Supports (MTSS) process is legally required for schools, it is not clear in either the statutes or the literature as to how these processes should be integrated with educational evaluations for ASD. This chapter provides a proprietary Best-Practice Approach for conducting a comprehensive ASD evaluation within an RtI or MTSS framework.

Keywords Autism in schools • Educational eligibility of autism • Educational diagnosis of ASD • RtI and MTSS and ASD • Multi-Tiered Systems of Support (MTSS) • School interventions for autism • Autism assessment in an RtI framework • Narrative coherence in ASD • Willard Imagery Observation Scales (WIOS) • Best practice ASD assessment in schools

It is important to clarify here that the precise approach schools should be employing for ASD identification is still under study around the country. Further, even a well-established and effective process must be considered in light of the legal mandates and limited resources that are constantly juggled by school teams. Thus, readers are advised to consider any of the guidance provided in this chapter carefully to ensure that the process aligns with district policy, state laws, and within the specific administrative rules and associated resources in the particular school and district where evaluations are conducted.

© Springer International Publishing Switzerland 2016

A.P. Kroncke et al., *Assessment of Autism Spectrum Disorder*, Contemporary Issues in Psychological Assessment, DOI 10.1007/978-3-319-25504-0_18

School: The First Frontier

School-based identification of ASD may come under scrutiny in some circles in light of the fact that school teams may not have been clinically trained to conduct evaluations. Many school districts have not been provided with the comprehensive training necessary to reliably administer the Autism Diagnostic Observation Schedule-Second Edition (ADOS-2) or the Autism Diagnostic Interview-Revised (ADI-R). However, as this chapter will point out, not only is it legally required that school teams conduct evaluations, the school environment may be one of the best opportunities for children with ASDs to be identified. Notice, the term "identified" is not considered equivalent to "diagnosed" and will not be used synonymously in this chapter. Rather, this discussion seeks to empower and instruct school teams to collect and analyze readily available data within the school environment to conduct a comprehensive evaluation. Further, the process provided here allows school teams to collect data, implement evidence-based interventions, and evaluate and identify students with ASD as a part of an RtI framework. Although the school identification process is much different than the clinical evaluation process, neither is considered inferior. School evaluation serves a different purpose in terms of both identification and provision of services, and schools are uniquely positioned to do just that.

So, how then is the school environment such a unique opportunity? During an assessment, it is necessary to look at each symptom, not only to understand whether or not it is pathologic, but also the impact of this symptom on the child's life. That is, in respecting a client's differences and autonomy, there are times where a certain trait or behavior, although atypical, is not really "getting in the way" of his or her life, dreams, or ambitions. In that case, it is not necessarily to be perceived as a symptom, but rather a difference, sometimes referred to as a "quirk"; other times as a "gift." In the home environment, it may be that the child's personality trait is seen more as a quirk; whereas in the school system when placed in context with social and academic demands, it is possible to see whether or not this trait occurs in the context of a disability.

For example, some children are very shy. Could shyness be a symptom of autism? Indeed it may be. The child is shy because he lacks the skills to socialize, communicate, and make friends. In this case, shyness could be a sign of ASD. However, shyness could also signal an introverted personality; someone who is happy spending time alone. In this case, shyness is not a symptom at all, but a personality trait which may actually contribute to his or her life. Perhaps, this introverted child may be highly productive; enjoying time reading, writing, drawing, or learning, in lieu of socializing.

The question becomes, when does a trait or behavior become a symptom or major concern? The answer generally comes down to this, to what degree is this trait or behavior *interfering* with the client's occupation, relationships, goals, and pursuit of happiness? If the symptom interferes, it is worthy of consideration for identification and treatment.

So what is a child's *occupation* then and how do we know if a symptom is interfering with it? "Student" is a child's occupation, or certainly one of them. Children spend much of their waking hours in a school building, where they live, learn, work, and grow. This is why school is referred to in this section as The First Frontier.

School is the place where children choose a path for their lives, make potentially lifelong friends, and navigate some of the decisions regarding career endeavors. Although earlier is always considered better, symptoms are likely to show up when the child first enters the academic world, perhaps in Kindergarten and First Grade. School professionals are wise to take a close look at early elementary school students to see if they are able to integrate and socialize with peers, initiate and maintain conversations, play with others at recess, follow classroom instructions, and access the learning environment. Particularly in the case where a child has never attended preschool, kindergarten and first grade may be the primary place where signs and symptoms are identified.

As this chapter will clearly delineate, the law requires that children from age birth to 21 are to be identified, evaluated, and provided with early intervention or special education services commensurate with their needs. The law does not require that the children solely be provided with academic supports (Colorado Department of Education (CDE) et al., 2014); school teams are to teach the life skills needed for participation in future endeavors such as college and career. Thus, these school-based evaluations are essential and critical such that individuals with ASD can obtain an accurate identification and begin the path for intervention and services. In order to provide a framework for understanding the requirements for school-based teams, the next section delineates the mandates from the IDEA and Child-Find. Also included later in this chapter is the RtI requirements for schools and the Appendix provides more specific information about Independent Educational Evaluations, IEP's and 504 Plans.

Legal Requirement for School-Based Teams

The purpose of this section is to examine federal statutes, regulations, and legal administrative guidelines involving the identification, assessment, and evaluation of students with Autism Spectrum Disorders for determination of eligibility for special education.

IDEA

The Individuals with Disabilities Education Act (IDEA) is the guiding federal statute regarding school-based assessments. IDEA 2004 puts forth that states must ensure that all students with disabilities, birth to age 21, in need of special education, or suspected of having disabilities are identified, located, and evaluated (IDEA Regulations, 34 C.F.R. § 300.220).

In determining eligibility for special education services, IDEA 2004 states that states shall not be required to take into consideration a severe discrepancy between ability and achievement. Furthermore, states must permit the use of "a process that determines if the child responds to scientific, research-based interventions" (IDEA Regulations, 34 C.F.R. § 300.307). This landmark legislation approved the use of response-to-intervention models, but did not prohibit the use of a discrepancy model in determining eligibility for special education. A discussion of response-to-intervention models can be found in a later section.

IDEA 2004 requires that a full, comprehensive, and individualized evaluation of the child's educational needs must be conducted to determine eligibility. Thus, a school-based evaluation is a critical step in providing special education. The evaluation must include all suspected areas of need, which may include: vision, hearing, and motor, assessment of social and emotional status, general intelligence, academic performance, and communicative abilities (IDEA Regulations 34 C.F.R. § 300.532[f]). Additionally, a comprehensive school-based evaluation shall include: (1) Applicable developmental information, (2) information from a student's family, (3) a consideration of student's ability to access and progress in general education, (4) classroom-based assessments, observations from teachers and other service providers (IDEA Regulations, 34 C.F.R. § 300.305). A school multi-disciplinary team, including professionals from special education, general education, and a family member, meets to review the evaluation and determine eligibility. An eligibility determination cannot be made if the present levels of performance are due to a lack of appropriate instruction in reading or math, or limited English proficiency.

Under the IDEA § 300.8 1(i), "Autism" is defined as such:

Autism means a developmental disability significantly affecting verbal and nonverbal communication and social interaction, generally evident before age three that adversely affects a child's educational performance. Other characteristics associated with autism are engaging in repetitive activities and stereotyped movements, resistance to environmental change or change in daily routines, and unusual responses to sensory experiences. The term autism does not apply if the child's educational performance is adversely affected primarily because the child has an emotional disturbance. A child who shows the characteristics of autism after age 3 could be diagnosed as having autism if the criteria above are satisfied (CDE et al., 2014).

ECEA

Most states, including Colorado, provide school teams with an Eligibility Checklist. Generally, these checklists are written in accordance with the guidelines provided under the Exceptional Children's Education Act Rules, as there exists a specific set of criteria for ASD evaluations in schools. The ECEA definition is clear, but state boards of education often define policies and write Rules to ensure administration of the ECEA Act and to align with IDEA. In this way, the school's process considers all areas defined to be important by both federal and state statutes.

First, the ECEA Act specifies that autism is:

"A child with a developmental disability significantly affecting verbal and nonverbal social communication and social interaction, generally evidenced by the age of three.

Other characteristics often associated with ASD are engagement in repetitive activities and stereotyped movements, resistance to environmental changes or changes in daily routines, and unusual responses to sensory experiences." (CDE et al., 2014)

The ECEA Act further specifies that the Autism Spectrum Disorder prevents the child from receiving reasonable educational benefit from general education as evidenced by at least one characteristic in each of the three areas. Listed below is a paraphrased and simplified version of the ECEA definition of ASD for the purposes of helping the IEP team to make sure that all of these areas are assessed during a comprehensive evaluation. This is NOT intended to replace or amend in any way the ECEA Act or Administration Rules. IEP teams are wise to read the rules provided by your state's educational regulating body and then ensure that the school team's process aligns closely with the language of the Rules and the IDEA. The following three areas must be assessed in an ASD evaluation under the Rules; a child who displays at least one characteristic in each of the following deficit areas is determined to have ASD under the ECEA.

1. Interacting with and **understanding people** and maintaining social relationships

    (a) Difficulty establishing and maintaining social–emotional reciprocal relationships
    (b) Lack of typical back and forth conversation
    (c) Deficits in understanding and using nonverbal communication including eye contact, facial expression, and gestures

2. Significant difficulties in other aspects of social **communication**, both receptively and expressively

    (a) An absence of verbal language OR
    (b) Lacking typical integrated use of eye contact and body language
    (c) Difficulty sharing and engaging in imaginative play and maintaining friendships

3. Child seeks consistency in environmental events to the point of **significant rigidity**

    (a) Shows marked distress over changes in routine
    (b) Significant preoccupation with objects or topics

In addition to these three areas, the ECEA Act indicates that there is a list of other characteristics that "may be present," but can "not be used as the sole basis" for eligibility determination. School teams are wise to consider some of these characteristics, but should focus primarily on the three areas defined above. The additional characteristics are: delay or regression in skills, advanced or precocious development in some areas while other skills are below typical levels, atypicality in thinking processes, unusual sensory responses, lacking the functional use of objects, or difficulty displaying a range of interests; and stereotyped motor movements (paraphrased from the ECEA ASD definition, CDE et al., 2014, p. 11). In Colorado, the eligibility checklist follows this guide precisely. The team is literally required to check off at least one characteristic in the top three areas provided by the ECEA rules. There is a separate section on the Colorado form which lists all of the potential associated features of ASD that are not to be used as the sole basis for eligibility.

Keep in mind that at the top of the form, before the initial discussion of these symptoms is the primary question: *"Can the child receive reasonable benefit from general education alone?"* Indeed, if the team checks "yes," the rest of the checklist cannot be completed. In this case, the team can and should provide a follow-up plan for interventions and supports that can be provided in general education or they may open the discussion about 504 eligibility. However, the discussion about an IEP is essentially over. However, if the team checks "No," then this checklist is filled out, considering the three primary areas at the top and the associated characteristics at the bottom. So, at the end of the evaluation, the team completes this checklist to make the eligibility determination. Every phase of the evaluation should be conducted to align with these Rules and to provide a body of evidence to complete the checklist at the IEP meeting.

It might be important to state here that the form can be fairly confusing because the language is complex in the checklist and the multiple areas that need to be checked off to make a decision. IEP teams are advised to take as much time as is necessary to explain the symptom categories to the family. This process is designed to be collaborative and the family is to be included as a member of the decision-making process. Indeed, "family involvement and support" is indicated as a part of high-quality programs in schools that are "legally defensible under the IDEA" (Schwartz & Davis, 2008a, 2008b, pp. 1519–1521). As such, it is essential that the family understands what these categories mean and the potential consequences of checking off certain boxes (for example the "reasonable benefit" box is critical). It may be necessary to use the guide provided above in this chapter that explains the ECEA Rules to the family in a simplified and paraphrased fashion.

In order to simplify the ASD Evaluation process, the following *Best Practice Screening and Assessment Process* is provided. This is adapted from many sources: the CDE guidelines, the process employed in various districts in Colorado, and the guidelines provided by multiple state's educational bodies in the form of whitepapers and guide-books, and the collective experiences of the authors. As previously stated, there exists no clearly defined process that is either federally mandated or has been implemented in most states nationwide. Instead, individual districts and state boards are diligently working to establish processes and procedures that align with ECEA and IDEA guidelines. To make matters more complex, there is no clear guide for how the ASD evaluation and identification process should fit into the Response to Intervention (RtI) or Multi-Tiered Systems of Supports (MTSS) framework. However, a tiered model is known as essential for high-quality school programs that support students with ASD. Experts in best-practice for school-based intervention in ASD say, "The overarching goal across all three tiers of the model and all levels of support is to increase independent functioning and meaningful progress toward important educational outcomes for those with ASD" (Schwartz & Davis, 2008a, 2008b, p. 1517).

The authors of this text provide a Best-Practice approach that follows nicely from this conceptual framework and is somewhat streamlined, but can be dynamically adapted based on the structure of the school and the individual being assessed. This is one potential method for determining eligibility under the ASD category. In order to begin this discussion, school teams should be well-informed that it is not only possible but is legally required that children suspected of having autism are identified in schools. The Child Find mandate makes this requirement abundantly clear.

Child Find

The Child Find mandate Part B falls under the Individuals with Disabilities in Education Act (IDEA) and should guide school-based clinician's decisions around educational identification. Child Find requires that public schools: *Identify, Locate, and Evaluate* children in the state who may need special education services, age birth to 21 (Yell, 2006, p. 256). This mandate includes children who are in migrant families, homeless children, and children attending private schools. The mandate recommends public awareness campaigns such as radio and television ads, mailings, and coordination between local agencies, as a means to locate these individuals. Thus, it is unequivocally clear that school professionals are to be involved in identifying students who may have a disability. Autism is clearly included in the list of disabilities under the IDEA (Yell, 2006). Therefore, school-based teams can and should be a part of the process in identifying children in their school district, who may have an ASD.

Removing the Fog for School-Based Professionals

It is often the case that school-based professionals are put into a bit of a bind when they suspect a child may have autism. School teams often have a plethora of helpful information for families regarding the potential that a child has autism and then be cautioned against using it; either by administrators, or as a matter of policy. Families and community members might believe that the reason school teams will not even utter the word "autism" to parents is because the school does not want to be burdened with the cost of an evaluation or sued for that cost if the child is later found to not have autism. Although these risks exist in some cases; generally, the decision to steer clear of diagnostic terms is made with integrity and sound ethics. That is, School Psychologists and other members of the support services teams are not qualified to diagnose and absolutely must keep all discussions with families centered around observable behaviors and symptoms that may interfere with school performance. Now couple that ethical responsibility to avoid diagnostic labels with the mandate to *find* and identify children with disabilities, and school professionals are placed in an awkward position.

Thus, the goal of this section is to "remove the fog" about autism identification. It is not only legally required for school teams to identify ASDs, but also it is the right thing to do to help the child, support the teacher, and maximize the child's potential for optimal outcomes. School teams should feel empowered to conduct these evaluations as they have the skills, access, and the most natural environment to do so. It will be clearly advanced in this chapter that school teams are legally required to identify children who are suspected of having an Autism Spectrum Disorder and that it is possible to do so while still maintaining the ethical requirement not to diagnose; as well as, enacting a comprehensive evaluation process which is very much in line with the IEP assessment process used for other disabilities such as Specific Learning Disabilities.

Tiered Systems of Support: Implications for Students with ASD

A paucity of research exists regarding the implications of RtI, Positive Behavioral Intervention and Supports (PBIS), and Multi-Tiered Systems of Support (MTSS) approaches in determining eligibility of services for students with ASD. This section presents information regarding the implications of RtI/MTSS in determining eligibility and providing services for students with ASD. Additionally, a tiered approach to interventions is utilized in the Best Practices model put forth in this chapter.

Alphabet Soup: What Are RtI, MTSS, PBIS, FSP?

RtI is a multi-tiered approach to support students' behavioral and academic needs, which highlights how well students respond to changes in instruction. Traditionally, delivered in three tiers: universal, secondary and tertiary, the essential elements of RtI approaches are: the provision of increasingly intense, evidence-based instruction and interventions and progress-monitoring outcome for the purposes of making educational decisions. As noted in the Best Practices for Best-Practice approach for ASD Screening and Identification put forth in this chapter, universal screening is a critical first step in the identification of children with ASD. If red flags are raised about core symptoms of ASD, Tiers 2 and 3 naturally follow.

Tier 1—universal: school-wide or district-wide screening of academics and behavior, to determine which students need additional interventions. Tier 1 interventions for ASD may include environmental arrangements, schedules, visuals, accommodations, and regular home-school communication (Schwartz & Davis, 2008a, 2008b).

Tier 2—secondary: students identified as "at-risk" receive interventions in areas of need; progress is monitored to determine if students are meeting goals. Tier 2 interventions for ASD might include social skills groups and small-group reading or academic intervention.

Tier 3—tertiary/intensive: students identified as having the greatest needs receive intensive interventions and more frequent progress monitoring. Individualized behavior plans, academic interventions, and in-classroom 1:1 support may be included at Tier 3 for individuals with ASD.

PBIS is an empirically supported, systemic approach to proactively support school-wide behavior based on an RtI model. This evidence-based practice has been described thusly, "PBIS is a systems approach for establishing a continuum of proactive, positive discipline procedures for all students and staff members in all types of school settings" (Eber, Sugai, Smith, and Scott 2002). Born out of a behavioral analysis, it is a function-based approach to reduce challenging behaviors and replace them with prosocial skills. Multi-Tiered Systems of Support (MTSS) is an RtI model that utilizes a three-tiered system combining the efforts of traditional RtI and PBIS. These authors will use the terms interchangeably when discussing any tiered system of student support.

A complimentary model that can be utilized in a best-practice approach within an RtI and PBIS framework is *Wraparound Services*, which is a collaborative planning method with foundations in the "systems of care paradigm," whereby community members provide integrated and comprehensive services through collaboration with families and community agencies (Eber et al., 2002, p. 172). Wraparound services will be covered more comprehensively in Chap. 19, where school-family-community partnerships are discussed. For now, readers are advised that RtI, PBIS, and Wraparound services are all best-practice frameworks that should be used to guide the work of school professionals in helping students succeed, while integrating supports throughout the school, home, and community.

Within an RtI framework, these authors advance that *family-centered practices*, which build on families' capacities as partners in promoting student success, are most critical (Sheridan, Taylor, and Woods 2008). This essential practice is captured in the term *Family School Partnerships (FSP)*. Christenson and Sheridan (2001) founded many of the principles of FSP, emphasizing the building of strong relationships with families through: open communication, respect, and trust. Lines, Miller, and Arthur-Stanley (2011) propose that the following vision underlies effective FSP practice: "(a) student school success is the center of family school partnering, (b) education is a shared responsibility between home and school, and (c) families and schools each bring unique experiences and cultures" (p. 28). They further advance that FSP is a natural part of the RtI and PBIS Framework, explaining, "RtI and PBIS exemplify educational best-practices: recognition of a continuum of needs in the population through the tiers, the importance of prevention and effective 'core curricula,' data-based decision making, and evidence-based practices" (Lines et al., 2011). All of these models: RtI, MTSS, PBIS & Wraparound, and FSP are best-practice approaches to supporting students and must be incorporated into effective interventions, identification, and services for students with ASD.

Supporting Students with ASD Within MTSS

A 2008 survey of 117 school psychologists revealed that 53.0 % of respondents indicated that RtI procedures were inappropriate for ASD eligibility determination (Allen, Robins, & Decker, 2008). Although MTSS procedures have improved greatly, many school-based practitioners experience challenges using MTSS to support students with ASD. Hammond, Campbell, and Ruble (2013) raise three issues of tiered interventions serving as part of a preventive framework for ASD: (1) delaying ASD identification; (2) complexity of a tiered interventions addressing social, communication, behavior, adaptive, and motor skills; and (3) first initiating the least intensive intervention instead of considering more intensive, comprehensive programming.

In contrast to a child with a specific learning disorder, such as dyslexia, for whom MTSS supports through small group instruction in an evidenced-based reading curriculum may correct and prevent challenges with reading, the expression of ASD is not prevented via interventions. Rather, a comprehensive individualized education plan will bolster strengths and improve areas of weakness. As such, these authors advocate for a hybrid approach between traditional individualized special education approaches and MTSS approaches for identification of children with ASD within schools.

For students with an existing diagnosis or overt pervasive symptomology, an expedited evaluation and eligibility determination is recommended. That said, for those students who are not already diagnosed or immediately identified, the results of universal screening should be the first step in identification. For example, if social and communication concerns are flagged on universal screeners, a second level of screening, such as an autism-specific parent and teacher measure should be the next step. If secondary screeners further raise concerns, an evaluation should be initiated. Within the MTSS framework, the child should receive evidence-based interventions such as social skills group, speech groups, and reading comprehension instruction simultaneous to the comprehensive evaluation. Thus, useful data is obtained without delaying an evaluation to determine if the student meets educational eligibility under an IEP or Section 504 Plan.

Given that school teams are not in the business of direct diagnosis, it is not necessarily important that the school teams be trained in highly sensitive diagnostic instruments such as the ADOS-2 and the ADI-R. When providing guidance to school teams who do not have access to diagnostic instruments, it is important to state here that children have a right to be evaluated and these authors advance that school teams have plenty of data available to make an accurate determination. It is vitally important to consider social justice. In the case that the child is suspected of having autism, and the school team does not have access to diagnostic instruments, the family should not be expected to secure a diagnosis from an outside agency due to the cost and time lost for educational supports.

Best Practice for Assessment Training

There is a current debate as to whether or not school teams should be administering the ADOS-2, or other clinical diagnostic measures. The ADOS-2 is a gold standard instrument and is critical to clinical evaluations; however, may not be as useful or effective in school evaluations (Hepburn, personal communications, 2015). That is, although these clinical instruments are ideal in clinical settings, sometimes school teams are hard-pressed to provide and maintain the training, and logistically, to assign school clinicians to do the evaluations, when they generally have another position within the school district. If school districts fail to provide the time for both training and the assessment time needed, school professionals are likely to quickly burn out and vacate their roles within the ASD assessment process. When this happens, school teams are taxed twice: first the cost of the training to the school teams, and second when the Autism Team is yet again left without qualified evaluators.

The authors of this book make no clear statement as to whether school teams should administer the ADOS-2; although it is optimal, the process advanced in this book does not require it. However, should school teams be provided with such clinical instruments, it is recommended that they become adequately trained. School professionals administering the ADOS should *at least* attend the 2-day WPS ADOS training and attend sessions locally with a clinically trained and well-versed clinician to assess for one's reliability of scoring and accuracy. Generally, although in clinical settings the ADOS-2 is administered by psychologists, in school evaluations an interdisciplinary team may conduct the instrument together, similarly to a play-based approach such as the Transdisciplinary Play-Based Assessment model (Linder, 2008). In that case, the team may be comprised of psychologists, speech-language pathologists, occupational therapists, audiologists, and special education teachers. Often, as in the case in Colorado, local agencies are willing to provide supervision or training on obtaining clinical reliability on the ADOS-2. It is important to be clear here that knowing how to give the measure is only a small part of the training needed for the ADOS-2, because the scoring and assessment of symptoms is perhaps the most nuanced and challenging part of giving the ADOS-2. For example, the clinician needs to be able to assess the quality of the rapport, the child's eye-contact, emotional awareness, response to joint attention, gesture use, social response, social overtures, flexibility or rigidity, repetitive speech and behaviors, restricted interests, reporting of events and a host of other symptoms, *in the moment* as the ADOS-2 is meant to be scored immediately following administration.

Given all of the above considerations, it may *seem* that the school should always err on the side of caution and complete an evaluation, just in case the child may have an ASD if a referral has been made. The authors want to make a clear and firm point that this is absolutely not the approach recommended here. Rather, these authors support autism identification, as with other disabilities, should only occur when the school team has considered whether or not the child can receive reasonable benefit from general education alone, and only after evidence-based interventions have been employed with fidelity. The child must always be placed in the Least Restrictive Environment (LRE), and as such, school teams are charged with

providing a supportive educational environment with first-best instruction provided by teachers in the education classroom, within consultation with support
services (as needed). It is time to look closely at what most ASD evaluations in
schools will entail. Every state looks a bit different but the process is similar in
terms of the primary elements from some sort of referral process to an eligibility
determination and initiation of services.

In Colorado, a collaborative relationship was established between the
Colorado Department of Education and JFK Partners, Center of Excellence for
Autism and Neurodevelopmental Disabilities in collaboration between The
Children's Hospital and the University of Colorado Medical School. Through
this partnership, a guidebook was written which describes a best-practice
approach for doing an autism evaluation in Colorado schools. This guidebook
describes the process thusly (interested readers are invited to read the guidebook
in detail—the reference is provided):

A. *Detect* phase, which is where the student is suspected of potentially having an
   ASD and the team begins collecting data. Next, the team makes a decision as to
   whether to conduct a screen for ASD.
B. A *Referral* is made when an ASD is suspected. At this point, the team may
   determine if the ASD is NOT suspected. Then, the team may end the process or
   consider eligibility for another disability if an ASD is suspected.
C. A *Screen* is conducted where the team meets with the family and autism screeners are completed. Next, a decision is made about whether or not ASD is suspected, which again, if ASD is NOT suspected, leads to either ending the process
   or initiating an evaluation for another potential disability if ASD is suspected
   after the screener.
D. *Evaluate*, where consent for an evaluation is obtained and the team determines
   which areas should be assessed.
E. *Collaborate* is the phase where the team meets to review all of the data from the
   various assessments conducted by the IEP team. Next, a decision is made about
   eligibility. If the child is determined to be eligible.

The final phase then is (G) *Activate* where the IEP program is put into place
and services begin (with parental consent). (Process taken directly from CDE
et al., 2014, p. 15).

In addition to the process presented above in Colorado, there are multiple similar
models throughout the country that include most of the same elements in somewhat
different configurations. One approach is offered and well-articulated by an excellent
online resource called Ohio Center for Autism and Low Incidence (OCALI), which
includes a free training module called, "Educational Evaluation of Autism: A team
approach." This approach flows thusly: Referral, Evaluation Plan, Observation,
Evaluation, Collaboration Team Reports, Meeting with team and family, Follow up."
As shown here, there are multiple approaches that can be considered. For this study,
Colorado, Ohio, California, and Oregon's processes were studied. Although these
processes are certainly all aligned with legal guidelines and would generally be considered appropriate, the authors did not find a process that comprehensively included
the RtI or Multi-Tiered System of Supports structures. As such, the procedures and

Best-Practice Approach for Screening and Assessment of ASDs in schools are provided here to aide schools in developing a process that aligns with universal screenings and evidence-based intervention procedures that are in place in most schools across the country (Fig. 18.1).

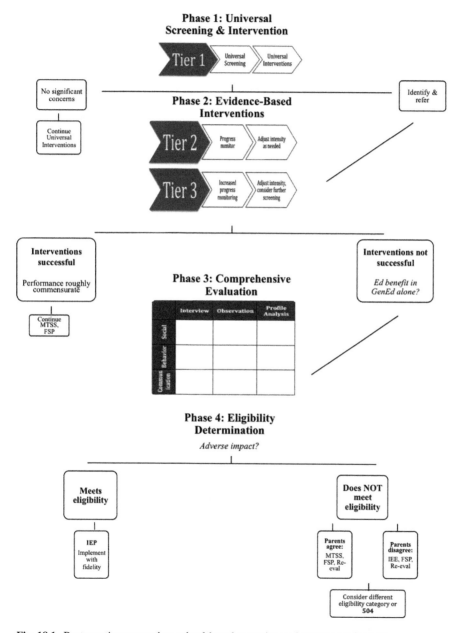

Fig. 18.1 Best practice approach to school-based screening and assessment for ASD

A Description of the Best-Practice Approach for ASD Screening and Identification

Phase 1: Universal Screening and Intervention

The first thing that happens in the ASD Identification process is that someone suspects the child has a disability or is concerned about the child's functioning in the classroom. Generally, this process is initiated by either the child's parents or teacher. It may be the case that the child is struggling in school. It is important to state that although IDEA mandates that the child must require specialized instruction for an IEP to be initiated, there is no legal mandate that the child's academic skills are impacted by the disability. Confusing as that sounds, the IDEA indicates that the Autism must "*adversely affect* a child's educational performance" (CDE et al., 2014). However, the law does not indicate that "academics" must be affected. Although this is difficult to interpret, most states take this to mean that any symptoms of the disability that interfere with the child's ability to participate and function within the school environment can show evidence of these adverse effects. Thus, school teams are wise to consider not only whether the child can do the work in the classroom, but also whether he or she can work in groups, go to recess and lunch, transition between classes, handle schedule changes and fire-drills, and socialize. That last point is of course a tricky one because not all kids with poor social skills need an IEP; however, social skills are perhaps the most significant factor in autism identification, so the child's social skills must be evaluated.

Tier 1: Universal Interventions

Within Phase 1, Universal Screening and Intervention must occur in order to support students suspected of having ASD in the general education classroom. Tier 1 interventions are available universally to all students and include such methods as PBIS (discussed previously), first-best instruction, compacted, and differentiated teaching. Interventions at the universal tier for ASD might include: classroom management strategies, enhancing clarity of instructions and school rules, establishing and nurturing Family School Partnerships (FSP), and interventions available through the Positive Behavior Interventions and Supports (PBIS) program at the school. For example, if the school offers "cougar tickets" for good behaviors, it may be that the teacher needs to incorporate more systematic use of these types of reinforcers to improve the participation and behavior of all students. Second Step classroom-wide social skills interventions can be employed in Tier 1.

Many students with ASD can benefit from Tier 1 supports. Schwartz and Davis (2008a, 2008b) indicate that some children with ASD may "do quite well" within a "high quality" educational program that includes "well-placed support and developmental surveillance" (p. 1517). However, most of the cases presented in this book are not comprehensively served within Tier 1 and require more intensive intervention.

Many children with autism need social skills groups (generally in Tier 2) and academic or behavioral intervention (generally in Tier 3). "While we know that children with ASD benefit from universal interventions, we understand that this level of support alone will be insufficient," report experts in school psychology best-practice (Schwartz & Davis, 2008a, 2008b, p. 1517). These authors argue that many children on the Spectrum can achieve adequately in Tier 1, but interventions designed to meet their unique needs, specifically in the face of social, behavioral, and academic failures, are often more effective within Tier 2 and Tier 3. Thus, the final step of Phase 1 is that the child is identified for increased support and referred to the RtI team. Although it is not required that a member of the IEP team formally sit on the RtI or problem-solving team, in an ASD eligibility, it is extremely helpful that some of the same individuals be involved from the initiation of observations and Tier 1 interventions through Tier 3 and the eligibility determination.

Screen, Identify, and Refer

The focus of this initial observation and screening generally involves an assessment of the child's functioning within the classroom. The focus of the observations is more universal as this screen is provided in part to see if there is anything at all to be concerned about; not to look for ASD. If the team is truly doing a formal observation for ASD, the data gathering should be more systematic; a process described later in this section.

Screening Observation Tools

The school team should screen the child through an informal observation during phase 1 of this model. In this observation, the school team can observe the child in multiple settings. It is preferred to have multiple observers (from various disciplines) so that different impressions can be compared. However, for a screening, it may only be possible to ask one of the team members to observe the child. The observer should look for levels of *participation, interaction with peers, ability to follow directions, perform academic tasks, on-task behavior,* and *communication skills*. At this point, no metrics are needed, but an observation form may be helpful and some states utilize specific observation guides to look for key areas (Southwest Ohio Regional Advisory Council, 2014). Another option for this screening might be to use a general observation tool such as the RIOT/ICEL matrix (Hosp, 2008). The RIOT/ICEL model is a "mental framework" that improves efficiency of data collection in determining the specific problems that may interfere with student learning or behavior. RIOT stands for Review, Interview, Observe, and Test and ICEL stands for Instruction, Curriculum, Environment, and Learner. This matrix allows school teams to collect the necessary information to identify the areas of concern for a student without going overboard to the extent that data are collected which are not truly essential to decision making (Wright, 2010). Interested readers are invited to the Intervention Central website where Jim Wright, a recognized RtI expert, describes the RIOT/ICEL matrix, as well as other RtI techniques in detail.

Phase 2: Evidence-Based Interventions

Once concerns have been uncovered, interventions should be designed and planning should occur with all stakeholders including: teachers, intervention team members, the classroom teacher, school psychologist or mental health provider, and parents. The FSP partnership model proposes that the FSP planning cycle involves the following components: Define, Plan, Implement, and Evaluate (Lines et al., 2011). The team evaluates the supports, interventions, and resources a child may need to be more successful in the classroom. This nicely flows from the screening observations that have been conducted as certain areas can quickly be identified for support. It is important to state that these interventions can begin immediately. Schwartz and Davis (2008a, 2008b) explain, "Additionally, these services should be put into place as soon as the team suspects that the child has an ASD. In other words, it is not necessary to wait for a medical or educational diagnosis to begin specialized intensive intervention" (p. 1519).

Tier 2 Interventions

Tier 2 interventions generally involve small groups of students and arc intended to address approximately 15 % of the school population. There are a number of interventions which may be helpful in Tier 2 to children with social skills, communication problems, or social skills deficits. Specifically, perspective taking lessons in a small group format, small group instruction for reading comprehension or other challenging subjects, pragmatic language groups with Speech Therapist, supports and supervision at recess and in the lunchroom, are recommended. Within Tier 2, Schwartz and Davis (2008a, 2008b) recommend that school teams look closely at social skills deficits that may not be immediately evident to teachers and recess monitors. They report, "Yet the lack of social skills is just as problematic to future independence and school success as outward aggression. While school teams may be looking [at tier 2] for delays in cognition and language, the child who is at grade level academically, but may have no friends or not know how to join a group on the playground, also needs additional supports" (p. 1520).

Social skills groups or lunch bunch with the Counselor or School Psychologist may be employed at Tier 2. Regarding development of best-practice social skills groups for children with social deficits, several useful models exist that the school team might consider. For younger children in preschool and early elementary, Wolfberg (2003) provides an evidence-based Integrated Playgroup (IPG) model which includes children on the Spectrum with typically developing peers. It encourages imagination and positive social skills through a series of organized play scenarios using toys and functional objects to facilitate more imaginative and symbolic play scenarios. With children in elementary (approximately in 2nd–5th grade) school students, the Super Flex Curriculum (Madrigal & Winner, 2008; Winner & Crooke, 2008) can be useful. This approach uses colorful "superhero" cartoon characters such as "Rock Brain" and "Was-Funny-Once" to encourage flexible thinking and social problem solving. A Collaborative Problem-Solving model such as those proposed by

Ross Greene can be helpful for social groups of upper elementary and middle school students (Greene, 2014; Greene & Ablon, 2005). For upper elementary school, middle school, and high school, the PEERS model (Laugeson, 2010) is an effective approach for teaching social skills.

Tier 3 Interventions

Individual interventions are employed at Tier 3 and are intended for roughly 5 % of the school population. The RtI team should discuss the problems that are interfering academically, socially, or behaviorally and identify priorities for intervention. If the child is struggling in reading or math, it may be helpful to pull progress-monitoring tools from Easy CBM or Intervention Central. For mild behavior problems such as trouble responding to transitions in the classroom, it may be helpful to provide the teacher with nonverbal prompting tools, visual schedules, or other reinforcement to aide in the transition process. Schwartz and Davis (2008a, 2008b) recommend the following at tier 3 for students with ASD, "The services are likely to include instruction that uses clear cues for responding (i.e., explicit), uses principles of ABA, provides multiple opportunities to practice across the day, is implemented consistently across the day, and is implemented consistently with some measure of fidelity" (p. 1520).

At this point, it may be helpful to develop a behavior plan to enable the child participate in class discussions. Consultation with the teacher and parents is often necessary to put supports in place such as visual checklists of tasks to complete for each subject, Daily Report Cards, Home-School Communication Notebooks, and regular collaboration with the family to ensure fluid and collaborative home-school supports.

A comprehensive approach to Family School Partnerships and collaboration is offered up by Lines et al. (2011) in the book, *The Power of Family-School Partnering (FSP): A Practical Guide for School Mental Health Professionals and Educators (School-Based Practice in Action)*. Interested readers are guided to this book which provides practical tools such as permission forms for RtI screeners or "diagnostic-prescriptive assessments"; as well as, data collection techniques, family communication sheets, family letters, and system-wide collaborative frameworks to aide in development of effective relationships with families.

Progress Monitor

The first question that can be answered with progress monitoring is, with the interventions, if the child doing better? That is, compare the child to his or her own baseline performance and assess growth. In order to evaluate "growth," there are a variety of measures that can be used. It is strongly encouraged that schools send a letter, such as that provided by the FSP book above, to obtain consent for any formal screeners within the progress-monitoring process.

Academic interventions: Intervention Central is an excellent online source for quick assessment probes that can be used to gather baseline data and progress monitor, primarily in reading and math. Chart Dog is a tool available through Intervention Central to graph the child's progress on the assessments. It also may be useful to work with a tool such as *Easy CBM* or *Aimsweb* in order to gather academic data within the RtI process.

Behavior interventions: to progress monitor behavior growth, generally some sort of behavioral tracker should be used. One such tool is called "Behavior-Snap" (previously, Behavior Lens), which is available inexpensively from the iTunes store and can be downloaded to an iPad. Behavior Snap allows school psychologists, behavior analysts, and social workers to evaluate the child's behavior both narratively and quantitatively. It provides an easy conversion to visual representations of data such as charts and graphs and includes the ability to email visual data to families and teachers. Behavioral progress monitoring may include a more formal assessment of on-task, off-task percentage, which would be collected pre-intervention, weekly or biweekly during the intervention, and as a summative tool at the end of the intervention. Another app is called "Motiv-Aider," which is an on-task, off-task self-monitoring tool. This application prompts the child on pre-set intervals (for example every 10 min) with the question, "Am I doing what I am supposed to be doing?" The child is then asked to mark "yes" or "no" on a simple T-Chart. At the end of the day, the number of "yes" responses can be totaled up for a prize.

There is also an app called "Class Dojo" which is a digital behavior chart where teachers can give the child either positive or negative points on certain identified behaviors such as participation and following directions. The app provides real-time reports of the child's percentage of positive as compared to negative behaviors. It includes cute avatar characters to represent the child and the students can adjust their avatar, as well as see their own points and progress. This is also extremely helpful for collaborating with families because parents can log-on and see their child's progress and text the teacher through the Class Dojo app with any questions or concerns.

Another option is a Daily Report Card to be completed by the classroom teacher where the child's performance is rated on a few key areas. For example, "Did I do my best work today," "Did I follow directions today," and "Did I have safe hands in class today." This would be rated by the teacher and ideally would be collaboratively "graded" by the teacher and student. Report card generators are available online: http://www.interventioncentral.org/tools/behavior-report-card-generator.

Closing the Gap

For behavior data and academic data, it is possible using any of these tools to compare baseline performance to the child's demonstration of positive behaviors during the intervention phase. Simply measuring baseline compared to current performance data is not the only measure of whether the intervention is successful. The other issue, and the *most important*, is whether or not the child's growth trajectory is sufficient to *close the gap* between the student and his or her peers. This means that the child's growth in any area, either academic, communication, or behavioral, must be considered as compared to the growth of a same-aged peer. It is not sufficient to consider whether or not the child is improving. The question for the intervention team to ask is whether or not the child's growth is eventually going to catch up to peers at the current level of support. That is, the child's line should not be parallel with peers, but should be projected to cross over the growth trajectory of typical peers. If indeed, the child is predicted to catch-up, an IEP evaluation may not be necessary. If, however, the lines are predicated to remain parallel or the child's skills appear to be somewhat flat-lined, it is time to initiate an IEP evaluation.

Determine If Interventions Are Successful

At this point in the RtI framework, there should exist data to make a determination as to the child's progress. The RtI methods used in the school building and district should lend nicely to the process highlighted here within an ASD identification model. A comprehensive explanation of progress-monitoring tools goes beyond the scope of this chapter; however, some simple guidelines have been provided above. If interventions are not successful, it is time to obtain consent to move to Phrase 3: A comprehensive evaluation.

Obtain Consent for Evaluation

At this point in the process, the intervention team has determined through a data-based process that the child is not responding to intervention. The question then becomes, at what point should the family be involved? Again the answer is complex and no clear answers are provided in the law, statutes, or Rules. It is generally considered best practice for the family to have early involvement and be informed of every phase of the RtI intervention process (Lines et al., 2011). However, there is no clear legal guideline that this is necessary. At times, the teacher may have a hunch that classroom interventions will be successful and may start small group supports for a targeted group of students. It is best practice to involve families when extra supports are provided (particularly in Tier 2 and beyond), but the rules vary by district in terms of what kinds of consents are needed. In some districts, families are invited to the RtI meetings, but the meeting goes on whether they choose to attend or not. Often, the families sign a letter indicating their consent for specific interventions and certainly for any formal screening tools to be conducted. At the point that an IEP evaluation is being considered, the family must sign their consent before any assessment data can be collected.

Obtain Consent for Evaluation

It is recommended that at least one member of the IEP team meet with the family to discuss the reasons for the evaluation and explain the process. After consent is obtained, the family should be provided with information on the process and soon after a meeting date should be set.

Notice of Meeting

The family should receive a Notice of Meeting that includes the type of assessments that will be done (Social, Emotional, Behavioral, Academic, Cognitive, Speech/Language, Motor and Sensory, and Autism-Specific testing); the date and time of the meeting, and all of the IEP meeting participants (Table 18.1).

Once the family has been informed of the evaluation and provided formal consent, the team must determine how a body of evidence will be collected for each of the three areas and should develop a preliminary plan for when the team will meet to review results as data are collected during the evaluation.

Phase 3: Comprehensive Evaluation

The Comprehensive Evaluation should include: *Interviews* of the child, family, and teacher; *Observations* of the child in multiple settings; and *Testing* that includes both formal assessments and informal tests such as Curriculum-Based Measures and work sampling.

Interviews

Parent Interview

This parent interview can and should be an ongoing, collaborative, and a fluid process; not occurring in one simple meeting but throughout the evaluation. The principles of Family School Partnerships (FSP) would dictate that collaboration with families promotes best outcomes, is essential to data-based decision making, and delivers the best prospect of bringing about meaningful results in educational,

Table 18.1 IEP meeting participants

Required participants	Optional participants
• Student's parents or guardians	• Related service providers (OT, PT, speech, ELL)
• Special education teacher (at least one)	• Assistive technology specialist
• General education teacher (at least one)	• Transition agency representative
• Representative of educational agency (to supervise the process)	• Part C provider (if child eligible)
• Person(s) to interpret results of evaluation	• Other persons at request of parent (including advocates and outside providers)
• Child (when appropriate and at transition meetings)	

Adapted from (Yell, 2012)

social, adaptive, and affective development for students. (Esler, Godber, & Christenson, 2008; Lines et al., 2011; Sheridan et al., 2008). These authors advance that any effective intervention in a school should include families as experts on their children. Families see their children in multiple contexts and there is strong evidence to support that parent participation brings about best outcomes for students (Jaynes, 2005). Sheridan et al. (2008) explain, "Families are the primary and essential facilitators of meaningful change that can have the most impact on a child's growth and development over time" (p. 995). Thus, school teams should consider this interview, not as a single "step"; but rather as an ongoing, conceptual framework for the entire process.

Formal Interview. Interviews with the family can be either formal or informal. A more formal interview may include the ADI-R (Lord, Rutter, & Le Couteur, 1994). Some estimates are that the ADI-R can take around an hour to complete (Indiana Resource Center, 2011). However, a word of caution here is that the ADI-R is considered a formal diagnostic tool and the team needs sufficient training and time to administer the measure. Another option would be a semi-structured interview in which the parents would be asked questions about the child's social skills, communication, and behavior at home. It may be possible to complete the Vineland Scales of Adaptive Behavior, Second Edition (Vineland-II) during this meeting (VABS: Sparrow, Cicchetti, Balla, 2005). School-based clinicians should be aware that parents may not understand the Vineland-II questions well; therefore, this assessment should be completed in a face-to-face meeting and must include a clear explanation of the intent behind the items. Parents should be aptly informed that their responses should capture not what the child is capable of doing, but rather the skills the child actually demonstrates on a consistent basis. At a minimum, the first meeting with the family should include (a) a clear explanation of the reasons for the evaluation and the process, (b) formal consent for evaluation, and (c) an opportunity for parents to share their concerns about their child.

Parent interview Questions: Consultation with the child's parents/guardians is an important task in a comprehensive evaluation. It is recommended to ask family about the student's behavior and social skills. For example:

- Child strengths?
- Developmental milestones (language/motor): met early, on-time, late?
- Family history of disabilities?
- Medications?
- How does he/she interact with peers in extra-curricular activities?
- How does he/she respond to changes in routine? Does child have rituals or non-functional routines?
- Does the child tantrum or have unusual responses to sensory stimuli?
- Does he/she know the difference between a friend and a classmate?
- Does the child have any restricted and repetitive interests?
- Can child follow social conversation and/or directions?

Child Interview

A child interview should include questions that evaluate a child's insight into his or her own feelings; as well as, the feelings and perspectives of others. Children with autism often struggle in these interviews to answer questions like, "If you could be any animal, what animal would you be?" Or, "If you had three wishes, what would you wish for?" The problem with questions like these is that they are open-ended, require imagination, and demand some degree of emotional insight. A typical student may be comfortable confidently stating an answer, while a child with ASD may refuse a response due to the fact that the questions have no clear answer and the relative level of challenge due to their different cognitive profile. An interview should also consider questions about the child's feelings. The interviewer could ask, "How do you feel most of the time" and "What are some things that make you feel sad, mad, anxious ..." The interviewer can get a sense from these questions about the child's level of emotional understanding. Another question to ask is about friends. A child with autism may have an extremely difficult time answering questions about friends. He or she may or may not have friends. Often, children with autism cannot name friends or even identify who they sit next to in class. They may not know how to tell a friend apart from a classmate. Any of these unique challenges should be noted in a clinical interview and considered part of an autism screening or evaluation.

Child Interview Questions: Clearly when assessing for symptoms of ASD, it is critical to interview the child and obtain information about his/her social skills and social reciprocity. For example:

- What are your greatest strengths?
- Tell me about your friends
- How is a friend different from a classmate?
- What do you do for fun?
- How can you tell if you are feeling happy? Mad? Sad?
- How can you tell if someone else is mad? Happy?

Teacher Interview

Teachers provide key data to the evaluation team in terms of how the child is interacting in class, whether or not he or she can follow directions and routines, and overall levels of participation. If the teacher sees the child as withdrawn, per-severative, rigid, sensory-sensitive, and behaviorally challenging, these data are essential red-flags that autism symptoms may be interfering with the child's per-formance. Bear in mind that teachers are not necessarily experts in autism; how-ever, they are subject matter experts in terms of evaluating the child's skills in comparison to typical peers.

Teacher Interview Questions

Consultation with the child's teachers and service providers is a critical piece in developing a comprehensive body of evidence. It is recommended to ask school staff who are familiar with the student about his/her behavior and social skills. Some sample questions include:

- Student strengths?
- Does the student know the difference between a friend and just a classmate?
- How does the student respond to changes in routine?
- Does the child have any restricted and repetitive interests?
- How does he/she interact with peers in specials and on the playground?
- Does the child behave differently in group work vs. individual work?
- Can child follow social conversation and/or directions?

Observations

Formal Observations

The school team or professionals on the district Autism Team should observe the child in multiple environments. It is important that observations are conducted by individuals with diverse training, for example, a school psychologist/ social worker, speech pathologist, and occupational therapist; completing three different observations would provide critical cross-discipline information about the child. Suggestions for team members and for the types of data to collect are provided below.

Observers:

- Mental Health Providers (School Psychologist, School Counselor, School Social Worker)
- Speech Language Therapists
- Motor (Physical Therapy or Occupational Therapy) Therapists
- Each professional conducts a separate observation

Observations should include:

- Description of social communication skills
- Social overtures to adults and peers (verbal and nonverbal)
- Social responses to adults and peers (verbal and nonverbal)
- Interactions (intensity, frequency, duration)
- Behaviors (repetitive, restricted)
- Adaptive functioning in the classroom

The observer should look for **Social Concerns** such as: eye contact, limited peer interaction, lack of spontaneous sharing of enjoyment with peers, lack of social reciprocity (CDE et al., 2014). The observer can look for how the student interacts with familiar and unfamiliar adults and peers. Key questions can guide this observation, such as, is the child withdrawn or avoiding interaction; does he take turns, or is he more interested in objects than people? (Southwest Ohio Regional Advisory Council, 2014). This would be a place to note whether or not the child prefers to spend much of class-time alone, refuses to work in groups, or "acts as if he is in his own world."

The observer would also consider **Communication Concerns** such as: delay or lack of verbal communication, refusal or failure to successfully initiate conversations, exchanges lacking the to and fro quality and reciprocal nature of typical peer interactions, lack of pretend play, or lack of social imitative play. Key questions to consider here are: what is the mean length of utterance, gesture use, and vocalizations; is there echolalia? What is the function of the communication? Is the focus on getting one's own needs met; or is he or she seeking friendships, or to express feelings, or ask for help? (Southwest Ohio Regional Advisory Council, 2014). It also may be helpful to consider having the speech therapist conduct a formal assessment of the child's pragmatic language skills, either by using a formal observation protocol in the classroom, or by way of clinical observations during the speech/language portion of the evaluation. This would be the place to consider if the child tends to focus only on his or her own interests, to monologue, or to ignore peers who attempt to initiate conversations. If the child rarely talks to peers or walks away when others are talking to him or her, this would be of note as a red flag for communication problems associated with autism.

The observer would then evaluate **Behavioral Concerns** such as: inflexibility and rigidity or insistence on non-functional routines or rituals, repetitive motor movements, aggressive behavior or outbursts, abnormal focus on topics or objects (seems "obsessed" with dinosaurs or volcanoes, Thomas the Train, or Minecraft for example). Key questions that may be considered here are frequency and duration of any repetitive motor movements; and what is the function of any undesired behavior? The observer can also assess how the student responds to change such as a new schedule; different clothing, food, or toys (Southwest Ohio Regional Advisory Council, 2014). This would be the place to note whether the child can generally function in the classroom. If the child seems to ignore directions, have tantrums, refuse to participate in group activities, or is highly disruptive in group activities, this could be a sign of ASD (this section adapted from CDE et al., 2014, p. 28). Again, the team should constantly bear in mind that the focus of these observations is not to determine whether the child has ASD; rather, does the child show symptoms in all three areas identified by the ECEA rules (social, communication, behavioral)? Spending a lot of time conversing with the teachers, parents, and team about other symptoms of autism may serve to be ultimately fruitless, because even if the child has ASD, he or she still may not qualify for an IEP.

Tests

Formal Assessments

At this point in the process, the team should be ready to complete any formal assessments. In terms of the areas to assess, it may be that from the Interview and Observation process conducted previously, the team has a clear picture of symptoms in one area. However, all three areas must be assessed (social, communication, and behavior/flexibility). In addition to these three, a Comprehensive Evaluation should include: IQ or Cognitive, Emotional, Adaptive, and Academic Testing. There are specific examples provided later in this chapter for how to use measures that are typically administered in any evaluation to assess for the areas of ASD.

Communication

The Speech Therapist may complete a Clinical Evaluation of Language Fundamentals, Fifth Edition (CELF-5) to evaluate the child's Core Language and any discrepancies between Receptive and Expressive Language. As mentioned previously, a significant discrepancy between Expressive and Receptive language where the Expressive language is much better then Receptive is a significant sign an ASD may be present (see Part 3 table: Data Analysis Framework).

Behavior

If the issues are more behavioral, the mental health team should carefully examine the areas of concern using formal or informal measures such as the BASC-SOS, Behavior Assessment Scales for Children, Student Observation System, and any data obtained during the Intervention phase using some of the data tracking tools mentioned previously. Additionally, if there are significant behavioral concerns, the team may conduct a Functional Behavioral Analysis or Functional Analysis to determine the function of the behavior and begin to develop a Behavior Intervention Plan.

Social and Adaptive

If the issues are social, it may be most helpful to look at Pragmatic Language measures, or to take data from the Vineland Scales of Adaptive Behavior, Second Edition. Social–Emotional testing might include measures like the Behavior Assessment System for Children, Second Edition (BASC-II) or the Child Behavior Checklist (Achenbach). On the Vineland-II, it might be important to consider all of the communication scales, interpersonal relationships, and any internalizing or externalizing behaviors. Further, interviews of teachers and parents are useful resources to educate behavior concerns. Regarding Adaptive skills on the Vineland-II, often children with autism struggle on coping skills and receptive language. Parents may report on the measure that their children do not follow multi-step directions, have emotional meltdowns over minor changes to the schedule, and prefer to play alone.

Cognitive

A formal cognitive evaluation provides critical information about the child's baseline skills. Although the law does not require it, generally it is considered best practice that all IEP initial evaluations include an IQ test, such as the Wechsler tests, Differential Ability Scales, Second Edition (DAS-II), Stanford Binet—V or Test of Nonverbal Intelligence (TONI-3: Brown, Sherbenou & Johnsen, 2001), or the Universal Nonverbal Intelligence Test, Second Edition (UNIT-II, see Chap. 8 for more information on this and other cognitive tests). The IQ test provides an overall measure of skills for all of the other instruments to be compared. Remember that on the Wechsler tests, children with ASD tend to score lowest on the Comprehension subtest as compared to all other tests. Even though the Comprehension test is not required on the WISC-V, it is recommended that this test always be administered in ASD evaluations. Children with autism tend to score lower on Coding, relative to Symbol Search. Their processing speed tends to be the lowest index. Children with ASD may perform especially well on Matrix Reasoning and Block Design. This cognitive profile should be seen as a sign that ASD may be relevant for this student.

Autism-Specific

Formal autism rating scales can be conducted such as the Gilliam Autism Rating Scale, Second Edition (Gilliam, 2006) or the Childhood Autism Rating Scale, Second Edition (Schopler, Van Bourgondien, Wellman, Love, 2010) The Autism Diagnostic Observation Schedule (Lord, Rutter, DiLavore, Risi, Gotham, & Bishop, 2012) may be included in the evaluation, if the tool and trained administrators are available in the district.

Academic

Academic testing must occur as well as is part of the IEP initial evaluation. For information specific to academic testing for children with autism, see the academic testing section later in this chapter. Remember that although the ASD symptoms must "adversely affect the child's educational performance," this is not defined to mean academic performance specifically. If the child's social, communication, and behavior are impaired, the child's symptoms are having an adverse effect on his education, regardless of academic performance.

Within academic areas, most often, autism symptoms tend to show up in the area of reading comprehension. Often, the child's narrative coherence (story telling) (Losh & Capps, 2003; Suh et al. 2014; Sutera et al. 2007; Willard, 2013) and writing skills can be impacted as well. Sometimes, children with autism struggle more in conceptual math and story problems than procedural math and math facts. The child may struggle with participation in academic tasks due to poor executive functioning and may have difficulty with task initiation, following directions, and work completion; these behaviors could potentially affect any area of academics. At a minimum, the evaluation should include a measure of reading, writing, and math. This may be accomplished through separate tests for each area (GORT-5 for reading; Key-Math-3 for math, and TOWL-4 for writing); or a general achievement test such as the WIAT-III.

Collaborate with IEP Team and Discuss Findings

Collaboration should happen throughout testing. It is certainly important to not meet as a team to predetermine eligibility because all of the eligibility discussion should occur at the IEP meeting. However, the IEP team should meet frequently to share data and compare results. For example, if the Verbal IQ came out Average or High on the Wechsler test administered by the school psychologist, while functional communication skills or Receptive Language administered by the Speech Language Pathologist are Low, this is a red flag for autism. In some school districts, the IEP team has a central depository for any data gathered, where the evaluators can regularly update the team on all of the information as it is scored and completed.

Phase 4: Eligibility Determination

This IEP meeting should proceed much like any traditional IEP Initial meeting. The parents should receive the Parent Rights document, participants should all sign in, and then all of the members of the team and IEP guests should be introduced. Next, all of the relevant data gathered during the evaluation should be provided to the family. Typically, the team allows the teachers to share first as they may need to get back to their classrooms. Next, the Learning Specialist or Special Educator generally shares all relevant academics. This may be followed by the School Psychologist or other Mental Health provider, who shares cognitive, adaptive, social-emotional, and behavioral data. Next, it may be the Speech Therapist who shares Core language results, Receptive versus Expressive Language, Pragmatic Language, and Articulation. Any other specialists can also share their results. Many teams include an audiologist (OCALI, 2014) as hearing issues can impact communication substantially. The team may also include autism specialists or behavior specialists who would share their results. It is important to keep the findings clear, concise, and relevant to the eligibility, so as to not overwhelm the family. One of the authors on this book cautions that IEP meetings can sometimes feel like a "data gun" that is being shot out at the family. Be careful not to use language the family does not understand and check in frequently to see that the family is clearly following all of the data presented.

During the eligibility meeting, as mentioned previously, the next step is to complete the ASD checklist. In some cases, the child may also be suspected of having an Intellectual Disability, Learning Disability, Significant Emotional Disability, and in that case, those checklists should be reviewed as well. As discussed in earlier parts of this chapter, the IEP checklist for ASD includes three primary symptom categories: (a) social understanding and maintenance of reciprocal social relationships, (b) communication, and (c) flexibility in handling changes to routine. There may also be a checklist of associated symptoms which are not part of eligibility determination, but can be used to further understand the child's symptom levels. If it is determined that:

1. The child CANNOT receive reasonable benefit from general education alone and requires specialized instruction
2. There are no other reasons he is not receiving reasonable benefit (exclusionary factors, such as excessive absence, lack of instruction, major medical conditions)
3. There is at least one symptom in each of the three categories (social, communication, behavior) listed on the checklist

Child Meets Eligibility

Then, the child is determined to be eligible for services under the IDEA and should receive special education, which includes the development of goals and associated services. This IEP will be reviewed annually at the IEP Annual Review meeting where goals are adjusted and progress is discussed. Every 3 years is the IEP Triennial Review where the entire comprehensive evaluation must be administered again and eligibility reevaluated. If the child is then able to receive reasonable benefit from general education alone, the services will be discontinued and the IEP will no longer be in place. If the child still needs services to be successful, the same eligibility checklists will be completed, new goals will be set, and service minutes can be adjusted to meet the new goals.

At the eligibility meeting, the parents sign consent to initiate services and these services are set to begin immediately. Services may be under an IEP or 504. The services should be aligned with the Least Restrictive Environment Mandate, which specifies that the child should be educated to the maximum extent appropriate with non-disabled peers. Often, services are provided in the classroom, whenever possible. This may include behavior supports for task initiation and participation, small reading groups, and social skills supports. Alternately, children may be pulled out of class for academic supports and interventions, social skills groups, mental health counseling, or behavioral intervention.

Child Does Not Meet Eligibility

School psychologists and mental health providers, such as school counselors and social workers, can provide critical supports to students who do not meet eligibility for an IEP. That may include social skills groups and counseling supports. Often, anxiety reduction strategies and coping skills supports can be helpful to students who do not meet eligibility criteria. It is also possible to consider whether or not the child meets criteria for another disability or to reevaluate in the future.

As shown on the Best-Practice Screening and Assessment graphic, the child may be determined ineligible for services. The child may be determined to be ineligible due to the lack or limited data supporting that he or she is unable to benefit from general education. The parents may or may not agree with this determination. In one of the author's experience, this happens a small percentage of the time and is likely due to poor information from outside clinicians or a lapse in communication between the school and family.

In the case that the family disagrees with the determination that the child is ineligible for services, parents can proceed in multiple ways. First, it may be appropriate to look at accommodations under a 504 Plan. Sometimes, these 504 Eligibility meetings can happen during the IEP Initial meeting, and in others, a separate eligibility is scheduled. Secondly, the family could consider pursuing an outside evaluation and then if the child is diagnosed with ASD or another eligible category of disability, the child could be evaluated again at school, using some of the existing data, and new testing as necessary. Finally, the family can request an Independent Educational Evaluation. A more comprehensive discussion regarding family rights and roles proceeds in the next chapter (Chap. 19). Generally, if the team keeps lines of communication open and does a thorough evaluation, with parent participation, this process is amicable and fluid. When discussions become tense, focus should always and exclusively be on the best interest of the child.

Remember that the law requires a Free and Appropriate Public Education; not "best possible" education and that means that given limited resources, there may be optimal services that, although potentially helpful, are not necessary for the child to receive reasonable benefit. In that case, the school district is not required to provide such services. However, the law is very clear that, if a service is necessary for the child to receive reasonable benefit and does not require a medical doctor to administer (Zero Reject Principle; Daniel RR Case: LRP Publications, 2007), the school must provide the service to the child. The essential question then for the family and the school to consider is whether any particular service is necessary for the child to receive reasonable educational benefit. If it is needed, the school district (not necessarily the home school) is obligated to provide the service, regardless of the cost.

Although all of these laws and ethical mandates may be daunting, the take-home message is that if the child needs services to receive reasonable benefit from his or her education, he or she is eligible for special education. However, it is important to state that if the child is determined ineligible, there is still plenty the school can do to support the child. There are a wide variety of supports that school teams can and should provide to support students, even outside of special education (Schwartz & Davis, 2008a, 2008b):

- Social skills groups
- Mental health support on informal basis
- Supported interactions with typically developing students
- Ongoing assessment and progress monitoring
- Speech and Language pragmatics groups
- Teacher consultation by IEP team or Mental Health provider
- Academic supports
- Reevaluate in a year

Comprehensive Information about Data Analysis during School Evaluations

Previously in this section, the evaluation process was outlined through four phases from identification or referral to eligibility determination. In order to keep the process clear, the specific information about reviewing data from school evaluation was not included in that section. Rather, following in the next section is a more comprehensive guide for considering signs and symptoms of ASD from data that is typically collected during an IEP initial evaluation. Although more comprehensive, this section could not possibly consider every evaluation instrument a school might conduct. There is a thorough look at evaluation instruments provided in Part III and in the associated table: Data Analysis Framework for Comprehensive Evaluation. However, this section offers a much more detailed account of academic information that can be used to screen for ASD symptoms, particularly in reading. In addition, this section provides a brief account of some of the informal tools and assessment instruments that may be available in schools and generally are not accessible by clinic teams. As stated early in this chapter, the school is uniquely positioned in many ways to understand how the child is functioning in their primary "occupation," which is generally considered to be "school." School psychologists and clinicians are uniquely positioned to gather collaborative data from home and school in order to inform evaluations and instruction (Esler et al., 2008). School teams may provide the essential information families need to understand their children's disabilities and to know how they can help them succeed in school and in life (Esler et al., 2008; Jaynes, 2005; Lines et al., 2011; Sheridan et al., 2008).

Detailed Description of School-Based Assessment Data That May Indicate ASD

Formal Assessment Types

Although some school teams have access to Gold Standard instruments such as the ADOS-2, generally school teams have a limited set of psychological instruments and screeners. This section will provide suggestions on how to use any of the screeners typically included during an IEP evaluation to do an Educational Identification of Autism. Similar to a clinic setting, school-based teams should consider the following, which they generally have access to in their buildings:

- Cognitive or IQ testing
- Social-Emotional rating scales such as the BASC-II, CDI, RCMAS
- Executive Functioning measures such as the BRIEF
- Academic testing such as the GORT-5, WIAT-III, WJ-IV
- Adaptive Scales such as the Vineland or SIB-R
- Speech and Language testing such as the CELF-V, or PPVT

In many districts in Colorado, school teams have access to: the Behavioral Assessment System for Children, Second Edition (BASC-II), the Vineland Scales of Adaptive Behavior (or other adaptive measure), and Wechsler Intelligence Scales for Children, Fourth or Fifth Edition (or other intelligence test). In addition to these, some schools have access to the Social Communication Questionnaire (SCQ), executive functioning measures like the BRIEF, and rating scales for autism such as the GARS.

Informal Assessment Types

In addition to standardized assessment, informal assessment is essential on school-based teams. In fact, it should be clearly stated here that school teams have a significant advantage over clinical teams in terms of informal assessment measures. Yell (2006) writes, "Far too often, unfortunately, evaluations of students for special education services focus exclusively on … standardized tests and ignores curriculum-based assessments, the informal tests, and direct observations that will lead directly to programming decisions" (p. 251). Considering this word of caution, a thorough autism assessment or screening can include the following:

- Student observations
- Work sampling
- Functional Analysis or Functional Behavioral Assessment
- Curriculum-Based Measurement
- Report card analysis
- Attendance Records
- Discipline and office referral data
- Standardized state achievement tests

Cognitive

Using IQ Test Data to Conduct a School-Based ASD Evaluation

A thorough review of the data that can be gathered from IQ tests was provided in Chap. 8, in the cognitive evaluation section. Interested readers will find a comprehensive approach to considering the child's approach to testing and problem-solving skills, the examiner–examinee interaction in Chap. 6 where facilitators/inhibitors are discussed. A brief highlight of areas to look for in a school-based autism screening is considered here.

One area to evaluate during an IQ test is the child's test behaviors. Sometimes children with autism are challenging to test during an IEP evaluation. The first red flag for autism would be an overarching difficulty establishing rapport with the child during the IQ test. The child may be aloof, defiant, or highly distractible, requiring inordinate administration strategies. Although not diagnostic, this should be noted as a sign of concern for symptoms related to autism or another neurodevelopmental disability.

Some of the primary markers for autism would first include low scores on the Comprehension subtest of the WISC-IV or V. This test has been shown in numerous studies (Mayes & Calhoun, 1999) to be the most difficult for children with autism. It is possible that the social complexity and abstract reasoning required for this test is difficult for children who present with difficulties in social understanding and communication problems. A study by Mayes and Calhoun in 1999 suggested that 33 % of young children who had IQ testing a year apart experienced significant change in IQ scores over time (Mayes & Calhoun, 2003). Thus, a degree of instability in IQ scores can be a marker for autism; the scores may increase or decrease more than would be expected for typically developing children. Another potential indicator is that some children with autism excel on tasks like Matrix Reasoning, which requires more nonverbal reasoning and limited verbal mediation strategies, as well as no time requirement. Children with autism tend to prefer nonverbal tasks, although they may not necessarily perform higher on the Perceptual Reasoning Index relative to the Verbal Comprehension Index, due partially to the fact that some of the nonverbal tests are timed.

Of note, children with autism generally tend to have unevenly developed skills, often requiring a General Ability Index due to problems with Processing Speed or Working Memory relative to stronger abilities on the Perceptual Reasoning or Verbal Comprehension indexes. Taken together, when screening for autism, consider the following: Quality of Rapport, Failure on the Comprehension test of the WISC-IV or V, Failure on Processing Speed or Working Memory, and relatively higher scores on Matrix Reasoning. Any of these findings should raise clinical concern in the school psychologist's mind and may be a part of an autism screener or assessment.

Social/Emotional

In order to conduct a thorough screening for autism, school-based clinicians should consider a clinical interview and a self-report emotional rating scale to be paramount. Children with autism present differently in many ways than children who are neurotypically developing and this is critical to conduct a personal interview; as well as, ask the child to rate his or her own emotions on standardized rating scale.

Essential data can be harvested from the child's self-report on screening instruments such as the Behavioral Assessment System for Children, Second Edition (BASC-II). An interesting pattern often emerges on this instrument. Children with autism may display this pattern: a frozen profile, coupled with clinically significant Atypicality. A "frozen profile" appears thusly: average ratings for Depression, Anxiety, School Problems, Learning Problems, and Relationships with Parents, etc. While certainly some students truly present this way, children with autism tend to simply not know how they feel. In order to assess this, a thorough screening would include a careful look at the examiner's own impressions, parent report, parent rating scales, and teacher interviews. If the child reports no symptoms in any area, but in fact teachers and parents are concerned about emotional problems, it is likely that the child has poor insight into his or her own feelings. This pattern should be considered a huge sign of concern for autism. It is highly likely that the child is experiencing clinically significant levels of emotional symptoms, but has such poor emotional understanding that he or she is unable to report it. Due to the fact that children with autism fail to fully develop in the emotional area of the brain, they generally are unable to successfully self-assess, regulate, or report on their feelings.

Further, children with autism often endorse clinically significant ratings on the Atypicality scale of the BASC-II. This scale includes items like, "I see things that others cannot see" or "I hear things that others cannot hear." In the author's experience, children with autism tend to endorse items like this because they are expressing either: their own personal experience, or their limited awareness of how another person's perspectives may be similar or different to one's own. When asked about these endorsements, one child with autism reported, on the item "I see things that others cannot see" with "I have an eagle eye." This assertion shows that the child does not fully understand the question, is interpreting quite literally, and may not have the ability to consider social desirability in his response. That is, he may not realize that it is considered odd or even pathologic to see things others cannot see. Instead, he "sees" this question literally and may believe his superhuman sight is an attribute, rather than a sign that he is different or "atypical" relative to peers his age.

In several cases, the authors have found that this "frozen profile" coupled with high scores in Atypicality is the very first indicator that autism may be present. Further, many children with autism may endorse concerns on the Attention Problems and Hyperactivity scales, due to the high comorbidity of autism and AD/HD symptoms (whether or not they meet full criteria for both disorders). School-based teams generally have screening tools such as the BASC-II at their disposal and patterns such as these are essential tools in an ASD eligibility.

Academic

Signs and Symptoms of ASD Using the WIAT-III

During academic assessment, in order to screen for autism, school-based clinicians may consider various areas of assessment and a child's performance in these areas. Reading comprehension assessment may provide useful information, as in some cases individuals with Autism Spectrum Disorders may perform poorly on these measures in comparison to overall reading performance. Reading assessment results that demonstrate an individual's struggle with making inferences, predicting, assessing emotions and motivations of characters, and summarizing or providing the main idea of a reading passage may be more likely to have autism. Children who prefer non-fiction and can provide detailed recall, sometimes wrote reporting of facts and information, but struggle with fiction, characters, and plot may have autism. This is not to say that most children with reading comprehension challenges have ASD, rather some may. An individual with challenges in this area could have a learning disability, a language disorder, or cognitive deficits.

When assessing academics, it is also useful to note significant performance discrepancies between areas like math, reading, writing, and oral language. Those with autism may have a very scattered profile academically, while a typically developing child is more likely to present with a more consistent profile (obviously those with learning disabilities will have area(s) that are much weaker than other areas depending on the disability). There may be language discrepancies when assessing expressive versus receptive domains in oral language. There exists a dearth of literature pertaining to challenges in mathematics in children with autism.

Because of a deliberate and slow response or processing style, those with ASDs often have challenges with fluency and will perform poorly on timed measures. Even when an individual with an ASD has solid academic performance on a standardized measure, he or she may struggle to break assignments into manageable parts, keep up with school work, or advocate for him or herself with teachers. The authors have observed that some children with ASD may struggle with the confine of a specific teaching method, for example, Common Core and other "show your work" methods. Curriculum-Based Measurements and classwork may show a child is struggling in subject such as math. On academic testing in which getting the correct answer is more important than "show your work," students may perform better than would be expected based on work samples. Overall, the significant rigidity and inflexibility often associated with ASD can impact the acquisition of academic skills. As such, it is important to monitor academic performance and provide support when it is needed to help individuals access an appropriate education.

Reading Tests

A primary predictor of autism found in the academic data is the "*hyperlexic*" reader profile. This means that the child is able to decode as well as or better than peers; whereas his reading *comprehension* is significantly impaired. A reading test, such as the GORT-5, provides an assessment of fluency, accuracy, and comprehension that can be used to assess this. Achievement tests can be utilized as well. It is also helpful to gather data from the classroom teacher on the child's reading performance. The hyperlexic pattern in autism is well-documented (Huemer & Mann, 2009; Mayes & Calhoun, 2007; Naples, 2010; Nation, Clarke, Wright, and Williams 2006; O'Connor & Klein, 2004; Snowling & Frith, 1986; Tager-Flusberg, 2006).

A range of comprehension problems have been identified in autism, including three primary areas of difficulty. First, children with autism tend to struggle to get the **main idea or the "gist"** of what they have read (Mayes & Calhoun, 2007; Nation et al., 2006; Nuske & Baven 2010). This failure to get the big picture is often referred to under a theory called "The Central Coherence Account" (Nuske, 2010; Tager-Flusberg, 2006). The Central Coherence Account is a conceptual model that sees the autistic brain as more compartmentalized and detail oriented, sometimes referred to as "finer grain size processing" (Naples, 201). A child with weak central coherence prefers local over global processing. It might be metaphorically represented thusly. A child may go on a field trip to a famous train station. He may recall the types of trains there, the wheels, the motors, the year make and model of the trains, and the train schedules. When asked after the trip, "where did you go?," he may struggle to provide the simple answer "it was a train station."

Similarly, when a child with autism reads a passage, even fluently and accurately, and is then asked, "what is this story basically about?," he cannot answer. Individuals with ASD may not be able to form a globally coherent mental model, a visual image, or a mental representation of text (Huemer & Mann, 2009; Nation et al., 2006). Thus, children with autism might be able to read fluently without gaining even a basic understanding of the passage, story, or book.

A second reading problem for children on the Spectrum is **"integration"** (Norbury & Bishop, 2002; Nuske & Baven, 2010). While typical children can relate parts of a story to another part, or integrate across multiple texts, children with ASD often find this difficult. Those with autism struggle to connect and integrate the information they read (Nuske & Baven, 2011; Wahlberg, 2001; White, Hill, Happe, & Frith, 2009). They are often unable to integrate their background knowledge with the new information gained from the text (Norbury & Bishop, 2002; Nuske & Baven, 2011; O'Connor & Klein, 2004; Wahlberg, 2001). Functional MRI analysis may reveal the reason for this poor integration. Children with autism appear to show what is termed "functional underconnectivity;" a term that refers to the fluid neuronal connections between the parts of the brain that process images and language, Broca's area, and Wernicke's area (Just, Cherkassky, Keller, and Minshew 2004). They explain,

"Note that our analysis shows that the activation between two areas is less synchronized in the autistic group specifically at the time that they are doing the sentence comprehension" (p. 1816).

In line with this research, on poor integration skills and functional underconnectivity, studies show that children with autism typically fail to understand or tell about *causal connections* in their stories (Losh & Capps, 2003; Willard, 2013). A related concern is difficulty with *sequencing*, which is seen in various autism assessment measures, such as "following multi-step directions" on adaptive scales, or the "following directions" subtest of the CELF-V. There seems to be a problem for children with autism in creating a mental story board; a difficulty understanding which events were significant and in which order they occurred.

These unique comprehension problems in autism lead to the third issue, **"narrative coherence"** (Diehl, Bennettto, and Young 2006; Losh & Gordon, 2014; Suh et al., 2014; Sutera et al., 2007; Tager-Flusberg, 2006; Willard, 2013). Narrative coherence is the ability to retell, summarize, or talk about a passage or event in their lives. Children with autism include irrelevant details, extraneous themes, and go off on-tangents when producing a narrative. Their narratives lack a logical sequence, a main idea, and are laden with irrelevant details. It is important to note that these differences exist, even controlling for the effect of IQ. Thus, although the children with autism may be able to logically understand the story as well as neurotypicals, they cannot put the story together and retell it in a coherent fashion.

Some studies have found that children with autism can tell stories from a simple picture book, but struggle more when the narratives include their own emotional experiences or when the narrative task is more demanding (Losh & Capps, 2003; Losh & Gordon, 2014). In line with this problem, children with autism tend to include their personal interests in the story, resulting in a lack of coherence with the overall narrative. For example, (Willard, 2013) found that one of the children with Asperger's told an elaborate story about diurnal and nocturnal turtles and tortoises when telling her story. In the picture, the main idea is not about the turtle itself, but about what the turtle is witnessing (flying frogs). Thus, although the child clearly had the cognitive ability to understand and tell about the picture, she did not focus on the main idea, rendering her narrative incoherent and hard to follow.

Taken together, children with autism tend to struggle to provide a globally coherent and logical narrative of what they read or experienced. Suh et al. (2014) studied the narrative coherence of individuals with autism as a potential predictor of optimal outcomes. They found several unique patterns in the narratives of children with ASD. Individuals with autism often included ambiguous pronoun referents in their narratives, meaning that they did not tend to know how to refer back to characters they had previously mentioned during their stories. The recognized autism experts on this study postulated that individuals with ASD may use ambiguous pronouns because they fail to consider the perspective of the listener during communication; therefore, not realizing whether or not the listener knows which character he or she is referring to in the narrative (Suh et al., 2014).

School-based clinicians are wise to consider difficulties with comprehension relative to average or better decoding skills, also known as "hyperlexia," as a red flag for autism. Problems with understanding the main idea of the story, challenges with sequencing and integration, and poor narrative coherence are all potential signs that an Autism Spectrum Disorder may be present.

Willard (2013) proposes that it is possible to use the story-telling task of the ADOS-2 as a means for evaluating reading comprehension patterns common to children with autism. The Willard Imagery Observation Scales (WIOS: Willard, 2013) is a patented assessment that can be used by clinicians to rate the narrative quality of the client's responses when telling the story, *Tuesday* during ADOS administration. Factor analysis and survey design techniques were incorporated into development of this innovative assessment approach for ASD. This use of the story telling task as a way of assessing narrative quality in autism has been used in other studies for different purposes, finding similar results (Suh et al., 2014). Both Willard (2013) and Suh (2014) found that children with autism were less likely to include the "gist" of the story and to name the story characters as typically developing children.

The first domain of the WIOS assesses a child's narratives in terms of the Main Idea of the story. The main idea domain was designed based on the Weak Central Coherence Account of autism described previously. The items within the Main Idea domain assess a child's ability to tell about: (1) Characters, (2) Actions, and (3) Sequence. The child's responses are rated 0-2, which is an assessment of the child's narrative quality and the degree to which it demonstrates imagery-related comprehension skills. The integration domain was designed based on the Functional-Underconnectivity theory of autism. The Integration domain assesses: (4) Gestures, (5) Emotions, (6) Perspective Taking, (7) Cause and Effect, and (8) Integrative Statements. Willard (2013) found through regression analysis on a sample of 71 children that the children with autism ($N=48$) scored significantly lower on the total score, the domain scores, and on all of the items, except "actions (#2)," as compared to typically developing children ($N=23$). This research indicates that children with autism struggle to identify the: characters, sequence, emotions, perspectives, and cause and effect relationships in stories. They have significant difficulty integrating across the text in their own narratives and using gestures in storytelling.

The WIOS allows examiners to evaluate the degree of comprehension difficulties shown in the child's narrative that are commonly seen in children with autism.

The child's imagery (ability to create a coherent mental representation of a story) is considered as a primary skill that is required for strong reading comprehension; a hypothesized weakness area in ASD. In utilizing the WIOS, responses are coded as to the narrative quality, imagery-related comprehension skills, the child's understanding of the character's emotions and perspectives, and the ability to put the story together. This WIOS screener can be used along with clinical observation and reading assessments to (a) clarify whether or not the child's narrative quality is characteristic of autism, and (b) whether or not the children's reading comprehension skills are likely to be affected by their disability of autism (Willard, 2013).

Concluding Remarks on School-Based Assessment

This concludes the section on how to conduct a school-based evaluation for ASD within an RtI framework. The reader was guided through a process of Informal Observations, Tier 1 interventions such as classroom accommodations for all students, Tier 2 interventions such as social skills groups, and Tier 3 interventions such as behavior plans. Next, the school team must go through a process, using progress-monitoring tools and summative evaluation to determine if the child is responding to these interventions and closing the gap with peers. If the child is not showing expected growth in the interventions, it is time to obtain consent and begin an IEP evaluation. The reader was guided through the process of collecting observations of Communication, Social, and Behavior skills. An approach was included for conducting interviews with parents, teachers, and students. Next, information regarding formal assessment of Cognitive, Social, Emotional, Adaptive, and Academic domains was provided.

Finally, the reader was guided through eligibility determinations. If the child is determined to be eligible, an Individual Education Plan is written that includes services and accommodations to meet the child's needs in the identified areas. If the child is determined not to be eligible, there are interventions and supports that can be put in place, the family can pursue an outside evaluation, or the team could consider a reevaluation in a year. When teams collaborate with each other and closely with the family, this process should be seamless and smooth. Children with ASD are well-served by school teams who conduct these comprehensive evaluations within an evidence-based RtI framework of this nature.

Chapter 19
School, Parent, and Community Partnerships

Abstract Children with ASD can be supported more comprehensively when school teams make a concerted and committed effort to collaborate with diagnostic clinics, community agencies, and families. In some cases, a clinical diagnosis may be needed and the school team might be able to reduce the time and cost of the evaluation by providing any screening data the school has on-hand to the diagnostic team. Specifically, if the school-based team has completed cognitive, social-emotional, and adaptive testing, sharing these data with a clinical evaluation team may conserve critical resources and may allow for more comprehensive testing of ASD and comorbid disorders. These types of collaborations fall nicely in line with the principles of effective family–school–community partnerships as these data-sharing opportunities are in the best interest of the child (*The power of family–school partnering (FSP): A practical guide for school mental health professionals and educators*, New York, 2011). It is the authors' firm belief that school teams should make every attempt to foster strong partnerships with families. This collaboration can be described as, "Partnering is a relationship involving close cooperation between parties having joint rights and responsibilities" (*Schools and families: Creating essential connections for learning*, New York, 2001). The continuation of care that is created when there is a symbiotic relationship between schools, parents, and community agencies can make a significant difference in empowering families to help their children to obtain the support they critically need across the many environments where they learn and live.

Keywords Family–school partnership (FSP) • Family–school–community partner-ships • Parental advocacy in ASD • School advocacy for families • School referrals to clinical evaluations in ASD • Parental anger, denial, and grief in ASD • Parental involvement in urban schools • FSP improves academic outcomes • Leffingwell • Wraparound services

Although different, neither school-based assessment nor clinical diagnosis is considered inferior; simply different processes for distinctly separate purposes. However, it is proposed in this chapter that it is entirely possible, and indeed, can be considered best practice for school teams to collaborate with outside providers such that both teams can inform each other and the child may be eligible for school-based services; as well as, considered for a clinical diagnosis. Schwartz and Davis (2008a,

2008b) explain, "A more appropriate role for most school psychologists is to act as the triage coordinator for the data coming out of the schools that can inform the diagnostic team" (p. 1518). Thus, in addition to the educational eligibility role defined in Chap. 18, school psychologists (and other school-based professionals) can serve as the liaison between the school, parents, and community clinicians in order to get families the critical help they need.

As shown in the table on the next page, the providers are different in a clinical evaluation; typically primarily conducted by a licensed psychologist and potentially other licensed professionals on an interdisciplinary team; in schools they are conducted by the IEP team. The outcome is different in that children who are assessed in a clinic may also be diagnosed with comorbid conditions; as well as autism; whereas school-based evaluations are only intended to determine eligibility for services. The evaluation tools are different as has been explained throughout Chap. 18; clinical tools are used for diagnostic assessments, while schools may utilize more informal assessments and observation protocols, as well as interviews and academic testing. The cost is entirely different as clinical evaluations tend to be at a significant cost to families; whereas school-based assessments are free to families as an obligation of FAPE. Finally, the location of the evaluation is different because clinics and hospitals conduct diagnostic assessments, while school-based assessments are conducted in the school or district building settings (Table 19.1).

The referral from a school-based professional can enact better outcomes for students. Indeed, Schwartz and Davis (2008a, 2008b) explain, "The key to work-

Table 19.1 Clinical diagnosis vs. educational identification of ASD

Clinical diagnostic evaluation	Eligibility determination
Provided by a licensed psychologist, pediatrician, or psychiatrist OR an arena evaluation may be multi-disciplinary including: Developmental Pediatrician, Neuropsychologist, Speech Therapist, Occupational Therapist, Doctoral Interns and Practicum Students in Psychology	Provided by a Child Find or IEP team which may include a school psychologist, speech therapist, occupational therapist, and special education teacher
Outcome is a Diagnosis of ASD and differential diagnosis of potential comorbid conditions such as ADHD, Anxiety, or Depression	Outcome is a determination of eligibility for services under the ASD criteria and creation of an Individualized Education Program (IEP)
Evaluation must utilize diagnostic tools such as the ADOS or ADI-R or both as well as clinical observation, interview, standardized assessment, and parent participation	Evaluation must use tools necessary to identify every area of potential special education need. This may include standardized assessment and informal measures but there is no requirement that diagnostic tools be used
Evaluation costs $1500–$3500 and may be covered by insurance	Evaluation is Free as a part of FAPE
Evaluation can occur in a medical clinic, hospital, or psychologist office, either local or out of state	Evaluation must be completed through local school district

Adapted from CDE et al. (2014)

ing with children with ASD and their families is for school psychologists to recognize when additional support is necessary and to know to provide, or make the appropriate referral to professionals who can provide, the type or amount of support needed to help the child succeed"(pp. 1517–1518). This means that school professionals should be prepared to not only support students and consider eligibility for an IEP, but also be ready to deliver appropriate referrals for clinical and community services, as needed.

Wraparound and Collaboration between School and Community Providers

In many cases, the school-based professional can best serve the client by providing a comprehensive support structure that includes home, school, and community providers. If a school is to receive a diagnosis from an outside clinic, the team has several obligations. The team *must consider* these data as a part of the eligibility review process (OCALI, 2014). At a minimum, the school team should consider whether or not the outside evaluation provides some evidence that an eligibility review at school is needed in order to determine services. Further, the outside evaluation may be used to expedite the school process in that if the outside evaluation includes standardized assessment data such as adaptive skill scores, cognitive scores, or emotional rating scales, the school team may not be required to repeat these assessments. Finally, in the case where the outside evaluation suggests the need for services, the school team can and should begin providing services (potentially Tier 2 or Tier 3 interventions), even before the eligibility meeting (Schwartz & Davis, 2008a, 2008b). Taken together, although the eligibility determination and medical diagnosis process are quite different and separate procedures, they can share a symbiotic and collaborative relationship, which is in the best interest of the child's need for services, both in and out of school.

In terms of this symbiotic relationship, the school team can also inform the diagnostic team in helping the child obtain a medical diagnosis and provision of services at home or in the community. For example, the school provider may conduct a screening process and these data may be shared with the diagnostic team by way of a letter or record review. It also may be that the school completes a full IEP evaluation for ASD, determines that the child is eligible for services, and then provides the diagnostic team with these data as a part of the outside evaluation.

This collaboration may allow for the family to obtain Cognitive Behavioral Therapy, Applied Behavior Analysis Therapy, parent consult services, or medication through a psychiatrist or pediatrician, under their insurance plan. When the child experiences significant impairments in multiple environments, this sort of collaboration can be critical in order to obtain better outcomes for students with ASD. Recognized experts in school-based services for ASD (Schwartz & Davis, 2008a, 2008b) explain, "Likewise, the literature suggests we may see more robust results (i.e., quicker acquisition and increased generalization) and provide better outcomes for children if we teach them new skills in a variety of settings (e.g., general education, community, and self-contained) and with a variety of materials" (1518). Given these factors, both a school evaluation and a clinic diagnostic assessment are needed, and again, the collaboration between both teams is extremely helpful to the family.

Collaboration and Partnership with Families

This section is written for school teams.

The importance of partnering with families cannot be overstated. Children make more progress and school professionals find increased success, when parents and school teams are on the same page. Lines, Miller, and Arthur-Stanley (2011), recognized experts in collaborative partnering with families, explain it thusly, "We believe that family-school partnering must be a 'non-negotiable' component of preschool through high-school transitions. There must be a pervasive 'no excuses' attitude" (p. 13).

It should be stated here that although there is certainly variation in symptoms, the families that school teams are tasked with helping generally have suffered a great deal on the part of their children's disabilities. Unfortunately, many parents of children with disabilities feel very much alone. To make matters worse, many parents feel blamed by school teams for their children's behavior problems. A recognized expert in the parental grief process (Moses, 1983) identifies the powerful feelings that parents experience "dramatically influence their relationships with professionals who work with their children" (p. 157). It may be that a well-meaning, hardworking, and under-resourced school professional is caught in the cross-hairs of parental grief, denial, guilt, and shattered dreams. This serves as no excuse for parents or school teams to give up on each other; rather, shared understanding and shared responsibility serve as the foundation for successful family–school partnerships (Christenson & Sheridan, 2001; Esler, Godber, & Christenson, 2008; Lines et al., 2011).

Parents are faced with modifying dreams and expectations for their children and deal with the "devastating and continuing loss of having an impaired child" (Moses, no date). However, even in the throes of this grief, school teams and parents can share an effective, collaborative, and essential relationship that is shown in the research to lead to best outcomes for kids. Indeed, parental involvement in school-based services has been shown in large-scale meta-analysis, including 41 studies, to be directly linked to better outcomes for students, including higher GPAs and academic test scores (Jaynes, 2005).

Parents of children with disabilities often experience anger, depression, and guilt. Many parents find that this guilt originates from identifying broken dreams and expectations; as well as, a lack of control over their children's behavior and outcomes. Moses (1983) explains, "When an initial diagnosis of developmental disabilities is received by a parent, a grief process begins. The parental dreams are almost always shattered by learning of the disability… the initial diagnosis often marks the destruction of a cherished and significant dream" (p. 157). Of course families may have all kinds of reactions to the news of their child's disabilities. Some parents may not experience broken dreams, but almost certainly there is a period of adjustment as parents are continually faced with having to adjust some of their plans and expectations for their children.

Now, putting oneself in the shoes of the school-based professional, it is important to think about calls home to families and what these "reports" might mean to them. The very sight of the phone ringing with a call from the school may set off a familiar pattern of grief, anxiety, and panic. "What did my child do now?" parents begin to think. One particular parent consulted on the writing of this book, indicating the importance of reaching out to families in a positive way (Leffingwell, Personal Communications, April 28, 2015). Leffingwell (2015) shares that a positive call from the school brings an indescribable sense of comfort and joy; not often experienced by parents of children with disabilities. Based on this conversation, one of the authors has included as part of her daily practice what she terms a "+1" call every day. That is, she makes it a point to call one family every day with entirely good news. Examples might be:

- I noticed how happy Joey seems today.
- I noticed that Margot was socially reciprocal in group today.
- I noticed that Christie was kind to another student today.
- I noticed how Micah got started right away on his math today.
- I noticed that Nicholas recovered from a setback today.
- I noticed how Mathew never gave up on a hard task today.

A statement like those mentioned above may be the first time a parent has ever heard something positive from the school. Sometimes just one "+1" phone call is the precise element that creates a family–school partnership, even when there might have been a contentious or challenging relationship in the past. When school professionals reach out like this, parents tend to believe that the school professional cares about their children and see the delight and magic that lies within them. Sometimes, this type of communication may empower families and help them find inner strength to endure the challenges that an autism diagnosis presents.

Alternately, when nothing but negative communication comes from school, this bond can be quickly broken, causing families to feel mistrustful, and alone in their fight for their children with autism. Moses (1983) defines the process thusly, "Like the other states of grieving, anger serves a unique function. One's sense of justice is violated when an unfair event such as parenting an impaired child befalls a person. Anger is the vehicle that permits the parent to restructure their concepts concerning justice … allowing that parent a more comfortable system that can better explain or accept life's unpredictable occurrences" (p. 163). Sometimes in the process of observing their child's suffering and pervasive challenges, parents of children with disabilities feel anger directed at school professionals is justified. However, even in the face of these seemingly unscalable mountains, family–school partnerships are possible. The authors of this book implore school professionals to remember that, "both school and home reciprocally influence and help determine the path children's development takes. Home-school collaboration reflects the critical interface these two vital, socializing systems have on children's learning" (Esler et al., 2008, p. 918). School-based practices such as the "+1 call" can be the impetus for family–school partnerships and make a monumental difference for families.

Another important role family–school partnerships can play is in a learning capacity regarding the child's needs in various settings. School professionals can offer expertise on learning needs, behavior management, peer relationships, and communication with teachers. Parents, as the experts on their children, can offer expertise on how the child functions at home; the child's wants and desires, background information on their child, challenges at home, and family dynamics. Schools are charged with learning from families to enhance services and practices.

It is generally the case in one author's experience that behavior plans that fail to include the parent's participation are generally unsuccessful. It is her firm belief that for children to successfully change their challenging behaviors, the parents and school teams must be working together. This might include point sheets that go home for a reward, daily feedback to families via email, or reinforcement systems that include a home–school component. For example, the parent might buy a book at the book-fair and leave it with the school psychologist to offer the child upon successful completion of an assignment in class. Alternately, the parents might contact the school team and share that the child did homework independently and be rewarded at school with a sticker, praise, or a marshmallow. There are a myriad of options school teams can discover here. The take-home message is this: to serve the child, school professionals MUST serve the family.

Collaboration and Partnership with Community Agencies

School-based teams are often charged with two tasks (although the clinical piece is not legally required) when they suspect a child may have an Autism Spectrum Disorder. First, they must determine whether or not the disability likely is having an educational impact, requiring specialized instruction and in that case an IEP evaluation must ensue. Second, the team needs to think about whether or not a full clinical diagnosis is needed. The first issue was addressed elsewhere in Chap. 18 where the elements of a school-based evaluation were discussed. The second issue about clinical diagnosis is considered here.

As mentioned in Chap. 18, *Wraparound* and Positive Behavioral Interventions and Supports share an integrated and best-practice context for supporting families in schools and community settings. Wraparound is often referred to as a service; however, wraparound is actually a planning approach that includes relevant community members in a collaborative relationship that serves to improve outcomes for students (Eber, Sugai, Smith, & Scott, 2002). Wraparound programs include essential elements to be effective for families. Eber and colleagues (2002) suggest these components: "(1) Community based, (2) Individualized and strengths based, (3) Culturally competent, (4) Families as full and active partners, (5) Team-based process involving family, child, natural supports, agencies, and community supports, (6) Flexible approach to funding, (7) Balance of formal and informal community resources, (8) Unconditional commitment, (9) Development of individualized services/support plan based on a community/neighborhood, interagency collaborative process, and (10) Outcomes determined and measured through the team process" (p. 73).

A school psychologist or other IEP team member with expertise in childhood disabilities should consider wraparound as an approach for understanding the needs of students within the larger systems of their lives, such as the home, neighborhoods, community, agencies, culture, and belief systems that are important to them. Wraparound can be defined as, "This process is used to build consensus within a team of professionals, family members, and natural support providers to improve the effectiveness, efficiency and relevance of supports and services developed for children and their families" (Eber et al., 2002, p. 73). In order to effectively incorporate best-practice wraparound programs into the school team's practice, it is important to know when children should be referred to community providers for support. Following in this next section are guidelines for determining when to make such referrals.

Guiding Questions for a Referral to Outside Providers

1. Does the child's potential disability have a pervasive impact on his or her life primarily outside of the school building?

   In this case, it could be that the child's disability does not impact his education significantly, but the parent's report concerns about friendships and extracurricular activities outside of school. Thus, a clinical diagnosis may be helpful to address the family's concerns. The school team could help with the evaluation process, but there is not necessarily a need to go forward with special education eligibility determination.

2. Does the child or family need intensive therapy that is likely to go well beyond the scope of what can be provided at school?

   It may be that the child clearly shows a need for Applied Behavior Analysis therapy, Cognitive Behavioral Therapy, or Family Systems Therapy (for example), which may not be available through the school. In this case, medical diagnosis may allow for insurance coverage for these therapies. One potentially complimentary service the school could provide in this case would be "lunch bunch" or social skills groups. In an ideal collaborative relationship, consistent with the wraparound approach, the outside therapist and the counselor or school psychologist could collaborate on the specific skills to address during social skills groups at school. This model has a distinct advantage over outside services in that the students in the group are the very peers who the therapist is trying to teach kids to interact with; aiding in generalizing of skills. The inclusion of typical peers who are trained to support students with ASDs can be a critically important factor in social skills groups (Baker, 2014a, 2014b; Wolfberg, 2003).

Further, lunch bunch and similar programs can provide a support group, which can protect against bullying and assist with navigating the social world at school.

Often, the authors have found that these lunch groups give the child with an ASD the opportunity to be exposed to appropriate peers who provide modeling and emotional support. Further, the facilitator can aide peers in the offering of feedback about any misconceptions of recent social situations. For example, one of the authors has found that the child with ASD feels "wronged" or rejected, when in fact, the peers report that it was he who did the rejecting due to misinterpretations. Thus, correcting these ill-constructed social models can have a truly therapeutic impact on students with ASDs in the school building.

3. Does the team suspect comorbid conditions such as ADHD, Anxiety, Depression, Bipolar, Attachment Disorder, or a Trauma- and Stressor-Related Disorder?

    In this case, it is highly likely that services beyond the school may be necessary. The only time when the inability to provide these services could be in conflict with FAPE would be when the child's emotional disability is adversely affecting his education. In that case, school services should be implemented; however, there is no requirement that the services be mutually exclusive. Indeed, it may be that the services provided by the school to address the emotional condition are developed and facilitated collaboratively with therapists in the community (again, this is consistent with principles of FSP and wraparound explained earlier). If the child's autism and comorbid emotional disability are significantly pervasive, it is reasonable that the school team has the requirement of meeting the child's school-related needs; the remaining supports can be provided in the community through more intensive therapies, which may necessitate a clinical diagnosis to secure.

4. Does the team suspect that the school tools may be insufficient to uncover whether or not the child's difficulties stem from ASD or another disability?

    Sometimes, the child's needs are so complex that the school team does not believe it is qualified to address all the areas of the child's needs. Legally, the school team must address the child's special education needs. However, it may be necessary for the school team to either: (A) contract with an outside clinician who is qualified to help the team evaluate the symptoms; or (B) provide a referral to an outside provider who can do an evaluation.

In highly complex cases, the family may request an **Independent Educational Evaluation (IEE)**. This would likely occur when the school's evaluation was deemed by the family to be insufficient in addressing all the child's areas of disability. In this case, an IEE is warranted at the public expense as a right under the IDEA, which means that the school district has to pay for the outside evaluation (LRP Pubs, 2007). The law reads 34 CFR 300.502 (a) (3) (i): "an evaluation conducted by a qualified examiner who is not employed by the public agency responsible for the evaluation of the child in question" (p. 134). Although the parent has the right to request an IEE, the school district can pursue a due process hearing and if the school's evaluation is considered sufficient, the parent still has the right to the IEE but the school district is not required to cover the cost. Even if the school district does not agree with the IEE, school teams are required to "consider" the evaluation when evaluating services. Although this issue of an IEE may be perceived as a combative or litigious process, in the authors' experience, the IEE can be collaborative and may result in the most peaceful and objective evaluation for certain complex cases.

Taken together, if the team has concerns that an eligibility meeting either: (A) is not warranted due to the fact that the entire team and family do not see any educational impact of the potential disability; or (B) the team is concerned that the eligibility meeting may not provide the families with all that they need in terms of services or diagnostic information; the clinical evaluation may be needed. In this case, it is recommended that the school team help the family with this process.

One way to help the family is for the school psychologist or IEP team to write a letter to the outside provider highlighting the concerns evidenced at school (sample letter provided at the end of this chapter). This letter can be as brief as one page, so long as it includes the following elements. First, the school psychologist should discuss the reason for the referral... although the "referral" is not directly made to any individual or agency. If the school district "refers" to individual agencies, the district could be liable for the cost of the evaluation or for any problems incurred during the evaluation, so it is important that the school team remain neutral and provide only lists of potential resources (as would occur if the family requests outside therapists). That said, principles of effective family–school partnership indicate that school may maintain a comprehensive list of numerous competent community resources for the purposes of providing families with referral options for "specific needs" (Lines et al., 2011). As such, due to the complexity of autism, schools should maintain lists of *multiple* options for evaluations when a clinical diagnosis of autism is suspected.

The letter should explain the relationship the school psychologist has with the student; including a comment about how long she or he has known the student and in what capacity (lunch bunch, individual counseling, or in the classroom). Then, there should be data provided about any screening instruments conducted and the findings of these. In the author's experience, the school psychologist might include information about the Social Responsiveness Scale (SRS), Social Communication Questionnaire (SCQ), the Behavioral Assessment System for Children, Second Edition (BASC-II), or the Revised Children's Manifest Anxiety Scales (RCMAS). In addition to these more clinical screeners, information about the child's academic performance can be included, such as the child's grades, teacher feedback, standardized test scores on state tests, curriculum-based measures, or work samples. The letter should conclude with the school psychologist's concerns about the student. In some cases, the letter may include a list of potential Rule-Out's for the diagnostic team to consider. To avoid inadvertently suggesting a diagnosis has been made at school, it is often preferred to make a list of symptoms, rather than to provide the rule-out categories specifically. In an appendix to this letter, the school psychologist can provide tables of scores for any instruments administered. At times, the outside agency may request more specific results from the BASC-II or WISC-V. This can be provided only when it is clear that these scores will only be provided and read by: a psychologist, psychiatrist, medical doctor, or other person qualified to interpret the scores.

In some cases, a letter may not be sufficient to report on all of the child's needs or to provide all necessary data to the diagnostic team or medical doctor. In that case, a "Psychoeducational Report" can be written. This is most helpful in cases where an outside team is requesting "school records." In order to respect confidentiality and test security, a report is the best way to make sure the family has what they need in terms of data but without provision of protocols or privacy protecting school records. In this case, the same data would be provided as listed above: Reason for Referral, Instruments Administered, Results, Conclusions, and an Appendix with test results. These reports are certainly not commonplace due to the fact that a letter or even a phone call may be sufficient to support the family in getting all pertinent school data to the psychologist or medical doctor. Further, it is strongly recommended that school administrators review any letters or reports before they are sent. Finally, it is important that the report goes directly to the family, who then provides it to the medical professionals of their choosing; rather than the school team sending it out based on the parent's request. Certainly, consent to share information would be signed to be clear that the family's intent is for these data to be shared; however, it is still best practice that the family "owns" the psychoeducational report and can choose where and when information is shared with outside providers.

A Word on Parental Advocacy

This section is written for families.

It is important to say a word about advocacy in the school environment here because there is so much controversy and misinformation about what parents must do to advocate for their children when the parents suspect the child may have autism. Too often, the authors of this book, who may even get involved in forensic cases against school districts, hear the following, "I had to fight the school but I got the following ___." Schools do have limited resources and lots of children to serve; however, many school teams are competent people who will do whatever they can to help students. It may be necessary to be persistent. Certainly, if the school professionals are not doing their jobs, it may be the parent's role to be a squeaky wheel; and in some cases, if the district refuses to do what is best for a child, then legal action or fierce advocacy may be needed.

However, an angry, litigious, and fighting approach should simply not be assumed as the posture of any parent advocate. Moses (1983) reminds parents that in their advocacy, anger may be a normal part of the process; however, just as we say to our children, feelings of anger are okay, but "acting out" towards others in anger is not acceptable; we must not allow angry feelings to result in mistreatment toward professionals. He explains, "Most professionals are hardworking, underpaid, sensitive people who are genuinely struggling with the same child who is offering you so much difficulty. They truly need your advice, suggestions, and help, but will have the same reactions to rejection, criticism, and emotional assault as you would, were they to behave that way toward you" (p. 165). Thus, parents are advised to be gentle with themselves; as well as, the people who are attempting to serve their children.

To make matters worse, parent groups sometimes might make a parent feel that he or she has somehow sold the child short if there was no "fight" with the school for any particular service. Generally, it is good practice to be involved, stay on top of the accommodations and services, and ensure that the school is doing what is needed for the child. However, assuming a combative posture may in fact be doing a disservice in not only energy wasted, but also arguing with the very people who parents need to help them. In the case that legal representation is warranted, consult the Forensic chapter (Chap. 17) of this book for more information. However, if parents feel reasonably assured that the school is doing their best to provide services to the child, there is no need to worry that parents are failing as advocates; it could in fact just be in a good school with professionals who know what they are doing — and this does happen!

All three authors on this book have the experience of being essentially on both sides of the table in advocating for a child. One side of the table would be the school team and the other side of the table would be the family and the family's advocate (s), if present. There are full books dedicated to helping families' advocate for kids and this is not intended to be a comprehensive guide. However, a few words of advocacy advice are offered below.

Know Your Rights

- Right to prior written notice and giving consent.
- Right to be involved in the evaluation and decision-making process.
- Right to obtain official copy of IEP or 504.
- Right to disagree.
- Right to adequate notice and multiple available times for IEP meetings.
- Right to an independent education evaluation (IEE).
- Right to engage in dispute resolution.

Do

- Do bring important documents and papers.
- Do share information with the school team regarding concerns, data from outside evaluations, family dynamics, and other data that could help the team make informed decisions.
- Do ask questions. Although parents are not always directly interviewed for IEP evaluations, this is certainly always an option parents can request. Parents can call and ask for a meeting during the evaluation process and provide any pertinent input.
- Do have an open mind and be honest with yourself.
- Do keep communication channels open.

Don't

- Don't be intimidated.
- Don't lose sight of the goal, which is to identify your child's needs and the appropriate services to meet those needs.

- Don't assume the school is trying to withhold services.
- Don't go into the evaluation, preparing for a "fight."
- Don't expect the school to "fix" everything.
- Don't quit!

More on Family Rights and Roles

Regarding the rights of families, it must be stated here that parents do have the right to a "comprehensive evaluation to discover all special education needs, whether or not linked to the disability category." That is, although the RtI process is recommended, this does not serve as a reason to delay an evaluation, if the family believes one is necessary. If families "formally request an IEP evaluation," the school has to provide it. Parents do not have the right to choose which assessments will be done. For example, just because parents would like an IQ test to be conducted, that does not necessitate the school to do one. It is generally considered best practice that all IEP initial evaluations include IQ testing, but there is no legal mandate that this be included. Or, if the parents would like an ADOS-2, for example, the school team does not have to administer this measure, provided that there is an alternative process by which autism symptoms can be assessed for the purposes of educational identification. If the child is determined to not be able to receive reasonable benefit from general education alone, an IEP or 504 plan must be put in place, given that certain exclusionary factors have been ruled out.

Parents should know that they have the right to be involved in the IEP Evaluation and decision-making process, as well as a right to obtain an official copy of the IEP document and any associated meeting minutes, including service minutes and any decisions made regarding the child during the IEP meeting. Although some evaluations may not require much in the way of parent interview or intense collaboration with families, parents should know that they have the right to be involved with the evaluation. Parents can check on the status of the evaluation, ask to be interviewed as part of the process, and can invite family members who are significant in the child's life to be interviewed as part of the evaluation or included as participants at the IEP meeting.

In some cases, families choose to provide letters to the IEP team from significant individuals in the child's life, highlighting concerns. In one author's practice, these letters have provided particularly useful data for more complex IEP evaluations. This allows the team to hear from multiple perspectives in the child's life that might otherwise be missed. In general, keep in mind that parents are experts on their children and school teams generally want to hear about the parent's thoughts and concerns as critical data during the evaluation. The school team has the expertise of knowing which services and accommodations may be helpful to the child and thus the IEP meetings are intended to be a collaborative process between families and school teams. In this way, letters and interview data from parents and extended family may serve as critical data in the evaluation process.

Parents have the right to disagree with the results of the evaluation. At the IEP meeting, parents are provided with the "Parent Rights" document. If parents need more information, they are advised to read this. It will tell the family of their rights in the IEP process and clearly explain what to do when there is disagreement over the evaluation or the provision of services. When there is disagreement, there are several options. The IEP team can do further evaluation if the assessment is not deemed to be "sufficiently comprehensive." Although this doesn't happen a lot, anyone on the IEP team, including parents, can decide that the evaluation was not comprehensive enough and then the school must continue evaluating (or demonstrate that the evaluation was comprehensive with a body of evidence).

Another option is for parents to request an IEE (explained earlier in this chapter). Finally, the parents and IEP team can simply discuss alternate services that may be more acceptable to the family. Keep in mind that just because that meeting is over, that does not mean the "case is closed." Parents can always request more meetings or refuse the services being offered. Even in the case where the team feels the child does not require an IEP and the parents feel that an IEP is needed, it may be that the team decides to reevaluate in a year in order to see if the symptoms are more or less significant with time for maturation and to try additional interventions. Finally, the family can alternately pursue a private clinical evaluation and then request that the school conduct an additional IEP evaluation in consideration of these results.

Keep in mind, as is stated repeatedly in this chapter, even if the outside evaluator determines the child has autism, and even if the clinical team recommends an IEP, the child does not automatically qualify for an IEP. The IEP team must determine that the symptoms have significant educational impact as well. Remember also that certain services, such as those received for reading and math disabilities, require a significantly low score on one or several standardized assessments in order to be eligible for services. Although this may seem like a "wait to fail" model or unfair in that the child has to be substantially struggling to receive services, bear in mind that these services are specifically designed for children who have such a substantially limiting disability that they cannot receive reasonable benefit from their education. These services are not intended to be the "best possible" educational services and they are not intended for children without disabilities.

Concluding Remarks on Family–School Partnerships

If parents feel confused, they are encouraged to ask questions. If they are still concerned, ask more. School teams tend to throw around acronyms and data points as if everyone would know what these mean; in fact, people don't. However, school teams are, as a rule, happy to sit down with parents and explain any part of the process to or provide more information. Generally, if lines of communication are lost, it is smart to open them back up. It may be that the team has lost sight of the family's needs or is unaware of the family's questions. However, if indeed the relationship with the school has flown south, it is time to get some answers. Parents can always ask to talk to a higher authority in the district and this is generally fairly transparent. There may be a director over special education or an assistant director to whom parents can ask their questions. Again, just as with any other organizational process, parents are advised to assume best intentions and seek to understand first. It is recommended that the parents ask the IEP team directly about pursuing a higher authority in the district before going this route. Often, the school team can clear up misunderstandings and there is no need for additional parties. Again, there are resources provided in this book for more serious cases where the school has trespassed on the rights of the child or the family, and in that instance, it may be necessary to have an entirely different approach (see Forensic Evaluation chapter). In summary, it is a good idea for parents to be familiar with some of the basic rights surrounding the IEP evaluation process and special education. However, it should not be assumed that this journey is arduous, combative, or litigious. At times, parents may have to advocate more fiercely, but parents are well-advised to assume positive intentions on the part of the school team and make every attempt to collaborate. Parents and families who engage in effective wraparound and Family–School Partnerships are participating in best-practice approaches, shown in the research to maximize the potential for optimal outcomes for students with disabilities.

Case Study (Willard, 2012)

Judy

Provided within this school assessment chapter was a review of many potential ways that assessment can share a symbiotic role with the Tiered models of intervention. In the case study provided here, Judy was a student at a school where one of the authors (Dr. Willard) was the school psychologist. Judy provided her enthusiastic consent to be included in this book and to have the chance to be recognized for her hard work during this particular RtI reading intervention. This intervention was designed to use a visual imagery strategy and proprietary assessment tool (WIOS, 2013) to aide in reading comprehension for students with ASDs. This case study report was provided to the family as part of the traditional academic intervention program at the school and is not considered to be research. However, the family signed consent before initiation of the intervention that with their consent, her story may be included in future papers or books regarding the intervention. This process from assessment to intervention and follow-up was developed by the team at the University of Denver, Child Family and School Psychology program in alignment with the requirements of the National Association of School Psychologists for providing academic interventions within an RtI model. The names have been changed for confidentiality. However, "Judy" is happy to share her story with readers of this book as a way to inspire and advocate for other children who have Autism Spectrum Disorders and Dyslexia. Dr. Willard and "Judy" hope that other students will see that with the right supports in place and hard work, great success can come.

RtI Academic Intervention Report
Temple Grandin School

Picture of "Judy's" Final Project during Reading Intervention (provided with consent)

Section 1: Identification

Referral

Judy is an 11-year-old girl in the sixth grade attending Temple Grandin School, a private school for children with Autism Spectrum Disorders. Judy's teacher and parents referred her for intervention at this time because of her seeming lack of motivation and effort in reading. Her participation in language arts has recently waned, resulting in unfinished homework, missed class time, and poor performance on tests. Judy's teacher would like for her to complete in-class assignments and improve her performance on comprehension tests. Judy's parents would like her to reengage in her coursework and to complete assignments more independently.

Background

Judy lives in Boulder with her parents and older sister. Judy speaks English as her first language. Her birth and developmental history were unremarkable, with the exception of a speech delay. At current, she is verbally fluent but struggles with reading and math. This is her first year at the Temple Grandin School; she attended public school from

Kindergarten through fifth grade. She has been diagnosed with Pervasive Developmental Disorder—Not Otherwise Specified (PDD-NOS), Mixed Anxiety Disorder with features of Obsessive Compulsive Disorder (300.09), and Dyslexia. She was placed on a 504 plan in elementary school which required some individualized instruction and accommodations. She received 2 years of support from the University of Colorado's Speech and Hearing program. Past reports reveal that she was removed from special education in fifth grade because of her progress on expressive language and reading. Although Judy no longer received services at school, her reading and mathematics skills were at the third grade level at that time, and her CSAP scores were Partially Proficient in all areas. At present, she is provided with individualized accommodations such as using the iPad for written work, frequent breaks, and support in organizing classroom materials. Her teachers report that she tends to make excuses to leave class and gives up easily on challenging tasks. They feel she could perform much better than she currently demonstrates. She participates in social skills intervention, the school's universal social skills program. There are no significant health, family, economic, or cultural issues that impact her school performance. Her strengths include her friendly and caring nature, and her enjoyment of dancing and theater. Teachers report that Judy is a pleasure to have in class and is well-liked by her classmates.

Baseline

Baseline data were taken using standardized tests, curriculum-based measures, interview, behavior observations, and brief reading probes. Regarding standardized measures, Judy completed the Gray Oral Reading Test (GORT). Judy demonstrated average scores in Rate (37th percentile) and Comprehension (75th percentile); however, her Accuracy (ninth percentile) and Fluency (ninth percentile) were below average; around the third to fourth grade level. Curriculum-Based Measures included grade level comprehension tests where Judy scored below grade level, averaging 66 % correct. During interviews, Judy indicated that she did not particularly enjoy the content of the reading assignments. She further explained that she is a visual learner and likes to have the opportunity to visualize; as well as, discuss her reading. Parent interviews revealed that Judy often refuses to read for homework, requiring a great deal of support at home. Further, they feel that it will be necessary to approach learning from a variety of modalities in order to "reach" her and ignite her interest in language arts. During brief reading probes, Judy showed the ability to recall some details from a passage; however, she struggled with her accuracy and comprehension on grade level passages. Judy was also administered a proprietary visual imagery reading measure, the Willard Imagery Observation Scales. She obtained a score of 9 out of 16 points possible. On this test, she demonstrated the ability to identify the characters, take the character's perspective, identify the character's actions, and the sequence of events in the story. However, she did not effectively identify emotions, make causal connections, or provide integrative statements to tie the story together. Gap analysis revealed that in order for Judy to reach grade level (80 % correct on comprehension), she would require direct intervention. As a result of this analysis,

Judy was moved to a Language Arts intervention with four other peers. All of the students participated in comprehension intervention.

Baseline levels of performance are variable on curriculum-based measures. Judy ranged from 56 % correct to 75 % correct on grade level comprehension tests (an average of 66 %). In order for her to close the gap with grade-level peers, she needs to obtain a score of 80 %. She was frequently observed engaging in a variety of avoidance strategies, often indicating that, "it is too hard," or "I can't handle it." This often resulted in her taking frequent breaks and missing critical content. In order to close the gap, Judy will need to improve her performance from 66 to 80 % correct over the next 6–10 weeks (by the end of the term).

Section 2: Analysis

Hypotheses

In order to understand the basis for Judy's difficulties in motivation and engagement in Language arts as well as her low performance on comprehension tests, the following hypotheses were developed.

Hypothesis #1: *Judy is not motivated because she is uninterested in the subject matter.* At the time of this intervention, the class was engaged in a difficult reading assignment about the holocaust. When interviewed, Judy described her dislike for the reading topic. To test this hypothesis, Judy was given the material ahead of class and provided with strategies to understand the reading. During class, she was allowed to discuss the reading aloud and instructed on how to use imagery to remember the story. Judy's interest immediately piqued, as demonstrated by her frequent and on-topic comments in class. She also improved her comprehension that day, as measured by a quick comprehension probe. *Hypothesis #1 was rejected.* It appeared, instead, that Judy's motivation was related to her understanding of the material, rather than her interest in the topic.

Hypothesis #2: *Judy is not engaged because she needs to be taught in different learning modalities.* Judy mentioned during an interview that she is a "visual thinker." She also described that she learns best when she has the opportunity to talk about the reading. Further, Judy's parents verified that Judy would likely respond best to a visual or verbal strategy. This hypothesis was tested through observation after employing visual and verbal teaching methods. Observations revealed, on multiple occasions, that she showed instantly improved motivation when allowed to use imagery and "think-alouds." *Hypothesis #2 was accepted.*

Hypothesis #3: *Judy is not engaged because of her difficulties with fluency and accuracy.* It was hypothesized that Judy was having trouble engaging with the reading because reading is hard for her, having been diagnosed with Dyslexia and having scored in the ninth percentile on the GORT. To test this hypothesis, Judy was allowed to read one-on-one with an adult before the class period in Language Arts. Her performance in Language Arts was then compared to Social Studies, where she was not provided with this support. Judy showed immediately enhanced performance in Language Arts, after having received one-on-one reading support. Her enhanced engagement was evidenced by answering questions in class and making frequent on-topic comments. In contrast, in Social Studies, Judy tended to drift, asked no questions, and made frequent off-topic comments to other students. *Hypothesis #3 was accepted.*

Goals

Goal #1: to address accepted hypothesis #2: Through the use of visual imagery and think-alouds; allowing her to utilize the visual and verbal learning modalities, Judy will improve her participation in class. This will be achieved when she is observed making 2–3 on-topic comments or asking 2–3 on-topic questions during each class period (as compared to 0–1 during baseline).

Goal #2 to address accepted hypothesis #3: In order to address Judy's identified weaknesses in reading fluency and accuracy, she will be provided with direct one-one-one reading support for all in-class assignments. The interventionist will use "neurological impress" whereby Judy is allowed to read with the interventionist; identify and practice unknown words, learn appropriate inflection and intonation, memorize sight words, and improve word-attack skills. This will allow her to feel prepared for classroom discussion and is expected to improve her comprehension. Further, Judy will be directly instructed to use a visual imagery strategy during language arts class. This goal will be measured by improved performance on comprehension tests. Judy will improve her performance from 66 % accuracy on comprehension tests to 80 % or better.

Section 3: Intervention

Intervention Selection & Description

In order to meet stated goals, an intervention was selected, collaboratively with Judy's Language Arts teacher. The intervention was specifically selected to work within the school schedule while maximizing the amount of intervention time available. First, Judy and a group of similarly struggling students were moved to a new language arts intervention class. This would allow her to receive the same classroom material; however, a higher dose of strategy instruction and intervention, than is provided in other courses. Next, during the student's study hall period, one-on-one intervention would be provided by the teacher, the classroom aide, or the interventionist, as available. Finally, frequent progress monitoring was developed to assess Judy's progress toward goals and to monitor intervention fidelity.

To address Judy's engagement in language arts and to improve her comprehension, a visual imagery strategy was selected. This strategy was chosen because research has repeatedly demonstrated that children with Autism Spectrum Disorders (ASD) tend to show significant deficiency in their use of imagery strategies (Joffe, Cain, & Maric, 2007; Kana et al., 2006). Further, research shows that children with Judy's profile show immediately enhanced comprehension when imagery strategies are directly taught and practiced (Nation, Clarke, Wright, & Williams, 2006; Nuske & Baven, 2011; Wahlberg, 2001).

In order to improve Judy's comprehension, Judy was provided with pre-reading intervention during study hall one-on-one with the interventionist or language arts teacher. Although the research regarding pre-reading for students is yet to demonstrate significant results (O'Connor & Klein, 2006), most studies show that children with ASD tend to respond to evidence-based reading instruction in general (Whalen, Otaiba, & Delano, 2009), which often includes pre-teaching. Pre-reading with an interventionist was expected to allow Judy to benefit more from time spent reading and to improve comprehension due to the fact that reading errors and miscues would be corrected. Research has shown that children with Dyslexia tend to show improved comprehension when provided with metacognitive strategies which can include pre-reading, questioning, and think alouds (Camahalan, 2006).

Intervention Delivery

The imagery intervention was delivered in one 60 min session per day, 4 days per week, for a period of 4 weeks. The pre-reading intervention was delivered for 30 min, once per week, for 4 weeks. Judy was provided with pre-reading time for 30 min, with the interventionist or teacher during study hall. During this time, the interventionist read with Judy for one paragraph, then Judy read one paragraph alone, and finally the interventionist read one paragraph. This allowed Judy to practice reading with the same rate and fluency as the interventionist, to practice reading independently while correcting miscues, and finally to listen to the text read aloud. Immediately following the reading, the interventionist captured any unknown words on flash cards, to practice during the next session. At this point, Judy practiced sight words on flash cards with the interventionist; mastery was demonstrated when Judy could read the word fluently over three trials. Finally, Judy was provided with the opportunity to "think aloud" about the text and to discuss comprehension questions.

Then, direct imagery intervention was delivered during Language Arts class. This intervention involved several discrete steps. The steps were employed in the same way and in the same order each time. First, the teacher wrote a list of five comprehension questions on the board. Judy (and other students) was asked to respond to the questions based on the pre-reading exercise. Next, the teacher read the text aloud and asked the students to "create pictures in their minds" as they listened. Then, the students each described or drew their images. Finally, the students were asked the same five comprehension questions again. Judy preferred to type her answers on her iPad and then describe her images aloud. In class, she tended to achieve about 60–70 % accuracy before using imagery and then almost perfect scores after the imagery practice. The materials used were grade-level reading texts; one was an assigned novel about the holocaust, called "The Boy in the Striped Pajamas," and the other was a literature book called, "The Day Book." These materials were chosen because baseline data were available, the teacher found the intervention more relevant and acceptable, and progress monitoring data could be collected without extensive modifications to the current testing procedures or curriculum.

Intervention Fidelity

Intervention fidelity was monitored using three distinct phases. First, the precise strategy was discussed one-on-one with the language arts teacher. During this phase, the Language Arts Teacher was provided with a one-page description of the elements of the intervention. She also took notes during the intervention instructions. Next, the interventionist modeled the intervention approach by teaching it to the language arts class, once per week, over 4 weeks. Finally, the teacher provided the intervention daily and had the opportunity to discuss questions with the interventionist weekly. Fidelity was also monitored based on Judy's descriptions of her imagery strategy use; as well as, performance on comprehension tests. Judy described herself as a "visual learner" and said that she loved using the imagery strategies. Further, she was proud of her improved performance on comprehension tests and attributed her performance to the use of these imagery strategies.

Section 4: Evaluation

Summary of Results

After a total of 16 imagery intervention sessions and four pre-reading intervention sessions, Judy's engagement in Language Arts improved significantly as did her performance on reading comprehension tests. Judy's engagement was measured by the number of questions and on-topic comments made during Language Arts class. These data were gathered weekly by the interventionist during observations. During the baseline phase, Judy provided 0 or 1 on-topic comment or question. During the intervention phase, her contributions increased to a rate of 5–7 per class period (60 min). Further, Judy left class an average of 2 times per class period during baseline. She did not leave class at all during the intervention phase. Thus, Goal #1 to increase Judy's engagement and participation in Language Arts class was reached.

Following the 16 imagery intervention sessions, Judy's comprehension improved significantly (see Fig. 19.1). Her performance was measured on progress monitoring probes and unit tests. The progress monitoring probes were short quizzes over the last week's reading. On these tests, Judy's performance ranged from 56 to 75 % accuracy. On the post-intervention probe, Judy achieved a score of 100 %. On the pre-intervention unit test, Judy achieved a score of 66 % correct. On the post-intervention test, Judy obtained a score of 103 % (including correct answers on

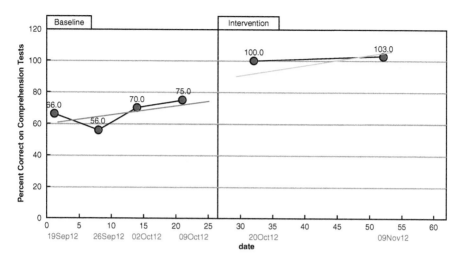

Fig. 19.1 Baseline and intervention results: comprehension CBM

extra credit items). Although the progress monitoring quizzes and unit tests were of different length, the types of questions and difficulty level were identical; and thus, the tests were used interchangeably for progress monitoring. Overall, her performance improved from 66 % correct to 100 % correct or better. Thus, Goal #2 for Judy to improve her comprehension to greater than 80 % correct was achieved. This change is significant and positive with a moderate effect size of .64. In summary, the intervention was effective in meeting the goals of improving Judy's engagement in language arts and her comprehension scores.

The intervention was employed with adequate fidelity, due in large part to the dedication of the classroom teacher to learn these strategies. Further, the student's own commitment to using imagery improved adherence to the intervention. Finally, the interventionist provided frequent check-ins and modeling sessions. The only change that occurred was the length of the intervention. After only 4 weeks, Judy's performance had improved to over 100 %. Initially, the intervention was expected to occur throughout the rest of the semester (10 weeks). However, Judy improved so quickly that it was collaboratively determined that the initial intervention be altered after 4 weeks. At present, the imagery intervention is employed daily; and a new strategy (SQ3R) is being introduced in the classroom simultaneously. Judy has been instructed to use both strategies to improve her comprehension. Over the last 2 weeks, Judy has responded positively to the use of Imagery and SQ3R during classroom exercises.

Overall Conclusions

Overall, the results of this intervention demonstrate the appropriateness of using pre-reading, think-alouds, and visual imagery to improve engagement and comprehension in a child with ASD and Dyslexia. The intervention was especially effective because the student described herself as a visual learner. Further, the intervention fidelity was improved substantially because of the firm commitment on the part of the classroom teacher. In conclusion, this type of intervention; involving pre-teaching, think-alouds, and visual imagery, is recommended for a child with the same referral concerns.

Sample letter to outside providers

Dear Psychologist,

This letter is to provide information regarding a student at our school, Joey Jones, here at Hidden Trails Elementary. He is in the second grade and has been recently struggling with his social skills and emotional regulation at school. His parents have requested that I write this letter highlighting my concerns and I am happy to do so. Joey was recently a part of our Response to Intervention process and he was able to make significant progress academically. At this time, he is fully participating and his performance in the classroom is roughly commensurate with his same age peers. However, our team wonders whether or not Joey may have a disability which interferes somewhat socially and emotionally, particularly in extra-curricular activities.

In school, he has significant difficulty adapting to changes in routine, such as school assemblies and fire-drills. He becomes so upset as to require time in the office with the school counselor so that he can calm down enough to return to class. He struggles at recess in that he often plays alone or spends time reading in lieu of playing with friends.

A set of school-based screeners was administered, revealing concerns in social communication, anxiety symptoms, and school problems. The student reports symptoms in the clinically significant range for Atypicality and Attention Problems on the BASC-II. The parent and teacher report clinically significant concerns about socialization, anxiety, and depression. The SCQ reveals a clinically significant score. Further, although Joey's grades are quite good, his scores on "scholarly habits" such as Perseverance and Teamwork were a "2" which means that he is approaching the standard (on a scale from 1 to 4).

Taken together, the school team wonders whether or not Joey may have a disability in social communication or a mood disorder. If a disability is identified and the family is open to sharing the results of your evaluation, we will be happy to incorporate any accommodations you recommend to support Joey's success at school. The school staff would like to learn of counseling and educational strategies that may be helpful to Joey. Please do not hesitate to call if you have any questions at the following number: 949-555-5555.

Sincerely,

Joe Smith, Ph.D.

School Psychologist

Legal Terms in School-Based Assessment

Legal Terms utilized in Educational Identification

Many legal terms and educational programs will be introduced in this chapter. Thus, it is critical to provide a primer of these terms, in order to avoid confusion. A comprehensive description of each term will be provided later in the chapter.

(Section) 504 Plan: falls under the Americans with Disability Act and ensures that a child who has an impairment that substantially limits a major life activity, such as Learning, Thinking, and Communicating, is provided with accommodations and educationally related services within general education (these services are distinctly different from those provided in special education on an IEP)

Child Find Program: requires school systems search for and evaluate children who may have a disability.

Curriculum-Based Measurements (CBM): standardized, reliable, short duration measurements which evaluate basic skills and the effects of interventions of: reading, math, and writing

Free Appropriate Public Education (FAPE): education for children with disabilities in the least restrictive environment, and at public expense.

Functional Behavior Analysis (FBA): an assessment of a student's behavior using principles of Applied Behavior Analysis.

Independent Educational Evaluation: An IEE is an evaluation conducted by a qualified examiner employed by an organization other than the school district responsible for the education of the student in question. Under the 2004 reauthorization of IDEA, parents have the right to request an IEE if they disagree with the results of the school district's evaluation. Upon parental request, the district must cover the costs of an IEE or file a due process complaint requesting hearing to try prove that the district's evaluation was appropriate (IDEA Regulations, 34 C.F.R. § 300.503).

Individualized Education Program (IEP): legal document that defines special education services between the school district and the parents.

Individuals with Disabilities Education Act (IDEA): a law that guarantees educational rights to all students with disabilities.

Part B of IDEA: the part of the IDEA 2004 that applies to school age children with disabilities (ages 3–21).

Part C of IDEA: the part of the IDEA 2004 that applies to infants and toddlers with disabilities (birth to age 3).

Least Restrictive Environment: the environment with the fewest restrictions in which children with disabilities can receive a reasonable education.

Positive Behavior Intervention and Support (PBIS): an approach, usually school-wide, to eliminate undesired behaviors and replace them with pro-social skills.

Response to Intervention (RTI): multi-step approach to providing educational supports and instruction to children who are struggling.

Screening: brief testing/observation that gives preliminary information on a child.

Chapter 20
Assessment Across the Lifespan

Abstract Autism assessment across the lifespan requires expertise in the unique way autism symptoms present in individuals of various ages. The assessment and feedback process look distinctly different when the evaluation is of a very young child as compared to an adult. Clinicians diagnosing children under the age of 2 should be prepared to manage toddler behaviors, engage with very young children, and obtain and analyze developmental data. Evaluating adults requires careful consideration of the quality of the interaction and the ease in developing rapport as well as the individual's own insights about why this assessment is necessary. During the feedback process, families may have different reactions to their child's diagnosis, depending on the age of the individual. Families with young to elementary-aged children ask about college and independent living after their children reach adulthood. Questions about employment, job satisfaction, marriage, and starting a family are often raised with older children and adults. The uncovering of a referral concern and eventual diagnosis may validate concerns in one parent, overwhelm another parent, or may trigger a cycle of grief in one or both parents as they consider hopes and plans for their child and are faced with modifying some of their expectations. This chapter will provide clinical guidance regarding the assessment, diagnosis, and feedback process across the lifespan, considering the distinctly different challenges faced by families depending on the age of diagnosis.

Keywords Assessing toddlers with ASD • How young can autism be diagnosed? • Assessing play skills in toddlers • ADOS-2—toddler module • ADOS-2—module 4 • Assessing adults with ASD • Autism across the lifespan • Impact of ASD on families • Gap: first concern to diagnosis in ASD • Advantages of early diagnosis

Implications for Assessing Toddlers

Early Identification Can Lead to Optimal Outcomes

Effective toddler assessment is critical in light of research showing that early intervention can lead to better outcomes (Helt et al., 2008; Horovitz, 2012). Research suggests that early diagnosis, strong cognitive abilities, and solid adaptive skills may be predictive of the best outcomes (Sutera et al., 2007). Some children assessed at 2,

© Springer International Publishing Switzerland 2016   437
A.P. Kroncke et al., *Assessment of Autism Spectrum Disorder*, Contemporary Issues in Psychological Assessment, DOI 10.1007/978-3-319-25504-0_20

and diagnosed with autism who demonstrated strong baseline skills in cognitive, adaptive, and motor domains, and who were provided treatment, did not meet criteria at age 4. Specifically one study shows that 39 % of a Pervasive Developmental Disorder group and 11 % of an Autistic group no longer met criteria at age 4 (Sutera et al., 2007). Research such as a study conducted by Deborah Fein's group at the University of Connecticut may indicate that solid baseline skills and early intervention can make the difference as to whether a school-aged child has strong peer relationships and is successfully able to participate in a mainstreamed school program. Thus, early identification can be a critical factor in optimal outcomes.

Often children assessed at a young age have been referred because they have an older sibling on the Autism Spectrum. The likelihood of having an Autism Spectrum Disorder may be approximately 1 in 5 when a sibling has been diagnosed. Studies show that even when family members do not meet criteria for ASD they are more likely to exhibit traits or symptoms such as stereotyped language or challenges with pretend play. This is sometimes referred to as "The Broader Autism Phenotype" or "subclinical symptoms of autism." One study showed that siblings were delayed on response to joint attention and general social skill development but only 15 % of those in the study met criteria for an ASD themselves (Yoder, Stone, Walden, & Malesa, 2009). Yoder et al. found that the best predictor of later ASD diagnosis was "Weighted Triatic Communication" or a combination of language use and frequency of communication (2009). Research indicates that between 7 and 20 % of siblings may have an Autism Spectrum Disorder themselves. This is compared to a rate of approximately 1.5 % or 1 in 68 children in the general population (Centers for Disease Control and Prevention, 2014). This risk is higher for boys than girls (Ozonoff et al., 2011).

Some clinicians express concern about diagnosing "too early" but outcome research indicates that with early diagnosis there seems to be a better likelihood of treating symptoms before social and communication demands increase. Sutera et al. found that 27 % of the 2-year-olds assessed at age 2 did not meet criteria at 4 (2007). This is a better rate than the data collected by Eaves and Ho in 2004 noting that 7 % of children assessed at 2 and again at 4 moved off the Autism Spectrum. Sutera et al. found that it is difficult to predict who will benefit most from early interventions and thus "it is crucial to provide all children with intensive early intervention" (Sutera et al., 2007, p. 106). The authors recommend that it is better to treat symptoms early and hope for a considerable recovery from symptoms rather than "wait and see" if the child will grow out of certain behaviors or gain appropriate skills outside of a therapeutic setting. Unfortunately, the "wait and see" model that is often suggested by pediatricians may lead to more significant symptoms that need more extensive treatment and poorer outcomes later. As mentioned earlier in this book, the temporal horn of the brain is developing in early life, which is where emotional insight and regulation begins. In the brain of a child with autism, this process simply does not develop as it should. With intervention, emotional development can be targeted and supported, thus allowing for the child's development to be more on-track with peers. Some studies are underway to better understand the structural and neuronal changes that when combined with maturation may change the brain and allow for optimal outcomes (Fein et al., 2013, p. 203). However, unidentified children are more likely to have visible social skills challenges and potentially develop other mental health conditions like anxiety or depression as well as oppositional behaviors, as they reach school age and social and communication demands increase. Further, time is of the essence because of the social opportunities that happen in early childhood. It is often said that a "child's work is a child's play." Indeed, these play experiences at the park, and in the preschool classroom, and at family gatherings, are the blueprint and cornerstone of later social development. Children who have not been provided with early intervention often are "in their own world" or are isolated from these opportunities due to feeling overwhelmed or anxious in social settings. As such, even as the child gains skills after a later diagnosis and subsequent intervention, he or she has a lot of catching up to do. This "catch-up" discrepancy is sometimes referred to as "The Shadow Effect," which simply means that the child has missed some of the learning opportunities that were available to non-disabled peers in early life.

It is the authors perspective that it is never too early to address parent concerns and provide evaluation data to assess progress and evaluate development in cognition, language, motor, social and behavioral domains. When evaluating very young children, who are often repetitive in language and play as part of typical development, there are a number of signs that may indicate the presence of ASD. First understanding the child's cognitive ability utilizing a scale like the Mullen, in relationship to social skills and communication can provide noteworthy data. For example a child who has very high cognitive abilities but lacks social engagement in the form of making eye contact, sharing, initiating and responding to joint attention, is displaying noteworthy symptoms. Also a pattern of high expressive language but low receptive language may be cause for concern. Another early language symptom is the expressive-receptive discrepancy coupled with pronoun reversals. For example, the child might say, "You want a cookie," when he means "I want a cookie." These are noteworthy language patterns and indicate that an autism diagnosis may be relevant.

Setting up for Success in the Assessment of Toddlers

Clinicians diagnosing children under the age of 2 should be prepared to manage toddler behaviors, engage with very young children, and to obtain or analyze developmental data obtained through a test like the Mullen or Bailey. These assessments can and ideally should go quickly in order to not fatigue the child, which can lead to behavioral problems and difficulty obtaining an accurate assessment of skills. Many psychologists utilize multiple clinicians during toddler assessment. One clinician provides materials and helps with scoring, while the other clinician conducts the assessment and maintains the connection with the child. The assistant must be familiar with all of the items and materials the examiner will need to make the assessment fluid and quick. When there are behavioral challenges two adults can better manage the environment so as not to reinforce undesired behavior. In special instances when a young child has a history of very intense self-injurious or dangerous behaviors clinicians recommend including an ABA therapist with a Board Certification in Behavior Analysis to assist in keeping the child safe.

In some cases, children who are referred this young have significant symptomology and this may be the reason a child is identified early. In other cases, the child may have a few symptoms but these may be subtle and complex to diagnose. In either case, the clinician should be clear on the developmental milestones expected of a child this young. The age tables provided by the Transdisciplinary Play-based Assessment manual (Linder, 2008) may be used to identify behaviors which are developmentally appropriate, slightly behind, or significantly delayed. It is also important in toddler assessment to consider anxiety, attachment-disorders, and trauma, as potential differential diagnostic considerations (see Part IV).

Setting up the evaluation room so that it is comfortable for parents to sit and a toddler to play is important. Remove all distractions and keep non-ADOS toys locked away to help the testing go smoothly. Providing snack and juice breaks and time to bounce on a toy trampoline or sit in a spinning chair can make the day more fun. These authors find that asking parents to bring a couple of preferred snacks on the day of the evaluation avoids food preference and allergy issues.

A session may last from an hour and a half to 3 h depending on a parent's preference and a child's behavior. At times the examiner may shorten a session and reschedule a part of the assessment for another day in an effort to encourage the best performance from the child. The ADOS-2 T must be completed in a single day of testing but a second day could be scheduled to complete a Vineland Adaptive Behavior Scale or Mullen Scales for example.

Assessing Toddlers with the ADOS-2 Toddler

The ADOS-2 Toddler module provides assessment guidelines, materials, and activities for children as young as 12 months of age. The ADOS-2 Toddler includes 11 tasks and takes usually up to an hour to administer (recommended 40–60 min). One or both parents must be present for the administration because parent–child as well as examiner–child interactions are scored. The authors of this text have found that many toddlers enjoy the ADOS-T activities as the play activities are filled with toys and tasks that are meant to be engaging. It is important to allow time for the toddler to warm up and see the evaluation room. Often by preparing parents in the initial session for what the testing day will entail an examiner can streamline this process and everyone is more comfortable.

Parent Role During Administration of ADOS-2 Toddler

It can be a useful strategy to tell the parents what their role will be in the assessment. The clinician can inform parents that it is helpful that they are available to comfort the child if he or she comes to them. However, the parent should remain neutral and not provide prompts to the child. The clinician can let the parents know that they will be asked some questions about the child's play preferences and about how the child's play and behavior compared to his or her typical play and interactions at home. The clinician can let the parent know that there may be times when they are asked to jump in, so as to engage or comfort the child during the assessment. However, parents should know that it is important for the clinician to have some time to get to know the child as well so the parents can best support the process by only assisting when asked by the examiner.

Testing Day: Administering the ADOS-2 Toddler

The ADOS-Toddler Activities include free play, blocking toy play, response to name, bubble play, anticipation of a routine with objects and social interaction, response to joint attention, responsive social smile, bath time, functional and symbolic imitation and snack (Lord et al., 2012). Tasks in the Toddler module are coded to give higher priority to a child's social responses and lesser priority to initiations than in other ADOS modules. Tasks assess a child's interests, language, facial expression, eye contact, play skills, the presence of repetitive behaviors, and note the child's response to his or her environment and to overtures from the examiner and the parent. Snacks can be used for the ADOS-2 T snack time and after activities are completed as reinforcers or breaks. The total time a toddler may be in the office will be shorter than the assessment time for an older child. The examiner codes the child's behavior and responses immediately following administration.

During the ADOS-T, although testing strategies may be needed to manage behaviors, it is important that the examiner only provides enough support as necessary to maintain the child's engagement. If the child wanders off for a minute, the examiner should allow this scenario to play out. Where does the child go? Does he or she go to the parent? Does he go to the door? Does he try to open a cabinet to find more toys? Does he hide under a table? That is, it is important that the examiner *not* "give" the child too much in the way of assistance on the tasks. The examiner should *not* work too hard in order to engage the child. If the child is very reserved and quiet, it is okay for the examiner to sit quietly and wait for the child to come over or to warm up on his or her terms. If the child is struggling with a task, and clearly does not initiate a request for help by pointing or giving the toy to the parents, simply wait and see if the child will do this on his or her own. It is easy for the examiner working with young children to fall into the trap of trying to assist the child too much by prompting, "help? Do you need help" Certainly, it is important to monitor the child's emotions and not allow for him or her to become very upset and frustrated, but in obtaining an accurate sample of the child's skills, it is vitally important that the clinician not "lead" the child. Rather, the clinician should allow the child to lead and in so doing the clinician is joining and engaging with the child's way of navigating and understanding his world. If the child says a certain word repeatedly, or makes a gleeful noise, the clinician can simply mirror that response by using the same tone of voice or repeating the word back to him or her.

As with any assessment for autism, it is important to take the time to experience and note what the interaction feels like, while taking observations on any difficulty the examiner is having connection with the examinee.

During the ADOS-2 T the authors of this text look carefully at the way a child communicates socially as opposed to functionally, i.e., getting wants and needs met. As with ADOS-2 modules for older children, it is important to see if the child uses the examiner or parent's hand as a tool, rather than obtaining eye contact, pointing, or giving the object to the parent for help. Again, if the Mullen or Bailey data indicate the child has average cognitive abilities, these social communication deficits are of greater concern.

Assessing Reciprocal Play During the ADOS-2 Toddler

Concerning Play Behaviors

During play, a child who focuses on the object or toy, mainly ignoring the examiner and parents, is displaying clinically significant signs of autism. Some children show or label toys, comment and make requests but do not reference caregivers or examiners. They may ignore questions asked by others and be slow to ask for help making a toy work. During administration of the Toddler module there are many opportunities for the examiner to initiate interaction with a child using a bubble toy, ball, shape sorter, peek-a-boo, jack-in-the-box, and other toys. It is important to be able to assess whether the child looks only at the toy during some of these playful interactions, rather than at the parent or examiner. These are red flags, indicating poor reciprocal play. Another opportunity to assess reciprocal play and social interaction is during the "teasing bubble play." The examiner is to first establish bubble play with the toddler and then offer the bubble toy or wand to the child with a playful "oops!" and then suddenly pull it away (Lord et al., 2012). By pulling the toy away, the examiner can assess whether the child looks to the examiner (versus the toy) with an expression that may read "hey, wait a minute!" or offers a smile and a laugh, indicating typical development. However, if the child simply looks at the bubble toy and treats the examiner as a tool to get what the child wants, this indicates concern about poor reciprocal play and social skills characteristic of ASD.

Pro-Social Reciprocal Play

Typically developing children watch or look to adults for cues on how to understand their environment. They may play repetitively with bubbles or make the same statement over and over but they appear engaged and aware of the social world and use these cues in the learning process. Eye contact, shared smiles, initiating joint attention by looking at an object, *checking in* with mom or dad and then looking back to the toy are evidence of appropriate reciprocal play. Responding to joint attention and then sharing enjoyment over a toy or game with another person is also a pro-social behavior. By using a task like bubble play, the examiner can determine whether the child views the examiner as a means to an end or as part of a social network.

One author has a 22-month-old nephew rather obsessed with his toy slide. He loves to slide night and day and can do this very repetitively. Some might view this as cause for concern, but repetitive play can be part of the learning process for typically developing children. This particular nephew is engaged socially with the process of sliding. He invites others to slide too, makes eye contact, laughs, claps, and giggles while initiating and responding to joint attention bids. The slide is repetitive but the child responds to and initiates social interaction during the process. The same child says "The frog jumped out!" a punch line to his favorite story, every time he sees his aunt on Skype, video chat. He is sharing the story of the surprised frog while probably remembering that it made people laugh initially and provided wanted attention. Thus, a toddler who enjoys repetitive play or language is somewhat typical. All repetitive behaviors are not necessarily indicative of the presence of autism. However, delayed language coupled with repetitive play, poor reciprocity, and significant delays in eye contact, sharing and joint attention, are red flags for ASD. Even a few of these symptoms with a family history for ASD is cause for concern.

Diagnosing a Toddler with ASD

The codes on the ADOS-2 T result in a range of concern. "Little to No Concern," "Mild-to-Moderate Concern," and "Moderate-to-Severe Concern" are the ranges considered. In the validation sample for this measure, only 3–6 % of children who scored in the moderate-to-severe range were false positives for the Autism Spectrum. These data show that when administered and used correctly, this measure is valid and reliable, as young as the age of 12 months. The manual reports that there was some controversy over differentiation between autism and Pervasive Developmental Disorder (Lord et al., 2012). Currently, the controversy is no longer a concern, with the Autism Spectrum Disorder dimensional categorization put forth in DSM-5.

This ADOS-2 Toddler administration is only a piece of the data collection and should be considered along with rating scale data, parent interview, and early cognitive development. A battery may include an interview like the ADI-R, an ADOS-2 T, a Vineland Parent/Caregiver Rating form and a Mullen Scales of Early Learning. It is then up to the clinician to determine whether enough data is present to provide a diagnosis. When a child is assessed at 12 months of age and diagnosed with an Autism Spectrum Disorder it is recommended that treatment begin immediately and in fact government waivers exist in many cases for children under 3 to help fund this treatment. Re-evaluation after a year can provide data to determine whether the child continues to meet diagnostic criteria or has made marked progress in treating symptoms to the extent that criteria are no longer met. In the author's experience, parents who have obtained an early diagnosis and treatment from a very young age, have seen their child make amazing growth and progress in just 1 year's time. The child may go from tantrums to communication; from sudden escalations to the ability to modulate emotions, and from disconnected, to connected. This is a major reason why early diagnosis and treatment are recommended.

With children 12–30 months, the ADOS-2 T is likely to be the best measure to assess autism symptoms. When children are older than 30 months, their level of expressive language can help a clinician determine whether Module 1 or 2 would be more appropriate. Once a child has expressive language above a 4-year-old level, Module 3, for school-aged children and younger adolescents can be administered. This module requires fluent language for administration. Module 1, Module 2, and Module 3 can provide detailed information on skill development during a re-evaluation or can be used in an initial evaluation for a child aged 30 months and older.

Although some clinicians are hesitant to diagnose very young children, the importance of early identification cannot be overstated. Families and referring clinicians are well advised to pursue an evaluation if any of the aforementioned symptoms are present or there is a family history of ASD. If symptoms are significant and the child is diagnosed, a family can embark on early treatment and begin building skills toward a brighter future. If not, the evaluation can bring peace of mind and recommendations to facilitate continued growth and development. Early consultation and evaluation when concerns are present provides answers and insights to families. It is sometimes important to remind families that simply pursuing an evaluation does not mean they are essentially creating a problem that was not there before. Sometimes people feel that they are "making mountains out of mole-hills" and they worry that if they go see a psychologist, they will receive an unnecessary diagnosis. To that, the authors say, "just like having a cancer screen does not give you cancer, having an autism assessment, doesn't give you autism." If the child does not have autism, clients will be sent home with either a clean bill of health, or some important suggestions to help the child obtain the skills needed to be happier and well-adjusted. Having spoken to many parents who malign themselves as "overly concerned" "crazy" or "too cautious" during the referral process, the authors have been able to see the benefit of evaluating these children and providing much needed answers. The authors find that parents can gain peace of mind in seeing that their concerns are quite valid no matter how many friends, relatives, and professionals have suggested they ought to "wait and see." Parents also gain peace of mind when presented with cognitive, language, and social data that is within age-expected ranges.

As the remainder of this book covers assessment of children and adolescents, it is unnecessary to cover those ages in this chapter regarding the lifespan. Most clinicians who work in the field of autism feel a level of comfort and familiarity with school-aged children. However, assessment of toddlers and adults is often intimidating to clinicians. As such, the next section provides a guide for accurate assessment and identification of adults with ASD.

Implications for Assessing Adults

Identifying the Need for Assessment in Adults Suspected of Having ASD

Assessment and diagnosis were less prevalent 30 years ago. Temple Grandin's story of her own diagnosis and treatment and her parents' fight to determine the best supports, schools, and social outlets is a unique one (Grandin, 1995). Quite often adults with social skills deficits were labeled odd or quirky, were picked on in high school, and either became anxious or depressed. Alternately, they may have coped the best they could, finding jobs with minimal social requirements and immersing themselves in more solitary or computer-based interests. Often these adults are referred by a significant other or spouse who wonders whether the social introversion, challenges with affective expression, and highly specific areas of interest may be indicative of autism.

Other times a child has been diagnosed and at feedback a mother or father shares, "you are describing me" or "I'd like to be evaluated too." In these cases a family may have more than one diagnosis on the Autism Spectrum in a short period of time. In other cases, an adult seeks an evaluation after a long fight with depression, massive social anxiety or challenges communicating with bosses and co-workers that impact job satisfaction and security. Sometimes these individuals have come across internet questionnaires and websites that lead them to believe they may have autism. Adults come seeking clarification as well as validation of who they are and the idea that they might not be alone. Diagnosing an adult can be powerful and helpful but it can also be painful. The diagnosis may shed light on a challenging marriage that has not been characterized by strong emotional support, understanding, and insight from the individual who has autism.

Assessing Adults: Testing Day

When evaluating an adult it is crucial to obtain as much detail as possible in the clinical and developmental interview so as to understand any early delays, social challenges, and restricted interests. When it is possible, interviewing a parent can be helpful, particularly if the adult is in his or her late teens or 20s. In this case, parents may provide recent insight as well as developmental history. Making the rule out between a social anxiety disorder, depression, OCD, and a personality disorder will require detailed consideration of development and the history of challenges. It can often be helpful when assessing an adult to talk to the individual's spouse or significant other, sibling, or other close relative. Further, the individual's own insights about why he or she feels this assessment is necessary can provide critical data for the evaluation.

The ADOS-2 Module 4 is best suited to evaluating adults with adequate cognitive and language abilities suspected of having an ASD. It involves an extensive interview of social practices, emotional awareness, self-care, and personal goals as well as history of friendships, occupation, and education. ADOS-2 Module 4 activities provide information on creativity, response to humor, emotional insight, use of gesture and facial expression, and perspective taking. This module requires fluent language skills to complete and must be viewed as part of a whole dataset in order to understand the impact of other potential emotional diagnoses like depression or anxiety. When administering this module, it is important to take careful note of the quality of the interaction and the ease or relative lack of ease in developing rapport. Often adults who have lived with autism a long time may have some appropriate communication skills in some areas or some compensatory strategies such as good manners, or pleasant small talk. However, an adult with autism will generally not be able to maintain the quality of the conversation beyond a few exchanges before becoming one-sided in the interaction, uncomfortable or confused, particularly, when the conversation veers into the domain of emotions, relationships, and abstract insights. For example, an adult with autism may be able to hold a relatively pleasant exchange but then suddenly freeze up when asked about friends, romantic relationships, or his or her own dreams and aspirations.

Adults with significantly impaired language or cognitive ability are often evaluated using the ADOS-2 Module 1 or 2. These modules offer a chance to assess reciprocity, social skills, and repetitive interests through play and creative tasks. This way, reciprocity can be evaluated without the confounding effects of language problems or an intellectual disability. Using the ADOS-2, Module 1 or 2 in addition to a language measure allows for a language disorder to be differentiated from autism. Catherine Lord and others are working on standard modifications to modules 1 and 2 so that these will be more appropriate for use with older adolescents and adults.

WPS the developer of the ADOS-2 is in the active development stages of Adapted Module 1 and Adapted Module 2 for use with adolescent and adult populations. At the time of this publication, the adapted modules are only being used for research populations and are not widely available for clinical use. Presently, modules included in the ADOS-2 are selected based on the client's expressive language levels. That said, persons of all ages including adults and adolescents with limited language will be administered Module 1 or 2. Activities, materials, and presses in both modules are geared toward younger children. Similarly, the present diagnostic algorithm was standardized on young children. The adapted modules include changes in materials, presses, and activities, as well as behavioral codes. Changes take into account developmental appropriateness and changes in symptom profiles over time (Vanessa Hus Bal, personal communication, April 17, 2015). For example, social routines are updated to be more appropriate for adult populations, materials are larger for older populations and materials are updated to match recent changes in science and technology. Again it is important to note that the adapted modules are only available for research use. At the time of publication, the precise activities and diagnostic algorithms of the adapted modules have not been standardized.

Emotional problems and mood disorders should be considered during an autism evaluation with an adult, particularly when test behaviors raise clinical concern in the examiner's mind. When using Module 4 these authors find that it is important to consider other emotional challenges like depression and anxiety as these may impact the flow of conversation, amount of reciprocity, use of gestures, and level of cooperation on creative tasks. Tasks like telling a story from a book and description of a picture can be very informative. If an individual really struggles to approach the story-telling task and shares comments like "I can't tell stories" or "I'm just not creative in this way" are red flags for ASD. Alternately, if he or she describes the picture with no character development, plot or emotional identification, this behavior may be consistent with ASD. When presented with the cartoon map, clinicians should take note of an individual who lists states and capitols or comments on how large the icons are in respect to the characters or states. This may be evidence of lack of insight into the playful, or humorous cartoon task. Challenges like these would not be explained by depressive symptoms. Similarly individuals who remark that they can't teach a task like driving or brushing teeth because they "aren't really a talker" or "don't really do a good job of brushing teeth anyway" are also exhibiting a remarkable challenge with social perspective taking and creativity that would not relate to depression.

Clinicians should bear in mind that poor performance on an ADOS task can be a symptom of autism or, rather, of emotional problems, depending on the specific presentation. By considering the ADOS-2 data in light of emotional questionnaires like the Beck Depression Inventory and Beck Anxiety Inventory, it is easier to determine whether mood and anxiety played a role in performance. For example, limited eye contact, conversation and gesture may be caused by depression. During administration of Module 4, it is important to take note of an adult's ability to describe goals, personal responsibility, and friendships. A person who is depressed may have few friends but he or she should be able to speak about the nature of social relationships and describe what a friend is. An adult who describes a common-law spouse of 20 years with whom he has two children as his "roommate" is clearly missing a somewhat basic understanding of social relationships.

Taken together, a detailed interview, developmental history, and close attention to ADOS-2 Module 4 tasks taken in the context of other data collected during the evaluation, does make it possible to assess for depression, anxiety, ASD, or another neurodevelopmental disability in an adult. Providing an adult with a diagnosis on the Autism Spectrum connects him or her with a community that includes resources and supports. This clarification can also lead to better self-awareness and improved self-esteem. In the case of an adult who is married and has a family, the diagnosis can help family members better understand how to communicate and introduce him or her to support groups and community resources that may help improve relationships and prevent conflict and divorce. This new found insight and understanding may enable spouses and family members to have more compassion and understanding for the individual with autism, which can allow for greater connection and overall functioning for the entire family.

Age of Diagnosis and the Impact on the Individual

The International Meeting for Autism Research in 2014 included a number of presentations regarding time of first parental concern to the age of diagnosis. This data was shocking to the authors. It is sad to see a broken system in which families express concern early, services are available and could have a considerable impact on optimal outcomes but diagnoses are not provided until years later. Published data (Daniels & Mandell, 2014) on age at diagnosis indicates that the mean age at the time of diagnosis ranges from 3 years 2 months old to 10 years old. This is a large range. Fortunately, meta-analysis studies indicate that the age is going down over the years. Daniels and Mandell (2014) considered 42 studies published from 1990 to 2012 to establish the age range 3–10. This is consistent with what the authors of this text see in practice. Sometimes children are diagnosed around age 2 and sometimes they do not present for an evaluation until the teen years, but generally many children are evaluated between 3 and 10. Factors identified by Daniels and Mandell that impact age at diagnosis include community resources, state policies, socioeconomic status, and severity of symptoms. Interestingly, although intelligence is implicated in optimal treatment outcomes, it can sometimes mask symptoms and lead to later diagnosis. Thus, intelligence can be a bit of a double-aged sword, in that it makes children more receptive to treatment and better outcomes, but also, leads to later diagnosis and treatment initiation. Children who have more diagnostic centers available in their city or state, whose families have resources, and who present with more severe symptoms are more likely to receive support.

Age of First Concern to Diagnosis

A study conducted by Jiang et al. in 2014 reports that parental concerns begin at 13 months of age. Wiggins et al. in 2006 also found concerns developing between 12 and 23 months. This study focused on a group of 8 year olds identified by the CDC database as having been diagnosed with ASD. Seventy-six percent of the children were diagnosed in clinical settings and 24 % were identified in schools. Most diagnoses were made by a clinician with a Ph.D. although neurologists, pediatricians, and psychiatrists also diagnosed autism. This study found that the concerns arose by 23 months, evaluations were conducted at a mean age of 48 months and diagnoses were actually provided at 61 months, or 5 years old. Wiggins et al. stated that the degree of impairment did impact the age at diagnosis. Taking the data together, this means that *at minimum* families are waiting 2–3 years from the time of first parental concern until diagnosis and comprehensive services are provided. In many cases families are waiting much longer.

Another study further examined and reviewed data on factors that impact age at diagnosis. This study by Mishaal, Ben-Itzchak, and Zachor (2014) focused on children aged 1–6 who had been diagnosed with ASD. The mean age at diagnosis for the sample was 30.9 months. The study used the ADOS, ADI-R, and Vineland-II with 551 children. The factors most correlated with early diagnosis in this study were the presence of developmental regression and a child not being first born. In this case a child was at least second born and the parents had a typically developing older child. Researchers postulated that parents who had seen autism before were more aware of which factors were developmentally problematic. The level of impairment in communication and social interaction also had an impact on the age of diagnosis. Although previous research (Fountain, King, & Bearman, 2011; Mandell et al., 2005) found a significant effect on the age of first diagnosis for high maternal education, high socioeconomic status, or stereotyped behaviors, Mishaal et al. (2014) did not find such an effect. Fountain et al. in 2011 found mixed reviews for parental education impacting age at the time of diagnosis. Conclusions of the Mishaal study (Mishaal et al., 2014) indicate that it is important to educate parents about warning signs for Autism Spectrum Disorder particularly when they are first-time parents.

Jang et al. considered racial and ethnic differences in the age of first parental concern to determine whether ethnic or racial differences impacted the age at which concerns were identified. No racial or ethnic differences exist in Jang et al.'s dataset, meaning that parental concerns developed around 1 year of age (13 months) for all families in the study whether their ethnicity was classified Caucasian, African American or Hispanic. The study also looked at age at diagnosis and found data comparable to Daniels and Mandell (2014), indicating that while concerns come for all families around 13 months, there are ethnic and racial differences in regard to age at diagnosis. By ethnicity, diagnosis happened earliest for Caucasian children with an average age of 6.3 years. African American children were diagnosed next at age 7.9 years and finally Hispanic children were diagnosed at age 8.8 years. Jang et al. concludes that there is a significant delay in first concern versus age of diagnosis and this is most concerning when considering treatment outcomes. This gap is even wider for Hispanic and African American children than it is for Caucasian children. Taken together, ethnicity does appear to be a factor in the age of diagnosis but not in the age at first concern. Social justice comes into play here as these data indicate children from minority groups are receiving later diagnosis, which impacts their opportunity for optimal outcomes significantly. This research points to the fact that mothers of all ethnicity groups should be informed of autism symptoms and provided guidance on how to seek an evaluation. Further, cost-effective assessment and treatment is critical for many families, particularly minority families from lower socioeconomic status groups. Jang et al. cites Horovitz et al. (2012) noting that best treatment outcomes come with early intervention.

In 2007 a "reliable" diagnosis could be made at 24 months (Lord et al.) and in 2012 the ADOS-2 Toddler Module suggested that moderate-to-severe concern could be established as young as 12-months-old with few false positives. Parental awareness of "red flags" and a physician referral to a specialist are very helpful variables. Interestingly children who saw a pediatrician were not more likely to be identified early but children referred to a specialist were (Jang et al., 2014). So in conclusion, research supports the notion that psychologists and psychiatrists are able to recognize and diagnose Autism Spectrum Disorders from a very young age. When parents understand what they are looking for and physicians are willing to make early referrals for evaluation, children are more likely to be diagnosed and to receive early intervention services. Sometimes these early interventions may make the difference between a marked decrease in symptomatology, even "recovery" referred to as "optimal outcomes." Later diagnosis, on the other hand, leads to an increase in social skills challenges, more difficulty in mainstream education, and risk for increased emotional symptoms like anxiety and depression. Thus, referring doctors and other specialists are well advised to identify and refer their patients whenever even modest concerns regarding autism are observed.

The 2–3 Year Gap from First Concern to Diagnosis: What Is the Impact?

Considering the data presented earlier in this chapter on early intervention and optimal outcomes, families are done a great disservice when it takes years to be diagnosed. Also, many states provide support to young children (for example with a diagnosis of autism in Colorado waiver support for speech, occupational therapy, and early childhood, special education may be provided at no cost to children on the Spectrum until age 3). Considering this data, very few children will be diagnosed before age 3 even considering that parents have been voicing concerns since a child turned one. This means that when the parent's concerns go unaddressed for 2 years, the window of opportunity for low cost or free early intervention services has closed. Due to the Child Find mandate, many early services are available to very young children from the age of 0–3. Around the age of 3, the child would need to obtain preschool-based services in order to receive state support. School-based services tend to look different and may not be available in-home. In-home supports can be extremely helpful, especially when it comes to utilization of ABA services, which may include setting up a home behavior plan, and in-home parent consultation. At the age of 3, and certainly by 5, many of these opportunities for state support of this nature have already passed by.

The 2–3 year gap between first concern and diagnosis represents a significant problem in the field of assessment; impacting individuals, families, and our society as a whole. The lifetime savings for a child who receives early intensive treatment services is considerable (Larsson, 2012). Again, this brings to bare the point that early diagnosis is critical to obtaining treatment and essential to the best possible outcomes. This wasted time that has been discovered in the literature should serve as a beacon to clinicians, pediatricians, and advocates everywhere to get families in for a diagnosis as soon as parents first indicate concern. The "wait and see" approach, which is often appropriate for other developmental or medical problems, is no longer to be utilized for ASD as the risk of assessment is low; whereas, the risk of waiting for 2 or 3 years is extremely high.

Diagnosis Across the Lifespan and the Impact on Families

Diagnosis may come with a different set of questions or concerns considering the age of the individual being evaluated. Nearly all families with young to elementary aged children ask about college and independent living after their children reach adulthood. Questions about employment, job satisfaction, marriage, and starting a family are often raised. Unfortunately much of the data we have now on adult outcomes points to poorer prognosis for those on the Autism Spectrum when compared to individuals with Down syndrome (Mailick, 2014; Smith, Mailick, & Greenberg, 2014). Studies show that adults often have access to fewer social supports and services and may tend to isolate themselves. Quality-of-life research conducted by Chiang and Wineman (2014) emphasizes the importance of leisure activities for both children and adults. Looking at adult data, individuals with fewer behavior problems and more leisure activities had a higher quality of life. Child quality of life data indicated a larger number of variables are implicated. Data also factored in age, severity of symptoms, social skills, adaptive skills, and education. The study also found that a small percentage of adults live independently and are gainfully employed. Before the year 2000, data indicated that 18 % of adults lived independently or semi-independently. From 2000 to 2011 Howlin and Moss (2012) report that data indicates this number is still below 20 %. There are some improved outcomes as fewer adults are in hospital care and 49 % are working at a job. Fifteen percent of adults are in a meaningful romantic relationship and 25 % report having at least one close friend. There is huge variation in the adult ASD literature but researchers agree we must work for better adult outcomes. Volkmar, Klin, and McPartland reported in the Overview for their book Asperger's Syndrome, Second Edition, that challenges may include poor adaptive skills, vocational issues, and comorbid psychiatric conditions (in Eds. Volkmar, Klin, & McPartland, 2014). Howlin and Moss reported that individuals with useful speech by five have better outcomes as adults; whereas, comorbid diagnosis can lead to worse outcomes. Adults in many of these studies are between the ages of 20 and 40. Howlin and Moss (2012) point out that participants did not have access to the level of supports and services provided for those diagnosed today and less intervention may also impact these adult data. Adult outcomes continue to be a huge area of research interest and more funding is being provided to ensure that adults have job training, social supports, and can hope to lead more independent and successful adult lives.

Howlin and Moss (2012) and other studies reported high levels of stress and depression in parents whose school-aged children have been diagnosed with an Autism Spectrum Disorder (Kelly et al., 2008). The most significant factors that affect families with ASD are: having two or more impacted children, parents who themselves display autism phenotype "traits"; stress, isolation, and financial demands. Children with ASD diagnoses experienced more bullying and poorer quality of friendships. Siblings of children on the Spectrum may have more social challenges (Howlin & Moss, 2011). Kelly et al. identified five areas of concern for school-aged children with ASD including: understanding and expressing emotion, perspective taking, sensory sensitivity, rigidity, and orientation towards narrow areas of knowledge. Thus, a child with ASD struggles more with the social communication, collaboration, and play skills needed for a successful school experience. Howlin and Moss (2011) also suggested that family conflict impacted the level of symptoms children demonstrated. Families who can secure services can be supported; and thus be supportive of their children and adolescents, they can have better outcomes. The age of diagnosis and service provision has an impact not only on the individual but on the family as a whole. The discussion that follows describes the impact diagnosis may have on a family when the individual diagnosed is a toddler, child, adolescent, or an adult.

Toddlers

When a toddler is diagnosed all the work falls on the parents. Parents of a toddler with ASD often immediately embark on a race to find and qualify for the needed services. It can be an insurance nightmare to determine whether Applied Behavior Analysis (ABA) is covered; whether the family may qualify for federal funds, and once these logistics are ironed out, then comes the issue of who can provide these services. Often when toddlers are diagnosed treatment in a range of 15–30 h per week of ASD, specific intervention is recommended. Some insurance plans, though not plans originating in Colorado and many other states (see below), may deny ABA services with an autism diagnosis. Currently 31 states mandate that insurance providers provide coverage for the treatment of autism (National Conference of State Legislatures, 2014). While there seem to be ways around these mandates for some insurance carriers, mandated treatment is a step in the right direction. Families also often are encouraged to contact school districts, speech therapists, occupational therapists, physical therapists, feeding therapists, neurologists, the list goes on.

A comprehensive evaluation provides a useful guide in terms of knowing which specific services are recommended for each child. The importance of a comprehensive assessment from a qualified clinician and careful consult regarding services cannot be overstated. Families have been thrown into a whole new world of services and therapies. Often in feedback sessions, clinicians and parents discuss treatment priorities. Depending on the needs of each child a clinician should be able to recommend first steps, the essentials, and then provide information on other services that may address specific deficit areas. Often ABA therapy and a preschool program with an emphasis on social skills and social interaction are first steps.

When securing resources for a toddler, families often feel vulnerable to a host of offerings for expensive treatment that "should" help their children. For example, many families who have come back to the authors on this book, indicate that motor therapy has been recommended to their child, when no motor concerns were identified in the evaluation. Similarly, every child with autism does not require speech therapy, sensory services, or ABA therapy. Bear in mind that parents will also be introduced to many unsupported treatments which may be available such as certain diets, complementary and alternative (CAM) treatments, medicinal oils, neuromassage, biofeedback, and acupuncture. Some of these alternative therapies do have positive impact on some children with ASD and as such, it is not appropriate to dismiss them out of hand. Rather, educate parents on how to know if the treatment is working. Tell parents to ask questions about what is the expected treatment outcome after 3 weeks, 6 weeks, or 10 weeks. Have the parents ask how the progress in treatment will be documented and tracked. If indeed, the child is getting better, continue with that treatment. If, after 6 weeks or more, the child does not show improvement, these precious and limited funds, are better spent elsewhere or saved until a time when other services are needed.

This advice is only appropriate for treatments that may not necessarily have research efficacy but are not expected to have harmful effects. Other therapies, such as chelation and more invasive treatments of this nature, have been shown to cause harm and even death to patients. In that case, clinicians should clarify to parents in a direct and data-based fashion, the risk of these therapies and the lack of evidence for their use in treatment of ASD.

During a feedback session with a parent of a toddler who has been diagnosed with ASD, questions abound. Parents stop to breathe and begin wondering "What will this look like in 1, 2, 5, and 10 years?" "Will my child recover?" "Will his symptoms be noticeable?" "Who should we tell?" "Who should see this written report?" Parents also often wonder "What about the baby (other child not diagnosed)?" or "What if we have more kids?" Parents experience grief and loss of "normality" or "what is typical." On the one hand, many of their suspicions have been validated and this provides relief; however, at the same time, the parent is flooded with worries about the future. Parents then begin the process of attempting to make a change to view strengths, weaknesses, and set goals for building language, social skills, and behavioral compliance.

After receiving a diagnosis, parents of toddlers often have to embrace a change in their own interaction with their child. They may hear "Don't be so quick to do it for your child." "Don't modify the environment so much to avoid conflict that he does not learn flexibility." or "Do not anticipate needs because then he does not have to use language to request." These skills can be modeled and statements can be presented in a gentler manner but the fact remains that a diagnosis likely means a change in parenting strategies and a need to work harder. Some children are just more challenging to parent and professional guidance can be helpful.

With early diagnosis comes hope of recovery, the advantage of brain plasticity and the optimal outcomes Deborah Fein speaks of. At the same time it is overwhelming and scary. As clinicians we must understand what parents face when diagnostic feedback is provided. Some parents dive right in with an action plan while others need time to process. Usually it is the parents who suspected ASD, hear the news of strong cognitive abilities, and have already begun to investigate services who hit the ground running. For other parents a diagnosis of ASD is a shock, they have little knowledge of the Spectrum and they do not have a plan formulated. For most parents there is a level of grief and loss or at the least a need for refocusing and redirection.

Emily Perl Kingsley wrote an essay in 1987 about the experience of parenting a child with Down syndrome. She went on to make sure children with Down syndrome were provided services, recognized in the public (via the show Sesame Street), and she worked to help parents understand the challenges and limitations of Down syndrome. She notes in her 1987 essay "Welcome to Holland," "What do you mean Holland? I signed up for Italy! I'm supposed to be in Italy. All my life I've dreamed of going to Italy" (Stray & House 1987). She later goes on to write about the beauty and joy of being in Holland, but the sentiment is that when a parent is presented with an unexpected change in course, it is not ultimately easy and may require an enormous shift in perspective as well as tireless hours of work to support your child. As clinicians it is important to be ready to support families as they hear a diagnosis and change the course of their life.

Children

The age of diagnosis can be impacted by IQ, rigidity, language ability, parenting and community factors and whether a sibling has been diagnosed. Often children diagnosed younger have more obvious symptoms (Mandell et al., 2005). This diagnosis of a child under 2 or 3, may be harder for a family than the diagnosis of an older child who has more subtle symptoms. Older children are generally in mainstreamed school when they present for an evaluation so parents do not worry about whether children can be in mainstream education, can carry on conversations, or can take care of personal needs like dressing and toileting. School-aged children have passed these milestones and are referred for social skills and executive functioning weaknesses more frequently than for language deficits and self-injurious or repetitive behavior.

Diagnosis in childhood may indicate that symptoms are less noticeable. For example, Giarelli et al. (2010) found that females with good cognitive skills were diagnosed later than those with more severe symptoms. Despite perhaps a better symptom profile, diagnosis comes with it, for parents, a reexamination of who their child is. A parent is asked to recognize skill and ability deficits (as well as strengths) and reexamine the comforting reassurance that they have likely heard from friends, neighbors, pediatricians, etc. that "all children develop differently." The "wait-and-see" motto leads parents to sometimes delay evaluation and then later question whether they are intervening soon enough. The concept of diagnostic delay can play a role and a child may have not just an Autism Spectrum Disorder but also anxiety, behavior problems, or depression that have developed in the wake of untreated Autism Spectrum.

A parent may hear the diagnosis of autism and remark "That's just fine. I was the same way. We do not need to label my child." Howlin and Moss (2011) wrote that traits of ASD are common in parents. A parent may not see these challenges as problematic because from the parent's viewpoint, socialization is less crucial and perhaps a weakness for parents as well. The problem here is that just because a certain symptom is well known in the family, or commonly observed in other members, this in no way indicates it is less pathologic. This analogy equates somewhat to families who may have an uncle or parent who is an alcoholic and everyone is aware that "This is just how he always has been. Everyone knows uncle Ed is like that." The familiarity of the symptoms in some ways lessen the family's awareness that they are pathologic. This discovery that some long-held family traits are actually pathologic can in turn lead to stress between parents and other family members like grandparents, aunts, and uncles. A parent shared "Autism is too harsh of a word. People hear autism and think Rain Man and padded helmets." In some cases, the parents simply may not be ready to receive the diagnosis. Often, if the clinicians are clear and consistent, the family will come back and reopen the discussion after some time to digest it or to see the symptoms for themselves. The same parent referenced earlier stated, "My child may have these challenges but I don't want to call it autism." Later his wife shared that she felt she was embarking on this journey alone without any support. She was perhaps the only "neurotypical" in the family. The stress of tackling parenting as well as the IEP process unsupported led to symptoms of anxiety and depression in this mother. Another parent shared "I didn't have friends in elementary school. I liked to read and to study. There is nothing wrong with that." At the same time, his fifth-grade child had crawled under the classroom table and was curled up next to his mother's leg. He was experiencing real social challenges that one parent did not recognize. While the mother saw this as problematic, the father did not. Research indicates that these kinds of family challenges impact quality of life for all family members (Howlin & Moss, 2011).

Those diagnosed in later elementary school are likely bright and compliant. Often more subtle symptoms result in more emotional barriers for the family to accept the diagnosis. Additionally teachers, other therapists, and physicians may react with surprise and lead parents to feel confused about the diagnosis. One author of this book diagnosed a bright 6-year-old with Asperger's a few years ago. His parents felt enlightened and sought psychotherapy, social skills intervention, and a 504 plan at school. The classroom teacher and school psychologist said "This is not autism." As mentioned earlier in the text, professionals who are not qualified to make the diagnosis are also not qualified to rule it out; but these professionals had not noticed the symptoms and were quick to say so. This child's parents handled the situation beautifully and did not back down. They maintained a strong relationship with the school and the child got a 504 plan. As a third grader now, his school psychologist works weekly on social interventions and perspective taking and he continues to see his therapist, now twice a month. He is doing well but no one doubts his high-functioning Autism Spectrum Disorder. For this child, there was very little diagnostic delay. He has some difficulty managing teasing and with flexibility in social situations but he has a few friends, good grades, and is emotionally quite stable.

Another set of parents of a newly diagnosed fifth grader were quizzical. They had been referred by the school and agreed that there were social issues in that setting but as an only child their son was fine at home. They were cheerful and eager to share the diagnosis at school. Their son was diagnosed with only an Autism Spectrum Disorder, no additional challenges presented. The mother noted "We're quirky. Thank goodness our child isn't typical." She was eager to provide what he needed, in fact the school psychologist called a week later to follow-up. These parents were not grieving. They saw their son as a happy 11-year-old who needed extra social skills and executive functioning skill support and were eager to provide it.

What Should a School-Aged Child Know About His or Her Diagnosis

For those diagnosed in adolescence and childhood, parents often quickly ask "How, when, or should I tell him or her?" They have a fear of middle school and complex social skills as well as teasing and bullying. They may not want peers to find out about the diagnosis and they do not want their child to be devastated or lose valuable self-esteem over the diagnosis. From the perspective of the authors, explaining a diagnosis as a piece of a child's pattern of strengths and weaknesses can be helpful in fostering a strong sense of self. By starting with strengths like great verbal skills, artistic talent, or memory skills it is easier to embark on discussion of social weaknesses. Older children and adolescents tend to respond favorably to being included in the feedback session when it is conducted in a respectful manner that highlights how to build on personal strengths and cope with the challenges of ASD. Clinicians and parents are encouraged to use the child or teenager's own words. For example if they say in the evaluation: "I'm unique. I don't like to just go with the crowd." Or "Socially I'm shy. I just don't know what to say." Or "I don't think about emotions at all, so I really don't know how I feel." It can be very useful to cite these examples, use their own words, and share that Autism Spectrum provides a framework from which to understand themselves as individuals and as part of a network of children who share some of their differences. Often after hearing this, older children and teenagers are instilled with "universality," the sense that they are not alone. Many children and adolescents are able to own the "label" and take pride in who they are. Clinicians can share the many famous figures thought to have been autistic like Albert Einstein, Temple Grandin, and many famous "computer or science geeks" struggled to fit in with the fabric of society but were still able to find great success in their lives. The third grader discussed above explained his differences poignantly, stating, that he "loves his smart brain" but he just needs "a little help with social stuff."

Adolescents

Examining the transition from childhood to adolescence one study reported that mothers experience increased rates of negative impact from autism as their children enter adolescence. Anecdotally, the authors agree with this finding. Often, autism presents new challenges with each new developmental phase, adolescence, perhaps being the most difficult. This varies with the education of the mother, her ethnicity, and her perception of ASD (Carr & Lord, 2012). This is a longitudinal study of perceived negative impact with factors including financial, social, and emotional burdens. This construct is inversely related to parental well-being. That is, parents who were struggling with an adolescent who had ASD, were more impacted if there were also financial or other personal struggles occurring in the parent's life. Lord and Carr measured these factors using a semi-structured interview and rating scales. Autism Spectrum Disorder was found to have perceived negative impact that was generally worse than for other disorders. Mothers with higher education reported more negative impact from ASD than mothers with lower education.

A diagnosis made in adolescence may mean the symptoms of autism are quite subtle; perhaps having flown under the radar, for many years. There are exceptions, for example, when parents fear a diagnosis and delay evaluation until it is necessary to discuss issues like guardianship and disability benefits. At these times it is particularly emotional to see the level of disability an adolescent is burdened with and wonder what progress could have been achieved with earlier intervention. Often adolescents present for testing of their own accord, having read about autism on the internet or heard about it on the news. Some teens report that their parents insisted they be evaluated.

A diagnosis at this point in development is shared with both teenagers and parents and sometimes the biggest challenge is on the teenager him or herself. The teen years are a time of figuring out who you are and how you fit in socially, academically, or athletically. Teenagers can be dramatic and self-critical and probably express some level of "adolescent ego-centrism" a term introduced by David Elkind to explain adolescents' challenges differentiating between what they perceive and what others think and notice. Often teens with Autism Spectrum Disorders are described by parents as "selfish" "not caring about others" or "not aware of what others think." For teenagers with ASD it is even more difficult to take perspective and understand others than it is for a "typical" teenager. While parents may express concern that hearing a diagnosis could harm their son or daughter's self-esteem, often having an explanation for what always felt "different" is somewhat of a relief for a teen. When discussed thoroughly and presented in a sensitive way, many adolescents take on the ASD identity as part of their uniqueness. Other teenagers may have more difficulty accepting the diagnosis, but often it becomes a point of self-exploration. A feedback session with a teenager can be a place for a clinician to appeal to the teenager's appreciation of facts, structure, concrete information, and data. Some teens with ASD really enjoy setting goals and making a plan to make progress socially.

In many cases for teens, ASD becomes evident as social and relationship demands increase to an advanced level. Teenagers with ASD may excel academically, have a well-formulated college and career plan but lack mature social relationships. Others may have a few friends but prefer to be alone, excel at videogames, have executive functioning challenges, and report that they have never thought about the future beyond high school. Often questions about college or career planning are met with a blank stare. Having a diagnosis can lead to treatment in the form of social skills intervention, individual therapy, and executive functioning support in planning, organizing, structuring school work and chores, so that things are completed in a timely manner. Therapy with teens often focuses quite a bit on self-advocating, a skill that is helpful as teenagers become adults and do not have consistent support and supervision. Sometimes a teen with a high IQ who does well in school in some areas but struggles in others, may find comfort on learning about his or her cognitive profile. Highly gifted adolescents with ASD, for example, often have a scattered profile, with extreme strengths in nonverbal reasoning, average to high-average verbal skills, and extremely low processing speed. Armed with this information, teachers and parents are able to find compassion and understanding for a smart child who appears unmotivated or fails to get his work done at school. Parent teacher conferences may constantly conclude with, "I know he can do it but he just doesn't apply himself." Hearing about the child's cognitive strengths and weaknesses can aide in developing supports and accommodations for teenagers who display this pattern in their school performance.

It is somewhat infrequent that the authors of this text evaluate adolescents for an initial diagnosis and find only an Autism Spectrum Disorder. Often with teenagers, the issue of diagnostic delay does present itself and there are other concerns at the time of diagnosis in addition to autism. Comorbid diagnosis is associated with worse outcomes in adulthood and must be addressed immediately (Howlin & Moss, 2011). At times an anxiety or depressive disorder is the primary concern and psychotherapy, school supports, medication, and family therapy are needed to assure that an adolescent is on the right track. At these times social skills training and planning for the future must be put on hold as other diagnoses and symptoms are addressed. For example a teenager who is diagnosed with dyslexia, AD/HD, depression, and ASD will have treatment focused on addressing symptoms of depression including suicidal thoughts before any other area of concern is visited in depth. Once her mood has improved learning disabilities and AD/HD are likely to be the area of most concern as academic demands continue to increase over the high school years. Once these have been treated it will be time to work on social perspective taking, emotional perspective taking, and building relationships. Of course all four diagnoses are related. Challenges with communication and relationship building lead to social isolation and rejection. Learning disabilities and AD/HD undermine confidence and lead to poorer school performance. Executive functioning challenges are present in both AD/HD and ASD. Also, there will be considerable overlap in treatment. Of utmost importance, in this example the complexity of the picture is much greater now than it may have been. Imagine that learning disabilities had been addressed in elementary school and social skills interventions implemented for ASD. With that early treatment it is likely that this teenage client would not be depressed now.

How to Conduct a Feedback with an Adolescent

Parents of adolescents diagnosed with ASD may present for a feedback session without their son or daughter, and they may experience stress over how to present the data to their child or what reaction their teenager might have. Frequently parents choose to set up a session for their adolescent to see the data, ask questions, and hear information "from the professionals." The parents may feel comfortable having some discussion in advance of that setting and others may not. Some parents have shared discomfort at sharing the diagnosis at all. In these cases, clinicians work to help families feel more comfortable giving their adolescent child choices and opportunities to formulate an opinion themselves. This may take time, but it is important for parents to be able to be open with their teenager as soon he or she will have the right to make decisions without parent consent. Feedback sessions often focus on plans for developing independence, adaptive skills, and goals for post-high school. Some teenagers with ASD have poor hygiene, expect parents to drive them everywhere (for fear of seeking a license), and refuse to cook, do laundry, or clean their rooms. Some level of messiness is common in many teenagers but teens with ASD may have significant needs for support in developing these skills. At times ABA therapy in home can help the motivated teenager improve these skills for increased independence. Parents often express concerns about their child graduating from college, maintaining employment, achieving success in life and finding a partner. At this point, parents should know that we do not have all the answers, but there is reason to have hope. While the research regarding outcomes for adults with ASD does not look very promising at this point, indicating that symptoms tend to worsen in adulthood, because of the paucity of services available after high school (Mailick, 2014), there is a trend toward greater numbers of providers and better adult services. The authors of this book are in the process of developing more education around the need for adult services; as well as, adding to the field by provision of best practice adult respite care and therapy. Although services are scarce, particularly in Colorado, awareness is increasing, and services are slowly expanding to the adult population. Also promising is the fact that many of the individuals who are being diagnosed now are accessing services at younger ages and with more intensity than the adult population at present. This means that although the research on current adult outcomes is generally discouraging, the future for adults with ASD may be much brighter in a decade or two. If we as clinicians and parents can scaffold skills and support teens and adults as they attend college, interview for jobs, and pursue romantic relationships, hopefully adult outcomes will improve.

Conversely, when parents do not share the diagnosis with an older teenager, an individual who is 15, 16, 17, for example, they run the risk of their child resenting this fact later. It is best to allow an adolescent to formulate his or her own opinion about the data, given he or she is cognitively able to do so, and provide input to parents, teachers, and clinicians on supports like an IEP or 504 plan. The authors of this text have found that it works best when a parent shares initial results, allows a teenager to express his or her own opinion and offers to schedule a one-on-one feedback session with the teen and a clinician who can show the data, explain the diagnoses, and answer questions. It is better to have a teenager who sees the data, shares "I do not agree with this" and can feel heard than to have a teenager who feels his or her parents are withholding information. If parents are uneasy or unsure of how to provide this information they can discuss this in the feedback session and even role-play scenarios. On occasion these clinicians have been asked to tell the teenager together with parents and this can work well too provided the teen has adequate time to process and ask questions and does not feel "ganged up on."

Adolescence: Sexuality

Another central issue to diagnosis in the teen years that causes some parents to cringe is the issue of sexuality. Issues of sexuality exist for teenagers on the Autism Spectrum no matter when they were diagnosed, and across all levels of functioning, and parents are likely to have questions about how to address these. While parents of individuals with significant cognitive delays may report their child is not mature enough for these considerations, the physical body is often maturing at a faster rate than they realize. With individuals who have intellectual disabilities it is important to teach about body parts, masturbation, privacy, and safety. While it may be uncomfortable for parents, teenagers, and children need names for body parts, rules about where and when it is okay to take off clothing or touch oneself and understanding that it is not okay for people who are not doctors to touch you or have you undress. Sometimes when parents are uncomfortable with topics like masturbation for example, they may choose to ignore these behaviors and fail to teach when and where they are appropriate. Baker (2006, 2014a, 2014b) has developed visual schedules and guides for parents and clinicians to use when discussing masturbation with teens on the Spectrum; as well as, an excellent guide for teens regarding having a fulfilling dating life. Baker (2006) provides suggestions on how to read the signs from girls regarding their interest in dating, how to ask a girl out, and what to do on a date. Teens need to clearly understand the rules around harassment of other children at school and public masturbation. A lack of knowledge on these issues can lead to criminal behavior and charges. Those with autism are at an increased risk for being charged with other sexual offenses related to inappropriate touching or stalking or offenses related to pornography. Setting rules and having open dialogue is really important. As Nick Dubin writes in his book "Autism, Sexuality and the Law" (Attwood, Henault & Dubin, 2014) it can be very challenging to get individuals with autism to discuss sexuality but it is crucial that these conversations happen. Mr. Dubin himself endured an excruciating legal battle after being charged with possession of child pornography. His story is an example of an otherwise bright individual with autism who lacked the sexual understanding and perspective-taking skills he needed as a sexual being. This led to significant consequences for Mr. Dubin and his family (Attwood et al., 2014).

When children are younger it is important to have clear and concrete discussions about sex-defining terms, setting boundaries, and discussing privacy. A 7-year-old client came to one of the authors with frustration that he did not understand "puberty." He had been having a meltdown over after-school care and his parents were baffled about the change in behavior. Upon further discussion it was evident that during after-school care, an older student was talking very openly about sex and sexual development and speaking in inappropriate terms. The 7-year-old had quite a lot of sexual knowledge that his parents were not aware of and he was confused by some terms that were being discussed. This client had not reported the comments to an adult because he rationalized that the older student would deny it and he would get in trouble for accusing him. After talking with his therapist and mother, the issue was addressed and handled. He no longer avoided after-school care, and he and his father had open discussions during which his questions were appropriately addressed.

With higher functioning, teenagers concerns form around how to talk to members of the opposite sex, pursue dating interest and communicate once in a relationship. What is it appropriate to talk about? How do you ask someone out? How can you tell someone is interested in going out with you? What do you do if they are not interested? It is important that parents of teens with ASD provide clear and concrete guidelines and support. A therapist can also help to play this role. With middle-school and high-school students these authors have encountered times when students were accused of "stalking" because they misread cues. Dates went poorly because an individual with ASD said the wrong thing, moved too quickly, or moved too slowly. College-aged students in relationships could not understand why their girlfriends did not like them to look at pornography. In one case a student who had never had treatment for his ASD made very inappropriate sexual advances to another teenager mistakenly believing that she would find his behavior arousing. When parents are unsure of how to address some of these topics, meeting with a therapist or reading material can be helpful. Baker's (2006) book entitled, Preparing for Life: the Complete Guide for Transitioning to Adulthood for those with Autism and Asperger's Syndrome, is an excellent resource for answering questions regarding dating in ASD. Lynn Koegel Ph.D. and parent Claire LaZebnik authored a text "Growing up on the Spectrum" (2009) with information on how to talk to teenagers and young adults about sex and relationships. Jerry and Mary Newport, adults with ASD, authored "Autism-Asperger's and Sexuality: Puberty and Beyond" (2002) sharing their own experiences growing up and advice for parents from the perspective of someone with autism.

There is little research on sexuality and Autism Spectrum; but one study by Brown-Lavoie et al. (2014) investigated sexual victimization in teenagers and adults on the spectrum. Subjects were diagnosed with High Functioning autism and aged 19–43. The study suggested that these individuals have age-appropriate interest in sexuality, but they have limited knowledge and social skills deficits. Studies like this one have shown that those with ASD have less sexual knowledge and less understanding of privacy. Parents lack confidence in discussing sex openly for fear that it will lead to increased interest in sex and increased sexual behavior (Konstartareas & Lunsky, 1997). The results of Brown-Lavoie et al.'s study indicated that those with ASD had less social sources for sexual information, meaning fewer peers, parents and teachers, and more sources that included books, internet, even pornography. ASD subjects reported in interviews that sexual knowledge came from television and "Making mistakes." Males on the spectrum had more perceived knowledge of sex than actual knowledge. Overall less sexual knowledge led to a higher incidence of at least one count of sexual victimization. For the control population, 47 % had experienced some victimization and for the ASD group, 78 % experienced victimization. Overall results of this research indicate that 19–43-year-olds with Autism Spectrum Disorders lack the sexual knowledge to protect them from sexually transmitted diseases, lack knowledge of sexually appropriate behavior, and lack the knowledge of how to have safe sex.

Adolescence: Diagnosis in the Family

Another issue with later diagnosis of ASD in adolescence concerns whether a parent may also have a Spectrum Disorder. Often when there is diagnostic delay it can be related to one or both parents missing the symptoms or feeling that the social and communication challenges that go with ASD are "normal" and not a cause for concern. A diagnosis in adolescence may open family wounds and shed light on relationship challenges. An ASD diagnosis can have a great impact on the family system and everyone within it. In these cases, having a strong individual therapist as well as parent consultation or family therapy may be the best recommendation. The journey can be a difficult one but ultimately by communicating and respecting each other families can grow and find peace.

The transition from adolescence to adulthood shows improvement in parental well-being for the parents of adults who have ASD. There is lower stress reported by African American mothers than for Caucasian moms. Overall parental stress at each transition point is impacted by the individual's level of impairment (including adaptive skills and history of restricted repetitive behaviors), the number of children in the family, and amount of social support available. Also relevant are behavior problems, the onset of puberty, and the amount of therapy provided (Lord & Carr, 2012).

Adults

When adults are diagnosed with an Autism Spectrum Disorder may be self-referred, meaning, the individual him or herself has presented for an evaluation; or the referral may come from a spouse or partner who has urged the individual to seek an evaluation based on his or her concerns. Family members such as siblings and parents can make referrals for adult evaluations as well. Some adults respond to a diagnosis with "I thought so! This explains so much." Other adults may feel more overwhelmed and pose questions that may include: "Who do I share this with?" "How will ASD impact my career?" "How do I find a partner?" "How can I give my partner more emotional support?" "Do I want to marry?" "Since this can be genetic, am I the parent of a child with ASD?" "Do I want kids?" Psychotherapy is an excellent venue to address these questions and to help develop skills. Like teenagers, adults diagnosed for the first time are likely to have experienced bullying/social rejection, to have been depressed or to suffer from anxiety. Some may have been misdiagnosed with personality disorders and labeled antisocial or narcissistic. Any and all of the questions posed above most need to be addressed on an individual basis by a clinician experienced in diagnosing ASD in adults. Additionally many state and local Autism Society chapters have groups for adults diagnosed with autism as well as for family members of those diagnosed. These can be great resources. The diagnosing clinician should be ready to listen and process with the client and be able to provide resources for adult and family services.

Adults: Marrying Someone with an Autism Spectrum Disorder. What Does Diagnosis Mean?

Increasingly, clinicians who provide autism treatment are coming to understand that there are many adults with Autism Spectrum Disorder (ASD) who may be struggling in their intimate relationships or marriages without realizing they have ASD. Many times it's the neurotypical partner who suddenly realizes he or she is lonely even while having a partner or spouse. Other times, the conflict in a relationship signals that there are significant problems but traditional marital therapy or counseling doesn't seem effective. How does a spouse know if his or her partner has ASD?

Signs that an individual or his or her spouse may have ASD vary widely but nonetheless have common characteristics. These qualities include: weak or absent emotional facial expressions or gestures, that leave the partner feeling unsupported, especially when they share an emotional experience. Adults with ASD often have difficulty recognizing or communicating their own emotions talking instead about events, logistical details, or activities without any reference to feelings. Such absence of emotions inevitably hurts a couple's opportunity to feel close to each other since emotions color relationships and without feelings a relationship tends to seem bland, platonic, or mechanical.

Other signs of ASD in an adult include rigidity or repetitiveness often seen in conversations whereby the adult with ASD really only converses on one or two topics that he or she is highly interested in. The individual with ASD may tend to wear the same clothes, eat the same foods, dine at the same restaurants, or insist on the same schedule week to week and bids from their partner to make significant changes are met with resistance. Many times adults with ASD have a subtle awkwardness in their speech such as speaking with a flat tone, volume that's too quiet or too loud, or an irregular, halting rhythm.

Last but not least, adults with ASD can evidence difficulty taking appropriate responsibility for some things even while being quite successful in other areas of their life. Problems with initiating, planning, or organizing can manifest in securing and maintaining a job, or remembering to take care of the yard, car, or housework. Adult parents with ASD may have trouble, raising children, helping them get organized for school in the morning, and responding to them with sensitivity and nurturing. Other times, adults with ASD are meticulous about certain domestic chores and predictably become upset or angry if things are not repeatedly done the way they want.

Many of the qualities discussed above are seen in adults who don't have ASD. People may be depressed, angry, narcissistic, or just lazy and manifest many of these same problems. A big difference between ASD and these more common challenges is traits of ASD are generally unchanging regardless of how the person feels. People with ASD exhibit the same voice qualities, rigidity, conversational tendencies, or emotional depravity regardless of what's going or how they feel. They generally show these same qualities on good days and bad; at work and at home; on vacation or when visiting their mother. Furthermore, typical counseling that focuses on improving communication and sharing feelings is not very effective.

Without a diagnosis, it's very likely that one or both partners in a relationship will increasingly get angry, and the marriage or partnership is likely to ultimately fail. An evaluation is a courageous step for anyone to take. It typically requires a lot of strength and humility for a person to be committed to better understanding him or herself and important relationships. Adults considering an evaluation for ASD may question whether they will still be the same person after the evaluation. A significant difference will likely be that an individual can come to understand why he's struggled, why intimate relationships are so hard to maintain successfully, and why a partner feels frustrated or lonely. An expert clinician will strive to help an adult answer these questions with complete sensitivity and respect. Similarly, the skilled clinician can coach the spouse in developing empathy and patience with a partner who has ASD; in terms of adapting to his or her limitations, needs, and struggles.

Incidence Within the Family: What Does Diagnosis Mean?

As was discussed in this chapter, parents and families of individuals with ASD do experienced increased levels of stress. Howlin and Moss (2011) noted that frequently there are two or more impacted children in the family and one or both parents have the autism phenotype or at least a few traits of autism. A parent with symptoms of autism may not be the best model for social skills and behavior for their child. The family dynamics and relationships may be strained or a parent may feel "This is appropriate behavior; my child is just like me." This can be a strain whether some members of the family are diagnosed or undiagnosed. A typically developing sibling may be depressed/anxious or feel unsupported as the family works to help the child with autism. This study (Howlin & Moss, 2011) also reported that typically developing siblings may have more social challenges in childhood than average. A study of 69 adult siblings around age 40 found that these individuals were doing well, employed, had relationships and families, etc. Howlin & Moss did find an increase in anxiety around the future for siblings and what would happen to their autistic sibling when the parents pass away.

Lifespan and Death: What Is Life Expectancy?

According to Howlin and Moss (2011) there is "indication" that death rates for Autism Spectrum Disorders are higher than those for the general population. There is not extensive data on life expectancy and at this time few researchers are following the elderly. In a talk at IMFAR 2014 Joseph Piven, M.D., a distinguished researcher with the University of North Carolina at Chapel Hill, reported that his team was following a cohort of older adults to study outcomes of ASD at this period in life. He unexpectedly identified an elderly gentleman within the UNC cohort from Leo Kanner's original autism study and cohort from the 1940s. His anecdote reminds us that autism is still a relatively new diagnosis and we may not have extensive data on mortality because many individuals are still living. This is certainly good news.

Looking at what data is available it is indicated that the death rate is higher for those with severe impairments in learning and cognition and/or those with epilepsy (Howlin & Moss, 2011). It is estimated that epilepsy may occur in 11–39 % of individuals with Autism Spectrum Disorders, which is a much higher rate than in the population as a whole. It appears that those with Autism Spectrum Disorders have fewer deaths associated with alcohol and smoking and more deaths associated with drowning; even in those with higher cognitive ability. It is known that those with ASD have more severe gastrointestinal, digestive, motor and sensory challenges. At this time researchers are not clear on the relationship between these variables and mortality (Howlin & Moss, 2011). Ten percent of autism cases have association with genetically determined disorders like Fragile X which brings with it associated health problems and risks. Chromosomal issues are present in 5 % of cases of ASD and the Autism Consortium on Clinical Genetics suggests that families pursue chromosomal microarray analysis to further explore possible genetic variables that could impact health (Howlin & Moss, 2011). Obviously those without the ability to describe physical health and symptoms are at greater risk for medical complications as issues may go undiagnosed. Finally the issue of comorbid diagnosis increases the risk associated with having ASD. Those with severe depression and ASD for example will have an increased risk for suicide than those in the general population.

Concluding Remarks on Assessment Across the Lifespan

Back to Joe Piven and his point at IMFAR 2014, the field is still young in terms of understanding the lifespan of people on the spectrum, and this process and now is the time to develop a model for how we hope for individuals with autism to age and progress. What do we want the trajectory to look like? Researchers and clinicians alike wish to improve quality of life, increase social and leisure activities, provide supported work possibilities, and increase the number of friendships and romantic relationships for individuals on the Autism Spectrum. A model focused on more treatment and early intervention and less comorbidity. If treatment can target many points across the lifespan including toddlers, children, adolescents, adults, and elderly hopefully the quality of life, lifespan, and mortality data shifts dramatically. As Howlin and Moss (2011) postulate those we study now did not have the treatment options we have for young people today.

Summary of Part VI: Assessment in Applied Settings and Special Testing Considerations

All of this research points back to the need to close that first concern and diagnosis gap and expand the availability of services for those from a young age across their lives. Optimal outcome data says that a percentage of children move off the Autism Spectrum with the right intervention. Assessment technology continues to improve and treatment options are expanding. This provides hope. As clinicians in schools, clinical, and forensic settings, it is crucial to diagnose and provide treatment early, carry this through adolescence and adulthood and strive for better outcomes and quality of life for individuals with ASD at all ages. Readers of this book are charged now with expanding the path that was forged by the researchers who came before, as these authors have done, to search ever fervently to find the treatments and supports needed to bring healing, comfort, and the promise of a brighter future to individuals with ASD and their families.

Vignettes: Assessing Adults

By Khalid Mohammad B.S.
    Relationship Challenges within the Family
    George Smith
    Age: 45 years old
    This case study illustrates some of the challenges that may come with a late diagnosis and with a family in which a parent and child are both diagnosed with an Autism Spectrum Disorder.

Background

George is a 45-year-old divorced, father of two. George reports he originally got married because it was "consistent with his life goals." His marriage served a functional purpose for him in a stepwise progression of what his life course should be: get married, buy house, decorate house, have children. For George the connection with his wife was never the purpose of their interactions. Problems initially started when he began noticing a disconnect between what his wife wanted in the relationship and what George wanted. Concrete goals were not her only focus. She wanted an emotional connection, and more specifically emotional support. Although problems were beginning to be evident in the relationship, the pair had two children. The concrete role of father was a strength for George. Between diaper schedules and bottle schedules, his image of being a father was being met. In early childhood George's daughter Paulina began showing signs of ASD. This did not conform to George's rigid view of fatherhood and he could not make that shift.

George reports that his wife was developing anxiety; Paulina's symptoms persisted and George demonstrated a lack of growth in his own role in the family. George reports that at the same time he did not understand his daughter's inability to respond well to "traditional parenting" and did not understand an exceptional child. George's daughter Paulina was diagnosed with an Autism Spectrum Disorder at Emerge. Shortly after that time George and his wife were divorced. His lack of flexibility, rigid approach to relationships, and parenting challenges were at the root of the marriage's failure. George began therapy at Emerge. The focus of therapy became George's parenting, as he was approaching the process as if Paulina was a neurotypical child. Begrudgingly, George participated in an evaluation at the age of 40; George was diagnosed with an Autism Spectrum Disorder also.

George participates in weekly psychotherapy at this time. Present therapy focuses include: his parenting approach and his relationship with his children. He seems to struggle most presently with his second daughter who is neurotypical. He does not understand her need for an emotional connection with her father. As his children are getting older and are able to speak maturely like adults, he expects them to have the emotional processes of adults. He commonly asks his children "why are you angry?" "what's wrong?" He lectures his children on every mistake they make on homework and reports not understanding why they do not appreciate this help. Furthermore, he continues to search for a wife, but has continually failed in his pursuit of a partner. He reports wanting an "immediate link" with a partner. Online dating, speed dating, and other pursuits have been implemented as attempts at being efficient in finding a partner. Through therapy, George is learning that he is not willing to take the time to build an intimate connection. He reports that dating has failed as he has yet to find the "link" and George reports "I should know in the first 5 min if we have a link." George also reports that he has not been intimate since his first marriage. Although, he indicates he does not have a sex drive, he does report wanting a spouse and wishing to have a child with that spouse because he wants to take on a "traditional father role" and wants "an intact family unit." Overall, George is making small gains in cognitive flexibility despite a late diagnosis of an Autism Spectrum Disorder. He has ways to go in developing his social perspective-taking skills and improving his emotional reciprocity. George may not find a spouse soon but he is seeing positive changes in his relationship with his two daughters.

Jennifer

Adult Outcomes Case: Hope after Educational Challenges

An Adult Evaluation and Treatment

Age: 19 years, 6 months

Assessments

Behavior Assessment System for Children—Second Edition, (BASC-2) Self & Parent Reports

Wechsler Adult Intelligence Scale, Fourth Edition (WAIS-IV)

Wechsler Memory Scale, Fourth Edition (WMS-IV)

Rey Auditory Verbal Learning Test (RAVLT)

Woodcock-Johnson Tests of Achievement, Third Edition, Normative Update (WJ-III, Ach, NU)

Test of Variables of Attention (TOVA)

Rey Complex Figure Test (RCFT)

Stroop Color and Word Test, Adult Version

Tower of London, Second Edition (TOL-II)

Rorschach Ink Blot Test

Beck Anxiety Inventory (BAI)

Beck Depression Inventory (BDI-II)

Minnesota Multiphasic Personality Inventory, Second Edition (MMPI-2)

Vineland Adaptive Behavior Scales—Second Edition, (VABS-II) Parent/
Caregiver Rating Form

Clinical Interview with Jennifer and her Parents

Clinical Observations of Jennifer

Jennifer, a young adult, and her parents sought a neuropsychological evaluation at Emerge to determine whether a diagnosis of an Autism Spectrum Disorder was relevant. Her parents wanted her to succeed as an independent young adult in college with the goal of transitioning out of the home and living independently. Jennifer had attended one semester of college before moving back home due to anxiety and somatization symptoms after being away from her parents.

Jennifer was previously diagnosed with Major Depression by her psychiatrist who prescribed Wellbutrin and Citalopram to manage symptoms. Jennifer was described as a shy and obedient child by her parents who first became concerned about her development in middle school with concerns continuing throughout high school to the present evaluation. These concerns included independent decision-making skills; such as what to wear or what activities to participate in, maturity, lack of motivation; which included sleeping 15 h a day, mood swings, distractibility, and social interaction with peers. When away from her parents Jennifer reported becoming ill with symptoms of nausea, headaches, and fever; which wouldn't resolve until she returned home. The thought of leaving the home for Jennifer caused significant anxiety. Additionally Jennifer struggled with emotional awareness and would become physical, pushing and bumping others when upset and during arguments. Academically Jennifer is a bright student with slow processing speed who worked best in a small and nurturing environment. During middle and high school Jennifer felt overwhelmed by the large schools and the increased academic and social demands which lead to depression. She began therapy during this time with medication management from her psychiatrist. Jennifer's experience in college was unsuccessful as she missed classes, failed to complete assignments, struggled to make friends with peers, and would stay in her dorm room feeling ill for the majority of the semester.

During the evaluation at Emerge Jennifer was observed to be somewhat fidgety, distracted, and impulsive at times. Her overall affect was flat, expressing no emotion when discussing her anxiety and social and academic difficulties. Jennifer discussed her love for animals and working at a vet clinic. Although she enjoys this work it is noteworthy that she didn't seek out relationships with peers or co-workers, endorsing statements that she doesn't spend time with people outside of the setting in which they share, such as the clinic or school, is indifferent to others, and prefers not to have close friends. Testing results indicated that Jennifer's cognitive profile was strong in the areas of verbal comprehension and perceptual reasoning skills with relatively weak processing speed which affects her ability to complete assignments within expected time limits. Academic and executive functioning measures provided data on significant struggles with math ability. A large discrepancy between her achievement in math and exceptional performance in writing and reading, her inattention and impulsivity, and skill deficits in shifting set, planning, and organizing; all warranted a diagnosis of Mathematics Disorder (315.1). Additional diagnoses included Autism Spectrum Disorder (299.00) based on observations during the ADOS-2 which included being a matter of fact and missing symbolic meaning, displaying limited emotional awareness, and weakness in social reciprocity. Furthermore, emotional testing indicated significant anxiety surrounding family stressors such as unpredictable changes in routine and relational conflict with her siblings. Jennifer struggled to cope with stress effectively and would often withdraw from others leading to depression, anxiety, and isolation. Additionally her poor insight into how she feels and reliance on family members to tell her how she should be feeling or acting contributed to her low adaptive skills. Based on her emotional profile Jennifer received diagnoses of Generalized Anxiety Disorder (300.2) and Major Depressive Disorder, In Partial Remission (296.25).

Following the evaluation at Emerge recommendations included weekly psychotherapy to improve emotional awareness and manage anxiety and coping skills, tutoring to improve executive functioning, Applied Behavior Analytic support to improve adaptive skills for independent living, family therapy for Jennifer's parents to understand how to support a young adult with an Autism Spectrum Disorder, a consult with a metabolic specialist to address low energy and somatization when away from home, and a medication review with her psychiatrist. Since Jennifer was more likely to work slower than her peers based on her processing speed, academic recommendations included an IEP for utilizing disability services. These supports included extra time to complete assignments and tests, a modified or quieter environment to stay focused, copies of notes for her courses, tutoring services for math and organization, and access to counseling and support for anxiety and development of social skills.

Since executive functioning skills are imperative for successful independent living, Jennifer participated in an intervention program designed to teach life skills in preparation for college living. Through these treatment recommendations and independent life coaching, Jennifer was successfully able to move toward independence; enrolling in college, achieving good grades, building strong relationships with peers, and remaining employed at the clinic. After proper intervention and supports, Jennifer had a positive outcome. Her case delineates some of the academic challenges that present in adolescents with cognitive and emotional profiles that are common in ASD and comorbid conditions. This combination of diagnoses affected Jennifer's ability to adapt and cope with the increased academic and social complexities that adolescents face when entering college and becoming independent. Jennifer is an intelligent adolescent whose difficulties with anxiety, depression, attention, and executive functioning prevented her from achieving in college at a level commensurate with her Average to Superior intellectual functioning. This case is provided to highlight the promising outcomes which can occur when accurate diagnoses are made and a clear picture of strengths and weaknesses are obtained to identify and implement appropriate recommendations. Jennifer's continued success following the evaluation depicts the therapeutic result hoped for by parents and treating clinicians.

Footnote—States with laws for autism treatment at time of publication (Alaska, Arizona, Arkansas, California, Colorado, Connecticut, Florida, Illinois, Indiana, Iowa, Kansas, Kentucky, Louisiana, Maine, Massachusetts, Michigan, Missouri, Montana, Nevada, New Hampshire, New Jersey, New Mexico, New York, Pennsylvania, Rhode Island, South Carolina, Texas, Vermont, Virginia, West Virginia, and Wisconsin)

Appendix: Measures and Psychometrics

Other Measures Used in Comprehensive Neuropsychological and Psychological Assessment: Psychometric Properties and Administration

Many studies indicate that a comprehensive battery of tests in combination with sound clinical judgment and ASD-specific measures like the ADOS-2, ADI-R, and rating scales make up the most useful assessment for ASDs and the comorbid conditions that are often present (articles on emotional/attention comorbidity Trammell, Wilczynski, Dale, & McIntosh, 2013). It is important to note that measures across cognitive, language, memory, mood, anxiety, etc. are not normed on individuals with ASD and thus results must be interpreted with caution. This is especially relevant in considering measures of mood and anxiety as often individuals with ASD have low emotional awareness and are uncomfortable in social situations because of poor social perspective taking. Studies indicate that it is important to use these measures in combination with interviews and strong clinical observations to make diagnostic conclusions. The domains discussed below are important parts of a comprehensive psychological and neuropsychological battery for ASD assessment. Measures discussed provide a sample of measures available to assess the domains covered. This list is not exhaustive but provides information on many of the measures available.

Cognitive Measures and Their Administration

Cognitive assessment provides data to indicate skills in areas often including verbal abilities, nonverbal reasoning skills, spatial skills, processing speed or cognitive efficiency, and memory. It is valuable to assess for cognitive deficits because the most common comorbid condition for individuals with ASDs is an

© Springer International Publishing Switzerland 2016
A.P. Kroncke et al., *Assessment of Autism Spectrum Disorder*, Contemporary Issues in Psychological Assessment, DOI 10.1007/978-3-319-25504-0

Intellectual Disability (Trammell et al., 2013). Additionally assessment of intellectual functioning allows for discussion of cognitive strengths and weaknesses and can lend to recommendations for both academic and community supports depending on areas of strength and weakness identified. Sixty-five percentage of individuals with ASD are not intellectually disabled (Trammell et al., 2013). However; cognitive profiles tend to be more scattered in individuals with ASDs than in the general population (Joseph, Tager-Flusberg, & Lord, 2002). What follows is a discussion of measures utilized to assess cognitive abilities across age ranges. It is important to note that cognitive abilities do not become stable until approximately school age (Sattler, 2008) but measures provide information on skills and abilities at the time of assessment. This discussion includes a number of widely used cognitive measures but this list is not exhaustive.

Toddlers and Young Children

Mullen Scales of Early Learning

The Mullen is an individually administered test that can be administered with individuals from birth to age 68 months. One or both parents are often present for administration and cognitive skills are measured in the domains of Visual Reception, Expressive Language, Receptive Language, Fine Motor and Gross Motor skills. Scores are converted to T scores and Standard scores with a composite score including all domains except Gross Motor skills. This measure is most often used with very young children. As noted previously often individuals with ASD have stronger expressive than receptive language skills. This measure allows a comparison of language development even in a child who is 1–2 years old. Visual Reception as a scale is predictive of later cognitive abilities. The reliability and validity data for the Mullen indicates adequate internal consistency with a median coefficient range for the five scales from .75 to .83 and a high median value of .91 for the Early Learning Composite. Test–retest reliability was measured across two age-group samples; a younger group aged 1–24 months and an older group aged 25–56 months. Data showed a high stability level over time especially for the younger age-group with coefficient values ranging from .82 to .85 for the younger age-group including a high value of .96 for the Gross Motor scale and a value range of .71–.79 for the older age-group. Inter-rater reliability was strong as well with a range of .91–.99. Construct validity is supported by the principal-factor loadings of general intelligence ranging from .55 to .90 for all scales with the highest loadings for the Receptive and Expressive Language scales. The Mullen has good reliability and specificity as a measure of general cognitive ability (Mullen, 1995).

Differential Ability Scales: Second Edition Upper and Lower Early Years Battery

The Differential Ability Scales—Second Edition (DAS-II) Early Years Battery is an individually administered measure of cognitive abilities normed for administration with individuals aged 2 years, 6 months to 6 years, 11 months. This measure has an Upper Years core and a Lower Years core. The Lower Years core consists of four subtests, two under a verbal and two under a nonverbal domain. The Upper Years core includes six subtests adding a test of Matrix Reasoning and Copying designs to tests of Verbal Comprehension, Naming Vocabulary, Picture Similarities, and Pattern Construction. A spatial domain is also included with the verbal and nonverbal domains. Standard scores (Mean = 100, Standard Deviation = 15) are calculated from Ability scores along with T scores (Mean = 50, Standard Deviation = 10) for each subtest in both core batteries. A General Conceptual Ability (GCA) score is provided along with a Special Nonverbal Composite (SNC) score available only for the Upper Years core. In addition, percentiles and age-equivalents are available. The measure uses a cognitive profile approach and domains are in accordance with the Cattell–Horn–Carroll (CHC) model of intelligence (Elliott, 1990, 1995). Reliability data for the DAS-II Early Years Battery indicates mean internal consistency values of .95 for the GCA and SNC. Mean test–retest reliability is high for the GCA and SNC with coefficients of .90 and .85, respectively. Inter-rater reliability on some of the subtests is very high with coefficients of .98–.99 (Elliott, 1995). The DAS-II Early Years Battery has sufficient concurrent validity with other measures which yielded moderate-to-high correlations of .80 on intelligence, .81 on academic achievement, and .62 on language measures (DAS-II; Elliott, 2007; Sattler, 2008).

School-Aged Children and Adults

Wechsler Intelligence Scale for Children: Fourth Edition

The Wechsler Intelligence Scale for Children—Fourth Edition (WISC-IV) is a measure of cognitive ability for those aged 6–16 years. Scores are standard scores with a mean of 100 and standard deviation of 15. The WISC-IV has 15 subtests with a core of 10 summarized into four composites including Verbal Comprehension, Perceptual Reasoning, Working Memory, and Processing Speed. Composites combine to form a Full-Scale Intelligence Quotient which is an overall measure of intellectual ability (WISC-IV; Wechsler, 2003). A General Ability Index can also be calculated utilizing the Verbal Comprehension and Perceptual Reasoning scores (cite from GAI paper). This allows for calculation of an intellectual ability without considering Working Memory and Processing Speed. The WISC-IV is known to have reliability ranging from .96 to .97 for the Full-Scale IQ and .81–.95 for other composites (Sattler, 2008). Test–retest reliability ranges from .84 to .93 and internal consistency reliability measures .68–.89. The WISC-IV was standardized on a sample of 2200 children from 11 age groups, equal males/females, and a wide variety of ethnicities. The test shows adequate criterion-related validity compared to other Wechsler tests (.73–.87) though Sattler (2008) notes that evidence would have been stronger if the test was compared to other cognitive tests from a different publisher. Factor analysis was conducted noting good construct validity (Sattler, 2008).

Differential Ability Scales: Second Edition School-Age Battery

The Differential Ability Scales—Second Edition (DAS-II) School-Age Battery is an individually administered assessment of cognitive ability in individuals aged 7–17 years, 11 months. Domains assessed include Verbal Ability, Nonverbal Reasoning Ability, and Spatial Ability. There are six subtests, two in each of the three domains: Word Definitions, Verbal Similarities, Matrices, Sequential and Quantitative Reasoning, Recall of Designs, and Pattern Construction. Standard scores (Mean = 100, Standard Deviation = 15) are calculated from Ability scores along with T scores (Mean = 50, Standard Deviation = 10) for each subtest. GCA and SNC scores are provided. In addition percentiles and age-equivalents are available. The measure uses a cognitive profile approach and domains are in accordance with CHC model of intelligence (Elliott, 1990, 1995). Reliability data for the DAS-II School-Age Battery indicates mean internal consistency values of .96 for the GCA and SNC. Mean test–retest reliability is high for the GCA and SNC with coefficients of .90 and .85, respectively. Inter-rater reliability on some of the subtests is very high with coefficients of .98–.99 (Elliott, 1995). The DAS-II School-Age Battery has sufficient concurrent validity with other measures which yielded moderate-to-high correlations of .80 on intelligence, .81 on academic achievement, and .62 on language measures (DAS-II; Elliott, 2007; Sattler, 2008).

Wechsler Adult Intelligence Scale: Fourth Edition

The WAIS-IV is used to assess individuals ranging in age from 16 years to 90 years 11 months. Indices assessed include Verbal Comprehension, Perceptual Reasoning, Working Memory, and Processing Speed. The WAIS-IV has a mean of 100 and standard deviation of 15. The WAIS-IV has 15 subtests with a core of 10 summarized into the four composites listed above. Each composite index combines to form the Full-Scale Intelligence Quotient which measures overall intellectual ability. Reliability for the Full-Scale IQ ranges from .97 to .98 across all age groups and .87–.98 for other composites. Test–retest reliability ranges from .87 to .96 across all five indices and inter-rater reliability measures .91–.99 (WAIS-IV: Wechsler, 2008). The WAIS-IV was standardized on a sample of 2200 individuals from 13 age groups with equal male to female ratios for all age groups except the five older age groups aged 65 years to 90 years, 11 months and also included a diversity in ethnic backgrounds, education levels, and geographic origins. The WAIS-IV shows strong criterion-related validity with composite correlations ranging from .83 to .94 when compared to the WAIS-III and .77–.91 when compared to the WISC-IV among other measure comparisons. Construct validity included average intercorrelations for the Full-Scale IQ with coefficients in the range of .54–.72. Correlation coefficients with the WISC-IV suggest a highly agreeable measure of similar constructs leading to strong construct validity (WAIS-IV: Wechsler, 2008).

Conclusions

The cognitive measures discussed all have adequate reliability and validity. The nonverbal measures do have some drawbacks but can provide useful information when used as part of a comprehensive battery. When assessing the cognitive skills of a nonverbal individual it is also possible to use nonverbal reasoning or spatial scales from one of the more comprehensive measures. It is important to provide some measure of cognitive ability both to rule out intellectual disabilities and to provide useful data to guide treatment planning and determine other areas to assess in a comprehensive battery. Significant splits in index scores on cognitive measures provide data on strengths and weaknesses and can lead to determination of other tests to include. Individual subtest score differences are also helpful to assess. Often individuals with ASDs have stronger rote verbal skills and weaker skills on comprehension measures. This is not always the case but significantly different scores may lead a clinician to give a pragmatic language measure or consider comprehensive language testing as discussed below. If an individual with an ASD has Very Superior verbal performance across domains, the language assessment may not be as useful. Individual subtest differences can be analyzed considering timed versus untimed measures and a person's performance across testing from the first to last administered subtest. Considering individual scores and composites can be most helpful in understanding a client and making comprehensive diagnostic decisions.

Assessing Language to Provide Diagnostic Information

Assessing language development particularly in young children and school-aged children can be very helpful as a part of the diagnostic assessment for ASD. Communication is a core deficit of Autism Spectrum Disorders and is an area that should be assessed directly and indirectly in a variety of ways for a comprehensive assessment. While some individuals may have particularly high scores across language measures, many individuals may have more varied patterns of language development. As noted above when Verbal Comprehension abilities are Very Superior and are equally high across subtests, a language measure like the CELF-4 may be less helpful than it would be for an individual with a more varied cognitive profile. In this case often noting the prosody, tone, and formality of language is most useful. When an individual has lower comprehension scores or a varied profile including working memory deficits it may be helpful to assess areas like expressive language, receptive language, language content, or language memory. The language and word structure tasks administered to children up to age 8 may provide useful information on language errors like pronoun reversal or incorrect use of irregulars. Speech Therapy and ABA Therapy may be prescribed for younger children to treat areas of language weakness.

Clinical Evaluation of Language Fundamentals: Fourth Edition

The Clinical Evaluation of Language Fundamentals—Fourth Edition (CELF-4) is an individually administered test of language and communication development that takes anywhere from 30 to 60 min to administer. It is used in the identification of language abilities and disorders for students in order to provide recommendations and determine eligibility for obtaining services like an IEP. The measure is administered to those aged 3–21 years and has a Preschool form for younger children 3–6 years. The CELF provides a Core Language assessment score as well as scores in the domains of Receptive Language, Expressive Language, Language Content, Language Structure, Language Memory, and Working Memory. There are 19 subtests that comprise the six indexes above. Many scores are utilized and include raw, scaled, standard, age-equivalent, and percentile scores. Age-equivalent scores are provided for the scaled and composite scores. The composite standard scores have a mean of 100 and standard deviation of 15 while the scaled scores have a mean of 10 and standard deviation of 3. The CELF Preschool is nearly identical with overlapping subtests and domains although some of the subtests and the Working Memory index are not included. The CELF assessment process model can be broken into four levels; Level 1: Identify whether or not there is a language disorder, Level 2: Describe the nature of the disorder, Level 3: Evaluate early classroom and literacy fundamentals, and Level 4: Evaluate language and communication in context. Each level comprises a specific set of subtests and can be used separately and in any order based on the individuals presenting profile and reason for referral allowing for flexibility in assessment. In addition the CELF test model assesses four broad aspects of language which are morphology and syntax, semantics, pragmatics, and phonological awareness. Test–retest reliability ranged from .71 to .86 for the subtests and .88–.92 for the composite scores. Internal consistency data indicates stable item content with value ranges of .69–.91 for subtests, and .87–.95 for composite scores. The inter-rater reliability for some of the subtests that require clinical judgment ranged from .88 to .99 indicating high inter-scorer agreement. Vast support and evidence of validity for the CELF is provided with high sensitivity and specificity for distinguishing the presence or absence of language disorders for tested populations (CELF-4; Wiig, Secord, & Semel, 2006).

Controlled Oral Word Association Test

The Controlled Oral Word Association Test (COWAT) is one of a number of subtests included in the Multilingual Aphasia Examination, Third Edition (MAE-III). The MAE-III is utilized in the evaluation of aphasic disorder and is normed for use with individuals ranging in age from 16 to 69 years. The COWAT is an oral fluency test whereby the examinee is instructed to make verbal associations to different letters by saying all the words they can think of which begin with that letter. The test structure includes two forms (A and B) each with three letters of increasing difficulty based on the amount of words which begin with each letter according to English language dictionaries. A practice letter is given prior to the first letter to confirm the subjects understanding of the test instructions. A raw score is totaled based on the sum of all correct response words from the three letters. In addition, the examinee's age, sex, and level of education can affect performance so adjustments in the total raw score are made accordingly. Psychometric data indicates a correlation coefficient between the COWAT and the Visual Naming subtest of the MAE-III of .56 indicating that both tests require retrieval of words. A value of .34 was obtained between the COWAT and Sentence Repetition indicating minimal common variance (MAE-III: Benton, Hamsher, & Sivan, 1994). Reliability data included internal consistency with a high correlation coefficient of .83 and a moderately high average intercorrelation of .61 for the items/number of words for each letter. Test–retest reliability was satisfactory with a correlation value of .74. Both measures of reliability provide evidence supporting the COWAT as a reliable and stable test (Ruff, Light, Parker, & Levin, 1996).

Expressive One-Word Picture Vocabulary Test: Fourth Edition

The Expressive One-Word Picture Vocabulary Test—Fourth Edition (EOWPVT-4) is an assessment of verbal expression and the ability to name and generate words for individuals who range in age from 2 to 80+ years. The EOWPVT-4 is frequently used across multiple disciplines to evaluate expressive vocabulary and usually takes 20 min to administer. The test is a counterpart to the Receptive One-Word Picture Vocabulary Test—Fourth Edition (ROWPVT-4) which examines understanding the meaning of words and scores can be compared to each other. There are 190 items which are colored pictures and illustrations in which the examinee is asked to name with one-word what is seen. The items are presented in a sequence that is developmentally appropriate. As a vocabulary test the EOWPVT-4 plays a role in child and adult cognition, language ability, and academic achievement and has been developed with regard to each of these areas. The EOWPVT-4 has outstanding reliability data. Internal consistency is high ranging from .93 to .97 for all age groups with a median of .95. Test–retest reliability coefficients for the raw scores is .98 and for standard scores is .97 suggesting consistent stability over time. Construct validity was tested by comparing EOWPVT-4 scores to other measures which included the WISC-IV VCI, EOWPVT-3, ROWPVT-4 standard scores, and ROWPVT-4 raw scores. The corresponding coefficients are as follows: .43, .95, .69, and .86. Results show the highest correlations between the EOWPVT-3 and ROWPVT-4 which is to be expected since these measures are testing very similar constructs. Criterion-related validity was tested by comparing the EOWPVT-4 to a reading and cognitive test. The STAR reading test yielded a value of .69 while the WISC-IV FSIQ yielded a value of .35. A positive but weak correlation to the WISC-IV is expected since the EOWPVT-3 is not an outright language measure and vocabulary is only one aspect of broader language abilities that are frequently incorporated in cognitive tests. Overall the data supports validity of the EOWPVT-4 in assessing vocabulary abilities (EOWPVT-4; Martin & Brownell, 2011).

Peabody Picture Vocabulary Test: Fourth Edition

The Peabody Picture Vocabulary Test—Fourth Edition (PPVT-4) is a measure used in the assessment of receptive vocabulary for individuals who are 2 years, 6 months through 90 years. The test examines the ability to understand spoken language and is used in a variety of applications including the identification of reading and language impairments requiring only 10–15 min for administration. There are two forms available for use each with 228 items. The examinee is instructed to choose one picture from four colored pictures on each page that goes best with the meaning of a spoken stimulus word by the examiner. All the items are grouped into 19 sets of 12 items each and organized by gradual increase in difficulty. The PPVT-4 is co-normed with another measure of expressive vocabulary, the Expressive Vocabulary Test—Second Edition (EVT-2). Both age and grade norms are available and various scores can be derived from the raw scores on the PPVT-4. These scores include a standard score, stanines, growth-scale values, normal curve equivalents, age and grade equivalents, and percentiles. The concept of vocabulary although strongly related to other areas such as cognition and reading comprehension is a unique and distinct form of achievement. Reliability is excellent and is evidenced by internal consistency coefficients in the high .90s across all ages and grades as well as test–retest coefficients that range from .92 to .96 with an average of .93. Construct validity studies included PPVT-4 score comparisons to the EVT-2 and parts of the CELF-4. A coefficient range of .80–.84 was obtained with a mean of .82 for the EVT-2 comparison while a range of .67–.75 was obtained for the CELF-4. The former indicates that both tests measure word retrieval, while the latter suggests a moderate relationship with abilities that are somewhat related but different. The reliability and validity data lend to strong support of the PPVT-4 as a measure of receptive vocabulary (PPVT-4; Dunn & Dunn, 2007).

Test of Pragmatic Language

The Test of Pragmatic Language (TOPL) is an individually administered measure of pragmatic or social language for those aged 5–13 years old and takes on average 30–45 min to administer. The TOPL uses standard scores with a mean of 100 and a standard deviation of 15. The test model for the TOPL uses a three-dimensional system comprised of two pragmatic modes of communication, two pragmatic components, and six pragmatic variables. The two modes of communication include *receptive language* or incoming information and *expressive language* or outgoing information. The first pragmatic component within this system is *context* which describes the environment of a conversation and the audience that conversation is directed towards. The second component is *message* or the actual communication itself which includes areas such as the topic, content, and purpose of the conversation. The third dimension houses six pragmatic variables which are: physical setting, audience, topic, purpose, visual-gestural cues, and abstraction. Reliability data indicates adequate internal consistency with a coefficient range for all ages from .74 to .89 with the .74 coefficient being the lowest for age 6. Additionally inter-rater reliability was good at .99. Validity data indicates a sufficient correlation coefficient value of .70 on a comparison of the TOPL to the language subtest of the Screening Children for Related Early Educational Needs (SCREEN) test lending to evidence of construct validity. Concurrent validity was also sufficient with a value of .82 (TOPL; Phelps-Terasaki & Phelps-Gunn, 1992).

Social Communication Questionnaire

The Social Communication Questionnaire (SCQ) is a screening measure of Autism symptomatology for individuals suspected of having an ASD who are 4 years and older and have a minimum mental age of at least 2 years. The SCQ assists in the decision to consider a more comprehensive assessment of ASD with measures such as the ADOS-2 and ADI-R and was originally developed as a companion to the ADI-R. The SCQ is a 40-item parent-report rating scale with "yes or no" questions that takes on average 15 min to complete and score. Two forms are available; one examines the individual's entire developmental history while the other form assesses their behavior across the most current 3-month period. The measure uses a Total score which is compared to a cutoff score of 15. Any score of 15 or higher is considered significant for a possible ASD and further assessment is recommended. The item selection on the SCQ is based on the ADI-R algorithm and focuses on three specific domains or areas of functioning: Reciprocal Social Interaction; Communication; and Restricted, Repetitive, and Stereotyped Patterns of Behavior. Factor analyses surveyed four distinct factors: Social Interaction, Communication, Abnormal Language, and Stereotyped Behavior. All factors were found to coincide with one or more of the three algorithm areas discussed above. Reliability coefficients were .90 for the total scale, .91 for the first factor, .71 for the second factor, .79 for the third factor, and .67 for the fourth factor. Concurrent validity is supported by a study from Norbury and Bishop (2002) comparing the ADI-R to the SCQ for each of the three ADI-R domains and indicated intercorrelations of .92, .73, and .89 for each respective area. Overall the SCQ is a good screening measure which provides a reasonable view of symptom severity for individuals with possible ASD (SCQ; Rutter, Bailey, & Lord, 2003).

Wepman's Auditory Discrimination Test: Second Edition

Wepman's Auditory Discrimination Test—Second Edition (ADT) is a quick assessment of a child's ability to discriminate between phonemes used in English and hear spoken language correctly. Auditory discrimination helps in the development of language and articulation in children and the ADT is used to measure this skill in those ages 4–8 years. It is commonly used in children with suspected learning, speech, and language difficulties. Word pairs are presented and the examinee is instructed to indicate verbally or nonverbally whether the two words are the same or different. The ADT is available in two forms for retesting and each form contains 40 pair word items. Thirty items are dissimilar by a single phoneme while the rest are identical. Calculated scores include a raw ADT Total score, a Qualitative score, T scores, and percentiles. There are also two scores used to check validity of responding. The Qualitative score ranges from −2 to +2 and is an estimate of discriminative ability level. The T scores have a mean of 50 and standard deviation of 10 with a score less than 40 indicative of a deficit in auditory discrimination. The ADT has excellent reliability with moderately high total correlations of .80 and .83 on both forms for internal consistency. Test–retest coefficients were also found to be high across three studies with values in the high 80s and 90s. Several studies examined criterion-related validity comparing the ADT to other tests of auditory processes. These tests included the Test of Nonverbal Auditory Discrimination (TENVAD), the Screening Test of Auditory Perception (STAP), and the Templin Sound Discrimination Test. Correlations were found to range from moderate to high for all these measures. In addition when the ADT was compared to tests of academic achievement and intelligence moderate correlations were found as well. Factor analyses identify a single factor labeled as auditory discrimination which is measured by the ADT yielding significant test validity (ADT; Reynolds, 1987).

Adaptive Skills

Assessing adaptive skills domains is important in a comprehensive evaluation for ASD because information on adaptive skills strengths and deficits can be important in guiding treatment and in making diagnoses. Often parents state something along the lines of "I know my child but I don't know what is "typical" development in these areas." Collecting parent-report data and sometimes teacher report data on adaptive skills allows a clinician to provide normative data on adaptive skills and inform parents of their child's progress in relation to peers.

Adaptive skill assessments such as the Vineland-2, SIB-R, and ABAS-II allow parents or caregivers to report skills across communication, daily living skills and social domains. The Vineland-II and SIB-R also collect data on problem behaviors. An adaptive assessment is the most important piece of data in determining an intellectual impairment and with ASD, adaptive skills assessment can provide specific data on weaknesses in domains like social interaction or personal self-care. Sometimes very bright individuals with ASD have poor hygiene, community living skills, or receptive communication. It is also helpful to know when individuals do not have these deficits. Some well-meaning parents may have unrealistic expectations for their children. For example a parent who expects a 2-year-old to eat a hamburger on a bun without issue when a plate is presented may be concerned because the child needs to have food cut into small pieces. This parent may be comforted to see that their child has age-appropriate daily living skills and to understand that more scaffolding of feeding is warranted.

Vineland Adaptive Behavior Scales: Second Edition

The Vineland Adaptive Behavior Scales—Second Edition (VABS-II) is an assessment system used to measure adaptive behavior with individuals from birth through 90 years. There are three versions available that include two survey forms, an Expanded Interview Form, and a Teacher Rating Form. The two survey forms consist of a Survey Interview and Parent/Caregiver Rating Form both of which assess behavior across four broad domains: Communication, Daily Living Skills, Socialization, and Motor Skills. Each domain coalesces to yield an Adaptive Behavior Composite. Additionally a Maladaptive Behavior domain is included in the evaluation of problem behaviors and is composed of three subscales: Internalizing, Externalizing, and Other. Overall the VABS-II contains 11 sub-domains which are grouped into the four broad domains above. Numerous scores are utilized and include raw scores, standard scores, stanines, v-scale scores, adaptive levels, age-equivalents, and percentiles. Each sub-domain uses a v-scale score which are summed to yield respective composite scores. The test structure is based on factor analyses which purport a three- or four-factor model to fit best with each factor classified as one of the broad domains previously discussed. Internal consistency reliability data for the sub-domains is overall moderate-to-high with most coefficients at .75 or greater. The domain coefficients are mostly high as well in the upper .80s to low .90s. Average test–retest coefficients for sub-domains were mostly high at .85 or greater. Domain coefficients ranged from .88 to .92 however, lower values were present for ages 14–21 across all domains. Inter-rater reliability data indicates values lower than test–retest values on the Survey Interview Form which suggests that there is an examiner effect on scores. Inter-rater data for the Parent/Caregiver Form was comparable to the Survey Interview Form results with moderate values suggesting it could be used across raters if they knew the individual well enough. Reliability data is also provided for the Maladaptive Behavior Index. Internal consistency coefficients ranged from .85 to .91. Test–retest coefficients were high exceeding .85. Inter-rater coefficients are moderate to high for both the Parent/Caregiver and Survey Interview Forms. When compared to the Behavior Symptoms Index on the BASC-2 there was a moderate correlation of the Maladaptive Index subscales with a coefficient of .69. Validity studies with a clinical group of children with ASD found Adaptive Behavior Composite scores to be more than two standard deviations below the mean when compared to the nonclinical control group. The lowest domain for the ASD group was Socialization which supports the diagnostic criteria of deficits in socialization and expressive communication for this population. Overall the VABS-II has good reliability and validity in its use as a tool in evaluating adaptive behavior (VABS-II; Sparrow, Cicchetti, & Balla, 2005).

Scales of Independent Behavior: Revised

The Scales of Independent Behavior—Revised (SIB-R) is a measure of adaptive functioning and problem behaviors across multiple everyday settings. Results can be used to guide program development and assist in obtaining access to required services. A very broad age inclusion starting from infancy through 80 years and older allows for its use in many populations where adaptive functional independence is of concern. The SIB-R offers convenient test flexibility with multiple forms available for administration including a Full Scale, Short Form, and Early Development Form. To examine problem behaviors, each form includes a Problem Behavior Scale. The Full Scale is comprised of 259 items subsumed under 14 subscales which are sorted into four adaptive behavior clusters: Motor, Social Interaction and Communication, Personal Living, and Community Living. The Short Form has 40 items which are from these subscales while the Early Development Form also has 40 items that pertain specifically to the development of young children. Both the Short Form and Early Development Form have raw scores that range from 0 to 120 and take on average 15–20 min to administer. Administration time for the Full Scale is longer at around 1 h. The Problem Behavior Scale is structured across eight areas which are organized into three broad maladaptive behavior indexes: Internalized, Asocial, and Externalized. The SIB-R contains item scores which are summed and converted into raw scores. The raw scores are then converted into derived scores. Standard scores with a mean of 100 and standard deviation of 15 and corresponding percentiles are utilized. Age-equivalent scores are also available for comparison by age. A combination measure of both Adaptive and Problem behaviors provides a Support score which ranges from 0 to 100 and indicates the level of support an individual may need. Other scores include a Maladaptive Index Score which ranges from +5 to −70 with an average of 0 and standard deviation of 10. More negative scores indicate that more serious behavior problems are present. Reliability data is discussed beginning with internal consistency and followed by test–retest and inter-rater. For all ages the Short Form coefficient was .76. For all ages the Full-Scale subscale range was .70–.88. On the cluster scores the median coefficients for all ages are as follows: Motor Skills (.88), Social Interaction and Communication Skills (.90), Personal Living Skills (.94), Community Living Skills (.91), and Broad Independence (.98). The Early Development Form had a value of .84. A study on internal consistency with disabled children aged 6–13 yielded high coefficient values with .97 for the Short Form, .92–.98 for the Full-Scale subscales, and .99 for all cluster scores except Social Interaction and Communication Skills which was .98. Reliability data continues with test–retest studies for children aged 6–13. The data indicates a value of .97 on the Short Form and a range of .83–.97 on the Full-Scale subscales. Cluster score values are .96, .96, .97, .96, and .98, respectively. One study presented a Support Score value of .96 with moderate-to-high Maladaptive Behavior Index values: Internalized (.83), Asocial (.83), Externalized (.80), and General (.83). The test–retest coefficient on the Early Development Form was high at .97 and Maladaptive Behavior coefficients are listed as follows: Internalized (.90), Asocial (.90), Externalized (.85), and General (.92). Final reliability data is presented through inter-rater studies between mother/father and teacher/teacher aides as raters. The data indicates consistently high correlation coefficients similar to the values presented above across different forms, raters, scales, subscales, and indexes. The studies on inter-rater reliability were conducted with children aged 6–13 and adolescents with and without intellectual disabilities. Numerous studies lend evidence to strong validity in all its applications. Overall the comprehensive reliability and validity data presented support the SIB-R as a strong measure of adaptive and problem behaviors.

Assessment of Emotional Functioning

Research indicates that mood and anxiety disorders are the most prevalent comorbid psychological diagnoses among those with ASD (Trammell et al., 2013). Measures used to assess psychopathology like the MMPI-2, Beck Depression Inventory, etc. often do not include individuals with ASDs in the standardization sample resulting in poor discriminant and predictive validity (Trammell et al., 2013). Trammell et al. goes on to say that the lack of instruments intended to assess mood and anxiety in individuals with ASD poses a challenge for clinicians. Individuals with ASDs often lack insight into their emotions and/or internal thought processes. They also tend to use more dichotomous adjectives like "always" or "never" to describe thought processes. Self-report measures must be used and interpreted with caution in this population (Deprey & Ozonoff, 2009).

The authors' experiences indicate that using a variety of instruments is best. Collecting teacher and parent rating scales, interviewing parents and taking behavior observations provide assessment of a child or adolescent's mood without asking them directly. Additionally rating scales, interviews, sentence completion measures, projective drawing or story measures can all provide insight into anxiety or depression.

Children's Depression Inventory: Second Edition (CDI-2)

The Children's Depression Inventory—Second Edition (CDI-2) is an instrument used to assess depressive symptoms in children and adolescents aged 7–17 years during the most recent 2-week period. The measure is available in hand and computer versions for individual and group administration. The CDI-2 is comprised of four forms. Two forms are self-rated scales and include a 28-item full CDI-2: SR form and a short CDI-2: SR(S) form. The other two forms are adult-rated scales and include a 17-item parent CDI-2: P form and a 12-item teacher CDI-2: T form. The CDI-2: SR(S) short form is employed for screening purposes. There is a three-point option per item on the CDI-2: SR form which ranges from (0=none) to (2=definite). For both of the adult-rated forms a four-point scale is used and ranges from (0=not at all) to (3=much or most of the time). Both of the adult-rated forms as well as the self-rated SR form have two scales: Emotional Problems and Functional Problems. Each of these scales includes two subscales: Negative Mood/Physical Symptoms, Negative Self-Esteem and Ineffectiveness, Interpersonal Problems, respectively. Scoring the CDI-2 involves summing the items to obtain raw scores which are then converted to T scores and percentiles based on specific age and gender groups. The groups are separated by male and female for two age groups: 7–12 and 13–17. Interpretation of the scores falls into five categories; Very Elevated, Elevated, High Average, Average, and Low, each with relative T scores and percentile ranks. The test structure for the CDI-2 is composed of the four sub-scales and two scales mentioned above, and a Total Depression score. Reliability data indicates an internal consistency coefficient range of .67–.91 across all forms, for the total score and all subscales, across all ages and genders. Test–retest reliability data indicates satisfactory short-term stability of the self-report forms although the adult-rated forms were not tested. Additionally, data is available for the construct validity of the CDI-2. On the SR form a high correlation of .77 was found between the two broad scales. A moderate correlation range was found for the subscales (Hong & O'Neil, 2001). The correlation between the Full and Short self-report forms was .95, while the adult-rated forms had moderate correlations of .61 and .65 on the Parent and Teacher forms, respectively. Convergent validity is supported through comparisons of the CDI-2 to the Beck Depression Inventory—Youth (BDI-Y) and the Conners Comprehensive Behavior Rating Scales (Conners CBRS) which found moderate values supporting the congruency of the CDI-2 with other tests which measure depression. This data suggests that the CDI-2 assesses the construct of depression and provides distinctive information obtained from various rater perspectives (Bae, 2012).

Revised Children's Manifest Anxiety Scale: Second Edition

The Revised Children's Manifest Anxiety Scale—Second Edition (RCMAS-2) is a self-report rating scale used to measure specific types of anxiety and associated severity in children aged 6–19 years. Normative data was obtained based on a sample of 2368 children from the United States. The RCMAS-2 is straightforward and can be completed quickly requiring only 10–15 min to complete. There are 49 items divided across six total scales. These six scales fall under two broad scale types which include Validity and Anxiety. The Validity Scale includes the Inconsistent Responding Index (INC) which is consisted of nine question pairs and the Defensiveness (DEF) Scale which consists of nine items. A Total Anxiety (TOT) Scale with 40 items is part of the Anxiety Scale. There are three anxiety scales; Physiological Anxiety (PHY), Worry (WOR), and Social Anxiety (SOC) which each have 12, 16, and 12 items, respectively. The RCMAS-2 converts total raw scores from each of the six scales to respective T scores and corresponding percentiles. Each score can be plotted for three distinct age groups; 6–8, 9–14, and 15–19. The test model incorporates years of research in anxiety and is built upon previous versions beginning with the original Manifest Anxiety Scale (MAS; Taylor, 1951) to the Children's Manifest Anxiety Scale (CMAS; Castaneda, McCandless, & Palermo, 1956) followed by the Revised Children's Manifest Anxiety Scale (RCMAS; Reynolds & Richmond, 2008) and culminating in the current version used today. The construct theory of trait anxiety is grounded in the RCMAS which describes a type of anxiety that is more enduring as individuals are predisposed across multiple settings. As part of the reliability data the internal consistency and test–retest coefficient values for the Total Anxiety (TOT) score suggest that it is the most stable measure at .92 and .76, respectively and as such should be utilized frequently. Correlation estimates for the other scale scores ranged from .75 to .86 and .54 to .73 for internal consistency and test–retest, respectively. Of note is the low .54 value obtained for the Short-Form Total Anxiety (SF-TOT) scale on test–retest. The authors state that a low value is to be expected given the briefness of the item format on the Short Form, however overall the reliability data lends support for general stability of test scores. Validity data includes factor-analytic evidence of a robust general anxiety factor (Ag) delineated from all the scales which are also not affected much by outside variables such as cognitive ability or gender. Additional support for construct validity of the RCMAS-2 as a measure of chronic manifest anxiety is obtained from comparisons to other measures of anxiety such as the State-Trait Anxiety Inventory for Children (STAIC) (RCMAS; Reynolds & Richmond, 2008).

Behavior Assessment System for Children: Second Edition

The Behavior Assessment System for Children—Second Edition (BASC-2) is a comprehensive multifaceted assessment of behaviors and internal perceptions of individuals aged 2–25 years. The system assists professionals with clinical differential diagnosis, educational classification, and planning of treatment services for individuals with emotional and behavioral disorders. The BASC-2 is comprised of rating scales and forms which include a Self-Report of Personality (SRP) scale, Parent Rating Scales (PRS), Teacher Rating Scales (TRS), a Structured Developmental History (SDH) form, and a Student Observation System (SOS) form. The rating scales are organized by rater type and specific age group and include a broad range of behavioral and emotional composites and scales which measure both positive (adaptive) and negative (clinical) aspects of behavior. When interpreting results, raw scores are converted to T scores with corresponding percentiles. Generally, reliability and validity data for the BASC-2 is satisfactory supporting its use in evaluating behaviors among children and young adults. The reliability and validity data for the BASC-2 is extensive and readers are encouraged to refer to the manual for detailed information on these psychometric properties (BASC-2; Reynolds & Kamphaus, 2004).

Beck Depression Inventory: Second Edition

The Beck Depression Inventory—Second Edition (BDI-II) is a self-report questionnaire utilized in the assessment of depression severity and symptomology for individuals aged 13–80 years. The BDI-II is comprised of 21 items which ask the individual about their depression during the most recent 2-week period. Test time is short requiring only 5–10 min to complete with manual or computer formats available. Each of the 21 items are rated on a four-point scale with (0 = not at all) on the low end, and (3 = severely, I could barely stand it) on the high end. The items are listed as follows: Sadness, Pessimism, Past failure, Loss of pleasure, Guilty feelings, Punishment feelings, Self-dislike, Self-criticalness, Suicidal thoughts, Crying, Agitation, Loss of interest, Indecisiveness, Worthlessness, Loss of energy, Changes in sleep, Irritability, Changes in appetite, Concentration, Tiredness/fatigue, and Loss of interest in sex. The items are subsequently summed to derive a total score between 0 and 63. T scores (mean = 50, standard deviation = 10), a percentile rank, a diagnostic range, and a clinical interpretation are also provided. Two factors are identified for the BDI-II both by Beck, Steer, and Brown (1996) as well as a study by Dozois, Dobson, and Ahnberg (1998). These factors are Cognitive-Affective and Somatic-Vegetative, with a correlation of .60 between both which was indicated by Dozois et al. (1998). Reliability data indicates high internal consistency. An alpha coefficient of .91 was indicated by Dozois et al. (1998) while coefficients by Beck et al. (1996) included .93 for a college student sample and .92 in an outpatient group. Data from Dozois et al. (1998) indicated item-total correlations which ranged from .41 to .62. These researchers also found high internal consistency based on gender with alpha coefficients of .91 and .92 for women and men, respectively. Results by Dozois et al. (1998) included support for convergent validity with a correlation of .93 between the BDI-II and the original BDI. While further research is needed to test other aspects of reliability and validity, the BDI-II has a coherent factor structure and is a strong measure of depression (Beck et al., 1996; Dozois et al., 1998).

Beck Anxiety Inventory

The Beck Anxiety Inventory (BAI) is a self-report questionnaire utilized in the assessment of anxiety severity, and symptomology for individuals aged 17–80 years. The BAI is comprised of 21 items which ask the individual about their anxiety during the most recent week, requiring only 5–10 min to complete. The test is available in a manual or a computer format and is useful in evaluating anxiety across various clinical populations. Each of the 21 items are rated on a four-point scale with (0 = not at all) on the low end, and (3 = severely, I could barely stand it) on the high end. The items are listed as follows: Numbness or tingling, Feeling hot, Wobbliness in legs, Unable to relax, Fear of the worst happening, Dizzy or lightheaded, Heart pounding or racing, Unsteady, Terrified, Nervous, Feelings of choking, Hands trembling, Shaky, Fear of losing control, Difficulty breathing,

Fear of dying, Scared, Indigestion, Faint, Face flushed, and Sweating (not due to heat). The items are subsequently summed to derive a total score between 0 and 63. *T* scores (mean = 50, standard deviation = 10), a percentile rank, a diagnostic range, and a clinical interpretation are also provided. Many studies have examined the factor structure of the BAI. One study by Hewitt and Norton (1993) found a two-factor structure present with items loading on either a cognitive or somatic factor. They do however note that some items load on a combination of both factors and not solely one or the other. This structure supports Beck, Epstein, Brown, and Steer's (1988) the original two-factor model although other researchers have found alternative models such as Beck and Steer's (1991) and Osman et al.'s (1993) four-factor models. Research by Osman, Kopper, Barrios, Osman, and Wade (1997) suggests both a four- and a second-order factor model fit the data well with a single score that can be extracted from the second-order factor model. Data from Osman et al. (1997) indicates adequate internal consistency with a Cronbach alpha value of .90 and correlations that range from .39 to .64 across all items. Reliability data from Beck et al. (1988) indicated a Cronbach alpha value of .92 with an item-total range of .30–.71 and a mean coefficient of .60. Additionally a test–retest coefficient of .75 was provided. Validity included convergent and discriminant data from Beck et al. (1988) which indicated a high correlation value of .51 when the BAI was compared to other measures of anxiety such as the Hamilton Anxiety Rating Scale—Revised (HARS-R) and the Cognition Checklist—Anxiety subscale (CCL-A). When the BAI was compared to other non-anxiety measures, discriminant validity was supported with low values of .25, .15, and .22 on the Hamilton Rating Scale for Depression—Revised (HRSD-R), Hopelessness Scale (HS), and the Cognition Checklist—Depression subscale (CCL-D), respectively. These results provide good evidence for the discriminative ability of the BAI between anxious and non-anxious groups. Additional validity data by Osman et al. (1997) strongly supports the BAI as a measure of state anxiety with higher correlations for a tested anxiety state scale.

Minnesota Multiphasic Personality Inventory, Second Edition, and Adolescent Edition

The MMPI-2 and MMPI-A may be administered to an adolescent between 14 and 18 or an adult 18 and above to assess emotional profiles and personality characteristics providing insights into an individual's level of emotional distress. This measure can play a role in making a diagnostic decision as to whether an individual with an ASD also experiences a mood or anxiety disorder. The MMPI has several criticisms associated with it and results must be interpreted cautiously. The MMPI does not provide data related to normal populations but items were rather gathered from psychiatric populations in comparison with "normals." The newer versions of the test have moderate reliability in temporal stability and internal consistency, extensive length, and problems related to scale construction including item overlap, high correlations between scales and multidimensional poorly defined variables (MMPI-2 book Butcher et al. 1989). Difficulties associated with reliability and the construction of scales has led to challenges with validity. Rodgers in 1972 referred to the original test as a "psychometric nightmare." Since that time-extensive validity studies and the research into two- and three-point code types have worked to establish validity. This measure can provide useful data in assessing individuals with ASDs when used in combination with other emotional measures and the additional components of a comprehensive evaluation.

Roberts: Second Edition

The Roberts—Second Edition (Roberts-2) is an assessment of social cognition via expressive language used with children and adolescents with social and emotional adjustment difficulties. The test is used as a supplement with other measures and evaluates two primary functions: developmental differences and differences in performance between groups. An age range of 6–18 years is appropriate for administration. The Roberts-2 is comprised of 16 card pictures each illustrating various social situations that are used by the examinee to tell a complete story. Scoring guidelines are used for each story with scales that probe different aspects of social cognition. The cards are used to assess both developmental changes as social experience increases and problems in these categories determined by unusual content. Twenty-eight scales are organized into seven scale categories for interpretation and include: Theme Overview, Available Resources, Problem Identification, Resolution, Emotion, Outcome, and Unusual or Atypical Responses. Raw scores from these scales are converted to T scores which are used to decide if an area is of clinical significance or concern. The authors state that the Roberts-2 is not a projective test. Although the test and its predecessor the Roberts Apperception Test for Children (RATC) are frequently described as and grouped into other projective instruments, the Robert-2 is not projective and is instead based on social cognitive skills. Reliability is tested through inter-rater and test–retest data. The median coefficient for inter-rater reliability across all scales for the combined clinical and nonclinical groups was .92. Adequate values were indicated across all scales with a median greater than .70 for both samples (.75 in the clinical sample) based on test–retest data. Validity is supported through statistical testing of each scale where only one scale (Depression) had no significant correlation to either of the two assessment functions. Furthermore validity of each scale was evaluated through mean score differences and effect sizes. The data supports the strong ability of the Roberts-2 to measure social understanding in children and adolescents across various developmental levels as well as groups, both clinical and nonclinical in nature (Roberts-2; Roberts & Gruber, 2005).

Attention

Interestingly, in the DSM-IV it is asserted that ASD and AD/HD cannot co-occur. This assumption was corrected in the DSM-V which does allow for comorbid diagnosis (Matson, Rieske, & Williams, 2013). Research indicates that AD/HD and ASDs are co-occurring 14–78 % (Gargaro et al., 2011). This is a wide range but indicates that many individuals with ASDs struggle with attention. For this reason it is very important to thoroughly assess attention skills when evaluating for an ASD. Mayes et al. in 2012 state that ASD and AD/HD are "neurobiological disorders with similar underlying neuropsychological deficits." (p. 283) Children with comorbid symptoms have more difficulty with inhibitory performance when compared with children who have ASD alone (Mannion & Leader, 2013). Those with ASD alone demonstrate better inhibition, flexibility, working memory, and planning skills than those with comorbid diagnosis (Sinzig, Bruning, Morsch, & Lehmkuhl, 2008). Deprey and Ozonoff (2009) found that hypervigilant attention and internal distractibility are more common in ASD while lack of focus and distractibility by external stimuli is characteristic of AD/HD. Studies have found similar structural brain abnormalities in those with ASD and AD/HD when compared to controls (Matson et al., 2013).

Along the lines of Deprey and Ozonoff's findings, the authors of this text observe that many children with ASD exhibit intermittent challenges with attention and executive functioning skills while those with comorbid diagnoses have significant deficits in sustained attention and focus. Individuals with AD/HD who do not have ASD may have some social challenges influenced by impulsivity, inattention, and hyperactivity. When focused individuals with only AD/HD should be able to engage in pretend play and creative activities like telling a story or acting out a cartoon. Sustained attention can be assessed via continuous performance testing and with rating scales completed by parents, teachers, and individuals. These may include the TOVA, BASC-2, or Conners AD/HD scales.

Test of Variables of Attention

The Tests of Variables of Attention (TOVA) are individually administered computerized tests of attention and impulse control that are used with both normal and clinical populations. The TOVA assists in the screening, diagnosis, and treatment monitoring of attention disorders like ADHD and is an objective, neurophysiological measure of attention as opposed to other measures of attention and behavior such as the Conners' three-rating scales. There are two versions of the TOVA for administration; a visual and an auditory format. Both versions involve sustaining attention in the absence of immediate reinforcement and utilizing a clicker to press a button when a target stimulus is either seen on screen or heard through speakers, and conversely, not pressing the button when presented with a non-target stimulus. For both versions the stimulus is present for 100 ms at 2000 ms intervals. On the visual format two geometric figures are centered on the computer screen. The TOVA tests have been normed for administration with individual's aged 4 to 80+ years. The tasks measure four distinct attention variables: response time variability, response time, impulsivity (commission errors), and inattention (omission errors). Each area is assessed across four quarters or two halves with each quarter taking 5.4 min for a total test time of 21.6 min. The actual test is administered following a

3 min practice test and in younger children aged 4–5, test time is shortened to only half of the full 21.6 min. The first half contains less target responses than non-target responses with a ratio of 36:126 for each quarter. In the second half, the opposite is the case with more target responses than non-target responses with a ratio of 126:36 for each quarter. Raw scores, standard scores, and percentiles are calculated based on the responses, nonresponses, and reaction times of the examinee. The standard scores have a mean of 100 and standard deviation of 15 and are provided for each variable by quarters, halves, as well as totals. Additional indices include anticipatory responses (guessing), multiple responses, post-commission response time (response time variability), d-prime (discriminability), and beta (response style) domains. An ADHD score is also provided which compares the performance of the examinee to an ADHD group to analyze how similar their performance is to a known ADHD profile. The TOVA is modeled on earlier versions of the original Continuous Performance Test (CPT) and has been developed over the years with the emergence of new technology and software and with the incorporation of hardware such as the clicker button. On each of the four main indices, internal consistency was high both between halves and for each half to the total. Response time coefficients ranged from .89 to .99, response time variability ranged from .70 to .99, commission values ranged from .71 to .96, and omission values ranged from .70 to .93. Test–retest reliability indicates moderate correlation although the sample used was an ADHD population where variability is expected. Correlation values were .51 and higher for the core domains. Overall validity was satisfactory with percentages of 84 and 90 for sensitivity and specificity, respectively (TOVA; Leark, Dupuy, et al., 2007).

Executive Function

Tower of London: Second Edition

The Tower of London—Second Edition (TOL-II) is a neuropsychological test used to assess executive functioning, specifically problem solving and planning. It is used in the evaluation of attention disorders and other executive functioning difficulties related to planning with both children and adults with frontal-executive dysfunction. The test can be administered to individuals who are 7–80 years. Tasks involve arranging red, green, and blue beads on a peg board to match the configuration of beads on the examiners peg board in as few moves as possible. Score categories include: Total Move, Total Correct, Total Rule Violation, Total Time Violation, Total Initiation Time, Total Execution Time, Total Problem-Solving, and Total Stimulus-Bound. Raw scores for each are based on either the number of moves made, the time it takes to complete each problem, or the amount of violations that are made. Each raw score is converted into standard scores with a mean of 100 and standard deviation of 15. These categories evaluate a specific aspect of executive planning, among other executive functions, which provides an overall profile of the individual being tested. Additionally the Stimulus-Bound score is only utilized for elderly examinees who are 60 years or older and occurs when the examinee attempts to solve a test item using the examiners peg board instead of their own. The TOL-II is a modified version of the original TOL by Shallice (1982) and has been extended and refined based on research concerning the development of executive functions throughout the lifespan. These findings point to the emergence of frontal lobe executive skills early on in childhood with maturation over time. The role of working memory has also informed test development citing literature from Barkley (1998), Levin et al. (1996), and Welsh, Satterlee-Cartmel, and Stine (1999). Test–retest reliability data was provided through a study with ADHD children 7–10 years for the Total Move, Total Correct, Total Time Violation, and Total Rule Violation scores. Data indicates a moderate-to-high coefficient of .80 for the Total Move score suggesting its sound stability over time. The Total Correct score had a value of .42 and the authors state that further studies are needed to determine its stability. For the Total Time Violation score, a moderate coefficient of .67 suggests that the speed of problem solving doesn't vary much across time. The last score analyzed was Total Rule Violation which had a very low coefficient value of .24 indicating poor stability and high vulnerability to change over time as evidenced by fewer violations committed during the retest trial. Other studies of reliability with a sample of patients with Parkinson's disease yielded coefficients that were mostly in the high range. Criterion-related validity was supported through many comparisons with other measures and control populations resulting in high intercorrelations. Factor analysis identified a four-factor model: Executive Concept Formation/Flexibility, Memory, Executive Planning/Control, and Psychometric Intelligence. These factor loadings coincide with other neuropsychological measures such as the WCST which lends to the sensitivity of the TOL-II as a test of executive problem-solving and planning and supports ongoing construct validity (TOL-II; Culbertson & Zillmer, 2001).

Wisconsin Card Sorting Test: Revised and Expanded

The Wisconsin Card Sorting Test—Revised and Expanded (WCST) is a neuropsychological assessment of abstract reasoning and executive functioning in clinical populations with suspected neurologic dysfunction. Specifically, the WCST assess a person's ability to both develop and shift problem-solving strategies based on changing environmental criteria. Normative data is available for use with those aged 6 years, 6 months to 89 years. The test consists of four stimulus cards and 128 response cards that have figures with different characteristic forms, colors, and numbers. There are a number of various scores which all convert a raw score into standard scores, T scores, and percentiles. These scores include: Total Number of Errors, Percent Errors, Perseverative Responses, Percent Perseverative Responses, Perseverative Errors, Percent Perseverative Errors, Nonperseverative Errors, Percent Nonperseverative Errors, and Percent Conceptual Level Responses. In addition, a Learning to Learn score can be calculated which is a measure of efficiency across test stages. The WCST was developed from early research into learning abilities of brain-lesioned and intact primates by (Settlage et al., 1948; Zable & Harlow, 1946) as a tool for investigating flexibility of thinking in humans (Grant & Berg, 1948). The measure is grounded in early human and animal studies regarding abstraction (Weigl, 1941) and the effects of frontal lobe lesions on maintaining set (Settlage, Zable, & Harlow, 1948; Teuber, Battersby, & Bender, 1951; Zable & Harlow, 1946). Current uses of the WCST are rooted in literature concerning sensitivity to brain dysfunction of the frontal lobes by (Drewe, 1974; Milner, 1963; Robinson, Heaton, Lehman, & Stilson, 1980; Weinberger, Berman, & Zec, 1986) among other interests. Reliability data indicates inter-rater coefficients of .93, .92, and .88 for Perseverative Responses, Perseverative Errors, and Nonperseverative Errors scores, respectively. A coefficient range of .89–1.00 was obtained for all WCST scores. Further reliability data includes a generalizability coefficient range for scores of .39–.72 with an average value of .57 and median value of .60. In this case, values of .60 and higher are considered good, indicating that most scores contributed to strong test reliability. Many studies with children, adolescents, and adults yield data that is supportive of construct validity concerning the measurement of executive functioning among neurologically impaired populations (WCST; Heaton, Chelune, et al., 1981; Heaton, Chelune, Talley, Kay, & Curtiss, 1993).

Stroop Color and Word Test: Adult Version

The Stroop Color and Word Test—Adult Version (Stroop) is a neuropsychological measure of cognitive processing and executive functions such as inhibition used in various populations to examine brain impairment, cognition, and psychopathology. The adult version of the Stroop can be given to individuals 15–90 years and takes around 5 min to administer. It is available for administration in both individual and group settings. The test uses three basic scores, a raw Word Score, a raw Color Score, and a raw Color-Word score. From these scores one derived Interference Score can be calculated. Raw scores are converted to T scores which are used for clinical interpretation along with associated percentiles. There are many theories regarding the Stroop although the authors state that it remains a bit ambiguous since no theory fully explains the range of behaviors and correlations exhibited. The current standard form of the Stroop is grounded in and developed from years of research from many earlier versions. Reliability has proved to remain highly consistent across different versions and forms of the test. Test–retest reliability coefficients by (Jensen, 1965) for the three basic raw scores (Word, Color, and Color-Word) were .88, .79, and .71, respectively. Coefficients from (Golden, 1975b) for all three scores from group and individual testing formats were .89, .84, .73 and .86, .82, .73, respectively. Values for individuals who took both the group and individual testing formats were .85, .81, and .69. For all the samples above, coefficient values for the raw interference score were in the .70s range. The manual cites many common patterns of test scores for clinical interpretation and a large amount of research is provided with regard to various subject areas and populations contributing to the ongoing validity of the Stroop (Stroop; Golden & Freshwater, 1998).

Comprehensive Trail-Making Test

The Comprehensive Trail-Making Test (CTMT) is a neuropsychological measure widely used to assess brain and executive function impairment. The CTMT has been standardized for use with individuals who are 8–74 years of age and provides *T* scores with a mean of 50 and a standard deviation of 10. Five trail-making tasks are utilized in which the examinee is instructed to connect numbers which are in numerical form or spelled out and letters in a predetermined order as fast as possible. A *T* score is derived from the raw score for each trail and these scores are summed to calculate a composite index *T* score. Reliability data for internal consistency ranges from .68 to .74 for all five trails and .91 for the composite index. Test–retest values range from .70 to .78 for all five trails and .84 for the composite index. Inter-scorer reliability for all five trails ranges from .96 to .98 with a high value of .99 for the composite index. Additionally overall validity is supported by adequate factor analyses and sufficient correlation coefficients when compared with other measures such as the Developmental Test of Visual Perception-Adolescents and Adults (CTMT: Reynolds, 2002).

Visual and Motor Skills

Visual-Motor Integration, Motor Coordination, and Visual Perception skills may be impacted in individuals with ASDs. While some individuals have strong nonverbal reasoning or visual-spatial skills, many individuals may have fine or gross motor skills deficits. In younger children cognitive measures like the Mullen Scales include motor skills assessment. The Vineland-2 also provides sections for parents to report motor skills from birth to age 6. Additional assessments like the Beery Sequence, informal drawing and writing tasks, the MVPT-III, and the Grooved Pegboard can provide information on fine motor and visual perception. As these skills have an impact on academics, these assessments can provide data that is helpful in understanding learning styles and perhaps explains problem behaviors. In some cases individuals may escape/avoid tasks that involve motor skills because this is an area of weakness.

Beery–Buktenica Developmental Tests of Visual-Motor Integration, Visual Perception, and Motor Coordination: Fifth Edition

The Beery–Buktenica Developmental Tests of Visual-Motor Integration, Visual Perception, and Motor Coordination—Fifth Edition (Beery VMI) is an assessment used to help identify difficulties with integration of visual and motor abilities (eye–hand coordination) and is designed to assess visual-motor integration difficulties in individual's aged 2–18 years. The test serves populations with cognitive developmental disorders and visual-motor deficits and has been shown through research to be culture-free. It is comprised of drawings of geometric forms arranged in order of increasing difficulty and requires individuals to copy, find, and trace them. There are four standardized tests; a Full Form Beery VMI with 30 items that can be either group or individually administered in 10–15 min, a Short Form Beery VMI with 21 items for children ages 2–7, a Visual Perception test used to compare VMI results with pure visual performance, and a Motor Coordination test used to compare VMI results with pure motor performance. The latter two tests (Visual Perception and Motor Coordination) are supplemental developmental tests that are part of the overall Beery VMI developmental test. Raw scores for each separate test can be converted into Standard and Scaled scores with appropriate percentiles. Since the test model for the Beery VMI evaluates developmental abilities, research has shown performance to correlate highly with chronological age and to a lesser extent intelligence, correlating more heavily with the nonverbal aspects of intelligence. Overall reliability is excellent with high coefficient values of .92, .91, and .90 for the Beery VMI, Visual Perception, and Motor Coordination tests, respectively. Specific reliability data indicates an internal consistency correlation coefficient of .82 overall. Inter-rater correlation values were .92, .98, and .93 for the Beery VMI, Visual Perception, and Motor Coordination tests, respectively. The test–retest reliability values were slightly lower at .89, .85, and .86 for each of the three tests, respectively. Content, concurrent, construct, and predictive validity are all strongly supported based on validity data (Beery VMI; Beery, 2004).

Motor-Free Visual Perception Test: Third Edition

The Motor-Free Visual Perception Test—Third Edition (MVPT-3) is an individually administered measure of overall visual processing and perceptual ability in the absence of motor action. The test can be used with a very broad range of individuals, aged 4 through 95+ years, making it ideal for use with children, adolescents, and adults alike. The MVPT-3 is designed to be utilized by many professionals as only a general overview of visual perception and not as a tool in identifying the specific cause of possible deficits. With that said, various populations can benefit from testing including individuals with brain damage and trauma, intellectual disability, and learning disabilities for example. The MVPT-3 takes roughly 25 min to administer and score and a single raw score is converted to a standard score, percentile, and age-equivalent. There is also the option to compare an individual's score to their same-aged peers or to an alternate reference group. The test model of the MVPT-3 is based on research from the most well-known empirically supported theoretical constructs of visual perception and is categorized into five types; Spatial Relationships, Visual Discrimination, Figure-Ground, Visual Closure, and Visual Memory. Reliability is supported through internal consistency data which indicates for ages 4–10 a correlation coefficient range of .69–.87 on items 1–40 with a median value of .80. For those older than 10 in the 11+ age group coefficients were based on items 14–65 and ranged from .86 to .90 with a median of .89. This data suggests solid stability for ages 5 and older and should be used only as a screener for 4-year-olds since they had the lowest correlation at .69. Test–retest reliability was sufficient at .87 in the 4–10-year age group and .92 in the 11 to 84+-year age group. Validity data

Week 5
13-15.

indicated good criterion-related validity particularly when scores were compared to another test of visual perception, the Developmental Test of Visual Perception—Second Edition (DTVP-2), which yielded a correlation coefficient of .78 for the General Visual Perception score. Construct validity data indicates a moderately high positive correlation for ages 4–10 at .72 when performance is compared to the age of the individual. For ages 11–39 a weaker positive correlation was found to be at .37. Ages 40+ had a negative correlation of −.46. The data suggests a rapid improvement in performance with early maturation from the ages of 4–10 years then a steady improvement till around age 39 where a subsequent decline begins to occur in visual ability each year thereafter. Data obtained comparing performance to both cognitive ability and academic achievement levels indicated a low correlation suggesting a minute effect from these variables on visual perception.

Grooved Pegboard Test

The Grooved Pegboard Test (GPT) is an individually administered measure of eye–hand coordination and motor speed that requires only 5 min on average to administer. Test use ranges in age from 5 to 70 years and is utilized with individuals with suspected lateralized brain damage, such as that in Parkinson's disease, or problems with manual dexterity. Scores are computed in seconds required for the patient to place all the pegs and is recorded separately for each hand. The raw time scores are then converted into z scores in order to find the corresponding T scores, Standard scores, and percentile ranks. The age of the patient greatly affects test scores with improvement in performance during childhood and a gradual decrease in performance as the patient gets older. Another factor affecting performance is hand preference with faster scores when the dominant or preferred hand is used. Research has shown that variables including gender and education level or IQ have little or negligible effects on scores. Research by Hardan et al. (2003) has provided evidence of reduced pegboard-placing speed in individuals with Autism. Reliability data is presented with test–retest coefficients that are moderately high from .67 to .86 in normal individuals aged 15 years and older with no information available for children younger than 15 years. Validity data is presented with correlation coefficients to comparisons of tapping speed (−.35), near visual acuity (−.62), attention (.31), perceptual speed using Digit Symbol (−.60), and nonverbal reasoning using Block Design (−.34) and Object Assembly (−.45) (Haaland & Delaney, 1981; Schear & Sato, 1989).

Sensory Processing

Sensory sensitivities are common in both ASDs and AD/HD. So frequently individuals present for an evaluation between ages 5 and 10 with a "diagnosis" of Sensory Processing Disorder. While sensory sensitivities are real and have a real impact on day-to-day functioning for many individuals, the DSM-V does not contain such a diagnosis. Rather sensory sensitivities are recognized as occurring in the context of other diagnoses. It would be ideal if professionals treating individuals for sensory impairments at a young age would refer those individuals for comprehensive evaluations. If this was standard practice, many children would receive the early intervention research indicates leads to best outcomes. Many occupational therapists do make these referrals and thus children may receive OT, Speech, and ABA therapy that lead to best outcomes. These providers are to be championed. Sadly, there are still providers who discourage parents from seeking other evaluations stating that occupational therapy must occur "first" and will "cure" behavior problems. This uninformed practice hurts young children who could be receiving comprehensive services. The authors' experience is that frequently parents seek evaluations after months or years of OT services that they express did not "cure" problem behaviors. While a diagnosis of SPD is not supported by the research comprehensive assessment of sensory sensitivities is a part of an assessment because individuals with ASDs do very frequently have sensory processing differences. Sometimes this makes concentrating in a busy classroom difficult. A large, crowded, noisy lunch room can be nearly impossible and certain clothing, lighting, and/or art materials may be overwhelming and uncomfortable to a child (or to an adult). In providing tools for success occupational therapy or OT consultations at school can be very valuable to assess the environment and make sensory modifications that may help individuals. Use of the Sensory Profile Questionnaire, Short Sensory Profile or direct questioning during parent and child interview can provide data that is useful in a comprehensive assessment.

Another thought on sensory processing is that for many parents it is much easier to hear and process that a child has Sensory Processing difficulties than it is to hear ASD or even AD/HD because of the stigma related to medication. It is so crucial for parents to understand that occupational therapy can play a valuable role in a child's treatment but unless the challenges are solely handwriting and pencil grip it is rarely going to be effective alone.

Sensory Profile

The Sensory Profile is a caregiver questionnaire concerned with sensory processing abilities and the effects of these abilities on daily functioning of children ages 5–10 years. The Sensory Profile can be used with children 3–4 years as well although precautions should be taken in the interpretation of scores. The Sensory Profile is available in a Full 125-item form and a Short 38-item form. Completion time for the Full and Short questionnaire is 30 and 10 min, respectively. All the items on the Full form are categorized into three broad sections. The first section is Sensory Processing which subsumes six areas, the second section is Modulation with five accompanying areas, and the last section is Behavioral and Emotional Responses which has three areas. The items across these three sections form nine important factors: Sensory Seeking, Emotionally Reactive, Low Endurance/Tone, Oral Sensory Sensitivity, Inattention/Distractibility, Poor Registration, Sensory

Sensitivity, Sedentary, and Fine Motor/Perceptual. These nine factors identify items which describe a child's level of responsiveness to sensory stimuli. The 38 items which comprise the Short form assess sensory Modulation specifically, using items that are most discriminating for the presence of sensory issues that require further assessment. The Sensory Profile uses raw scores which are summed and compared to cut off score categories which fall into three classifications: Typical Performance, Probable Difference, and Definite Difference. The test model is formulated on neuroscience literature reviewing neurological thresholds and the behavioral responses to those thresholds. The research suggests a continuation of both which interact together to determine how children process sensory information. The neurological threshold is the amount of stimuli required for neurons in the brain to engage and fire. Behavioral response describes the way a person behaves in response to their thresholds, either going along or going against the response of their nervous system. Based on this joint interaction, there are four outcomes which manifest: poor registration, sensitivity to stimuli, sensation seeking, and sensation avoiding. Reliability data indicates an internal consistency range on the Full form of .47–.91 across the nine factors and three broad sections. The internal consistency range on the Short form was .70–.90. Validity data indicates that content validity was established by confirming the test sampled all sensory behaviors exhibited by children. On the Short form, internal validity ranged from .25 to .76 which indicates the use of unique constructs and supports the factor structure in place. Construct validity was established through convergent and discriminant studies which compared sensory scores to a separate measure called the School Function Assessment. Additionally clinical group comparisons with Autism and ADHD populations helped validate the Sensory Profile as a good measure of sensory differences in children (Sensory Profile; Dunn, 1999).

Memory

Assessment of memory provides valuable data in a comprehensive ASD evaluation. Studies have considered the correlations between language skills in individuals with ASDs and verbal memory (Tyson et al., 2014). While the CELF-4 and the WAIS-IV/WISC-IV, previously discussed, do provide some assessment of auditory and verbal memory, additional memory measures can provide additional information particularly when memory is an area of reported difficulty. Measures like the CVLT and RAVLT are relatively brief language memory measures that can provide useful information on auditory learning and memory, perseveration and use of memory strategies. Additional measures that may be more time consuming but provide comprehensive data on working memory, learning and delayed memory include the WMS-IV and the TOMAL. When considering memory profiles it can provide guidance for treatment if an individual understands his or her memory strengths and can develop ways to cope with deficits.

Wechsler Memory Scale: Fourth Edition

The Wechsler Memory Scale—Fourth Edition (WMS-IV) is an individually administered assessment of memory functions primarily involving working memory and of declarative episodic nature. The test is used with individuals suffering from neurodevelopmental, neuropsychiatric, and neurological conditions that impair memory. The WMS-IV is divided into two batteries; the first is an Adult battery that covers ages 16–69 years and the second is an Older Adult battery which covers ages 65–90 years. The Adult battery has five indexes: Auditory Memory, Visual Memory, Visual Working Memory, Immediate Memory, and Delayed Memory. Its subtests include Logical Memory I and II, Verbal Paired Associates I and II, Designs I and II, Visual Reproduction I and II, Spatial Addition, and Symbol Span. On the Older Adult battery there are four indexes: Auditory Memory, Visual Memory, Immediate Memory, and Delayed Memory. Its subtests include Logical Memory I and II, Verbal Paired Associates I and II, Visual Reproduction I and II, and Symbol Span. Information is presented through the use of standard scores with a mean of 100 and standard deviation of 15 for each index, scaled scores with a mean of 10 and standard deviation of three for each subtest as well as cumulative percentages which are sorted into seven percentile groups. In addition there are contrast-scaled scores and process-scaled scores that can be computed. The contrast-scaled scores are used to adjust one score based on performance on another particular variable which provides a different scope in understanding performance. Process-scaled scores are available for some subtests as well and provide information on specific aspects of performance. The theoretical model for the WMS-IV test is based on a thorough review of the literature on memory, which includes research on the current theories of long-term memory and corresponding branches of declarative episodic memory by Squire and Butters (1992) and Szpunar and McDermott (2008) and research from Baddeley (2000) and Gathercole (2008) on working memory. Reliability data is provided for both test batteries. The internal consistency subtest and index average coefficient ranges for the Adult battery were .74–.97 and .93–.96, respectively. Internal consistency for the Older Adult battery had average subtest and index value ranges of .74–.96 and .92–.97, respectively. Coefficients were also available for special clinical groups with average subtest and index value ranges of .86–.97 and .93–.98, respectively. Test–retest data for the Adult battery indicates subtest and index coefficient ranges of .59–.77 and .81–.83, respectively. Value ranges on the Older Adult battery were .69–.81 and .80–.87 for subtest and index scores, respectively. Inter-rater reliability was very high for most subtests at .98–.99. Numerous studies indicate sufficient support for the validity of the WMS-IV and factor analysis tested two models; a two-factor and three-factor model. Results indicate both models fit the data well and the three-factor model was chosen to delineate the tests core index structure. Concurrent validity was supported through many studies comparing WMS-IV test scores to a number of other measures which included the California Verbal Learning Test—Second Edition and Delis-Kaplan Executive Function System (WMS-IV; Wechsler, 2009a, 2009b).

Rey–Osterrieth Complex Figure Test and Recognition Trial

The Rey Complex Figure Test (RCFT) is a neuropsychological measure employed in the assessment of visuospatial memory and constructional ability for adults aged 18–89 years. The test is most commonly used in populations with suspected neurologic impairment and memory disorders such as traumatic brain injury and Alzheimer's disease. Four separate trials structure the RCFT beginning with a Copy trial in which the examinee copies a complex figure from a stimulus card, then after 3 min the examinee draws the figure from memory in the Immediate Recall trial. Thirty minutes after the Copy trial is completed, the examinee again draws the figure from memory in the Delayed Recall trial. Finally a Recognition trial is completed immediately after the Delayed Recall trial where the examinee tries to recognize 12 of 24 items which are from the stimulus figure with the other 12 items serving as distractors. The RCFT converts raw scores for the Immediate Recall, Delayed Recall, and Recognition Total Correct scales into T scores and corresponding percentile scores. Memory profile patterns can also be discerned from the pattern of scores across these three RCFT scales. These memory patterns provide additional interpretive data and include Attention, Encoding, Storage, Retrieval, and Normal profiles. The RCFT test model is supported by factor analyses which delineate five domains of cognitive functioning: visuospatial recall memory, visuospatial recognition memory, response bias, processing speed, and visuospatial constructional ability. The RCFT has excellent inter-rater reliability with a range of .93–.99 and median of .94 for Total Raw scores. Other reliability data indicates test–retest correlation coefficients of .75 for Immediate Recall, .88 for Delayed Recall, and .87 for Recognition Total Correct scores. Validity data indicates sufficient construct validity of the RCFT as a measure of visuospatial memory and constructional ability based on intercorrelations between the RCFT and other measures such as the Wechsler Adult Intelligence Scale—Revised (WAIS-R) and neuropsychological measures like the Controlled Oral Word Association Test and Benton Visual Retention Test (RCFT; Meyers & Meyers, 1995).

Rey Auditory Verbal Learning Test

The RAVLT requires an individual to remember a list of 15 words repeated over five trials. Then another list of 15 words is presented to potentially interfere with the first list. After a 30 min delay the individual is again asked to recall the original word list. Finally a recognition trial is administered using a story or list of words and asking the examinee to check words from the original list. The RAVLT provides T score and Standard score data and provides metanorms as well as various specific alternative norms. The RAVLT has best normative data for those aged 13 and older. For assessing younger children the *Children's Auditory Verbal Learning Test* uses the same format and provides normative data for children. Test–retest reliability for the RAVLT was best at .70 after 1 year for the total number of words recalled after five trials. Overall test–retest reliability was moderate at .55. Research has shown that those with frontal lobe challenges may have difficulty with the five trial recall but score within age-expected ranges on the recognition trial (Screening and Assessing for Neuropsychological Impairment-book). The challenges may be more related to retrieving and organizing. Individuals with ASDs may have these executive functioning challenges, which is important to note. Individuals may also have very strong memory skills and recall the list verbatim in only a few trials. It is helpful to note the process and report whether an individual simply memorizes the list in order or whether he or she groups related words or uses another memory strategy. Individuals with ASD may have strong verbal memory and more challenges with working memory (Assessed on the WISC-IV) or visual memory (WMS-IV, TOMAL, or RCFT). This greater reliance on verbal memory has been demonstrated in research and is linked to strong language abilities (Tyson et al., 2014). Understanding strengths and weaknesses across memory and learning can provide information to an individual on what strategies or teaching modalities may work best. Sometimes individuals with ASD have poor insight into their own emotions and learning processes (Trammell et al., 2014) so this data can be valuable to support vocational or school success and learning.

Test of Memory and Learning

The Test of Memory and Learning (TOMAL) is a comprehensive measure of memory ability in individuals aged 5 years old up to 19 years, 11 months, 30 days old. The test is composed of 10 core subtest, five verbal which form the Verbal Memory Scale, and five nonverbal that form the Nonverbal Memory Scale. Four supplementary subtests are included. Core Indexes include: Verbal Memory Index (VMI), Nonverbal Memory Index (NMI), Composite Memory Index (CMI), and the Delayed Recall Index (DRI). Additionally five supplementary indexes are included: Sequential Recall Index (SRI), Free Recall Index (FRI), Associative Recall Index (ARI), Learning Index (LI), and the Attention/Concentration Index (ACI). The TOMAL uses standard scores for all indexes with a mean of 100 and standard deviation of 15. Reliability data was presented through internal consistency and test–retest coefficients which ranged from .85 to .98 and .81 to .92, respectively, for all measure indexes. Validity data suggests strong construct and criterion-related validity (TOMAL: Reynolds & Bigler, 1994).

Academic Achievement

Woodcock–Johnson Test of Achievement: Third Edition Normative Update

The Woodcock–Johnson Tests of Achievement—Third Edition, Normative Update (WJ-III ACH, NU) is a test used to measure academic performance, provide information on academic strengths and weaknesses, and assist in educational programming with individuals aged 2 through 90+ years. The WJ-III ACH, NU is comprised of four curricular domains: Reading, Math, Oral Language, and Written Language. There are six general clusters: Reading, Math, Oral Language, Written Language, Academic Knowledge, and a Special Purpose cluster. Each area is broken down into specific clusters which are broken down further into tests that assess more targeted abilities within each area. There are 12 tests in the Standard Battery, 11 tests in the Extended Battery, and 9 tests in the Brief Battery. The WJ-III ACH, NU like the WJ-III COG uses the CHC theories of the structure of intelligence. Five intelligence factors that are derived from this model are Reading–Writing, Mathematics, Comprehension-Knowledge, Auditory Processing, and Long-Term Retrieval. The WJ-III ACH, NU yields standard scores, confidence intervals, and percentile ranks for the clusters and individual tests. Confidence intervals and percentile ranks on the WJ-III ACH, NU can be reported based on same-grade comparisons with an individual's peers as well as with their same-aged peers. Stability coefficients for test–retest reliability range from .69 to .96 for test scores across all ages with the Handwriting test having the lowest stability. Cluster coefficients for all ages ranged from .93 to .99 with the Total Achievement cluster having the highest stability. Reliability is generally high with most of the other values at or exceeding .80. Factor analyses support the CHC model with developmental growth curve data supporting the factor structure. Data pertaining to a population of ASD children indicated that Processing Speed, Brief Reading, Brief Math, Brief Writing, and Academic Knowledge were weak areas of performance (WJ-III ACH, NU; Woodcock, Shrank, McGrew, & Mather, 2007).

Gray Oral Reading Tests: Fifth Edition

The Gray Oral Reading Tests—Fifth Edition (GORT-5) is an individually administered assessment of oral reading with accompanying strengths and weaknesses for individuals 6–23 years, 11 months. The test is most commonly used with students who are falling behind their same-aged peers in reading. It consists of two forms with 16 different stories on each form that an individual must read in order to determine their scores in various domains. Five comprehension questions follow each story and the stories are ranged from lowest to highest in terms of reading level. Starting points are determined based on the child's current grade in school and it takes anywhere from 15 to 45 min to administer. The GORT-5 is composed of five scores: Rate, Accuracy, Fluency, Comprehension, and a composite Oral Reading Index score. For Rate, Accuracy, and Fluency, raw and scaled scores (mean = 10, standard deviation = 3) are provided along with age and grade equivalents and corresponding percentiles. The Oral Reading Index uses standard scores with a mean of 100 and standard deviation of 15 and accompanying percentile ranks. In addition an optional method for calculating the percentage of miscue substitutions and other deviations from print is available. The GORT has a long history and the latest revision improves upon previous editions while maintaining a similar framework for evaluating oral reading. The GORT-5 has exceptional reliability. Internal consistency is very high with a coefficient range for all five scores, across both forms, averaged for all ages, at .91–.97. Test–retest reliability data indicates a range of .82–.90 for all five scores across both forms in a combined grade sample. Inter-rater reliability is excellent across both forms for all five scores with values at .99 or higher. Validity was tested with criterion-related data comparing GORT-5 scores to the index scores of five other separate tests used in the assessment of reading. A coefficient range of .68–.77 was present across all other measures indicating satis-factory support of criterion-predictive validity. Construct validity was also tested by comparing the GORT-5 to intelligence and academic achievement tests. Validity data indicates a moderate correlation of GORT-5 scores with the WISC-IV FSIQ especially with the Oral Reading Index composite. A strong relationship was also indicated between GORT-5 scores and an academic achievement test called the Iowa Test of Basic Skills (ITBS) with a value range of .61–.74. Overall reliability and validity data substantiates the GORT-5 as a highly reliable and valid measure of reading ability (GORT-5; Wiederholt & Bryant, 2012).

Wechsler Individual Achievement Test: Third Edition

The Wechsler Individual Achievement Test—Third Edition (WIAT-III) is a test used to measure academic skills, provide information on academic strengths and weaknesses, and assist in educational programming with individuals aged 4–19 years, 11 months. The test is used across multiple settings to evaluate student achievement from Pre-Kindergarten up to grade 12. Administration time varies widely depending on the examinee and which subtests are given, anywhere from 30 min to 2.5 h. The WIAT-III is comprised of 16 subtests organized across eight composite scores. The composite scores are listed as follows: Oral Language, Total Reading, Basic Reading, Reading Comprehension and Fluency, Written Expression, Mathematics, Math Fluency, and Total Achievement. The WIAT-III yields standard scores (mean = 100, standard deviation = 15) percentile ranks, normal curve equiva-lents, growth-scale values, and stanine scores. Additionally age and grade equiva-lents can be calculated for comparisons to peers. The WIAT-III test model works well with the response to intervention (RTI) model as well as with Individualized Education Program (IEP) goals. The test is also consistent with the No Child Left Behind (NCLB) and Individuals with Disabilities Education Act (IDEA) legisla-tion. Reliability data indicates a high internal consistency coefficient range of .91–.98. This value range applied for composite scores which were based on age as well as grade (fall and spring semesters). Test–retest reliability is moderate to high. Data is provided for pre-kindergarten through twelfth grade. For grades Pre-K to 5 the composite scores had a coefficient range of .83–.97. For grades 6–12, the composite scores had a coefficient range of .90–.97. Across all grades, the average coefficient range was .87–.96 for the composite scores. Inter-rater reliability was high with values greater than .90 across the board for subtests. Support for validity included data based on internal structure, which indicated intercorrelations for composite scores across age and all grades ranging from .46 to .93. Comparisons to the WIAT-II were also made indicating similar constructs are measured with corrected values between common subtests at .62–.86 and a range of .76–.93 for composites. Additionally the WIAT-III was compared to several other ability measures providing evidence of divergent validity which indicates that the test measures different constructs. Correlations of .60–.82 support this finding, although some overlap in cognitive skills is seen. Studies with special groups support appropriate test sensitivity and specificity (WIAT-III; Wechsler, 2009a, 2009b; Vaughan-Jensen, Adame, McLean, & Gámez, 2011).

Additional Measures for Comprehensive Assessment of Autism Spectrum Disorders Not Reviewed Specifically in the Text

ASD Measures

Autism Spectrum Rating Scales (ASRS)
Gilliam Autism Rating Scale—Third Edition (GARS-3)
Childhood Autism Rating Scale—Second Edition (CARS-2)
Social Responsiveness Scale—Second Edition (SRS-2)
Gilliam Asperger's Disorder Scale (GADS)
Asperger Syndrome Diagnostic Scale (ASDS)
Monteiro Interview Guidelines for Diagnosing Asperger's Syndrome (MIGDAS)
Checklist for Autism Spectrum Disorder (CASD)
Autism Screening Instrument for Educational Planning—Third Edition (ASIEP-3)
PDD Behavior Inventory (PDDBI)
Assessment of Functional Living Skills (AFLS)
Verbal Behavior Milestones Assessment and Placement Program (VB-MAPP)
Assessment of Basic Language and Learning Skills—Revised (ABLLS-R)
Psychoeducational Profile—Third Edition (PEP-3)

Cognitive Measures

Bayley Scales of Infant & Toddler Development—Third Edition (Bayley-III)
Wechsler Preschool and Primary Scale of Intelligence (WPPSI-IV)
Slosson Intelligence Test—Primary (SIT-P)
Shipley Institute of Living Scale—Second Edition (Shipley-2)
Cognitive Assessment of Young Children (CAYC)
Developmental Assessment of Young Children—Second Edition (DAYC-2)
Stanford–Binet Intelligence Scales—Fifth Edition (SB5)
Woodcock Johnson—Fourth Edition Tests of Cognitive Abilities (WJ-IV COG)
Kaufman Assessment Battery for Children—Second Edition (KABC-II)
Kaufman Brief Intelligence Test—Second Edition (KBIT-2)
Cognitive Assessment System—Second Edition (CAS-2)
Detroit Tests of Learning Aptitude—Fourth Edition (DTLA-4)

Reynolds Intellectual Assessment Scales (RIAS)
Slosson Intelligence Test—Revised (SIT-R)
Wide Range Intelligence Test (WRIT)
Structure of Intellect Learning Abilities Test (SOI-LA)
Primary Test of Nonverbal Intelligence (PTONI)
Universal Nonverbal Intelligence Test (UNIT)
Comprehensive Test of Nonverbal Intelligence—Second Edition (CTONI-II)
Wechsler Nonverbal Scale of Ability (WNV)
Test of Nonverbal Intelligence—Third Edition (TONI-3)
Leiter International Performance Scale—Revised (Leiter-R)
Raven's Progressive Matrices

Speech and Language Measures

Comprehensive Test of Phonological Processes—Second Edition (CTOPP-2)
Test of Auditory Processing Skills—Third Edition (TAPS-3)
Comprehensive Assessment of Spoken Language (CASL)
Oral and Written Language Scales—Second Edition (OWLS-II)
Test of Early Communication and Emerging Language (TECEL)
Comprehensive Receptive and Expressive Vocabulary Test—Third Edition (CREVT-3)
Receptive One-Word Picture Vocabulary Test—Fourth Edition (ROWPVT-4)
Test of Written Language—Fourth Edition (TOWL-4)
Test of Early Written Language—Third Edition (TEWL-3)
Arizona Articulation Proficiency Scale—Third Revision (Arizona-3)
Test of Language Development—Fourth Edition (TOLD-4)
Language Processing Test—Elementary (LPT-3)
Auditory Processing Abilities Test (APAT)
Test for Auditory Comprehension of Language—Third Edition (TACL-3)
Speech and Language Development Chart and Poster Pack—Third Edition
Sequenced Inventory of Communication Development—Revised (SICD-R)
Kaufman Survey of Early Academic and Language Skills (K-SEALS)
Vocabulary Assessment Scales—Receptive & Expressive (VAS-R) (VAS-E)
Test of Nonverbal Auditory Discrimination (TENVAD)
Screening Test of Auditory Perception (STAP)
Templin Sound Discrimination Test

Behavior Measures

Adaptive Behavior Assessment System—Second Edition (ABAS-II)
Conners Comprehensive Behavior Rating Scales (Conners CBRS)
Conners Clinical Index (Conners CI)
Conners Early Childhood (Conners EC)
Conners Early Childhood Global Index (Conners ECGI)
Behavior Intervention Monitoring Assessment System (BIMAS)
The Devereux Early Childhood Assessment Clinical Form (DECA-C)
Devereux Student Strengths Assessment (DESSA)
Burks Behavior Rating Scales—Second Edition (BBRS-2)

Adaptive Behavior Scale-School—Second Edition (ABS-S:2)
Developmental Profile—Third Edition (DP-3)
Developmental Assessment for Students with Severe Disabilities—Third Edition (DASH-3)
Early Childhood Development Chart and Mini-Poster Pack—Third Edition

Emotional Functioning Measures

Multidimensional Anxiety Scale for Children—Second Edition (MASC-2)
Carroll Depression Scales (CDS)
Adult Manifest Anxiety Scale (AMAS)
State-Trait Anxiety Inventory (STAI)
Davidson Trauma Scale (DTS)
Children's Depression Rating Scale—Revised (CDRS-R)
Multiscore Depression Inventory for Children (MDI-C)
Reynolds Adolescent Depression Scale—Second Edition (RADS-2)
Feelings, Attitudes, and Behaviors Scale for Children (FAB-C)
Student Behavior Survey (SBS)
Thematic Apperception Test (TAT)

Personality and Psychopathology Measures

Personality Inventory for Children—Second Edition (PIC-2)
Personality Inventory for Youth (PIY)
Personality Assessment Inventory (PAI)
Trauma Symptom Checklist for Young Children (TSCYC)
Trauma Symptom Checklist for Children (TSCC)
Trauma and Attachment Belief Scale (TABS)
Trauma Symptom Inventory—Second Edition (TSI-2)
Holden Psychological Screening Inventory (HPSI)
Rorschach Inkblot Test
Jesness Inventory—Revised (JI-R)
Jesness Behavior Checklist (JBC)

Attention Measures

Conners' 3 ADHD Index (Conners' 3AI)
Conners' 3 Global Index (Conners' 3GI)
Conners' Kiddie Continuous Performance Test Version 5 (K-CPT V.5)
Conners'—March Developmental Questionnaire (CMDQ)
Conners' Continuous Performance Test—Third Edition (Conners' CPT 3)
Conners' Continuous Auditory Test of Attention (Conners' CATA)
Conners' Adult ADHD Rating Scales (CAARS)

Executive Functioning Measures

Behavior Rating Inventory of Executive Function (BRIEF)
Paced Auditory Serial Addition Test (PASAT)
Comprehensive Executive Function Inventory (CEFI)

Category Test (CAT)
Quick Neurological Screening Test—Third Edition (QNST-3)
Children's Psychological Processes Scale (CPPS)
Nonverbal Stroop Card Sorting Test (NSCST)
Test of Information Processing Skills (TIPS)
Symbol Digit Modalities Test (SDMT)
Neuropsychological Impairment Scale (NIS)
Brief Neuropsychological Cognitive Examination (BNCE)
Hooper Visual Organization Test (VOT)
WPS Electronic Tapping Test

Visual and Motor Measures

Bender Visual-Motor Gestalt Test—Second Edition (Bender-Gestalt II)
Koppitz Developmental Scoring System for the Bender-Gestalt Test—Second Edition (KOPPITZ-2)
Developmental Test of Visual Perception—Third Edition (DTVP-3)
Test of Visual-Motor Skills—Third Edition (TVMS-3)
Test of Visual Perceptual Skills (non-motor)—Third Edition (TVPS-3)
Wide Range Assessment of Visual-Motor Ability (WRAVMA)
Peabody Developmental Motor Scales—Second Edition (PDMS-2)
Goal-Oriented Assessment of Lifeskills (GOAL)

Sensory Processing Measures

Sensory Processing Measure (SPM)
Sensory Processing Measure—Preschool (SPM-P)
Sensory Integration and Praxis Tests (SIPT)
Test of Sensory Functions in Infants (TSFI)
DeGangi–Berk Test of Sensory Integration (TSI)

Memory Measures

Test of Memory and Learning—Senior Edition (TOMAL-SE)
Wide Range Assessment of Memory and Learning—Second Edition (WRAML-2)
Recognition Memory Test (RMT)

Academic and Achievement Measures

Learning Disabilities Diagnostic Inventory (LDDI)
Psychological Processing Checklist—Revised (PPC-R)
Jordan Left–Right Reversal Test—Third Edition (Jordan-3)
School Motivation and Learning Strategies Inventory (SMALSI)
Diagnostic Achievement Battery—Third Edition (DAB-3)
Diagnostic Achievement Battery—Intermediate (DAB-I)
Test of Silent Contextual Reading Fluency—Second Edition (TOSCRF-2)
Test of Silent Word Reading Fluency—Second Edition (TOSWRF-2)
Diagnostic Assessments of Reading—Second Edition (DAR-2)
Early Reading Assessment (ERA)

Decoding–Encoding Screener for Dyslexia (DESD)
Test of Word Reading Efficiency—Second Edition (TOWRE-2)
Test of Written Spelling—Fifth Edition (TWS-5)
Test of Silent Reading Efficiency and Comprehension (TOSREC)
Test of Mathematical Abilities—Third Edition (TOMA-3)
Test of Early Mathematics Ability—Third Edition (TEMA-3)
The Reading Observation Scale (ROS)
The Nelson-Denny Reading Test (NDRT)
Screening Test for Educational Prerequisite Skills (STEPS)
Young Children's Achievement Test (YCAT)
Test of Early Reading Ability—Third Edition (TERA-3)
Test of Reading Comprehension—Fourth Edition (TORC-4)
Gray Diagnostic Reading Tests—Second Edition (GDRT-2)
Test of Handwriting Skills—Revised (THS-R)
Norris Educational Achievement Test (NEAT)
Wide Range Achievement Test—Fourth Edition (WRAT-4)

References

Ainsworth, M. S. (1979). Infant–mother attachment. *American Psychologist, 34*(10), 932.

Allen, R. A., Robins, D. L., & Decker, S. L. (2008). Autism spectrum disorders: Neurobiology and current assessment practices. *Psychology in the Schools, 45*(10), 905–917.

American Psychiatric Association. (2000a). *Practice guidelines for the treatment of patients with eating disorders* (2nd ed.). Washington, DC: American Psychiatric Association.

American Psychiatric Association. (2000b). *Diagnostic and statistical manual of mental disorders* (4th ed., text rev.). Washington, DC: American Psychiatric Association.

American Psychiatric Association. (2000). *Diagnostic and statistical manual of mental disorders* (4th ed., text revision). Washington, DC: Author.

American Psychiatric Association. (2013). *Diagnostic and statistical manual of mental disorders* (5th ed.). Arlington, VA: American Psychiatric Association.

Anderson, J. S., Druzgal, T. J., Froehlich, A., DuBray, M. B., Lange, N., Alexander, A. L., … Lainhart, J. E. (2011). Decreased interhemispheric functional connectivity in autism. *Cerebral Cortex, 21*(5), 1134–1146. doi:10.1093/cercor/bhq190.

Anderson, J. S., Nielsen, J. A., Froehlich, A. L., DuBray, M. B., Druzgal, T. J., Cariello, A. N., … Lainhart, J. E. (2011). Functional connectivity magnetic resonance imaging classification of autism. *Brain, 134*(Pt 12), 3742–3754. doi: 10.1093/brain/awr263.

Ankenman, K., Elgin, J., Sullivan, K., Vincent, L., & Bernier, R. (2014). Nonverbal and verbal cognitive discrepancy profiles in autism spectrum disorders: Influence of age and gender. *American Journal on Intellectual and Developmental Disabilities, 119*, 84–89.

Attwood, F. (2014). *Mainstreaming sex: The sexualization of Western culture.* London: England: IB Tauris.

Attwood, A., Frith, U., & Hamelin, B. (1988). The understanding and use of interpersonal gestures by autistic and Down's syndrome children. *Journal of Autism and Developmental Disorders, 18*(2), 241–257.

Author. (2005). Harvard clinic scientist finds cut and autism link. In *Proceedings from the Oasis 2001 Conference for Autism.* Author. Retrieved April 4, 2010, from http://enzymestuff.com

Ayres, A. J. (2005). *Sensory integration and the child: Understanding hidden sensory challenges* (25th anniversary ed., rev. and updated/by Pediatric Therapy Network ed.). Los Angeles, CA: WPS.

Bachmeyer, M. H. (2009). Treatment of selective and inadequate food intake in children: A review and practical guide. *Behavior Analysis in Practice, 2*(1), 43.

Baddeley, A. D. (2001). Is working memory still working? *The American Psychologist, 56*(11), 851–864.

Bae, Y. (2012). Review of children's depression inventory 2 (CDI 2). *Journal of Psychoeducational Assessment, 30*(3), 304–308. Retrieved from http://dx.doi.org/10.1177/0734282911426407.

© Springer International Publishing Switzerland 2016

A.P. Kroncke et al., *Assessment of Autism Spectrum Disorder*, Contemporary Issues in Psychological Assessment, DOI 10.1007/978-3-319-25504-0

Bailey, A., Palferman, S., Heavey, L., & Le Couteur, A. (1998). Autism: The phenotype in relatives. *Journal of Autism and Developmental Disorders, 28*(5), 369–392.

Baker, J. (2006). *Preparing for life: The complete guide for transitioning to adulthood for those with Autism and Asperger's Syndrome.* Arlington, TX: Future Horizons.

Baker, J. (2014a). Children with social skills deficits and challenging behaviors. In *JFK Partners Annual Autism Conference, October 10, 2014.* Aurora, CO: JFK Partners.

Baker, J. (2014b). Effective interventions for behavioral and social challenges. In *Presented at the Second Annual Autism Disorders Conference, October 10, 2014.* Aurora, CO: JFK Partners.

Baranek, G. T. (1999). Autism during infancy: A retrospective video analysis of sensory-motor and social behaviors at 9–12 months of age. *Journal of Autism and Developmental Disorders, 29*(3), 213–224.

Baranek, G. T., Boyd, B. A., Poe, M. D., David, F. J., & Watson, L. R. (2007). Hyperresponsive sensory patterns in young children with autism, developmental delay, and typical development. *American Journal of Mental Retardation, 112*, 233–245.

Barkley, R. A. (1998). *Attention-deficit hyperactivity disorder: A handbook for diagnosis and treatment* (2nd ed.). New York, NY: Guilford Press.

Barkley, R. A. (2006). *Attention-deficit hyperactivity disorder: A handbook for diagnosis and treatment* (3rd ed.). New York, NY: Guilford Press.

Barkley, R. A., & Lombroso, P. J. (2000). Genetics of childhood disorders: XVII. ADHD, Part 1: The executive functions and ADHD. *Journal of the American Academy of Child & Adolescent Psychiatry, 39*(8), 1064–1068.

Barlow, J. S. (2002). *The cerebellum and adaptive control.* Cambridge, England: Cambridge University Press.

Barnhill, G., Hagiwara, T., Smith Myles, B., & Simpson, R. L. (2000). Asperger syndrome: A study of the cognitive profiles of 37 children and adolescents. *Focus on Autism and Other Developmental Disabilities, 15*, 146–153.

Baron-Cohen, S. (2004). The cognitive neuroscience of autism. *Journal of Neurology, Neurosurgery & Psychiatry, 75*(7), 945–948. Retrieved from http://dx.doi.org/10.1136/jnnp.2003.018713.

Baron-Cohen, S., & Belmonte, M. K. (2005). Autism: A window onto the development of the social and the analytic brain. *Annual Review of Neuroscience, 28*, 109–126. doi:10.1146/annurev.neuro.27.070203.144137.

Barry, M., Moran, A., Anglim, M., Conway, E. V., & Guerin, S. (2013). Examining IQ among a clinical sample of preschool children with autism spectrum disorder over time. *Irish Journal of Psychological Medicine, 30*(3), 179–186. Retrieved from http://dx.doi.org/10.1017/ipm.2013.26.

Beck, A. T., Epstein, N., Brown, G., & Steer, R. A. (1988). An inventory for measuring clinical anxiety: Psychometric properties. *Journal of Consulting and Clinical Psychology, 56*(6), 893–897.

Beck, A. T., & Steer, R. A. (1991). Relationship between the beck anxiety inventory and the Hamilton anxiety rating scale with anxious outpatients. *Journal of Anxiety Disorders, 5*(3), 213–223.

Beck, A. T., Steer, R. A., & Brown, G. K. (1996). *Beck depression inventory manual* (2nd ed.). San Antonio, TX: Psychological Corporation.

Beery, K. E. (2004). *The Beery-Buktenica developmental test of visual-motor integration: Beery VMI, with supplemental developmental tests of visual perception and motor coordination, and stepping stones age norms from birth to age six.* Minneapolis, MN: NCS Pearson.

Belmonte, M. K., Saxena-Chandhok, T., Cherian, R., Muneer, R., George, L., & Karanth, P. (2013). Oral motor deficits in speech-impaired children with autism. *Frontiers in Integrative Neuroscience, 7.* Retrieved from http://search.proquest.com/docview/1431014381?accountid=14506

Ben-Itzchak, E., Watson, L. R., & Zachor, D. A. (2014, May). *Cognitive ability is associated with different outcome trajectories in autism spectrum disorders.* Poster presented at the 13th Annual International Meeting for Autism Research, Atlanta, GA.

Benton, L. A., Hamsher, K., & Sivan, A. B. (1994). *Controlled oral word association test. Multilingual aphasia examination.* Iowa City, IA: AJA.

Billington, J., Baron-Cohen, S., & Wheelwright, S. (2007). Cognitive style predicts entry into physical sciences and humanities: Questionnaire and performance tests of empathy and systemizing. *Learning and Individual Differences, 17*, 260–268.

Blair, R., Frith, U., Smith, N., Abell, F., & Cipolotti, L. (2002). Fractionation of visual memory: Agency detection and its impairment in autism. *Neuropsychologia, 40*, 108–118.

Boucher, J., Mayes, A. R., & Bigham, S. (2008). Memory language and intellectual ability in low functioning autism. In J. Boucher & D. M. Bowler (Eds.), *Memory in autism: Theories and evidence* (pp. 268–290). Cambridge, England: Cambridge University Press.

Boucher, J., Mayes, A., & Bigham, S. (2012). Memory in autistic spectrum disorder. *Psychological Bulletin, 138*(3), 458.

Bowler, D. M., Gaigg, S. B., & Gardiner, J. M. (2009). Free recall learning of hierarchically organized lists by adults with Asperger's syndrome: Additional evidence for diminished relational processing. *Journal of Autism and Developmental Disorders, 39*, 589–595.

Broad Institute of MIT and Harvard. (2012, April 4). DNA sequencing consortium unveils patterns of mutations in autism. *ScienceDaily*. Retrieved April 9, 2012, from http://www.sciencedaily.com/releases/2012/04/120404133658.htm

Brown-Lavoie, S. M., Viecili, M. A., & Weiss, J. A. (2014). Sexual knowledge and victimization in adults with autism spectrum disorders. *Journal of Autism and Developmental Disorders, 44*(9), 2185–2196.

Buescher, A. V., Cidav, Z., Knapp, M., & Mandell, D. S. (2014). Costs of autism spectrum disorders in the United Kingdom and the United States. *JAMA Pediatrics, 168*(8), 721–728.

Burner, K. M., Sterling, L. J., Munson, J., Estes, A. M., Dawson, G., & Webb, S. J. (2014, May). *A longitudinal study of emotion processing in ASD and the relation with other clinical symptoms: The Cpea early development study of autism.* Paper presented at the 13th Annual International Meeting for Autism Research, Atlanta, GA.

Butcher, J. N., Dahlstrom, W. G., Graham, J., Tellegen, A. M., & Kreammer, B. (1989). *The Minnesota Multiphasic Personality Inventory-2 (Mmpi-2): Manual for administration and scoring.* Minneapolis, MN: University of Minnesota Press.

Camahalan, F.M.G. (2006). Effects of a metacognitive reading program on the reading achievement and metacognitive strategies of students with cases of dyslexia. *Reading Improvement 43*(2),77–92.

Caron, M.-J., Mottron, L., Berthiaume, C., & Dawson, M. (2006). Cognitive mechanisms, specificity and neural underpinnings of visuospatial peaks in autism. *Brain: A Journal of Neurology, 129*(7), 1789–1802. Retrieved from http://dx.doi.org/10.1093/brain/awl072.

Carr, T., & Lord, C. (2013). Longitudinal study of perceived negative impact in African American and Caucasian mothers of children with autism spectrum disorder. *Autism, 17*(4), 405–417.

Carter, A. S., Volkmar, F. R., Sparrow, S. S., Wang, J., Lord, C., Dawson, G., … Schopler, E. (1998). The Vineland Adaptive Behavior Scales: Supplementary norms for individuals with autism. *Journal of Autism and Developmental Disorders, 28*(4), 287–302.

Castaneda, A., McCandless, B. R., & Palermo, D. S. (1956). The children's form of the manifest anxiety scale. *Child Development, 27*(3), 317.

Centers for Disease Control and Prevention. (2012). Prevalence of autism spectrum disorders— Autism and developmental disabilities monitoring network. *Morbidity and Mortality Weekly Report (MMWR), 61*, 1–19.

Centers for Disease Control and Prevention. (2014). Prevalence of autism spectrum disorders among children aged 8 years—Autism and developmental disabilities monitoring network. *Morbidity and Mortality Weekly Report, 63*, 1–21. Retrieved from http://www.cdc.gov/ncbddd/autism/data.html.

Cervantes, P., Matson, J. L., Tureck, K., & Adams, H. L. (2013). The relationship of comorbid anxiety symptom severity and challenging behaviors in infants and toddlers with autism spectrum disorder. *Research in Autism Spectrum Disorders, 7*(12), 1528–1534.

Chen, Y., Rodgers, J., & McConachie, H. (2009). Restricted and repetitive behaviors, sensory processing and cognitive style in children with autism spectrum disorders. *Journal of Autism and Developmental Disorders, 39*, 635–642.

Chiang, H. M., & Lin, Y. H. (2007). Reading comprehension instruction for students with autism spectrum disorders: A review of the literature. *Focus on Autism and Other Developmental Disabilities, 22*(4), 259–267.

Chiang, H. M., & Wineman, I. (2014). Factors associated with quality of life in individuals with autism spectrum disorders: A review of literature. *Research in Autism Spectrum Disorders, 8*(8), 974–986.

Chlebowski, C., Fein, D. A., & Robins, D. (2014, May). *ASD screening at 18 and 24 months: Incremental validity and characteristics of screen positive cases.* Poster presented at the 13th Annual International Meeting for Autism Research, Atlanta, GA.

Christ, S. E., Kester, L. E., Bodner, K. E., & Miles, J. H. (2011). Evidence for selective inhibitory impairment in individuals with autism spectrum disorder. *Neuropsychology, 25*(6), 690–701. doi:10.1037/a0024256.

Christenson, S. L., & Sheridan, S. M. (2001). *Schools and families: Creating essential connections for learning.* New York, NY: Guilford.

Coe, D. A., Matson, J. L., Russell, D. W., Slifer, K. J., Capone, G. T., Baglio, C., et al. (1999). Behavior problems of children with Down syndrome and life events. *Journal of Autism and Developmental Disorders, 29*(2), 149–156.

Cohen, H., Amerine-Dickens, M., & Smith, T. (2006). Early intensive behavioral treatment: Replication of the UCLA model in a community setting. *Journal of Developmental & Behavioral Pediatrics, 27*(2), 145–155.

Colorado Department of Education (CDE) & JFK Partners of the University of Colorado, Anschutz Medical Campus; Hepburn, S., Kaider, K., & Graham, M. (2014, February). *Guidelines for the evaluation of autism spectrum disorder: Exceptional student services unit.* The Office of Special Education.

Constantino, J. N., Gruber, C. P., Davis, S., Hayes, S., Passanante, N., & Przybeck, T. (2004). The factor structure of autistic traits. *Journal of Child Psychology and Psychiatry, 45*(4), 719–726.

Coolican, J., Bryson, S. E., & Zwaigenbaum, L. (2008). Brief report: Data on the Stanford-Binet intelligence scales (5th ed.) in children with autism spectrum disorder. *Journal of Autism and Developmental Disorders, 38*, 190–197.

Cooper, J. O., Heron, T. E., & Heward, W. L. (2013). *Applied behavior analysis.* Upper Saddle River, NJ: Pearson.

Corbett, B. A., Constantine, L. J., Hendren, R., Rocke, D., & Ozonoff, S. (2009). Examining executive functioning in children with autism spectrum disorder, attention deficit hyperactivity disorder and typical development. *Psychiatry Research, 166*(2), 210–222.

Courchesne, E., Townsend, J., Akshoomoff, N. A., Saitoh, O., Yeung-Courchesne, R., Lincoln, A. J., … Lau, L. (1994). Impairment in shifting attention in autistic and cerebellar patients. *Behavioral Neuroscience, 108(5)*, 848.

Cox, A., Klein, K., Charman, T., Baird, G., Baron-Cohen, S., Sweetenham, J., … Wheelwright, S. (1999). Autism spectrum disorders at 10 and 42 months of age: Stability of clinical and ADI-R diagnoses. *Journal of Child Psychology and Psychiatry, 40*, 719–742.

Cronbach, L. J. (1970). *Essentials of psychological testing* (3rd ed.). New York, NY: Harper & Row.

Culbertson, W. C., & Zillmer, E. A. (2001). *Tower of London—Drexel University, (TOLDX). Technical manual* (2nd ed.). North Tonawanda, NY: MHS.

Cycowicz, Y. M., Friedman, D., & Rothstein, M. (1996). An ERP developmental study of repetition priming by auditory novel stimuli. *Psychophysiology, 33*(6), 680–690.

D'Amelio, M., Ricci, I., Sacco, R., Liu, X., Arguma, L., Musarella, L. A., … Persico, A. M. (2005). Paraoxonase gene variants associated with autism in North America but not in Italy: Possible regional specificity in gene-environment interactions. *Molecular Psychiatry, 10*, 1006–1016.

D'Eufemia, P., Celli, M., Finocchiaro, R., Pacifico, L., Viozzi, L., Zaccagini, M., … Giardini, O. (1996). Abnormal intestinal permeability in children with autism. *Acta Paediatrica, 85*(9), 1076–1079.

Daniel, M. H. (2013). *User survey on Q-interactive examinee behavior* (pp. 1–10). Bloomington, MN: Pearson (published on Hello q.com).

Daniels, A. M., & Mandell, D. S. (2014). Explaining differences in age at autism spectrum disorder diagnosis: A critical review. *Autism, 18*, 583–597.

Day, J. J., & Sweatt, J. D. (2011). Epigenetic mechanisms in cognition. *Neuron, 70*(5), 813–829. doi:10.1016/j.neuron.2011.05.019.

Deer, B. (2009, February 13). *MMR doctor Andrew Wakefield fixed data on autism* [Electronic version]. UK Times Limited, p. 1.

DeFelice, K. (2008). *Enzymes for autism and other neurological conditions* (3rd ed.). Johnston, IA: ThunderSnow Interactive.

Denmark, J., Feldman, M. A., & Holden, J. A. (2003). Behavioral relationship between autism and fragile X syndrome. *American Journal on Mental Retardation, 108*(5), 314–326.

Denmark, J. (n.d.). The relationship between autism and Fragile X syndrome: A review of the research. *Journal*, 29–43. Retrieved March 21, 2015.

Deprey, L., & Ozonoff, S. (2009). Assessment of comorbid psychiatric conditions in autism spectrum disorders. In S. Goldstein, J. A. Naglieri, & S. Ozonoff (Eds.), *Assessment of autism spectrum disorders* (pp. 290–317). New York, NY: Guilford Press.

Diehl, J., Bennettto, L., & Young, E. C. (2006). Story recall and narrative coherence of high-functioning children with autism spectrum disorders. *Journal of Abnormal Child Psychology, 34*(1), 87–101.

Dietz, C., Swinkels, S. H., Buitelaar, J. K., van Daalen, E., & van Engeland, H. (2007). Stability and change of IQ scores in preschool children diagnosed with autistic spectrum disorder. *European Child and Adolescent Psychiatry, 16*(6), 405–410. doi:10.1007/s00787-007-0614-3.

DiLavore, P. C., Lord, C., & Rutter, M. (1995). Pre-linguistic autism diagnostic observation schedule. *Journal of Autism and Developmental Disorders, 25*(4), 355–379.

Doubleday, E. K., King, P., & Papageorgiou, C. (2002). Relationship between fluid intelligence and ability to benefit from cognitive-behavioural therapy in older adults: A preliminary investigation. *British Journal of Clinical Psychology, 41*, 423–428.

Dover, C. J., & Le Couteur, A. (2007). How to diagnose autism. *Archives of Disease in Childhood, 92*(6), 540–545.

Dowd, A. M., McGinley, J. L., Taffe, J. R., & Rinehart, N. J. (2012). Do planning and visual integration difficulties underpin motor dysfunction in autism? A kinematic study of young children with autism. *Journal of Autism and Developmental Disorders, 42*(8), 1539–1548. doi:10.1007/s10803-011-1385-8.

Dowell, L. R., Mahone, E., & Mostofsky, S. H. (2009). Associations of postural knowledge and basic motor skill with dyspraxia in autism: Implication for abnormalities in distributed connectivity and motor learning. *Neuropsychology, 23*(5), 563–570.

Dozois, D. J. A., Dobson, K. S., & Ahnberg, J. L. (1998). A psychometric evaluation of the Beck Depression Inventory-II. *Psychological Assessment, 10*(2), 83–89. Retrieved from http://dx.doi.org/10.1037/1040-3590.10.2.83.

Drewe, E. A. (1975). An experimental investigation of Luria's theory on the effects of frontal lobe lesions in man. *Neuropsychologia, 13*(4), 421–429. doi:10.1016/0028-3932(75)90065-2.

Dunn, W. (1999). *The sensory profile manual.* San Antonio, TX: The Psychological Corporation.

Dunn, L. M., & Dunn, D. M. (2007). *Peabody picture vocabulary test* (4th ed.). Bloomington, MN: Pearson Assessments.

DuPaul, G. J., & Stoner, G. (2003). *ADHD in the schools: Assessment and intervention strategies* (2nd ed.). New York, NY: Guilford Press.

Dykstra, J. R. (2014, May). *Engagement of students with ASD in elementary and middle school classrooms.* Oral presentation at International Meeting for Autism Research (IMFAR), Atlanta, GA.

Dziuk, M., Larson, J., Apostu, A., Mahone, E., Denckla, M., & Mostofsky, S. (2007). Dyspraxia in autism: Association with motor, social, and communicative deficits. *Developmental Medicine and Child Neurology, 49*(10), 734–739.

Eaves, L. C., & Ho, H. H. (2004). The very early identification of autism: Outcome to age 4 1/2–5. *Journal of Autism and Developmental Disorders, 34*(4), 367–378.

Eber, L., Sugai, G., Smith, C. R., & Scott, T. M. (2002). Wraparound and positive behavioral interventions and supports in the schools. *Journal of Emotional and Behavioral Disorders, 10*(3), 171–179.

Edwards, L. A., Masyn, K. E., Luyster, R., & Nelson, C. A. (2014, May). *Early developmental trajectories of social communication in infants at risk for ASD.* Poster presented at the 13th Annual International Meeting for Autism Research, Atlanta, GA.

Eigsti, I. (2011). Executive Functions in ASD. In D. A. Fein (Ed.), *The neuropsychology of autism* (pp. 185–203). New York, NY: Oxford University.

Eigsti, I., de Marchena, A. B., Schuh, J. M., & Kelley, E. (2011). Language acquisition in autism spectrum disorders: A developmental review. *Research in Autism Spectrum Disorders, 5*(2), 681–691. Retrieved from http://dx.doi.org/10.1016/j.rasd.2010.09.001.

Elliott, C. D. (1990). *Differential ability scales.* San Antonio, TX: The Psychological Corporation.

Elliott, C. D. (2007). *Differential ability scales: Introductory and technical handbook* (2nd ed.). San Antonio, TX: Pearson.

Esler, A. N., Godber, Y., & Christenson, S. L. (2008). Best practices in supporting family-school partnerships. In A. Thomas & J. Grimes (Eds.), *Best practices in school psychology V* (pp. 917–929). Bethesda, MD: NASP.

Falkmer, T., Anderson, K., Falkmer, M., & Horlin, C. (2013). Diagnostic procedures in autism spectrum disorders: A systematic literature review. *European Child and Adolescent Psychiatry, 22*(6), 329–340. doi:10.1007/s00787-013-0375-0.

Fein, D. (Ed.). (2011). *The neuropsychology of autism.* Oxford, England: Oxford University Press.

Fein, D., Barton, M., Eigsti, I. M., Kelley, E., Naigles, L., Schultz, R. T., … Tyson, K. (2013). Optimal outcome in individuals with a history of autism. *Journal of Child Psychology and Psychiatry, 54*(2), 195–205. doi: 10.1111/jcpp.12037.

Fein, D., Barton, M., Eigsti, I. M., Kelley, E., Naigles, L., Schultz, R. T., & Tyson, K. (2013). Optimal outcome in individuals with a history of autism. *Journal of Child Psychology and Psychiatry, 54*(2), 195–205. doi:10.1111/jcpp.12037.

Filipek, P. A., Accardo, P. J., Baranek, G. T., Cook, E. H., Jr., Dawson, G., Gordon, B., … Volkmar, F. R. (1999). The screening and diagnosis of autistic spectrum disorders. *Journal of Autism and Developmental Disorders, 29*(6), 439–484. Retrieved from http://dx.doi.org/10.1023/A:1021943802493.

Fischbach, G. D. (2007, December 7). Retrieved May 5, 2014, from http://sfari.org/news-and-opinion/classic-paper-reviews/2007/leo-kanners-1943-paper-on-autism-commentary-by-gerald-fischbach

Flanagan, D. P., & Kaufman, A. S. (2004). *Essentials of WISC-IV assessment.* Hoboken, NJ: Wiley.

Foley-Nicpon, M., Assouline, S. G., & Stinson, R. D. (2012). Cognitive and academic distinctions between gifted students with autism and Asperger syndrome. *Gifted Child Quarterly, 56*(2), 77–89.

Foss-Feig, J. H., Heacock, J. L., & Cascio, C. J. (2012). Tactile responsiveness patterns and their association with core features in autism spectrum disorders. *Research in Autism Spectrum Disorders, 6*, 337–344.

Foundation, S. (2014). National. *Fragile X Foundation, 2014.* Retrieved from https://fragilex.org.

Fountain, C., King, M. D., & Bearman, P. S. (2011). Age of diagnosis for autism: individual and community factors across 10 birth cohorts. *Journal of Epidemiology and Community Health, 65*(6), 503–510.

Fragile X. (2014). National. *Fragile X Foundation, 2014.* Retrieved from https://fragilex.org.

Fragile, X., & National Fragile, X. (2014). *Foundation.* Retrieved from https://fragilex.org.

Freeman, B. J., Ritvo, E. R., Needleman, R., & Yokota, A. (1985). The stability of cognitive and linguistic parameters in autism: A five-year prospective study. *Journal of the American Academy of Child Psychiatry, 24*(4), 459–464.

Freitag, C. M., Kleser, C., Schneider, M., & von Gontard, A. (2007). Quantitative assessment of neuromotor function in adolescents with high functioning autism and Asperger Syndrome. *Journal of Autism and Developmental Disorders, 37*(5), 948–959. doi:10.1007/s10803-006-0235-6.

Frith, C. (2004). Is autism a disconnection disorder? *The Lancet Neurology, 3*(10), 577.

Fuller, C. G., & Sabatino, D. A. (1998). Diagnosis and treatment considerations with comorbid developmentally disabled populations. *Journal of Clinical Psychology, 54*(1), 1–10.

Gabig, C. S. (2008). Verbal working memory and story retelling in school-age children with autism. *Language, Speech, and Hearing Services in Schools, 39*(4), 498–511.

Gaigg, S. B., Bird, G., & Bowler, D. M. (2014, May). *Alexithymia in autism: psychophysiological correlates and a possible route to anxiety.* Paper presented at the 13th Annual International Meeting for Autism Research, Atlanta, GA.

Gaigg, S. B., & Bowler, D. M. (2008). Free recall and forgetting of emotionally arousing words in autism spectrum disorder. *Neuropsychologia, 46*(9), 2336–2343.

Gargaro, B. A., Rinehart, N. J., Bradshaw, J. L., Tonge, B. J., & Sheppard, D. M. (2011). Autism and ADHD: how far have we come in the comorbidity debate? *Neuroscience & Biobehavioral Reviews, 35*(5), 1081–1088.

Garretson, H. B., Fein, D., & Waterhouse, L. (1990). Sustained attention in children with autism. *Journal of Autism and Developmental Disorders, 20*(1), 101–114.

Georgiades, S., Szatmari, P., Zwaigenbaum, L., Duku, E., Bryson, S., Roberts, W., … Mahoney, W. (2007). Structure of the autism symptom phenotype: A proposed multidimensional model. *Journal of the American Academy of Child & Adolescent Psychiatry, 46*(2), 188–196. doi: 10.1097/01.chi.0000242236.90763.7f.

Ghaziuddin, M. (2011). Asperger disorder in the DSM-V: sacrificing utility for validity. *Journal of the American Academy of Child and Adolescent Psychiatry, 50*(2), 192–193.

Giarelli, E., Wiggins, L. D., Rice, C. E., Levy, S. E., Kirby, R. S., Pinto-Martin, J., & Mandell, D. (2010). Sex differences in the evaluation and diagnosis of autism spectrum disorders among children. *Disability and Health Journal, 3*(2), 107–116.

Gilliam, J. (2006). *Gilliam autism rating scale* (2nd ed.). Austin, TX: PRO-ED.

Golden, C. J. (1975). The measurement of creativity by the Stroop color and word test. *Journal of Personality Assessment, 39*(5), 502–506.

Golden, C. J. (2003). The adult Luria-Nebraska neuropsychological battery. In G. Goldstein, S. R. Beers, & M. Hersen (Eds.), *Comprehensive handbook of psychological assessment: Intellectual and neuropsychological assessment* (Vol. 1). Hoboken, NJ: Wiley. doi:10.1002/9780471726753.ch9.

Golden, C. J., & Freshwater, S. M. (1998). *Stroop color and word test.* Chicago, IL: Stoelting. (Original work published 1978)

Gordon, B., & Stark, S. (2007). Procedural learning of a visual sequence in individuals with autism. *Focus on Autism and Other Developmental Disabilities, 22,* 14–22.

Gotham, K., Bishop, S. L., & Lord, C. (2011). Diagnosis of autism spectrum disorders. In D. G. Amaral, G. Dawson, & D. H. Geschwind (Eds.), *Autism spectrum disorders* (pp. 30–43). New York, NY: Oxford University Press.

Gould, S. J. (1996). *The mismeasure of man.* New York, NY: Norton.

Grandin, T. (1995). *Thinking in pictures: And other reports from my life with autism.* New York, NY: Doubleday.

Grant, D. A., & Berg, E. (1948). A behavioral analysis of degree of reinforcement and ease of shifting to new responses in a Weigl-type card-sorting problem. *Journal of Experimental Psychology, 38*(4), 404–411.

Green, D., Charman, T., Pickles, A., Chandler, S., Loucas, T., Simonoff, E., & Baird, G. (2009). Impairment in movement skills of children with autistic spectrum disorders. *Developmental Medicine & Child Neurology, 51*(4), 311–316. doi: 10.1111/j.1469-8749.2008.03242.x.

Greene, R. (2014). *Lost in school: Why our kids with behavioral challenges are falling through the cracks and how we can help them.* New York, NY: Scribner.

Greene, R., & Ablon, S. (2005). *Treating explosive kids: The collaborative problem-solving approach.* New York, NY: Guilford Press.

Haist, F., Adamo, M., Westerfield, M., Courchesne, E., & Townsend, J. (2005). The functional neuroanatomy of spatial attention in autism spectrum disorder. *Developmental Neuropsychology, 27*(3), 425–458.

Hamilton, L. M. (2009). *Facing autism: Giving parents reasons for hope and guidance for help.* Colorado Springs, CO: WaterBrook Press.

Hammond, R. K., Campbell, J. M., & Ruble, L. A. (2013). Considering identification and service provision for students with autism spectrum disorders within the context of response to intervention. *Exceptionality, 21*(1), 34–50.

Happé, F., & Frith, U. (2006). The weak coherence account: Detail-focused cognitive style in autism spectrum disorders. *Journal of Autism and Developmental Disorders, 36*(1), 5–25. doi:10.1007/s10803-005-0039-0.

Hardan, A. Y., Kilpatrick, M., Keshavan, M. S., & Minshew, N. J. (2003). Motor performance and anatomic magnetic resonance imaging (MRI) of the basal ganglia in autism. *Journal of Child Neurology, 18*(5), 317–324.

Hare, D. J., Mellor, C., & Azmi, S. (2007). Episodic memory in adults with autistic spectrum disorders: Recall for self-versus other-experienced events. *Research in Developmental Disabilities, 28*, 317–329.

Harmon, A. (2012, April 8). The autism wars. *The New York Times*, SR3.

Hart, B., & Risley, T. R. (1995). *Meaningful differences in the everyday experience of young American children*. Boston, MA: Brookes.

Heaton, R. K., Chelune, G. J., Talley, J. L., Kay, G. G., & Curtiss, G. (1993). *Wisconsin card sorting test manual revised and expanded*. Lutz, FL: Psychological Assessment Resources.

Helt, M., Kelley, E., Kinsbourne, M., Pandey, J., Boorstein, H., Herbert, M., & Fein, D. (2008). Can children with autism recover? If so, how? *Neuropsychology Review, 18*(4), 339–366. doi: 10.1007/s11065-008-9075-9.

Hepburn, S. (2015, April 17). Co-occurrence of down syndrome and autism spectrum disorder: Implications of assessment & intervention. In *JFK Partners 50th Anniversary Symposium, Aurora, CO*.

Hepburn, S., & Katz, N. (2009, October 14). *Screening and assessment of autism spectrum disorders*. Unpublished lecture, University of Colorado at Denver Medical School, Aurora, CO.

Hewitt, P. L., & Norton, G. R. (1993). The Beck Anxiety Inventory: A psychometric analysis. *Psychological Assessment, 5*(4), 408–412. Retrieved from http://dx.doi.org/10.1037/1040-3590.5.4.408.

Hnida, D. (2006). *Father's age may be linked to autism*. Retrieved February 9, 2009, from http://cbs4denver.com/local/Colorado.News.Denver.2.552125.html

Hofvander, B., Delorme, R., Chaste, P., Nyden, A., Wentz, E., Stahlberg, O., … Leboyer, M. (2009). Psychiatric and psychosocial problems in adults with normal intelligence autism spectrum disorders. *BMC Psychiatry, 9*, 35.

Horovitz, M., Matson, J. L., Turygin, N., & Beighley, J. S. (2012). The relationship between gender and age of first concern in toddlers with autism spectrum disorders. *Research in Autism Spectrum Disorders, 6*(1), 466–471.

Horvath, K., Papadimitriou, J. C., Rabsztyn, A., Drachenberg, C., & Tildon, J. T. (1999). Gastrointestinal abnormalities in children with autistic disorder. *Journal of Pediatrics, 135*, 559–563.

Hosp, J. L. (2008). Best practices in aligning academic assessment with instruction. In A. Thomas & J. Grimes (Eds.), *Best practices in school psychology V* (pp. 363–376). Bethesda, MD: National Association of School Psychologists.

Howlin, P., Wing, L., & Gould, J. (1995). The recognition of autism in children with down syndrome-implications for intervention and some speculations about pathology. *Developmental Medicine & Child Neurology, 37*(5), 406–414.

Huckabee, H. (2003). *Correspondence of DSM-IV criteria for autistic spectrum disorders with standardized language measures of intelligence and language*. Unpublished dissertation, University of Houston, Presented April, 2003.

Huemer, S. V., & Mann, V. (2009). A comprehensive profile of decoding and comprehension in autism spectrum disorders. *Journal of Autism and Developmental Disorders, 40*(4), 485–493. doi:10.1007/s10803-009-0892-3.

Huerta, M., Bishop, S. L., Duncan, A., Hus, V., & Lord, C. (2012). Application of DSM-5 criteria for autism spectrum disorder to three samples of children with DSM-IV diagnoses of pervasive developmental disorders. *American Journal of Psychiatry, 169*(10), 1056–1064. doi:10.1176/appi.ajp.2012.12020276.

Inbar-Feigenberg, M., Grafodatskaya, D., Choufani, S., Chung, B. H. Y., Roberts, L. J., Russell, C., … Weksberg, R. (2013). Social skills impairments in girls with Turner syndrome. In *63rd ASHG Annual Meeting 2013*. Boston, MA: The American Society of Human Genetics.

Indiana Resource Center. (2011). *Assessment process for autism spectrum disorders: Purpose and procedures*. Retrieved August, 2014, from http://www.iidc.indiana.edu/index.php?pageId=365

Individuals with Disabilities Education Act (IDEA). (2004). 20 U.S.C. § 1400 et seq. Individuals with Disabilities Education Act Regulations, 34 C.F.R. § 300.1 et seq.

Iwata, B. A., Pace, G. M., Dorsey, M. F., Zarcone, J. R., Vollmer, T. R., Smith, R. G., … Willis, K. D. (1994). The functions of self-injurious behavior: An experimental epidemiological analysis. *Journal of Applied Behavior Analysis, 27*(2), 215–240.

Iwata, B. A., Vollmer, T. R., & Zarcone, J. R. (1990). The experimental (functional) analysis of behavior disorders: Methodology, applications, and limitations. In A. C. Repp & N. N. Singh (Eds.), *Perspectives on the use of nonaversive and aversive interventions for persons with developmental disabilities* (pp. 301–330). Sycamore, IL: Sycamore.

Joffe, V. L., Cain, K., & Maric, N. (2007). Comprehension problems in children with specific language impairment: Does mental imagery training help? *International Journal of Language & Communication Disorders, 42*(6), 648–664.

Jang, J., Matson, J. L., Cervantes, P. E., & Konst, M. J. (2014). The relationship between ethnicity and age of first concern in toddlers with autism spectrum disorder. *Research in Autism Spectrum Disorders, 8*(7), 925–932.

Jang, J., Matson, J. L., Williams, L. W., Tureck, K., Goldin, R. L., & Cervantes, P. E. (2013). Rates of comorbid symptoms in children with ASD, ADHD, and comorbid ASD and ADHD. *Research in Developmental Disabilities, 34*(8), 2369–2378. Retrieved from http://dx.doi.org/10.1016/j.ridd.2013.04.021.

Jaynes, W. H. (2005). A meta-analysis of the relation of parental involvement to urban elementary school student academic achievement. *Urban Education, 40*(3), 237–269.

Jensen, A. R. (1965). Scoring the Stroop test. *Acta Psychologica, 24*(5), 398–408.

Jiang, Y. V., Capistrano, C. G., & Palm, B. E. (2014). Spatial working memory in children with high-functioning autism: Intact configural processing but impaired capacity. *Journal of Abnormal Psychology, 123*(1), 248.

Jones, C. R., Happé, F., Pickles, A., Marsden, A. J., Tregay, J., Baird, G., & Charman, T. (2011). 'Everyday memory' impairments in autism spectrum disorders. *Journal of Autism and Developmental Disorders, 41*(4), 455–464. doi: 10.1007/s10803-010-1067-y.

Joseph, R. M., Tager-Flusberg, H., & Lord, C. (2002). Cognitive profiles and social-communicative functioning in children with autism spectrum disorder. *Journal of Child Psychology and Psychiatry, 43*(6), 807–821.

Just, M. A., Cherkassky, V. L., Keller, T. A., Kana, R. K., & Minshew, N. J. (2007). Functional and anatomical cortical underconnectivity in autism: Evidence from an FMRI study of an executive function task and corpus callosum morphometry. *Cerebral Cortex, 17*(4), 951–961. doi:10.1093/cercor/bhl006.

Just, M. A., Cherkassky, V. L., Keller, T. A., & Minshew, N. J. (2004). Cortical activation and synchronization during sentence comprehension in high-functioning autism: Evidence of underconnectivity. *Brain, 127*, 1811–1821.

Kamp-Becker, I., Smidt, J., Ghahreman, M., Heinzel-Gutenbrunner, M., Becker, K., & Remschmidt, H. (2010). Categorical and dimensional structure of autism spectrum disorders: The nosologic validity of Asperger Syndrome. *Journal of Autism and Developmental Disorders, 40*(8), 921–929. doi:10.1007/s10803-010-0939-5.

Kamphaus, R. W., & Campbell, J. M. (2006). *Psychodiagnostic assessment of children: Dimensional and categorical approaches*. Hoboken, NJ: Wiley.

Kana, R. K., Keller, T. A., Cherkassky, V. L., Minshew, N. J., & Just, M. A. (2006). Sentence comprehension in autism: Thinking in pictures with decreased functional connectivity. *Brain, 129*(9), 2484–2493.

Kandel, E., Schwartz, J., & Jessell, T. (1991). *The principles of neural science* (3rd ed.). Norwalk, CT: Appleton and Lange.

Kanne, S. M., Randolph, J. K., & Farmer, J. E. (2008). Diagnostic and assessment findings: A bridge to academic planning for children with autism spectrum disorders. *Neuropsychology Review, 18*(4), 367–384.

Kanner, L. (1943). Autistic disturbances of affective contact. *Nervous Child, 2,* 217–250.

Kaye, J. A., del Mar Melero-Montes, M., & Jick, H. (2001). Mumps, measles, and rubella vaccine and the incidence of autism recorded by general practitioners. *Western Journal of Medicine, 174*(6), 387–390.

Keehn, B., Lincoln, A. J., Müller, R. A., & Townsend, J. (2010). Attentional networks in children and adolescents with autism spectrum disorder. *Journal of Child Psychology and Psychiatry, 51*(11), 1251–1259.

Keehn, B., Müller, R. A., & Townsend, J. (2013). Atypical attentional networks and the emergence of autism. *Neuroscience & Biobehavioral Reviews, 37*(2), 164–183. doi:10.1016/j.neubiorev.2012.11.014.

Keehn, B., Shih, P., Brenner, L. A., Townsend, J., & Müller, R. A. (2013). Functional connectivity for an "Island of sparing" in autism spectrum disorder: An fMRI study of visual search. *Human Brain Mapping, 34*(10), 2524–2537.

Kelley, E., Naigles, L., & Fein, D. (2010). An in-depth examination of optimal outcome children with a history of autism spectrum disorders. *Research in Autism Spectrum Disorders, 4*(3), 526–538. Retrieved from http://dx.doi.org/10.1016/j.rasd.2009.12.001.

Kelly, A. B., Garnett, M. S., Attwood, T., & Peterson, C. (2008). Autism spectrum symptomatology in children: The impact of family and peer relationships. *Journal of Abnormal Child Psychology, 36*(7), 1069–1081.

Kent, R. G., Carrington, S. J., Le Couteur, A., Gould, J., Wing, L., Maljaars, J., … Leekam, S. R. (2013). Diagnosing autism spectrum disorder: Who will get a DSM-5 diagnosis? *Journal of Child Psychology and Psychiatry, 54*(11), 1242–1250. doi: 10.1111/jcpp.12085.

Kientz, J. A., Goodwin, M. S., Hayes, G. R., & Abowd, G. D. (2013). Interactive technologies for autism. *Synthesis Lectures on Assistive, Rehabilitative, and Health-Preserving Technologies, 2*(2), 1–177.

Kim, Y. S., Leventhal, B. L., Koh, Y., Fombonne, E., Laska, E., Lim, E., … Grinker, R. R. (2011). Prevalence of autism spectrum disorders in a total population sample. *The American Journal of Psychiatry, 168*(9), 904–912. Retrieved from http://dx.doi.org/10.1176/appi.ajp.2011.10101532.

Kingsbury, B. (2009). The concept of 'law' in global administrative law. *European Journal of International Law, 20*(1), 23–57.

Klin, A., Carter, A., Volkmar, F. R., Cohen, D. J., Marans, W. D., & Sparrow, S. S. (1997). Developmentally based assessments. In D. J. Cohen & F. R. Volkmar (Eds.), *Handbook of autism and pervasive developmental disorders* (2nd ed.). New York, NY: Wiley.

Klin, A., Saulnier, C. A., Sparrow, S. S., Cicchettti, D. V., Volkmar, F. R., & Lord, C. (2007). Social and communication abilities and disabilities in higher functioning individuals with autism spectrum disorders: The Vineland and the ADOS. *Journal of Autism and Developmental Disorders, 37*(4), 748–759.

Koegel, L. K., & LaZebnik, C. S. (2009). *Growing up on the spectrum: A guide to life, love, and learning for teens and young adults with autism and Asperger's.* New York, NY: Penguin Books.

Koegel, L. K., & LaZebnik, C. (2014). *Overcoming autism: Finding the answers, strategies, and hope that can transform a child's life.* New York, NY: Penguin.

Konstantareas, M. M., & Lunsky, Y. J. (1997). Sociosexual knowledge, experience, attitudes, and interests of individuals with autistic disorder and developmental delay. *Journal of Autism and Developmental Disorders, 27*(4), 397–413.

Koshino, H., Kana, R. K., Keller, T. A., Cherkassky, V. L., Minshew, N. J., & Just, M. A. (2008). fMRI investigation of working memory for faces in autism: Visual coding and underconnectivity with frontal areas. *Cerebral Cortex, 18*(2), 289–300. doi:10.1093/cercor/bhm054.

Krakowiak, P., Walker, C. K., Bremer, A. A., Baker, A. S., Ozonoff, S., Hansen, R. L., & Hertz-Picciotto, I. (2012, April 9). Maternal metabolic conditions and risk for autism and other neurodevelopmental disorders. *Pediatrics.* Retrieved April 9, 2012, from http://pediatrics.aappublications.org

Kulage, K. M., Smaldone, A. M., & Cohn, E. G. (2014). How will DSM-5 affect autism diagnosis? A systematic literature review and meta-analysis. *Journal of Autism and Developmental Disorders, 44*, 1918–1932. doi:10.1007/s10803-014-2065-2.

Kuschner, E. S., Bodner, K. E., & Minshew, N. J. (2009). Local vs. global approaches to reproducing the Rey Osterrieth complex figure by children, adolescents, and adults with high-functioning autism. *Autism Research, 2*(6), 348–358. Retrieved from http://search.proquest.com/docview/759134043?accountid=14506.

Kushki, A., Chau, T., & Anagnostou, E. (2011). Handwriting difficulties in children with autism spectrum disorders: A scoping review. *Journal of Autism and Developmental Disorders, 41*(12), 1706–1716.

Lahiri, D. K., Sokol, D. K., Erickson, C., Ray, B., Ho, C. Y., & Maloney, B. (2013). Autism as early neurodevelopmental disorder: Evidence for an sAPPα-mediated anabolic pathway. *Frontiers in Cellular Neuroscience, 7*, 94.

Laidler, J. R. (2004). *The "Refrigerator Mother" hypothesis of autism.* Retrieved May 25, 2014, from http://www.autism-watch.org/causes/rm.shtml

Landry, R., & Bryson, S. E. (2004). Impaired disengagement of attention in young children with autism. *Journal of Child Psychology and Psychiatry, 45*(6), 1115–1122.

Lane, A. E., Young, R. L., Baker, A. E. Z., & Angley, M. T. (2010). Sensory processing subtypes in autism: Association with adaptive behavior. *Journal of Autism and Developmental Disorders, 40*, 112–122.

Lang, R., O'Reilly, M., Healy, O., Rispoli, M., Lydon, H., Streusand, W., … Giesbers, G. (2012). Sensory integration therapy for autism spectrum disorders: A systematic review. *Research in Autism Spectrum Disorders, 6*(3), 1004–1018.

Laugeson, E. A. (2010). *Social skills for teenagers with developmental and autism spectrum disorders: The PEERS treatment manual.* New York, NY: Taylor and Francis Group.

Le Couteur, A., Rutter, M., Lord, C., Rios, P., Robertson, S., Holdgrafer, M., & Minderaa, R. (1989). Autism diagnostic interview: A standardized investigator-based instrument. *Journal of Autism and Developmental Disorders, 19*(3), 363–387.

Leark, R. A., Greenberg, L., Kindschi, C., Dupuy, T., & Hughes, S. J. (2007). *Test of variables of attention: Professional manual.* Los Alamitos, CA: Universal Attention Disorders.

Lehnhardt, F., Gawronski, A., Pfeiffer, K., Kockler, H., Schilbach, L., & Vogeley, K. (2013). The investigation and differential diagnosis of Asperger syndrome in adults. *Deutsches Ärzteblatt International, 110*(45), 755–762. Retrieved from http://search.proquest.com/docview/1475576449?accountid=14506.

Levin, E. D., Christopher, N. C., Briggs, S. J., & Auman, J. T. (1996). Chronic nicotine-induced improvement of spatial working memory and D2 dopamine effects in rats. *Drug Development Research, 39*(1), 29–35.

Lin, C. C. H., Hsiao, C. K., & Chen, W. J. (1999). Development of sustained attention assessed using the continuous performance test among children 6–15 years of age. *Journal of Abnormal Child Psychology, 27*(5), 403.

Lind, S. E., Williams, D. M., Raber, J., Peel, A., & Bowler, D. M. (2013). Spatial navigation impairments among intellectually high-functioning adults with autism spectrum disorder: Exploring relations with theory of mind, episodic memory, and episodic future thinking. *Journal of Abnormal Psychology, 122*(4), 1189–1199. doi:10.1037/a0034819.

Linder, T. (2008). *Transdisciplinary play-based assessment* (2nd ed.). Baltimore, MD: Brookes.

Lines, C., Miller, G. B., & Arthur-Stanley, A. (2011). *The power of family-school partnering (FSP): A practical guide for school mental health professionals and educators.* New York, NY: Routledge.

Liss, M., Saulnier, C., Fein, D., & Kinsbourne, M. (2006). Sensory and attention abnormalities in autistic spectrum disorders. *Autism, 10*(2), 155–172.

Lloyd, M., MacDonald, M., & Lord, C. (2013). Motor skills of toddlers with autism spectrum disorders. *Autism, 17*(2), 133–146. Retrieved from http://dx.doi.org/10.1177/1362361311402230.

Lord, C., Cook, E. H., Leventhal, B. L., & Amaral, D. G. (2000). Autism spectrum disorders. *Neuron, 28*(2), 355–363.

Lord, C., & Jones, R. M. (2012). Re-thinking the classification of autism spectrum disorders. *Journal of Child Psychology and Psychiatry, and Allied Disciplines, 53*(5), 490–509. http://doi.org/10.1111/j.1469-7610.2012.02547.x.

Lord, C., Risi, S., Lambrecht, L., Cook Jr, E. H., Leventhal, B. L., DiLavore, P. C., … Rutter, M. (2000). The autism diagnostic observation schedule—generic: A standard measure of social and communication deficits associated with the spectrum of autism. *Journal of Autism and Developmental Disorders, 30(3)*, 205-223.

Lord, C., Rutter, M., DiLavore, P. C., Risi, S., Gotham, K., & Bishop, S. L. (2012). *Autism diagnostic observation schedule*, (2nd ed., ADOS-2). Torrance, CA: Western Psychological Services.

Lord, C., Rutter, M., DiLavore, P. C., & Risi, S. (1999). *Autism diagnostic observation schedule-WPS (ADOS-WPS)*. Los Angeles, CA: Western Psychological Services.

Lord, C., Rutter, M., & Le Couteur, A. (1994). Autism diagnostic interview—Revised: A revised version of a diagnostic interview for caregivers of individuals with possible pervasive developmental disorders. *Journal of Autism and Developmental Disorders, 24*(5), 659–685.

Lord, C., & Schopler, E. (1989). Stability of assessment results of autistic and non-autistic language-impaired children from preschool years to early school age. *Journal of Child Psychology and Psychiatry, 30*(4), 575–590.

Losh, M., & Capps, L. (2003). Narrative ability in high-functioning children with autism or Asperger's syndrome. *Journal of Autism and Developmental Disorders, 33*(3), 239–251.

Losh, M., & Gordon, P. C. (2014). Qualifying narrative ability in autism spectrum disorder. A computational linguistic analysis of narrative coherence. *Journal of Autism and Developmental Disorders, 44*, 3016–3025.

Lugnegard, T., Hallerback, M. U., & Gillberg, C. (2012). Personality disorders and autism spectrum disorders: What are the connections? *Comprehensive Psychiatry, 53*, 333–340.

Maccow, G. (2015). *Advanced interpretation of the WISC-V [slides]*. Retrieved from http://downloads.pearsonclinical.com/videos/WISC-V-020515/WISC-V-Advanced-Webinar-Handout-020515.pdf

Madrigal, S., & Winner, M. G. (2008). *Superflex. A superhero social thinking curriculum*. San Jose, CA: Think Social.

Maestro, S., Muratori, F., Cavallaro, M. C., Pei, F., Stern, D., Golse, B., et al. (2002). Attentional skills during the first 6 months of age in autism spectrum disorder. *Journal of the American Academy of Child & Adolescent Psychiatry, 41*(10), 1239–1245.

Mailick, M. R. (2014, May). *Adolescents and adults with ASD and their families: Life course development and bi-directional effects*. Paper presented at the 13th Annual International Meeting for Autism Research, Atlanta, GA.

Maister, L., Simons, J. S., & Plaisted-Grant, K. (2013). Executive functions are employed to process episodic and relational memories in children with autism spectrum disorders. *Neuropsychology, 27*(6), 615–627. doi:10.1037/a0034492.

Mandell, D. S., Novak, M. M., & Zubritsky, C. D. (2005). Factors associated with age of diagnosis among children with autism spectrum disorders. *Pediatrics, 116*(6), 1480–1486.

Mandy, W. P., Charman, T., & Skuse, D. H. (2012). Testing the construct validity of proposed criteria for DSM-5 autism spectrum disorder. *Journal of the American Academy of Child and Adolescent Psychiatry, 51*(1), 41–50. doi:10.1016/j.jaac.2011.10.013.

Mangun, G. R., & Hillyard, S. A. (1988). Spatial gradients of visual attention: behavioral and electrophysiological evidence. *Electroencephalography and Clinical Neurophysiology, 70*(5), 417–428.

Mannion, A., & Leader, G. (2013). Comorbidity in autism spectrum disorder: A literature review. *Research in Autism Spectrum Disorders, 7*(12), 1595–1616. Retrieved from http://dx.doi.org/10.1016/j.rasd.2013.09.006.

Martin, N., & Brownell, R. (2011). *Expressive one-word picture vocabulary test* (4th ed.). Novato, CA: Academic Therapy Publications.

Matson, J. L., Nebel-Schwalm, M., & Matson, M. L. (2007). A review of methodological issues in the differential diagnosis of autism spectrum disorders in children. *Research in Autism Spectrum Disorders, 1*, 38–54.

Matson, J. L., Rieske, R. D., & Williams, L. W. (2013). The relationship between autism spectrum disorders and attention-deficit/hyperactivity disorder: An overview. *Research in Developmental Disability, 34*(9), 2475–2484. doi:10.1016/j.ridd.2013.05.021.

Matson, J. L., & Shoemaker, M. (2009). Intellectual disability and its relationship to autism spectrum disorders. *Research in Developmental Disabilities, 30*(6), 1107–1114. Retrieved from http://dx.doi.org/10.1016/j.ridd.2009.06.003.

Matthews, N. L., Pollard, E., Ober-Reynolds, S., Kirwan, J., Malligo, A., & Smith, C. J. (2015). Revisiting cognitive and adaptive functioning in children and adolescents with autism spectrum disorder. *Journal of Autism and Developmental Disorders, 45*, 138–156.

Maurice, C. E., Green, G. E., & Luce, S. C. (1996). *Behavioral intervention for young children with autism: A manual for parents and professionals*. Austin, TX: PRO-ED.

Mayes, S. D., & Calhoun, S. L. (2003). Ability profiles in children with autism: Influence of age and IQ. *Autism, 7*(1), 65–80. Retrieved from http://dx.doi.org/10.1177/1362361303007001006.

Mayes, S. D., & Calhoun, S. L. (2007). Learning, attention, writing, and processing speed in typical children and children with ADHD, autism, anxiety, depression, and oppositional-defiant disorder. *Child Neuropsychology, 13*(6), 469–493.

Mayes, S. S., & Calhoun, S. L. (2008). WISC-IV and WIAT-II profiles in children with high-functioning autism. *Journal of Autism and Developmental Disorders, 38*(3), 428–439.

Mayes, S. D., Calhoun, S. L., Mayes, R. D., & Molitoris, S. (2011). *Autism and ADHD: Overlapping and discriminating symptoms*. Research in Autism Spectrum Disorders.

Mayes, S. D., Calhoun, S. L., Mayes, R. D., & Molitoris, S. (2012). Autism and ADHD: Overlapping and discriminating symptoms. *Research in Autism Spectrum Disorders, 6*(1), 277–285.

Mazefsky, C. A., Herrington, J., Siegel, M., Scarpa, A., Maddox, B. B., Scahill, L., & White, S. W. (2013). The role of emotion regulation in autism spectrum disorder. *Journal of the American Academy of Child & Adolescent Psychiatry, 52(7)*, 679-688.

Mazefsky, C. A., & Oswald, D. P. (2006). The discriminative ability and diagnostic utility of the ADOS-G, ADI-R, and GARS for children in a clinical setting. *Autism, 10*(6), 533–549. doi:10.1177/1362361306068505.

McCandless, J. (2009). *Children with starving brains: A medical treatment guide for autism spectrum disorder*. North Bergen, NJ: Bramble Books. (Original work published 2002)

Mehtar, M., & Mukaddes, N. M. (2011). Posttraumatic stress disorder in individuals with diagnoses of autism spectrum disorders. *Research in Autism Spectrum Disorders, 5*, 539–546.

Meyer, N. (2014, December 26). *MIT researcher's new warning: At today's rate, half of all U.S. children will be autistic by 2025*. Retrieved January 3, 2015, from www.earthweareone.com

Meyers, J. E., & Meyers, K. R. (1995). *Rey complex figure test and recognition trial: Professional manual*. Odessa, Ukraine: Psychological Assessment Resources.

Mezzacappa, E. (2004). Alerting, orienting, and executive attention: Developmental properties and sociodemographic correlates in an epidemiological sample of young, urban children. *Child Development, 75*(5), 1373–1386.

Ming, X., Brimacombe, M., & Wagner, G. C. (2007). Prevalence of motor impairment in autism spectrum disorders. *Brain and Development, 29*(9), 565–570. doi:10.1016/j.braindev.2007.03.002.

Minshew, N., & Goldstein, G. (1993). Is autism an amnesic disorder? Evidence from the California verbal learning test. *Neuropsychology, 7*, 209–216.

Minshew, N., & Goldstein, G. (2001). The pattern of intact and impaired memory functions in autism. *Journal of Child Psychology and Psychiatry, 42*, 1095–1101.

Minshew, N. J., Goldstein, G., Taylor, H. G., & Siegel, D. J. (1994). Academic achievement in high functioning autistic individuals. *Journal of Clinical and Experimental Neuropsychology, 16*(2), 261–270.

Minshew, N. J., Luna, B., & Sweeney, J. A. (1999). Oculomotor evidence for neocortical systems but not cerebellar dysfunction in autism. *Neurology, 52*(5), 917–917.

Mishaal, R. A., Ben-Itzchak, E., & Zachor, D. A. (2014). Age of autism spectrum disorder diagnosis is associated with child's variables and parental experience. *Research in Autism Spectrum Disorders, 8*(7), 873–880.

Moses, K. (1983). The impact of initial diagnosis: Mobilizing family resources. In J. A. Mulick & S. M. Pueschel (Eds.), *Parent-professional partnerships in developmental disabilities.* Cambridge, MA: Academic Guild.

Mostofsky, S. H., Dubey, P., Jerath, V. K., Jansiewicz, E. M., Goldberg, M. C., & Denckla, M. B. (2006). Developmental dyspraxia is not limited to imitation in children with autism spectrum disorders. *Journal of the International Neuropsychological Society, 12*, 314–326.

Moulton, E., Fein, D., Barton, M., & Robins, D. L. (2014, May). *Early characteristics of children who lose their ASD diagnosis between age 2 and 4.* Poster presented at the 13th Annual International Meeting for Autism Research, Atlanta, GA.

Mullen, E. M. (1995). *Mullen scales of early learning.* Circle Pines, MN: American Guidance Service.

Naples. (2010). *Variability in reading ability.* PhD Dissertation, Yale University, CT. Retrieved November 16, 2010, from Dissertations and Theses: Full Text (Publication No. AAT 3395801).

Nash, J. M. (2002). The secrets of autism: The number of children with autism and Asperger's in the U.S. is exploding. Why? *Time, 159*, 47–56.

Nation, K., Clarke, P., Wright, B., & Williams, C. (2006). Patterns of reading ability in children with autism spectrum disorder. *Journal of Autism and Developmental Disorders, 36*(7), 911–919.

Norbury, C. F., & Bishop, D. V. M. (2002). Inferential processing and story recall in children with communication problems: A comparison of specific language impairment, pragmatic language impairment and high-functioning autism. *International Journal of Language & Communication Disorders, 37*(3), 227–251.

Noterdaeme, M., Mildenberger, K., Minow, F., & Amorosa, H. (2002). Evaluation of neuromotor deficits in children with autism and children with a specific speech and language disorder. *European Child & Adolescent Psychiatry, 11*(5), 219–225.

Nowell, K. P., Schanding, G. T., Jr., Kanne, S. M., & Goin-Kochel, R. P. (2015). Cognitive profiles in youth with autism spectrum disorder: An investigation of base rate discrepancies using the differential ability scales, second edition. *Journal of Autism and Developmental Disorders, 45*, 1978–1988. doi:10.1007/s10803-014-2356-7.

Nuske, H. J., & Baven, E. L. (2010). Narrative comprehension in 4–7 year old children with autism: Testing the weak central coherence account. *International Journal of Language & Communication Disorders, 46*, 108–119.

O'Connor, I., & Klein, P. (2004). Explorations of strategies for facilitating the reading comprehension of high-functioning students with autism spectrum disorders. *Journal of Autism and Developmental Disorders, 34*(2), 115–127.

O'Hara, N. H., & Szakacs, G. M. (2008). The recovery of a child with autism spectrum disorder through biomedical interventions. *Alternative Therapies in Health and Medicine, 14*(6), 42.

OCALI: Ohio Center for Autism and Low Incidence. (2014). *Educational assessment of autism.* Retrieved August, 2014, from http://www.ocali.org/project/educational_assessment_of_autism

Osman, A., Barrios, F. X., Aukes, D., Osman, J. R., & Markway, K. (1993). The beck anxiety inventory: Psychometric properties in a community population. *Journal of Psychopathology and Behavioral Assessment, 15*(4), 287–297.

Osman, A., Kopper, B. A., Barrios, F. X., Osman, J. R., & Wade, T. (1997). The Beck Anxiety Inventory: Reexamination of factor structure and psychometric properties. *Journal of Clinical Psychology, 53*(1), 7–14.

Osterling, J., & Dawson, G. (1994). Early recognition of children with autism: A study of first birthday home videotapes. *Journal of Autism and Developmental Disorders, 24*(3), 247–257.

Osterling, J. A., Dawson, G., & Munson, J. A. (2002). Early recognition of 1-year-old infants with autism spectrum disorder versus mental retardation. *Development and Psychopathology, 14*(02), 239–251.

Ozonoff, S. (1995). Reliability and validity of the Wisconsin Card Sorting Test in studies of autism. *Neuropsychology, 9*(4), 491–500. Retrieved from http://dx.doi.org/10.1037/0894-4105.9.4.491.

Ozonoff, S. (2012). Editorial perspective: Autism spectrum disorders in DSM-5—An historical perspective and the need for change. *Journal of Child Psychology and Psychiatry, 53*(10), 1092–1094. doi:10.1111/j.1469-7610.2012.02614.x.

Ozonoff, S. (2014, May). *Parent report of onset status: prospective versus retrospective methods.* Session presented at the International Meeting for Autism Research, Atlanta, GA.

Ozonoff, S., Garcia, N., Clark, E., & Lainhart, J. (2005). MMPI-2 personality profiles of high-functioning adults with autism spectrum disorders. *Assessment, 12*, 86–95.

Ozonoff, S., Goodlin-Jones, B. L., & Solomon, M. (2005). Evidence-based assessment of autism spectrum disorders in children and adolescents. *Journal of Clinical Child & Adolescent Psychology, 34*(3), 523–540.

Ozonoff, S., & Strayer, D. L. (2001). Further evidence of intact working memory in autism. *Journal of Autism and Developmental Disorders, 31*(3), 257–263.

Ozonoff, S., Young, G. S., Carter, A., Messinger, D., Yirmiya, N., Zwaigenbaum, L., & Stone, W. L. (2011). Recurrence risk for autism spectrum disorders: A Baby Siblings Research Consortium study. *Pediatrics, 128*(3), e488–e495.

Pastor, P. N., & Reuben, C. A. (2008). Diagnosed attention deficit hyperactivity disorder and learning disability: United States, 2004–2006. *Vital Health Statistics, 10*, 1–14.

Pavlov, I. P. (1927). *Conditioned reflexes: An investigation of the physiological activity of the cerebral cortex* (translated by G.V. Anrep). London, England: Oxford University Press.

Pennington, B. F. (1997). Dimensions of executive functions in normal and abnormal development. In N. A. Krasnegor, G. R. Lyon, & P. S. Goldman-Rakic (Eds.), *Development of the Prefrontal Cortex* (pp. 265–381). Baltimore, MD: Paul H. Brookes.

Pennington, B. F. (2002). *The development of psychopathology: Nature and nurture.* New York, NY: The Guilford Press.

Pennington, B. F., & Ozonoff, S. (1996). Executive functions and developmental psychology. *Journal of Child Psychiatry, 37*, 51–87.

Petersen, S. E., & Posner, M. I. (2012). The attention system of the human brain: 20 years after. *Annual Review of Neuroscience, 35*, 73.

Phelps-Terasaki, D., & Phelps-Gunn, T. (1992). *Test of pragmatic language.* East Moline, IL: Linguisystems.

Polanczyk, G., Silva, D. L., Bernardo, L. H., Biederman, J., & Rohde, L. A. (2007). The worldwide prevalence of ADHD: A systematic review and metaregression analysis. *The American Journal of Psychiatry, 164*(6), 942–948.

Posner, M. I., & Petersen, S. E. (1989). *The attention system of the human brain* (No. TR-89-1). St. Louis, MO: Department of Neurology, Washington University.

Posner, M. I., Walker, J. A., Friedrich, F. J., & Rafal, R. D. (1984). Effects of parietal injury on covert orienting of attention. *Journal of Neuroscience, 4*, 1863–1874.

Prior, M., Eisenmajer, R., Leekam, S., Wing, L., Gould, J., Ong, B., & Dowe, D. (1998). Are there subgroups within the autistic spectrum? A cluster analysis of a group of children with autistic spectrum disorders. *Journal of Child Psychology and Psychiatry, 39*(6), 893–902. Retrieved from http://dx.doi.org/10.1111/1469-7610.00389.

Reaven, J. (2015, April 17). Co-occurring psychiatric symptoms in children and adolescents with autism spectrum disorder: Implications for identification and treatment. In *JFK Partners 50th Anniversary Symposium, Aurora, CO.*

Reaven, J. A., Hepburn, S. L., & Ross, R. G. (2008). Use of the ADOS and ADI-R in children with psychosis: Importance of clinical judgment. *Clinical Child Psychology and Psychiatry, 13*(1), 81–94.

Reid, J. S. (2004). Can enzymes help your child with autism? *The Exceptional Parent, 34*(2), 25.

Reiss, S., & Szyszko, J. (1983). Diagnostic overshadowing and professional experience with mentally retarded persons. *American Journal of Mental Deficiency, 87*(4), 396–402.

Reszka, S. S., Boyd, B. A., McBee, M., Hume, K. A., & Odom, S. L. (2014). Brief report: Concurrent validity of autism symptom severity measures. *Journal of Autism and Developmental Disorders, 44*(2), 466–470. doi:10.1007/s10803-013-1879-7.

Reynolds, C. R. (2002). *Comprehensive trail making test (CTMT).* Austin, TX: Pro-Ed.

Reynolds, C. R., & Bigler, E. D. (1994). *Test of memory and learning (TOMAL).* Austin, TX: Pro-Ed.

Reynolds, C. R., & Kamphaus, R. W. (2004). *Behavior assessment system for children manual (BASC-2)* (2nd ed.). Circle Pines, MN: AGS.

Reynolds, C. R., & Richmond, B. O. (2008). *Revised children's manifest anxiety scale (RCMAS)*. Los Angeles, CA: Western Psychological Services. (Original work published 1985)

Reynolds, W. M., & Rubin, M. (1987). National standardization of the auditory discrimination test: Normative and reliability results. *Archives of Clinical Neuropsychology, 2*(1), 67–79.

Richards, J. E. (1997). Peripheral stimulus localization by infants: Attention, age, and individual differences in heart rate variability. *Journal of Experimental Psychology: Human Perception and Performance, 23*(3), 667.

Roberts, G. E., & Gruber, C. (2005). *Roberts-2*. Los Angeles, CA: Western Psychological Services.

Robertson, J. M., Tanguay, P. E., L'Ecuyer, S., Sims, A., & Waltrip, C. (1999). Domains of social communication handicap in autism spectrum disorder. *Journal of the American Academy of Child & Adolescent Psychiatry, 38*(6), 738–745.

Robinson, A. L., Heaton, R. K., Lehman, R. A., & Stilson, D. W. (1980). The utility of the Wisconsin card sorting test in detecting and localizing frontal lobe lesions. *Journal of Consulting and Clinical Psychology, 48*(5), 605–614.

Rogers, S. (2010, October). *Autism: A closer look*. Paper presented at the Rosenberry Conference: Denver. Aurora, CO: The Children's Hospital.

Rogers, S. (2015, April 17). Past, present and future of early intervention: A view through the ASD lens. In *JFK Partners 50th Anniversary Symposium, Aurora, CO*.

Rogers, S., & Vismara, L. (2008). Evidence-based comprehensive treatments for early autism. *Journal of Clinical Child & Adolescent Psychology, 37*, 8–38.

Roid, G. (2003). *Interpretive manual: Expanded guide to the interpretation of the SB5 test results*. Austin, TX: Pro-Ed.

Rosenthal, M., Wallace, G. L., Lawson, R., Wills, M. C., Dixon, E., Yerys, B. E., & Kenworthy, L. (2013). Impairments in real-world executive function increase from childhood to adolescence in autism spectrum disorders. *Neuropsychology, 27*(1), 13–18. doi: 10.1037/a0031299.

Rudy, L. J. (2013, July). *Is autism on the rise?* Retrieved May 9, 2015, from http://about.com

Rueda, M. R., Fan, J., McCandliss, B. D., Halparin, J. D., Gruber, D. B., Lercari, L. P., & Posner, M. I. (2004). Development of attentional networks in childhood. *Neuropsychologia, 42*(8), 1029–1040.

Ruff, R. M., Light, R. H., Parker, S. B., & Levin, H. S. (1996). Benton controlled oral word association test: Reliability and updated norms. *Archives of Clinical Neuropsychology, 11*(4), 329–338.

Russell, J., Jarrold, C., & Hood, B. (1999). Two intact executive capacities in children with autism: Implications for the core executive dysfunctions in the disorder. *Journal of Autism and Developmental Disorders, 29*(2), 103–112.

Rutherford, M. D., Young, G. S., Hepburn, S., & Rogers, S. J. (2007). A longitudinal study of pretend play in autism. *Journal of Developmental Disorders, 37*, 1024–1039.

Rutter, M. (2011a). Research review: Child psychiatric diagnosis and classification: Concepts, findings, challenges and potential. *Journal of Child Psychology and Psychiatry, 52*(6), 647–660. doi:10.1111/j.1469-7610.2011.02367.x.

Rutter, M. L. (2011b). Progress in understanding autism: 2007–2010. *Journal of Autism and Developmental Disorders, 41*(4), 395–404. doi:10.1007/s10803-011-1184-2.

Rutter, M., Bailey, A., & Lord, C. (2003). *The social communication questionnaire: Manual*. Los Angeles, CA: Western Psychological Services.

Ryden, E., & Bejerot, S. (2008). Autism spectrum disorders in an adult psychiatric population. A naturalistic cross-sectional controlled study. *Clinical Neuropsychiatry, 5*(1), 13–21.

Sachse, M., Schlitt, S., Hainz, D., Ciaramidaro, A., Schirman, S., Walter, H., … Freitag, C. M. (2013). Executive and visuo-motor function in adolescents and adults with autism spectrum disorder. *Journal of Autism and Developmental Disorders, 43*(5), 1222–1235. doi: 10.1007/s10803-012-1668-8.

Sadiq, F. A., Slator, L., Skuse, D., Law, J., Gillberg, C., & Minnis, H. (2012). Social use of language in children with reactive attachment disorder and autism spectrum disorders. *European Child and Adolescent Psychiatry, 21*, 267–276.

Salzberg, S. (2015). *Large study finds MMR vaccine doesn't cause autism, and may lower autism risk.* Retrieved May 9, 2015, from http://www.forbes.com

Samsel, A., & Seneff, S. (2013). Glyphosate's suppression of cytochrome P450 enzymes and amino acid biosynthesis by the gut microbiome: Pathways to modern diseases. *Entropy, 15*(4), 1416–1463. doi:10.3390/e15041416.

Samson, A. C., Hardan, A. Y., Podell, R. W., Phillips, J. M., & Gross, J. J. (2014). Emotion regulation in children and adolescents with autism spectrum disorder. *Autism Research, 8*(1), 9–18.

Sanders, S., Murtha, M. T., Gupta, A. R., Murdoch, J. D., Raubeson, M. J., Willsey, A. J., … State, M. W. (2012). De novo mutations revealed by whole-exome sequencing are strongly associated with autism. *Nature, 485*(7397), 237–241. doi:10.1038/nature10945.

Santangelo, S. L. (2014, May). *How can genetic research inform current psychiatric diagnostic practice?* Paper presented at the 13th Annual International Meeting for Autism Research, Atlanta, GA.

Sattler, J. M. (2001). *Assessment of children: Cognitive applications* (4th ed.). San Diego: Jerome M. Sattler.

Sattler, J. M. (2008). *Assessment of children: Cognitive foundations* (5th ed.). San Diego, CA: Jerome M. Sattler.

Saulnier, C. A., & Ventola, P. E. (2012). *Essentials of autism spectrum disorders evaluation and assessment.* Hoboken, NJ: Wiley.

Schear, J. M., & Sato, S. D. (1989). Effects of visual acuity and visual motor speed and dexterity on cognitive test performance. *Archives of Clinical Neuropsychology, 4*(1), 25–32.

Schedule—WPS (ADOS-WPS). Los Angeles, CA: Western Psychological Services.

Schneider, W., Niklas, F., & Schmiedeler, S. (2014). Intellectual development from early childhood to early adulthood: The impact of early IQ differences on stability and change over time. *Learning and Individual Differences, 32*, 156–162.

Schoen, S. A., Miller, L. J., Brett-Green, B. A., & Nielsen, D. M. (2009). Physiological and behavioral differences in sensory processing: A comparison of children with autism spectrum disorder and sensory modulation disorder. *Frontiers in Integrative Neuroscience, 3*, 1–11.

Schopler, E., Van Bourgondien, M. E., Wellman, G. J., & Love, S. R. (2010). Childhood autism rating scale (2nd ed.). Los Angeles, CA: Western Psychological Services.

Schreibman, L., Dufek, S., & Cunningham, A. B. (2011a). Identifying moderators of treatment outcome for children with autism. In J. L. Matson & P. Sturmey (Eds.), *International handbook of autism and pervasive developmental disorders* (pp. 295–305). New York, NY: Springer. Retrieved from http://dx.doi.org/10.1007/978-1-4419-8065-6_18.

Schreibman, L., Stahmer, A. C., Barlett, V. C., & Dufek, S. (2009). Brief report: Toward refinement of a predictive behavioral profile for treatment outcome in children with autism. *Research in Autism Spectrum Disorders, 3*(1), 163–172. doi:10.1016/j.rasd.2008.04.008.

Schubert, C. (2008). Male biological clock possibly linked to autism, other disorders. *Nature, 14*, 1170. doi:10.1038/nm1108-1170a.

Schwartz, I. S., & Davis, C. A. (2008). Effective services for young children with autism spectrum disorders. In A. Thomas & J. Grimes (Eds.), *Best practices in school psychology V* (Vol. 4, pp. 1517–1529). Bethesda, MD: NASP.

Seneff, S. (2014, June) *Is roundup the toxic chemical that's making us all sick?* Slideshow Presented at the Autism One Conference December, 2014. MIT: CSAIL.

Seneff, S. MIT: CSAIL. (2014, June). *Is roundup the toxic chemical that's making us all sick?* Slideshow presented at the Autism One conference December, 2014. Campbell Performing Arts Center, Groton, MA.

Settlage, P., Zable, M., & Harflow, H. F. (1948). Problem solution by monkeys following bilateral removal of the prefrontal areas; performance on tests requiring contradictory reactions to similar and to identical stimuli. *Journal of Experimental Psychology, 38*(1), 50.

Shallice, T. (1982). Specific impairments of planning. *Philosophical Transactions of the Royal Society of London, Biology, 298*, 199–209.

Sheridan, S. M., Taylor, A. M., & Woods, K. E. (2008). Best practices for working with families: Instilling a family-centered approach. In A. Thomas & J. Grimes (Eds.), *Best practices in school psychology V* (pp. 995–1008). Bethesda, MD: NASP.

Siegel, D. J., Minshew, N. J., & Goldstein, G. (1996). Wechsler IQ profiles in diagnosis of high-functioning autism. *Journal of Autism and Developmental Disorders, 4,* 389–406.

Simon's Foundation. (2014). National Fragile X Foundation, 2014, Retrieved from https://fragilex.org.

Simonoff, E., Pickles, A., Charman, T., Chandler, S., Loucas, T., & Baird, G. (2008). Psychiatric disorders in children with autism spectrum disorders: Prevalence, comorbidity, and associated factors in a population-derived sample. *Journal of the American Academy of Child & Adolescent Psychiatry, 47*(8), 921–929. Retrieved from http://dx.doi.org/10.1097/CHI.0b013e318179964f.

Sinzig, J., Bruning, N., Morsch, D., & Lehmkuhl, G. (2008). Attention profiles in autistic children with and without comorbid hyperactivity and attention problems. *Acta Neuropsychiatrica, 20*(4), 207–215.

Skuse, D. H. (2012). DSM-5's conceptualization of autistic disorders. *Journal of the American Academy of Child and Adolescent Psychiatry, 51,* 344–346.

Smith, L. E., Mailick, M. R., & Greenberg, J. (2014, May). *Transitioning together: A multi-family group psychoeducation program for adolescents with ASD and their parents.* Paper presented at the 13th Annual International Meeting for Autism Research, Atlanta, GA.

Snowling, M., & Frith, U. (1986). Comprehension in 'hyperlexic' readers. *Journal of Experimental Child Psychology, 42*(3), 392–414.

National Down Syndrome Society. (2012). *Down syndrome.* Retrieved from www.ndss.org.

Soloman, A. (2012). *Far from the tree: Parents, children, and the search for identity.* New York, NY: Scribner/Simon & Schuster.

Southwest Ohio Regional Advisory Council. (2014). *Guiding questions: When considering educational identification of autism spectrum disorder.* Retrieved August, 2014.

Sparrow, S. (2008). *Vineland Adaptive Behavior Scales, second edition (Vineland II).* Livonia, MN: Pearson. (Original work published 2005, 2006)

Sparrow, S. S., Cicchetti, D. V., & Balla, D. A. (2005). *Vineland Adaptive Behavior Scales* (2nd ed.). Circle Pines, MN: American Guidance Service.

Speaks, A. (2010). *Facts about autism.* Retrieved August 12, 2011, from http://www.autismspeaks.org/what-autism/facts-about-autism.

Squire, L. R., & Butters, N. (1992). *Neuropsychology of memory* (2nd ed.). New York: Guilford Press.

Steele, S. D., Minshew, N. J., Luna, B., & Sweeney, J. A. (2007). Spatial working memory deficits in autism. *Journal of Autism and Developmental Disorders, 37*(4), 605–612.

Stevens, M. C., Fein, D. A., Dunn, M., Allen, D., Waterhouse, L. H., Feinstein, C., & Rapin, I. (2000). Subgroups of children with autism by cluster analysis: a longitudinal examination. *Journal of the American Academy of Child and Adolescent Psychiatry, 39*(3), 346–352. doi: 10.1097/00004583-200003000-00017.

Stone, W. L., Lee, E. B., Ashford, L., Brissie, J., Hepburn, S. L., Coonrod, E. E., & Weiss, B. H. (1999). Can autism be diagnosed accurately in children under 3 years? *Journal of Child Psychology and Psychiatry, 40*(2), 219–226.

Stray, G. K., & House, W. (1987). *Babies with Down syndrome: A new parents guide.* Bethesda, MD: Woodbine House.

Suh, J., Eigsti, I., Naigles, L., Barton, M., Kelley, E., & Fein, D. (2014). Narrative performance of optimal outcome children and adolescents with a history of an autism spectrum disorder (ASD). *Journal of Autism and Developmental Disorders, 44*(7), 1681–1694.

Summers, J., & Craik, F. (1994). The effect of subject-performed tasks on the memory performance of verbal autistic children. *Journal of Autism and Developmental Disorders, 24,* 773–783.

Sundberg, M. L. (2008). *Verbal behavior milestones assessment and placement program: The VB-MAPP.* Concord, CA: AVB Press.

Sutera, S., Pandey, J., Esser, E. L., Rosenthal, M. A., Wilson, L. B., Barton, M., … Fein, D. (2007). Predictors of optimal outcome in toddlers diagnosed with autism spectrum disorders. *Journal of Autism and Developmental Disorders, 37*(1), 98–107. doi: 10.1007/s10803-006-0340-6.

Sweeney, J. A. (2014, May). *Brain circuits and functions across psychiatric disorders*. Paper presented at the 13th Annual International Meeting for Autism Research, Atlanta, GA.

Szatmari, P. Bryson, S. Duku, E. Vaccarella, L. Zwaigenbaum, L. Bennett, T. & Boyle, M. (2009). Similar developmental trajectories in autism and Asperger syndrome: From early childhood to adolescence. *J Child Psychology and Psychiatry, 50*(12), 1459–1467.

Szpunar, K. K., & McDermott, K. B. (2008). Episodic future thought and its relation to remembering: Evidence from ratings of subjective experience. *Consciousness and Cognition, 17*(1), 330–334.

Tager-Flusberg, H. (1991). Semantic processing in the free recall of autistic children: Further evidence of a cognitive deficit. In G. Dawson (Ed.), *Autism: Nature, diagnosis, and treatment* (pp. 92–109). New York, NY: Guilford Press.

Tager-Flusberg, H. (2006). Defining language phenotypes in autism. *Clinical Neuroscience Research, 6*, 219–224.

Tanguay, P. E. (2000). Pervasive developmental disorders: A 10-year review. *Journal of the American Academy of Child & Adolescent Psychiatry, 39*(9), 1079–1095.

Tanguay, P. E. (2011). Autism in the DSM-5. *American Journal of Psychiatry, 168*, 1142–1144.

Tanguay, P. E., Robertson, J., & Derrick, A. (1998). A dimensional classification of autism spectrum disorder by social communication domains. *Journal of the American Academy of Child and Adolescent Psychiatry, 37*(3), 271–277. doi:10.1097/00004583-199803000-00011.

Taylor, J. A. (1951). The relationship of anxiety to the conditioned eyelid response. *Journal of Experimental Psychology, 42*, 183–188.

Teuber, H. L., Battersby, W. S., & Bender, M. B. (1951). Performance of complex visual tasks after cerebral lesions. *The Journal of Nervous and Mental Disease, 114*(5), 413.

Thiel, C. M., Zilles, K., & Fink, G. R. (2005). Nicotine modulates reorienting of visuospatial attention and neural activity in human parietal cortex. *Neuropsychopharmacology, 30*(4), 810–820.

Thomas, C. C. (1960, July 25). Medicine: the child is father. *Time, 111*, 167.

Toal, F., Bloemen, O. J. N., Deeley, Q., Tunstall, N., Daly, E. M., Page, L., … Murphy, D. G. M. (2009). Psychosis and autism: Magnetic resonance imaging study of brain anatomy. *The British Journal of Psychiatry, 194*(5), 418–425. Retrieved from http://dx.doi.org/10.1192/bjp.bp.107.049007.

Toichi, M. (2008). Episodic memory, semantic memory and self-awareness in high-functioning autism. In J. Boucher & D. Bowler (Eds.), *Memory in autism: Theory and evidence* (pp. 143–165). Cambridge, England: Cambridge University Press.

Toichi, M., & Kamio, Y. (2002). Long-term memory and levels-of-processing in autism. *Neuropsychologia, 40*(7), 964–969.

Trammell, B., Wilczynski, S. M., Dale, B., & McIntosh, D. E. (2013). Assessment and differential diagnosis of comorbid conditions in adolescents and adults with autism spectrum disorders. *Psychology in the Schools, 50*(9), 936–946. Retrieved from http://dx.doi.org/10.1002/pits.21720.

Troyb, E., Orinstein, A., Tyson, K., Helt, M., Eigsti, I. M., Stevens, M., & Fein, D. (2014). Academic abilities in children and adolescents with a history of autism spectrum disorders who have achieved optimal outcomes. *Autism, 18*(3), 233–243. doi: 10.1177/1362361312473519.

Tsai, L. Y., & Ghaziuddin, M. (2014). DSM-5 ASD moves forward into the past. *Journal of Autism and Developmental Disorders, 44*(2), 321–330. doi:10.1007/s10803-013-1870-3.

Tulving, E. (1984). How many memory systems are there? *American Psychologist, 40*, 385–398.

Turner Syndrome Society. (2013). *Turner syndrome*. Retrieved from www.turnersyndrome.org.

Tye, C., Asherson, P., Ashwood, K. L., Azadi, B., Bolton, P., & McLoughlin, G. (2013). Attention and inhibition in children with ASD, ADHD and co-morbid ASD+ ADHD: An event-related potential study. *Psychological Medicine, 15*, 1–16. doi:10.1017/S0033291713001049.

Tyson, K., Kelley, E., Fein, D., Orinstein, A., Troyb, E., Barton, M., … Rosenthal, M. (2014). Language and verbal memory in individuals with a history of autism spectrum disorders who have achieved optimal outcomes. *Journal of Autism and Developmental Disorders, 44*(3), 648–663. doi: 10.1007/s10803-013-1921-9.

Uhlmann, V., Martin, C. M., Sheils, O., Pilkington, L., Silva, I., Killalea, A., … O'Leary, J. J. (2002). Potential viral pathogenic mechanism for new variant inflammatory bowel disease. *Journal of Clinical Pathology: Molecular Pathology, 55*, 84–90.

van Ijzendoorn, M. H., Rutgers, A. H., Bakermans-Kranenburg, M. J., Swinkels, S. H., van Daalen, E., Dietz, C., … van Engeland, H. (2007). Parental sensitivity and attachment in children with autism spectrum disorder: Comparison with children with mental retardation, with language delays, and with typical development. *Child Development, 78*(2), 597–608.

Vannorsdall, T. D., Maroof, D. A., Gordon, B., & Schretlen, D. J. (2012). Ideational fluency as a domain of human cognition. *Neuropsychology, 26*(3), 400–405. doi:10.1037/a0027989.

Vaughan-Jensen, J., Adame, C., McLean, L., & Gámez, B. (2011). Test review of Wechsler individual achievement test (3rd ed.). *Journal of Psychoeducational Assessment, 29*(3), 286–291. Retrieved from http://dx.doi.org/10.1177/0734282910385645.

Veenstra-VanderWeele, J., Christian, S. L., & Cook, E. H., Jr. (2004). Autism as a paradigmatic complex genetic disorder. *Annual Review of Genomics and Human Genetics, 5*, 379–405. doi:10.1146/annurev.genom.5.061903.180050.

Vohra, R., Madhavan, S., Sambamoorthi, U., & St Peter, C. (2014). Access to services, quality of care, and family impact for children with autism, other developmental disabilities, and other mental health conditions. *Autism, 18*(7), 815–826.

Volkmar, F. R. (1998). Categorical approaches to the diagnosis of autism: An overview of DSM-IV and ICD-10. *Autism, 2*(1), 45–59. Retrieved from http://dx.doi.org/10.1177/1362361398021005.

Volkmar, F. R., Klin, A., Siegel, B., Szatmari, P., Lord, C., Campbell, M., … Kline W. (1994). Field trial for autistic disorder in DSM-IV. *American Journal of Psychiatry, 151*(9), 1361–1367.

Volkmar, F. R., Klin, A., & McPartland, J. C. (2014). Asperger syndrome: An overview. In J. C. McPartland, A. Klin, & F. R. Volkmar (Eds.), *Asperger syndrome: Assessing and treating high-functioning autism spectrum disorders* (2nd ed.). New York, NY: Guilford Press.

Volkmar, F. R., Sparrow, S. A., Goudreau, D., Cicchetti, D. V., Paul, R., & Cohen, D. J. (1987). Social deficits in autism: An operational approach using the Vineland Adaptive Behavior Scales. *Journal of the American Academy of Child and Adolescent Psychiatry, 26*, 156–161.

Volkmar, F. R., & Wiesner, L. A. (2009). *A practical guide to autism: What every parent, family member, and teacher needs to know*. Hoboken, NJ: Wiley.

Wahlberg, T. (2001). Language development and text comprehension in individuals with autism. *Advances in Special Education, 14*, 133–150.

Wahlstrom, D. (2014, June). *Telephone interview regarding Q interactive test format*.

Wahstrom, D. (2015, May 14). Phone interview: Autism profiles on the WISC-V. Pearson assessments.

Wallis, C. (2006, May 15). New insights into the hidden world of autism. *Time, 167*, 42–51.

Wallis, C. (2006, May 15). *TIME, New Insights into the hidden world of autism*.

Wallis, C. (2006, May 7). A wealth of new brain research—And poignant testimony from people who have autism—Is lifting the veil on this mysterious condition. TIME.

Wechsler, D. (2003). *Wechsler intelligence scale for children: Technical and interpretive manual* (4th ed.). San Antonio, TX: The Psychological Corporation.

Wechsler, D. (2008). *Wechsler adult intelligence scale* (4th ed.). San Antonio, TX: Pearson.

Wechsler, D. (2009a). *Wechsler individual achievement test* (3rd ed.). San Antonio, TX: Pearson.

Wechsler, D. (2009b). *Wechsler memory scale: Administration and scoring manual* (4th ed.). San Antonio, TX: Pearson.

Weigl, E. (1941). On the psychology of so-called processes of abstraction. *The Journal of Abnormal and Social Psychology, 36*(1), 3–33.

Weissman, J. R., Kelley, R. I., Bauman, M. L., Cohen, B. H., Murray, K. F., Mitchell, R. L., … Natowicz, M. R. (2008). Mitochondrial disease in autism spectrum disorder patients: a cohort analysis. *PLoS One, 3*(11), e3815.

Weitlauf, A. S., Gotham, K. O., Vehorn, A. C., & Warren, Z. E. (2014). Brief report: DSM-5 "levels of support:" A comment on discrepant conceptualizations of severity in ASD. *Journal of Autism and Developmental Disorders, 44*(2), 471–476. doi:10.1007/s10803-013-1882-z.

Welsh, M. C., Satterlee-Cartmell, T., & Stine, M. (1999). Towers of Hanoi and London: Contribution of working memory and inhibition to performance. *Brain and Cognition, 41*(2), 231–242.

Whalen, K., Otaiba, S., Delano, M. (2009). Evidence-based reading instruction for individuals with autism spectrum disorders. *Focus on Autism and Other Developmental Disabilities, 24*(1), 3–16.

White, S., Hill, E., Happe, F., & Frith, U. (2009). Revisiting the strange stories: Revealing mentalizing impairments in autism. *Child Development, 80*(4), 1097–1117.

Wiederholt, J. L., & Bryant, B. R. (2012). *Gray oral reading tests (GORT-5)* (5th ed.). Austin, TX: Pro-Ed.

Wiggins, L. D., Baio, J. O. N., & Rice, C. (2006). Examination of the time between first evaluation and first autism spectrum diagnosis in a population-based sample. *Journal of Developmental & Behavioral Pediatrics, 27*(2), S79–S87.

Wiig, E. H., Secord, W. A., & Semel, E. (2006). *Clinical evaluation of language fundamentals preschool* (2nd ed.). San Antonio, TX: Pearson Education.

Willard, M. (2013). *Development of an integrative comprehension imagery scale for children with and without autism.* Proquest: Dissertations and Theses (PQDT) University of Denver, 177 pages. Retrieved from http://digitaldu.coalliance.org/.../Willard.../Willard_denver_0061D_10648.pdf

Willcutt, E. G., Doyle, A. E., Nigg, J. T., Faraone, S. V., & Pennington, B. F. (2005). Validity of the executive function theory of attention-deficit/hyperactivity disorder: A meta-analytic review. *Biological Psychiatry, 57*(11), 1336–1346.

Willemsen-Swinkels, S. H. N., Buitelaar, J. K., Dekker, M., & van Engeland, H. (1998). Subtyping stereotypic behavior in children: The association between stereotypic behavior, mood, and heart rate. *Journal of Autism and Developmental Disorders, 28*, 547–557.

Williams, D. L., Goldstein, G., & Minshew, N. J. (2006). The profile of memory function in children with autism. *Neuropsychology, 20*(1), 21–29. doi:10.1037/0894-4105.20.1.21.

Williams, D. M., Jarrold, C., Grainger, C., & Lind, S. E. (2014). Diminished time-based, but undiminished event-based, prospective memory among intellectually high-functioning adults with autism spectrum disorder: Relation to working memory ability. *Neuropsychology, 28*(1), 30–42. doi:10.1037/neu0000008.

Wilson, C., Kenworthy, L., Anthony, L., Eisenberg, I. W., Orionzi, B., Martin, A., & Wallace, G. L. (2014, May). *Exploratory profile of high functioning adolescents and young adults with autism spectrum disorders experiencing subthreshold psychotic symptoms.* Poster presented at the 13th Annual International Meeting for Autism Research, Atlanta, GA.

Wing, L. (1969). The handicaps of autistic children—A comparative study. *Journal of Child Psychology and Psychiatry, 10*(1), 1–40.

Wing, L., & Gould, J. (1979). Severe impairments of social interaction and associated abnormalities in children: Epidemiology and classification. *Journal of Autism and Development Disorders, 9*, 11–29.

Wing, L., Gould, J., & Gillberg, C. (2011). Autism spectrum disorders in the DSM-V: Better or worse than the DSM-IV? *Research in Developmental Disabilities, 32*(2), 768–773. Retrieved from http://dx.doi.org/10.1016/j.ridd.2010.11.003.

Winner, M. G., & Crooke, P. (2008). *You are a social detective.* San Jose, CA: Think Social.

Witwer, A. N., & Lecavalier, L. (2010). Validity of comorbid psychiatric disorders in youngsters with autism spectrum disorders. *Journal of Developmental and Physical Disabilities, 22*(4), 367–380. Retrieved from http://dx.doi.org/10.1007/s10882-010-9194-0.

Wojcik, D. Z., Moulin, C. J., & Souchay, C. (2013). Metamemory in children with autism: Exploring "feeling-of-knowing" in episodic and semantic memory. *Neuropsychology, 27*(1), 19–27. doi:10.1037/a0030526.

Wolfberg, P. J. (2003). *Peer play and the autism spectrum: The art of guiding children's socialization and imagination (Integrated play groups field manual).* Shawnee Mission, KS: Autism Asperger.

Woodcock, R. W., Shrank, F. A., McGrew, K. S., & Mather, N. (2007). *Woodcock-Johnson III normative update (WJ III NU).* Rolling Meadows, IL: Riverside.

Wright, J. (2010). *'How RtI works' series*. Whitepaper for interventioncentral.org (pp. 1–6). Retrieved April 19, 2015.

Yell, M. L. (2006). *The law and special education* (2nd ed.). Upper Saddle River, NJ: Pearson/Merrill/Prentice Hall.

Yell, M. L. (2012). *The law and special education* (3rd ed.). Upper Saddle River, NJ: Pearson.

Yerys, B. E., Kenworthy, L., Jankowski, K. F., Strang, J., & Wallace, G. L. (2013). Separate components of emotional go/no-go performance relate to autism versus attention symptoms in children with autism. *Neuropsychology, 27*(5), 537–545. doi:10.1037/a0033615.

Yirmiya, N., & Charman, T. (2010). The prodrome of autism: Early behavioral and biological signs, regression, peri- and post-natal developments and genetics. *Journal of Child Psychology and Psychiatry, 51*(4), 432–458.

Yoder, P., Stone, W. L., Walden, T., & Malesa, E. (2009). Predicting social impairment and ASD diagnosis in younger siblings of children with autism spectrum disorder. *Journal of Autism and Developmental Disorders, 39*(10), 1381–1391.

York Haaland, K., & Delaney, H. D. (1981). Motor deficits after left or right hemisphere damage due to stroke or tumor. *Neuropsychologia, 19*(1), 17–27.

Young, R. L., & Rodi, M. L. (2014). Redefining autism spectrum disorder using DSM-5: The implications of the proposed DSM-5 criteria for autism spectrum disorders. *Journal of Autism and Developmental Disorders, 44*(4), 758–765. doi:10.1007/s10803-013-1927-3.

Zable, M., & Harlow, H. F. (1946). The performance of rhesus monkeys on series of object-quality and positional discriminations and discrimination reversals. *Journal of Comparative Psychology, 39*(1), 13–23.

Zimmer, M., & Desch, L. (2012). Sensory integration therapies for children with developmental and behavioral disorders. *Pediatrics, 129*(6), 1186–1189.

Zimmerman, A. (2008). *Autism: Current theories and evidence*. In D. Tarsay (Series Ed.). Totowa, NJ: Humana Press.

Zwaigenbaum, L., Bryson, S., Rogers, T., Roberts, W., Brian, J., & Szatmari, P. (2005). Behavioral manifestations of autism in the first year of life. *International Journal of Developmental Neuroscience, 23*(2), 143–152.

Index

© Springer International Publishing Switzerland 2016
A.P. Kroncke et al., *Assessment of Autism Spectrum Disorder*, Contemporary
Issues in Psychological Assessment, DOI 10.1007/978-3-319-25504-0

Printed by Printforce, the Netherlands